MW01615521

LENNON

ALSO BY TIM RILEY

Tell Me Why: A Beatles Commentary

Hard Rain: A Dylan Commentary

Madonna: Illustrated

Fever: How Rock 'n' Roll Transformed Gender in America

LENNON

The Man, the Myth, the Music—The Definitive Life

Tim Riley

NEW YORK

Copyright © 2011 Tim Riley

All rights reserved. No part of this book may be used or reproduced in any manner whatsoever without the written permission of the Publisher. Printed in the United States of America. For information address Hyperion, 114 Fifth Avenue, New York, New York 10011.

The photo credits on p. 766 constitute a continuation of this copyright page.

ISBN-13: 978-1-61793-848-1

Book design by Fearn Cutler de Vicq

For Sara Laschever, my hero

Contents

PART THREE

Beyond Beatles, 1970–1980

Preface

When two great Saints meet, it is a humbling experience. The long
battles to prove he was a saint . . .

PAUL McCARTNEY, DEDICATION TO *Two Virgins*, 1968

WHEN JOHN LENNON PRESENTED HIS FELLOW BEATLES WITH THE
cover art for *Unfinished Music No. 1: Two Virgins* in November
of 1968, everybody recoiled. McCartney's quote sat beneath Lennon and
his lover, Yoko Ono, holding hands naked in their bedroom with postco-
ital grins. EMI's lordly chairman, Sir Joseph Lockwood, refused to distribute the record, pronouncing John and Yoko "ugly." In America,
Capitol Records balked, and even when the album was shipped through
an independent distributor, New Jersey authorities confiscated thirty
thousand copies, declaring the cover "obscene." Controversy subsumed
the record's experimental sounds. Nobody could understand why Lennon
would deliberately extend the public-relations debacle he had already
created by leaving his British wife and child for the Japanese-American
"conceptual artist," especially on the eve of the first Beatles album in
eighteen months, the double *White Album* (originally *The Beatles*).

Time has papered over the photograph's insolence: Lennon was
pouring acid on the Beatle myth, demonstrating how shallow and ridiculous pop stardom seemed even as his band hit new creative peaks. This

would be just the first of many media campaigns he waged to kick his way out of the Beatles.

That July of 1968, when this insouciant photograph was taken, the Beatles were slogging through the "poisonous" *White Album* sessions that prompted EMI engineer Geoff Emerick to quit in a huff. Drummer Ringo Starr walked out soon thereafter. The Lennon and McCartney songwriting collaboration had long since trailed off into independent work, even though the songs still bore the trademark Lennon-McCartney authorship. Increasingly, their partnership had graduated from aesthetic one-upmanship to outright conflict: in that same hectic period, the band vetoed Lennon's first rendition of "Revolution" as too slow, and even the blazing remake sat on the flip side of McCartney's "Hey Jude," the band's revitalizing summer single.

To the others, this widening rift coincided with Yoko Ono's divisive presence. Lennon could not have chosen a more passive-aggressive way to disrupt the group's chemistry. Yoko planted herself not only at recording sessions but at private group demos and Apple business meetings, offering comments as if she were a de facto member of the band. Not even the "Beatle wives" had ever been granted such access. She roamed the EMI studios unfettered, without so much as an introduction to George Martin, the band's producer.

But whatever resentments among the band, the bond between Lennon and Ono was already immune to protest.

BY NOW, SOME FORTY YEARS AFTER the group's breakup, the Lennon legend has graduated into myth of an entirely different order than the one that turned him into an international rock star, the one he retired from for the last five years of his life to raise his son Sean. On the radio, he sings to us from some idealized Tower of Song, frozen in time and memory like Buddy Holly or Eddie Cochran, those creative martyrs who haunted his own impressionable adolescence.

The remaining three Beatles reunited in the mid-1990s to tell their own version of their story with the *Anthology* video and book, the band's story tunneled into nostalgia. In 2000, the greatest-hits album *1* became the fastest-selling CD in history, reached number one in twenty-eight countries, and went on to sell more than thirty-one million copies worldwide, the best-selling album of the decade in the United States. At decade's end, the Beatles became the best-selling band of the new millennium. (This would be the last release guitarist George Harrison oversaw directly; he died in November of 2001.) In 2006, the Cirque du Soleil's *Love* began selling out six shows a week in a Las Vegas theater with a customized sound system by producer George Martin and his son, Giles. Its remashed sound track became still another huge hit.

Lennon's own story, of course, had passed through rock's looking glass long before. He hovered over every frame of the *Anthology,* and his familiar quotes heaved with subtext: it was hard to imagine Lennon participating in such a whitewashed, sentimental project devoted to enshrining a myth he had done so much to puncture during his lifetime. His post-Beatle revolts linked the personal with the aesthetic: he first ran off with Yoko Ono, then married her the week after McCartney married Linda Eastman, then howled at the demise of the Beatles (on 1970's blistering *Plastic Ono Band*) even as he subtly helped to engineer it. He rebuilt his peacenik/politico façade while ridiculing his former partner McCartney (in "How Do You Sleep?"), before careening into a hackneyed drunken-celebrity "lost weekend" in the early 1970s. Finally, after winning a long immigration battle with the Nixon administration, he washed up onto the shores of storybook "monogamy" and parenthood during a five-year sabbatical. His assassination in 1980 quelled Beatle reunion rumors, but only temporarily.

In the fall of 2009, the Beatles' entire sixties recording catalog was remastered in luminous digital audio, updating the flat CD mixes that had circulated since the late 1980s. These joint releases sent both Lennon's myth and his Beatle legacy into yet another orbit, reigniting stalwart fans and breeding a vast young listenership. Scholars who had studied these recordings for decades suddenly heard previously unnoticed details, alongside a new vocal and instrumental physicality. New ideas came to the fore, and lingering contradictions commanded fresh attention. The finely blended close harmonies on "This Boy" and "Nowhere Man" took on new immediacy; McCartney's guitar solos on "Taxman" and "Good

Morning Good Morning" suddenly seemed richer, grittier, and down-right contemporary. Alongside elaborately detailed sessionographies like *The Complete Beatles Recording Sessions* by Mark Lewisohn (1992) and *Recording the Beatles* by Kevin Ryan and Brian Kehew (2006), these remasters confirmed how profoundly the Lennon-McCartney recording catalog transcended its era.

Britons have come to rank the Beatles just after Shakespeare as a core element of their national identity, but few feel challenged to explain how a rock career, once culture's most defiled profession, now sits comfortably next to one of Western culture's highest achievements. Lennon's childhood is generally known to be "traumatic," but even some of the better biographers give his primal separation scene (between his father, Alfred Lennon, and his mother, Julia Stanley Lennon, in an uncle's Blackpool home in June of 1946) a paragraph at most. This black hole of emotional loss swallows up all his intimacies. He spent his life adopting father figures and mourning his mother, who died in an accident when he was seventeen. "I lost my mother twice," he once said; and like a lot of his lyrics, these words are truer than many fans appreciate.

In many of his key intimate relationships—with songwriting partner Paul McCartney, manager Brian Epstein, drummer Ringo Starr, and first wife Cynthia Powell—Lennon balanced alliances with fragile affections; he seemed to spend almost two-thirds of his Beatle tenure surrounded by people he wished to avoid. As his first marriage fell apart, Lennon's reliance on McCartney also began to fall away, even as McCartney's support for his eccentricities strengthened. (One intriguing subtext of "Hey Jude" involves McCartney's affection for Cynthia and his fatherly sympathy toward Julian.) Their showbiz feud over control of their publishing catalog belies their friendship. And Lennon's influence on McCartney is far more pronounced, and remarked upon, than McCartney's subtler influence on Lennon. As they entered their epic feud, Lennon made sure Ringo Starr drummed on his 1970 "divorce" album, *Plastic Ono Band;* but Lennon never appeared on a single McCartney solo album, or vice versa.

These relationships inflect Lennon's music in chimerical ways: he does some of his best writing while strung out on drugs as his first marriage collapses throughout 1966 ("She Said She Said," "Tomorrow Never Knows," "Strawberry Fields Forever"). Alternatively, the late period (1975–80), where he commits himself to fathering and private life, sees a lull in musical craft. How best to understand Lennon's music in regard to his life? Where does the music illuminate the life, and where does it veer off into myth?

Beyond his music, Lennon's talent as a cartoonist, illustrator, lithographer, and collage artist influenced every aspect of his work. His songs carve out richly textured spaces of sound, which spring from a lifelong interest in pop and modern art. With his art-school classmate Stu Sutcliffe, Lennon roamed Hamburg's museums in 1960, talking about how rock 'n' roll seemed poised to fulfill modern art's promise. One night, Sutcliffe recognized the artist Eduardo Paolozzi at a nightclub with students, and approached him about his work, long before Paolozzi became a touchstone for Andy Warhol. This visual arc runs from Sutcliffe on through the classic Beatle pop art of Peter Blake (the *Sgt. Pepper* cover) and Richard Hamilton (the *White Album* package) and the Magritte-inspired Apple logo, and gives Lennon's second marriage, to New York City–based conceptual artist Ono, hints of fate.

In chasing down all these threads of Lennon's story, several important sources have fallen out of print and general notice. Pete Shotton, Lennon's childhood friend from Woolton, wrote a memoir back in 1982 called *In My Life,* which details many fascinating scrapes and insights into Julia Stanley's sister, Aunt Mimi, the prim hypocrite who wound up raising John. Alfred Lennon's 1991 memoir, *Daddy Come Home,* relates his side of the child's story, the Blackpool episode, and the brief skirmishes between father and son as adults.

Beyond the music, many journalists dismiss the counterculture Lennon helped inspire, or how his songs snared key youth movement tensions (from "You Can't Do That" and "And Your Bird Can Sing" on through "Revolution," "Imagine," "Woman Is the Nigger of the World," and "Beautiful Boy"). This would be like covering Muhammad Ali without referencing his immense civil rights status. The new era of scholarship ushered in by EMI's 2009 remasters, compressed onto a single green USB flash drive, earned comparison of Beatle recordings to popular work by Charlie Chaplin, Alfred Hitchcock, Duke Ellington, and Louis Armstrong. Surely Lennon would chuckle at how "respectable" the rock world has become since his death, which might be the price of his music's resilience.

With his Beatles and beyond, Lennon remains a defining legend for our time: we return to it to tell ourselves our most cherished stories about how we grew up, came of age, and became adults. The music, of course, remains enchanting enough to revisit Lennon and the Beatles as a source of meaning in the modern era. But how much can it really tell us about Lennon's intellectual and emotional life? Where does his life align with his art, and where does his songwriting balloon into grandiose self-mythology? Can the music begin to tell us how it felt to be Lennon, or just how he wanted us to experience him? Can the British "John Lennon" be reconciled with his American persona? What do the overlaps and contradictions tell us about his accomplishment? These biographical questions beguile a music critic, and exploring these tensions has only made Lennon's songs seem richer, more demanding, less encumbered by the tensions of his era.

Tim Riley
Concord, Massachusetts
2011

LENNON

PART ONE

PRE-BEATLES

1940–1959

I

No Reply

The worst pain is that of not being wanted, of realizing your parents do not need you in the way you need them. When I was a child I experienced moments of not wanting to see the ugliness. . . . This lack of love went into my eyes and into my mind.

—JOHN LENNON, 1971[1]

L IVERPOOL WAS A DESPERATE PLACE ON OCTOBER 9, 1940, WHEN JU-
lia Stanley Lennon gave birth to her first and only son, at the Oxford Maternity Home. For the third month in a row, the Nazis were
raining bombs on the city, trying to disrupt supply lines through Liverpool's sprawling port system, with its direct access to the Irish Sea. Built
up around the River Mersey's deep estuary, thirty miles across at its wid-
est point and navigable by oceangoing vessels, the Port of Liverpool was
a critical point of entry for the beleaguered nation's food and fuel; the
Allies called it their "Atlantic approach." In targeting Liverpool, Hitler
hoped to starve Britain into submission and yoke the island into his
European conquests.

The first bombs fell on Liverpool in August, a mere two months
before Julia gave birth. Hitler dropped 454 tons of high explosives and
1,029 tons of incendiaries on the town, more than the Luftwaffe dropped
on any other British city that month, including London. Throughout

the following weeks, in a relentless barrage, the German bombs savaged dockyards, factories, and airfields, destroyed both a children's convalescent home and a jail. The wreckage left thousands of Julia Stanley Lennon's neighbors homeless, more than half of them from "the Bootle," the hardest-hit neighborhood and home of most of the docks' workforce. Many of these workers relocated to outlying towns, and ten thousand commuted back to the wharves daily to keep the docks running for the rest of the war.[2]

The terrified population buckled down to maintain some semblance of normal life, tending their shops and gardens, unsure how long the bombing would last. Remarkably, most historians report high morale throughout that fall.[3] But underneath, Liverpool, not to mention the rest of England, was panicked by what the war might bring: whether Britain would still be Britain or, like most of Europe and much of North Africa, a Vichy-like satellite or appendage to the Third Reich.

On October 8, 1940, the day before John Lennon was born, the BBC radio broadcast Prime Minister Winston Churchill's address to the House of Commons. Churchill promised that the cities devastated by German bombs would "rise from their ruins, more healthy, and, I hope, more beautiful."[4] In Liverpool and cities like it, where the bombing seemed endless, Churchill's words injected the careworn citizenry with a newly found courage. "So hypnotic was the force of his words," Isaiah Berlin later wrote, "so strong his faith, that by the sheer intensity of his eloquence he bound his spell upon them until it seemed to them he was indeed speaking what was in their hearts and minds. If it was there, it was largely dormant until he had awoken it within them."[5]

Julia Stanley Lennon—called Judy by her four sisters—was raised in a stable middle-class family. Her paternal grandfather, William Henry Stanley, had been a solicitor's clerk and an amateur musician, who taught his musical granddaughter Judy how to play the banjo. William Henry had moved his family out of the dockyard slums by the time his son George married Annie Jane Milward. George and Annie moved one step farther out, to Toxteth, then a neighborhood of row houses, semi-detached "cottages," and tidy parks south of the city center. The family lived within walking distance of the Queen and Albert docks, where

George worked at the Liverpool and Glasgow Salvage Association, initially as a diver and then as the leader of a salvage crew, raising sunken vessels from the ocean floor. Judy, the fourth daughter of five girls, arrived in 1914, after Mimi, Elizabeth, and Anne but ahead of Harriet. George's work, however, was so arduous and required such long, relentless hours that his daughters regarded him as another man at sea. Like so many Liverpool families in similar situations, the Stanleys functioned as a typical dockside matriarchy.

George never owned property, which made the Stanleys' respectability tenuous and that much more precious. In England's tenaciously class-conscious society, in which one's "place" was finely parsed and underlined by every interaction with one's "betters," the worst thing you could be was "common." Having escaped that fate, the Stanleys were determined never to slip back. John Lennon's first wife, Cynthia, recalled that his aunt Mimi's harshest reproof was to not be *common*.[6]

The Stanleys' status anxiety reflected Liverpool's own social insecurity. A grimy city filled with transients and immigrants, descendants of slave traders, Americans from the nearby Burtonwood Air Force Base, and the occupants of some disreputable rooming houses, Liverpool was perceived by England's ruling elite as a sorry by-product of the Industrial Revolution. The city was useful because of its bustling port but, even compared with nearby Manchester, Liverpool was short on cultural prestige and beneath the notice of the country's aristocracy. "It was in England but not exactly of it," observes Jan Morris, "being a boisterous and sometimes explosive mix of nationalities—Irish, Welsh, Chinese, African and many more—and it had been built upon the most ruthless kind of capitalist enterprise."[7] As the hub of the North American slave trade, Liverpool nursed long-standing moral and class resentments.

Long before the city was ravaged by the war, the prevailing Liverpool character carried a chip on its shoulder, conveyed in an embittered, comic language studded with class antipathy—the perfect incubator for John's personality. Dockers spoke a thickly accented brogue called Scouse, immediately recognizable as a working-class tongue, rich with suggestive street slang, its own obscenities and many colorful non sequiturs. Often mistaken for London Cockney, a garden-variety low-class accent, Scouse more resembles the rich tonal inflections of its Irish ancestry. The ends of declamatory sentences often rise up like questions, which lends Scouse conversation musicality and innate self-mockery. As an adult, even though he had not grown up on the docks and his accent was far less pronounced, Lennon often spoke Scouse to "take the piss out of" someone whom he thought ridiculous. Like most Scousers, he enjoyed confirming people's worst assumptions about low-class northerners. All Scousers nursed a fierce local pride—one that Lennon adopted as his own.

During Liverpool's shipbuilding heyday, which lasted from 1881 to 1921, the local elite had erected an array of monumental public buildings proclaiming the respectability of the city and its leading citizens. During those same decades of prosperity, Liverpool sprouted a ring of leafy suburbs, claimed from fallow fields that had been overfarmed for two centuries and no longer supported the dairy trade that had anchored the region's economy since the Middle Ages. With prosperity, the city's population grew, spawning a new class of teachers, accountants, tailors, clerks, watchmakers, and grocers who strove toward a higher standard of living—and to separate themselves from the nation's common image of working-class Liverpudlians.

George Stanley's brood joined this great social migration toward middle-class respectability, but fun-loving Judy had no interest in abiding by the rules of decorum that governed "respectable" people. Self-confident and self-absorbed, small-boned and pretty, she cut a striking figure with her high heels, gleaming red nail polish, and auburn hair cut in stylish imitation of the movie stars of the day. "People used to turn back for another look at her," John's cousin Leila Harvey reported. "When some cheeky boy gave her a wolf whistle, she would say, 'Hmmm, not bad yourself.'"[8] Judy Stanley was determined to do as she pleased, and one thing she liked to do was provoke her parents. Alfred Lennon, a young man with no skills, no connections, and no "class," was ready-made to outrage the Stanleys' carefully wrought propriety.

Alfred was born in 1912, the fourth of six surviving children of Jack Lennon Jr., an Irish shipping clerk. Jack was musical, and had spent the 1890s touring the United States as a singer with Andrew Robertson's "Kentucky Minstrels," a traveling act that played vaudeville venues and country fairs. Although little information survives about this troupe, the act donned blackface to perform popular minstrel material to American audiences for an uncanny musical foreshadow.

Around 1900, John's paternal grandfather moved back to Britain with an American wife, whose name has been lost. Rather than return to Ireland, Jack Jr. found work as a shipping clerk in Liverpool, which by then was known as "Little Ireland."⁹ After the death of his first wife, Jack married his Irish housekeeper, Mary "Polly" McGuire, who bore him eight children, six of whom survived. In 1917, after a life spent clerking, singing, touring, and drinking, Jack fell dead at sixty-two from "liver disease," the era's polite euphemism for advanced alcoholism. Polly was overwhelmed. Alone now, with four children to support (her eldest, George, was sixteen and old enough to work) and another on the way, she gave five-year-old Alf and his two-year-old sister, Edith, over to the Blue Coat Orphanage, a charitable institution for children of the poor, in an act of desperation that would be repeated a generation later. From then on, young Alf and Edith saw their mother and other siblings only on holidays, although their brothers Sydney and Charles remained constant figures throughout Alf's life. Although no Dickensian workhouse, the Blue Coat adhered to strict regimens—especially tough by today's standards—which prompted Alf to attempt more than one escape.¹⁰

From the start, young Alf also had health problems. As a boy playing in the soot-darkened streets of industrial Liverpool, he'd developed rickets, a disease caused by inadequate exposure to the sun's ultraviolet rays and made worse by poor diet. Rickets shorten and deform the weight-bearing limbs, and the orphanage put Alf in leg braces for straightening until he was twelve. Even so, as a full-grown man he was only five feet, two inches tall, six inches shorter than his famous son, and both his legs curved outward (think Charlie Chaplin's Tramp, whose bowlegs symbolized privation).

Like his father, Jack, Alf loved to sing. When he was fourteen and out on a weekend pass from the Blue Coat, his brother Sydney took him backstage after hearing the Will Murray Gang, a song-and-dance act at the Liverpool Empire. Alf plunged into a rendition of "I Do Like to Be Beside the Seaside," and his plucky presentation persuaded Murray to offer him a slot in the show. The next day, Alf grabbed his harmonica, fled the orphanage, and headed to Glasgow to join the band.

Orphanage officers quickly caught up with him and dragged him back, berating him in front of his classmates. None of this quenched Alf's thirst for freedom and fun, which marked the rest of his life and echoed down into his son's persona.[11] In this break from the narrow confines of his childhood, Alf, the stunted child, the unwanted boy who'd been sent away and locked into leg braces, ran, as his son later would, toward all the things that his life at the orphanage lacked—adventure, independence, music. He would be on the run, more or less, for the rest of his days, chasing a long string of small-time scams, always looking for the "big break" that would free him from a perpetual hand-to-mouth existence.

ALF MET JUDY IN 1927, when she was thirteen and he was fifteen. Their meeting, though entirely accidental, seemed almost foreordained. He was strolling in Sefton Park, one of Liverpool's ample expanses of public green, south of the Toxteth Park Cemetery near the Penny Lane roundabout. After ten years and two escape attempts, he'd finally left the Blue Coat for good and found work as a bellboy at the Adelphi Hotel. He was taking a stroll, seeing what else the world had to offer. "I had just bought myself a cigarette holder and a bowler hat and I fancied my chances," Julia's daughter and namesake quotes Alf as saying in her memoirs.[12]

A friend was teaching Alf how to pick up girls when they spotted the pretty redhead lounging on a bench by the boat lake. Before Alf even had a chance to try his new moves, the girl called out to him, telling him he looked silly. He responded that she looked lovely and sat down on the bench. If he wanted to sit next to her, the girl said, he'd have to take off his hat. Without hesitating, Alf Lennon stood up and threw his new hat into the lake, which made Judy Stanley laugh. With that impulsive flourish, he won her over.[13]

They suited each other's needs. Besides sharing a wayward sense of fun, they were both trying to eclipse their pasts: Alf was on the lam from the deprivations of the orphanage, while Judy wanted to slip free of the claustrophobic, post-Victorian embrace of her respectable parents. What better way for Alf to exercise his independence than by hooking up with a stylish, fun-loving girl determined to defy her family? The Stanleys saw themselves as much higher-class than an orphan-bred boy with no family to speak of. To Judy, this only made Alf more desirable. She enjoyed his irreverence and off-color sense of humor while at the same time taunting her family. They dated on and off for the next several years, touring the pubs and dance halls (although Alf's crippled legs meant he more often sang than danced), including several near the docks that were frequented by sailors—establishments where "nice girls" just didn't go. Pops Stanley forbade their courtship for a time, but this didn't deter Judy—it just prompted the two of them to be more ingenious and secretive about their rendezvous.

In Liverpool in those years, a loafer could always find work as a merchant seaman by lining up at the dockyard gates ("the pools") every morning to see if any boats were hiring. With no engineering training, navigation experience, or ability to manage accounts or track inventory, the best Alf could do was scramble for jobs as cook and steward. He never knew until he'd signed on whether he'd be at sea for three weeks or three months, and the work was strictly job-by-job—steady employment was rare. After every voyage, he had to start from scratch, hanging out at the pools or going from one shipping office to another looking for his next assignment. With no job security and lousy pay, Alf quickly learned to supplement his income by gambling and by smuggling hard-to-find goods to sell on the black market.[14]

AFTER EIGHT YEARS of peripatetic dating, Alf and Judy were finally married on Saturday, December 3, 1938. He'd saved up for three weeks to pay for their marriage license. Why they finally decided to marry is unclear. Alf's second wife and widow, Pauline Lennon, edited Alf's memoirs after he died and published them as *Daddy Come Home* in 1990.[15] As she tells it, Judy dared him to "put up the banns"—the old practice of publicly announcing one's intention to marry three weeks ahead of time. This allowed any interested party a chance to object. Alf supposedly took the dare. Beatle historian and Lennon's art school classmate Bill Harry suggests another reason: with work scarce, Alf needed a marriage certificate to get on the dole.[16] Whatever the prompt, Alf and Judy tied the knot at the Mount Pleasant Registry Office with Alf's older brother Sydney as their witness. Afterward, they went to the Trocadero Cinema on Camden Street, where Judy worked off and on as an usherette, and watched Mickey Rooney in *The Boy from Barnardo's* (as *Lord Jeff* was called in England). They laughingly called this their honeymoon. She was twenty-four and Alf was twenty-five.

"That's it! I've gone and married him then!" Judy announced as she made her entrance at the family house in Toxteth that night. While the length of their courtship testifies to the strength of their bond, Alf and Judy's whimsical nuptials suggest that what each prized most about the other may have been a shared love of frivolity and a deep aversion to being serious.

Judy and Alf made unconventional newlyweds, even for England on the cusp of World War II. Alf shipped out soon after the wedding while Judy continued to live with her parents, working sporadically as a waitress and as an usherette at the Trocadero. In 1939, with an almost empty nest, George and Annie Stanley relinquished their Toxteth home for a more modest apartment at 9 Newcastle Road in Wavertree, near Alf's Blue Coat Orphanage, and Judy moved in with them. With Alf at sea, the Stanleys may have figured that he wouldn't be sharing the space much, and their other four daughters had already married and moved out. Although Judy had no apparent interest in becoming a mother, John was conceived "on a cold January afternoon in 1940 on the kitchen floor," Alf recalled, just as rationing became a way of wartime life.[17]

NINE MONTHS LATER, Judy went alone to the hospital to have her baby. Whether she didn't tell her family where she was going or they stayed home because of the bombing (or they didn't want to risk their necks for Alf Lennon's child), no one held her hand or sat in the waiting room, worried about her safety, or expressed any interest in greeting her child. The following evening, October 9, at 6:30 P.M., after thirty hours of difficult labor, Judy—alone and exhausted—finally gave birth to a healthy seven-pound, eight-ounce boy. It's hard to imagine the complicated feelings she must have felt when, bereft of her husband, she first held her son. She was twenty-six and liked her freedom—what was she going to do with a baby? She named him John, after Alf's father and grandfather. With Churchill's radio speech from the day before ringing in her ears, she selected "Winston" for his middle name. "Winston" spoke to Judy's ambivalent class attitudes, only to confound her son's "Working Class Hero" legacy.

Later that night, a nurse called the Stanley house to announce, "Mrs. Lennon has had a boy." Galvanized by this news, her oldest sister, Mimi Smith, raced to see the infant. Mimi later wrote:

> I was dodging in doorways between running as fast as my legs would carry me. . . . I was literally terrified. Transport had stopped because the bombs began always at dusk. There was shrapnel falling and gunfire and when there was a little lull I ran into the hospital ward and there was this beautiful little baby.[18]

Mimi's memory might be the only place in town where bombs actually fell that night—there was certainly a curfew, and the buses were not running, but records indicate bombs fell on London and another "northwest town," but not on Liverpool.[19] Nonetheless, Mimi's memory defined Lennon's story: he grew up believing he was born during an air raid, and felt branded by Churchill's name as a reminder. Regardless, as soon as Mimi picked John up, the air-raid sirens screamed again. The hospital staff insisted that she go down to the basement or go home. Mimi chose to go home. Judy, worn out, stayed put. "John, like the other babies, was put underneath the bed."[20]

In the brief moments, however, when she held him, Mimi literally fell in love. Whether it was because she was one of five sisters and he was a boy, or because she herself, the oldest Stanley daughter, was childless, John's arrival answered some need in Mimi. It was a need that she would play out—often at the expense of the boy she believed she was protecting—throughout her nephew's childhood. For the rest of her life, she claimed that the moment she saw John in the hospital she knew that *she* was supposed to be his mother, not Judy. "Does that sound awful?" she asked when she related this story to Bill Harry. "It isn't really," she explained, "because Julia accepted it as something perfectly natural. She used to say, 'You're his real mother. All I did was give birth.'"[21] Judy, though she had little appetite for motherhood, didn't hand him over outright—not yet. After the standard week of "lying in," she took her son home to the family apartment on Newcastle Road to meet his grandparents. On October 12, the *Liverpool Echo* ran the following birth announcement: "Lennon—October 9th, in hospital to Julia (née Stanley) wife of ALFRED LENNON, Merchant Navy (at sea), a son. 9 Newcastle Road."

Three weeks later, the *Empress of Canada* docked in Liverpool, and Alf Lennon met his son for the first time. He spent several weeks with his wife and child before leaving again, and those first few weeks of John Lennon's life were the only time that he and his parents lived peacefully together under the same roof—albeit with Judy's parents. During the next five years, Alf would spend barely a total of three months in Liverpool, and much of that time he spent in air-raid shelters with his wife and child or at the docks "fire watching" during raids.[22]

THE NAZI BOMBING PEAKED the following May, when the Germans dropped 2,315 high-explosive bombs and 119 other incendiaries on Liverpool, putting half the docks out of action, killing 1,741 people, and injuring 1,154. On May 3, the Germans blew up the *Makaland,* docked in Liverpool and loaded with more than a thousand tons of bombs and explosives. When the dust cleared, 2,500 Liverpudlians had been killed outright, and more than 50,000 more were homeless; another 50,000 were relocated outside the imperiled metropolis. The children who remained in the city, many of them orphaned, grew up amid ruins. John remembered playing in bomb craters.

In June of 1941, Judy's mother, Annie, died at age seventy, leaving George—"Pop"—alone in the Newcastle Road apartment with Judy and John.[23] Despite the presence of her father, Judy continued to take a lackadaisical approach to raising her son and honoring her marriage vows. With soldiers and sailors streaming through the city and wartime romances commonplace, Judy found various opportunities to escape the rationing, divert herself from the air raids, and shrug off the war's gloom. Although Alf sent home most of his wages to support his family, he often returned to find John stashed at Mimi's and to discover traces of other men. Having told his wife to "go out and have a good time" while he was gone, and probably not averse to the standard merchant marines' "favors" in foreign ports himself, Alf at first took Judy's infidelities in stride.

The following year, when John was two, Mimi invited Judy and John to move into her Woolton cottage at 120A Allerton Road, behind the house called Mendips where she had settled with her husband, George Smith. Judy jumped at the chance to get away from her father's disapproving presence. But Alf's next visit was rocky. Judy had become accustomed to her routine of trolling the pubs and dance halls each night, and soon after Alf's return she left John behind with him—"for a change," in her words—and went out by herself. Brushing past the protesting Alf, Judy left the house with her friends.[24]

The next morning Alf confronted her: her mother, he said, would have been ashamed of her behavior. Judy poured a cup of hot tea over his head, and Alf responded by slapping her across the face—the only reported account of his striking her.[25] Alf's blast gave Judy a nosebleed, and he called to Mimi to "set things straight." But things were never quite the same again. His next job brought Alf a promotion: to chief steward on the *Berengaria,* bound for New York. Although he thought his career was on the upswing, this trip turned out to be a prolonged disaster. It would be another eighteen months before Alf saw Liverpool, or his family, again.

SHORTLY AFTER ALF LEFT, for reasons that remain unclear, Pop Stanley relocated with other relatives, and Judy moved back into a previous apartment at 9 Newcastle Road with John, by then an active three-year-old. For the rest of the war, Judy remained in this apartment, and at some point she even had her father's name on the lease replaced by Alf's. Mother and son lived on the money Alf sent home, and Judy continued her rambunctious pub life, often coming home drunk. She seems to have had no compunction about bringing men home and sleeping with them with her son in the house, perhaps even the same bed. "Mummy being Mummy, she naturally just tucked him in beside her each night in their large double bed," John's half sister, Julia, later explained.[26]

Aboard the *Berengaria,* Alf's singing made him the star attraction at the Pig and Whistle, the crew's bar, where even passengers sought entrance to watch the crewmen perform. Merchant shipping at the time supported a healthy show-business subculture, complete with elaborate variety shows and drag queens. Belowdecks was one place in British culture where gay men openly expressed themselves, even inventing a pidgin language called "Parole," a witty offshoot of Scouser slang.

Alf often played master of ceremonies, recruiting the talent and hosting the show and singing his own numbers between sketches. When four-year-old John began asking whether his father would come home for Christmas, Judy gave him a program that Alf had enclosed in his last letter to her, with Alf listed singing "Begin the Beguine." John was tantalized, but Judy hid an unspoken worry: the letters—and checks—had stopped coming. During the war, most merchant ships carried supplies and munitions for the military effort. Targeted by Nazi U-boats and submarines, the merchant ships were shepherded from port to port in large convoys, and one in twenty such "commercial" ships were sunk during the war.[27] Alf was as much a target as any military sailor.

LUCKILY, IT WAS carousing that got Alf into trouble, not Nazi torpedoes. In New York, having been dropped by the *Berengaria,* Alf was scheduled to ship out on a trawler called the *Middle East,* but he missed the ship's departure after a long night of singing at a dockside bar. (In *Daddy Come Home,* Alf claims it was all an elaborate scam, in which ship owners persuaded workers to take reduced pay with promises of promotion and then conned them out of work once they reached New York.) With no visa and no job, Alf was interned at Ellis Island by the U.S. Immigration Service, and from there he was unable to get word to his wife. Judy went down to collect her monthly check only to be told that her husband had "jumped ship." Strapped for cash, she assumed the worst about Alf: that he had jumped the marriage or was lost at sea—or dead. The Stanleys, including Mimi, shook their heads knowingly. Even if he was alive, wasn't Alf just the sort to skip out on his responsibilities? Without Alf's checks, Judy had little means of support, especially since her father was no longer living with her on Newcastle Road. Unsubstantiated rumors, strongly denied years later by her daughter, swirled around her that she started sleeping with men for money during this time.[28] Whether or not this is true, concern for her son's welfare does not seem to have rated high on Judy's list of priorities.

Meanwhile, in New York, the British consulate found Alf a job on a steamer called the *Sammex,* which kept him from being charged with desertion by the U.S. authorities. But he had to take a demotion, and the *Sammex* was loaded with "hot" cargo—booze and cigarettes. When police boarded the boat in North Africa, the loot was confiscated and Alf was taken into custody for "stealing and finding," and thrown into prison for three months, unable to send money to Judy. He finally found his way home to Liverpool on a ship called the *Monarch of Bermuda,* which docked as the war was winding down in mid-1945.

If Alf envisioned a happy homecoming, he was disappointed. At Newcastle Road, Judy was nowhere to be found, and neighbors were watching his son. When Judy returned home around midnight, quite pregnant with another baby, she informed a stupefied Alf that she'd been raped by a soldier. Initially, she refused to give up his name, but Alf pressed her. Once Judy relented, Alf headed straight off to the Cheshire barracks and dragged the man, one "Taffy" Williams, back to Liverpool to "sort things out." Williams denied raping Judy and pledged his undying love. The rape story quickly unraveled: apparently the two had been seeing each other for well over nine months. But when Alf brought them face-to-face, Judy laughed and threw Williams out of the house.

This second baby realigned family politics. Alf, ever forgiving, offered to stick by Judy and help raise the new child, but Judy refused. Mysteriously, Pop Stanley supported her in this. Ignoring Alf's, Mimi's, and even Williams's offers to bring up the child, and unhappy at the prospect of two fatherless children being raised by an absent, careless mother, Pop insisted that Judy put the new baby up for adoption. Mimi arranged for Judy to stay at Elmswood, a Salvation Army hostel in North Mossley Hill Road. She gave birth to a little girl on June 19, 1944, less than two weeks after D-Day, named her Victoria Elizabeth (did such respectable, patriotic names help Judy legitimize her offspring?), and turned her over for adoption by a Norwegian sailor. (In 1998, a Norwegian woman named Ingrid Pedersen made plausible claims that she was John Lennon's half sister.)[29] Judy forbade Alf ever to mention the baby again. Alf, in his memoirs, describes her personality as forever changed by the giving up of this child; and his emphasis on this moment suggests that he saw it as central to her turning away from the marriage. From most other accounts, though, it appears that Judy remained the same old Judy—a woman who had begun moving on from Alf long before.

There is disagreement among family histories about whether John, almost five, knew that his mother was pregnant and understood what had happened to the baby she bore. Most five-year-olds today know what it means when a woman is pregnant and recognize a pregnant woman when they see one. Many people have described Lennon as an alert, bright, and curious child; it seems unlikely that he would have been oblivious to such a big event. Although Mimi Smith insists that the truth was kept from him, this may have been what Mimi needed to believe. If John did understand what was happening, it can only have increased his feeling that his place in the world was uncertain, even perilous. His mother had given away another child; mightn't she one day give him away, too?

Just before John turned five in autumn 1945, Mimi, stepping into the mother's role, enrolled him in the Mosspits Lane Infant School, the neighborhood kindergarten. That following spring, however, the school dismissed him for severe behavioral problems, which suggests that he was already confused and angry, even before he watched his mother carry another baby and give her away. Nigel Walley, a childhood schoolmate, remembers a scuffle: "John was expelled for being disruptive. . . . I remember he bullied a girl called Polly Hipshaw."[30]

After the birth of Victoria, Alf returned to sea, assuming that his on-again, off-again marriage was back on. But he was gone a long time, and when he returned to Newcastle Road in March 1946 the situation had changed again: Pop Stanley was back in the apartment and had had Alf's name removed from the lease. Someone else was living in the apartment, too: Judy's new boyfriend, a waiter named Bobby Dykins, who worked at the same hotel, the Adelphi, where Alf once had been a bellhop. Why Pop Stanley would tolerate living in the same apartment with his married daughter's lover remains a mystery, unless his distaste for Alf outweighed his disapproval of Dykins.

Coming back to this new arrangement, Alf responded by throwing Dykins out and telling Pops to move out the next day. He was still sending home money to support Judy and John and figured that gave him certain rights. But this time Judy rebelled, announcing that she was moving out, too. Alf didn't take her seriously until he woke up the next morning to find half the furniture on its way out the door. He pleaded with his wife to stay for John's sake, if not for his own. In his memoirs—which offer the only version we have of this conversation—Alf described Judy's response: "What difference will it make to him?" John rarely saw his father anyway, she pointed out. "The sea has always been more important to you than we have." She blamed the rift that had opened between them on his misadventures in New York and Morocco. "You can't just disappear for eighteen months and expect things to be the same."³¹

Taking John with her, Judy went to live with Dykins in a tiny one-bedroom flat across town in Gateacre. Convinced that the marriage was truly over and enraged by his wife's behavior, Alf followed his brother Sydney's advice and hired a lawyer to place notices in the local papers declaring that Alfred Lennon was no longer responsible for his wife's debts.³² But the Gateacre arrangement was short-lived: within months, Judy, John, and Bobby Dykins had moved back into 9 Newcastle Road.

The drama didn't end there. In May of 1946, hours before Alf was due to sail for two weeks on the *Queen Mary* out of Southampton as a night steward, he received a long-distance call from Mimi Smith. Mimi told Alf that John had just walked two miles from Newcastle Road to Mendips because he didn't like living with Judy and Dykins. Mimi put John on the phone to plead with his father not to leave, but Alf said he'd lose his job if he didn't sail—he was still earning back the good faith of his employers after his jail time in New York and Africa. Alf told John to stay with his aunt Mimi and promised he'd be back soon.[33]

When Alf returned to England in June, he docked at Southampton and traveled straight to Mendips to find John. Mimi had already put John down for bed, so she invited Alf back to her kitchen for tea and began itemizing her expenses for taking care of the little boy. Alf gave Mimi a twenty-pound note and accepted her invitation to spend the night. After retiring, he made a momentous decision: he would take John with him. The following morning, he told Mimi he was going to take John for a short holiday at Blackpool, a resort town about thirty miles up the northwest coast from Liverpool. Mimi hesitated. Judy was out of town on "a short trip"—there's no record of where she went or with whom. In Alf's memoirs, Mimi revealed that John had been living with her on and off for about nine months. She may have begun to feel as though she could finally keep him. With Judy out of town, Mimi had misgivings about letting the boy go. But Alf was his father, and perhaps, after taking his money, she didn't feel she could refuse.

When John woke up the next morning, Mimi told him that Alf had come to see his boy and had spent the night. John raced upstairs and jumped on his father in bed. John knew his father, of course, but until that day Alf's visits had always devolved into arguments with Judy, disruption of John's routine, and often a move. With Alf's infrequent time ashore during John's first five years, John had had no chance to form an attachment. Judy had told John stories of their ten-year courtship, "always larking around and laughing." And Alf's letters and postcards had filled John's head with images of his exotic travels. Now his father was finally there, and he told John that they were going on a fabulous holiday.

Did any five-year-old ever get a more irresistible invitation? John begged his aunt to let him go. Mimi packed a small bag for him, and the little boy followed Alf into what must have seemed like a waking dream.

BLACKPOOL HAD LONG BEEN the preferred seaside resort for workers, sailors, and their families in the region's industrial towns, an Atlantic

City on Britain's western shore, complete with a promenade, rides, games, and vendors. Its 1894 Tower replicated the Eiffel Tower in Paris, and three piers were lined with concessions. Holiday goers liked to promenade on its boardwalk, romp in the waves, and visit its amusement park built in an American Style.[34] Although past its prime in 1946, Blackpool still had carnival rides, games to play, donkeys to ride, and prizes to win. Playwright John Osborne set his 1957 play *The Entertainer* in an unnamed Blackpool to symbolize the end of empire during the Suez crisis of 1956. In one of his great, self-lacerating roles (immortalized in Tony Richardson's 1960 film), Laurence Olivier portrayed the repulsive, over-the-hill music-hall comic Archie Rice, and there was a lot of Archie Rice in Alf—a ham past his prime, working his racket in a town sinking from its own faded glory.

To a five-year-old boy accustomed to wartime rationing, however, Blackpool must have seemed like paradise. Alf had abruptly removed John from the physical and emotional rubble of his life in Liverpool to a sunny seaside where he could eat treats and play all day. Now that the war was over, a father finally had time for his boy.

Alf had misrepresented his intentions to Mimi, however. One of his shipmates, a man named Billy Hall, was planning to relocate to New Zealand, and this became Alf's plan, too: he would take his son to New Zealand and start a new life. Having finished two stints in prison and given up on reconciling with Judy, Alf was ready for a big change. Judy wasn't taking proper care of the boy, anyway. In his memoir he wrote, "I set off with John for Blackpool—intending never to come back."

Alf took John with him to Billy Hall's parents' place in Blackpool and set about getting ready for the big move. To fund the trip, though, he and Billy needed to unload some swag. "You couldn't go wrong in those days, just after the war," Alf wrote later. "I was on lots of rackets, mainly bringing back black market stockings. They're probably still selling the stuff in Blackpool I brought over."[35] At some point, Alf needed to leave town for several days, and he took John to stay with his brother Sydney, who had a summer house nearby—a familiar experience for John, whom Judy had handed off several times to Sydney's home in Liverpool. When Alf returned, he was full of talk about their new life abroad.

Alf's point of view has been given little credence in most Lennon histories; he didn't get his say until his second wife published his memoirs in 1990, almost fourteen years after his own death and ten years after John's. For years, Mimi Smith's version of events stood unchallenged. In her version, Alf was a low-class lout who impregnated Judy and then lived the life he'd always lived: as a drifter with no real prospects. He went to Blackpool to run an undergarment black market with his no-good buddy Hall and left John with his brother. In Mimi's view, far from rescuing John, Alf was dumping him with family the same way Judy had. And if John was going to be dumped with a relative, Mimi wanted it to be her.

From Alf's vantage point, Judy gave few signs that she cared much for their son. Alf seems to have truly loved her, however, and even took some responsibility for her behavior. At each juncture, he was willing to carry on with her in spite of a sequence of betrayals. Once she'd decided firmly against him, Alf concluded that he had just as much right to raise their son—he couldn't do any worse than she had. Since he never had the chance to try, we can't say for certain whether he would have made a go of it, but he had no personal experience of a stable home himself. At one point during the Blackpool holiday, he stopped to light a cigarette and John, running ahead, fell into a deep gully in the sand and couldn't climb out. Alf was sufficiently far behind not to have seen where he fell, and he ran up and down the beach for five minutes before discovering the boy at the bottom of the hole, frightened but unhurt.[36] Although this incident reflects badly on Alf, his reporting of it gives the rest of his story added credibility.

The length of the Blackpool holiday is in dispute, but it appears to have lasted three weeks at most. It came to an abrupt end on June 26, when Judy knocked on Billy Hall's door. She'd tracked down her husband through the local "pools"—the dockworkers' work log—and she'd come to retrieve *her* son. Alf was stunned: he was days away from setting off for New Zealand, and the last person he expected to get in his way was his carefree wife.

Dykins had accompanied Judy to the house, and waited nervously by the gate as she went in. In Alf's recollection, Judy didn't seem quite herself; she wouldn't meet his eyes. Her manner was uncharacteristically meek; her spirited and challenging personality seemed muted. She always dressed with panache, but on that day she wore an "ill-shaped" getup that made her look positively matronly—and was definitely out of character for the girl Alf knew and the "wickedly" irresponsible mother Mimi had described to him.[37] Did Judy dress more conservatively to impress Alf with her new commitment to family? Were her awkwardness and subdued manner products of her ambivalence about making the trip—about insisting that Alf give John back? Did she bring Dykins along for moral support, to keep her from being swayed by Alf's charm, or to remind herself that she had another life she wanted to go back to, one that had nothing to do with this man and his child?

Alf sent John into the kitchen to wait with Hall's parents while he and Judy talked in the front room. He begged Judy to get back together with him, told her that he still loved her, and said making up would be good for the boy. The three of them could get a fresh start in New Zealand together. "I could tell she still loved me," he wrote in his memoir. But Judy refused. A reconciliation with Alf was out of the question. She presented herself as newly stable, anxious to finally prove herself and give John the home he deserved. She had set herself up with a new man and planned to make her own fresh start, including having more children, with Dykins.

After they reached this stalemate, the two adults who should have taken the most care to protect their son and choose the best life for him instead did something shockingly cruel. Alf called John in, and the boy ran out from the kitchen and jumped onto his father's lap. John asked if his mother was going to stay with them, if they'd all be going away together. Alf said no. John would have to decide which parent he wanted to go with. Whom did he prefer, his father or his mother? Would he rather stay with his father and travel abroad and have a wonderful adventure in New Zealand, or go back home with his mother (to gray Liverpool) and the life he knew (of not belonging)?

As these two adults sat there, expecting their five-year-old to make his choice, perfectly willing to accept whatever he decided, the ground must have opened up beneath the child. If you've never had a real father and your mother is fun and tenderhearted but unreliable and self-absorbed; if your father is a glamorous adventurer but never around; if you love your mother because she's your mother, but she's distracted (though compellingly mysterious); if you know that choosing your mother doesn't really mean *having* your mother, and choosing your father means . . . what?; if you've watched your mother give away another child; if you've been having a great holiday with the first and only man who has belonged specially to you—whom do you choose? At some level John, consistently described as a sensitive child, may have intuited that either option was essentially tragic: that either choice was simply more abandonment in different clothes.

John chose Alf. He was sitting on Alf's lap; he'd just spent the happiest weeks of his life with his father, and what Alf was offering, speculative though it truly was, probably seemed more enticing than anything he had experienced with his mother. Judy asked again; and when John repeated his choice, she got up and said good-bye. She joined Dykins at the gate and headed up the street. Having left it to a confused five-year-old to decide his own fate, Judy was content to walk off with another man and abandon her child completely—to let him travel halfway around the world, perhaps never to see him again.

Within seconds, panicking, John ran out of the house after Judy. What five-year-old could watch his mother, even a careless mother like Judy, walk away forever and not call her back? He ran after her. And this time it was Alf who turned away. He didn't try to stop the boy. He'd shown the kid a good time, showered him with treats and toys, and John didn't want to go with him. That was that. Alf didn't change his plans and stay in England to be near his son. He went off to New Zealand with Hall and continued to travel as he had before. His own mother had abandoned him when he was young—it was clearly acceptable to walk away from your children and leave them to other people to raise. He'd given the boy a chance to have a father, and the boy had chosen against him; and for Alf, that was decisive. That night at his pub, he recalled, he sang Al Jolson's number, "My Little Pal," as "My Little John," with tears in his eyes. But he never made another attempt to contact John until his son had become famous, when Alf approached him—eighteen years later—on the set of *A Hard Day's Night*.[38]

THIS BLACKPOOL TRAUMA ricocheted one last time back in Liverpool. Mimi may have deputized Judy to go to Blackpool and retrieve John, but she still felt as though John belonged to her. She hated that Judy had moved in with another man while she was still legally married to Alf and raising his son. Even if this suited Judy—what about the child? It was as if Judy didn't give a hang about the Stanleys' hard-won reputation. Mimi decided to claim her nephew even if it meant wrenching him from his mother. Surely, a home with both a father and a mother figure would be preferable to a broken home with an illegal, live-in stepfather. Even before the Blackpool trip, hadn't John run away (at least once that we know of) to demonstrate his discomfort with Judy's new boyfriend?

Mimi alerted Liverpool Social Services, telling them that her sister was an "unfit mother." Although a social worker visited the Newcastle Road apartment twice during that summer of 1946, it wasn't until the second visit that John's lack of a bed seemed to register with the officials. When Social Services insisted that she find an alternative situation for the boy or they would be forced to take him from her, Judy handed off her son to Mimi for the last time. For Judy, giving John to Mimi was both an abdication of parenthood and a surrender to Mimi's driving will—and one Dykins favored, with his natural desire for a family of his own.[39]

Mimi Smith had good reason to be concerned about John's home life, but her motives mixed simple compassion with self-interest, creating a second complicated layer of possession and competition for John as he turned six years old that October of 1946. The questions a child wrestles with at this age of psychological development—Where do I belong? Who will take care of me? Where can I feel safe?—were hardwired as confusion into John's young mind. Born into a failing marriage between a heedless girl-about-town and a perpetually absent seafaring father, John Lennon began his life rootless. Shuttled from dwelling to dwelling, handed off repeatedly to a possessive aunt or to one of his uncles, he was relocated more than half a dozen times before he was five. Despite his troublemaking at school, many adults who met John at the time describe him as a charming, cheerful little boy. Several people besides Mimi Smith offered to adopt him, including his uncle Sydney and Billy Hall's parents. Nonetheless, he was, in a fundamental and obvious way, unclaimed.

Lennon was installed in his familiar bedroom in Mendips the autumn of 1946, and for years afterward he saw his mother only sporadically. Mimi Smith later said that at first John wanted to know where his mother was, but she dodged his questions. "I didn't want to tell him any details," she said. "How could I? He was so happy. It would have been wrong to say your father's no good and your mother's found someone else."[40] Although Lennon himself never described the Blackpool episode in any of his interviews or writings, he did report on its aftermath. "I soon forgot my father," he said. "It was like he was dead. But I did see my mother now and again and my feeling never died off for her. I often thought about her, though I never realized that all the time she was living no more than five or ten miles away. Mimi never told me. She said she was a long, long way away."[41]

In quick order, Judy and Dykins moved out of the tiny Newcastle Road apartment into a larger one in Allerton, where they raised two girls of their own, Julia, born in 1947, and Jacqueline, two years later, but the couple never married. This apartment, at 1 Blomfield Road in a council-estate development called Spring Wood, was across the Allerton Golf Course from Mendips, not far from the newer council houses where a family named McCartney would soon settle.

Something to Hide

THERE'S NO MORE MISLEADING LENNON MYTH THAN THE ONE SPUN from his 1970 song "Working Class Hero," which every self-respecting Liverpudlian renounces as a sham. "He was solidly *middle-class*," they'll tell you proudly, as if Lennon's ironic broadside insults all the hard work that town did after the war to give him a proper upbringing. Widely misheard as an ode to the rewards of hard work, a homage to the mean streets of Merseyside, the song dissects class pretensions and the stigma of being labeled "common." Lennon wrote it for his Beatle "divorce" album, *Plastic Ono Band* (1970), and he repeats the line "A working class hero is something to be." But his voice drops to sardonic resignation on its rejoinder: "If you want to be a hero well just follow me."

A working-class hero *would* be something to be, but he's not one of them. Rather than a paean to the moral superiority of a hard-earned work ethic, the song spins an emphatic, unsentimental rejoinder to such cant. Of all the lingering fictions surrounding Lennon's persona as his myth enters history, this one deserves the strongest riposte. A suburban kid who had become one of the world's most famous men by the time he was twenty-three, Lennon used "Working Class Hero" to push back at the idea that hard work brings honor to a man, that it's the key to success and self-respect, and a form of heroism in and of itself. In the song, he turns that cliché into a curse, the irony bent by experience: "There's room at the top they are telling you still/But first you must learn how to smile as you kill." Like the sugarcoated agnosticism of "Imagine," Lennon's most famously misinterpreted song, "Working Class Hero" undermines the very truism it purports to celebrate. Liverpudlians scoff at the idea of Lennon's rough-and-tumble childhood, especially when compared to the other three Beatles'. And Lennon played both sides of this line.

Raised by his auntie in Woolton, in a semidetached house eight miles in from the docks, he became infatuated with rock 'n' roll poetry the way Andy Warhol was drawn to advertising. Lennon was easily the most privileged of the four Beatles, but he strove hard to hide it beneath his contempt for class hypocrisy.

The Woolton house in which Lennon grew up with the Smiths was named Mendips after the Mendip Hills, a stretch of low-rolling curves in the comfortably middle-class region between Bristol and Wells in Somerset, southeast of the Bristol Channel.[1] Joined to a row of "comfortable" dwellings, similar to an American duplex or side-by-side two-family, Mendips overlooked Menlove Avenue, a main thoroughfare through Woolton Village. Menlove Avenue branched off a main avenue, Ullet Road, after Penny Lane, and curved around Calderstones Park and the Allerton Golf Course. A semidetached house was a big step up from the thousands of attached council row houses—state housing projects—that snaked through the dockworkers' neighborhoods. While not as luxurious as the single-family homes just up the Church Road near St. Peter's, Mendips was built of solid red sandstone from the local quarry and was regarded as an upper-middle-class dwelling. During John's childhood, the mayor of Woolton, in fact, lived next door.[2]

Woolton and its adjacent suburbs attracted the professional classes— doctors, lawyers, politicians—as well as prosperous retailers like the Epstein family, who lived in nearby Childwall and whose youngest son, Brian, would play a critical role in Lennon's future. The prouder Woolton residents even claimed their own dialect, far removed from the docker's Scouse, an Anglo-Saxon variant that resembled the better accents of South Lancashire and Cheshire.

Although built in 1933, Mendips possessed a certain old-world charm, including a small portico between the front porch and front hall made of glass brick. On the right side of a central hallway, a brick fireplace dominated the front room, which had leaded glass windows. On the left of the front hall, stairs led to two bedrooms. In the back of the house, a small sitting room, used as a dining space, abutted a kitchen with broad terraced windows, both of which looked out on Mimi Smith's prized side garden. The garden, the house's "proper" front hallway and vestibule, the fireplace lined with books, the cozy sitting room—all were middle-class accoutrements. John's small bedroom on the second floor faced the house's sole bathroom, or "water closet," which had a pull-chain toilet and tiny bath. None of the other Beatles had indoor toilets; all three lived in neighborhoods that relied on unheated outhouses. Compared to the houses in most dockside neighborhoods, such as the Dingle, where Ringo's family lived, Mendips seemed vast.

The American notion of "suburb" has far more expanse and roominess—ranch houses, broad lawns. Woolton houses were pitched much closer together, but the neighborhood was quiet and safe. The town also hosted plenty of undeveloped land that kids explored on foot and by bicycle, including the hilly area around St. Peter's Church and cemetery called Woolton Hills; the grounds of the Strawberry Field Salvation Army home for problem children; and the playing fields surrounding the Quarry Bank High School on Harthill Road, which John would later attend. While Lennon was growing up, the Allerton golf course literally spilled across Menlove Avenue just beyond his front gate; he could spy the pond from his living-room window.

JOHN MOVED INTO Mendips permanently in July or August of 1946, and his aunt took charge. His life became more stable psychologically—he didn't need to adapt to the moods and personality of a different adult every few months. He could let himself become attached to the household's pets—two cats, Tich and Tim, and a mutt named Sally whom he adored. "Mimi was a cat lover," schoolmate Len Garry remembers. "She loved her cats more than she loved kids, that's for sure. She was a frightening woman.

She wasn't homely—she was more like a headmistress, librarian-type person. And you were frightened to knock on that Mendips front door."[3]

John eventually added a fourth animal to the brood, Sam, a stray cat that he brought home one evening. He also played regularly with his cousins, the children of Judy's other three sisters. Elizabeth, the second of the five Stanley girls, had married a man named Charles Parkes, who died during the war. Their son, Stanley Parkes, was seven years John's senior and looked out for his younger cousin, holding his hand when they went to the park. John was also close to his cousin Leila,[4] three years older than John and later the widow of an Egyptian named Ali Hafez. Stanley remembers the three of them playing outside at Mendips while their mothers visited:

> Little Leila, John and myself would go to Mimi's and play in the garden there and then go round to Aunt Harriet's cottage which was half of Uncle George's farm. Mimi owned half of the farmhouse, which was known as The Cottage to us, and we'd sit there and we'd play records—all kinds of records. Harriet had one of the old-fashioned wind-up HMV gramophones and she had a vast collection of records and we'd spend hours playing them.[5]

Stanley called Mimi "strict but all right":

> She had an orchard in the back of her garden with apple trees and pear trees and she would bake lovely apple pies for us and we'd have picnics. She had a garden shed in the back garden and as I say, being strict, she was very strict on our table manners, but she said "Alright you can go and eat out in the garden shed." To us it was a great adventure going out into this shed, and just to be naughty we would eat with our hands with no knives and forks. Just devilment you know.

In the summers, Mimi sent John up to Edinburgh, where his aunt Elizabeth, called "Mater," had settled with Bertie Sutherland, a dentist, who became Stanley's stepfather. Elizabeth and Bertie took in all the Stanley cousins during the summer, including Leila and, later, Judy's two daughters with Dykins, Julia and Jacqui, Lennon's half sisters. Early on, Stanley played the big brother:

> When I first moved up to Scotland, I would go down to bring John up because Mary [Mimi] wouldn't let him go anywhere unchaperoned, but as he grew a little bit older she did relent and let him come up on the bus. . . . I'd meet him off the bus at Edinburgh bus depot and take him to my parents' home at Murrayfield in Edinburgh. He'd stay there a week or so and then off we'd go up to the Sutherland family croft up in Durness in Sutherland at Cape Wrath, which is the most fartherly north west tip of Scotland.

ALTHOUGH JOHN BENEFITED from Mimi's steadiness, her predictable schedules and reliable husband, he'd also landed in the home of a domineering, anxious woman who could not have been more different from his mother. To those who knew them both, John's character resembled Judy's—his moods swung between cocky and funny to pensive and remote. Many describe a level gaze and a self-possession unusual for a boy. He had a penchant for practical jokes and theatrical gestures, and enjoyed shocking his peers. His cousin Stanley recounted: "Leila had a lovely little doll's pram and one time she was walking round the garden with this doll's pram and John and I climbed up on the top of this garden shed and John said 'Watch this!' and he jumped off the shed clean through the bottom of Leila's pram! She was mortified over that."

Where Mimi was authoritarian, her husband, George Smith, was soft-spoken and affectionate, and universally beloved. "George was a gentle giant," recalls Julia Dykins Baird in the first of her two memoirs, *John Lennon, My Brother*. "Six foot tall with a mound of silver hair, who often hit the door frame when he walked into a room. He was the most kind, pleasant, and unaggressive man with not a cross word to say."[6] Even before John moved in with them, George would sit the little boy on his lap in the evening and read through all the *Liverpool Echo* headlines with him. "Syllable by syllable," Mimi remembered, "George would work at him till he got it right. John couldn't spell at that age, of course, but he could get down what he wanted. My husband went through all the headlines in the newspaper with John every night."[7]

While Smith, with his brother, inherited his family's dairy, he struggled with a problem that had already marked Lennon's life: he was a drinker—not a violent or a sloppy drunk, but one who was sufficiently handicapped by his drinking that he couldn't keep his business thriving. Cynthia Powell Lennon later reported Mimi complaining about his "gambling," and Mimi often took student boarders to make ends meet.[8] To accommodate this arrangement, Mimi slept in the sitting room off the kitchen, turning the front living room into the only shared common room.

At one point, a group of George's friends from the neighborhood— his pub crowd—gave him a half-grandfather clock with "George Toogood Smith" inscribed on its face, which was actually his christened name. This clock stood on the mantel in the sitting room off the kitchen at Mendips throughout John's childhood, a reminder of Mimi's ideal man, the kind she had chosen to marry. The men in Mimi's house needed to be better than just good—they needed to be *too* good. And the pressure to be "too good" took its toll, on George and, over time, on John, too.

In the fall of 1946, Mimi enrolled John in the Dovedale Primary School in Allerton. To get there, Lennon took a long bus ride down the main Menlove thoroughfare with a change at Penny Lane (with Mimi trailing him from behind), or walked through the vast stretch of Calderstones Park—or sometimes a combination of the two routes, depending on the season. The headmaster there, a man named Bond, told Mimi: "There's no need to worry about him. He's sharp as a needle. But he won't do anything he doesn't want to."[9] The school uniforms put John in a tie, black blazer, a badge with a dove, and gray shorts. Lennon's classmates remember his tie constantly askew and his shirt deliberately untucked.

Comedian Jimmy Tarbuck, one of his Dovedale classmates, says of Lennon at the time, "He wasn't easily missed at school—he wasn't the sort of kid to stand in corners, studiously reading his books. Oh no, he had a load of energy even then. . . . If there was a playground fight, he'd be involved in it."[10] At the end of Lennon's first year at Dovedale, Fred Bolt, one of his teachers, took several students for a brief summer jaunt to the Isle of Man, off the coast of Britain in the Irish Sea. A photo survives of Lennon and Tarbuck and a group of boys horsing around in the surf at Port Erin, near the isle's ferry dock. John and Jimmy dominate the picture: Jimmy's fists are clenched, his right arm pulled up as if threatening a punch, his face seized by a prankster's grin. He looks ready to pounce on the photographer. To his left, Lennon wears a question mark. Mimi had trimmed his hair close on the sides, and his left hand is extended downward instead of up in the air like Jimmy's. Of the eight boys, John alone is not laughing, an early and rare instance of a camera catching a fleeting vulnerability.

When John was eight, Mimi enrolled him in the Sunday school at St. Peter's, the local Anglican church, where John sang in the choir. Two friends from his neighborhood, Ivan Vaughan and Nigel Walley, remember Lennon teaching them to palm pennies from the St. Peter's collection plate so that they could buy bubble gum. Vaughan and Walley lived nearby on Vale Road, which ran parallel to Menlove Avenue, one street behind. Also at church school were Rod Davis, a future Quarryman, and Barbara Baker, one of John's earliest girlfriends.

AT DOVEDALE, JOHN BECAME fast friends with Pete Shotton, a towheaded boy whose family also lived on Vale Road and attended St. Peter's. Everyone who knew them at Dovedale remembers them as inseparable. Pete, teasing John about his high-toned middle name, called him "Winnie," which John hated. Lennon tagged Shotton "Snowball" for his blonder-than-blond hair. As they grew closer ("our relationship came to resemble that of Siamese twins"), John referred to them as "Shennon and Lotton."[11]

In the beginning, John, the more aggressive of the two, pushed Pete around. Only after standing up to him did Shotton earn Lennon's respect. In his memoir, *John Lennon: In My Life* (written with Nicholas

Schaffner in 1983), Shotton describes recognizing that the only way he could stay friends with Lennon and keep his self-respect was to stick up for himself after one of Lennon's barbs. One day after science lab, when John had ribbed Shotton mercilessly in front of others, Pete confronted him: "If you want to be like that, I'm not fucking playing with you anymore." Apparently unfazed, Lennon started tapping Shotton on the head with a bicycle pump, asking, "Getting the egg, are you? Getting the egg, then, Shotton?"—roughly translated, "Am I making you angry?" At this point, Shotton realized, he had to make a choice: face up to Lennon's bullying or forever be bullied by him. So he socked John in the nose.

Though Shotton never expected that to put an end to it, Lennon let the matter go with a dismissal that left them both smiling, and he never humiliated Shotton again. "I really respected you for that," Lennon later told Shotton. "I knew you were in awe of me, and yet you had the guts to turn round and say 'That's enough!' The last thing I ever expected you to do was to hit me—that was one of the biggest surprises of my life. . . . I'd really thought I had you sussed."[12]

From early on, Shotton reported, Lennon had more nerve and guile than most kids, so other boys quickly followed his lead. In class, Lennon passed around funny caricatures of the teacher and other students, daring his friends to keep a straight face as his pictures made the rounds. Fooling around one evening on the site of a new housing development being built in the neighborhood, Lennon and Shotton let the nightwatchman chase them into an empty, darkened house. Unable to find them in the dark, the frustrated man planted his feet and called out, commanding the boys to leave at once. Lennon began howling like a ghost, and the poor man fled downstairs, while Lennon and Shotton burst into peals of triumphant laughter.[13]

Another local friend, David Ashton, remembers Lennon as "alluring and beguiling, even bewitching to be with or near sometimes, even spellbinding and never boring," a Liverpudlian Huckleberry Finn. "He knew things or found them out and if he liked you he got you into trouble!" One day Ashton was playing football with Lennon, Shotton, Vaughan, and Walley in a cow field near Woolton Hill when a "posh" boy named Robert Bancroft showed up and started playing rugby. Ashton remembers scrambling to learn the rules, with Lennon instructing him on tackling: "Grab him, pull down his 'keks' (trousers) and rub his balls with cowpat."[14]

Lennon moved up to the Dovedale Junior School for boys in 1948. By the time Lennon was ten, Shotton remembers he was talking about "[popular British children's author] Richmal Crompton, Edgar Allan Poe, James Thurber, Edward Lear, Kenneth Grahame (*Wind in the Willows*), Robert Louis Stevenson, and Lewis Carroll." Shotton says that *Alice in Wonderland* and *Through the Looking-Glass* were particular favorites—"like the Bible to us both." John loved Lewis Carroll's fantastical gibberish "Jabberwocky." "John's ultimate ambition," Shotton says, "was to one day 'write an *Alice* himself.' "[15]

The Reverend Morris Pryce-Jones, rector of St. Peter's Church, also took his Sunday-school classes on various school trips. When he took them to Llandudno, a seaside resort on the northern Welsh coast, the boys marveled at the water's "turquoise-blue" hues: "It was clean!" David Ashton recalls. "We choirboys were used to the grimy, dirty River Mersey water as it was then (it's much cleaner nowadays). John Lennon's comment was 'Shakespeare said "The quality of Mersey is not pure" ' and I got in to trouble at school later for saying it and had to write out a hundred times the correct Shakespeare quotation 'The quality of Mercy is not strained.' "[16]

Lennon took his 11-plus exam at Dovedale in 1952. With the passage of the Education Act of 1944, the British school system began sorting older students using a "tripartite" system: grammar school for the most gifted, secondary school for most kids, and technical college for vocational training. Assignments were based on the 11-plus, an all-important comprehensive exam, named for the age cutoff that determined each child's intellectual capacities and future prospects. John seems to have passed the test without much preparation or study.

"I do remember him at Dovedale as not making a lot of effort," said Michael Isaacson, another classmate. "But he had obvious talent, because getting through the 11-plus in those days wasn't an easy task. Only the minority passed."[17] Lennon may not have been especially studious, but he was an avid reader, according to his aunt. "I had twenty volumes of the world's best short stories and we had a love of books in common," claimed Mimi Smith. "John used to go back and read them over and over again, particularly Balzac. I thought there was a lot of Balzac in his song writing later on. Anyway, he'd read most of the classics by the time he was ten. He had such imagination and built up the stories himself when he and I talked them over."[18]

By the time he was eleven or twelve, Lennon had developed a passion for drawing, and soon he was churning out savagely funny cartoons and precocious political satire. Lennon's jokes, puns, and cartoons soon leapt from his notebook into a stapled flyer he edited called the *Daily Howl*.[19] The headlines whir past in Lennon's mock-authoritative voice, many of them nonsensical, inscrutable, yet irresistible: QUEENE ANNE IS DEAD reads a typical headline from 1950 (the year of Princess Anne's birth, on August 15) surrounded by musical notes dancing to and fro. STOP PRESS: DAVID NIXON IS GETTING A TONY CURTIS, reads another, referring to a then-famous children's TV magician getting either a haircut or a movie career. ARE YOU A CATYLIST . . . OR A PRETESTANT, OR A CHRISTIAN? a third headline asks provocatively. Throughout this absurdist wordplay, with jumbled names and spellings and wacky rhymes, Lennon illustrated people with swollen heads, dogs with spectacles, and wide-eyed figures twisted into pretzel poses. His publication circulated around the class as much to baffle as to entertain his schoolmates.

Crude yet compelling, the *Howl* window-frames Lennon's careening adolescent mind. An acutely engaged personality already in full-tilt rebellion, Lennon ridicules the emphatic irrationality of grown-ups and casts politics as so much light entertainment. His adults are the type only kids can see: wearing funny costumes and making ridiculous pronouncements in their overserious voices. It was the *Liverpool Echo* and the mighty BBC News tossed about like pies in a food fight, celebrity pretense deflated with affectionate disdain.

Passing his 11-plus exam qualified Lennon to enroll at one of the preferred grammar schools, and Mimi selected the Quarry Bank High School, even though it was considered less prestigious academically than other secondary schools in the area—such as Prescot, Liverpool Colle-giate, and the Liverpool Institute. But it had a reputation for discipline, and John, she thought, needed that. The other boys called it "the Army." When he entered Quarry Bank in 1952 at age eleven, Lennon was primed to rebel against the school's conservative style. In response to Quarry Bank's rote method of teaching, Lennon made it his mission to disrupt and disobey. Pete Shotton remembered John tying string on the doors of old ladies' houses to keep them shut,[20] setting alarm clocks to go off during lectures, rigging blackboards to collapse when a master turned to write on them, filling bicycle pumps with ink,[21] and cadging unused lunch tickets to turn into cash.[22] Lennon later reported, with some pride, that "most of the masters hated me like shit." Former school-mates remember him as a troublemaker, the ringleader in planning pranks, with a cruel streak. His caricatures were particularly abusive to cripples and the mentally retarded; he had a troubling impulse to strike out at people weaker than him.

Lennon and his friends also enjoyed rafting in the pond at Foster's Field, which was adjacent to the Strawberry Field home, and to fool Aunt Mimi they'd build a bonfire and dry their clothes before returning home, "a process we found so amusing that we began setting fires just for the sake of it," said Pete Shotton.[23] Also common were ongoing rival-ries with groups of Catholic kids, who went to Sunday school next door to St. Peter's, at St. Anne's, and carried on the battles of their Irish ances-tors. "We called [the Protestant kids] the 'Orange Protties,'" one Catho-lic resident remembered, "and there were very real pockets of prejudice in some households."[24]

AT GRAMMAR SCHOOL, Lennon's reputation for daring spread. Every year on Guy Fawkes Day, November 5, the Woolton Tip, a former pond that had been filled in after the war, was the site of a community bon-fire. Hanging out on the day before the event with Pete Shotton, Ivan Vaughan, Len Garry, Bill Turner, and another friend, Lennon had a brainstorm. The wood was all piled up for the bonfire—why not light it a day early? That would turn some heads! The others quickly agreed.

Shotton ran home to retrieve some matches, which they then "applied to the great heap of combustibles." Once the fire was set, the boys retreated to the embankment across Menlove Avenue and waited for the commotion.

Suddenly, the whole of young Woolton emerged from their houses, attracted by the blaze, some with buckets of water, trying to put it out. Celebration quickly turned to panic, and Lennon and his mates streaked across the Allerton Golf Course for fear of catching the blame. But the gods were smiling. "The next day, to his horror," Shotton wrote, "Bill Turner was accosted in his schoolyard by Brian Halliday, the local bully. 'If I ever find out who it was that lit our fucking bonfire,'" Shotton recalled him saying to Turner, "'I'm gonna fucking KILL 'em!' 'Right, Bri,' Bill agreed, expecting his own voice to betray him any second. 'That was a really rotten trick, wasn't it, Bri?' Fortunately for us, we all managed to keep our cool (and our secret)."[25]

To distinguish himself from his peers, Lennon adopted the trendy "Teddy Boy" garb, named for its satiric use of Edwardian jackets over flagrantly colorful shirts and tight jeans ("drainpipes")—think of Elvis's pink shirts and greased-back hair filtered through turn-of-the-century British dandies. One of Lennon's Quarry Bank classmates, Michael Hill, remembers that Lennon "managed to look like a Teddy Boy even in uniform."[26] Peter Blake's famous *Self-Portrait with Badges,* from 1961, depicts a typical British youth in his backyard who looks at the viewer with aghast silence, wearing a fruit salad of buttons on his denim jacket, holding an Elvis movie magazine, pledging his undying visual devotion to American culture—as if by adopting the insignia of the prevailing postwar power, he might adopt some of its confidence for himself. Blake's subtext is Thomas Gainsborough's *Blue Boy* ravaged by American wealth.

The "Teddies" fused their own cultural heritage with the American Beats. The word "beatnik" was a derogatory term coined by the reactionary San Francisco columnist Herb Caen in 1958, the "nik" suffix tacked onto the root word to echo "Sputnik" and brand the scene as un-American. Poet Allen Ginsberg, the author of *Howl,* responded to Caen's meretricious term in the *New York Times*: "The foul word beatnik," Ginsberg wrote, was already media simplification of a thriving counterculture. "If beatniks and not illuminated Beat poets overrun this country, they will have been created not by Kerouac but by industries of mass communication which continue to brainwash man."²⁷

Lennon encountered the Beat sensibility through movies like *The Wild One* (1953) with Marlon Brando and, later, books like Jack Keruoac's *On the Road* (1957)—both of which Shotton mentions as Lennon favorites. Of course, Hollywood quickly reduced "beatniks" to a series of clichés: goatees, shades, black turtlenecks, coffee houses, "crazy, man" jargon, and the like. Maynard G. Krebs, the goofball *Dobie Gillis* TV character played by Bob Denver, before he became Gilligan, typified this beatnik stereotype. But cultural historian Ray Carney writes how false this idea was: "Beat culture was a state of mind, not a matter of how you dressed or talked or where you lived. In fact, Beat culture was far from monolithic. It was many different, conflicting, shifting states of mind."²⁸

For British youth, this attitude—the cool persona in ironic, turn-of-the-century Edwardian clothes—overlapped with the notion of a rising class of "angry young men," first depicted in John Osborne's fearsome play *Look Back in Anger* (1956). Jimmy Porter, Osborne's hero, voiced underclass resentments about the limited opportunities and the constraints of life in cash-strapped, post-Empire Britain. While much of the rhetoric in Osborne's play sounds dated now, at the time its language splashed cold water on polite British society's façade.

Britain's Teds echoed their American Beat counterparts with a ritualized dress code to look cool; but Teddy Boys were strictly a teenage phenomenon, and more about style than either art or politics. Lennon's Teddy-Boy image served several purposes. It set him apart as an outsider, rebelling against his school, his aunt, and the establishment tastes and values they represented, although his actual rebellions were pretty minor. "The sort of gang I [ran with] went in for things like shoplifting and pulling girls' knickers down," Lennon said years later. "I was scared at the time, but Mimi was the only parent who never found out." Emboldened by their Guy Fawkes Day triumph, Lennon and his buddies became more daring, and moved on from shoplifting candy to stealing things they could sell, such as cigarettes.

Taking on the image of a Teddy Boy also allowed Lennon to express a creative exuberance in his dress that monotonous school uniforms never allowed. Most of all, it made him look tough—which his insecurities made him desperate to do. Lennon needed his Teddy-Boy image, he later told his first wife, Cynthia, precisely because he didn't feel strong at all on the inside. He believed he had a better chance of avoiding a run-in with genuinely tough kids if he simply looked fierce enough. "If he was really pushed," however, she reported, "he could fight as dirty as his attackers and frequently did in the old days. . . . [But] John was a self-confessed coward [and] he would use every trick in the book to avoid a confrontation."[29] Lennon was so successful at creating a tough image for himself that he became notorious for it. Paul McCartney remembers hearing about Lennon before actually meeting him: "John was the local Ted. You saw him rather than met him."[30]

According to Quarry Bank's conservative headmaster of the early 1950s, E. R. Taylor, Lennon was easily the most unruly student he had to deal with in his career. Taylor's replacement, William Ernest Pobjoy, who took over in Lennon's second year—and famously abolished corporal punishment at the school—adopted a more progressive outlook. "John was a very talented lad, but from junior school he had taken a delight in mischief," Pobjoy later recalled. "Things were different in those days, and I remember one of the remarks on his report was a complaint from a teacher about John, who had been caught gambling on the cricket field during a house match. Cricket was taken very seriously in those days. I remember that the last thing written on his final report was that he could go far."[31] Busy with his personal and stylistic rebellion, Lennon brushed off classes and, at sixteen, failed the next round of exams in the British diagnostic pyramid, the O-levels.

Lennon's early pranks had conceptual flair. One term Lennon was miffed to learn that his friends Garry and Turner, students at the Liverpool Institute, would get a day off for "teachers' training" while Quarry Bank was still in session. Taking Lennon's dare, the two of them showed up at Lennon's art class in their Institute uniforms, claiming to be new students who'd just enrolled and whose parents had bought them the wrong clothes. As the instructor, a man named Martin, started writing down their names, in walked Pete Shotton, anxious to see how the ruse was going. He told Martin he was retrieving his pen from Lennon, who protested with mock self-righteousness: "I haven't seen your pen. Furthermore I strongly object to you coming in and disturbing me working. And I am sure I speak on behalf of Mr. Martin as well." "I must say I agree with Lennon on this occasion," Martin responded. "Shotton, you will write out 500 lines saying 'I must not interrupt Mr. Martin's Art Class,' and let me have them in the morning." "A week later," Len Garry recalled, "in our morning assembly at the Institute, the headmaster . . . mentioned in passing about an incident in which Quarry Bank had been 'infiltrated by the enemy.' We were later given a sharp reprimand by the head—but we got knowing smiles from the other teachers. For the rest of that term, we were heroes in the school."[32]

Rod Davis remembers how many teachers made a distinction between their admiration for Lennon's talent and their role as his superiors. "These stories would get around the teachers' staff room, but I don't think Lennon appreciated that the teachers really thought a lot of him. The last thing they could possibly do is admit it!"[33]

Shotton remembered another teacher, Mr. McDermott, who could never be bothered to read student essays; he simply put a red check mark in the margin and handed them back. For an assignment on St. Paul's journey to Damascus, Lennon wrote, "On the road to Damascus, a burning pie flew out of the window and hit St. Paul right between the eyes and when he came to he was blind forever." McDermott returned the essay with his usual mark.

"What McDermott really wants is a class full of fucking vicars," Lennon told Shotton. "Why not give it to him?" Together they cut forty cardboard "dog collars" out of cereal boxes and gave one to every student in his class. That day McDermott came in, opened his briefcase, pulled out his papers, and started to read "in his boring religious voice." When he finally looked up at his class, he froze, dropping his jaw midsentence. "And then he laughs and laughs and laughs," Shotton remembered. "His enormous frame shakes so much I thought he'd have a seizure. 'That was terrific, boys,' he says. 'What a prank.' He enjoyed it so much he made us keep on our dog collars for the rest of the lesson."[34]

As he began having his head, Lennon skipped class often. On his 1956 Christmas report card, where the "absent" marks go right down the page, his math teacher, Mr. Nixon—known as "Old Nick," according to Rod Davis—wrote: "Term mark: 17 percent. If he continues like this, this boy's bound to fail!" Davis explains how this remark got misinterpreted: "So this is December 1956, and in July he's going to be taking his maths GCE exam, right? [It's] a perfectly reasonable statement to make after all these absences!" But that "bound to fail" remark proved irresistible to biographers. Lennon himself bandied it around with interviewers, and it's trailed him ever since.

Lennon lumped Quarry Bank into his larger story about his troubles with Aunt Mimi and his restless adolescence. But some of his school friends argue that it wasn't so bad and that Lennon painted his Quarry Bank teachers with a very broad brush. "Many of them had served in the war and were wonderful characters and storytellers," Davis recalled, citing a math teacher named Fred Yule, "who had been a bomber navigator and sported a metal leg which creaked so that you could hear him coming for some distance! He was so strong that he once lifted Lennon clean off the ground by his lapels!"[35]

Despite his carefree attitude, Lennon paid more attention than he let on. Convinced he was smarter than the snobs who controlled his days, Lennon resolved to drop out of school as soon as he could. In the meantime, in an offhanded way, he designed his own program of education—reading, drawing, and soaking up knowledge from the emergent pop culture of Liverpool and Britain in the 1950s. His Quarry Bank grades and teachers' notes show high marks in History and Geography.[36] Moreover, Pobjoy, the Quarry Bank headmaster, became John's chief advocate in getting him into art college after graduation despite being, along with the teachers, the occasional target of Lennon's caricatures. Davis recalled an annual fair at St. Peter's where the Quarry Bank boys were operating booths. "John had done these drawings of the teachers. . . . If you got three darts on your favorite master, you won something. These caricatures were absolutely brilliant. I've got a copy of the *Sunday Express* magazine which has copies of these, and they are still brilliant when you look at them now. And this was when he was in fourth year!"

Lennon always spoke about how marginalized he felt, and how few teachers seemed to believe in him. But Davis thinks this gets overblown: Lennon received high marks when he paid attention, and many enjoyed his cartoons and practical jokes. Davis insists the teachers felt conflicted about Lennon. At Quarry Bank, "everybody considered themselves part of the 'top slice,' the most promising young minds with the most promising futures." The faculty, he says, "couldn't very well encourage his rebellions—otherwise, the entire fabric of what was going on would fall apart." Reigning cultural mores simply didn't allow them to reward his antics. Davis chortles when he remembers how they felt: "Apart from locking him up, there wasn't a lot they could do with him!"[37]

She Said She Said

Lennon's teenage years paralleled Britain's postwar penury. Rock 'n' roll was not quite a rumor on the English music scene. The Marshall Plan had swept into Europe in 1948, resurrecting the Continent and rebuilding destroyed cities, but Britain hardly shared in its bounty. With war debt still dragging on the economy, interest rates held at punitive. The country was barely able to service its existing obligations, never mind borrow more for rebuilding. As historian Paul Johnson writes in *Modern Times:*

> The war had cost [the UK] $30 billion, a quarter of her net wealth. She had sold $5 billion of foreign assets and accumulated $12 billion of foreign debts. America had given her a post-war loan, but this did not cover the gap in her trade—exports in 1945 were less than a third of the 1938 figure—nor her outgoings as a slender pillar of stability in Europe, the Mediterranean and the Middle East.[1]

At the same time, in response to international pressure, Britain began dismantling its empire, which meant writing off revenues from former colonies. Struggling to mend its battered cities and absorbing the loss of a previous generation's imperial glory, the British populace experienced the first decade after the war as a time of prolonged shortages.

TIM RILEY | 43

The shelling had stopped, but food rationing continued until 1954. During the same period—the years between Lennon's move into Mimi Smith's house and his embrace of rock 'n' roll ten years later—the United States experienced an unprecedented level of economic expansion, giving American teenagers more free time and more cash to spend on their own amusement. Teens in postwar Britain, however, suffered privation far removed from the American boom. This cultural gap had profound effects on how early rock 'n' roll history played out.

The underfunded, state-run British Broadcasting Corporation (BBC) didn't even launch a television news service until 1954. Only in 1955 did England finally see glimmers of an economic resurgence similar to the one broadcast from the United States. That same year, the Independent Television Network (ITV) was launched, with the aim of providing more lively, up-to-date, and entertaining programming. Still, at that time, only 30 percent of Britons owned television sets (compared to more than 50 percent in the U.S.), and working- and lower-middle-class kids in Liverpool families were not among them. Luckily for John, Pete Shotton's policeman father had bought one of the first televisions in the neighborhood, and Pete lived only one block over, on Vale Road. The 1953 coronation of Queen Elizabeth would be the medium's first broadcast event in England well before any boom.

This postwar privation caused British adolescents to experience the mid-1950s rock explosion much differently from their American counterparts. The BBC Light Programme played mainstream standards, Tin Pan Alley tunes, and occasional big band music, but Liverpool ears sought out many more styles than dreamt of by the BBC. If anything, its bustling seaport resembled the Memphis train junction, with new products and influences streaming in daily. Once a haven for hundreds of thousands of Irish fleeing the great potato famine and a hub for slave traders during the mid-nineteenth century, Merseyside also housed Europe's first Chinatown. "Liverpool is where the Irish came when they ran out of potatoes, and it's where black people were left or worked as slaves or whatever," Lennon remembered. "We were a great amount of Irish descent and blacks and Chinamen, all sorts."[2]

This polyglot culture sprouted diverse and lively entertainments.

American sailors on the Cunard lines brought in early rhythm-and-blues and country-and-western records to sell on the black market in advance of European distributors.[3] In his book *Magical Mystery Tours,* Tony Bramwell, George Harrison's friend who became a Beatle publicist, describes huge weekend record swaps near the docks. Americans stationed at the nearby Burtonwood base invited locals into their homes to drink Coca-Cola and spin American records on their turntables.[4] "All the girls would head up to Burtonwood for the dances," Quarrymen drummer Colin Hanton remembered.[5] Travelers also brought back European releases of American music that had not yet been picked up by British labels. Lennon had strong memories of Liverpool's country-and-western scene, and knew about the local folk and blues clubs well before the rock 'n' roll tide came in. By 1955, Liverpudlians had already been exposed to a dense variety of cultural influences. As a result, they boasted the least parochial taste in Britain, and their Scouser pride celebrated stylistic variety. "The people there—" Lennon said, "the Irish in Ireland are the same—they take their music very seriously."[6]

In this atmosphere, alternative radio became a pipeline to the American scene. Radio Luxembourg, launched in 1931 to play military band music and passed through Nazi and then Allied hands during and after the war, transformed itself in the 1950s. Its 208-meter wavelength ("2-0-8 Power Play") couldn't reach far beyond Germany during the day, but at night the signal had greater reach, and much of the UK could tune in. The station began broadcasting a 7 P.M. English service in 1950. Against the BBC's relatively meager light fare, it stood out as the only signal that carried American R&B, country, and rock 'n' roll. Nobody with the slightest interest in music could live without it, and its oracular nighttime-only reception gave it the insider status of an "offshore," or pirate, station.

There's not much mentioned when it comes to Aunt Mimi's taste in music; like a lot of parents of her generation, she simply thought guitars were so much "noise." Her sister Judy, however, ran wires connecting her gramophone to remote speakers in different rooms of her home—commonplace now but unheard of at the time. Lennon copied this setup at Mendips, stringing wire from the living-room radio up to his bedroom, where he installed a speaker so he could listen to adventurous DJs like Jimmy Savile and Jack Jackson on Radio Luxembourg at night.⁷ Listening to Radio Luxembourg, Lennon heard whispers of the emergent rock 'n' roll style during the spring of 1955, just as it began to surface in the United States. Lennon's and the UK's introduction to early rock 'n' roll, however, came through the unlikely figure of Lonnie Donegan, a Scottish banjo player and guitarist from Chris Barber's jazz band. During intermissions, Donegan organized a small "skiffle" combo to entertain audiences (Barber, a trombonist, sat in on upright bass or harmonica). Skiffle (derived from "skiffle party," a synonym for "rent party") grew out of the original Dixieland and ragtime styles to turn common household items into instruments, typically an old-fashioned wooden washboard strummed in time with a sewing thimble, along with a guitar and a harmonica. (If you were really fancy, you could add drums.) The style enjoyed a couple of stateside hits following World War I, with Jimmy O'Bryant and the Chicago Skifflers, and a brief revival from Dan Burley and His Skiffle Boys, featuring guitarists Brownie and Stick McGhee, in 1948. Through Donegan, this stateside novelty style enjoyed its first and only craze.

In late 1954, Donegan recorded a skiffle version of the American blues singer Leadbelly's "Rock Island Line." Drained of Leadbelly's authority, Donegan's cover sparked an infectious, do-it-yourself spirit that British teens responded to. The skinny style sounded completely unpretentious and winning, as if its jumping rhythms could leap tall buildings, with no pretense at skill, unlike all the stuffy orchestras and big-band arrangements the BBC played. Released in early 1955 as a 45 rpm extended-play (EP) single, along with Donegan's cover of another Leadbelly track, "John Henry," and Royal Festival Hall concert recordings of "I Don't Care Where They Bury My Body" and "Digging My Potatoes," it conquered the UK charts, selling three million copies in six months. Stranger still, "Rock Island Line" leapt clear across the pond to reach number eight in America in March 1956.

Donegan's lighthearted audience rapport and bouncing rhythms set off a run on Britain's guitars and unused washboards. Perhaps the UK required something tamer than Elvis to make way for rock's more aggressive rhythms; perhaps the protracted effort to market Elvis world-wide simply delayed his impact. At the time, it turned Donegan into a major UK star; history has since cast him in the role of England's John the Baptist.

In Barber's jazz lineup, Donegan played the banjo, but he switched to guitar for skiffle. Lennon took note of that connection. Julia had taught him the banjo, so here was the leap to guitar made plain: if you could play one, you could play the other. Donegan had simply gone in the opposite direction: "Chris Barber wanted me to join him on banjo, so I bought one," Donegan remembered. "He said 'Put your fingers in the middle and do something.' "[8]

Although not much of a looker, Donegan helped himself to clothes from his previous job as a department-store window dresser.[9] Fan enough to adopt a black musician's name (pianist Lonnie Johnson, for whom Donegan had opened back in 1952), he played the dandy without the looks, and a lot of his appeal lay in how he defined himself against current norms. "If he looked like a used car salesman offstage," wrote rock historian Alan Clayson, "[he] could be mesmeric in concert, creating true hand-biting excitement as he piled into numbers his group didn't know; took on and resolved risky extemporizations, and generated a sweaty, exhilarating intensity."[10] "Puttin' On the Style," a 1926 number he put out in 1957, sketched this persona out and became an early teen dress-up anthem: "She's putting on the agony, putting on the style/That's what all the young folks are doing all the while."

Upward of five thousand skiffle groups formed in the UK during 1955 and 1956. Even Mick Jagger, who would later deny it, got his start as a member of the Barber-Colyer Skiffle Band in London, when Chris Barber lost Donegan to a solo career and started another group. Van Morrison joined Belfast's Sputniks.[11] The almost fourteen-year-old Paul McCartney and the thirteen-year-old George Harrison both heard Donegan perform at Liverpool's Empire Theatre in May 1956, at the height of his popularity; McCartney waited by the stage door to get Donegan's autograph, and the star's personable demeanor with fans made a lasting impression.[12]

In Britain, Donegan's influence is hard to overstate: he had eight top-thirty UK hits in 1956 stores, and twenty-two more before 1962, ranging from Woody Guthrie material like "Grand Coulee Dam" to Leadbelly's "Bring a Little Water, Sylvie" and Riley Puckett and Gid Tanner's 1924 "Cumberland Gap." The following year brought the novelty "Does Your Chewing Gum Lose It's [sic] Flavor (on the Bedpost Over Night)?" (from a 1924 hit by Billy Jones and Ernest Hare) and a cover of the Carter Family's "My Dixie Darling." The Carters' country-and-western connection is tied in with skiffle's do-it-yourself ethos: skiffle groups were originally called "spasm bands" when they surfaced in New Orleans. You had to have chops to play trad jazz, but skiffle offered the immediate gratification of a style anybody could copy, and washboards and tea chests were just lying around people's houses. Quarryman Hanton remembers more music shops getting robbed than jewelers.[13] "The question wasn't 'is your brother in a skiffle band?'" Julia Baird recalled, "it was 'which skiffle band is he in?'"[14]

LENNON BOUGHT and cherished "Rock Island Line," one of his first records, a prized possession that he eventually passed on to his Quarry Bank schoolmate Rod Davis. Julia Baird remembers, "My father's big wind-up gramophone was the highlight of social evenings at home. That's how Jacqui, John and I first became acquainted with the strange new music from America called rock 'n' roll, which the local seamen had brought back with them."[15] Rock's early mysteries unfolded through coded slang, borrowed from black rhythm and blues, which suddenly took on new meanings among a wider, and younger, audience. The music cut a swath through the world, separating teenagers from adults, hips from squares, those who heard the call and those it baffled. This introduced a new layer of complication between Judy, who "got it," and her sister Mimi, who didn't—and never would.

In the middle of this battle, one figure remained constant: George Smith, John's most important ally as a child. Then, abruptly, one Sunday in June of 1955, George collapsed and was rushed to Sefton Hospital, diagnosed with cirrhosis of the liver. He died the next day from a brain hemorrhage at the age of fifty-two. Nobody, apparently, so much as suspected that George was ill. Although he must have been in chronic pain for months before he died, he hid his ailment from those who loved him most. John, four months short of his fifteenth birthday, had just left for his summer holiday in Scotland. He turned around immediately and headed home. His cousin Leila, sixteen at the time, traveled back with him, and later described the scene to Julia Baird: "It was a terrible shock to us all, but especially to John who looked on him as a father. . . . He and John always had little secrets going on between the two of them. He was so affectionate. John always used to insist on giving him 'squeakers,' his name for kisses, before George put him to bed."[16]

None of the reports of George's sudden death address the causes of his cirrhosis, but the likelihood is that he, like John's paternal grandfather, Jack Lennon Jr., died from alcoholic liver disease, still one of the leading causes of mortality throughout the world. Whatever his failings, George Smith's love for his nephew was one of the few uncomplicated attachments of Lennon's early life. When Mimi sent John up to his room for misbehaving, it was George who would tiptoe up with cake to leave by his door to smooth things over. When John was older, George sneaked him off to the movies despite Mimi's disapproval. George, the more passive personality in the house, had long since replaced Alf as his father figure.

As relatives started to stream through for Smith's funeral, John hid upstairs in his bedroom with Leila, giggling hysterically rather than crying. This eruption, now treated as a perfectly "normal" grief response, tormented his conscience for years. To have good relations with a "stepfather" was triumph enough for a boy whose father had left him at age five. And George, quiet in his influence but a kind and merry man, had loved him unconditionally, made few demands on him, and protected him from his aunt's harsh and unpredictable temper. Compounding John's pain, Alfred Lennon reappeared briefly during this phase and contacted his son to suggest a meeting. Pete Shotton reported that John was "electrified by the prospect of encountering [his father] face to face—and felt cruelly cheated when the plans ultimately fell through." Thereafter, John rarely spoke of him "except to note, without any apparent resentment, that his old man had 'run away to sea.'"[17]

After George's death, Lennon, alone in Mimi's household with only his beloved dog, Sally, to comfort him, tumbled into an emotional free-fall. Rock 'n' roll came along right as grief ambushed his life again, echoing all the way down to those fearsome, ten-year-old Blackpool separation anxieties.

Lennon began to follow the music's progress in the papers throughout 1956. He begged Judy for a guitar, which she bought him: a second-hand Egmond, which cost her five pounds. Judy tuned the guitar's top four strings as if it were a banjo (ignoring the low E and A strings), and Lennon taught himself to play from his mother's banjo chords, trying at first to imitate Donegan's sound.

Several forces began gathering in Lennon's world to form the perfect Elvis storm; Presley's rhythms were swift, but his UK ascent happened gradually. Bill Haley's "Rock Around the Clock" got slapped on as an afterthought to the sound track of *Blackboard Jungle* in 1955; Haley didn't appear in the movie, but the song became huge. Lennon rushed to see it with Len Garry and Pete Shotton at the Woolton cinema, only to be disappointed. He had read all about teenage riots, but he took in a lousy teen-exploitation movie, saddled with a sound track by an overweight, middle-aged white guy with a phony curl on his forehead fronting yesterday's big band, trying too hard to swing. "Just to be cheeky, Lennon and Shotton suddenly threw a fight out of boredom, right in the middle of the film. They turned on the lights and there was a big scene—but it was all just a laugh. I don't even remember the film, just Lennon causing a scene," said Garry.[18]

Even so, a lot of tedium still clogged the British charts. Throughout 1955, pop still propped up Frankie Laine, the cloying singer who recorded with the Paul Weston or Mitch Miller Orchestra and the Norman Luboff Choir on throwback material like "In the Beginning," "Cool Water," and "Strange Lady in Town" (all from 1955). Like many rock fans, Lennon recoiled when Pat Boone smoothed over Fats Domino's original "Ain't That a Shame," which he knew from Radio Luxembourg. To Lennon, the racial contrast on those two records mattered less than aesthetics: Domino outsang Boone by a factor of at least ten. Hearing hard-core rock 'n' rollers push their way up the charts through layers of treacle boasted dramatic intrigue with a visceral kick; shouting down pop was half of rock 'n' roll's mission. In the United States, "Cherry Pink (and Apple Blossom White)," as recorded by Perez Prado, spent ten weeks at the fore while Presley began to see regional chart action in the South with "That's All Right," buttressed by appearances on the popular *Louisiana Hayride* on radio and television.

Presley didn't break wide in England until "Heartbreak Hotel," in the spring of 1956. In cultural terms, Britain trailed behind America, but the lag worked in Presley's favor: that summer, "Heartbreak Hotel," "Blue Suede Shoes," "I Want You, I Need You, I Love You," and "Hound Dog" crowded the UK charts. Carl Perkins, Fats Domino, and Little Richard also scored hits in the UK later in 1956, while Buddy Holly, Jerry Lee Lewis, and Chuck Berry began to win fans there in early 1957.

In fact, Lennon remembered reading about Elvis Presley before actually hearing his voice. Julia Baird claims that her mother first played Elvis for John;[19] while his memory held on to his classmate Don Beatty's sharing an article about Presley in the *New Musical Express*. The hype made Lennon suspicious.

> The music papers were saying that Presley was fantastic, and at first I expected someone like Perry Como or Sinatra. "Heartbreak Hotel" seemed a corny title and his name seemed strange in those days. But then, when I heard it, it was the end for me. I first heard it on Radio Luxembourg. He turned out to be fantastic. I remember rushing home with the record and saying, "He sounds like Frankie Laine *and* Johnnie Ray *and* Tennessee Ernie Ford!"[20]

Lennon identified three distinct Elvis influences to make key musical connections. In Presley's vocal style, he recognized aspects of Laine's vaguely country "Hawk-Eye" (1955) and "Sixteen Tons" (1956), Ray's smooth R&B hustle in "Hey There" and "Such a Night" (both from 1954), and Ford's stately pop delivery in "Give Me Your Word" and "The Ballad of Davy Crockett" (both 1955). That these three styles were previously unconnected dots seemed far-fetched in the extreme; that Presley linked their diverse audiences remains his triumph.

ELVIS PRESLEY WAS the great linchpin of early rock 'n' roll, the figure every Beatle bows down before. "Before Elvis there was nothing" became Lennon's koan. "Suddenly it was like . . . the *Messiah* has come," Paul McCartney said. "Oh God I loved him, you have no idea," Ringo Starr proclaimed well into middle age.

For his breakthrough, Presley's "Heartbreak Hotel" delivered a fast, peculiar thrill and left a dizzying afterglow. Every verse teased and threatened, and then he wound down slowly into melodramatic, agonizingly quiet refrains. Finally, as if overwhelmed, he turned guitarist Scotty Moore loose for a solo. The song turned Presley into an emotional pretzel—too much longing, too much desire, too much seduction clanging up against too much self-knowledge—and by seizing its challenge, he walked away King. All by itself, "Heartbreak Hotel" sucked you into a torrid affair that was too tempting to resist but too doomed to succeed; it was altogether thrilling, forbidden, and flamboyantly condemned. In telling the story, Elvis sounded like he had way too much to express, and the music coursed through his body like a religious passion inculcating a new believer. Metaphorically, the record brewed up backwoods emotional hooch that made you loopy at first gulp. Imagine the emotionally hungry John Lennon tasting this forbidden fruit.

Once this sound got in your head, the beat was colossal, but that booming Elvis voice was even bigger, and seemed to dominate worlds outside the song. The record seeped into Lennon's life, and everybody else's, like a virus, whether you had just played it or hadn't heard it in a week. Once Presley grabbed hold, he spoke like an oracle, your new teen mentor, sitting on your shoulder, urging you to embrace romance, kiss that girl, and take a thousand other risks, even as his doubt and hesitation whispered uncertainty and dread. Presley's daring was emphatic: it was almost as if this tremulous sound told you to take risks because not to take them meant certain defeat—playing meant winning. All you had to do was find him on your radio, or get his musical juices flowing in your walk and your talk, and you, too, could tap the Elvis within by strutting with a hero's stride and living out the sound.

Most Americans were introduced to Elvis on their living-room televisions, via the Dorsey brothers' *Stage Show, The Milton Berle Show, The Steve Allen Show,* and finally *The Ed Sullivan Show* in September 1956, as Presley systematically smashed everybody's perceived notions about Southerners. Presley was beautiful, sure; but until he opened his mouth and the music took hold of his body, he was an overconfident rube. Surprise was all: to the broad middle class, here was a new kind of hick, transformed by sheer self-respect, redeemed by a glowering self-confidence.

Presley's musical stature oozed poetry. As the quintessential American, the truck driver who transcended his own rags-to-riches dream-coming-true, he fleshed out a musical answer to actors like Montgomery Clift, James Dean, and Marlon Brando and quickly enfolded them into a larger notion about America, not just its music, but its very idea of itself. Presley's confidence in adopting black music somehow transcended self-assurance to pose a bigger threat to Jim Crow customs than any *Brown v. Board of Education* ruling (1954). After Elvis, many other performers sounded vaguely show-biz, acts with mannerisms where his curled, charismatic lips and unruly hips elevated his singing into pure symbolism, recklessness as style that trumped entertainment.

To Lennon and his British friends, however, a lot of these American cultural associations simply evaporated. To them, Presley was more than just a poor kid from the provinces who made it big in the city; he carried a more universal charge as the charismatic misfit from "nowhere" who changed the way people heard and saw things quite literally all over the world. All during his ascent that year, Presley made everything that was limiting and oppressive about being young in a throwback town seem charged with possibility, change, full of dares too enticing to defy. When Elvis let loose, physically as well as vocally, he threw off a thousand invisible conventions, from all the customary ways white men should sing and move their bodies to all the customs entertainers were supposed to observe in public. He was the classless truck driver, the talent who was too big to be contained by mere records, too popular to be mere celebrity, and too magical to be mere Southerner, hillbilly, hick, rube, teen singer, or flash in the pan. Everyday life, in all its tiresome expectations, suddenly pulsed to Elvis Presley's hips.

If Donegan flung open the door, Presley turned on the lights and started a rumpus that lit up the whole dreary neighborhood. Yes, there was the sheer thrill of hearing an American youth set loose new metaphors of freedom on such a grand scale—racial, sexual, gender, and generational. But Lennon, and those he gathered around him at the time, also sensed a larger, overarching promise in Presley's success: in the guilty pleasures of "Heartbreak Hotel," the infinite joyride of "Hound Dog," and the wry self-deprecation of "I Forgot to Remember to Forget," Presley was quickly a symbol of how this new music stretched out endlessly. If this Memphis hick could, in critic Greil Marcus's words, "imagine himself King," so could you—especially if the rest of the world saw you as a common Scouser from a nowhere northern dock town. "I'm an Elvis fan because it was Elvis who really got me out of Liverpool," Lennon later said. Once he heard Elvis sing, "that was life, there was no other thing. I thought of nothing else but rock 'n' roll."[21]

Presley's first UK sortie came in May of 1956 with "Blue Suede Shoes," on the heels of Lonnie Donegan and the skiffle boom, like two relay runners passing a magical baton; and once he got a toehold on the British charts, he kept right on gunning until he had outlapped Donegan as well, each hit another rabbit from his hat, until Christmas brought the gooey *Love Me Tender,* his first film and a consolidation of his fame. "Blue Suede Shoes," "Heartbreak Hotel," and "Hound Dog" were so popular they kept returning to the top ten every few weeks that year, volleying for primacy, and when September rolled around, a rerelease of "Heartbreak Hotel" gave Presley his first UK number one. It was Presley's UK year, but Frankie Lymon and the Teenagers' doo-wop "Why Do Fools Fall in Love" also peaked that July, and among the other records Lennon bought and devoured in 1956 were Carl Perkins's hellbound rockabilly "Blue Suede Shoes," Little Richard's powder-keg "Rip It Up," and Fats Domino's slow-rolling "Blueberry Hill." All the while, Frankie Laine was serenading UK listeners with his cowboy drivel. He kept having hits, but once RCA started marketing Presley in England and Europe, Laine's presence shriveled in the newcomer's glare.

Every time parents, or the prim Aunt Mimi, denounced Presley, his authority swelled. Lennon's adoration must have felt boundless. Everything about Elvis had flash and humor, every gesture an element of self-mockery ("I Want You, I Need You, I Love You" alone snickered at every other sticky valentine while delivering its own affection). He could go all slurpy in "Love Me Tender" or "Love Me," but these sentimental ballads never detracted from his toughness, the guileless humor and illicit thrills of his streak through the first six months of 1957 hits: "Mystery Train," "Rip It Up," "Too Much," "All Shook Up," "(Let Me Be Your) Teddy Bear." In a flash, pop music posed pictures of integration beyond anything American or British culture had yet seen in real life.

LENNON'S CLASSMATE MICHAEL HILL remembers taking lunch breaks from school at his empty house (his mother worked), where he, Lennon, and two or three other friends smoked cigarettes, drank hot chocolate, and ate potato chips while listening to the latest records. Since rock received little mainstream airplay at the time, whenever one of the group acquired a new 45 it quickly became a shared secret. One sunny spring day in 1956, five of them biked over to Hill's house for their movable listening party. Hill himself was late to the rock trend, and eager to confirm his credentials as a guy in the know by showing off his latest acquisition from Holland, where he'd just been on a school trip. He doesn't remember what led him to buy this particular record, but he does remember its yellow label, and the old family radiogram—a record player, and radio, and speakers housed in the same wooden cabinet.

The record Hill boasted about was a 78 rpm by Little Richard that had been released on the Ronnex label, a small Belgian firm that imported American R&B to Europe. (It was also a rarity: Little Richard didn't score a UK hit with this record until 1957.) And Hill was quite confident that he had scored big. All the other guys were dead (read: extreme) Elvis fans; "Heartbreak Hotel" had made such a searing impression that his status as King was unassailable. Hill made an outlandish boast before playing the single: he proclaimed this new singer "better than Elvis." That riled Lennon—until the needle dropped into the grooves and Little Richard began to sing "Long Tall Sally." "I rarely remember him losing his composure," Hill recalls. "But that day he dropped his guard completely. . . . He was clearly stunned at what he heard. He didn't want to be convinced that Little Richard was better than Elvis. We played it over and over again, and I must say it was one of the few times any of us ever saw Lennon completely lose his tough veneer."[22]

Years later, Lennon described hearing "Long Tall Sally" for the first time as a pivotal moment in his musical development. "When I heard it, it was so great I couldn't speak." This was a matter of the utmost gravity to him: who could dare challenge the King? Hill's claim was blasphemy. And yet the power of "Long Tall Sally" was irrefutable, indomitable. "How could they be happening in my life, *both* of them?" Lennon remembered thinking of the two singers. At last, to break the tension, one member of the group pointed out that Little Richard was "a nigger," using the forbidden word to be cool; and somehow this solved Lennon's dilemma. Revealing his limited exposure to the cultural universe outside his part of Liverpool, he said, "I didn't know Negroes sang." In his mind, the difference between a white man and a black was so fundamental that they could never compete with each other. They belonged in different categories. "Thank you, God," he told himself, relieved that this showdown had some kind of resolution, that one needn't displace the other. Even better: the sound proclaimed how much room there was for *both* rock characters—and more, too.

The labels on "Heartbreak Hotel" and "Long Tall Sally" were different colors, and swirled around Lennon's early impressions of these two vocal characters, setting off obsessive thoughts about the music's packaging even before he'd seen how Little Richard's screams unraveled his bouffant.

A BRIGHT BOY like John could not fail to see through his aunt Mimi's deceptions. Mimi had concealed her sister's close proximity until John was eleven or twelve, and as they became reacquainted, Judy treated him more like a nephew than a son. Revelations since Mimi's death in 1991 intensify the possessive undercurrents between the two Stanley sisters. With Dykins, her new common-law husband, Judy had finally settled into motherhood and family life in her thirties, as her son would do in his own life. Judy seems to have relinquished most of the important decisions about young John's upbringing and education to Mimi, and only welcomed him back to her new home as he entered adolescence. The anxious maternal voltage between these sisters—one with children, one without—crackled straight through John's internal fuse box.

Once he started Quarry Bank and built his reputation as a tough, Lennon battled more and more against Mimi's iron hand. Judy lived just two miles from Mendips, and as he came of age, her more relaxed household became a refuge from the stultifying Aunt Mimi, and her daughters adopted John as an older brother once removed. The laughter and music in Judy's house became an oasis. With her charismatic, elusive personality, he began to identify with her as the real mother he'd longed for since she gave him up. Unlike Mimi, Judy also enjoyed watching John embrace the new Teddy-Boy trend, and she "gave me my first colored shirt," Lennon remembered. "I started going to visit her at her house. I met her new bloke and didn't think much of him. I called him Twitchy. Julia became a sort of young aunt to me, or a big sister. As I got bigger and had more rows with Mimi, I used to go and live with Julia for a weekend."[23]

Most narratives stress Lennon's patronizing attitude toward the "new bloke," Bobby Dykins. Yet Julia Dykins Baird claims that they were an extended family in every sense. It was Dykins's "funny little nervous cough" that inspired John to nickname him "Twitchy," Baird wrote, but "never to his face. He actually called him Bobby, as our mother did."[24] Dykins occasionally found John odd jobs at the Adelphi—the same hotel where Alf Lennon had been working as a bellboy when he met Judy Stanley. An only child in the Smith household, John enjoyed playing big brother to his younger half sisters. "We certainly weren't the only family in our street with odd domestic arrangements," Julia Baird recalled. "There was one family with nine children, two of whom lived with their grandmother. . . . The children of another family were looked after by their father because their mother only came home at weekends. . . . She worked in London."²⁵

Judy's home attracted Lennon for other reasons. Mother and son both craved music and laughter. Julia Baird described her mother walking down the street with her panties fashioned around her head like a scarf. Judy clearly preferred the sisterly role to the maternal, and relished the chance to participate in John's adolescence. As Judy's satellite home welcomed him in, she reentered his life in the way she felt most comfortable—almost as a peer.

EVENTUALLY, JUDY GAVE John his first guitar. But his first instrument was an old harmonica—or mouth organ, as it was called. The Smiths "used to take in students," Lennon recalled, "and one of them had a mouth organ and said he'd buy me one if I could learn a tune by the next morning. So I learnt two. I was somewhere between eight and twelve at the time; in short pants, anyway."²⁶ Julia Baird recalled that the instrument swiftly became "his most treasured possession. He took it with him everywhere, not wanting to lose sight of it for a single moment."²⁷

John's cousin Stanley Parkes remembers him having a cheap little harmonica that he played constantly, driving everyone crazy. On one of his bus trips up to Scotland, he played it the whole way, impressing the driver, who singled him out for praise when they arrived in Edinburgh. A previous passenger had left a harmonica on the bus some months back, he told John, who returned for it the following day. "He had it for years," Parkes recalled, "and in fact he played it on some of his records. Eventually he took it to America and had it in the Dakota building in New York, I believe."²⁸

At some point during this period, Stanley let John try out his own pint accordion. For Stanley, the instrument felt awkward, "like playing the piano sideways," but John "strapped it on his shoulder and just took to it like a duck takes to water." "How the heck did you do that," Stanley cried. " 'Oh, I don't know,' he said, 'I just do it.' He took it home and he had it for quite a while."²⁹

On this small keyboard, and later at Judy's piano (and using only his right hand), Lennon taught himself to play the same songs that he'd learned to play on the mouth organ, middlebrow standards such as Alfven's "Swedish Rhapsody," the "Theme from *Moulin Rouge,*" "Greensleeves," and a tune that later showed up in Beatle sets, "The *Third Man* Theme," from the 1949 Carol Reed movie starring Orson Welles.[30] Where Mimi would shush him up, at Judy's place he could play harmonica and poke out tunes at the piano, to Judy's delight. She even joined in with him. Why wouldn't he feel like spending more time with her?

PREVIOUS BEATLE HISTORIANS have placed a halo around Mimi's head because she rescued the neglected John, gave his life structure and stability, and provided him with a kindly stepfather. Mimi was free to cast herself in this role, however, because she was the one telling the story— Julia Stanley Lennon didn't live long enough to record her own version of events. And the reality turns out to be far more tangled. In Mimi's mind, she'd loved John since he was born, rescued him from his hapless parents, and felt wounded when he began to display a preference for the mother who had abandoned him. Pete Shotton remembered growing rows between Lennon and his aunt once John began spending weekends at his mother's, and the parental tug-of-war that had traumatized him when he was five escalated anew between the two Stanley sisters, who behaved very much like a divorced couple competing for their child.

The more Mimi tried to reassert her dominance in his life, the longer John would stay over at his mother's. After a big fight, Shotton said, "sometimes he'd inform his aunt he was 'running away' for good."[31] Mimi couldn't help feeling slighted—she did all the work, Judy had all the fun—but her anger at John's (quite natural) adolescent rebelliousness revealed a nasty side that long went unreported. One story in particular stands out. After "running away" to Judy's for a few days, John returned to Mendips to discover that Mimi had retaliated by having his beloved dog, Sally, put down. Shotton recalled this as one of the few times he ever saw Lennon cry. According to Shotton, Mimi justified disposing of the healthy animal because John had vowed never to return to Mendips.

"Since John wasn't going to be around to walk the dog, she argued, he'd left her with no choice but to have it destroyed."[32]

"Looking back," wrote Julia Baird, "I realize we became a refuge for John in his ever increasing struggle to live with Mimi amicably. Mimi, the aunt, was forced into the role of the heavy-handed mother, which allowed Julia, the mother, to become the indulgent aunt. Besides, at heart, Julia was still almost a teenager herself who easily identified with John and his friends."[33]

FOR JOHN, AFTER George's death, Judy became something more than a respite from her martinet sister. Mother and son's shared passion for the new, clandestine music hitting Radio Luxembourg led to an even stronger bond. Julia Baird remembers her mother as a "wonderful piano player," "twice as musically talented than Lennon himself"—a pretty bold claim, even adjusting for a daughter's hyperbole.[34] In 1955, Judy strutted around as one of the few forty-two-year-old mothers who not only knew about rock 'n' roll but proclaimed herself a fan. Like many parents, Mimi worried that rock 'n' roll would corrupt her rebellious nephew into a "juvenile delinquent." The fun-loving Judy named her cat Elvis.

If you were a teenager and the music grabbed you, you picked up instruments and imitated the sounds you loved; Lennon's gang was suddenly a band. Rod Davis remembers the lineup: "Bill Smith was on teachest; I played banjo; Eric Griffiths was on guitar; while Len Garry, Ivan Vaughan, Nigel Walley alternated on bass . . . Pete Shotton on washboard, and of course Lennon played guitar." Vaughan went so far as to paint the words "Jive with Ive, the ace on the bass" on his washtub.[35]

Shotton had qualms about joining; he didn't have any talent, he claimed. "Well, John always wanted somebody next to him," Len Garry remembers, "he always wanted some sort of support."[36] For Lennon, though, there was simply no question: musical ability counted far less than friendship. "Come on, don't be daft," he told Shotton. "Of course you can take part, anyone can."[37] Last to join was Colin Hanton, a trad jazz buff who played drums. As for singing, Lennon was always the lead; whatever the others lacked as musicians, he "could hold an audience."[38] And once he'd formed his first band, he behaved like the ultimate den mother: his devotion to the "group" long predated the Beatles.

They called themselves the Black Jacks at first, with Lennon fronting in his Teddy Boy garb. After months of rehearsing, they made an appearance on the back of a flatbed truck on June 22, 1957. An early Lennon debut came, with afternoon and evening sets, during street celebrations for Empire Day, when Liverpool celebrated its 550th anniversary.[39] According to Julia Baird, her mother helped fashion the Black Jacks' wardrobe. She remembered the scene:

> We found John and his four friends perched up on a lorry parked across the middle of the street, playing their hearts out in a frenzy of rock and roll. . . . My mother was the group's unofficial wardrobe mistress. She went to Garston open air market to buy the colored shirts they wore at that gig. The Teddy Boy look was the big fashion and they wore shoestring ties and took in their trousers to make them drainpipes. If their mothers could be talked into it, they got themselves DA [duck's arse] haircuts.[40]

The next month Pete Shotton's mother, Bessie, a planning committee member at St. Peter's, arranged for the band to play at the annual summer "Garden Fête" on Saturday, July 6. By that time they had settled on a more permanent name: the Quarrymen. This had simplicity, sounded tough enough, and referenced their school while snubbing the very idea of school spirit: Lennon's reputation was such that nobody could presume they meant the band's name as anything but a rebuke. The day-long event included a set on the back of another parade lorry, an afternoon set in the churchyard, and an evening dance.

The scene is lovingly recreated in Jim O'Donnell's fever-dream book *The Day John Met Paul,* a writer's obsessive fleshing-out of the day's few known details. Building on the foundations of a story that has long since entered the realm of myth, O'Donnell makes the plausible seem almost fated—as if a documentary film crew happened to be recording it all in the writer's mind. The fifteen-year-old McCartney, a slender, dark-

haired kid with soft features and twinkling brown eyes, came along at
the behest of his friend Ivan Vaughan. McCartney remembers donning
a "naff"—uncool—white jacket to impress the girls, inspired by Terry
Dene's hit that month, "A White Sport Coat (and a Pink Carnation)".
He heard Lennon at the microphone singing "Come Go with Me" by
the Del Vikings, a McCartney favorite from earlier that year. He remembers seeing the lead singer with his "curly, blondish hair, wearing a
checked shirt—looking pretty good and quite fashionable." According
to his affectionate yet spotty memory, Lennon kept "forgetting the words"
and making up nonsense on the spot to fill in the blanks:

> There's a little refrain which goes, 'Come little darlin', come and
> go with me, I love you darling.' John was singing, 'Down, down,
> down to the penitentiary.' He was filling in with blues lines, I
> thought that was good, and he was singing well. There was a
> skiffle group around him: tea-chest bass, drums, banjo, quite a
> higgledy-piggledy lot. . . . I quite liked them.[41]

Rod Davis insists that McCartney remembers wrong: Lennon wasn't
making up lyrics, he was simply vamping on the final refrain as the song
faded out, rhyming "penitentiary" with the original lyrics while they
brought the song to an artificial fade-out. Lennon's interest in the Del
Vikings carries more significance. This biracial group from a Pittsburgh
air force base combined doo-wop with rock 'n' roll for a brew far beyond
the scope of Donegan's skiffle; the group's doo-wop vocal arrangements
soared over muscular R&B beats. By his second public performance,
Lennon's interests had progressed far past skiffle toward doo-wop, R&B,
and rockabilly—the harder stuff. Other songs in the set included "Cumberland Gap," "Freight Train," "Midnight Special," and "Worried Man
Blues." But this Del Vikings number conveys especially discriminating
taste, both for what it signals about rock 'n' roll's development and how
it pricked up McCartney's ears. Lennon's omnivorous listening habits
already had moved the Quarrymen far from being a "mere" skiffle band.
    The music caught Mimi Smith's ears as well: she was drawn to the
"racket" and dumbstruck to see her charge fronting the noise in his

"drainies" and ducktail. Lennon, seeing her coming, undermined her glare by ad-libbing: "Uh-oh, here comes Mimi down the path . . ." Mimi joined Judy in the crowd, one sister scowling, the other beaming.

Between the afternoon set and the evening dance, Ivan introduced Paul to John, who seemed a bit tipsy to him ("breathing boozily").[42] Lennon feigned indifference when McCartney lit into Eddie Cochran's "Twenty Flight Rock" on Lennon's guitar—which he'd turned upside down. Lennon was impressed, but didn't let on just how much. Then McCartney dashed off a Little Richard medley, calling Lennon's bluff: Lennon had just led his own band through its second public appearance, and here was some new kid from Allerton upstaging him with chords, tunings, and lyrics. The two briefly discussed fingerings (the left-handed McCartney deciphered the banjo-chord formations on Lennon's right-hand guitar), and Paul cheerfully scribbled down Cochran's words.

Details surrounding this meeting remain in dispute. None of the surviving original Quarrymen, for instance, remembers Lennon, or anybody else, having anything to drink that day. "We wouldn't have," Colin Hanton says. "Where would we have gotten it? Nobody had any money."[43] And Rod Davis has no recollection of McCartney's "white jacket," which he's sure would have made an impression. Here, perhaps, it's McCartney's mind that's playing tricks: Lennon was twenty months his senior, after all, and the cockier presence, and he might have been acting smug and juiced just to put on a good front. As for McCartney's white jacket, and the Terry Dene hit that was going through his head, these seem to have blurred together for an image nobody can confirm.

That night's dance was interrupted by a power outage and heavy rain. Pete Shotton remembered walking home during a vivid lightning storm. Lennon's musical debut slammed up against Mimi's certain scolding; Judy's presence at that particular show would prove a talisman. The following week, following Lennon's instructions, Pete Shotton spotted Paul on his bike and invited him to join the Quarrymen.

4

Nobody Told Me

M cCARTNEY PLAYED STRAIGHT MAN TO LENNON'S LUNATIC, THE romantic to his skeptic, the "librarian" to his primitive. While there was always a power struggle over whose sensibilities would ultimately "define" the Beatles, with a chemistry beguiled by imbalance they began as fast friends, a bond created and fueled by the music's riches. Lennon often acknowledged McCartney's preeminence in technical proficiency, and McCartney immediately began sharing his notebooks with Lennon, intuiting a collaborator behind the bully.

By itself, McCartney's biography touches the tragic, but it positively glows against Lennon's childhood. The McCartney family came from the village of Everton, the dense Liverpool suburb known as "Little Dublin," named after the Irish refugees who had settled there by the 1880s. Like Lennon's grandfather Jack Lennon Jr., Paul's paternal grandfather, Joe McCartney, cut a musical profile in family lore. Joe played the E-flat bass horn, a cousin to the tuba, in the Territorial Army band at the outdoor concerts at Stanley Park in neighboring Anfield, and was an opera hound. Paul's father, Jim, was one of Joe's three sons and four daughters, and he played the trumpet, growing up to lead his own ragtime band, Jim Mac's Jazz Band, at local clubs in the 1920s. He even wrote a song, "Walking in the Park with Eloise," often requested at family house parties. At age fourteen, Jim went to work for A. Hannay & Co., the cotton traders, which became the Royal Cotton Commission during the war. He would work there on and off for the next twenty-eight years.

A confirmed bachelor at age thirty-six, Jim met a soft-spoken nurse, Mary Mohan, thirty-one, at his sister Jin's house in West Derby Village in 1938.[1] They married in 1941, at St. Swithin's Roman Catholic Chapel in Gillmoss, West Derby, to please Mary's Catholic parents. A lifetime teetotaler who went to bed promptly at ten each night, Jim moonlighted supervising garbage attendants to supplement the unsteady cotton trade. Mary supplemented his earnings working part-time as a midwife, riding her bike around town at all hours to deliver babies. It was a stressful life, with both parents working, but Mary's "nurse sister" status at Walton Hospital qualified them for a government housing subsidy.

The newlyweds moved to 92 Broadway in Wallasey, across the water from Liverpool. One year after their wedding, James Paul McCartney was born, on June 18, 1942. Another boy, Peter Michael, came along two years later. After a five-year series of moves, the McCartneys settled in at 20 Forthlin Road in Allerton for 6d a week, discounted for Mary's hospital seniority. This home sat across the expansive golf course from Mendips, and less than a mile from where Judy had set up house with Bobby Dykins.

The McCartneys' hard work began to pay off just as their boys were reaching adolescence: their stable family home hosted extended family gatherings, and they cherished their front garden and parlor piano. Jim's brothers and sisters gathered regularly for "pound nights" (rent parties), where aunts, uncles, and cousins gathered to pool pounds of sugar, tea, and goods, and continued a family tradition of weekly sing-alongs. Dykins and his two daughters were never quite welcome at Mimi's home; an extended Stanley family sing-along was for dreamers.

JIM DID THE crossword puzzles and helped his boys plunk out tunes on the piano. Paul's cousin Bett Robbins showed them ukulele chords when she babysat. For his fourteenth birthday, Jim gave Paul a trumpet, which he traded in for a guitar because of his growing attachment to Radio Luxembourg's evening broadcasts. This radio station alone was enough to cement a fast friendship with Lennon. Much like Judy had done with

her speakers, Jim hooked up an extension cord for the downstairs radiogram so that Paul could listen from his bed upstairs via a pair of
headphones.

Being left-handed, Paul struggled to figure out exactly how to master the guitar's fret board. At first, he learned upside down, forming
chords backwards with his right hand. "It wasn't until I found a picture
of Slim Whitman, who was also left-handed [that I realized] I had the
guitar the wrong way round," McCartney remembers.[2] Restringing the
guitar to reverse the high and low strings, and relearning his right-hand
chords, got him sorted out.

Barely a year into their new Allerton home, Mary, then forty-six,
took ill. After months of ignoring symptoms of fatigue and indigestion,
a wrenching pain took hold of her coming home from a visit to her boys
at their Scout camp in August 1956. Even then, she simply popped an
indigestion tablet and kept moving. But the attacks became more frequent, and more painful. Privately, Mary feared the worst about the lump
she had discovered in her breast. Finally she consented to see a doctor.
She asked Jim's sister to accompany her to the hospital, and when Dill
Mohan arrived at Forthlin Road on the morning of October 30, 1956,
she found Mary cleaning house. Dill remembers thinking how Forthlin
Road looked like "a pin in paper," a Scouse colloquialism for "impecca-
bly tidy." Mary had laid out the boys' clothes on their beds for the next
day's school, "in case I don't come back."[3]

By the time she went under the knife, later that same day, the cancer
was long past inoperable. Mary had seen enough cases to know her prog-
nosis. Paul and Michael were taken in to visit her in recovery and were
shocked to see her transformation from upbeat mother to unrecogniz-
ably ravaged victim. That night, at about 9:30 P.M., Jim arrived unannounced at the Eagle Hotel, on Paradise Street, where his friends the
Mohans were tending bar in the backroom of their half-filled pub. He
was physically wasted and distraught; all he could manage to say was
"She's gone." Mary had suffered an embolism and died shortly after the
boys left. Paul was only fourteen. "What are we going to do without her
money?" he blurted out to his father.[4] McCartney has obsessed over this
quote ever since, an outburst of financial anxiety in the midst of trauma

that shows not just how narrowly they were getting by, but how conscious the boys were of their predicament. Distraught, Jim took Paul and Michael to stay with his sister Jin in Huyton, North Liverpool. Auntie Jin tucked them into a single bed, where they cried themselves to sleep. Within weeks, McCartney had written his first song: "I Lost My Little Girl."

AFTER SEVERAL MONTHS of songwriting, McCartney met Lennon at the St. Peter's Garden Fête. The friendship between the two boys blossomed, to the consternation of their elders. "Aunt Mimi disapproved because she thought Paul was a working-class lad who was encouraging her nephew to devote time to his guitar which should have been spent studying," writes McCartney's authorized biographer, Barry Miles. And Jim McCartney smelled something funny about Lennon: "After one meeting he told Paul, 'He'll get you into trouble, son.'"[5]

But McCartney's early recollections of John zeroed in on some of the things his dad couldn't see: for one thing, his living-room walls were lined with books, and while Lennon may have been boasting about having read "all of them," it was clear he'd read quite a few. McCartney observed another unusual Lennon accoutrement: "I used to go round to Aunt Mimi's house and John would be at the typewriter, which was fairly unusual in Liverpool. None of my mates even knew what a typewriter was. Well, they knew what one was, but they didn't have one. *Nobody* had a typewriter."[6]

Mostly, though, they listened to 45s and talked about music. "We spent hours just listening to the stars we admired," John recalled. "We'd sit round and look all intent and intense and then . . . try and reproduce the same sort of sounds for ourselves."[7]

McCartney remembers the time fondly:

We'd often get in the little glass-paneled porch on the front door looking out on to the front garden and Menlove Avenue. There was a good acoustic there, like a bathroom acoustic, and also it was the only place Mimi would let us make noise. We were relegated to the vestibule. I remember singing "Blue Moon" in there, the Elvis version, trying to figure out the chords. . . . Then we'd go up to John's room and we'd sit on the bed and play records, Fats Domino, Jerry Lee Lewis, Chuck Berry. It's a wonderful memory: I don't often get nostalgic, but the memory of sitting listening to records in John's bedroom is so lovely, a nice nostalgic feeling, because I realise just how close I was to John.[8]

ONE OF MIMI SMITH's great strokes of parenting coincided with the budding Lennon-and-McCartney partnership in 1957. John had flunked out of Quarry Bank during his senior year, and shortly after the St. Peter's fête, he and Nigel Walley capped off a night of drinking by signing up for the merchant marine at first light. When Mimi found out about it, she marched down to the recruitment office and had John's name scratched.[9]

Desperate to get John into a more secure situation, Mimi lobbied hard to get her nephew an interview at Liverpool Art College. She found an ally in Quarry Bank's headmaster, Mr. Pobjoy, who wrote a letter of recommendation, which until now has been trotted out as a classic of faint praise, with its claim that despite his borderline O-level scores, Lennon was "not beyond redemption." In tandem with that "bound to fail" quote, from a Quarry Bank math teacher, it seemed to render Lennon's performance indistinguishable from his promise, fudging the more complicated reality.

Lennon's portfolio of drawings and cartoons squeaked his art-school application through, along with the advantage that he could commute from Woolton and the college wouldn't need to find him housing. For Lennon's generation, art college was Britain's relief hatch for creative kids of all stripes, outsiders who didn't fit conventional career molds, as a short list of English rockers testifies: Keith Richards (Sidcup Art College); Ron Wood, Pete Townshend, Ray Davies, Thunderclap Newman, and Freddie Mercury (Ealing); Eric Clapton (Kingston), Syd Barrett (Camberwell); Roger Waters (Regent Street Polytechnic); Jimmy Page (Sutton), Charlie Watts (Harrow); Cat Stevens (Hammersmith). Mimi assumed Lennon would learn a trade, and in a roundabout way, he did; these institutions wound up training the British Invasion.[10]

THIS SAME YEAR, 1957, saw the UK rock 'n' roll scene bust open with new singers and material that convinced fans how wrong the skeptics were. Following that initial ballast of Lonnie Donegan setting skiffle's mousetrap for Elvis Presley, everything seemed to unfold in a parade of unlikely yet inevitable new characters telling new stories in outrageously new ways. Between 1955 and 1958, Presley led a seemingly unending parade of titans like Little Richard, Chuck Berry, Gene Vincent, Eddie Cochran, the Platters, Carl Perkins, Jerry Lee Lewis, Sam Cooke, the Everly Brothers, and the Coasters, supported by a slew of sideshows like the Teddy Bears (with Phil Spector). In relatively no time at all, here was a sea change of fresh sounds and ideas, with songs like "Blue Suede Shoes" and "Whole Lotta Shakin' Goin' On" and "To Know Her Is to Love Her," hatching soulful innocence from desperate possibility, fathomless certitude from gaping inexperience. Along the way, certain American characters passed through the UK's cultural looking glass for personas that often outstripped what they enjoyed at home.

Buddy Holly appeared just as Lennon and McCartney struck up their musical friendship, and they worshipped him as only teenagers could, devouring his records and studying them the way some geeks take apart clocks, just to see how they work: Holly's recordings were so cleverly layered that to learn and perform them comprised a tutorial in rock form. In doing so, Lennon sponged as much from Holly's persona as from his music. Holly's untouchable lyricism in their minds also influenced Lennon's choice of the melodious McCartney as writing partner, like a tyrant who leans on his diplomat. Holly had started out in a country-and-western duo called Buddy and Bob, which opened for Elvis Presley in early 1955 at the Fair Park Coliseum in Lubbock, Texas. When Presley passed through town again five months later, Holly offered to drive him around: Buddy and Elvis, cruising around Lubbock together, talking trash. Holly started doing Presley songs in sets with his new band, which became the Crickets. His "That'll Be the Day" hit the

American airwaves in July 1957; he had cribbed the song's title from a catchphrase of John Wayne's in John Ford's *The Searchers* (1956). Once Presley's career gained traction, rock 'n' roll records began to leap across the Atlantic like fire across rooftops. When "That'll Be the Day" topped the UK charts in September 1957, this new stylistic coup gained momentum.

In Britain, the Presley fad spawned predictable imitators, pretenders like Tommy Steele and Cliff Richard, who smiled their good looks and nonthreatening attitudes into domesticated frames; their pale imitations made Elvis seem all the more dangerous. But most Americans still don't appreciate Holly's impact on British ears. His "square" looks and verbal fluency made him the most English of early rockers, and his UK listeners adored him for completely different reasons. Naming their band after Holly's Crickets laced Lennon and McCartney's ambition with clairvoyance; they drew from both Holly's sound and his image. To begin with, Holly created a space to stand within Presley's shadow without being the slightest bit derivative. "That'll Be the Day" was an angry song, sure—Buddy Holly was telling his girl off, to get a clue—but he did it without the trademark Presley sneer. In fact, announcing his love so boldly set Buddy Holly free, and gave his awkward stance some heft and swagger. He hiccupped his hormones out loud, and those thick plastic glasses, the facial equivalent of pocket protectors, only accented his normalcy, as if he'd put quotes around it. In doing so, Holly flipped everybody's high-school jitters into metaphor.

Holly's genius sidestepped Presley's sexual confidence. Male fans like Lennon thrilled to Presley's rebellious flight but found his sexual bravado, his self-confidence with women, out of reach. Where Presley was at ease singing to and about women, Holly romanced with a stuttering resolve that spoke more to male vulnerability and insecurity: "Uh well-uh, well-uh, well-uh, the little things you say and do . . ." If an awkward kid like Holly could approach women with stutters and baby talk, his gawky façade suddenly rebounded as an asset. Metaphorically, Holly's persona glowed with possibility—through his songs, you didn't have to be a smoothy like Elvis to score on the dance floor. In Holly, the young Lennon learned how tough didn't have to mean a lack of cheer, that seemingly white-bread sensibilities could master the grittiest R&B material (Holly even did Chuck Berry's "Brown Eyed Handsome Man"), and that good humor could make even the most looming threat irresistible ("I'm gonna tell you how it's gonna be/You're gonna give your love to me . . .").

Once his sound pulled you in, Holly's appearance yanked a chain to make everyday stuff seem radical. At first, Holly wore traditional wire-framed glasses, but after trying contact lenses he switched over to even thicker, all-plastic frames: horn-rimmed, of the type archconservative Arizona senator Barry Goldwater wore. Lennon, embarrassingly short-sighted, wore glasses only offstage—and then only when necessary—until 1966. And Holly wore those thin Texas neckties atop his politely buttoned shirts. He made no attempt to mimic Presley's suave hip movements. If he sounded awkward on record, his stage presence was positively stiff—and yet oddly self-possessed, as if his innate, wiry physicality had panache all its own.

Like Presley's, Holly's singles quickly crossed over to R&B charts, with a strong appeal to black listeners. The Crickets played Hank Ballard and the Midnighters' salacious "Work with Me Annie." Both Holly and Presley, two lily-white Southern boys, effortlessly won over black listeners with their own style—a feat that eluded Gene Vincent and Eddie Cochran, for example.

On top of all this, Holly toyed with his medium in more elaborate and self-conscious ways than Presley. Long before multitrack recording machines became standard, Holly added voices or instruments to tape by simply rolling the existing tape as a backdrop and performing live on top of it—duetting with his voice via tape recorder. "Words of Love," the only Holly song the Beatles recorded, had drums, bass, rhythm guitar, and a vocal before Holly added lead guitar and two more vocal lines on top of it. "By the time the recording was completed," wrote John Goldrosen and John Beecher, "the drumming had receded into the background, providing a distant, rolling rhythm which can be felt and heard but does not obscure the vocal or guitar patterns. Similarly, recording the vocal last gave the song a close, intimate feeling, by placing the vocal in front of the varying guitar patterns."[11]

Another defining feature of Holly's appeal to Lennon was almost invisible; it was described by Holly's friend and touring companion Phil Everly, who watched the men file into the audience after the girls. "As it progressed to the evening, it filled up with men and if you were getting a lot of girl reaction, like screams and things, it would start to wane. You had to really deliver when the men got there. . . . Buddy Holly was an exception—he would go over more on those evenings when there was a bigger male audience."[12]

Lennon's insecurities would be tweaked onstage by standing next to McCartney, Central Casting's ideal Matinee Idol. Taking Holly's cue, Lennon turned male anxiety into a central theme. He became obsessed with Holly's "That'll Be the Day." Judy helped him learn Holly's song, displaying "endless patience" until he "managed to work out all the chords," he later said. "She was a perfectionist. She made me go right through it over and over again until I had it right. I remember her slowing down the record so that I could scribble out the words. First hearing Buddy absolutely knocked me for a loop. . . . And to think it was my own mother who was turning me on it all," Lennon marveled.[13]

Holly's chart action wedged a creative infinity into two years, from 1957 up to his plane crash on February 3, 1959. British listeners were among his most fervent fans. Lennon always regretted missing Holly's only tour of England, in March 1958, when he passed through Liverpool for two shows at Philharmonic Hall. But there's a good chance Lennon caught Holly singing "That'll Be the Day," "Peggy Sue," and "Oh Boy!" on TV at Pete Shotton's, on either *Saturday Night at the London Palladium* or the BBC's *Off the Record*. Liverpool classmate Tony Bramwell recalls the years of ribbing he took from the Quarrymen for winning a school prize and attending both of Holly's Liverpool shows, and shaking Holly's hand in between sets.[14] From the moment "That'll Be the Day" entered the British charts, Lennon followed the rest of Holly's career, from his split with the Crickets to his last recordings with "pop" strings. Holly didn't just develop, he made the idea of a self-contained act meaningful. Even singing songs written by other people (like "Oh Boy!," "Rave On," and "It Doesn't Matter Anymore"), Holly turned in defining work that extended and enlarged his persona.

As Holly's star rose, Elvis Presley got a crew cut and joined the army. Rock 'n' roll began extending its early explosive impact into a long-running style, carried forward in unpredictable ways by each new performer. With Holly, the outsider as insider, Lennon identified with a whole new concept of how sound might counter image. In a letter to a Holly fan much later, Lennon wrote, "He made it O.K. to wear glasses. I was Buddy Holly."[15]

McCARTNEY ALREADY HAD a notebook with original song lyrics and chord changes when he met Lennon. Since he didn't know how to write music on a staff, he sketched out lyrics with chords to remind him of their melodies. When McCartney showed up at his first Quarrymen rehearsal, drummer Colin Hanton remembers him spouting ideas: "He set right in telling me how to play and what to do. There was no shyness about him." Once he joined the Quarrymen, his notebook began bulging with titles, ideas that he and Lennon worked on, embryos of the Lennon-McCartney catalog: "I Lost My Little Girl," "That's My Woman," "Thinking of Linking," "Years Roll Along," "Keep Looking That Way," "Just Fun," and "Too Bad About Sorrows"—efforts that mixed the derivative with the yet-to-come, the soft products of McCartney's pre-Lennon imagination. And with his new partner, the list began to sprout instrumentals: one called "Looking Glass" (perhaps a product of Lennon's early love of *Alice in Wonderland*) and another named "Winston's Walk" (spoofing Lennon's middle name).

From this repository of ideas, McCartney and Lennon produced the first songs that listeners would soon recognize as Beatle material, difficult to date precisely, but somewhere between their meeting in 1957 and their first trip to Hamburg in 1960: "One After 909," "Hello Little Girl," "When I'm Sixty-four," "Hot as Sun," "Catswalk," and McCartney's most harmonically ambitious early work, "I'll Follow the Sun." This suggests McCartney already had some writing chops Lennon had yet to form, and that he may have mentored his new partner early on. Some of these songs seemed to write themselves, and were finished off quickly; others were toted around and tinkered with for years. Most significantly, the songs veered between tightly bound duets ("One After 909") and individual numbers (McCartney's "When I'm Sixty-four"), a pendulum set swinging between Lennon and McCartney harmonizing together and pursuing separate interests. Their defining duets always traveled this intriguing mix of togetherness and individuality, support and inimitability ("There's a Place" and "If I Fell" on through to "Eight Days a Week" and "Don't Let Me Down"). The existing evidence points to McCartney's lead in this solo vein. Many of these early notebooks have been lost—but not accidentally thrown away by Jane Asher, as reported by some.

The Quarrymen played their first paid gig August 7, 1957, downstairs at the Cavern Club on Mathew Street in downtown Liverpool. (McCartney, however, was absent, away at Scout camp with his brother, Michael, in the village of Hathersage, seventy-one miles east.) A trad-jazz fan named Alan Sytner had started the club the previous January as a hangout for like-minded purists, and he was wary that rock 'n' roll would attract rough customers. (In America, there was a lot of talk among adults about rock 'n' roll promoting "juvenile delinquency," code for the interracial mixing and degraded behavior that would inevitably result from this musical miscegenation.) Nigel Walley arranged the booking through his job as an apprentice golf caddie at Lee Park. Alan Sytner's father, a doctor who played golf at Lee Park, liked Walley and put him in touch with his son. Sytner agreed to book the band, but only provisionally, as an opening act. Skiffle was fine, but Sytner gave the Quarrymen stern orders not to stray. Stylistic tribes were as passionate as religious denominations, even at that early stage.

Disregarding Sytner's instructions, Lennon played not just the Del Vikings' "Come Go with Me," but Presley's "Hound Dog" and "Blue Suede Shoes." Sytner sent a curt note from the bar: "Cut out the bloody rock!"[16] They were not invited back. Sytner joined the line of skeptics to be converted.

A FEW WEEKS LATER, Lennon entered Liverpool Art College. At sixteen in September of 1957, his persona had all the bluster of a full-blown

Teddy Boy: greased hair, drainpipe pants hugging his skinny legs, all framing a loutish attitude. His look struck many of his new college peers as ridiculous, since most of the other students styled themselves as turtle-necked bohemians and weren't hung up on looking tough. McCartney was a year behind Lennon and still in school at the Liverpool Institute, which was right next door to the art college. Daily music sessions continued without a hitch.

The intermediate art curriculum Lennon enrolled in followed tradi-tional lines: he would spend the first two years studying lettering, draw-ing, composition and perspective, and life drawing; once he'd mastered the basics, his final two years would concentrate on independent work. Art history was not required, and an emphasis on representation and body form was the rule. Most students hoped to go into commercial graphics or design. The most popular classes involved life drawing of nudes, and one day Lennon reportedly sat on model June Furlong's naked lap. The curriculum offered no classes in cartooning, and Liverpool Art College had yet to catch up with the modernist movements—abstract expressionism, conceptual art, pop art—exploding in New York and Lon-don. For the first two-year course, students were expected to attend classes, submit portfolios for review in their chosen specialization, and consult with tutors about their future direction. Upon graduation, a na-tional diploma in art and design was conferred, with various ranks awarded for different levels of accomplishment.

If Lennon stood out as a Ted, Stuart Sutcliffe, who exuded a quiet charisma through black leather, quickly trumped his image. Sutcliffe was by far the most talented painter in the class, the kind of standout even the faculty deferred to. Having just turned seventeen, he was at least a year younger than most of the other students, admitted early for his stunning portfolio. Lennon quickly gravitated toward him. Soon af-ter McCartney became Lennon's musical intimate, Stuart became his artistic soul mate.

Sutcliffe took the bus in from Huyton, across the Mersey from Liver-pool, a neighborhood regarded by most Liverpudlians as the "tony" side of town. His childhood years were stable yet complicated. Sutcliffe's mother, née Martha Cronin, called Millie, fell in love with Charles Ferguson

Sutcliffe while he was still married to his first wife. But that was only their first hurdle: where the creative and strong-minded Millie was Catholic, Charles was a Protestant, the same vast cultural gulf Jim and Mary McCartney traversed. Once Charles divorced his first wife, both families disowned them, which gives Millie some resemblance to Julia Stanley. The couple moved to London and Manchester before settling in Edinburgh, where Charles worked as a marine engineer for the John Brown shipyard. Stuart came along shortly after they settled in their "elegant, sophisticated" home on Chalmers Street in 1940; sister Joyce followed in 1942. The following year, Stuart's father was drafted as "an essential war worker" by the Cammell Laird shipyard in Birkenhead. He brought his family down to Merseyside and moved them into public housing on Sedbergh Drive, Huyton, in 1943.[17] Another sister, Pauline, was born there, on January 8, 1944—Elvis Presley's birthday, as Stu liked to point out. This youngest child wrote two important memoirs, *Backbeat,* in 1994, followed by *The Beatles' Shadow: Stuart Sutcliffe and His Lonely Hearts Club,* in 2002.

The Sutcliffe household could not have been more different from Mimi Smith's house. The Sutcliffe parents were not especially concerned about traditional notions of respectability and conventional behavior, and they prized the arts and intellectual fields. "We grew up surrounded by books, paintings and music," Pauline Sutcliffe writes in *The Beatles' Shadow.* "My parents had studied piano as small children and were always playing, and my father did his turn [as pianist] in a dance band and at the cinema for the silent movies."[18] Like John's mother, Julia, Millie was an original. An asthmatic who never stopped smoking, she worked as a Roman Catholic schoolteacher, traveling across Liverpool to her school by tram with her inhaler and pills to treat her sudden attacks. For her, domestic duties were "boring"; she preferred recording the minutes of Labour Party meetings in Huyton, where she befriended future prime minister Harold Wilson.

Like John, Stu attended Sunday school, although the Roman Catholic variety; and he sang in the church choir at St. Gabriel's in Huyton "until his voice broke."[19] Pauline recalls lively household discussions: "I could tell the distinctions between a Bevanite and a Gaitskellite [Scottish

Labour Party factions] as easily as the distinction between an Elvis or a Cliff Richard fan."²⁰ All three children took piano lessons.

SUTCLIFFE'S PRODIGIOUS TALENT and painterly mind-set stirred something new in Lennon. While he took art school about as seriously as he'd taken the rest of his formal education, he glimpsed something larger in Sutcliffe's dedication to painting, and adopted romantic heroes like Van Gogh as his own. In the subversive Scouser style, Lennon became as suspicious of art-school self-importance as he did of musical elitism: to him, anything that smacked of pretension was all guff. Jazz was a favorite target, especially since most jazz musicians and fans sneered at early rock. "We were always anti-jazz," Lennon later told Hunter Davies:

> I think it is shit music, even more stupid than rock and roll, followed by people like students in cheap pullovers. Jazz never gets anywhere, never does anything, it's always the same and all they do is drink pints of beer. We hated jazz particularly because in the early days they wouldn't let us play at clubs, as they only wanted jazz. We'd never get auditions because of the jazz bands.²¹

To Lennon, rock 'n' roll was loaded with ideas, and was all the more attractive because "intellectuals" found it so easy to dismiss. (And note that disarming bit of Lennon dismissing jazzers as drunks.) Soon Lennon was hanging out with his art crowd at all hours of the day and night, in the common room or the cafeteria, at the pubs Ye Cracke, the Philharmonic down Hope Street from the art college, or the Jacaranda coffee bar, which was run by a raffish twenty-nine-year-old Welshman, Allan Williams, in his converted basement. Williams hired a group called the Royal Caribbean Band to play into the night, and turned "the Jac" into a hub of after-hours student life.

Since the Liverpool Institute ("the Innie") sat just next door, McCartney would stop by the Liverpool Art College canteen at lunchtime, which became a key rehearsal period for the Quarrymen. McCartney made his debut with the group on October 18, 1957, at New Clubmoor Hall, the Conservative Club in (Back) Broadway, Liverpool. This gig was booked by Charlie McBain, who also booked Wilson Hall in the working-class suburb of Garston, the Garston Swimming Baths (renowned as "the Blood Baths," where rival gangs would often erupt into fighting), Holyake Hall in Wavertree, and Wavertree Town Hall. McBain wound up giving the Beatles plenty of work in the next five years.[22] Also that same fall of 1957, the Quarrymen entered the Carroll Levis talent show at the Empire Theatre, without advancing.

It was at one of these Liverpool venues, purportedly Wilson Hall, in February 1958, that George Harrison first heard the group play.[23] Harrison was only fourteen, one of four children who lived way out in Speke, where the McCartneys once had lived. George's father was a bus driver named Harold, and his mother, Louise, liked to tune the family radio to hear special BBC broadcasts of Indian classical music.

Harrison had attended Dovedale Primary School several years behind Lennon without meeting him and was now a year behind McCartney at the Liverpool Institute. Paul and George already played Lonnie Donegan numbers together informally at Harrison's house, and continued meeting up on their daily bus to the Innie. George sat at the back and noodled on his guitar. One day, McCartney heard him mimic "Raunchy," the loping Western instrumental made popular by Memphis guitarist Bill Justis's guitarist Sid Manker. Justis had supervised Sun Records sessions for Jerry Lee Lewis, Roy Orbison, and Johnny Cash. The instrumental spent an unlikely fourteen weeks on the U.S. charts in the fall of 1957, making it Sun's biggest-selling instrumental to date. "Raunchy" (originally called "Backwoods") featured a guitar lead on the lower strings, a reversal of most high E-string leads. Justis's early use of reverb caught a weirdly suggestive new sound, among the many that began pouring from the new electric technology. McCartney heard Harrison reaching for both the melody and its long sustain, even though he played it on an acoustic guitar. Impressed, McCartney had Harrison play "Raunchy" for Lennon, who admitted a grudging respect for his abilities. Although Harrison was already playing guitar for a jazz group called the Les Stewart Quartet, he joined up with the Quarrymen. Soon after, he brought them a gig: the band played for the wedding of George's brother Harry at the Harrisons' house in Speke in December 1958.

THE QUARRYMEN BUMPED along like many an amateur outfit during this phase, stringing together appearances at family events and hitting up employers. After Harry Harrison's wedding reception on December 20, 1958, they brought in New Year's Day, 1959, playing for Harrison's father's Speke Bus Depot Social Club's belated Christmas party at Wilson Hall in Garston. That summer they learned about a new club opening up in West Derby called the Casbah Coffee Club—a project driven by a local eccentric named Mona Best, who decided the local youth culture could use some juice and turned her large basement into a dance hall. Born in India, the daughter of a British army officer, Mona had married Joe Best, a sportswriter for the *Liverpool Echo*. Together they raised two boys, Pete, who wore a huge pompadour atop smoldering good looks, and Rory, three years younger. Pete Best, who went on to become "the Lost Beatle," later would write his memoirs, *Beatle!*, with numerous vivid descriptions of the Merseyside music scene and its characters. The *Liverpool Echo* ran a story announcing the "Kasbah's" opening, along with a photo of McCartney and Lennon performing as Cynthia Powell looked on adoringly.[24]

The Quarrymen's shot at the Casbah had a last-minute twist straight out of some Andy Hardy movie. Ken Brown, bassist for the Les Stewart Quartet, got into an argument with Stewart, who walked out on the opening-night gig. Desperate, Brown asked Harrison if he knew any musicians who might be willing to fill in at the last minute. Harrison "rounded up" Paul and John, invited Brown into the band, and the Quarrymen played the Casbah that night and every Saturday slot through October 10, 1959, for three pounds per performance—seventy-five pence per member. Brown's last night as a Quarryman came when Mona Best tried to pay him for a set he had sat out upstairs due to illness. (Why he bothered to show up with a heavy cold goes unexplained.) McCartney protested: why should Brown get paid when he didn't even perform?

John, Paul, and George closed ranks, and that ended their alliance with Brown and, for the moment, the Casbah.[25]

After their seven weeks as the Casbah's main draw, the band (calling themselves, for the occasion, Johnny and the Moondogs) once more entered the Carroll Levis *TV Star Search* at the Empire Theatre. This time they advanced through two appearances into the finals and performed for the concluding show in Manchester, thirty miles from Liverpool, on November 15. The finale awarded a giant prize at the end of the long evening, based on the readings of an applause meter brought on after all the acts had performed. This arrangement worked against the group: by the time Johnny and the Moondogs were summoned to the stage for their meter reading, John, Paul, and George had boarded the last train home, without enough cash to stay overnight.

As the three Quarrymen who would become Beatles began to venture into songwriting, they became students of some of the best in the business, tracking composers regardless of who performed their material. While they particularly admired writer-performers like Chuck Berry and Buddy Holly, they also tracked Brill Building tunesmiths like Atlantic's Jerry Leiber and Mike Stoller, whose credits dominated recordings by Elvis Presley ("Hound Dog" and "Jailhouse Rock"), Little Richard ("Kansas City"), and the Coasters ("Searchin'" and "Yakety Yak"), all of which rolled right into the Quarrymen's set lists. Along the way, learning these numbers taught them not just how to play but how to write, arrange, and harmonize.

Unfortunately, many of the home tapes from this embryonic period have been lost, with one exception. A certain Bob Molyneaux recorded the Quarrymen—pre-McCartney—playing at the St. Peter's fête in July 1957. (This recording was first heard commercially more than forty years later, on *Anthology 1*.) The Grundig reels made by Colin Hanton's neighbors Geraldine and Colette Davis and another fan, Arthur Wong, all have since been lost or wiped. Some April 1960 recordings from the McCartney home on Forthlin Road have leaked, but not "When I'm Sixty-four."

The Quarrymen cut their first piece of vinyl, with McCartney and Harrison, in the drawing room of Percy Phillips's house in the late spring or early summer of 1958. Phillips, a local inventor and tinkerer, had invested in a primitive disc-cutting setup: a reel-to-reel tape recorder, an amplifier, a four-channel mixer, and a disc cutter that carved the results into hot lacquer. Local acts were recorded in Phillips's living room while he monitored the bulky machine; then he transferred the analog recording onto a ten-inch shellac, a thick plastic disc. Harrison found out about the setup through his friend Johnny Byrne, a local guitarist who had made a record there earlier that year. Once it became apparent that you could sign up, pay your money, and take home an actual platter, the idea was irresistible: an actual record they could pass around . . . perhaps even send off to London and impress a label. "It was a big deal for all of us," Colin Hanton remembered many years later.[26]

Paul and John jointly decided to lead with "That'll Be the Day." Hanton played drums, George played guitar, John and Paul sang lead, and they asked another friend, John Lowe, to round out the sound with some honky-tonk piano. Phillips persuaded them that they'd achieve higher quality if they recorded their two songs to tape and then transferred them to disc, a process that would let them edit out a sloppy cutoff or false start. One version says John and Paul balked because Phillips wanted an extra pound for that service, but finally assented. Another version has them skipping the tape to cut out the extra fee. Each band member wound up paying seventeen shillings and sixpence to make the two-sided, ten-inch 78 rpm disc.

"That'll Be the Day" gets over on high spirits, with all the winning humor of Lennon's enthusiasm and none of the finesse of Holly's original: they completely miss those distinctive triplet rhythmic kicks on the final refrain. (Since this was the number he'd learned from Judy, it's tempting to think that he, as Presley did with "Old Shep," sang his first record for his mother.) For the B side, there was a quarrel about which song to do—until McCartney simply counted off "In Spite of All the Danger," a slow-tempo original which they never had actually rehearsed. Hanton and Lowe simply joined in, pretending to know their parts, as McCartney and Harrison banged out the tune they had fixed up together and Lennon chimed in.

For a group of mid-teenagers, at a time when the most successful acts typically did not write their own songs, it was beyond hubris to include one of their own compositions on a demo they hoped would get them a recording contract. "In Spite of All the Danger," a simple ditty that aims toward country peril with none of the pathos, gives you a good idea of their rough but earnest level of playing by this stage: some practiced guitar licks from George, and the hints of a vocal blend between John and Paul that would sound different with every record. As the only song ever credited jointly to Paul McCartney and George Harrison, it sets up an intrigue within the group, the first indication of a triangular power struggle. The song was largely McCartney's, but George's guitar solo lent a lanky ambition to the sound, and McCartney shared songwriting credit with Harrison as recognition. For the first time, all three Beatles are singing: Lennon and McCartney duetting, with Harrison providing backup "aaah"s and meek yet precise guitar work.

From then on, all the early original songs the group released were credited to Lennon and McCartney, which begs the question: did Lennon suddenly realize that he longed for that songwriting credit? (One early number, "Cry for a Shadow," gets attributed to Lennon and Harrison.) In the *Anthology,* McCartney recalls a conversation considering a three-way songwriting partnership with Harrison, "but we decided no, it would just be us two." Either McCartney quickly decided that Harrison's solo shouldn't amount to a writing credit, or his kinship with Lennon, and their productive chemistry, simply settled this question.

All the high hopes around making their own piece of shellac didn't take them very far: they passed it around the band and their friends— each member got to have it for a week's time—but nobody sent it off to London. The platter hid in John Lowe's linen drawer until McCartney bought it back in July 1981.[27] The "Danger" heard on *Anthology 1,* with forty-two seconds (a verse and chorus) edited out and heavy noise reduction applied, is a distant, tinny chorus waving at us from the other side of the myth.

LENNON'S POST–QUARRY Bank routine avoided Mendips as much as possible. Days were spent at art college, cadging cigarettes and wedging in lunchtime sing-alongs with McCartney and Harrison; afternoons and evenings were whiled away at coffee bars like the Jac, gabbing about art and getting fresh with girls. And he kept visiting Judy's household, acting as a big brother to his two stepsisters, Julia and Jacqui, often staying over on weekends, as if the Dykins house felt more like home than Aunt Mimi's.

On the evening of July 15, 1958, Lennon and Dykins were in the kitchen at the Blomfield Road residence cleaning up after tea; Julia was on her bike in the front garden, and Jacqui had been put to bed upstairs. As a sunny afternoon faded into dusk on that summer Tuesday, Judy called out to her daughter, "Just going to see Mimi, lovey," and set off down the road toward the bus stop. Dykins's mother—Nana to the children—stopped to talk with her on her way out, and Julia, then eleven years old, heard them both laugh. Julia remembered a premonition coming over her:

> Tonight, for no reason at all, I began to feel it wasn't quite the same. Suddenly, I knew something was terribly wrong. How does a child feel panic? My recollection is that my chest felt uncomfortably tight and I wanted to retch. Waves of fear swept through me, as if someone was standing over me, threatening me with a huge, hard fist. Without thinking, I threw down my bike and ran faster than I ever had to the top of the road, to try and catch my mother before she got on the bus. It was too late. When I turned the corner she was gone.[28]

After a long chat with Mimi, Judy left Mendips between 9:30 and 10 P.M. "Normally," her daughter says, "Mimi walked with her across Menlove Avenue to the bus stop. Tonight Mimi said, 'I won't walk you tonight, Julia. I'll see you tomorrow.'" Just as Judy was leaving the house, Nigel Walley came by looking for John. She invited him to join her on the bus ride and meet with John at her house. Walley declined, but offered to walk her to the bus stop at the intersection of Vale Road, where he waved good-bye as she crossed the street. "She had just started across the other side when a car hurled her up into the air," Baird wrote. "She was killed instantly. She was just forty-four."[29] After hearing a thud, Walley turned back to see Julia's body flying through the air. "I ran back to get Mimi, and we rushed to wait for the ambulance . . . white with terror, and crying in hysterics."[30] Years later, Walley told a *Liverpool Echo* reporter: "I must have been about 15 yards up the road when I heard a car skidding. I turned round to see John's mum going through the air. I rushed over but she had been killed instantly. . . . I had nightmares about it for years. I can see it today—Julia lying there with her hair fluttering over her face."[31]

"Many years passed," Baird wrote, "before John could bring himself to talk about that night," and then his words still carried the gaping agony of the nightmare that engulfed his life:

An hour or so after it happened a copper came to the door to let us know about the accident. It was awful, like some dreadful film where they ask you if you're the victim's son and all that. Well, I was, and I can tell you it was absolutely the worst night of my entire life.

. . . Anyway, Bobby [Dykins] and I got a cab over to Sefton General Hospital where she was lying dead. I remember rabbiting on hysterically to the cabbie all the way there. Of course, there was no way I could ever bear to look at her. Bobby went in to see her for a few minutes, but it turned out to be too much for the poor sod and he finally broke down in my arms out in the lobby. I couldn't seem to cry, not then anyway. I suppose I was just frozen inside.[32]

John's cousin Leila, with whom he'd spent summers in Scotland, was in medical school at Edinburgh University. Mimi sent a telegram which read: JUDY CAR ACCIDENT. DIED FRIDAY. FUNERAL TUESDAY. Leila rushed down to Mendips and went to Julia's funeral "in a complete daze . . . I couldn't stand it. I hated the funeral and everybody there. It was impossible to believe it was Julia in that box." The normally loquacious Lennon turned white and clammed up; being around people was the last thing he wanted in the days that followed. At the reception in the Cottage (where Julia had briefly set up house with John as an infant during the war), Leila sat with John, his head on her lap. "I never said a word. I can't even recall telling him I was sorry. There *was* nothing you could say. We were both numb with anguish."[33]

Part of Lennon's estrangement can be gleaned from the way Julia's daughters were treated: Dykins shuttled them off to relatives before the funeral, and they were not even told of their mother's death for several weeks. Lennon already felt himself in some strange purgatory farther from that Dykins family orbit. Mimi, of course, was shocked, most likely blamed herself for not walking Judy to the bus, and was still slogging through the long, lonely tunnel of her husband George's collapse. And given the tension between these sisters, Mimi had proven herself the last person Lennon might confide in about losing his mother for a second time. On top of Blackpool and losing his uncle George, here opens up a black hole of anguish and fury inside Lennon's pride.

Beyond the personal trauma, Julia's accident proved a travesty of justice. The driver was an off-duty cop named Eric Clague, who was racing into work after oversleeping—he had yet to pass his driving test. An inquest established his lack of a license, and Nigel Walley was called as a witness, but Clague got off with a reprimand and suspension from duty. John, Bobby Dykins, and Mimi attended the hearing, devastated. Beatle historian Bill Harry reports that Mimi cried out "Murderer!" in the courtroom.[34]

Many quotes from McCartney reveal how observant he was of Lennon's complicated relationship with Judy, and how much the loss solidified their musical connection:

> His mum lived right near where I lived. I had lost my mum, that's one thing, but for your mum to actually be living somewhere else and for you to be a teenage boy and not living with her is very sad. It's horrible. I remember him not liking it at all. John and I would go and visit her and she'd be very nice but when we left there was always a tinge of sadness about John. On the way back I could always tell that he loved the visit and he loved her but was very sad that he didn't live with her.[35]

Of course, both boys were already conditioned to keep such feelings hidden, which only intensified the shared emotion. Judy's death fed a strange, intimate currency between the two musicians, a private space they both used to underline their resentments against the world. McCartney remembered:

> Now we were both in this; both losing our mothers. This was a bond for us, something of ours, a special thing. We'd both gone through that trauma and both come out the other side and we could actually laugh about it in the sick humor of the day. Once or twice when someone said, "Is your mother gonna come?," we'd say, in a sad voice, "She died." We actually used to put people through that. We could look at each other and know.[36]

Although Beatle fans know her only through stories and her son's music, Julia Lennon lived long enough to catch whispers of John's early Beatles with the Quarrymen, watch his first year at art college, and glimpse his early partnerships with Stu Sutcliffe and Paul McCartney. She heard John perform live more than a few times. She bought him his first guitar, taught him banjo chords, shared rock 'n' roll through Buddy Holly and Elvis Presley, and designed his first colorful stage shirts. One scene that doesn't seem to have a first-person testimony is the day John brought Judy his band's first homemade recording, of "That'll Be the Day," a prize accomplishment. Her pleasure at coaxing Lennon's creativity contrasted with Mimi's disapproval; in many ways, Judy and John both used the new style to rebel against Mimi. History still wonders: besides "Julia," how many songs did John Lennon sing to the only grown-up in his world with an ear for rock 'n' roll?

Pools of Sorrow

I N THE MONTHS FOLLOWING JUDY'S DEATH, LENNON SPIRALED INTO AN emotional tunnel that left defining scars, and made nearsighted decisions that reaped long-term consequences. Perhaps this loss simply confirmed what Lennon had suspected since Blackpool: that his mother never was his, and never would be. Now this suspicion assumed a terrible immediacy just as his creativity began to win attention. Her loss made him lunge more toward release and meaning in art, one of the few comforts in a world of stiff-upper-lip platitudes. Three outlets stemmed his rage, trapdoors that could only simulate family stability: music, booze, and womanizing.

With all the loss thickening the Mendips air around Aunt Mimi, he moved in with Stu Sutcliffe and used the art college as a branch office for his music. The public-address system was pirated as the band's equipment, and Lennon talked Sutcliffe's painting teacher, Arthur Ballard, who ran the Student Union committee, into purchasing a reel-to-reel tape recorder. This Grundig machine was rarely on campus after the school bought it: Lennon and Sutcliffe began recording Presley songs and mimicking their favorite *Goon Show* radio routines at one of Sutcliffe's early apartments at 9 Percy Street: "Lennon was Peter Sellers, skinny Stuart was Harry Secombe, Rod [Davis] was Michael Bentine and Spike Milligan," writes Pauline Sutcliffe.[1] (These tapes have been lost.)

Given Lennon's poor showing his first year, it's a wonder they let him stay. "I mean, in England, if you're lucky you get into art school," he remembered. "It's somewhere they put you if they can't put you anywhere else."[2] Few at Quarry Bank seemed to sense they were getting razzed by a top-shelf comic talent; at least at art college, a few caught on to Lennon's routine, including Sutcliffe and perhaps Ballard, who remarked of Sutcliffe that he "seemed more a mentor to Lennon than best friend."[3] Early on, Ballard advocated for Stuart's painting, and hoped his talent might rub off on Lennon. Sutcliffe was "always helping him get back up to standard and fill out his notebooks with the required research notes and essays."[4]

At first, Lennon burrowed down into painting to follow Sutcliffe's lead. Then, after bedding around like the sailors who streamed through the docks, he fixed on a steady girlfriend from his lettering class, a docile brunette named Cynthia Powell. They recognized each other as blind bats too proud to wear glasses; their myopia became destiny. Powell commuted into Liverpool from Huyton, a suburb north of Woolton, where Sutcliffe had grown up. Their mutual friends were stupefied by the romance: Lennon the tough, cynical crackpot soon made her over as a blond, short-skirted Brigitte Bardot, the garish opposite of her subdued personality. "Cynthia was so quiet," a former girlfriend of John's, Thelma Pickles, told biographer Hunter Davies, "completely different type from us. She came from over the water, the posh part, from a middle-class area. She wore a twin set [a prim matching outfit]. She was very nice, but I just couldn't see her suiting John. He used to go on about her, telling us how marvelous she was. I just couldn't see it."[5] A "twin set" is what the Royals wore; it blared a prudishness both behavioral and, more important, philosophical. Pickles herself had just jumped off Lennon's romantic whirligig, screeching, "Don't blame me that your mother's dead!" one night in the Jacaranda.[6] Cynthia's attitude was different. Powell's family was what the British called "respectable," the next-best thing the middle class had to stature or power (or money); that is to say, she was bred in all particulars to be put off by someone of Lennon's coarseness—so she fell particularly hard. If Mimi Smith hadn't practiced such a smothering attachment to her nephew, you can almost imagine her approving of Cynthia, because she came from the right station. But escaping Aunt Mimi's clutches, Lennon anchored down in the first port that would take him.

He would speak disparagingly of this relationship, one of his longest, and he rarely was faithful to Cynthia. But the two somehow endured Beatlemania's early typhoon, and Lennon's affectionate letters read profoundly sincere. First reprinted in Ray Coleman's 1984 biography, they teem with "I love you"s and "XXX"s. Cynthia's insights across two books trace revealing strands of Lennon's private character. Both Powell memoirs, *A Twist of Lennon* (1982) and *John* (2005), can at first ring naïve— she seems not to have shared the slightest interest in rock 'n' roll. But dwelling inside Lennon's shadow, Powell gets underestimated: in the UK, she's viewed as the stalwart, salt-of-the-earth shotgun wife who anchored all of Lennon's wayward excesses, before and after his fame swallowed them both. (After all, even Yoko Ono kicked this guy out after a few years of marriage.) And Powell makes uncannily brutal remarks as the union ends: The first is her simple suggestion that he'd be happier with "someone like Yoko" even as he's figuring it out for himself. The second concerns his Beatles: "You seem to need them even more than they need you." That kind of observation is enough to bring many a husband running back into the speaker's arms. Cynthia's choices were guided by abiding love and forgiveness beyond all self-respect.

When Lennon first approached her to dance at an art-college mixer, Cynthia demurred, saying she had a boyfriend in Huyton. "Well, I wasn't asking you to marry me then, was I?"[7] Lennon shot back. Later, with Hunter Davies in 1967, she reflected on their early courtship: "I wasn't in a hurry to introduce John to my mother," Cynthia told him. "I wanted to prepare her for the shock. . . . Molly, the cleaning woman, once caught John hitting me, really clouting me. She said I was a silly girl to get mixed up with someone like that."[8] Some of her earliest memories of courtship include his drubbings.

Lennon's unconscious emotional radar led him to a more stable counterpart as he thrashed about against the death of his mother. "I was in a sort of blind rage for two years," he said. "I was either drunk or fighting. It had been the same with other girl friends I'd had. There was something the matter with me."[9] Picking up where Mimi left off, there was plenty of mothering for the old-fashioned Cynthia to do.

Lennon had spent his first year at art college still living at Mendips, shuttling to classes on the bus and crashing at Sutcliffe's apartment on Percy Street. By his second year, even his rows with Mimi had grown stale, beyond repair, and perhaps Mendips couldn't hold their combined grief.

"John was mesmerized by Stuart, who was always a noted stylist, crossing the boundaries between high and low art," wrote Pauline Sutcliffe.[10] Sutcliffe's influence on Lennon cannot be overstated: there existed no gap between the painters Sutcliffe admired and the music Lennon kept going on about; for them, art had both aesthetic and commercial attributes—something the Beatles would synthesize through album covers. Ballard remembered Sutcliffe as "wistful yet tough,"[11] and when Sutcliffe moved from Percy Street to a new flat on Gambier Terrace, Lennon followed—it was the one place where he and Cynthia found any privacy.

Bill Harry remembers hanging out at Sutcliffe's flat going on about modernism, painters like Nicolas de Staël, novelists like Albert Camus, and actors like Zbigniew Cybulski, "the Polish James Dean." Sutcliffe's own paintings adopted the late-impressionistic style of Van Gogh, another tragic hero. In the tradition of beatnik pretense, remembers Pauline Sutcliffe, "at times, it was a game to find characters, new and from the past, who they would consider worthy of their adulation, and it seemed that the more obscure your choice, the cooler you were."[12] In London in 1956, a sweeping collage built from American magazine ads by the young Richard Hamilton, called *Just What Is It That Makes Today's Homes So Different, So Appealing?*, had raised a stir at the This Is Tomorrow exhibition by the Independent Group at the Whitechapel Art Gallery. A new British impulse venerating fantasies of American consumerism began disrupting formal art circles and was later dubbed pop art. Like Sutcliffe, Hamilton demonstrated how many art students viewed painting—a traditional "high" art—as part of the same continuum as popular arts like movies, pop music, commercial fiction, and even advertising.

Meanwhile, the Quarrymen gigged sporadically at private parties, and McCartney, Harrison, and Lennon gathered with their guitars at the school cafeteria, the Jacaranda, or the McCartney home, but seldom at Mendips. Musically, they made headway in fits and starts, learned new records, chased down solos and vocal harmonies.

WINNING OVER RAKISH audiences became a defining scene at Quarrymen appearances, as rough-and-ready skiffle expanded into fisticuffs rock. Colin Hanton remembers a night in Wilson Hall when "a massive Teddy Boy, who'd had too much to drink, climbed up on stage. I thought he was going to thump John but he went up to Paul and eye-balled him, nose to nose. 'I want you to do Little Richard.' Paul certainly wasn't going to argue with this hulking drunk, so he announced that our next song would be 'Long Tall Sally.'" They hadn't planned on playing it, so Paul invented and then repeated a lot of lyrics. "He was brilliant at it," Hanton recalls. "And the drunk was happy."[13]

Learning how to thrive in such settings measured any musician's mettle, where girls itching to dance and boys itching to fight clashed in spasms of class rage. In a place like Garston or Litherland, when word got around that one of these Quarrymen hailed from a snob town like Woolton, the Teds, who needed very little encouragement, pulled out razors and bicycle chains and sent many dances careening into violence. The idea that Lennon, this tough Woolton "phony," with his ducktail and drainies, would show up and make music was barely tolerable; that their own girlfriends screamed for the band only bolstered their motivation. The irony of grammar-school boys striving to sound a notch *beneath* their station seems to have been lost on them. Here lies the crux of Lennon's class puzzle. After all, what was the future author of "Working Class Hero" to do—tell them his Woolton auntie took in students to make ends meet?

Anyway, the music was simply a prelude; the fight often became the main event. In this intensely working-class culture, throwing fists was a defining behavior of budding manhood, where a wrong look could get you a shiner. One evening in Prescot, Lancashire, the band won such crowd response during the first set that the manager opened up the bar for them and promised them more steady work. It was a big mistake: the second set degenerated into too much drink, with Lennon heckling both manager and audience from the stage. Colin Hanton, tired of Lennon's loutish inclinations, hauled his kit off the bus on the way home, never to return. He couldn't tell which was worse: the self-defeating carousing or the lost shot at some prime bookings. It was the beginning of the band's drummer's curse.

LENNON AND McCARTNEY were always on the make for gigs. At the Jacaranda coffee bar, where students gabbed into the night, they pestered Allan Williams, who still had the steel-drum band playing in his joint: why not some rock 'n' roll? He hired the band briefly for engagements at his new strip club, the Blue Angel, originally called the Wyvern Social Club. Meanwhile at the end of 1959, Sutcliffe won a painting award from more than two thousand entries, for a piece called *Summer Painting,* from John Moores, the Liverpool patron. Early in 1960, Lennon and McCartney persuaded him to spend his prize money, sixty-five pounds, for a deposit on rock's least glamorous instrument, the electric bass. With the others pressing him, Sutcliffe went to Hessy's on Whitechapel and purchased a Höfner bass guitar—the hollow-bodied, violin-shaped brand McCartney would make famous. Sutcliffe had been cultivating his own major rock 'n' roll fixation—his sister describes his Elvis obsession—and seemed genuinely torn between painting and the musical thrills Lennon coaxed out of him. "We were an Elvis family," Pauline Sutcliffe writes, "although we were also keen on Billy Fury and Johnny Kidd and the Pirates ('Shakin All Over')."[14] Hanton's departure had left the group drummerless. Now they could at least boast of a bassist, and with the borrowed PA equipment from the art college, they had some semblance of a unit. "The rhythm's in the guitars," they kept insisting.

Sutcliffe's hallowed status at the art college had shaped a mystique around him. His moody-painter pose, his sheer attitude, attracted Lennon almost as much as the paintings themselves; it was as if both of them discovered how similar sensibilities could be conveyed through different mediums, guitar and canvas. These motives were tangled for Lennon: while his best friend would necessarily be a member of his musical group (and get talked into spending money on equipment), Sutcliffe's friendship outweighed the musical partnership, which eventually would cause a bitter falling-out. Lennon, branching out from his drawings and cartoons, began sponging off his friend as a painting tutor. Cynthia would be "ordered to wait in a corner until these private lessons were over."[15]

Pauline Sutcliffe described a novel Stuart began in this period, where a character named Nhoke is the thinly veiled composite of Lennon and Sutcliffe, "an artist living in horrid rooms in Puke Street." She remembered how Stuart wrote of the "terrible change in John" in the months after they met, mirroring the loss of his mother: "He was capricious, incalculable and self-centered, yet at the same time he was always a loyal friend. A frustrated and misunderstood child not given its due need of affection ends as a man without roots, in rebellion or bewilderment, almost embittered."[16]

Most Beatle historians claim that Sutcliffe's verbal and painterly articulacy was absent from his bass playing. Many simplistically conclude that he couldn't have done that well, too, and that Lennon's loyalty to him outweighed his musical skills. But this enfeebled musicianship doesn't jibe with the historical record. Across many stages, to audiences both rapt and oblivious, Sutcliffe regularly performed "Love Me Tender" as a Quarryman. If Sutcliffe's charisma was "dry," putting over a contemporary Presley number like that takes pluck, not to say panache. And with his background in church choir and his boyhood piano lessons, there's good reason to assume he held his own on bass. The musically astute Cavern Club deejay Bob Wooler later argued that "the Beatles carried no passengers"; and in spite of Paul and George's avid competition for John's musical attention, Sutcliffe played with the band for just over a year.[17]

One way for McCartney and Harrison to badger Lennon was to complain about Sutcliffe's skill, but it's just as likely they were clamoring for more of Lennon's respect. "John and Stuart were top dogs and that was always a problem for Paul and George," wrote Pauline Sutcliffe, "for they did not feel totally included in everything that was happening." Lennon's bond with Stuart was artistic and intellectual, while his friendship with McCartney bridged onstage musical rapport with practical stuff like cadging 45s, deciphering lyrics, and figuring out chords. "Looking back on it now," McCartney told Pauline Sutcliffe, "I think it was little tinges of jealousy because Stu was John's friend. There was always a little jealousy among the group as to who would be John's friend. He was like the guy you aspired to."[18] By most accounts McCartney and Sutcliffe were like oil and water. Again, it speaks to Lennon's magnetism that they coexisted for as long as they did. Ironically, it's Sutcliffe's artier aspect, not anyone's playing, that seems to have shaped the band—its look, its attitude, its image—as they gained ensemble proficiency. Early on, their growing idea of themselves as Artists, with particular garb and matching attitudes, was ahead of their musicianship, both as individuals and as a group. With Sutcliffe, they latched on to an attitude and nurtured it into a sound.

There's a marked lag in live performances between two late Christmas parties in January of 1959, just before Buddy Holly died, and the opening the next August 29 of the Casbah Coffee Club, where the Quarrymen won a regular Saturday slot (and eventually picked up a new drummer). But this lag resembles their 1958 schedule, when by Beatle scholar Mark Lewisohn's scrupulous count the Quarrymen played only five gigs, with none at all between March and December.[19] Despite the gaps between performances, Lennon spent the bulk of his time practicing, learning chords, harmonizing, and writing songs with McCartney, as his studies tarried. In between gigs, his refusal to do anything serious with his art studies was pronounced. The motivating principle to his life was music, right down to the nitty-gritty of where to get gigs and how to snag equipment, combing the charts for new material, immersing himself in the playlists of Radio Luxembourg, and honing his skills on the guitar. As a musician at an art school, his daily interactions brought all kinds of new metaphors into play, and he began to think of rock 'n' roll as part of a larger story.

This larger picture started coming into view as the wheels began to spin off some major rock careers. Jerry Lee Lewis's success crashed into scandal after he married wife number three in December 1957: his cousin, Myra Gale Brown, aged thirteen. (His band swore she was only twelve.) Early the next year, Elvis Presley answered the peacetime draft by joining the army: he was inducted March 24, 1958, and bused from Memphis to Fort Chaffee, Arkansas, before getting assigned to the Third Armored Division and shipped to basic training at Fort Hood in Texas. On August 14, Presley's beloved mother, Gladys, died in Memphis. Julia Stanley's death dates almost exactly one month earlier.[20]

Presley's teenage glow had such force in Lennon's mind that he always took the King's drafting as a de facto enlistment: "Elvis died when he went into the army," he said as late as 1980.[21] At seventeen, he couldn't square the flashing neon Elvis with the straight-arrow enlisted soldier, who put his rebellion on hold to suit up during peacetime. The press covered it as an event, or a bad omen, as if the music itself might not survive.

It got worse from there. Early in 1959, after two weeks sleeping on subzero overnight treks in their broken-down tour bus, Buddy Holly chartered a plane and, along with J. P. Richardson ("the Big Bopper") and Ritchie Valens, raced ahead from Mason City, Iowa, to the Winter Dance Party tour's next gig, in Moorhead, Minnesota. Richardson had caught a nasty flu and had begged his seat off Holly's bass player, Waylon Jennings. "Well, I hope your ol' bus freezes up," Holly told Jennings. "Well, I hope your ol' plane crashes," Jennings shot back. When the plane went down shortly after takeoff in the early hours of February 3, everyone on board perished. Holly's "Heartbeat" had just entered the British charts. A month later, fans stopped short to hear Holly singing Paul Anka's "It Doesn't Matter Anymore," his last record, defying its syrupy strings to create a new, existential subgenre: the posthumous hit.

The year closed with Chuck Berry's prison sentence for violating the Mann Act—the same law used to hound heavyweight boxer Jack Johnson decades before. In Berry's case, a fourteen-year-old Apache prostitute complained to police after he fired her from his St. Louis nightclub.[22] With Carl Perkins's music in disrepair since his 1956 car crash, Little Richard enrolled at a seminary, and others downed by fate, racist persecution, and dumb bad luck, the gods seemed to be frowning on rock's staying power. American historians invariably describe the period between 1959 and 1963 as "fallow," which is really a measure of how differently Americans and Britons perceived the style.

To Liverpool fans, the rock 'n' roll juggernaut seemed less fallow than tragic. Rockabilly star Gene Vincent bucked and swayed on the new ITV network's show *Boy Meets Girls* in December 1959, and soon producer Jack Good imported a pal of Vincent's, the surly, ferocious Eddie Cochran, who streaked across TV screens in late January and February. Larry Parnes, a well-known London promoter, booked the Cochran-and-Vincent bill for a tour of the UK. Lennon and Sutcliffe caught the show at the Empire in Liverpool in March, and Pauline Sutcliffe remembers that "John was furious—what a colossal irony—when the screams of female fans drowned out his idols."[23]

Soon afterward, Allan Williams contacted Parnes to coproduce a second, even bigger package at Liverpool Stadium in May. ("I could smell money . . . lots of it," Williams recalled.)[24] The bill was slated to include, besides Cochran and Vincent, Peter Wynne, Lance Fortune, Nero and the Gladiators, Cass and the Casanovas, and Rory Storm and the Hurricanes (with a drummer named Ringo Starr). But late on April 16, after scandalizing Bristol's Hippodrome, Cochran hired a taxi back to London for his flight home. Just before midnight, his driver swerved into a lamppost outside Chippenham, Wiltshire. Cochran's fiancée, Sharon Sheeley, who had flown over to be with him on her twentieth birthday, suffered a broken pelvis. Gene Vincent survived with broken ribs and collarbone and further harm to an already damaged leg.[25] Thrown from the car and suffering severe head injuries, Cochran died the next afternoon at St. Martin's Hospital in Bath.

Singer Vince Eager (né Roy Taylor) told biographer Alan Clayson: "Larry Parnes rang to say that I ought to get down to the hospital in Bath, where Eddie was on the danger list. . . . There, the surgeon told me that Eddie was unlikely to survive. I was extremely upset, but when I emerged from the hospital, there was Parnes with the press and half his bloody pop stars, ready for a photo opportunity. I just drove off and refused to speak to Larry, who even before Eddie died had told the newspapers (a) about the 'irony' of Eddie's latest release, 'Three Steps to Heaven'—which was in fact the B-side then—and (b) that I was off to fly back to America with the coffin."²⁶ All the same, on May 3 the Liverpool show went on as scheduled, padded out with extra performers. The Quarrymen were there, forced to sit and watch, eager to perform yet still drummerless.

Cochran's death had a profound impact on British Invasion rockers, who remember him as a larger presence than most Americans do. "Twenty Flight Rock" was the first song Lennon heard McCartney sing, and by this point they had added Cochran's "C'mon Everybody," "Teenage Heaven," and "I Remember" to their sets. For Lennon, the tragedy struck especially close to home, since he'd just caught Cochran and Vincent's show at the Empire. This all happened in the shadow of Julia's accident in the summer of 1958. All of Lennon's teenage giants had stumbled, strayed, or failed to cheat death: Presley joined the army, Little Richard defected to the pulpit, and the ghost of Buddy Holly whispered, "It Doesn't Matter Anymore." "Let us remember that Eddie Cochran died for rock 'n' roll on the playing fields of England," Andrew Loog Oldham would write, voicing what Lennon surely felt after catching Cochran's only British tour.²⁷

As a manager for Lennon's group, Allan Williams was a stand-in for Alf Lennon—always scheming for a score. He had coaxed Larry Parnes to hire some of "his" groups to play for the May 3 show, and Parnes was impressed enough with the surging Liverpool beat scene to return the following week to audition support for singers in his stable, whose names blared his show-biz banality: Billy Fury, Johnny Gentle, Duffy Power, and the best-known of these, Tommy Steele. The "Silver Beetles," a name Sutcliffe first devised, were among the local groups that got the call, recruiting for the occasion a middle–aged drummer, Tommy Moore. Billy Fury, about to launch a short tour, attended the audition at the Wyvern, and he and Parnes offered the booking to Lennon, McCartney, Harrison, and Moore, urging them to drop Sutcliffe from the lineup. When they refused, Fury hired another band, and the Silver Beetles suffered another rejection.

But a week later, Parnes called Williams back with work for the group in Scotland, this time backing Johnny Gentle. Everybody dropped his school commitments and headed up to Alloa on May 20, 1960. Lennon skipped his art college exams; McCartney convinced his father that the trip would actually *help* him prepare for his A-level exams. Moore's tenure with the band would be even shorter than Hanton's: he got into a car accident in Scotland and had to race to a show from the hospital, where Lennon had howled at his injuries and insisted he play the gig. Moore quit shortly after the nine-day engagement was through. The band landed back in Liverpool having had a hard-core touring experience that only made them want more. Nobody else seemed to understand why. They eventually played Williams's new strip venue, the New Cabaret Artist's Club on Upper Parliament Street. The space was similar to the Jacaranda—a dim basement room with tables. But it sported a singular Liverpool character, the black and mysterious Lord Woodbine, named for his favorite brand of cigarettes, tending bar.

HAMBURG, GERMANY, BECAME the cultural crucible, the place where the Beatles invented themselves and discovered the riches of investing themselves in nightly work. But the job proved the most far-fetched yet in a string of unlikely breaks. In June the Royal Caribbean Band suddenly disappeared from the Jacaranda, leaving a string of expletives sputtering from Williams's stocky frame. Word filtered back that they had fled to Hamburg; Williams started getting letters from the band about the scene there. Once again, he smelled a percentage, and he headed across the Channel to check things out.

Hamburg was Williams's kind of place. Bands could do stints here, Williams reasoned, send a percentage home, and return with the kind of clubbing experience needed to gain more work. The steel drummers introduced Williams to Bruno Koschmider, owner of a club called the Kaiserkeller. A few months later, by sheer happenstance, he ran into Koschmider again at a London club, where he pitched the band Derry and the Seniors (with saxist Howie Casey). Koshchmider booked them, and within weeks wrote Williams asking for another act. In the meantime, Lennon's itch to play with words had him tweaking the band's name again: dropping "Silver" and respelling "Beetles" with an "a" to accentuate the pun on "beat." Now Williams turned to the Beatles.

He thought of them for Hamburg as much to shut them up as anything else. But for Lennon, McCartney, Harrison, and Sutcliffe, Hamburg was a much bigger break than touring Scotland as a backup band. The wages were decent (fifteen pounds a week, more than some of their parents were making), the work was steady, and it validated everything they had been working toward up to that point: the chance to dig down into what they previously had only flirted with in their ensemble, in front of a nightly audience. Of course, these assumptions were naïve; that's what made them so tempting. They had little idea that the Hamburg they were entering would shape their world from this point on in ways both practical and aesthetic, and alter their outlook decisively. But there was a hole to plug before they could go: they still needed a drummer. The answer seemed obvious: since Pete Best had been sitting in with them at his mother's place, the Casbah, and looked mutable, not to say gullible, they gambled and offered him the slot. Finally, the unsteady ensemble they had steered since Colin Hanton hauled his kit off that bus found some traction.

Here marks an early turning point in Lennon's professional identity, where fate and circumstance thrust him into a scene he could barely have imagined for himself before leaving Merseyside. Hamburg calls down through rock history as the great defining stage in Lennon's public character, a cauldron of noise and rude poetry, raising up his harebrained persona through the music as if hypnotized by some fierce, cackling joke. Only in retrospect can we trace how Lennon's earlier, more intimate defeats receded into the rearview mirror of a larger, infinitely more seductive musical epic. As he climbed into Williams's van with the others on August 16, perhaps, at least temporarily, it felt as if such defeats might be left behind, if not redeemed.

Although Harrison was underage at seventeen, Williams told them simply to flash their driver's licenses as government IDs and present themselves as tourists. The troupe included Williams's Chinese wife, Beryl; her brother Barry Chang; and Lord Woodbine, whose rock-star shades gave him the look of distant fortune. Lennon stole a harmonica from

Arnhem's Bergmann Muzick, and working their way north through the Netherlands, they stopped to pose in front of the Arnhem War Memorial. Tired and bedraggled, the musicians channeled their outrageous ambition into expressions of deadpan calm for Chang's camera, oblivious to the tombstone's World War II inscription: THEIR NAME LIVETH FOR EVERMORE. Apart from the photographer, one other figure is missing, Lennon. You can almost hear him snoring from the van.

PART TWO

BEATLEHOOD

1960–1969

Well Well Well

In the postwar years, before the Beatles arrived, Hamburg sprang back to life fitfully. The city had been virtually obliterated by RAF raids and was occupied by British forces until 1951. Hamburg was then, as now, known for its red-light district, the Reeperbahn, which sprawled for a mile along its port; locals called it "*die sündige Meile*" (the sinful mile), or simply "*der Kiez*" (the 'hood). By 1960, the Marshall Plan reconstruction provided for Germany and France in ways that must have stumped British youth—suddenly, they felt less like victors than victims. Up to this point, most had had no perspective on how far behind Britain lagged.

Hamburg's dock culture rang familiar to Liverpudlians, but these hard-bitten German lives, playing out the endgames of losing a disastrous war, were of a different breed than they probably grasped. Its decadent nightlife economy made Liverpool seem coy. Gangsters fleeing Communism in the East controlled the rackets, and neon signs flooded streets lined with brothels and gambling dens. While the Beatles grew up with bomb craters, and endless tales of national sacrifice and rebuilding, a huge portion of Germany nursed its war shame and twenty million casualties through profligacy; Hamburg, the northernmost major city, was its pre-Castro Havana. In the first few weeks of their first major club gig, these five teenage boys took young gulps of easy sex, weekly cash, and pills by the fistful. Unlike Amsterdam's De Wallen, Hamburg's red-light district was closed off with a large gate; juveniles and nonworking females were forbidden entry. As employees, the Beatles waltzed right through. "I might have been born in Liverpool," goes Lennon's famous quote, "but I grew up in Hamburg." Many of his remarks regarding his club days reek of a piercing self-awareness about both his lack of street smarts and how Scouser dock culture had shaped his outlook: "We were scared by it all at first," Lennon reflected, "being in the middle of the tough club land. But we felt cocky, being from Liverpool, at least believing the myth about Liverpool producing cocky people."[1]

Bruno Koschmider met Williams and the five Beatles on the Reeperbahn in the "St. Pauli" district the evening of August 17, 1960, and installed them in living quarters barely above impoverished: two rooms nested adjacent to the Bambi Kino, the B-movie theater he ran next door to his club the Indra. "We were put in this pigsty, like a toilet it was, in a cinema, a rundown sort of fleapit," Lennon recalled.

> *We were living in a toilet,* like right next to the ladies' toilet. We would go to bed late and be woken up the next day by the sound of the cinema show. We'd try to get into the ladies' first, which was the cleanest of the cinema's lavatories, but fat old German women would push past us. We'd wake up in the morning and there would be old German fraus pissing next door. That was where we washed. That was our bathroom. It was a bit of a shock in a way.[2]

Rosa, the Indra's basement "custodian," took a shine to the boys and pampered them with clean towels and "Prellies," diet-pill uppers (nonprescription Preludin).

Like many in this closely knit nightlife circle, Rosa became a fast friend. The backstage crew of barmaids, thugs, and prostitutes were daily acquaintances, and they dubbed the Beatles "Peedles," affectionate street slang for "penis," punning tribute to their budding appetites. Like most red-light subcultures, this Hamburg scene was an extended family and a reliable grapevine about rough customers. The boys dubbed Rosa "Mutti" (German slang for "Mother"), and Prellies circulated like candy.

Pills fueled Beatle stage antics as they revved up song tempos. Horst Fascher, a towering ex-boxer, worked as Koschmider's heavy, a bouncer skilled at tossing out the louder drunks once the booze animated their fists; the Beatles charmed Fascher into being their protector as well. After six to eight hours of playing, the Beatles burned off alcohol and amphetamines on through morning before collapsing in their bunks.

Williams stayed on for a week getting the boys settled, which quickly tilted him into their father-protector, a blurring of roles the Beatles assigned most of their future business partners. He made at least one trip back, in the fall of 1960, when his ten years' further experience in such matters had him holding the boys' urine up to the light to check for discoloration, the poor man's STD test.[3] An early Williams-Koschmider negotiation included blankets for their beds. Lennon remembered Koschmider approaching him as the band's leader to get the mood pumping:

> And of course whenever there was any pressure point I had to get us out of it. The guys said, "Well, OK John, you're the leader." When nothing was going on they'd say, "Uh-uh, no leader, fuck it," but if anything happened, it was like, "You're the leader, you get up and do a show." . . . So I put my guitar down and I did Gene Vincent all night: banging and lying on the floor and throwing the mike about and pretending I had a bad leg.[4]

Whoever coined it, Koschmider adopted *"Mach schau!"* ("Make a show!") as his refrain if ever a crowd lacked enthusiasm; it became the withering lash that propelled their music on several levels. On an off night when business was slow, Koschmider reminded his musicians from the floor why he had hired them in the first place: to keep the drinks flowing. That was a basic of bar-band life: earn your fee by holding customers' attention and selling ale. Hacks take their cue from the audience and adopt a listless affect if the crowd isn't buzzing. The stern subtext of *"Mach schau!"* is "Earn your keep!" The only reason club owners hire bands in the first place is to sell drinks. "We all did 'mach shauing' all the time from then on," Lennon said.[5]

Any working musician will tell you that playing a club nightly is grinding, unmerciful work. Their Hamburg gigs forced the Beatles to fall back on literally every song they could think of, whether they had rehearsed it or not. So Koschmider's "*Mach schau!*" doubled as a musical directive: stirring up the crowd could mean any number of things, from turning up the amps to hitting the drums harder, crashing the cymbals more often, speeding up tempos, baiting the audience, or coaxing requests if nobody responded to the numbers they'd already played. "Eventually, out of this, we built a little audience," McCartney remembered.[6] Within a few weeks, the Beatles were commandeering off nights and making them rousing affairs. Necessity turned them into pros.

Encouraging Lennon in this direction was probably redundant. Rock lore bulges with stories of his soused charades, performing with a toilet seat around his neck, goading the Germans by calling them "Nazi murderers," and pissing from the roof onto nuns on the street.[7] While mythic, enough of them come from credible sources to assume most are true—most of them are too good not to be. Howie Casey, saxist for Derry and the Seniors, who were playing Koschmider's larger room down the street, the Kaiserkeller, showed his Liverpool mates the ropes: places like the British Seaman's Mission on the docks, where they gathered most early afternoons for a corn-flake "breakfast."[8] "We were corn-flake buffs," Pete Best recalled. Casey vividly remembers Lennon vomiting in the same spot on his bedroom floor for weeks on end, building up a bizarre, putrid sculpture of regurgitated ale as a squalid protest to their condition.[9]

The peculiar theater he found himself in sharpened Lennon's nose for the absurd: performing American rock 'n' roll for drunken Krauts, his stage patter wove thick sarcasm into crass non sequiturs. Imagine a British band performing brash Yankee tunes to an Iraqi audience today and multiply it by the Holocaust, bomb-crater playgrounds, Hamburg's Marshall Plan fruits, the UK rationing and national debt the Beatles grew up under, and you'll sense the volatile cultural tensions between band and audience. Since the crowd barely understood the band's thickly accented English, Lennon taunted them: "This is a record by Chuck Berry," he declared, "a Liverpool-born white singer with bandy legs and no hair!"[10]

Aware of their cocky Liverpudlian image, the band lived up to some idea of dockside bravado while flexing their rock muscles. Realizing that Williams had installed them at the smallest club on the bottom of the local circuit's food chain, they immediately set their sights on the top-ten venues down the street, where Casey introduced them to the local legend Tony Sheridan (née Anthony Esmond Sheridan McGinnity), another Brit, whom Lennon remembered from the TV show *Oh Boy!* Sheridan drew crowds with guitar flash and cantankerous showmanship, cursing his backup band, the Jets, onstage. Beatle historian Bob Spitz quotes musicians comparing Sheridan to Jimi Hendrix, Eric Clapton, and Duane Allman, a showboating virtuoso ahead of his time.[11] In Sheridan's act, the Beatles glimpsed the next rung on Hamburg's ladder. Copping a lot of what worked for him, they earned a steady stream of regulars at the Indra, jumped about until they had demolished its rickety "stage," charmed their way into the local art clique, and broke their first contract.

IF LIVERPOOL SOCIALIZED THE SKEPTICISM and humor in the Beatles' attitude, their five stints priming Hamburg's brazen bar scene echoed through their records for the next eight years in both sound and attitude (McCartney's "Helter Skelter," a grinding, dead-of-night orgy, or Lennon's "I'm So Tired," a grinding, morning-after hangover). In his piercing reevaluation of their catalog, *Magic Circles: The Beatles in Dream and History*, Devin McKinney opens with an extended metaphor: "The Beatles music," he says, "is the very sound of the toilet."[12] The raucous St. Pauli clubs shaped Lennon's approach to the stage in defining ways, sharpened both his cynicism and his charm, and fueled the barely contained euphoria—of youth, possibility, and change—that the Beatles unleashed on the world. Winning over these hard-core ruffians on these terms made much that came after seem both easy and relatively deserved.

As a culture, Hamburg was a netherworld, a lawless haven where they could defy their parents' Victorian sexual ghosts. Of course, Lennon might not have been as shocked by this scene as the average American: his mother had set a high bar for snubbing convention; still, he worked hard to maintain his bad-boy status among his peers. For most

Liverpool teenagers, Hamburg signified liberty of a style unimagined by their parents. Set loose on the playground of the former enemy, who had shot and bombed their fathers and uncles in the war, these children saw abundance where their parents saw vice; freedom where their parents saw excess; and joy and exuberance in behavior their elders could only think of as immoral. In a parallel Lennon would have hated, he was living the life of a young jazz player in turn-of-the-century New Orleans, when Scott Joplin's ragtime was played in brothels, and syncopation was a rhythmic metaphor for loose morals. Plunging headlong into rock 'n' roll in Hamburg, Lennon and his Beatles were playing out similar fantasies unimagined by their emotionally remote, and quite literally absent, parents: of freedom to indulge in all manner of appetites, and of teenage life as a testing ground for exploring all manner of identities.

At first, the sexual candor and promiscuity must have felt like joining a cosmically libertine frat house; pills and beer fueled their all-night rants, and the Beatles proved themselves equal to the appetites of the swarthiest sailors. To frequent the Reeperbahn was to confront hard living on a daily basis, ward off hardened criminals, and come back for more. Entertainers were minor celebrities in this milieu: freebies were frequent from working girls, and the seventeen-year-old George Harrison lost his cherry as his bunkmates pretended to be asleep.[13] (As McCartney says in the *Anthology,* "Can you imagine the peer pressure?") To teenagers turned loose in this world, rock 'n' roll's glorious contradictions suddenly made surprising, persuasive sense, while at the same time the music seemed suddenly tame, even harmless, compared to the behavior of its hard-core audience. Like the young Presley taking the stage at the Hi-Hat and Bon Air clubs in downtown Memphis, Lennon and the Beatles were carried along by the music as the most redemptive aspect of a brutal subculture.[14] Far from corrupt, rock 'n' roll was easily the least harmless of Hamburg's vices.

THE BEATLES' ORIGINAL INDRA CLUB booking had them as opening act for Rory Storm and the Hurricanes, Liverpool's steadiest working band. Bonding as expatriates do in a foreign country, and sharing the same stage with the goal of literally bashing its wooden platform to bits, players swapped instruments, shared arrangements and tunings, and sat in with one another as needed. Down the street, Derry and the Seniors also backed up Sheridan, and the Beatles became part of this loose pool of alliances and favors, joining in the musical chairs. To Lennon, Sheridan was a god, even though he was playing Hamburg on the way down: with no chart success, his middling popularity in Britain had waned. All these players became drinking buddies after finishing their sets in the wee hours, and once the Seniors learned the Beatles were in town, they visited their friends' sets as well.

As the set list grew, the Beatles padded out standards with the flair the audiences hungered for. "What I'd Say," the Ray Charles smash from 1959, began with a tantalizing, understated Wurlitzer electric piano and got stretched out into a half-hour set piece, with Paul singing lead and Lennon leading the audience up and down to elongate the song the way they imagined Charles did with his audience. Somewhere along the line, they learned how trading vocal leads let them save their voices. Eventually, Pete Best handed the drums over to McCartney to sing lead on "Peppermint Twist"; Stu Sutcliffe did "Love Me Tender" in his prescription sunglasses, milking its sentimentality; and Harrison did Carl Perkins's "Matchbox." This gave Lennon and McCartney a break as it gave the audience simple variety, accented the group dynamics at work in the sound, and touted different aspects of the rock catalog the band was creating, from slick pop to hard-bucking rockabilly, Hollywood twaddle to gobbledygook outrage.

Few set lists remain from these shows, but song sequences took shape and were then tweaked from evening to evening, audience to audience. They could soon depend on Chuck Berry's "Rock and Roll Music" or "Roll Over Beethoven" to close, and Little Richard's "Long Tall Sally" became a short-fuse opener. Later, "A Taste of Honey" emerged as a McCartney set piece; he remembered joining the others in three-part harmony "on the little echo mikes, and we made a fairly good job of it."[15]

Lennon learned to swim in these waters quickly and, as he had back in Merseyside, marked out the extremes his bandmates measured themselves against. Between the roughnecks, who brandished guns and sent champagne to the stage even if it was 5 A.M., and the hardening mood of a crowd as they grew collectively drunker, the scene lived up to every cockeyed rock ideal Lennon had ever dreamed of. On night after unforgiving night, charming a surly crowd into a rousing choir could mean the difference between a handful of cash and a fistfight—it was a balance he enjoyed toying with, as the best of the music had its own violent rewards. "I used to be so pissed I'd be lying on the floor behind the piano, drunk, while the rest of the group was playing. I'd be on stage, fast asleep," Lennon remembered. "And we always ate on stage, too, because we never had time to eat. So it was a real scene. . . . It would be a far-out show now: eating and smoking and swearing and going to sleep on stage when you were tired."[16]

PETE BEST'S MEMOIRS CONTAIN the best day-to-day detail about how the Beatles adapted to Hamburg's nightlife, studded with incidents that would otherwise be lost. As the cold moved in, Lennon got himself a pair of baggy long johns, so when Harrison dared him to go for a stroll, "Lennon didn't hesitate. He picked up an English newspaper he had been reading earlier, tucked it under one arm, kicked open the crash doors, strode out into the middle of the street—crowded with weekend visitors to St. Pauli—and just stood there reading the paper."[17] This primitive performance piece has a dash of Julia Stanley's lens-free glasses. "Window-shopping" the ladies on the Herbertstrasse became a daily routine—"our morning booster," wrote Best. The band, he said, "injected a new style of entertainment to the Reeperbahn. For the sheer hell of it we would start at the top of the street and work our way to the bottom of it—playing leap-frog. We would keep going until we almost collapsed, not even bothering to stop when a traffic light showed red." Sometimes, the scene grew as Germans joined to create "a long trail . . . of varying ages . . . all leap-frogging behind us: it was complete madness."[18]

In the early flush of success, with one of his first paychecks Lennon bought a 1958 Rickenbacker model 325 guitar, which became a cherished Hamburg relic. Harrison remembered the two of them seeing it in a shop window and how Lennon mentioned that Jean "Toots" Thielemans, then a member of the George Shearing Quintet, used the same model. That Thielemans reference gives away Lennon's anti-jazz rants as sheer pretension—Shearing was an English pianist who had broken into the American scene, which made him heroic to Lennon no matter what style he played. In addition, the Rickenbacker's shortened (three-quarter-size) neck appealed to his guitarist insecurities. Playing bar chords forces your fingers all the way up and behind the fret board; playing them all night on a longer neck can make your wrists sore. Economizing that simple repetitive motion helped Lennon develop sharper, spikier attacks.[19] This abbreviated Rickenbacker design turned Lennon into a fireplug rhythm guitarist (think of "I'm Happy Just to Dance with You" or "You Can't Do That").

Simplifying his guitar work turned his mind to other matters. Everything Lennon learned from Hamburg's mean streets made its way right into the act, although there was a curious disconnect between some of his offstage moods and onstage provocations. Pete Best remembered a particular fascination with cripples, and howling impersonations of them onstage, which managed to offend even some in this tough crowd. Offstage, however,

the mere sight of deformed or disabled people sickened him physically and he could never bear to be in their company. More than once I was with him in a Hamburg café when suddenly he would discover that the occupant of a nearby table was a war veteran, minus a limb or disfigured in some way. John would leap up from his seat and scurry out into the street.... He never tried to explain this odd behavior or his reasons for devoting so much of his artistic talent to depicting distorted characters. Somewhere deep down I felt that perhaps he nursed a sort of sadness for them.[20]

The Beatles quickly became a popular local attraction, complete with groupies, both professional and amateur. Open flirtation and conquest became inseparable from the musical banter:

The more brazen of the girls ... would simply stand up and point at the Beatle she wanted and give the well-known sign.

You know—the bending of the elbow of one arm across the wrist of the other in a sharp upward movement that suggested an erection. "Wheee!" the girl would shout at the same time. Or later, as they got to know us more intimately, "Gazunka!," which was the Beatles' own war cry. We would fall about on stage whenever a fraulein gave out this routine, but she was never kidding.[21]

Within the first few weeks of their Indra stint, a Hamburg art student named Klaus Voormann was out walking off an argument he'd had with his lover, Astrid Kirchherr. They had been on again, off again for several months, and Voormann took his sour mood down to the St. Pauli district to drink off some resentment. Perhaps he'd done this bar crawl before and knew the Reeperbahn as an excellent source of distraction. For whatever reason, on this evening in the fall of 1960, the sounds pouring out of the Indra drew Voormann down inside. Here he encountered full-throttle rock 'n' roll of the kind he heard on Radio Luxembourg. He was astonished to chance upon such a thing in Hamburg, an underworld rearing up in his backyard.

Rory Storm was onstage, and Voormann sheepishly took a chair by a band of leather-clad boys waiting to go on: the Beatles. He was drawn in by the Hurricanes, but stuck around to hear the whole Beatle set, and couldn't stop talking about it to Astrid the next day. She refused to go back with him, so he returned alone with a record sleeve: a musician hobbyist, he wanted to design original album covers with art that captured the spirit of the music, and he carried an example of a sleeve he had designed for the Ventures' "Walk—Don't Run." "He gave it to John," Pauline Sutcliffe wrote, "who instantly handed it to Stuart."[22]

The third night Voormann brought another art buddy, Jürgen Vollmer, and afterward the two of them pestered Astrid to join them. When Astrid finally trespassed and descended the Indra's steps, in early October 1960, she was quickly swept up in the same magical roar that had seduced Voormann.

"I fell in love with Stuart that very first night," she told Philip Norman. "He was so tiny but perfect, every feature. So pale, but very, very beautiful. He was like a character from a story by Edgar Allan Poe."²³ Astrid was a stylish blonde, and there was some internal jockeying over who would win her over, but Stuart was clearly her favorite. Pauline Sutcliffe regards Kirchherr's sense of style as key to the band's whole development: "Astrid was much more than a girl we all fell in love with. She was a catalyst; her effect on everybody was such that it brought out the best in them, musically as well as personally. It was a very, very magical atmosphere in Hamburg at that time."²⁴

Within days Kirchherr took the band to the Dom, an empty fairground, to pose them for her camera. Her photos framed the Beatles in leather jackets and slicked-back hair, their baby faces and worldly expressions looking as though they'd already conquered something frightening and majestic. This aura of cool certainty became the shadowy subtext of their cheery mop-top image, their unfazed expressions already confiding unfathomable mysteries. Lennon and Sutcliffe (in shades) posed alone and together, hard stares concealing their insecurities, with Lennon hugging his new Rickenbacker. The certitude in their eyes is inescapable: the sense that for them, rock 'n' roll was fated, fraught with significance, that it would dishonor the music not to adopt its attitude in all things, even as unknowns. Like the most eccentric, self-absorbed art students', their expressions announced how every other pursuit paled by comparison. That Astrid and Klaus saw so much in the Beatles' image this early on speaks to their artistic foresight; imagine the sound that inspired these looks, and her pictures, and you get an inkling of their early authority.

Afterward, Astrid invited everyone to her family home in suburban Altona for tea. Once she developed her photos, the Beatles raved about her eye. She "captured the very quality," wrote Norman, "which attracted intellectuals like Klaus and her—the paradox of Teddy Boys with child faces; of would-be toughness and undisguisable, all-protecting innocence."²⁵ Of course, Kirchherr and Voormann had no idea that Liverpool's Teddy Boys were thugs—from their vantage, these guys were simply Brits adopting Americanesque rock poses, pretenders to Presley. But somehow the leather, the ducktails, and the formidable expressions gave them the confidence to transcend their circumstances. Astrid and the band quickly bonded, ventured off into more photo shoots, and she began learning English, the better to make her feelings known to Stuart. All of them became lifelong friends, wrote Cynthia Lennon. "During their stays in Hamburg, Astrid shot reel after reel of film of the boys. . . . I think only Paul ever smiled, the diplomat as ever. John wouldn't do anything he didn't want to, but Paul even in those early days could have earned a living in public relations." George was as "hungry-looking, with a broad, toothy grin . . . very quiet." But Lennon "emerged as the leader whenever a leader was wanted. He wasn't elected, he just was without question."[26]

At twenty-two, Astrid played big sister to most of the band. Just as she had done with Voormann, she gave Stuart a "French" hairstyle with bangs—a cut she herself wore, which made her look indescribably chic and self-possessed. How apt that Sutcliffe's girlfriend should model the band's haircut.

Within a few days they were all experimenting with their hair— except for Best. Now, instead of tough Liverpool Teds, the Beatles resembled the mod European art-student elite. This added another layer to their mystique. "Lennon moved from wearing a rock hairstyle to shock the art school world to wearing an art school hairstyle to shock the pop world," wrote Simon Frith.[27] Like the "duck's arse" haircut among Woolton grammar schoolers, this image trickled down from Hamburg's suburban middle-class art students who longed to be perceived beneath their station—who heard the art in the flash and bravura of sweaty rock 'n' roll filtered through Liverpool expats for Kraut sailors, and discovered the most exciting part of themselves through the Beatles' humors and desires. By November of 1960, a month after meeting, Stuart and Astrid had become engaged, and the Kirchherrs invited him to move into their Altona home, turning the attic into a live-in studio.[28] "We fell in love very quickly," Kirchherr remembered many years later. "It was very simple, and very powerful."[29]

The Beatles' adoption by the Hamburg art scene can't be overstated.

This small band of arty types read philosophy, called themselves the "Exis" (for "Existentialists"), and Voormann, Kirchherr, and Vollmer heard these esoteric values in song—to their ears, rock 'n' roll was a supreme act of aesthetic defiance, the aural analog to all the rebelliousness they admired in modernism, Dada, surrealism, conceptualism, and pop art collage and painting.

Of course, strictly speaking, theirs was a "student" brand of Nietzsche's God-is-dead, existence-is-meaningless, we're-alone-in-the-universe philosophy. The subversive spirit of the idea rang truer than its particulars: their middle-class upbringing seemed out of phase with the world they came of age in; what their parents dubbed "immoral" was far more complicated and intriguing than they'd expected. Like the rest of the Beatles' audience, they had grown up absurd, to use Paul Goodman's phrase, with a gnawing sense that there was more to life than the warweary stoicism of their parents.[30]

Here was another group of listeners who fancied themselves privy to a private joke, an absurdist-arty experiment in rock 'n' roll pretension mixed with rebel politics that set the Beatles apart. Here in Hamburg, as early as the fall of 1960, you have the alchemy of the band's success: highminded and arty rock 'n' roll performed amid squalor, adored by both sides of the cultural divide—the working stiffs who eked out a living busting up bar fights, and the educated students who found the music and persona overwhelmingly appealing *as art.* Iain Softley's 1994 film *Backbeat,* based in part on Pauline Sutcliffe's memoirs, carves out this high-low turf and presents the Beatles as mini-celebrities in the Hamburg subculture they helped create. This art influence fed Lennon's ambition and gave him growing confidence—it confirmed his strong intuition that rock 'n' roll was a new kind of poetry, exploding with ideas that "respectable" aesthetes simply hadn't noticed yet. It also seeded the puzzlement at the gulf between high and low culture that he expressed throughout his career.

ALTHOUGH HE WROTE to Cynthia every week, reporting on their growing repertoire and circle of friends, Lennon played the single man in

Hamburg: he put together an implacable macho façade. And as a restless teenager with oceans of testosterone rolling off him daily, he was just as quickly out of his depth. One evening, a huge German sailor started sending drinks up to the stage and motioned the band over to talk between sets. A waiter brought the message that he loved the music and wanted to treat the band to a late dinner after their set. Now here was a perk: a free meal with drinks sponsored by a wealthy patron who enjoyed spending. As he excused himself for a trip to the john, Lennon and Best agreed to jump him and filch his fat wallet on their way home. "Drunken sailors had always been considered fair game in Hamburg amongst the pickpockets and waiter fraternity in the early hours of the morning," Best recalled. "If ever there was a suitable case for mugging— this sailor was it."[31]

Sutcliffe had already gone home with Astrid, and after dinner McCartney and Harrison peeled off to head back to their bunks. Lennon and Best kept walking with their mark. Once they worked up the nerve, Best and Lennon pounced on the sailor and pinned up against a car park gate. He sobered up quickly and began fighting back. A Lennon punch felled him to his knees, and Best dove for the mark's wallet. But the man fought back, of course, much harder than the two amateur thieves had anticipated.

Finally, once Best finagled the wallet, the sailor pulled out a pistol and waved it threateningly. There was no way of telling whether it was loaded, so they charged him one last time as he fired into the air while falling back. They lashed him as hard as they could and then scrambled off, happy to be alive. Once that gun appeared, they forgot their thievery.[32]

Recounting the story back at the Bambi Kino bunks, McCartney and Harrison howled at their nonexistent spoils. That didn't stop them from worrying furiously about whether the sailor might reappear to have his revenge. He never did, but this incident provided fodder for people who wanted to believe Lennon kept murder as his darkest secret. This would be difficult to prove, but still more difficult to believe that any cops who found a dead sailor on the street wouldn't have traced his steps back to the restaurant and the club where he'd started out his evening, the band that played that club, and the long list of witnesses who'd spotted them dining together afterward. This incident joins a long list of might-have-happened things on Lennon's docket that get so easily inflated into actuality to prove a fatuous psychological profile, as if a robbery-turned-accidental-manslaughter might help explain the psychic gnarl of "Happiness Is a Warm Gun." Lennon was more confessional than the most melodramatic singer-songwriters he inspired; he recounted lapses of taste and morality in reams of interviews. The likelihood that he told an L.A. session guitarist like Jesse Ed Davis his guilt over such an incident—and nobody else, not Cynthia, Yoko, or even McCartney—is beyond remote.

Like most bands, the Beatles made their musical strides alongside increasingly thorny ensemble politics. Pete Best stuck to the remote drummer's role—moody and distant, a passive charm to contrast with John and Paul's antics. But by this point, Best stood aloof from the others in several ways: he didn't partake of pills; he was the first to wander off alone instead of hitting the after-hours clubs. His adventure with Lennon was atypical. He met the constant chatter and one-upmanship with nonchalant quiet. Lennon and McCartney dominated as lead singers; Sutcliffe and Harrison settled into supporting roles. Sutcliffe got piled on as the least adept with his instrument, chided mercilessly both onstage and off.

While Lennon obviously carried deep feelings for Sutcliffe, many remember him as cruel toward Sutcliffe's playing. It became a rift in their relationship: Sutcliffe had joined the band out of friendship for Lennon, but Lennon and the others had long since outpaced him musically. McCartney began to treat Sutcliffe coldly, out of both rivalry and his own booming musicianship; Paul came alive onstage, where Sutcliffe had to work at his public face. "When John and Stu had a row," Astrid said, "you could still feel the affection that was there. But when Paul and Stu had a row, you could tell Paul hated him."[33] Still, Norman's idea that McCartney wanted to play bass is stretching things—the bass still had a stigma, not the guitarist glamour McCartney lusted after. Hounding Stu out of the band would have meant a dicey game of straws as to who would have to give up guitar, and McCartney must have known it wouldn't be John—after all, he had a new Rickenbacker.

Lennon folded his rivalry with McCartney right into the act. Pete Best recalled: "John would play seriously for a while as Paul gave his emotional all to the song: then John would suddenly start to pull a grotesque face or adopt his wicked hunchback pose against the piano, head tucked into his shoulders, features contorted. Eyes in the audience would begin to stray from Paul and some laughter would follow, gathering pace at John's antics."[34] This would anger Paul at first, but then he'd join in the clowning, dousing the song's sincerity. Lennon would also sabotage McCartney numbers with intrusive squawks and wrong notes from his guitar, feigning innocence as Paul became distracted. Where Best delighted in such larks, Sutcliffe began to tire of them. He found all the self-indulgence wearisome, as his letters home detailed: "Hamburg has little quality, except the kind you would find in an analysis of a test tube of sewer water. It's nothing but a vast amoral jungle."[35]

Hamburg has a distorted space in rock history because of the Beatles. "What you have to remember also is that there were more Liverpool groups going to the American bases in France than there ever were to Hamburg," Bill Harry told music writer Paul Du Noyer,[36] including Rory Storm and the Hurricanes, who worked in France for several stretches in between Hamburg gigs. "We'd heard about musicians getting gigs in Stuttgart," said George Harrison, "where there were American army bases. We knew that those kinds of gigs were available around Germany, so it was an exciting thought."[37] In this larger context, Hamburg was actually a small pond where the Beatles grew to be big fish. After the Beatles came Gerry and the Pacemakers and a few others, but the Liverpool connection seems to have been limited to Koschmider and Williams's acts, and operational for only a couple seasons, especially since the Beatles wrested themselves free from Koschmider's contract the first chance they got.

The Hurricanes, by this point, were a gimmicky act, complete with dance steps, a proper song set list, and matching outfits and handkerchiefs. (Tony Bramwell likened the Hurricanes' act to an unironic Sha Na Na, mired in stage patter.)[38] They also had a drummer who oozed confidence to the point where the Beatles were wary of him at first. "I was still a Teddy Boy and I only found out later from John that they were a bit scared of me," Ringo Starr remembered in the *Anthology*.[39] "There was another thing," Harrison recalled. "Pete would never hang out with us. When we finished doing the gig, Pete would go off on his own and we three [John, Paul, and George] would hang out together, and then when Ringo was around it was like a full unit, both on and off the stage. . . . With Ringo, it felt rocking."[40] Sutcliffe wrote home: "We have improved a thousand fold since our arrival and Allan Williams, who is here at the moment, tells us that there is no band in Liverpool to touch us."[41]

THE POWER STRUGGLE within the band suddenly collapsed under St. Pauli's neighborhood politics. At the end of November, the police closed the Indra due to noise complaints from an elderly neighbor and the church across the street, so Koschmider installed his promising young band at his Kaiserkeller, where they succeeded the Seniors during the second week in October, in time for Lennon to celebrate his twentieth birthday on October 9. Where the Indra resembled the Cavern—low-ceilinged, with space for 150 patrons at most—the new room was spacious, boasted a large dance floor, and the band traded sets with Rory Storm and the Hurricanes for twelve hours, alternating one-hour sets back and forth, six hours apiece. This must have felt like an early arrival: busting out of the back streets onto the main stage, holding their own with an established St. Pauli act, and gaining more and more listeners in a competitive market.

But later that month things fell apart when a new rival challenged Koschmider. An Englishman named Peter Eckhorn recruited bouncer Horst Fascher from the Indra to help remodel his father's large underground warehouse, the Hippodrome, which had enjoyed a prewar heyday by featuring nudes on horseback. Soon other Koschmider employees defected: first Tony Sheridan from the Kaiserkeller, then Mutti, the Indra's WC attendant, and finally the Beatles. At first they simply appeared onstage backing Sheridan at Eckhorn's Top Ten Club soon after its grand opening in November 1960. Koschmider quickly lectured them on the finer points of their contract, which forbade performances at any competing club even without billing. He threatened physical harm if it happened again, but with Fascher on their side, and a large contingent of disgruntled Indra workers, they made the leap: there were no sentimental feelings about ditching the Indra. From the Beatles' perspective, Koschmider was only getting what he deserved: the lodgings he'd provided hadn't earned him any special allegiance, and he'd managed to lose more than half his staff once Eckhorn opened his new club. The Top Ten Club was huge: it held five times as many patrons as the Indra, so its cash take was thicker, and its aura was more "respectable," in St. Pauli terms. There didn't seem to be any point in trying to bash down this stage, whereas at the Indra it was a matter of pride.

There was another wrinkle: climbing the local entertainment ladder, and seizing a new business opportunity, the Beatles negotiated with Eckhorn for a higher fee. Having represented themselves, they wrote Allan Williams telling him they didn't intend to pay him a percentage on their new job. Williams wrote several letters in protest that went unanswered.

But Koschmider was the local businessman with pull, and he played his trump card: he called the police to look into George Harrison's work permit, which his English-speaking son, George Steiner, had vouched for originally. Once the police discovered Harrison's age, they immediately deported him. Stuart and Astrid put the dazed George on the train to England with a sandwich bag full of snacks. The remaining Beatles played a few more nights without him at the Top Ten. After a couple of days, McCartney and Best wandered back to their rooms above the Bambi Kino to get some of their things, which they found untouched. Depending on who's telling the story, McCartney either lit a match for light in the dark hallway or set fire to some condoms tacked to the wall as a farewell gesture to Koschmider. A minor fire was quashed as they escaped.

The next day, police arrested McCartney and Best at the Kaiserkeller and hauled them down to the station for questioning: Koschmider threatened to charge them with arson. Two more Beatles were promptly deported, although Koschmider didn't press charges. Lennon left by train the day after that, Rickenbacker slung over his shoulder; Sutcliffe holed up in Astrid's attic until February 1961. By then, he had begun to make plans to settle in Hamburg, continue his art studies, and marry.

Everybody had underestimated Koschmider's revenge impulse. Back in Liverpool on December 10, 1960, Lennon threw stones at Aunt Mimi's window to wake her upon his early morning arrival at Mendips. "Where's the £100 a week, then?" she said as he hit her up for his cab fare.[42]

JUST AS THE BEATLES returned from Germany, Allan Williams launched a brand-new club, named after Eckhorn's: Liverpool's own Top Ten. The grand opening was on December 1, 1960, and featured Terry Dene and Garry Mills. But five days later, a week after the fire in Hamburg, the club burned to the ground. With Williams, the talk inevitably turned to arson: whether a rival club owner settled a score or he botched his own insurance scam, Williams found himself belly-up again. The crime went unsolved.

The Beatles, who watched a sure gig go up in smoke, started nagging anybody and everybody at the Jac for work. One day, Bob Wooler, a local music collector who had quit his railway-office job to emcee at Williams's now-defunct Top Ten, took pity. He rang up Brian Kelly, who booked them for a show after Christmas at Litherland Town Hall in North Liverpool. (In the parallel movie of how the Beatles never saw worldwide fame, Wooler is the well-meaning but small-time manager who could never break them out of their local market.) Kelly reminded Wooler that the Beatles had burned him the previous spring, when they had stiffed him on a Lathom Hall booking to traipse up to Scotland with Johnny Gentle. Wooler persisted—and negotiated the fee up from four to six pounds.

So even though Lennon only got back to town on December 10, by the following week, having hired one Chas Newby to fill in for Sutcliffe on bass, the Beatles had gigs back at the Casbah (December 17 and 31), the Grosvenor Ballroom in Liscard, Wallasey (December 19, booked by Williams), and Litherland Town Hall (December 27), none of which paid very much, but all of which testified to the Beatles' determination to show off their Hamburg chops. Few in Liverpool had yet heard whispers of their progress or of their Hamburg reputation.

By far the most important gig was the one at Litherland Town Hall, which billed them as "Direct from Hamburg." Half of the kids who showed up were impressed to hear the band sing such good English. A futuristic new "glitter ball" hung from the ceiling, spraying down colored patterns on the dance floor during the show. Except that this evening there didn't turn out to be all that much dancing. Wooler put them in the prime center slot, between the Deltones and the Searchers, and instructed them to hit their first song as the curtains opened.

McCartney's voice cut Wooler off before he was done, before the curtain had even moved. With a death-defying leap into Little Richard's "Long Tall Sally," the band charged in behind him, a thunderbolt of sound that quickly dashed all preconceptions. The Hamburg feistiness and grit poured forth as a new, unspeakable force on the Litherland stage—the Beatles' command of the room left their Liverpool audience gasping. The crowd lunged for the stage; the promoters thought a riot had broken out. If they had ever heard this band before, it would have been playing skiffle as the Quarrymen, or in Best's basement at the Casbah. But few had: most local listeners that night had never heard of the Beatles, never mind music this driven, passionate, and brutal. The impact set loose something fierce and unknowable, and the volume of their amps only hinted at the intensity. Beatlemania was more than two years off, but Hamburg rock 'n' roll fever suddenly swept this local crowd, rekindling both buzz and expectations.

Everybody who was there swears they saw the Second Coming. Tony Bramwell happened upon George Harrison on the 81 bus, George's father's route, carrying his guitar, and latched on to him as a free pass: he had known the group before Hamburg and was curious to see how they sounded. He came away astonished, with a peculiar memory of their music's effect:

On stage that long-ago night in 1960 the audience seemed to sense that the Beatles were different from the other Liverpool bands. They seemed more aware, they had an edge, you felt they were dangerous. Part of the mystique was that they were different. You could jive when they played R&B, or Elvis hits . . . but it was almost impossible to dance when they played their own songs. It was totally the wrong rhythm, so we'd just cluster around the stage and watch.[43]

Lennon himself remembered the gig vividly: "Suddenly we were a wow. It was that evening that we really came out of our shell and let go. We stood there being cheered for the first time. This was when we began to think that we were good."[44]

After his initial shock, Kelly quickly forgot past complaints and hired the Beatles for another thirty-five dances in the region through March of 1961, which built them a local following and more gigs as word spread. Here, suddenly, was music limned with new vigor and authority, a band suddenly recast as an act, with personalities crowding the microphone and an ensemble pitching at greatness. Among all the unrecorded milestones in rock history, the Litherland Town Hall gig tops everybody's Beatles list.

LEAVING HIS FIANCÉE in Hamburg early in the new year, 1961, Sutcliffe returned to Liverpool to tell his family about his bride. He stepped back in on bass as the band continued gigging and building up their new reputation, but he "was always a target because of his small stature," Pete Best wrote.

One night at Lathom Hall . . . Stu was jumped on by a bunch of thugs and was taking considerable punishment when two girl fans breathless dashed up to [John and me] with the news. Lathom Hall was a two-tier dance hall in a tough area and the Teds had been able to trap Stu backstage. John and I doubled back and in usual style put our heads down and charged into the fray, freeing Stu and collecting our fair share of knocks along the way. Lennon broke a finger belting a Ted and had to play guitar for a while wearing a splint.[45]

When they rescued Stu, he was bleeding from the head. They brought him home to his distraught mother, but Sutcliffe was adamant that she not call the doctor.

HAMBURG'S CLUB SCENE had changed since the Beatles' first Indra booking. Eckhorn's club, the Top Ten, thrived during their absence with the tame yet eager Gerry Marsden and the Pacemakers. A return visit booked for April 1961 promised fourteen weeks to build upon what the Beatles had begun the previous fall. This time, however, the Beatles would share the bill as veterans with Rory Storm and the Hurricanes and were welcomed back into the scene as contenders by the old Koschmider crew. Launching into sets on the new stage, without fear of Koschmider's reprisals, they honed their skills and settled into a professional nightly routine they had barely grasped before getting run out of town: long sets, a big dance floor, and a more agreeable employer. Their prospects quickened. During this spring stint, Tony Sheridan brought a producer in to give them a listen: Bert Kaempfert, who booked them to back Sheridan on their first professional recording sessions.

One morning Kaempfert simply drove them over to an elementary school where he had rented out the auditorium. The boys set up their equipment onstage and he closed the curtains to create the "studio." He became the first producer to record the band (June 22–24, 1961), and their sessions backing Tony Sheridan led to their first singles: "My Bonnie," "The Saints (When the Saints Go Marching In)," and "Why." At this stage in his career, Kaempfert had enough label clout to try a quick cash-in on rock 'n' roll. Lennon, McCartney, and Harrison were aware of his industry stature: after all, he had cowritten Presley's recent hit "Wooden Heart." (Later, his ship would come in with Frank Sinatra's smash "Strangers in the Night.") The closest American analog to the pop stature Kaempfert held at the time might be Mitch Miller: a middle-aged label power stuck in Tin Pan Alley, cynically rearranging old songs as rock 'n' roll "jive." Kaempfert conducted his own pop orchestra on the radio and freelanced as a producer for Polydor. He even had been voted "Man of the Year" by *Cashbox* in 1959, coming off a huge international hit called "Wonderland by Night," a "sound portrait of Manhattan."[46]

As students of the genre, it is easy to imagine the Beatles pressing Kaempfert for details about the Presley sessions. Naturally, they hit him up to include their own material; but he only rolled tape during George Harrison's instrumental "Cry for a Shadow." The song veered between Cliff Richard tribute and parody, but Kaempfert heard it as more than a curiosity. For one number, "Ain't She Sweet," he let Lennon sing lead; he also did some takes singing lead on "My Bonnie." Kaempfert billed them as the Beat Brothers, hoping to sidestep the "Peedles" pun; Sheridan was framed as the star.

"Ain't She Sweet" survives as a good example of how Hamburg conditions shaped their jaunty sound. In all likelihood, they chose this standard because of Gene Vincent's modest hit with the song in 1960. But Vincent's rendition is a third again as slow, and Lennon's delivery combines a showman's verve with an arch suavity—while the band bustles alongside, siphoning energy off the sly confidence in his voice. At this remove it's difficult to understand any resistance to this sound: Lennon's lead already needles that mischievous interplay of sincerity and self-mocking irony. The beat isn't hard, but it's certainly not soft, and the band is keyed into the varied meanings that slide off Lennon's delivery: he's singing about a girl, but he's also singing about how silly it feels to give in to such feelings.

This single also presents the best evidence in favor of Pete Best's drumming: while not showy, the beat is steady, and gives the lie to those who say he couldn't drum. Best was not a bad drummer in any sense; whether he was up to the others' level was becoming the key question.

Most of the Beatles' tracks sat in the vault; Kaempfert released only "My Bonnie" backed with "The Saints," which gave the Beatles their first commercial pressing, even if their name didn't appear on the label. The single sold twenty thousand copies in Germany within two weeks that summer, landing at number five on a regional chart, alongside a

remake of Joey Dee's "Peppermint Twist," Charly Cotton's "Liebe-
straumals Twist," and the Oliver Twist Band's "Steller Zahn." But it
disappeared quickly.

AS THE BAND'S CAREER found a toehold with a recording, Sutcliffe continued romancing Kirchherr. One night he recognized the pop artist
Eduardo Paolozzi ("I Was A Rich Man's Plaything," 1947) surrounded
by German art students at a club. He introduced himself and made an
appointment for Paolozzi to view his work. With his focus on love and
his prospects as an artist, Sutcliffe's interest in the band began to wane
just as things were falling into place. In Sutcliffe's mind, living in his fiancée's house, and painting under a new mentor, it wasn't really much of
a choice at all.

I Found Out

HAMBURG HAD SEASONED THE BEATLES' LIVE SHOW AND BOOSTED their opportunities—on the Reeperbahn they enjoyed celebrity status. Back on their home turf, however, they returned to anonymity. For the uncertain stretch between the Litherland Town Hall concert in December 1960 and a professional manager's handshake in December 1961, they dug in for twelve months of solid slogging: long winter treks sleeping on top of one another in a van belonging to Pete Best's friend Neil Aspinall, trying to stay warm while shuttling between Derbyshire and Kent and Hull and Portsmouth and back again, pushing fifty miles an hour on Britain's winding, two-lane motorways. After these grueling hinterland gigs, Lennon famously hectored the others: "Where are we going, boys?" "To the top, Johnny!" "Where?" "To the toppermost of the poppermost!"[1] They were a small-time operation, but they were afloat.

In March 1961, Bob Wooler began booking them several times a week downstairs at the Cavern Club on the winding alleyway called Mathew Street, first for lunchtime breaks and then for evening slots. The club's original owner, Alan Sytner, had sold the club to Ray McFall in late 1959, and the former "trad-jazz" venue relented to the growing beat scene. At first the Cavern faced stiff competition from other clubs, like the Iron Door and the Casanova Club, booked by Sam Leach, but the Cavern soon became the best known. That year alone, the Beatles played three to eight Cavern sets per week, often twice in the same day, complete with groupies clamoring for front-row seats.

The music propelled them even through new political tension. By the time Lennon turned twenty-one in October 1961, Sutcliffe had been living with Astrid in the Kirchherrs' Hamburg home for a year. Engaged to the hippest German art student imaginable, he returned to his canvases and accepted a prestigious invitation to enroll in Eduardo Paolozzi's class at the German Hochschule. A giant from the cultural world had reached down and blessed Sutcliffe's work, making his choice obvious.

Even after all he'd been through before that, Lennon must have experienced his twenty-first year as his longest. By this point, he had gambled everything on rock 'n' roll. In professional terms, 1961 saw the Beatles snare a German contract with Polydor backing Sheridan, a Kaempfert session, even a modest hit on the German charts. By that November, the proprietor of Liverpool's biggest record shop, North End Music Stores (NEMS), had come knocking with ambitious plans for a UK record contract. In between, the band worked on expanding its set list, even though hopes far outran their success.

Their embrace of rock 'n' roll (which had grown to include C&W, gritty R&B, and hard-bashing Little Richard, as well as the cornball Hollywood stuff that McCartney seemed to get off on) served and challenged Liverpool's wide-ranging stylistic palate. The Mersey scene thrived on an uncommonly generous and self-propulsive flow of musical ideas. As the music got bigger, the gigs increased, the set lists mushroomed, and the culture constantly renewed itself; the larger project benefited them all. The spirit was both craven and hilarious; but even so, very few other acts had as large a song list as the Beatles. All these bands hunted down obscure B-sides for material, and the test was to see who could come to "own" certain numbers, the way standup comics fingerprint their routines.

Some songs entered several bands' set lists: Chan Romero's "Hippy Hippy Shake," for example, which became a hit for the swinging Blue Jeans in 1963. Others, like "Twist and Shout," became exclusive Beatle territory: with Lennon's spread-legged stance, smiling eyes, and slashing vocal, he bored holes in the song night after night to the point where a lesser piece of material might have emerged in tatters. The wonder was that the more they dug in, the more this song repaid their investment. And this was the story of how just one of their covers became one of many signatures. The larger game among bands was to keep everybody guessing, change the set list frequently, and toss surprises out when rivals were spotted in the audience. Bands like the Fourmost and the Mersey Beats were dim refractions of Beatle energy; but the Big Three thumped some serious beat (with numbers like Richie Barrett's "Some Other Guy" and Chuck Berry's "Reelin' and Rockin'"); the Swinging Blue Jeans had both oomph and swing; the Remo Four were known for hard-driving tempos; and Cass and the Casanovas specialized in vocal harmonies.

Sam Leach began booking the Beatles for several Liverpool Jazz Society events ("jazz" in name only), all-night marathons featuring twelve groups over twelve hours between eight o'clock Saturday night and eight the next morning. The first gig, held at the Aintree Institute on March 11, squeezed two thousand kids into a Temple Street cellar, capacity one thousand. By October, again at the Litherland Town Hall, the Beatles merged with Gerry's Pacemakers to form the Beatmakers, the supergroup as musical demo derby. Sharing the bill only goaded acts to play harder in front of each other; stealing material from other bands depended on the ability to top them. The Beatles developed group dynamics, alternating lead singers and projecting big personalities. If McCartney played the softy, the pretty boy in leathers fronting a bunch of toughs, that bill's Gerry Marsden made the "cute one" look demonic. Marsden did "You'll Never Walk Alone," Rodgers and Hammerstein's *Carousel* warhorse, and irony did not know his address. Many, many others fueled and fed off the Beatles' energy, which made their triumphs the scene's triumphs, until success quickly snowballed beyond all fathoming. Acts doubled up for marathons (a famous Rory Storm and the Wild Ones, Beatles, and Pacemakers bill appeared at the Liverpool Jazz Society in March), all-night Cavern blowouts, and last-minute subs and trade-offs when a band arrived at a gig a player short. In early spring of 1961, the Beatles returned to their Hamburg cash retreat, hungry for more.

SUTCLIFFE WENT TO Hamburg ahead of the others on March 15, 1961, to be with Astrid. He had been elected ambassador to the police: down at the station, he smoothed over the Beatles' return. He wrote the others: "The lifting of a deportation ban is only valid for 1 year, then you can have it renewed. One thing they made clear, if you have any trouble with the Police, no matter how small, you've had it forever. (Drunkenness, fighting, women etc.)"[2] But during this thirteen-week engagement at the Top Ten Club, Sutcliffe finally decided to leave the band. After struggling with the others to rise up through Hamburg's stages, Sutcliffe was drawn back into art by Astrid, and paintings began pouring out of him. This itself was loss enough for Lennon, and Pauline Sutcliffe detailed letters from her brother describing how troubled John was by Stu's circling back to art. Although his paintings are now dubbed merely "promising," Sutcliffe was a born painter; he couldn't put down his brush even when seized by illness.

But the group's politics were not neutral. Even Lennon now joined the others when bemoaning Sutcliffe's bass playing. "Stuart looked miserable onstage—if he turned up . . . ," Pauline Sutcliffe wrote. "[He] was never going to get any better on bass, for he wasn't trying. It was all an irritating fanfare in John's mind, according to Stuart. He said John did not want the aggravation; he wanted to maintain the status quo. But Stuart wanted to go off with Astrid, go off and paint, to leave the Beatles, to desert John."[3]

According to Pauline, Tony Sheridan remarked how much John envied Stuart's choices: the band had finally hit some stride, and now a key symbolic member had options even the resolute Lennon sympathized with. "Stuart and John liked to spend the day together at the museum, where they talked about all kinds of art," Astrid Kirchherr remembers. John and Stuart discussed the idea of them both leaving the Beatles and picking up their studies at art school back in Liverpool, Pauline wrote. But for Lennon this would have meant giving up the weekly cash and the sexual perks, a manner of living he had grown attached to. Letting go of Sutcliffe meant another wrenching loss, just three years after Julia's accident—this one to a beautiful fiancée and promising art career. Even more than McCartney, Sutcliffe was someone who would confront Lennon with his flaws and push back at his flashes of cruelty.

"They knew Paolozzi's work in pop art, and Stuart was very excited to meet him," Kirchherr recalls.[4] Paolozzi represented a huge leap from Sutcliffe's Liverpool Art College training. There, he was a big fish in a provincial pond. At his new digs, he got to study with a leading European artist who had made a splash with his nervy collages of consumer images, seeds of what became known as pop art.[5] The underside of Sutcliffe's big break stoked Lennon's envy: if his best friend knew himself well enough to make the right choice, Lennon's options seemed less clear. And while Kirchherr denies it, Lennon must have had a crush on her, like everybody else did. Sutcliffe had a strong enough ego around his art to choose it as a career. In Sutcliffe's blonde fiancée, and his new passion for visual work, Lennon likely saw a more developed version of himself. His best friend had suddenly sprinted out ahead in life.

Complicated by the strides the Beatles were making onstage, it must have seemed harshly ironic to Lennon that his best friend from art school, whom he had recruited into rock 'n' roll, was now stepping off stage back to the painting for which Lennon first admired him. As described by Pauline, Lennon's reaction measures the strength of his feelings:

> Late one evening it all got out of control. It was John at his most random. He and Stuart were talking in the street in Hamburg and suddenly Stuart was lying on the pavement having been punched by John. He had no time to even attempt to protect himself. The brakes were not working for John and he was taken over by one of his uncontrollable rages: he kicked out at Stuart again and again and kicked him in the head. There was blood streaming down from Stuart's head when John finally came to his senses. John looked down at Stuart—and fled, disgusted and terrified by his attack. He could not confront what he had done.[6]

In Pauline's account, McCartney witnessed this episode, incapable of intervening in this sudden, inexplicable burst of violence. As the Beatles took over Lennon's life, finishing Liverpool Art College seemed pointless. Everybody knew the move was right for Stuart, even though it scrambled the group. The unforeseen consequence of this move, one of rock 'n' roll's great tricks of fate, happened almost invisibly: McCartney drew the short straw and picked up Sutcliffe's bass.

THE SUMMER OF 1961 set Lennon's art vs. music dilemma against Cold War tensions that leapt into space. John F. Kennedy took the presidential oath in January, created the Peace Corps in March, sent five hundred "military advisors" to Vietnam in May, and met Nikita Khrushchev at a Vienna summit in June. Also in May, the first Freedom Riders descended from their bus in Jackson, Mississippi, and were promptly arrested for "disturbing the peace." As London erected its 581-foot Post Office Tower, Berlin built its Wall. The first manned spaceship orbited the earth, with the Soviet Union's Yuri Gagarin, in April. America's Alan Shepard followed in May, prompting Kennedy to announce an unimaginable goal: a man on the moon by the end of the decade.

The Beatles hit the Cavern stage in July for a routine that turned them into a house act: lunchtime sets let them hit outlying areas for evening slots. More listeners started showing up, and their dogged work soon brought them sweeping local stature by word of mouth. Lunchtime queues snaked around lower downtown's winding alleyways, and the venue emerged as a temple, a sweaty shrine, a contagion of hopes writhing amid a sardine scene of hormones.

A swarthy, genial bouncer named Paddy Delaney presided over the Cavern crowd, his gate funneling beehives and their boyfriends down eighteen steep steps into a noisy brick cloister. The Cavern was quite literally a cave divided into six parallel halls, joined at their centers by a spine of seats to form the unlikely shape of a triple cross. The band was jammed onto a wooden platform at the top, holding court at the altar of an adolescent underworld. At any given time, half of the patrons had no sight lines to the band. Those who were there still cherish the Cavern's heyday, with give-and-take between stage and audience that took on the air of ritual, followed by phone calls to Beatle houses with tomorrow's song requests. Half-eaten sandwiches topped the band's bruised amplifiers. During count-offs, lit ciggies got wedged in between guitar strings up by their tuning pegs like candles, and began dipping and swaying with the music.

The first thing Cavern regulars talk about is the smell: the highest hurdle the music cleared was how it redeemed the stench. A former vegetable warehouse, the Cavern sat atop an underground water system built during the nineteenth century as a storage house for dock shipments. Several aromas competed for dominance: distant cabbage remnants, human perspiration, spilled soda, and leftover snacks, all mingled with the overhang from a nightly Clorox scrub. Humidity seeped up from the underground waterways. Cokes and jam butties (butter sandwich squares) were the meager fare, and the drench gave patrons mononucleosis (the "kissing disease"). More than one Cavern regular remembers the walls seeming to sweat; and the beads of perspiration that seeped through McCartney's shirts during the opening numbers signaled a fierce musical commitment: music poured out of the Beatles like laughter, and the crowd roared back as if tickled. Local employers scowled at all the typists and mail boys who returned to their downtown offices drenched and dizzy.

The Beatles began to rule the Whitechapel district, logging more than two hundred Cavern sets during 1961 and 1962 while shuttling around regional dance halls and churches at night. Bill Harry started *Mersey Beat* to track all the groups, filling a newspaper devoted to a scene that by his count numbered between 300 and 350 bands, a number that locals still inflate to 400 or 500—this in a metropolis that was over 700,000 but in a slow, steady decline since wartime. *Mersey Beat's* first issue, dated July 6, 1961, featured Lennon's now-famous essay "Being a Short Diversion on the Dubious Origins of Beatles—Translated from the John Lennon" ("A man came with a flaming pie and said/You Shall be Beatles with an 'A' . . ."). "[Lennon] was so delighted he gave me everything he'd ever written," Harry recalled, "about 250 poems, stories, drawings, and I used them as a column called *Beatcomber*."[7] Harry remembered Lennon dropping off scads of paper, teeming with verbal cartoons and cackling wordplay, reminiscent of his *Daily Howl* material. A lot of this wound up in his first collection, *In His Own Write,* which Penguin scrambled to put out in 1964. The rest was inadvertently thrown away by Harry's girlfriend during an office move.

As Harry ran Lennon's "prose," Lennon dashed off running jokes in the personals section, updating his *Daily Howl* with more absurdist darts at British propriety: royalty, politicians, establishment showbiz. Interspersed among the typical Mersey entreaties for guitarists, scattershot localisms knocked up against randy innuendo: "Accrington welcomes Hot Lips and Red Nose. Whistling Jock Lennon wishes to contact Hot Nose. Red Scunthorpe wishes to jock Hot Accrington." History wonders at the secret nicknames and private jokes embedded throughout.[8]

Lennon's "Beatcomber" column was more of the same, with a guide to the local clubs doubling as a razor combing finer gradations of "cool." Exploding gags mixed with shaggy-dog punch lines to ridiculous effect, as though Lennon couldn't resist stringing his readers along for the sheer effrontery of his noodling:

> The Jackarandy—*Membrains only.* . . . La Matumba—*For a cheap heal.* . . . The Dodd Spot—Watch out for details.[9]

Who knows how many inside jokes mock history in such lines.

And "Small Sam," which never made it into Lennon's books, reads like the inspiration for the running tall-vs.-short gag that screenwriter Alun Owen nabbed for manager Norm and roadie Shake in *A Hard Day's Night.* In Lennon's micro-fable, Stan (sic), though small, is "highly regarded," but one day Stan "saw an adverse" in the "Mersey Bean" for "quickly grow your boots." Now the passers-by all remark on Stan's footwear: "Is not that small Stan wearing a pair of those clubs you quickly grow you boots?' And it is."[10]

Cavern patrons remember Lennon improvising such word fizzle from the stage. The Goons were the most obvious influence, with a head writer like Spike Milligan, whose *Silly Verse for Kids* (1958) and *Dustbin of Milligan* (1961) had found popularity as books. He'd also spawned a second BBC show, called *The Idiot Weekly*. But there were other sources: Stanley Unwin, the radio comic from Pretoria, had come out with his LP *Rotatey Diskers with Unwin* (1960) and his book *The Miscillian Manuscript* (1961), which offered up a similar mashed English, which he called "Unwinese" and everybody else called "gobbledygook." In time, Lennon gave musical color to his verbal dexterity ("I Am the Walrus," "I Dig a Pony"), but on the Cavern stage, his macho, tough-guy stance played off of his wordplay. He was goaded in this pursuit by Wooler, who was an unbearable punster, always on the prowl for catchy ways to introduce the acts at "the best of cellars." Coming from his haughty frame, his feet firmly planted, knees bent for an up-and-down swagger, Lennon's tart verbal riffs offset his musical arrogance.

THE BEATLES' STATURE as Liverpool's reigning scenesters was crowned by a towering set list. Lennon and McCartney's range and reach of material mushroomed to the point where they seemed to know every song worth knowing, and a few more each time out. The roughly 150 numbers that Mark Lewisohn lists for 1961 would come to be seen as an essential rock catalog that framed Chuck Berry, Buddy Holly, Carl Perkins, Eddie Cochran, and Gene Vincent together with the Olympics, the Coasters, and UK players like the Vipers (London skifflers) and Johnny Kidd and the Pirates (who scored with the low-rumble Goth of "Shakin' All Over" in June of 1960).

Paul McCartney had become Lennon's staunch musical sounding board and writing partner, in his front room at Allerton Road or in the vestibule at Mendips. Paul's younger brother, Mike, took pictures of the two hunched over their guitars, which jutted out in opposite directions, writing down words and chords in their notebooks. The more they wrote, the more the music posed riddles too good not to solve. By this point, they had worked at least sixteen originals into their set list, including Lennon singing "Hello Little Girl," the duet on "One After 909," McCartney doing "Like Dreamers Do," "Love of the Loved," and "Hold Me Tight," and some stray instrumentals (Harrison's "Cry for a

Shadow" got recorded in Germany, but "Winston's Walk" and "Looking Glass" never made it to the studio). So as early as this, their own songs counted more heavily than any other songwriter's, including Chuck Berry (the most covered, with eleven), Buddy Holly (nine), Carl Perkins (nine), Larry Williams (eight), and Leiber and Stoller (eight). They fiddled with their own numbers constantly. ("Love Me Do" and "Please Please Me," once considered two of their earliest tunes, weren't written until 1962.)[11]

The band's repertoire stretched all the way back to Arthur Smith's "Guitar Boogie," the 1946 number which George still played, but cut a wide swath through rock 'n' roll, R&B, C&W, and pop, even if the usual heavyweights cast long shadows: Elvis Presley was the performer they most covered, with fifteen songs based on his recordings, including "Mean Woman Blues," which Jerry Lee Lewis covered the same year as the King, 1957. Carl Perkins ranked second with eleven numbers, and another telling overlap: "Blue Suede Shoes" has two famous versions, Perkins's original wayward pass and the King's touchdown interception; it was a bit as if Perkins turned an insult into a hook and lobbed it to Elvis, whose wild-eyed sprint dodged comparisons to reveal the song's cockeyed philosophy. Then came Chuck Berry (eleven), Buddy Holly (nine), Larry Williams, Little Richard, and Lonnie Donegan with six each (although most of Donegan's stuff had probably dropped out of their sets by 1961), and the Coasters, Eddie Cochran, and Jerry Lee Lewis at five numbers each.

Among both the performers and the songwriters whose output the Beatles covered, Berry stood out, and not just because to many critics he ranks as the all-time great rock 'n' roller. Along with Buddy Holly's, his was the career Lennon and McCartney most admired. Even Berry's jail stint burnished his subversive prestige. His open-grill burgers, drive-in diners, and teenage cruisers were nothing if not all-American, but Lennon's genius located the universal pleasure impulse in Berry's writing and animated it as his own. Nearly every Mersey band had some Berry numbers in their set, but Lennon would be the UK's answer to Chuck Berry, and his songwriting hero's best interpreter.

As much as Lennon admired Berry, he placed him inside a larger frame. The great St. Louis duck-walker would never have picked up on some of the numbers this troupe specialized in: movie stuff like "The *Third Man* Theme" (a Lennon harmonica solo), Marlene Dietrich's "Falling in Love Again," and "Over the Rainbow" (based on Gene Vincent's version);[12] "Maggie Mae," the Liverpool sea shanty that became a Vipers hit in 1957 (produced by George Martin); "Summertime," the Gershwin standard from *Porgy and Bess;* and Ray Charles's "Don't Let the Sun Catch You Crying." Lennon, who sang eight out of their eleven Chuck Berry songs, also plucked "You Win Again," the Hank Williams song done by Jerry Lee Lewis, and "Fools Like Me"—country stuff that would have gotten laughed out of most London pubs. A growing musical confidence meant a willingness to embrace the strange, the foreign, and the downright wacky. To Lennon's ear, Berry was among the more inventive and direct writers in a larger continuum.

Learning this material was as simple as hitting the NEMS music store on Whitechapel, just up the block from the Cavern and the White Grapes pub across the street, ogling the latest singles, and monopolizing a listening booth where John and Paul could scribble lyrics. The cost came in stern looks from the buttoned-down manager, but only when he descended from his office to work the floor. (There were rumors about him anyway.) At the rate they were going, on a good week they could harvest between five and ten songs from stylus to stage: cadging verse, learning chords, then working out intros, transitions, and vocal harmonies back home. The following top forty hits from 1960 quickly entered their sets: "I Just Don't Understand," Ann-Margret's lingering pout, which Paul adapted; "I Wish I Could Shimmy Like My Sister Kate," by the Olympics (better known for "Hully Gully" and "Well . . . [Baby Please Don't Go]"); and "New Orleans," by Gary U.S. Bonds.

The NEMS shop was a song bank, and their education amounted to an advanced degree in rock music history, before there was such a thing. Simply by sponging all their favorite sounds up together, Lennon and McCartney skilled themselves in both writing and recorded sound, and began to frame the music inside their own higher tastes and guilty pleasures. All of it fed an ambition to write, even if the few songs emerging at this point felt strained and awkward; their appetite could barely keep up with their obsession. Like playing, where new songs gave them new ideas about ensemble, this feverish listening and thieving took root in ways they couldn't predict, stoking a songwriting muse that simmered for another year or more before boiling over with tunes. They paid back the interest on their NEMS account when its high-flown store manager, the neatly tailored square with the precious smile, finally took notice.

A Man You Must Believe

A MONG LENNON'S TANGLED BONDS WITH OLDER MEN, ECHOING IN the gaps left by Alf Lennon and George Smith, his relationship with Brian Epstein may be the most daunting, intriguing, and quixotically inspired—second only to his friendship with the only slightly older Stuart Sutcliffe. But Epstein's influence on Lennon is at once simpler and more complicated than prevailing myths explain. A closeted gay man whose Jewish family had triumphed in local retail, Epstein was just six years older than Lennon, and had recently given up on his own show business aspirations after a depressing year at the Royal Academy of Dramatic Art in London. Harry Epstein, his father, raised his sons, Brian and Clive, to take over his successful appliance stores. But Brian, the elder, had proven a troubled prospect, jumping from school to school, failing in the army, and utterly disinterested in inventory and receipts.

When asked if he was born in Liverpool, Epstein famously replied, "Yes. I'd say it was essential," and he meant this more poetically than intended. His homosexuality troubled him from his earliest school days, hardly surprising for a sensitive boy born in England in 1934. And every Jew in British culture suffered keen prejudice, far worse than in America. "Brian was a bit different to many friends because he did have this slightly curious background," remembered his friend Geoffrey Ellis. "He'd been an unhappy child at school, he'd had an unhappy period in the army, which he'd left rather prematurely to the relief of both sides,

and he was really still trying to find his feet at that time."[1] No wonder
Epstein took pride in his BBC English: as a Jewish outsider with an un-
mentionable secret, he had had to work extra-hard to perfect his trust-
worthy, "acceptable" public façade.

Epstein's creative streak led him down several vocational dead ends,
frustrating his father's expectations that he, as the elder son, "grow up."
It took a good while before Epstein was ready, however, to settle for his
father's expectations. His stint at the prestigious Royal Academy of Dramatic Art came only after years of what his parents felt was indulgence,
and it was their final favor to him, his last chance to turn his creative
impulse into something worthwhile. His father disdained the theatrical
profession, so when Brian soured on London's cliquish theatrical scene,
he had to hold to his end of the bargain: "When I left RADA," he remembered, "I was determined to throw myself into the family business
and make an increasing and lifelong success of it. It was 1957—I was
twenty-three and full of resolve to do well for my own and my parents'
sake. My brother Clive had now joined the firm and my father hoped for
great expansion."[2] His father misjudged the son's ambition: soon after
taking the reins, he lapped his brother by creating the most successful
music-retailer storefront in Britain—and launching the most famous act
in show business history.

The main Epstein furniture store was in Walton, expanding to a
Charlotte Street address in downtown Liverpool in 1957. Two-thirds of
this space was electrical appliances, "white goods" like washers and dryers,
managed by Clive. Brian was given the upstairs floor for music. When
he finished with it, it was filled to bursting with records, with album
covers papering the ceilings and crowded listening booths where teenagers gathered to listen and socialize.

To his father's surprise, the music business quickly outpaced appliances, to the point where they needed to open a second music shop devoted
entirely to records. When the Whitechapel store opened in 1959, Epstein
booked Britain's biggest pop star of the day, Anthony Newley, for an in-
person appearance at the grand opening. A former child screen star who
had graduated to adult roles, he had recently crossed over into singing:
his top-ten hits included "I've Waited So Long" (from his popular movie

Idol on Parade) and "Personality." Newley was the kind of all-round entertainer Epstein would groom his Beatles to be: pop records would be a launching pad for him to the upper tiers of film, TV—*The Strange World of Gurney Slade*—and clubbing.

Epstein made his way down the Cavern steps on November 9, 1961—one month after Lennon turned twenty-one.[3] There are several slants to this famous story, the most likely being that one Raymond Jones had made his way into the NEMS shop at the end of October to request a record by the Beatles. (How apt that the first retail request for a Beatle record came from a guy. Jones, like a lot of Cavern regulars, had heard Bob Wooler hawk the disc in between Beatle sets. On a return visit, Epstein informed him that he would happily order the record, which was probably German, by which time two more requests—from women—had come in.

The story captures Epstein's nose for trends, his marketing knowledge, and his rock 'n' roll blind spot. As a retailer, he was a classical snob who used his pop sales to support deep stock in symphonies, trad jazz, and bebop. But he tracked down the Polydor import of "My Bonnie," featuring Tony Sheridan backed by "the Beat Brothers," and ordered twenty-five, which sold out immediately, and then fifty more. In his 1964 memoir, *A Cellarful of Noise* (ghostwritten by press agent Derek Taylor), Epstein claimed he hadn't yet heard of the Beatles, yet this seems highly implausible. For some reason, Epstein wanted his Beatlemaniac readers to believe that he didn't read anything in *Mersey Beat* except his own ads. This belies several solid business tactics that had already made NEMS a runaway success: if he didn't scour *Mersey Beat* for ads and local shows by the bands whose records he was selling, what did he think his record buyers were listening to at their own clubs? Colin Hanton doubts Epstein's premise: "Well, it's like the story where he asked someone to take him to the Cavern 'cause he didn't know where it was," he remembered. "But the guy who owned the Cavern was his next-door neighbor." Epstein had even hired the Swinging Blue Jeans to play for his twenty-seventh birthday party there. "He must have known about it," Hanton insists.[4]

The muddled circumstances surrounding Epstein's discovery even led his assistant Alistair Taylor to claim (much later) that it was *he* who invented Raymond Jones, and put it in the NEMS log as a customer requesting a Beatle record, in order to draw Brian's attention to the local phenomenon. This is vanity: as the clerk who advised his boss on jazz titles, why wouldn't Taylor have simply ordered up the record himself, played it for Epstein, and told him the Beatles were a Cavern staple? In retrospect, Taylor drew himself a smaller role by fibbing than he may have actually performed. Spencer Leigh went so far as to publish a photograph of Jones in his book, *The Best of Fellas: The Story of Bob Wooler*.

And Bill Harry, *Mersey Beat*'s editor, maintains he had been chatting up Epstein about the Beatles as part of his newspaper's success. "Epstein took advertising in *Mersey Beat*," Harry said. "He asked me to arrange for him to go to the Cavern. In his book he comes up with this thing about a guy coming into the shop and asking for 'My Bonnie' but he'd been discussing the Beatles with me for months already."[5]

If Epstein really hadn't heard of the Beatles by that point, he clearly should have: in *Mersey Beat*'s debut issue, which sold swiftly in the NEMS shop, Lennon's piece appeared on the front page. The second issue featured the blaring headline BEATLES SIGN RECORDING CONTRACT (regarding the German Polydor sessions with Sheridan). As editor, Bill Harry aimed to cover the entire scene, but he was clearly a fan, and touted the Beatles at every opportunity.

By issue three, Epstein himself was a columnist, contributing a dashed-off tip sheet about pop releases like Presley's "I Feel So Bad," Bobby Rydell's "The Fish," and Chubby Checker's "Let's Twist Again." Epstein's prose, by the way, bespoke bleached-out taste: Peggy Lee's "Mañana" is dubbed "superb," while Del Shannon's "Hats Off to Larry," his September follow-up to April's number-one "Runaway," is merely "bright."[6] Also in that issue, he mentions George Martin's pop act Matt Monro, who had a new single, "Love Is the Same Everywhere." Just below his copy was a Cavern calendar listing the Beatles.

Epstein was simply too proud to miss the Cavern scene for which his shop supplied material. Alistair Taylor reports how Epstein had an "amazing talent" for sniffing out hits. Record labels began to follow his moves: if he ordered five hundred copies of a record for his two shops in Liverpool, labels ordered more pressings. Taylor remembered several instances of Epstein's ear tuning into hits long before they even hit radio, including Ray Charles's "Georgia on My Mind," his first UK hit, in December 1960, and John Leyton's "Johnny, Remember Me," which hit number one in August 1961. Taylor recognized the Beatles as the leather-clad "scallywags" who frequented the shop to monopolize listening booths with their notebooks. Epstein was not the kind of man who would miss such things.

He also paid attention to Taylor and his clerks. Taylor and others recall NEMS stocking the entire Blue Note catalog, then in its postbop heyday (featuring established scions like McCoy Tyner, Art Blakey, Horace Silver, and Jimmy Smith, with free-jazz radicals like Eric Dolphy on the horizon). Liverpool jazz collectors must have worshipped at Epstein's feet. Taylor recalled:

> He wasn't a hard taskmaster, but he wasn't easy. He could be awkward and he was a real stickler that everything had to be right. After all, he was running the best record store in the northwest of England. Then it became the north of England. Then it became the whole of England. He was the first man to stock the whole of the Blue Note jazz catalogue. Because he knew I loved jazz, he invited me to share a box at the [Liverpool] Philharmonic Hall to hear Art Blakey and Thelonious Monk.[7]

In his taste for bop titans like Monk and Blakey, Taylor was an adventurous jazz buff, outpacing the trad-jazz types who had frequented the original Cavern. He was among the Europeans who were these Americans' main support: Monk was becoming a revered figure, and Greenwich Village devotees were arguing about his heavyweight status even as John Coltrane passed through his band in 1957. Taylor was the kind of stuck-up jazz hound Lennon derided because of their disdain for rock 'n' roll's "simplicity." Still, Epstein had enough pride in his business sense to trust Taylor's judgment, attend jazz concerts, and appreciate the improvisations he heard, even if his own sensibility tended toward late-romantic sincerity. His ear was sophisticated enough to tell the difference between pedestrian and progressive, and it's crucial to Lennon's story. He was enough of a classical buff to call himself a "Sibelius hound," which is roughly like saying you're a proud somber fart: except for maybe the high religiosity of Bruckner, Sibelius is the least humorous of all the romantic symphonists. There's reason to believe that the Epstein ear enjoyed Lennon's dismissal of jazz, knowing that the brash confidence of such a shrewd rock 'n' roller could only help advance the popular style.

When Epstein finally made his way down Mathew Street, from the proper shop district through the winding alleyways crowded two centuries before with slave traders, he found the beehive-and-leather crowd queued around the corner. (In his mind, of course, this was the after-hours district he cruised for pickups. The lunchtime scene was supposedly new to him.) In his uniquely British biography, Alan Clayson claims Epstein had already caught the Beatles in Hamburg, become intoxicated with their look and sound, and feared getting caught up in a dangerous obsession. More likely, he felt snobbish about pop and probably rock, but shrewd about how trending styles supported folk, classical, and jazz. And like any good retailer, his ears constantly sought next season's hits.

There are Liverpudlians who remember well the day Brian Epstein came down into the Cavern: his natty suit, neatly folded breast-pocket handkerchief, and combed-back hair made him stand out like a teacher among truants, a suit among bohos. "He came in with his red tie," one observer remembers. "Everybody knew who he was, and Wooler even made an announcement, so there was this strange self-consciousness in the air about his appearance. It was as if the schoolmaster had come down to take a look round."[8] The Beatles, like their Cavern audience, recognized "Eppy" as the slick (read: Jewish) manager of Liverpool's largest and best local record store.

Did Lennon's aggressive stance and menacing grin trigger a surge of feeling in Epstein? Or was it simpler than that: did his business instincts kick in as the dank surge of the crowd surrounded him and he began to smell potential? There was certainly a bit of both. To underplay the homosexual attraction would dismiss part of his truest nature. But to over-emphasize his crush on Lennon trivializes his equally strong ambition to be a show-business player.

He approached the stage after their set and found the Beatles imperturbable. "What brings Mr. Epstein down the Cavern, then?" George Harrison drolly asked him, as if Epstein were hopelessly out of place. The way he stood out there made Epstein feel even more painfully self-conscious than usual. He stood baffled by how his ears suddenly trumped his eyes. These disheveled, grotty teenagers, smoking and swearing at their own audience, jolted the self-proclaimed "dapper" retailer. Maybe, too, he saw the band as rough trade, the kind of trouble that tempted him in the gay underground. Taylor also claimed that his lunch with Epstein after their first Cavern outing brought a firm offer of half ownership in the future management business that suddenly had formed in his mind. This was probably a Taylor fiction: Epstein had never managed an act before, never even spoke of such a notion, and it's doubtful that if he had wanted a partner, he'd have turned to a subordinate. At the same time, the story speaks to some of Epstein's tactics, especially his tendency to reveal his position and discuss figures way too early in negotiations. Perhaps, on some level, Epstein felt what he had heard was so big he simply couldn't handle it all by himself, and he had already learned to trust Taylor's ear through Thelonious Monk.

Even discounting Taylor's self-flattering firsthand account, Epstein's reaction to the Beatles was instantaneous; after introducing himself to them after their set, he invited them up to his NEMS offices for a meeting. "It was very awe-inspiring, being let into this big record shop after hours with no one there," McCartney remembers. "It felt like a cathedral."[9] There, from behind his desk, Epstein proposed acting as their manager and told them he was certain he could promise them a recording contract, or at the very least tend to their bookings and secure them better fees. How different this was from the strip-club pretensions of Allan Williams, whom they had to beg for work: the shopkeeper of the area's most successful record store was approaching *them* about management. From Epstein's vantage point, here was a chance to fuse himself with the most macho of young men to compensate for his effeminacy. A deep, subliminal sexual attraction would find expression through a professional relationship. It took him about a week to win over their skepticism.

Although he was only twenty-seven at the time, even to the haughty young Lennon Epstein had an air of success, of a grown-up who knew what he was about. He drove a sleek yet genteel Zodiac, Ford's luxury variant of its sporty Zephyr. McCartney remembered this as decisive: "The big impressive thing about Brian was his car. He had a bigger car than anyone we knew."[10] After Epstein made his pitch, "there was a pause," Alistair Taylor wrote. "The four Beatles—John, Paul, George, and Pete—exchanged glances. Then John said, emphatically, 'Yes.' He exhaled a sigh of relief. 'We would like you to manage us, Mr. Epstein.'"[11]

LIVING A SECRET LIFE as a homosexual in this era meant scrambling around in a shameful rat maze. A covert yet thriving subculture, the gay underworld promised a tragic and painful existence, and Epstein grappled with a double whammy, Jewishness and sexual preference, an almost unimaginable handicap then compared with today's perspective. But even in this narrow realm, Epstein created a unique persona for himself. He developed keen social skills to cope with all the homophobia, and an even more intricate private self among his peers.

"There's lots of beliefs amongst tough men that so-called poofs or pansies and people like that have a harder time," recalled club owner Yankel Feather. "There were slack-arsed trimmers, as the Liverpudlians called them, around the clubs and the odd sailor would come in, but it wasn't always the poofs who were the passive ones and it wasn't always the sailors and the slack-arsed trimmers who were the tough ones."[12]

The flip side of Epstein's finesse was his taste for rough trade, the seedier type he trolled for one-night stands with near the docks. Alistair Taylor described a typical encounter:

One night, he'd left my house about ten o'clock for wherever he was going. By about a quarter to midnight he was back on my doorstep. He left my house in a beautiful white shirt . . . and when he came back on my doorstep it was a brilliant red. He'd been knocked about so much that he didn't even come back in his car. . . . [Some] person had left him in this state. I bathed him.

I got him right. He stayed the night and went back home or wherever he went the next morning looking reasonably good.[13]

Long before he met Lennon, Epstein trafficked in a network of secrets and back-alley trysts that always threatened to erupt into blackmail. In an era not as far removed from Oscar Wilde's as a contemporary reader might think, Epstein was accustomed to duplicity in both personal and business affairs. In fact, pop music and theater would have been about the only two professions to account for any openness at all in terms of sexual preference. His father's business could have been brought down by such scandal. His friend Geoffrey Ellis recalled that Epstein "behaved sometimes in a way which was very dangerous, and he was conscious of this. In some ways, he sought out danger. It gave him a thrill, but of course led him into many very awkward situations from time to time. I think deep down he didn't want to be homosexual but paradoxically he enjoyed his homosexual experiences very much indeed."[14]

The duality of Epstein's personality was the first thing most took note of. As Cynthia Powell described him:

A very complex character was Brian. He was a most generous man, thoughtful to the point of embarrassment at times, shy and gregarious at the same instant, but if John ever refused him a request he could behave like a spoilt child and throw tantrums, even stamping his feet with frustration, tears in his eyes. And no one could frustrate Brian more than John. I think he reveled in his power to make Brian squirm and lose his temper, even though he admired Brian as manager and godfather to our son.[15]

To Lennon, here was a man who had been around the block a few times, in more ways than Lennon might have comprehended; and for all the talk of how Epstein's affection for Lennon transcended the music, Lennon's return "attraction" to Epstein was a complicated mix of desire, ambition, uncertainty, and arrogance. His conditioning told him that "Jews make money!"; his overconfident sexuality made him uneasy but also flattered to be fussed over and gazed at. Here, finally, was an older man who openly adored Lennon, and spoke of promoting him and his music.

EPSTEIN'S EFFECT ON the band could be felt immediately. He obsessed over his initial contract with "the boys," and pushed all four to sign it even when he knew that no court would honor it, with three band members under twenty-one. Just as Colonel Tom Parker visited Gladys Presley in Memphis to ingratiate himself with Elvis, Epstein, like a gentleman caller, courted Beatle parents, bringing Mimi Smith chocolates and impressing Jim McCartney with his sincerity. Epstein knew these locals harbored a reflexive anti-Semitism and that he would have to work doubly hard to win their favor. Ironically, his ethnicity worked to his advantage. "My dad," McCartney remembered, "when he heard about Brian wanting to manage us, said, 'This could be a very good thing.' He thought Jewish people were very good with money. This was the common wisdom," McCartney remembered.[16]

The Beatles' ambivalence about signing became evident when they gathered to meet Epstein to ink their first formal contract: retold with various details by Hunter Davies, Peter Brown, Ray Coleman, and others, the prime elements seem to be the long wait they made Epstein endure in his office before arriving, and once three of the four of them were there, having to ring up McCartney, who was at home taking a bath. "This is disgraceful!" Epstein spurted, "He'll be very late!" "Late . . . but very clean," came Harrison's response. Peter Brown has Lennon dragging Bob Wooler along and spontaneously introducing him as "Dad," which gave the tardiness a wry, formal edge, as if Lennon were self-consciously pitting his latest father figures against each other to see how they measured up.

Alistair Taylor remembered that first agreement, which amounted to a boilerplate for similar contracts of the era, until the final clause. "The first contract was effective from 1 February 1962 for a five-year period. But the Beatles and Brian were each able to give the other three months' notice if things went wrong. Brian was on 10 per cent of the

Beatles' income up to £1500, then Brian's percentage increased to 15 per cent. I don't think there has ever been anyone in the history of pop music who's had a fairer contract than the Beatles. Brian's percentage went up to 25 per cent in later contracts."[17] Consider the unguarded tone of that quote: no sooner has Taylor pronounced Epstein the fairest man in show business than he relates how heavily the later Epstein encroached on the Beatles' enormous earnings. If Epstein's sincerity in the beginning is unmistakable, his overreach during 1966 and 1967 is equally undeniable.

Even before he left his signature famously blank on that first contract, Epstein had begun pounding pavement. He settled "the boys'" equipment debt at Hessy's music shop, and had them "all doffed up" at Horner Brothers, the classiest hairdresser in town, to manicure their already distinctive haircuts. "John grinned that his Aunt Mimi would think he had turned over a completely new leaf," Taylor recalled.[18]

If the Beatles hadn't made an indelible first impression on Epstein at NEMS, they certainly made one when they visited his family home in Woolton. Somehow underscoring the classic gay trope, "Eppy" still lived there, devoted to his mother, Malka, nicknamed "Queenie." "I saw the boys coming . . . on a Sunday morning when I was in my garden," attorney Rex Makin, a neighbor of the Epsteins, recalled. "They came and they looked what we term in Liverpool a set of scallywags—untidily dressed and all the rest of it and not quite the thing for the genteel atmosphere of the part of Queens Drive where we lived."[19] Both father and mother were tolerant but suspicious about their son's latest obsession. He should be happy enough as the most successful retailer in the north; why this sudden interest in pop music, which he had so long considered beneath him? A scheme like this could end in embarrassment and failure, upsetting the family's careful reputation.

Within weeks, Epstein had "packaged" the Beatles, so his ideas formed quickly: How best to translate this raw energy into the all-round entertainers needed to please the BBC set, the middle classes, the Sunday-night TV audience? "Lose the leather, gum, ciggies and swearing, tidy up the hair, perhaps, but its length was somehow intriguing . . . and put them in matching suits. That should do." Did such ambitious thoughts run through his mind? Or did he simply gape at the spectacle, follow the heat and noise of the Cavern's underground temple as it carried him to some new, unknowable place?

BRIAN EPSTEIN'S IMPACT on Lennon's professional life was second only to George Martin's. Of course, Epstein came first, and his enthusiasm persuaded Martin to hear the band after a string of industry refusals, so you could argue that his impact was larger. And Lennon's relationship with Epstein trailed his partnership with McCartney in terms of male intimacies. He knew McCartney longer and won a place in pop history with their songwriting collaboration; but, knowingly and unknowingly, he may have trusted Epstein more, at least at the beginning. Epstein took on the role Lennon had looked for in vain in Allan Williams: that of the elder male figure who would manage all his affairs, from bookings to housing, to let him concentrate on music. McCartney was always a peer first, and a younger peer at that; Epstein drove a fancy car and ran his own business. Lennon looked up to Epstein's self-sufficiency and success even as he exploited his personal insecurities and belief in the band. Lennon was never as close to George Martin on a personal level; and Epstein brought the added complication of being privately gay yet relatively open about his affection for Lennon the man. Lennon had already denied talk of his bond with Stu Sutcliffe, which prompted even Sutcliffe's sister to speculate a physical intimacy. And art school had certainly put him in touch with queer life, which was half of how young macho men built themselves up, through ridicule and disdain. Epstein brought experience and sophistication to the band's ideas about gayness, even though they cackled about him behind his back.

Epstein's affection for Lennon seems to have been an open matter to everybody, even Lennon, who enjoyed ribbing him even more than he did McCartney or Harrison. Epstein's torment was to blush easily, and Lennon delighted in "taking the piss" out of him, just to watch his face go red. He could be cruel with his anti-Semitic remarks, although, like his "*Sieg heil!*" salutes and goose-step marches in his Hamburg act, they're naïve pronouncements of rebellion. There's ample evidence that Lennon was perfectly tolerant of Epstein's homosexuality and his ethnicity.[20]

Lennon himself spoke frankly about the topic: "Well, it was almost a love affair, but not quite. It was never consummated—but it was a pretty intense relationship."[21] (How many rock stars refer to their managerial relationships as unconsummated?) From his end, Epstein seems to have been extremely insecure about his feelings for Lennon, which tilted between romantic enchantment, affectionate listening, and sincere personal devotion. Lennon described a more platonic love affair, which can be even stronger and last longer than sexual relationships, where the "love" was subsumed into the professional "marriage." In Lennon's circle, Epstein became a new boundary to bounce off of, a close friend who doubled as a bumper car into which Lennon rammed his macho bluster.

Epstein's heritage, background, and troubled history of not fitting in comprised a charged, charismatic personality, the kind of agent gifted at recognizing genius in others, exploiting it, then envying the notoriety he had helped them win. With every strength came a flaw: he gave show business its biggest act ever, but ultimately sold them out for a relative pittance; he did deals that brought EMI and his clients vast fortunes, but left them poised to lose their most valuable asset—the Lennon-McCartney publishing fortune. As the pivotal link between Liverpool and the world, Epstein broke the Beatles wide open, but he was never a full-fledged member of the band, and in late 1966 he was distraught at their decision to stop touring. He confided in several people that he felt his role marginalized.

For all the short-term solutions he got right, however, he got several larger, long-term deals done terribly wrong. In the most immediate sense, Epstein steered the Beatles out of their regional market, but he was also the greenest of managers in terms of the critical contracts they engaged in as they took the world's stage from 1962 to 1964. Within a month of their meeting, he had Decca A&R man Mike Smith travel up from London to hear their set at the Cavern, and began booking shows in proper clubs like the Kingsway in Southport and Manchester's Oasis.

When he gets painted as a meticulous shopkeeper who excelled at window displays, Beatle historians reduce his role to some hoary, outdated

gay cliché. Still, he approached the Beatles as both a manager and a tai-
lor. His visual frame was exactly what they needed at this point to get
over, in direct conflict with what Lennon, Sutcliffe, and McCartney had
assembled without him: from Epstein's vantage point, their shoddy stage
presentation distracted from the music. ("We looked like four Gene
Vincents—only younger," McCartney would say later on.)[22] But in dressing up the Beatles, Epstein also dressed up rock 'n' roll, which tells just
how much he heard in their sound.

Epstein removed the leather, ciggies, curse words, and pissing about
between songs. Presenting the band in suits and ties, tightening up their
set pace, he insisted on punctuality and a minimum of audience interaction (which reveals just how loose and abiding this rapport was). Where
the Hamburg Beatles personified rock 'n' roll animism, complete with
leering jokes, German gibberish, toilet seats, and Nazi baiting fueled by
nationalist revenge, Epstein overlaid his version of what a respectable
show-biz outfit might look like: ties, combed hair, and natty jackets—only
at the humid Cavern did Eppy allow vests. He had them clip all their loose
guitar strings, which splayed from the ends of their guitar necks like so
many overgrown toenails. In short, he spiffed them right up into the prevailing norm needed to impress the London show-biz establishment.

In hindsight, this brief, pre-Beatlemania period, this Epstein package, gave the Beatles a schizoid personality: the music stayed fierce while
the image softened. Lennon would famously regret his capitulation to
Epstein's makeover, but at age twenty-one his ambition told him to swallow his pride and play along. The unintended consequence of his sardonic grin and obdurate stage stance rattled the very frame he'd been
put in, and offset McCartney's boyishness with a forbidding irony. The
tension must have been jarring: Were these hoodlums in suits? Did they
still run with knives? In one of their first professional photography
sessions, where they posed around Liverpool bomb ruins, they exuded
brash naïveté, an utterly serious cunning, and were at once lofty and
down-to-earth, grandly ambitious and beyond status-mongering.

Far from "selling out," as Lennon most feared, the tailoring only
added to their menace. The matching suits didn't fool teenagers; they
simply made their tough expressions, especially Lennon's, seem arch and

vaguely coy. The bangs and creeping-over-the-ears locks stayed: all by itself, this signaled defiance, and an eccentricity that synced up eerily with their sound. And topping jackets and ties, the haircuts assumed a surprising formality; rather than subdue them for television, their matching uniforms made them seem untamable. To hear them during this period was to witness the coming together of a sublime, two-headed musical ensemble, Lennon angling off McCartney; but the visual effect alone conveyed tension and intrigue. You had the sense, many fans remember, that these early Liverpool years were precious, that this town could not long contain these personalities, let alone their music.

What most historians miss in Epstein's doting makeover is that it was almost all visual. Theories abound about the precise source of their haircuts, and those bangs host an array of influences. Just before they met Epstein, in October 1961, Lennon used his twenty-first-birthday money, a cool hundred pounds from his aunt Harrie in Scotland, to hitchhike to Paris with McCartney. There they ran into Jürgen Vollmer, their Hamburg mate, on the street. One story has Vollmer giving them the new haircuts they returned with. Considering they attended a concert by Johnny Hallyday and found a crowd of French teens sporting the look, this makes sense. It also makes for a logical extension of their German-art-crowd identification in Hamburg and the haircut Astrid herself wore and gave Sutcliffe. But Bob Wooler had some insight on this as well:

> Brian put the Beatles into suits and he liked the idea of a Beatle haircut. Joe Flannery [another Merseyside manager] carries a photograph of his mother and says, "Look at her haircut. John liked my mother and copied her hairstyle." It's not impossible, but you could just as easily say it came from watching the Three Stooges. My theory is that Stu and Astrid saw the Peter Pan statue by George Frampton in Sefton Park. This was erected in 1928 and Peter Pan has a Beatle haircut, a Beatle bob if you like. She gave Stu that haircut and the rest followed on from that.[23]

According to Liverpool historian Spencer Leigh, "Epstein's biggest triumph was in leaving the Beatles' music alone."[24] Long before Lennon told him to get lost in the studio (with his famous retort "We'll look after the music"), Epstein sensed the musicality dripping off their personalities. Through trial and error, Lennon and McCartney gained leverage over their audition set lists as time and experience proved them right. This became another layer of how strong personalities vied for control.

Even though Epstein's personal rebellion included a polished ruling-class accent, he brought all the show-biz establishment's provincial prejudice into play. But in a curious way, he also joined with the band's outsider rock 'n' roll identification simply by turning himself into their advance man. Part of his refrain, however, courted sneers: his boys were going to be "bigger than Elvis," which by then was laughable hype, the worn-out, shooting-too-high, never-gonna-happen line that desperate agents rehearsed to slamming doors. "Bigger than Elvis" became Epstein's ruse, his dare, his personal mantra—and his epitaph. Finally, the Elvis line became the knife Epstein twisted into the pop industry before it instinctively twisted back. Most of the A&R people he met with seemed intrigued at how such a dapper, well-heeled retailer reeled off such fervent gospel about some beat group from up north.

Epstein began calling his record-label contracts with a simple ploy: he told them he wanted to arrange new discounts on his wholesale rates. He had invested enough in his reputation as the north's most successful record retailer to turn it into leverage as he approached London labels. Once face-to-face, however, he neatly dismissed this idea and played his record. He urged his listener to filter out the singer on "My Bonnie," Tony Sheridan, and focus on the backup band. Reluctantly, the label suits listened, if only to avoid being rude to a crucial link in their supply chain. Epstein's approach had the dual effect of setting the client at ease when he was poised to drive a hard bargain and putting them at a disadvantage when listening to Epstein's wares—a new gambit in his dealings. It was a clever approach that was in all ways polite and gentlemanly: how could anybody take offense at a prized retailer dismissing new margins on his stock?

His first trip to London with the "My Bonnie" single carried two goals: to secure a recording audition and to convince Polydor to release the single in Britain. His first call was to Decca, described by Rolling

Stones manager Andrew Loog Oldham in his indispensable sixties memoir, *Stoned:*

> Taciturn businessmen controlled Decca, with an apparent aversion to style reflected in the ruthlessly staid Decca offices. They did not even appear to like or listen to pop music—they could have been selling baked beans for all they cared. Their interest was in the tins. . . . The UK business turned a blind eye to the reality of America. The British recording establishment wishfully hoped the Furys and Wildes would all disappear and we'd return to the pre-hula-hoop safety of lush Mantovani.[25]

Among Epstein's many letters was one to Tony Barrow at Decca, who wrote under the pseudonym "Disker" for the *Liverpool Echo* from his office in London. When they met in person, Barrow politely told Epstein that he only covered new records, not live scenes; but he alerted Decca chief Dick Rowe to the fact that an important client was peddling a band, and Rowe gave him an appointment to maintain courteous business relations.

"My Bonnie" wasn't the greatest calling card, and Epstein got the industry runaround wherever he went. Epstein was far too generous in assuming that A&R stooges had ears anything like a retailer's. Instructing the men in suits to listen to the band behind Tony Sheridan was way too much to ask: in those days, the front man was the act. Familiar with stalling techniques, most labels pointed out that the band probably had a German contract that would need investigating before they gave serious consideration. EMI passed the record along to several staff producers, who all declined. But when Epstein called back at Decca, a suit named Mike Smith expressed enough interest to schedule a trip to the Cavern to hear the Beatles live. This all happened as November 1961 became December, because Smith was in the Cavern audience on December 13 to hear the Beatles, and everybody was aware of a London talent scout in their midst. Bob Wooler even made an announcement from the stage.

So within weeks Epstein had convinced the band that his skills were advancing their cause: not even a month had passed from his first hearing them and he brought in a Decca man to hear their live set. By many accounts, Smith visited on the same day the Beatles signed their management contract—the one Epstein himself didn't sign. When Alistair Taylor asked Epstein about this, he replied that he "didn't want the Beatles to feel tied to him in any way."[26] Almost exactly a year later, after they had recorded their second single, Epstein signed his first legally sound contract with them, which hiked up his fee to 25 percent of all earnings.

Only Decca showed interest at first, but an EMI contact offered to have the Polydor contract translated from German so Epstein could decipher its terms. This may have been a delay tactic to politely put off a retailer with stars in his eyes, but it did send Epstein to the Polydor offices to contact Bert Kaempfert. Kaempfert replied by letter in very gentlemanly terms, allowing the Beatles the freedom to sign in their home country as long as he was able to rebook them for recording when they returned to Hamburg in the spring. This was both expedient and revealing: Kaempfert was expressing faith in the band without trying to monopolize the product; he was anxious to record follow-up hits for his own market, but happy to let Epstein do the heavy lifting in the UK.

Once Smith returned to London, it took ages for Epstein to hear whether Decca might sign, so he simply carried on shopping "My Bonnie" around. Polydor agreed to market the disc in England (probably based on NEMS's own sales figures), and Epstein kept pounding. Finally, after weeks that seemed like years, Smith recommended a second "audition," which would be taped in a studio in London, and a date was set for January 1, 1962. This was fairly quick by modern standards: mere weeks after Smith trekked up to Liverpool, he had enough pull to schedule a studio session to convince his manager, Dick Rowe, that the live act would translate onto tape. It must have gotten the band's hopes up, which is exactly what Epstein wanted to do after Allan Williams had told him not to touch them "with a *fucking barge pole*."[27]

TRAINING DOWN TO London with high hopes on the last day of 1961, the Beatles felt the northerner's self-consciousness arriving in the staid capi-

TIM RILEY | 157

tal. Unlike their adopted second home in Hamburg, which taught them there were places even rougher than Liverpool, London loomed in their imaginations as the seat of national government, home to the Royals and the British Broadcasting Corporation, where celebrities walked more exalted ground than seaport docks. In Britain's highly segregated class system, Scousers roaming London streets were like Memphis rubes set loose in New York City. The class distinctions were foremost, but regional chauvinism gave them at least as much to prove.

This first London session, on the heady New Year's Day of 1962, was called an "audition," but it's gone down in history as a tape that proves how oblivious the labels were to the volcano they were sitting on. Epstein, suspecting the "audition" was probably as much a chance for him to get a better demo tape tracing the group's repertoire, helped select the set list. The material invites speculation: this was certainly not the kind of set the band played at the Cavern, and not the kind of bombast they went for in Hamburg. It's tempting to read Epstein's hand in the song choices, as well as that of Bob Wooler, whose fondness for Tin Pan Alley standards encouraged McCartney's shtick. But stacked up next to a club gig in Manchester a month later, whose set list Epstein typed out, those arguments shrivel.

Decca audition tape, London, January 1, 1962	Oasis Club, Manchester, February 2, 1962
"Like Dreamers Do" (Lennon-McCartney)	"Hippy Hippy Shake" (Romero)
"Money" (Gordy-Bradford)	"Sweet Little Sixteen" (Berry)
"To Know Her Is to Love Her" (Spector)	"The Sheik of Araby" (Smith-Wheeler-Snyder)
"Memphis, Tennessee" (Berry)	"September in the Rain" (Warren-Dubin)
"Till There Was You" (Wilson)	"Dizzy Miss Lizzie" (Williams)
"Sure to Fall" (Perkins)	"Take Good Care of My Baby" (Goffin-King)

Decca audition tape, London, January 1, 1962	Oasis Club, Manchester, February 2, 1962
"Bésame Mucho" (Velázquez)	"Till There Was You" (Willson)
"Love of the Loved" (Lennon-McCartney)	"Memphis, Tennessee" (Berry)
"Hello Little Girl" (Lennon-McCartney)	"What a Crazy World We Live In" (Klein)
"Three Cool Cats" (Leiber-Stoller)	"Like Dreamers Do" (Lennon-McCartney)
"September in the Rain" (Warren-Dubin)	"Money" (Gordy-Bradford)
"Take Good Care of My Baby" (Goffin-King)	"Young Blood" (Leiber-Stoller)
"Crying, Waiting, Hoping" (Holly)	"Honeymoon Song" (Theodorakis-Sansom)
"The Sheik of Araby" (Smith-Wheeler-Snyder)	"Hello Little Girl" (Lennon-McCartney)
"Searchin'" (Leiber-Stoller)	"So How Come" (Bryant)
	"Ooh! My Soul" (Penniman)
	"To Know Her Is to Love Her" (Spector) or "Hully Gully" (Smith-Goldsmith)
	"Roll Over Beethoven" (Berry)
	"Love of the Loved" (Lennon-McCartney)
	"Dance/Twist in the Streets" (Medley, possibly "Twist and Shout" with another unknown number)
	"Dream" (Mercer)
	"Searchin'" (Leiber-Stoller) [28]

Much later, Lennon went on record as being very put out that they softened up their sound for Decca instead of thumping those clueless men in suits into submission. He was firmly of the mind that his was a rock 'n' roll band, and felt humiliated whenever they pretended to be something else, or producers pointed them in the direction of Cliff Richard or the Shadows, who for Lennon personified pop phoniness. And yet immediately after McCartney sang an original, "Like Dreamers Do," Lennon became a human firehouse for "Money," which would slam their second album shut like a frying pan to the head. This set up a classic dialectic: the creative impulse vs. the corporate need to package, which Lennon could only acknowledge with irony or contempt. His vocal on "Money" pinned necessity down with ambition.

Arguments thrive over this selection of material, and how it distorted or defined the way the Beatles were seeing themselves as a band. What the Decca session dramatizes most conclusively, however, is how Pete Best's flat beat compares with Ringo Starr's livelier kicks: on "Money," Best lays low on the tom-toms, but the last two refrains don't go anywhere; in Ringo's version from the following year, he jacks each refrain up, higher and higher, until the band is playing chicken in a hot-rod race with Lennon's vocal. This audition version of "Money" never gets danger in its sights. Still, Lennon probably overworried the "middle-of-the-road" slant of this material: for full-bore rock 'n' roll, you can count the Chuck Berry ("Memphis, Tennessee"), two Coasters numbers ("Three Cool Cats" and "Searchin'"), a hilarious, lickety-split novelty for George ("The Sheik of Araby"), and three originals ("Dreamers," "Love of the Loved," and "Hello Little Girl"), although the softer side of McCartney leads the original numbers, and the set boasts a respectable balance of slick and ballast.

Was Lennon's insecurity about the softer numbers just so much McCartney envy? Since the audition didn't lead to the contract the band so desired, it must have been easy in retrospect for Lennon to blame Eppy or Paulie for the failure. It's the kind of second-guessing that goes on all the time with auditions and can never really be quantified. At this level, it's a subjective game; if a listener wasn't hip to this band's range, he didn't deserve to be signing bands.

Legend has it that Rowe passed on this audition, which he heard only on tape, with the quote "Guitar bands are on their way out," which shows you how easy it is to sneak fiction into a myth: instead, he signed another "guitar band," the bland mayonnaise Brian Poole and the Tremeloes, chiefly because they lived in a London suburb and would be easier to book for studio time. Even more revealing is the way George Harrison, at least, remembered Rowe when he met up with him at a Rolling Stones concert in 1963 and urged him to sign the band, bearing no resentment about the Beatles being passed over. Lennon was not so generous. McCartney is said to have remarked, "He must be kicking himself about now." Lennon's response: "I hope he kicks himself to death!"[29]

The leading perplexity for the label producers at this stage, stuck in prepackaged mode and resistant to innovation, seems to have been the alternating vocalists: this was a completely different model than the traditional lead singer with backing, and at first it befuddled rather than impressed the A&R dweebs. Even George Martin, the squarest open mind in music at the time, picked McCartney as the lead singer at first; perhaps Lennon's attack was still too forceful, too threatening, for how these suits thought of mainstream pop.

WITHIN TWO MONTHS after his trip to the Cavern, the band's Decca audition gave Epstein a whole new reel of songs to peddle. Moreover, Polydor released "My Bonnie" in the United Kingdom, correcting the label from "the Beat Brothers" to "the Beatles"; and on January 4 *Mersey Beat* released the results of its first annual contest, proclaiming BEATLES TOP POLL! (McCartney remembered filling out scads of ballots voting for the band.)

This was lightning-fast work, though short of a recording contract, and it kept "the boys" upbeat during the next six months of disappointment. Epstein increased their booking fees and crammed their calendar while he himself made frequent treks down to London. John and Paul often met him at the train station for coffee upon his return. Epstein found these meetings grueling, dealing face-to-face with the talent he had promised so much to. At one point he even sought counsel from Bob Wooler:

Following a Cavern midday session, he would invite me for lunch
to the Peacock in nearby Hackins Hey, and he would say, "What
am I doing wrong? Why aren't the record companies responding?" All I could say was, "I can't believe it, Brian. They should
come and see what the Beatles are doing to audiences." In those
days, the A&R men didn't hurry to a provincial town to see a
group. . . . Brian was so disappointed but he was persistent and
determined to make a breakthrough.[30]

In February 1962, Epstein returned to Dick Rowe's Decca office only
to be politely rebuffed with more finality. He took his two reel-to-reel
Decca audition tapes, fifteen songs, for more disappointment at Pye, and
then Oriole. In early February, he called Bob Boast, the manager of
EMI's HMV retail shop on Oxford Street in London, whom he had met
the previous year at the Deutsche Grammophon Convention in Hamburg. Here the Beatles story merges coincidence with fate. Boast listened
to the tapes and suggested Epstein go upstairs to cut a few discs, or vinyl
acetates, which would be easier to share with producers than his worn
reel-to-reel tapes. Upstairs at the lacquer machine, the material caught
the ear of engineer Brian Foy, who was impressed to learn that three
of the numbers ("Like Dreamers Do," "Love of the Loved," and "Hello
Little Girl") were original. Foy suggested Epstein contact a publisher,
the back door into the business through which writers gain a foothold by
selling songs instead of performances. It's curious that Epstein hadn't
already thought of this. Foy called upstairs to Sid Coleman's office at
Ardmore & Beechwood, and Coleman came down, gave a listen, and invited Epstein upstairs. From his office, Coleman gave his friend Parlophone's George Martin a ring; his secretary made an appointment with
Epstein for the following Tuesday. Thus in one morning did Epstein get
the final no from Decca only to get a good start on some new yesses
from both a major publishing and a major recording firm.

Epstein's pitch was polished at that Tuesday meeting, and Martin
remembers being more charmed by the band's manager than persuaded
by his samples. Still, he suggested a meeting with the group, intrigued
by something in the sound he couldn't articulate. That was enough for

Brian, who returned to Liverpool to ready the band for more Hamburg dates.

In the meantime, the Beatles' bookings grew in number and reputation. On February 15 at the Night Tower Ballroom in New Brighton, Wallasey, an extraordinary crowd of thirty-five hundred showed up to hear them. In early March, another gear in Epstein's strategy kicked in: they made their first radio appearance on the BBC Light Programme show *Teenager's Turn—Here We Go,* taping "Dream Baby," "Memphis, Tennessee," and "Please Mister Postman." Once the broadcasts became more frequent, fan letters kept return visits flowing; a year later they launched their own show, *Pop Go the Beatles!* Eventually, through 1965, they would perform more than 275 numbers on the air. BBC exposure vaulted their considerable Hamburg repertoire onto the airwaves, since their songwriting hadn't yet fully kicked in: playing the numbers they had developed at the Indra and the Top Ten, the Beatles filled BBC airtime with numbers like Buddy Holly's "Crying, Waiting, Hoping" and Little Eva's "Keep Your Hands Off My Baby." Finally, the band was reaching listeners, who found their way to live shows once they came to town, solidifying their reputation.[31]

Now that they had a manager, this time they flew into Hamburg looking to show off all their good fortune. They knew the scene, had a bucketful of songs, and strutted with new confidence. John, Paul, and Pete arrived at the airport on April 11, 1962, full of high expectations and higher spirits, eager to reclaim their title as titans of the Reeperbahn. But their first priority was to catch up with Stuart. (George Harrison would join them there the next day.)

Ever since Stuart's Liverpool visit with Astrid over Christmas of 1961, the Sutcliffe family had been receiving disturbing letters. A letter of Astrid's to Pauline spoke of Stuart's recurring headaches and pale skin, and told of a fainting spell in Paolozzi's master class. His headaches came as fierce attacks and had taken on epic proportions—the pain intensified until he blacked out, and he began to fear he was going mad. Astrid and her mother shuttled him around to Hamburg doctors, but nothing helped. Stuart would camp out for days in the attic, painting ferociously without sleep or food. Another fainting episode at school forced the Kirchherr family to move him into a private bedroom and hire a nurse. They commissioned X-rays, which seemed to disprove the theory that a tumor had appeared. For days at a stretch he felt completely normal. Then the headaches returned, and his condition worsened, with periods of blindness, throughout March.

The day before the Beatles landed, Astrid's mother called her at her studio and beckoned her home. She returned to find Stuart suffering yet another wrenching headache, and she called the hospital. An ambulance arrived, and Astrid jumped in next to him. The headache attacks seemed doubly unlucky to Astrid since Sutcliffe's painting had recently blossomed onto scads of canvases in the attic, sprawling oils that roared darkness and chaos, as if he could somehow push back against the pain through paint. Within a matter of months, Astrid's devotion to Stuart had turned from idyllic romance into dreadful consolation; the force of his headaches had reduced him to a suffering child, mocking all the ferocity that flowed through his brush.

When he'd last seen Stuart, Lennon's envy had been palpable: his best friend had left the band, choosing art over music, moving in with Hamburg's classiest, artiest scenester in the process. The news about his "headaches" hadn't seemed serious. Now Astrid met the band at the Hamburg airport with news she could barely deliver, never mind bear herself: Stuart, only twenty-one years old, had died next to her in the ambulance only the day before. Instead of their returning to Hamburg as conquering heroes, the ground suddenly opened up beneath them. McCartney and Best burst out crying; Lennon went silent.

It's hard to imagine the depths Sutcliffe's death sent Lennon into. He already had lost his best friend to painting and a hip fiancée, whom Lennon both admired and envied—he could only express his knot of emotions with his fists, and perhaps neither he nor Stuart could explain their friendship after that drunken blast. There is testimony to Lennon's stony refusal to admit his feelings; but by now he must have felt an awful intimacy with loss. It was as if premature death grafted itself as a bar code onto his life story. To him, life must have seemed terribly precarious—he had to act fast, for tragedy could appear at any turn. The Blackpool scene at age five had frozen inside him as insoluble unbelonging; his stepfather, the kindly George Toogood Smith, died when he was fourteen, leaving him alone in the house with an unforgiving Aunt Mimi; his adoring mother, Julia, had died just three years later. Now, just as his career began to get some traction, his best friend had been snatched from him before they could reconnect. He already had lost his mother twice; now he lost his best friend for a second time, too.

"I had a lot of people die on me," Lennon would say later. To him people didn't just die, they died *on* him. And with so many people he had trusted piled up cold, how else could he have taken it? He must have felt as though steeling himself sane was the only coping mechanism for losses he could barely comprehend. "Processing" all this grief was barely a psychological concept on some distant, more "evolved" horizon.

"I looked up to Stu. I depended on him to tell me the truth," Lennon later reflected. "Stu would tell me something was good and I'd believe him."

The Beatles hit the stage in front of yet another loud, drunken Hamburg throng at the brand-new Star-Club on Friday the thirteenth, contracted to do the impossible: play upbeat music from inside a black hole. From ambitious teenagers, they had to transform themselves into pros, especially since this booking paired them with their god Gene Vincent for two out of seven weeks. The day after John, Paul, and Pete flew in, Epstein arrived with George Harrison, joined by Millie Sutcliffe, who came to return her son's body to Liverpool. McCartney, once Sutcliffe's rival for Lennon's intimacy, was wracked with guilt about his musical disputes with Stu. "We ended up good friends, but we'd had a few ding-dongs, partly out of jealousy for John's friendship," he remembered. "We all rather competed for John's friendship, and Stuart, being his mate from art school, had a lot of his time and we were jealous of that."[32]

Many biographers dote on the fierce quiet that descended on Lennon after Sutcliffe's death, but that only fits his atypical grieving style: he beat himself constantly for "laughing hysterically" after George and Julia died; if he "showed no emotion" in Hamburg at this scene, there are a variety of complications that might have led to this response. For starters, he had envied Sutcliffe's attachment to Astrid. With Stu gone, he may have felt that keeping it together when the others were falling apart was part of his job as a band's leader. There was also the macho persona to prop up: there is no talk of him crying in front of McCartney or Sutcliffe, his two best friends, when his mother died. There are more descriptions of him "disappearing" for a couple of weeks. That was more the gruff, manly way of coping.

The cause of Sutcliffe's suffering and death are still in dispute. Certainly, drinking heavily while getting off pills would exacerbate any existing brain condition. One report has a German X-ray returned to Liverpool eighteen months later, where a small tumor revealed itself. Millie and Pauline traced the indenture of the skull found there back to the bloody fisticuffs that Lennon and Best rescued him from in 1959 (an episode reimagined at the opening of *Backbeat*). But a two-and-a-half-year calm before a final half year of accelerated suffering doesn't make as much sense as a possible injury from the 1961 brawl after a gig at Seaforth's Lathom Hall.

Pauline Sutcliffe, Stu's younger sister, has written about the possibility that Lennon's own Reeperbahn fight with Sutcliffe upon leaving the band (April 1961) may have contributed to his condition. This theory presumes a lifelong sense of guilt in Lennon, who never seems to have discussed it with anybody.[33] Just as plausible, though, was no injury at all: perhaps a simple, inexplicable aneurysm created an inoperable blood clot.

Paradoxically, the person to speak most glowingly of Lennon's mood after Sutcliffe's death was Astrid, who as late as 2005 remembered his warmth, empathy, and good counsel. Lennon soothed Astrid almost as if he knew too well how to console a grieving lover. Unlike George or Paul, who tried to reassure her by saying "everything will be fine," Lennon spoke without sentimentality, or the superficial cant that many people trade off as comfort. In his words to Astrid, you can hear what Lennon told himself:

"Well, you have got to decide what you want: do you want to live or do you want to die? Decide that, but be honest." And that helped me tremendously to go on. And then he said that there are so many things we haven't even discovered yet, and life has got to go on, and you can't sit down and cry all the time, you have got to get on, and if it's not for me, he said, it's for Stuart. And he said that in a very harsh voice, not like nice and sweet, but very directly.[34]

Already intimate with death, Lennon knew how the bereaving soul clutches at reality, however dim, beyond the hollow platitudes that infect misguided small talk. The loss of Stuart, as both a friend and an artist, was unbearable, and would remain unbearable, for as long as anyone would remember. For the rest of her life, even though she married, Astrid slept with a picture of Stuart at her bedside. Tellingly, Epstein had talked about having Sutcliffe do design work for the band; and later, his face was immortalized on the cover of *Sgt. Pepper's* menagerie of celebrities and as part of Richard Hamilton's *White Album* collage. And he earned himself a hallowed place in Lennon's heart. Lennon, typically described as cool and remote during this episode, made the most sentimental request: he asked for Sutcliffe's winter scarf, which, like his uncle George's tattered overcoat, he wore for years afterward.

9

Isolation

The Beatles' first British recording contract and sessions came fitfully, after great persistence from Epstein, through a comedy label. An impossibly long three months passed before Epstein heard back from George Martin, which he took as one more bad omen. Martin had simply been busy with sessions, and returned Epstein's message to schedule a second appointment for May 1962. Lennon fumed about the missed opportunity at Decca, and played out his lingering disappointment through a telling political omission: he, McCartney, and Harrison never told Pete Best that Decca had turned them down. For all Best knew, or couldn't be bothered to find out, the slow wheels of industry were still turning. The drummer's freeze-out was well under way before George Martin heard Best play live.

Leaving the Beatles in Hamburg, Epstein returned from the Sutcliffe trauma in mid-April to a welcome surprise in London: Martin finally offered him an EMI recording contract on an accelerated schedule. Instead of hearing the band perform for him in person, Martin's ears felt confident enough in his early impressions to book a studio date and take care of some paperwork along the way. This sudden reversal mystifies historians, especially since it inexplicably trips recording history forward. For a long time there was confusion about whether this "studio" session was an audition or an actual recording date, with tape rolling for a possible release. Epstein and the Beatles clearly viewed it as a professional session. Martin may have booked it as such, but probably looked at it more as an "artist test," an engineering audition where they figured out the ideal setup and levels for instruments and vocals.[1] This was customary, but parties remember these details differently. Did Martin conceal the true nature of this booking to capture the Beatles off guard, wind them up before making his commitment?

This was an unusual way of proceeding, but Martin had unusual powers. He had been made head of Parlophone in 1955, at age twenty-nine, and in those days that was quite young—especially within EMI, a company that prided itself on being even stuffier than Decca. In its lofty EMI offices in Manchester Square, Parlophone was looked on not so much as a boutique label as eccentric, an unlikely imprint to become a pop dynamo. The label was branded not with a fancy pound sign (£), as many assumed, but with a German L, for Carl Lindström, the man who founded the imprint.[2]

MARTIN HAD GROWN UP in London's Drayton Park. Unlike Lennon, he enjoyed a stable, working-class home; his father was a wood machinist. Young George taught himself the piano, and composed his first piece at the age of seven ("The Spider's Dance"). He dreamed of piloting airplanes for the elite Royal Air Force, and settled for the Fleet Air Arm. His timing was bad: after he was commissioned in 1945, the war suddenly ended, and he spent a year as a clerk before entering the Guildhall School of Music on a veteran's grant. There he picked up the oboe and studied orchestration, theory, and conducting, but his real education came in the recording studio. While Martin's full biography still awaits serious scholarly attention, some highlights of his early career seem like blueprints for his later work with Lennon.

After Guildhall, he cataloged scores for the BBC for a few months in 1950 before being hired as an assistant by Parlophone's Oscar Preuss, at age twenty-four. Parlophone also suffered bad timing: during the war, its big-label classical acts had been siphoned off by Columbia and HMV, leaving the roster lean. Even with the label's relatively thin catalog, though, the early years at Preuss's side exposed Martin to every mode of the era's recording practice: from soloists to orchestras, jazz groups to children's choirs and remote recordings in Scotland of Jimmy Shand's country dance band using EMI's mobile recording van. As the oddball division of Britain's largest recording firm, Parlophone hovered one rung on EMI's corporate ladder above its Salvation Army Band imprint, Regal Zonophone.

The hardscrabble streets of Liverpool were a long way from London's illustrious St. John's Wood. Previous decades saw giant composers and conductors like Sir Edward Elgar, Sir Malcolm Sargent, and Sir Thomas Beecham stroll down from their stately homes in lush Westminster to record with the London and Royal Philharmonics inside the enormous Georgian town house at 3 Abbey Road. This huge EMI building, with its humble domestic façade, dated back to 1830. Martin routinely shared recording studios there with the other subsidiaries, and the high-ceilinged, wood-paneled rooms were as likely to host the London Symphony Orchestra as they had swing bands like the Glenn Miller Orchestra or piano soloists like Arthur Rubinstein. In this rotation, Martin was the wild card. Preuss gradually handed over more and more responsibility to his able assistant, who was virtually running the label on his own by 1955. When Preuss retired in the spring of that year, Martin, at age twenty-nine, stepped in to replace him, making him the youngest label head in Britain. Martin realized that to keep the imprint afloat— and to keep himself employed—Parlophone needed to compete. While not forsaking its usual material, he carved a niche for the label through comedy and novelties.

With Preuss's encouragement, Martin had begun exploring the possibilities of the relatively new medium of magnetic recording tape as early as 1951, when the two coproduced a recording with bandleader Jack Parnell. "The White Suit Samba," the theme from Alec Guinness's *The Man in the White Suit* (1951), utilized an electronic sound effect from the movie as a rhythmic element. Here Martin dressed the tape experiments of the French avant-garde's *musique concrète* in the guise of a pop instrumental. A Peter Ustinov single followed in 1952, "Mock Mozart," wherein Martin painstakingly overdubbed the vocals by recording on one mono tape, then playing that recording to another machine while simultaneously recording another vocal part. Repeating this process, he stacked up four harmonizing parts.

Alongside comedy, Martin recorded a number of well-known children's records in the 1950s, including "Nellie the Elephant" and "Little Red Monkey," and in 1953, with Peter Sellers, he attempted a children's space-fantasy record called "Jakka and the Flying Saucers." An ambitious production, Martin treated it with the same primitive overdubs as the Ustinov single, as well as numerous tape edits, sound effects, and variable-speed recording. The record bombed; as technical experiment, though, "Jakka" was an advance on "Mock Mozart."

Most biographers rank Martin one of music's luckiest producers. His background tells a more nuanced story about how preparation met opportunity. Long before he ever met Lennon's Beatles, Martin was skilled in an emergent new medium that took the art of recording from live performance to the recording of multiple performances atop one another to create a detailed, layered production. Far from simply sticking a microphone in front of comics, or feeding radio broadcasts directly onto a master tape, Martin liked to tinker. As the EMI front office dragged its heels during the industry's transition from direct-to-disc lacquers to analog tape, and from 78s to twelve-inch LPs and seven-inch 45s, throughout the late 1940s and early fifties, Martin dabbled with how comparatively elastic the new tape medium was. Beyond all this, Martin was not satisfied with tape editing, and often tweaked his productions with variable-speed recording and evocative effects like compression to create what he would later call "sound pictures." Martin's skill lay somewhere between "live-to-radio" and "performance-on-tape."

Once Martin took over Parlophone, his recording studio increasingly resembled a workshop, a place where chasing sounds led to serendipitous accidents. To Martin's ear, comedy presented the perfect foil for tape tricks, allowing him to incorporate outlandish production ideas to ornament scatterbrained voices and gags. Before he became a movie star, the young Peter Sellers became a partner in this pursuit, scoring hits with a skiffle parody, "Any Old Iron," in 1957 and then with a ten-inch LP entitled *The Best of Sellers* in 1958.

Also in 1957, Martin issued an LP of a popular West End revue featuring Michael Flanders and Donald Swann called *At the Drop of a Hat*. More Sellers singles and two Sellers LPs followed in 1959 and 1960, each increasingly ambitious in scope. In 1961, Martin spent three days splicing together the tapes for an LP of another revue, *Beyond the Fringe*, which would launch the coming "satire boom" in British comedy. At the same time, he produced Charlie Drake's hit "My Boomerang Won't Come Back." The silliness of "Boomerang," which reached number 14, belied its sharp arrangement. The next year brought hits with Bernard Cribbins, most significantly "Right Said Fred," and two LPs that revealed just how far Martin's production skills had come. None of these records would have been nearly as funny without his careful attention to sonic detail, and he filed every skill into his database of tricks for his work to come.

For one of those 1962 LPs, Martin and former Goon Michael Bentine fashioned an album out of Bentine's absurdist television show *It's a Square World,* using multiple overdubs on the new four-track EMI machines, sound effects, and clever editing. The other LP contained a full-length parody of *The Bridge on the River Kwai,* produced during the second half of the year, when Martin began working with the Beatles. It benefited from an elaborate yet subtle production of overdubbed effects Martin constructed to bring the scenes behind the dialogue to life. (The album was ultimately renamed, nonsensically, *The Bridge on the River Wye,* because of a threatened lawsuit.) In an era when the British music industry was still in thrall of whatever was happening in the United States, Martin's comedy records were the product of homegrown talent of a particularly English sensibility. Even if the rest of the industry looked down their noses at these records, they were hits, and the savvier ears in the business heard ingenuity behind the laughs.

Inside EMI, Martin was the "suit" who courted trouble. In 1956 he made a recording with the Goons called "Unchained Melody," an elaborate parody of Les Baxter's American hit from the movie *Unchained.* As was the custom, other acts quickly hopped the same train; Jimmy Young, Al Hibbler, and Liberace all had top-ten UK hits with the tune that spring. But EMI feared the Goon demolition would result in a lawsuit from the publisher and refused to release it. Incensed, Spike Milligan went to Decca, which had no problem releasing a record tied to the BBC's most popular radio show. The label promptly scored two top-ten Goon hits: "I'm Walking Backwards for Christmas" in June and "The Ying Tong Song" in September. Lennon treasured his copy of the loopy "Ying Tong Song," most likely bought (or pilfered) from Epstein's Whitechapel shop.

Even on novelties Martin left his fingerprints. Ditties like John Dankworth's "Experiments with Mice," a top-ten hit in 1957, fused jazz with comedy. The Temperance Seven earned him his first number-one hit in 1961 with "You're Driving Me Crazy." Perhaps most tellingly, Martin worked with the Vipers, a skiffle outfit that rode the Donegan wave to produce successful covers of "Cumberland Gap," a song Lennon sang with the Quarrymen, and its B side, "Maggie Mae" (the Scouser prostitute ditty immortalized by Lennon's outburst on the *Let It Be* soundtrack). When Martin signed the Vipers in early 1956, he took a pass on their lead singer, Tommy Steele, who jumped to Decca and became a rock idol. While he probably regretted letting Steele slip by, Martin still squeezed hits from his band. Unlike Rowe and all the others, Martin could tell the difference between a lead singer and backup band. (Martin's decision regarding the Beatles in this matter would be finely nuanced.)

The Vipers also scored with a non-skiffle treatment of Bobby Helm's country song "No Other Baby," in 1958, which featured the slap-back echo Lennon adored from the Sun-label Memphis rockabilly of Elvis Presley and Carl Perkins. Another producer, like HMV's Walter J. Ridley, might have assigned the Vipers something on the order of "The Birds and the Bees," which Ridley chose as the surefire follow-up to Johnny Kidd and the Pirates' "Shakin' All Over" in 1960 (with Joe Moretti's ominous, forbidding guitar). It bombed. By contrast, the classically trained Martin had no problem letting skiffle be skiffle.

WHEN EPSTEIN FIRST called from Coleman's office, Martin was attending to singers like Matt Monro, whose "When Love Comes Along" became the follow-up to his February hit, "Softly As I Leave You" (which had reached number ten, his third top-ten hit since late 1960). Like most EMI producers, Martin's formal office was at EMI headquarters across town in Manchester Square, where the Beatles posed for their first album cover.

In this pre-rock era, pop was an afterthought, never mind taken at all seriously. It was seen as a necessary sop to the public which helped pay for the loftier classical product, much the same way Epstein financed his jazz and classical stock at NEMS. Martin was not even a member of London's "pop" circle, really—the hits he had came mostly from novelties—and while sturdy in terms of engineering practice, as a producer he was among the least likely men in the recording industry to be pegged a "comer." In retrospect, it's uncanny that the man who signed on the Beatles, and helped shape their work, had this dual background in comedy and, in BBC terms, "Light Programme" classical music. Martin's early interest in aeronautic engineering sprouted into technical wizardry when applied to sound, while his background as an oboe player gave him a flair for winds.

For Lennon, Martin's connection to the Goons proved compelling. But inside EMI, this comedy-classical connection was double-edged: while relatively free of the typical pop constraints, Martin didn't enjoy pop budgets to develop talent. Then again, the whole idea of "pop development"—giving a band three or four records to find their way in the medium—barely existed. His profile gave him the freedom he needed to take a chance on just such a band as the Beatles, unproven yet promising—the kind of gamble that might pay off if the planets aligned. It's still unclear how much attention Martin paid to the charts at the time, whether he cared where rock 'n' roll came from or where it might be headed. He was happy for the hits, even if they didn't buy him credibility at his own label. But he didn't have a vision for where the music could go. Martin's taste was probably closer to Epstein's: that of an educated man who went home to listen to classical records, not teenage stuff or R&B or C&W. So in this context, Martin was not signing what he thought was the next huge pop act. He heard the Beatles as a regional fad that just might break wider. And he picked up on their comic edge: if they stalled, he could always steer them toward novelties.

EPSTEIN AND MARTIN recognized each other in ways that transcended musical taste. Martin was charmed by Epstein's affection for the band; he seems to have capitulated more to Epstein's charisma than to the Decca lacquers. Of course, his colleague Coleman had arranged for a publishing deal, a strong referral: if a publisher thought this band's material had value, that was already one vote from a trusted ear.

And Epstein doubtless admired Martin's gentlemanly bearing and BBC English. He was the kind of gentleman Epstein saw himself as: intelligent, well-spoken, courteous, officious, and yet open-minded, willing to learn, a professional in the best sense; somebody who was not just out to make a buck, but devoted to his product, who had earned a certain standing by taking care with what he put his name on. Epstein's homework probably told him that Martin had a serious reputation in an industry where there was almost no such thing: to the EMI brass he was eccentric, but if Martin "stooped" to comedy, he had pretty much invented that market; and among sound enthusiasts it was clear he knew what he was doing. Surely Epstein would have made some calls and figured this out; at the very least he would have recognized Martin's stable from stocking records by the Vipers, Peter Sellers, and Matt Monro. Epstein also noted Martin's connections with the BBC.

Lennon's relationship with Martin would be entirely professional, or as professional as trusting someone to transcribe your personal abstractions onto tape can be. As studious and disciplined a technician as Martin was, he was more an arranger and facilitator than a collaborator—to Martin's ear, after a time Lennon didn't need any help writing, just translating his songs into recordings. And so a creative triangle formed outside the band: between Lennon and Epstein, where the sexual currents ran hot and forbidden; and Lennon and Martin, a meeting of prodigy and sympathetic mentor.

Between Epstein and Martin, a completely civil business relationship was born—Martin's squabbles would be with EMI, not Epstein. And it seems unlikely that Martin knew the nature of Epstein's lopsided Beatle contracts and NEMS foibles: although he gladly took on other of Epstein's Mersey artists (within eighteen months he recorded Gerry and the Pacemakers, Billy J. Kramer, and Cilla Black), his terms with the Beatles were on a completely different business track. Epstein had a preexisting arrangement with the Beatles; Martin saw no need for comment. That Epstein delivered Lennon to Martin must have earned him major stripes in Lennon's mind.

Martin's initial offer to Epstein was a huge boon for Epstein, Lennon, and the others, but posed little risk to Parlophone. As contracts go, it had all its era's boilerplate clauses, putting all the risk on the band and leaving EMI plenty of wiggle room if their music didn't chart. On May 9, Epstein dashed off two telegrams, the first to the band at the Star-Club:

CONGRATULATIONS BOYS. EMI REQUEST RECORD-
ING SESSION. PLEASE REHEARSE NEW MATERIAL.

and the second to Bill Harry at *Mersey Beat:*

HAVE SECURED CONTRACT FOR BEATLES TO
RECORD FOR EMI ON PARLAPHONE [SIC] LABEL
1st RECORDING DATE SET FOR JUNE 6TH
——BRIAN EPSTEIN[3]

It was the telegram the band had been dreaming about, and it arrived just weeks after Stuart's death.

WHEN HE RETURNED to Liverpool, Epstein had fires to put out. In another of the serendipitous ways in which he was perfectly suited to handle this band, the shameful underworld of homosexuality made his boys' indiscretions seem tame. Alistair Taylor reported in his memoirs that a young girl named Jennifer, no more than seventeen, came into the NEMS offices one day with both her parents. "Our Jennifer is five months pregnant," the mother said emphatically, "and the father is one of your Beatles—John."

It wasn't right, she insisted; their girl was "taken advantage of." She would miss her exams and the family was already strapped for money. Now they had a child to plan for. Epstein's "resolution" was a £200 pay-off and a signed agreement to stay quiet. Over the years several sources close to the Beatles have testified to many such complaints—more than just a handful—few of which ever made the papers or seemed to cause anybody overt stabs of conscience.[4] In Epstein's mind it became part of the cost of running the show: his "boys" belonged to their fans, nobody else. In those days, boys would simply be boys, the birth control pill was not yet widespread, and the entertainment business had relaxed customs on such matters. They were simply looked after the way quiz shows coached their contestants or politicians wheeled out their wives in wool coats: the show was upheld at all costs, a delicate fantasy that required constant maintenance. Backstage might be depravity, but the public persona was zealously guarded. After all, it was what people wanted to believe in that was being sold, not anything that resembled reality. Few acts have been as knowing about this as the Beatles, and few agents were as well suited to pitching such a fantasy as Epstein.

Shopping a band for less than two years is now a relative honeymoon. But what looks clean and swift in retrospect seemed unending for Epstein, Lennon, McCartney, Harrison, and Best. And while the Hamburg gig replenished the coffers and gave them perspective on how far they'd come, the cost was beyond measure: for Lennon, Sutcliffe's death put a pall on everything. The cost of "holding it together" would be high. His character hardened, his booze bingeing became epic, his fatalism cemented. For Lennon, success became something like the opposite of F. Scott Fitzgerald's "capacity for wonder"—it was tinged with the embittered personal resolutions he made to himself in the darkest of nights, to take his revenge, to climb on top of all these deaths and conquer everything and anybody that might hold him back.

THAT FIRST WEEK in June 1962, the international news wires were jumping. At the end of May, astronaut Scott Carpenter had orbited the earth three times. Adolf Eichmann was hanged in Israel on May 31. An Air

France charter flight, the *Château de Sully,* crashed when it overran its runway at Orly Airport in Paris; only two flight attendants survived amid 130 fatalities, most of them cultural and civic leaders from Atlanta, Georgia. President John F. Kennedy prepared to deliver the commencement address at West Point, and the Students for a Democratic Society would soon meet in Michigan to write the Port Huron Statement.

The morning of June 6 saw Neil Aspinall drive the Beatles in his van down to London, where they met with George Martin's assistant Ron Richards, his engineer Norman Smith, and "button pusher" (tape operator) Chris Neal around 5 P.M. in preparation for a two-hour session in Studio 2 starting at seven. They were tired from their Star-Club dates, which ended on June 2, and had spent their two days off running down songs in afternoon Cavern rehearsals. Six months had passed since their Decca audition, and the debate about material was piqued. Lennon argued that Epstein had made them sound "soft" for Decca, and he was determined to play a tougher hand this time around. After all, he argued, Decca had passed—that proved Epstein had blundered their set list, right? (This argument followed them into the studio and their career before evolving into a larger, ongoing debate about the nature of the band's legacy.)

"I remember Martin taking a quick look at them and leaving for tea," remembered technical assistant Ken Townsend.[5] (Others report Martin was simply out to dinner with his secretary, Judy Lockhart-Smith.) Ron Richards filled in as producer, as he did for many of Martin's pop artists. Norman Smith, however, says he summoned Martin back to the control room when the band started "Love Me Do." He stayed for the rest of the session.

For the hayseeds from Liverpool, problems emerged almost immediately. For starters, the Beatles' equipment gave off a ghastly buzz, especially McCartney's bass amp. The technicians didn't think much of Lennon and Harrison's guitar getups, but that bass amp was simply hopeless. While the band had tea, Townsend and Smith improvised an amp and speaker from the basement to get rid of the droning.

They taped four songs, beginning with "Besame Mucho," with which Jet Harris was just then enjoying a hit. (According to standard

EMI policy at the time, their first session tape was wiped for reuse, and only a private reel of "Besame Mucho," discovered in 1980, has survived.)[6] Harris, a former member of Cliff Richard's Shadows, was gunning for success by covering a marginal Coasters hit from 1960 (when it peaked in the UK at number seventy). The Coasters, of course, were songwriting powerhouse Leiber and Stoller's New York outfit, whom the Beatles adored (they also did "Searchin'," "Youngblood," and "Three Cool Cats"). The Coasters had sped up the pace of Jimmy Dorsey's hit from 1944 with a touch of Nat King Cole's version.

The Beatles, however, had a hard time taking this stuff seriously: they spanked the Coasters' version up to a sweaty gallop. Not only were they covering a current hit, proving to Martin they could master a top-ten sound, they drilled straight into the song's insipidness, puncturing its bathos for self-mockery. Theirs was a knowing, self-conscious arrangement that said, "We can do this stuff . . . but only by exposing its complete *fraudulence!*" The tempo alone snubbed convention, and it worked chiefly as comic fizz. It had the same sardonic ring as Lennon singing "Ain't She Sweet" as a "rock" song—a hilarious surface upended by its dismissive subtext.

The other three numbers were all original, meaning Lennon and McCartney won the argument with Epstein about material. (Or did they agree on a song list with Epstein, and then veer from it out of cheek?) For this new producer, they were intent on proving themselves not just as a band but as writers, which meant they not only had confidence in their chops but belief in their muse. "Love Me Do" sprouted a soaring harmonica from Lennon, an early signature. It gave Smith a start, and this is where George Martin entered the booth (either summoned by Smith or back from dinner). Although sketchy, it caught enough of what Lennon had in mind when he wrote it. Then came "P.S. I Love You," another original, a sticky McCartney valentine, and "Ask Me Why," with a querulous Lennon lead. All three of these songs made giant strides beyond "Love of the Loved" and "Like Dreamers Do," the originals they had played five months previously for Decca. Both "P.S. I Love You" and "Ask Me Why" boasted a new songwriting confidence, the latter in particular, which seesawed between playful "woo-woo-woo"s and tense silences. The distance between their Decca audition (January) and this first Parlophone session (June) could be measured by how far they had traveled as songwriters.

Martin stepped out from the control room to talk with the band before inviting them in to hear their performances. He gave them rookie coaching about their microphones and other technical matters (then as now, certain recording mics were "bidirectional," or two-sided, in that they responded better to a sidelong angle than to a direct frontal attack). The mood was suspicious as he gave his instructions, and the haggard Beatles seemed to listen without much response. They felt patronized. Only when Martin asked if they had any comments was there a mood change. "Look, I've laid into you for quite a time, you haven't responded," Smith recalled Martin saying. "Is there anything you don't like?" "They all looked at each other for a long while, shuffling their feet," Smith remembered, "then George Harrison said, 'Yeah, I don't like your tie.' "[7]

At some point during this session, or on the telephone with Epstein shortly thereafter, Martin aired his doubts about drummer Pete Best. McCartney remembers it opening up an ensemble rift that had been interrupted by the death of Sutcliffe: "If he wasn't up to the mark (*slightly* in our eyes, and *definitely* in the producer's eyes) then there was no choice. But it was still very difficult. One of the most difficult things we ever had to do."[8]

No further sessions were booked yet, but the contract got passed around for signatures. "What have I got to lose?" Martin remembers thinking after the session. He signed the contract and predated it June 4. The agreement called for four sides, or two double-sided 45-rpm singles, at a penny per single (not side). This included three one-year options with an increase of a quarter of a penny at the end of the first year and another halfpenny after the second (half that amount for overseas sales). If that weren't exploitative enough, a twelve-track album would count as only six tracks. With nothing up front, it was a risk-free arrangement for Martin; and Epstein, counting himself grateful after so much disappointment, didn't push back for better terms. If it fell within the ballpark of going industry contracts, it was still corporate theft.[9]

The Beatles returned to Liverpool for a week straight at the Cavern, where their "Welcome Home" gig on June 9 broke attendance records: nine hundred kids did the sardine routine in the sweltering basement to greet the band after two months away. Meanwhile, Martin had some thinking to do: which of these new songs would make the strongest debut? There were no uptempo numbers, and you can't break a pop act with a ballad. Here was a dilemma for Lennon: he ached to feature the band as a hard-rock act but had written only softer numbers for the original material they were determined to bank. ("One After 909" had been shelved due to weak lyrics.) The Beatles were clearly a beat group, steeped in R&B, but this early decision about how to position them vexed even Martin. Something had to change. Epstein's idea was obvious: suit them up and give teenage girls some matinee idols. Martin's thought process was more complicated: should he lead with McCartney, who had both the golden voice and the baby face, or Lennon, who had the "big personality"? "In the end it became obvious," he allowed. With "My Bonnie," Epstein had urged Martin to listen beyond Tony Sheridan's vocal to the Beatles in the background; now Martin realized he was dealing with a totality, not just a typical singer with backup group. His genius as a producer at this point boasted simplicity and taste: why choose between Lennon and McCartney when he could have both? This might have emerged eventually, but Martin's decision here shows keen sensitivity to what his ears were telling him: the Beatles had two front men.

THAT FIRST EMI SESSION took place in the midst of hectic travel as word of mouth spread and the band's BBC appearances gained popularity. Recording with a professional London producer, signing a major-label contract, put more than a gust in their sails. They began to taste success through a heavy daily grind, building up a national profile by slogging from town to town, wearing down the tires on Aspinall's van: 175 miles down to Swindon and Stroud; 28 miles across to Northwich in Cheshire; 42 miles down to Rhyl; 92 miles across the Pennines to Doncaster; 164 miles south to Lydney, in Gloucestershire; and 64 miles up to Morecambe, in the north of Lancashire. The June–July schedule alone was packed with sixty-two live dates, launched with the Parlophone recording session and their second appearance on the BBC.

Two days after the band got back to Liverpool, fans hired a coach to accompany them to Manchester, where they played "Ask Me Why," "Besame Mucho," and "A Picture of You" for the *Teenager's Turn—Here We Go!* show, broadcast on June 15. In the crowd scene that erupted in the streets outside the Playhouse Theatre, Pete Best got lost and the coach returned to Liverpool without him. It was portentous on any number of levels: an overwhelming spectacle of screams and affection that would snowball around the world over the next two years had the early and accidental side effect of leaving Best in the dust. In Liverpool, the Beatles had created a scene by digging in at the Cavern and working their fingers sore. Now, suddenly, they were far bigger in Manchester than simply a neighboring town's favorites. Beatlemania starts here.

That summer of 1962 swept past in a blur of swift changes and half-baked decisions on a grand scale. Aunt Mimi had met Cynthia Powell, of course, but chose to remain oblivious to the extent of her relationship with John. That changed when John used some of his gigging cash to buy his girl a black fur coat she'd been eyeing at C&A Modes department store. When they brought it home with a cooked chicken for dinner at Mendips to celebrate, Mimi threw a fit about it—the same competitiveness that flared up whenever another woman captured John's affection. Cynthia recalled:

> She screamed at John that he'd spent his money on a "gangster's moll" (even with Mimi yelling at us it was funny) and hurled first the chicken, which she grabbed from me, then a hand mirror at John. "Do you think you can butter me up with a chicken when you've spent all your money on this?" she screamed. "Get out." The color drained from John's face. "What the fuck's the matter with you? Are you totally crazy?" he shouted. I was rooted to the spot.[10]

John apologized to Cynthia, saying, "All she cares about is fucking money and cats!" He rode Cyn home on the bus. This was not the first time Mimi had attacked him, Powell later wrote, but it was the "first time she'd done it in front of someone else," and the incident left

Lennon "ashamed as well as angry." There's a small bomb of a revelation: "It wasn't the first time Mimi had attacked him violently."[11] John had confided in his future wife some alarming secrets about his auntie, secrets that would not emerge until long after her death: her stern will was matched by Victorian corporeal discipline. Since Mimi's death, we've learned she put down John's dog to punish him, and threw things at him in front of his fiancée, which would naturally create oceans of anger in the gentlest of souls. No wonder Judy had a tough time with her sister. The young Lennon's tough façade was not just a social persona created for other toughs; it was a condition of his self-respect within Mimi's four walls. Mimi's outburst revealed yet more to Cynthia about John's layered insecurities.

In July, Cynthia told John she was pregnant. They had never used birth control, Cynthia wrote later.

Of course we knew how babies were made and that pregnancy could be prevented, but the level of our ignorance was such that we honestly thought it would never happen to us. Until it did.

When I realized my period was late I didn't know who to turn to. Eventually I told [her close friend] Phyl, who agreed to go with me to the doctor. The female GP I saw was frosty and patronizing. She examined me, confirmed my fears, then delivered a stern lecture on morals. I left the surgery [sic] feeling utterly bleak. What on earth had I done? I didn't want a baby, not yet. I wanted a career, marriage and a life before children. Now I'd messed everything up.[12]

Crying alone at her bedsit (studio apartment), after the era's stereotypical elderly gynecology lecture, Cynthia dreaded her mother's forthcoming visit from Canada almost as much as she dreaded telling Lennon the news. When she finally did "pluck up all [her] courage," she had no idea exactly how he would react—and she feared the worst. Lennon surprised her, saying, "There's only one thing for it, Cyn. We'll have to get married." She pressed him to make sure it was what he wanted, and he reassured her, telling her, "I love you. I'm not going to leave you now."[13] Here is a side of Lennon's provincial good manners and rectitude that underlay his rock 'n' roll bluster. He could no more walk away from a pregnant girlfriend than he could confront the auntie to whom he felt so beholden. And echoes of Lennon's own birth ring in this decision: he would be different; he would show everybody how a father should act; he wouldn't pull an Alf and disappear.

John first told Epstein, who probably gulped hard and smiled. Then John went to Mendips, taking along his half-sister Julia for protection, knowing Mimi would be furious. "You don't understand, Mimi. I love Cyn, I *want* to marry her," Cynthia remembered John saying. But Mimi was convinced Cynthia had trapped him, and shadows cast by Judy and Alf prejudiced her strongly against what she sensed was a tired rerun.

In Lennon's young mind, Cynthia's pregnancy seemed less of a career threat than the trouble brewing around Pete Best. Before the band met up with George Martin again in London, they had to make a decision about their drummer. Lennon, McCartney, and Harrison turned the task over to Epstein.

Pete Best roams the outer circles of Beatles literature as the unlucky sod who got left behind. Even Best's suicide attempt in 1965 gets over-shadowed by Rory Storm's double suicide with his mother that same year—at least the Best legend pulled back from the gothic. History, as usual, tells a more complicated story. Years later, the remaining Beatles made sure that the *Anthology* project brought royalties, rumored in the amount of £1 million, to set up the drummer's family for life. But at the time it happened, Best's ousting was as much of a shock to him and his fans as it was a boon for Ringo and, more to the point, the music itself. And the deck was not even reshuffled before the band had to break a new player in to all their arrangements while threading the next needle Martin had sent from London: an execrable song demo for the band to learn called "How Do You Do It?"

The Beatles certainly didn't replace Best to please their fans: the Mathew Street fallout was far worse than they had expected, and landed George Harrison with a black eye—an early sign of fan idolatry curdling into violence. Everyone had his motives, some of them overt, some of them covert: Epstein was quoted as saying he couldn't take any more phone calls from Mona Best, who considered herself the band's first manager, with exclusive rights to positioning and opinions. But there was also tension surrounding Neil Aspinall's affair with Mona, which by then had turned his status from houseguest into full-blown home-wrecker. In Lennon's mind, the calculus must have gone something like this: if they severed ties with Best, would the trusted Aspinall side with his lover and her son or with his mates? How could they possibly maintain good relations with Aspinall when they knew he still resided at the home of their axed drummer, the son of the club owner who had given them their first steady employment and kept on booking them at her Casbah and elsewhere until Epstein came along?

Best's bad luck was earned: he had worked hard onstage with these players, and they had found him wanting. Lennon's assessment is cutting: "This myth built up over the years that he was great and Paul was jealous of him because he was pretty and all that crap. They didn't get on that much together, but it was partly because Pete was a bit slow. He was a harmless guy, but he was not quick. All of us had quick minds, but he never picked that up."[14] Such group tensions are typical when three musicians decide their fourth is weak and needs replacing: the fourth may disagree, but also may have no clue what the other three are on about; there are some musical abilities that aren't just difficult but impossible to teach. "The reason he got into the group in the first place," Lennon recalled, "was because we had to have a drummer to get to Hamburg. We were always going to dump him when we could find a decent drummer, but by the time we were back from Germany we'd trained him to keep a stick going up and down (four-in-the-bar, he couldn't do much else.)"[15] McCartney, less bluntly, remembered, "We really started to think we needed 'the greatest drummer in Liverpool,' and the greatest drummer in our eyes was a guy, Ringo Starr, who had changed his name before any of us, who had a beard and was grown up and was known to have a Zephyr Zodiac"—the same luxury wheels as Epstein's.[16]

Besides the musicianship, there were entrenched personality differences, Harrison argued: "Pete would never hang out with us. When we finished doing the gig, Pete would go off on his own and we three would hang out together, and then when Ringo was around it was like a full unit, both on and off the stage. When there were the four of us with Ringo, it felt rocking."[17] Pete had gotten married to his girlfriend, Kathy, in the spring of 1962, and this created another wedge. Others have tried to argue that since Best was the most popular Beatle with the women, McCartney, Lennon, and Harrison took him down out of envy. This contradicts the logic of their ambition: why get rid of a popular character unless he didn't share the same musical space? Martin wasn't even asking them to dump Best; he had simply told them he intended to hire a stick man for studio sessions. Even Bob Wooler, a nonmusician, noted this tension between Best and the rest of the Beatles. He remembers overhearing McCartney showing Best how he wanted certain patterns played and thinking to himself, "That's pushing it a bit." And to Wooler, Pete had "no show about him," even though he seemed to come alive for photo sessions.[18]

Mike McCartney, a drummer himself, had a better explanation—the only one that makes any sense: "I used to go home and tell Paul about Ringo who I often saw playing with Rory Storm and the Hurricanes. He certainly hadn't Pete's looks, but he was an amazing drummer; he went at the drums like crazy. He didn't just hit them, he invented new sounds."[19]

WHILE EPSTEIN DROPPED the bomb on Best at his NEMS offices, Lennon and McCartney headed straight to Butlins in Wales to collect Ringo. Ringo was amenable, even flattered, but had to fulfill Rory Storm's request and finish up two more nights at the camp. "Then one day, a Wednesday," Ringo recalled, ". . . Brian called and said, 'Would you join the band for good?' I wasn't aware that it had been in the cards for a while, because I was busy playing. In fact, the guys had been talking to Brian, and George had been hustling for me."[20] To Ringo, a record contract and an acetate song demo were plunder.

Initially, Best was in such a shock at Epstein's news that he agreed to honor their commitments for the next couple of gigs while they went after Ringo. By the evening, though, he was a no-show, and Johnny Hutchinson of the Big Three subbed for two nights. Ringo joined full-time on August 18, his first Cavern gig; Granada Television cameras from Manchester showed up on August 22 for the first and only footage of the band at the Cavern, performing a calm, authoritative "Some Other Guy" and "Kansas City/Hey, Hey, Hey, Hey" for a show called *Know the North*.

SACKING A DRUMMER and learning Martin's choice for a first single preoccupied Lennon as he leaped into marriage. Like his parents before him, he had to sneak off and do it without Mimi's blessing. Epstein served as best man, McCartney and Harrison giggled nervously, and Ringo was too new even to be included. Noticeably missing were Mimi, Bobby Dykins, and Lennon's two younger half sisters, Julia and Jacqui Dykins. Although he swore John and Cynthia to secrecy, Epstein took the couple in hand and made the wedding day something more respectable than it might have been. Cynthia remembers a threatening downpour, and Paul and George pacing about awkwardly in the waiting room. "They were all alarmingly formal in black suits, white shirts and ties—the only smart outfits they had. George and Paul had made a big effort to look the part and clearly felt it was their role to support John, who was sitting between them, white-faced." To the bride, they looked more as if they were attending a funeral. The paperwork in the registrar's office took place as a workman roared away with his pneumatic drill in the opposite backyard. The registrar shouted the vows, and the couple had to shout back to be heard above the din.

Always the gentleman, Epstein took them all to lunch afterward in the pouring rain. Cynthia remembers his gift, something they were too naïve to ask for: an apartment. "He announced that we couldn't possibly live in my bedsit and that he had a flat he seldom used, which we could live in for as long as we needed it. John looked at him in amazement and I was so excited by his kindness that I threw my arms around him. . . . Brian told us he used it from time to time to entertain clients and we didn't question it. In fact, we later realized, it was his bolthole."[21]

The wedding party laughed their way through the jackhammer ceremony and lunch, but the honeymoon was put on hold. That night the Beatles honored their gig in Chester, playing the Riverpark Ballroom. "At one point," Tony Bramwell recalls, "John did say that he hadn't really wanted to get married and felt pushed into it. (He even had another regular girlfriend he was besotted with, Ida Holly . . . not to mention a string of one-night stands)."[22] Lennon's sincere urge to do right by Cynthia, in spite of the brain trapped inside his pants, was a blip in the middle of tremendous career excitement. It lit a slow fuse that erupted almost five years later.

AT FIRST, MARRIAGE must have seemed like just another car on a train that was moving too decisively to jump off: Lennon hired a new drummer on a Thursday, and the following Friday he married his pregnant girlfriend out of a mixture of duty and honor. Epstein forced the couple to keep their nuptials under wraps lest the fans think they'd been outgrown. This was an old-school tradition of maintaining the teenage façade in pop even as babies began popping out. In practical terms, it meant harsher separation for Cynthia, especially after she had Julian, than ever before.

Lennon barely had time to focus. Now he had to deal with his new producer, George Martin, who had sent along a new song to rehearse: Mitch Murray's "How Do You Do It?" The demo was originally pitched for Adam Faith, sung by Barry Mason, and backed by players who would become the Dave Clark Five. Martin pushed this number as the ideal debut single for a young band: a slight yet sturdy jingle featuring both lead singers in an intricate duet. But the song reeked of a hack's cleverness ("Wish I knew how you did it to me, I'd do it to you"), which Lennon recoiled against as more of the swill rock 'n' roll should vanquish. Amid the tides of Lennon's emotional life, something told him that working up "How Do You Do It?" might give him leverage when pitching his own song. For at the same moment he asserted himself as group boss by firing Best and hiring Ringo, and defied his aunt Mimi by marrying Cynthia, Lennon confronted a new authority, a father figure of a producer who might yet gamble on their writing. Everything the band had worked for up to this point compelled this confrontation with George Martin: a debut single simply wouldn't feel like theirs unless it featured original material.

For a newly signed act, this was a radical, not to say self-defeating, notion: Martin had done his homework and found his hard-luck northerners a potential hit that could have delivered them to the radio and the charts and gained them pop visibility. And "Love Me Do," while the band's own, was not even up to the shopworn "How Do You Do It?" To appease Martin, and strengthen their resolve, they worked up an arrangement of Murray's song, flew to London, and rehearsed it in Abbey Road's Studio 2 on the afternoon of September 4.

That day's sessions were awkward and didn't yield anything publishable. In a move that reflects poorly on Epstein, Ringo Starr's appearance came as a complete surprise: Martin expected Best again, but had not yet booked a studio drummer. In effect, Ringo got an on-the-spot tryout. Lennon and McCartney urged Martin to hear their new arrangement of "Love Me Do," but Martin asked for "How Do You Do It?" first, which they laid down with respectable if perfunctory punch. Many historians ridicule this Beatles take on the song as subpar, but it has plenty of spring and juice—and an even bolder subtext that screams, "We're better than this!"

Satisfied with the band's homework, Martin then agreed to hear the new, quicker "Love Me Do," with Lennon's keening harmonica. This impressed Martin enough to give it fifteen takes—fourteen more than "How Do You Do It?" He reworked the harmonica line to return at the end of each chorus, giving McCartney those title-line vocal breaks. By the end of the session Martin had a new drummer and a new song to mull over, and a stubbornly assertive songwriting team.

Martin called Epstein and for security set up another session a week later, on September 11: here an experienced producer's gut instinct merged with skill. Martin booked a studio pro, drummer Andy White, but at the session alternated White with Starr: this way he could compare them back to back. Starr had won the Beatles' confidence; in this session he won Martin's. Starr gave him grief forever after.

The band hunkered down, determined to give Martin what he asked for. Starr and White traded off on drums, and Ringo picked up the tambourine for White's takes. Two different versions hit the racks.[23] But Martin's insistence on getting it right, combined with Lennon and McCartney's belief in their own material, gives these September 11 takes of "Love Me Do" an ambition that outstrips the song's flimsy construction. The song has one recurring smarmy moment, lit by its songwriters' bouncing vocal on the word "plea—ea—ea—ease" setting up a delicious silence. They caught a heady Everly Brothers echo in that bounce, and a new idea took shape: a smooth, nuanced harmony atop a firm, propulsive beat—a new twist on C&W crossed with R&B.

The structure of "Love Me Do" became a metaphor for all the innocence and yearning the Beatles held out for pop. It lived on as a slight yet enigmatic entrance for their career. They pulled it off by digging a shared promise from the song that far outcharmed its delicate frame, or that of any hack tune that blared anonymity. The ears that confronted this single, without any other evidence, heard enough in this sound to point toward a future that suddenly sounded unpredictable, like the beginning of a new mystery plot, bolder than anything British rockers had yet imagined for themselves. The message blared defiance: "We play our own material, just like Buddy Holly!" This gave the name "Beatles" distinct rock 'n' roll heroics, a reach that held out a brash new confidence in the music, both its British claims on the Presley, Cochrane, Vincent, Berry, and Perkins records that had illuminated their lives, and the explosive new possibilities that suddenly leapt from the simplest of beats. That enticing silence just before the title phrase hinted at untold thrills to come, a lover's pause before a blissful first kiss.

EPSTEIN ORDERED BOXES and boxes of the single for his shop, hanging on every chart to watch its ascent. George Harrison remembered that hearing it for the first time on the radio "sent me shivery all over. It was the best buzz of all time. We knew it was going to be on Radio Luxembourg at something like 7:30 on Thursday night. I was in my house in Speke and we all listened in. That was great, but after having got to 17, I don't recall what happened to it . . . but what it meant was that the next time we went to EMI, they were more friendly: 'Oh, hello lads. Come in.' "[24]

The week "Love Me Do" hit number seventeen, they bused back to London to record the follow-up: a Roy Orbison–style lament they had sped up as "Please Please Me," done in eighteen takes on November 26. Now the ensemble entered a new space: Ringo suddenly seemed inseparable from the others, and while this new song built on another Lennon harmonica solo and a soaring vocal duet, the tempo hit gusts of pure bliss, especially on the repeated "Please" in the refrain, when McCartney leapt toward a deliriously high harmony.

Mersey Beat columnist Alan Smith attended the session and was bowled over by the band's progress. "It has everything, from the hypnotic harmonica sound that came over so well in 'Love Me Do' to the kind of tune you can remember after one hearing," he wrote in the January issue.[25] "This time the harmonica sounds much bolder, too. It almost jumps out at you. And in the background, there's the solid, insistent beat, defying you not to get up and dance." The number still soars on rhythmic poetry—bouncing melodies rest atop fluid meters, like a thought caught in a slipstream. Lennon spoke frankly to Smith about the song's impetus: "I tried to make it as simple as possible. Some of the stuff I've written has been a bit way out, but we did this one strictly for the hit parade. Now we're keeping our fingers crossed."[26]

Smith also quoted George Martin as saying the group resembled " 'a male Shirelles,' " the girl group whose songs the Beatles already had mastered in their set lists ("Baby, It's You," "Mama Said," and "Boys"). Perhaps Martin's ear knew more about rock than his accent let on. This intimacy Lennon and McCartney hinted at in their vocal harmonies suggested an enticing idea about the rapture between band and audience. As his confidence in the band grew, Martin determined to follow them up to their home turf. Perhaps Epstein was right: you had to hear them at the Cavern to get the full impact of their sound.

"I'm thinking of recording their first LP at the Cavern," Martin said, "but obviously I'm going to have to come to see the club before I make a

October 9, 1944. One of a series of forty-eight photos—shot in rapid succession—from a Polyfoto contact sheet, taken on John's fourth birthday.

Summer 1949. Rockferry, Cheshire. John with his mother, Julia, at the Ardmore house of her older sister Anne Georgina ("Nanny").

Summer 1949. In Nanny's garden. From left to right: cousins Michael, Leila, David, half-sister Julia Baird (in hat), and John. John's clothing suggests this was taken on the same day as the photo with his mother.

Summer 1951. The Isle of Man. The Dovedale Primary School trip. Future comedian Jimmy Tarbuck has his fists raised while John stands just left of center.

1950s. Liverpool. A rare photo of Aunt Mimi and Uncle George Smith in the backyard at Mendips. This is also one of the few photographs of Mimi laughing.

June 6, 1957. Liverpool. The Quarrymen travel to the Woolton Parish Church Garden on the back of a lorry. From left to right: Eric Griffiths, Pete Shotton, Len Garry (standing), John Lennon, Colin Hanton, and Rod Davis (adjusting his glasses). This photo was discovered by Rod Davis in 2009 in a box of negatives shot by his father, James Davis.

June 6, 1957. Liverpool. The Quarrymen play at the Woolton Parish Church Garden Fete. From left to right: Eric Griffiths (guitar), Colin Hanton (in back, drums), Rod Davis (banjo), John Lennon, Pete Shotton (washboard), and Len Garry (tea-chest bass). Both Mimi and Julia attend this performance, one scowling, the other beaming. Later that day, Lennon meets Ivan Vaughan's friend Paul McCartney.

November 23, 1957. Liverpool. The Quarrymen at New Clubmoor Hall. From left to right: Colin Hanton, Paul McCartney, Len Garry, John Lennon, and Eric Griffiths.

August 9, 1959. West Derby, Liverpool. The Quarrymen play the Casbah Coffee Club. As John focuses on his guitar, Paul wins a grin from Cynthia Powell (center, with dark hair).

August 17, 1960. Holland. En route to Hamburg, everyone stops for a photo in front of the Arnhem War Memorial. From left to right: Allan and Beryl Williams, Lord Woodbine, Stuart Sutcliffe, Paul McCartney, George Harrison, and Pete Best; John sleeps in the van.

Autumn 1960. Hamburg, Germany. The Beatles on stage at the Indra Club. From left to right: Stuart Sutcliffe, Paul McCartney, George Harrison, John, and Pete Best.

November 1960. Heiligengeistfeld Square, Hamburg. George, Stuart, and John in one of a series of brilliantly styled photos by Astrid Kirchherr.

November 1960. Another of Astrid Kirchherr's photos at Heiligengeistfeld Square, with Stuart in the background.

left: Late 1960. Hamburg. Astrid Kirchherr snaps a picture of herself with fiancé Stuart Sutcliffe.

June 1961. Hamburg. On stage at the Top Ten Club, John sings lead flanked by Stuart (left) and George.

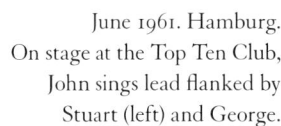

Spring 1962. Hamburg. A formal Kirchherr portrait taken in her parents' attic where Stuart Sutcliffe had made a studio for himself.

August 22, 1962. The Cavern Club, Liverpool. The Beatles after Epstein put them in suits. Only in the sweltering basement club were they allowed to remove their jackets. Ringo, obscured behind Paul, had just joined the band on August 18. This day's performance marked the first time television cameras filmed the Beatles, performing "Some Other Guy." John married Cynthia the following day.

decision. If we can't get the right sound we might do the recording somewhere else in Liverpool, or bring an invited audience into the studio in London. They've told me they work better in front of an audience." This "Please Please Me" session included several takes of "Ask Me Why," and another Lennon-McCartney original, "Tip of My Tongue," which they shelved and gave to Tommy Quickly the following summer. (The Beatles' attempts at this number appear to have been lost.) This meant the second single could also sport two Lennon-McCartney songs, with no hint of a fallback on "outside" material.

"Please Please Me" sounded less like a follow-up to "Love Me Do" than a career fuse getting lit. Press quotes started pouring in: in the *New Musical Express,* Keith Fordyce gushed about the record's "beat, vigour and vitality,"[27] and the material took on that wondrous effect of motivating listeners to run out and buy the record. EMI, true to its staid reputation, gave the record a "no plug" (read: no support) rating, even though it flew out of stores. The label committed to "two plugs per week for three weeks on Radio Lux," reported Sean O'Mahoney, who went on to publish the *Beatles Fan Club Monthly.* By comparison, the Shadows got seven plugs a week. "Epstein threatened to take all his business away from EMI, so eventually somebody said 'yes.'"[28] At their own record company, Epstein was still pushing irresistible material up a hill.

Martin now recommended a business associate to Epstein to improve their publishing arrangements: Dick James. James had started out as a singer, and written a couple of songs with Martin. After an early deal for "Love Me Do" with the firm Ardmore and Beechwood, Epstein sought more aggressive presence for his songwriting team. An acetate of "Please Please Me" persuaded James to take on Lennon and McCartney, and when he played the song over the phone for a contact at *Thank Your Lucky Stars,* Epstein left his office with a TV booking for January 1963. This was just the type of publishing action Epstein sought. James soon set up a new company, Northern Songs, to handle the Lennon and McCartney catalog, and Epstein granted James the then standard 50 percent royalty rate. The other half was split between NEMS, Lennon, and McCartney in lieu of Epstein's management commission.[29]

After finally getting some traction with recordings, and watching

"Love Me Do" make the charts, Epstein insisted the act meet all their previous obligations, even if it meant two gigs in a single day and hustling back from Wales for a Cavern lunch set. This meant more and more slogging even as they began to hear themselves on the radio almost daily. With "Please Please Me" in the can, Martin and Epstein knew they had a hit single at the ready, and an album needed scheduling amid a relentless performance calendar. December saw them mime "Love Me Do" and either "P.S. I Love You" or "Twist and Shout" for three decisive TV broadcasts, first from Bristol, Somerset, then London (ITV's *Tuesday Rendezvous*), and then Granada's *People and Places,* which beamed their surging confidence to their largest audiences yet. The Beatles surfed on a moment that caught an inexplicable serendipity between band, material, and audience. Playing "Love Me Do" after nailing "Please Please Me," the knowing glances they gave one another got bolstered by the increasing authority in their ensemble—had rock 'n' roll suddenly turned so irresistible so quickly?

Martin traveled up from London to catch the band at the Cavern on December 12, a year after Decca's Mike Smith had made the trip. But he decided against recording them there, because the space was too tight for the players, let alone engineers, and the acoustics were decidedly unworkable.

The next week, celebrating their second-year win topping the *Mersey Beat* poll, they played a regular gig at Birkenhead and then raced back to the Cavern at four in the morning for an all-night blowout thrown by Bill Harry. This all led to an anticlimactic final run of thirteen nights to close out 1962 back at the Star-Club in Hamburg, with the ghost of Sutcliffe haunting their return; they honored the engagement despite all their momentum back home. The pay was decent, 750DM (£67) per man per week, but they resented the grind, and another agent might have weaseled them out of it somehow. On their home turf their music had finally busted loose; in Hamburg they were a big deal playing yesterday's rooms.

Tapes of these Hamburg gigs, recorded off a single microphone hanging over the stage, only came to light in the late 1970s, when Allan Williams shopped them for release after years in local musician Ted

"Kingsize" Taylor's collection.[30] The Beatles never approved publication, as much for the patchy, unsympathetic fidelity as for the uneven performances. But the tapes reveal many ongoing developments in the Beatles' progress, including Ringo's assimilation into their ensemble, Harrison's rockabilly verve, and some stray songs that never found release in any other form. When the tapes actually deliver several songs in a row, without choppy breaks, the pacing has a sloppy geniality; the band yaps at the audience and trades inside jokes between songs, with the bedraggled insouciance Epstein had tried to sift from their Cavern shows.

At some points, botched lyrics drive songs right into the ditch: a game attempt at "Road Runner" simply stops before erupting into a magnificent "Hippy Hippy Shake," which comes to an abrupt finish only to erupt again, as if they can't help themselves. Having too much fun in Hamburg sounds like a good excuse to conquer the world, or at least grab the brass ring within their reach and swing for a good long time. There are moments, especially atop Chuck Berry's "Talking 'Bout You" and "Little Queenie," Fats Waller's "Your Feet's Too Big," and a new Lennon-McCartney number, "I Saw Her Standing There," where the world sounds tantalizingly theirs, so sure is their mastery of unhinged rock 'n' roll. Elsewhere, they blend right in with an audience determined to get trashed. It's an off-night with clues to how they mined later greatness.

For one of these sets, bouncer Horst Fascher and his waiter brother, Fred, lead off singing "Be-Bop-A-Lula" and "Hallelujah, I Just Love Her So," Lennon and McCartney vocal platforms by turn. Then the band lights up "I Saw Her Standing There," complete with Lennon's lower harmonies and Ringo's tom-tom swirls, and the number sounds finished down to the most particular detail, from the way they hit their trademark "ooh"s to the closing kicks. It has the uncanny feel of an original that might turn into a standard. Starr jacks their ensemble up several notches: each song section gets heightened definition, from corners and transitions to several jokey cutoffs. It's hard to imagine Best giving this number all it deserves.

Lennon and McCartney cast such long shadows in Beatle history, it's striking to hear how prominently Harrison sings and plays throughout these sets. His Carl Perkins rockabilly numbers, "Nothin' Shakin' (but the Leaves on the Trees)," "Matchbox," and "Everybody's Trying to Be My Baby," have a more frenetic pace and feel than any of the BBC or EMI takes, raising the question as to whether his talent ever translated well at all in the studio. Even singing the midtempo "Matchbox," which became a Ringo number, Harrison dominates the band as both singer and guitarist. He ambles around through the lyrics like he's taking Old Paint out for a trot, and his solo digs into the grooves like a rusty spur. Overall, Harrison's guitar work has more fluidity than it does on some early recordings, especially on "Long Tall Sally." Everywhere, his guitar stings and sails, goads the ensemble into taking reckless rhythmic risks. When he sings as he plays in "Roll Over Beethoven," he spits the curl to ride waves of ambition. If you came to this music unaware, you might not count Harrison out as a third front man. There's a chemistry between him and Starr here that unfolds in the way the guitar overtakes McCartney in Chuck Berry's "Little Queenie" and Ringo leaps into the mix as if Harrison's the hand and he's the happy puppet. This juices McCartney to crank up the final verse into a tirade.

The many and various vocal harmonies from the stage cement the Beatle band ideal, embedded in both guitar and voice. The McCartney ballads prove he always was a bit too fond of sentimentality—"Falling in Love Again," the Marlene Dietrich staple, works only because he fakes such a winning lyric. Three versions of "A Taste of Honey" exist, all mimeograph copies of one another, each with full-throated commitment from the lead and backup vocalists. Perhaps the cost of such literal sincerity helped them cut loose more on faster numbers; perhaps McCartney really thinks the song has some charm only he can squeeze out. Or perhaps it was a crowd favorite, an easy way to win girls, something they did without thinking. Every bar band has numbers they can relax through as a mental break. When McCartney turned to "Till There Was You," Lennon minced his sincerity into hash, answering every doe-eyed line with a riposte ("He never saw them at all/Wonderful roses . . ."). The harmonies get all the more impressive when you realize how faintly they could hear themselves.

Several stray songs reveal abiding affinities and lost chances. Lennon sings "Where Have You Been," another Arthur Alexander number, to make you wish they had at least done it for the BBC. "Your Feet's Too Big" finds McCartney doing Fats Waller in a beguiling example of garage-band compression. Waller defined himself by his heft at the keys; his piano anchored his recordings with lofty twitters and growling chuckles. Mounting the number onstage with only guitars takes nerve; what comes through is not just the band's maniacal belief that such translations can work but how quickly they're forgotten amid the delirium.

Several other numbers give off palpable heat, almost enough to forgive the poor sound. This final Hamburg stint, their fifth, may have yanked them backward to where they had paid their dues, but the momentum in these numbers propels them forward, into a future that starts to approximate the music's capacity for meaningful thrills. Lennon turns in Chuck Berry's "Sweet Little Sixteen," another BBC highlight, and "Talking 'Bout You," which drops from their set shortly after this. These grooves have the inexplicable primacy of later studio recordings like "Money," "Rock 'n' Roll Music," and "I'm Down." This is the sound Lennon spoke of when he proclaimed, "There was nobody to touch us in Britain." It doubled as the sound of a nation on the verge of renewal, clawing its way back from war, looking to pop-culture youth for a new image of itself.

Hold On

THE CONSERVATIVE PARTY'S HAROLD MACMILLAN CAME TO POWER as prime minister in 1957 by proclaiming, "You've never had it so good." The average UK income was finally on the rise, and discretionary spending began to pump up the economy. By 1963, this optimism hid its customary blind spots: Britain's balance of payments, propped up in the past by tributary products from its former colonies, still led to wage freezes in 1961, which cost Conservatives substantially in the 1962 parliamentary election. Panicking, Macmillan flushed out his cabinet that July by sacking eight junior ministers—"the night of long knives." (If only he had sacked John Profumo . . .)

Musically, Britain's charts leaned heavily on American product. Exceptions proved this rule: Cliff Richard and the Shadows stole space from predominant Yankee acts like Roy Orbison, Del Shannon, and Ray Charles. Tellingly, the Temperance Seven, George Martin's stiff, 1920s-style jazz outfit, found success briefly as beat groups readied their onslaught—the type of last-gasp popularity that tipped off how irrefutably passé trad jazz had become.

Rising fortunes suddenly brought about enormous cultural flux, shifting the tectonic plates between public and private life that had been in place since the Victorian era. London had spent the early stretch of Macmillan's term consumed by the *Lady Chatterley's Lover* obscenity trial at the Old Bailey courthouse. D. H. Lawrence's novel had been banned in Britain since its private publication in 1928, but had sold widely with the naughty bits chopped out. Prosecuting the new Obscene Publications Act, solicitor Mervyn Griffith-Jones became one of those unbearably bewigged foghorns of propriety. The outrage over "frank" depictions of sexuality in fiction seemed simply farcical to many; the defendant, Penguin Books, sold two million copies of the novel in the ensuing months. In *Can't Buy Me Love*, Beatle scholar Jonathan Gould points out how D. H. Lawrence's characters prefigure John Osborne's "angry young man" sensibility, which packed mid-fifties West End theaters:[1] Lawrence's plot revolved around a genteel lady who beds down with her gamekeeper—a servant named Oliver Mellors. The court case labored on about what people were flocking to see and read.

Now, as 1963 began, the same prosperity fueled a juicy political scandal, the worst news for politicians since the Suez crisis in 1956. The story began with the arrest of a young black Jamaican named John Edgecombe, who in December had fired shots into the Wimpole Mews front door of a wealthy London doctor, Stephen Ward. There, twenty-year-old Christine Keeler was visiting her friend Mandy Rice-Davies, who happened to be living with Ward, which was racy enough; Edgecombe's shots were part of a love triangle between Keeler and another Jamaican lover named Aloysius "Lucky" Gordon. If this had been the extent of it, it would have made for a racially charged blip on the inside pages. But once it hit the news, a *Sunday Mirror* check for £1,000 inspired Keeler to talk, and the story unraveled from there. Keeler boasted of a 1961 affair with John Profumo, Macmillan's secretary of state for war, then married to a former movie star, Valerie Hobson. Keeler also let it drop that she had attended some of Ward's wild orgies, complete with marijuana, for an elite set of socialites at Lord Astor's estate, Cliveden. Roll over Lady Chatterley.

This was scandalous not just because Keeler was an unrepentant "showgirl"[2] or because Ward's scene underlined all those clichés about the decadence of the rich, but because Keeler had also been dallying with a Soviet naval attaché, Yevgeny Ivanov, at the same time she was seeing Profumo.[3] Keeler's account of all this spooled out later beneath Lewis Morley's coolly seductive front-page photograph of her posing naked on a designer chair, camouflaging her breasts, seducing viewers into questioning their own "proprieties" in one of the era's iconic images. Her expression mixed pride of notoriety with contempt for her exploiters—in her victimless eyes, the whole thing was simply luscious. Lennon would draw a cartoon of Keeler for his first book, *In His Own Write,* and included a cryptic pun on her name in a salutation at the end of "A Letter": "We hope this fires you keeler . . ."[4] To Lennon, Keeler might as well have been transplanted from Hamburg, a service worker to the ruling class.

Keeler's *Mirror* gaze stared down Macmillan's Tory government as an emblem of corruption. The scandal sold many, many newspapers, and laid waste not just to Profumo but to the entire Conservative administration. Called before a House of Commons inquiry in March 1963, Profumo held that there was "no impropriety whatsoever," but by June he had recanted his perjury, and in July he resigned, with many calling for Macmillan's resignation as well.

Suddenly, "You've never had it so good" boomeranged with irony. After a summer of sensational revelations that rocked Parliament, Macmillan looked more and more as if he didn't know about things he should have and hadn't acted swiftly enough to control the damage. He stepped aside at the Conservative Party Conference in Blackpool that October, and the Labour Party won the next general election.

Sparked by this upheaval, Beatlemania's entrance on the scene played like a comic-relief valve to political cynicism; the band's ascent was woven into the Profumo scandal as if mapped out by a clever screenwriter. At the beginning of 1963, the Beatles had not yet entered the top ten or appeared on BBC television; by the end of the year they were a runaway phenomenon, dominating all the British charts, newspapers, and radio with two long-playing albums and a barrage of singles, each one better than the last, that turned them into pop Olympians. That fall they consolidated their success on national television, first on *Sunday Night at the London Palladium,* a cornerstone of the British entertainment establishment, and then on the telecast of the annual Royal Variety Performance, in front of the old guard's prim and dignified Queen Elizabeth II.

By autumn, of course, this was simply Buckingham Palace's way of hitching its wagon to the runaway train of adoration and mayhem that followed Lennon, McCartney, Harrison, and Starr wherever they went. Although Epstein didn't receive the royal invitation until August, by that point the ruling powers simply genuflected to fate. It was quickly understood, even by the older generation, that whatever you made of these Beatles, this act transcended show business and created the kind of heat even royals ought to rub up against. These political and cultural gusts vied with one another so that it was quickly hard to distinguish between teen screams and tabloid headers; the band's immense symbolic aura quickly turned into cultural semaphore for England's modern era. "This isn't show business," Lennon told his quickie *Love Me Do!* biographer, Michael Braun, that season, "this is something else."[5]

As if there were any doubt, the Royal Variety Performance went beyond established show-biz blessing in Britain: it conferred surpassing, supercelebrity status. The hypocrisy of the ruling class had reached such heights that the Beatles seemed not just a necessary tonic but an all-conquering elixir. With their winning comic charisma and clear disdain for show business as usual, it was almost as if the Beatles led the way out of a public crisis, relegating Profumo to the tawdry clichés of political potboilers, with an unmistakable subtext: "What do you expect from a bunch of . . . *stuffed shirts?*" There are very few examples in pop-culture history where the establishment and the radical agents of change shook hands so eagerly. The British government needed a distraction even more than the Beatles needed joke material. Right from the beginning, there was a very self-conscious aspect to Beatlemania that held up this collision of past and future—and there was very little question who the winner was. It made the band's cultural sovereignty both swift and absolute; and at key moments, like his Royal Variety Performance "rattle your jewelry" quip, Lennon's smirk summed up its attitude.

GETTING SWEPT UP in such a pop explosion is disorienting, even if you've been working as hard and waiting as long as the Beatles. The most appealing thing about their breakthrough, and the most important thing they had internalized by the time they landed in New York in February 1964, was a steadfast yet charismatic nonchalance about the mania. Their ambivalence about show business only made the act more tempting. To understand the scale of this breakthrough, bear in mind how northerners were held in even lower esteem by ruling-class Londoners than Tennessee boys were by the New York elite.

The term "Beatlemania" didn't enter the Fleet Street lexicon until the fall; but beginning in May 1963, all the papers charted the phenomenon as the world's most hard-bitten cynics swooned in unison. Beatlemania was even better than a scandal: an episodic rags-to-riches story about a slaphappy band of northern rubes whose energy and ideas announced a postwar boom. As rich as the Beatles were in musical terms, they may have been even richer in this symbolic sense: as an umbrella metaphor for youth, change, dynamism, aggression, lust, passion, and healthy irreverence. Each successive Beatles record became synonymous with this new national spirit, a souvenir of how good things might still get. Before they became "imaginary Americans," in literary critic Leslie Fiedler's enchanted phrase, the Beatles were intensely British, not just an emblem of the national spirit but its economic stimulant.[6]

The playfulness they brought to fame was more than appealing; it was probably the only sane reaction to an audience hyped up beyond all imagining. If the Profumo affair sponged off *Lady Chatterley* fumes, Beatlemania had a distinctly American-influenced, forward-looking twist. Even before they broke stateside, the Beatles trumped that sovereign American export known as celebrity: here was Valentino- and Sinatra- and Presley-style hero worship cranked up a few notches, multiplied by four; and it quickly shot Lennon's life soaring into a parallel universe of celebrity privilege and detachment, as far from ordinary as Alice was through the looking glass. Surprising even themselves, the Beatles had a knack for it—they made all the chaos seem like the tail of a cultural comet. Even in the beginning, they behaved as if their centering the culture's vortex wasn't just inevitable but richly deserved; and the more their records stormed the charts, the less audacious that seemed. More than a few commentators dismissed them as a passing fad, which only fed their determination to outlive their own hype. And all of this fed the "meta" aspect of Beatlemania, where everybody was not only experiencing its hurricane force but talking about it, analyzing it, aware of it as a unique moment in cultural history.

By the time the Americans jumped aboard, the band's momentum had made their act irresistible. As cultural critic Greil Marcus put it, "Excitement wasn't in the air, it *was* the air."[7] When this 1963 storm whooshed into America in 1964, it gained speed and intensity as it crossed the Atlantic. After a youth spent in thrall to rock 'n' roll culture, which sprang from Elvis Presley winning over black audiences in the Memphis Beale Street clubs, getting the United States to catch up to *them*—with music forged on the crucible of American racism—was an irony Lennon savored.

As 1963 BEGAN, the Beatles returned from their hangdog New Year's Eve gig in Hamburg only to slog anticlimactically north again to Scotland on January 2 for a five-day tour. After a storm canceled their opening gig in Keith, Banffshire, Lennon flew home for a few hours with his pregnant wife, returning the next morning for the gig in Elgin, Morayshire. This was the first time the band had been this far north since backing Johnny Gentle in 1960; and for all the gains they had made in the fall, there were still major questions chasing them as they pressed on. Now that Lennon and McCartney were writing songs Dick James would publish, their material was quickly in demand: Epstein wanted numbers for Billy J. Kramer, the Liverpool singer he'd plopped in front of a Manchester band, the Dakotas. Lennon and McCartney passed along "Do You Want to Know a Secret?" and eventually "Bad to Me," "I'll Keep You Satisfied," and "From a Window," an early draft of Lennon's "No Reply" narrative. Kramer tracked "Secret" and another Lennon/McCartney number, "I'll Be on My Way," in March. Epstein's ambitions had grown with his band's: as a retailer, he intuited how the Beatle tide could lift other Merseyside boats. (Many years later, Kramer remembered Lennon's apology demo for "Secret": "After he played the song, he apologized and said he'd looked all over the building for an empty room and this was the only place he could find. Then a toilet flushed.")[8]

Television would be the final push for their next single, and Epstein and the Beatles all knew it could mean the difference between a hit and a lost opportunity. After finishing the short tour, on January 8, they visited Scottish Television in Glasgow to mime "Please Please Me" for local broadcast, a warmup for some UK appearances in the coming weeks that would break the song wide open. On January 13 the Beatles were in Birmingham for their first *Thank Your Lucky Stars* appearance, and Andrew Loog Oldham caught the rehearsal.[9] A shark who was not easily impressed, he described the scene as it unfolded:

> Watching in the wings, I was spellbound by a new British group making their first appearance on national television. . . . I can clearly recall the buzz of watching them rehearse. They weren't that different in appearance from the other acts—they were all wearing suits and ties. What was unusual was their attitude: they exuded a "Fuck you, we're good and we know it" attitude. You normally didn't see that in an act making its first TV appearance.

In Oldham's mind, the Beatles' music and personal presence seemed both "omniscient and naïve" and gave off something "hypnotic and life-giving." The act reminded him of Bob Dylan, the young American singer he'd met during a brief BBC appearance the previous year.[10] "I realized these sixties were not only happening to me," Oldham thought. He was particularly impressed with Epstein, who wore an immaculate overcoat with a paisley scarf and hired Oldham on the spot. "Maybe they did need somebody pounding the pavements for them in . . . London," Oldham writes, "which he pronounced like a man getting rid of phlegm in his throat or a stone from his shoe."[11]

Oldham was known in London circles as a comer, a brash stylist with game who literally knocked on everybody's door asking for work. He had bounced around the fashion industry and found pop music managers positively Neanderthal. The Beatles fleshed out his mission to bring the flash and daring of fashion into pop. Epstein was just a couple of steps ahead of him. "When you sat down with Brian," Oldham recalled, echoing many descriptions of this manager's maniac faith in his act, "you knew you were dealing with a man who had a vision for the Beatles and nobody was going to get in the way of that vision. He was convinced that eventually everybody was going to agree with him. That gave him the power to make people listen." Oldham noted how Epstein's polished persona enveloped his whole enterprise: "That he was somewhat to the manor born gave him both a self-assurance and an entrée with the stubbornly middle-class label managers he had to deal with." Epstein's personal luster and the Beatles' musical daring fed off each other. Simply standing to watch his "boys" at *Thank Your Lucky Stars,* Epstein's belief in them seemed to permeate the room. "In those early days," Oldham wrote, "Brian's presence, the Beatles' irreverence and their mutual pleasure all conveniently merged."[12]

The first week in February the Beatles went out on a package tour as a supporting act to Helen Shapiro, then promoting her top-forty hit "Queen for Tonight." "I had a huge crush on John," Shapiro remembered, "but I was only sixteen! He treated me like a little sister."[13] The previous spring, Shapiro had starred in director Richard Lester's *It's Trad, Dad,* singing her top-ten hit "Let's Talk About Love." Lester's film took place in a television studio and now screens like a working draft of *A Hard Day's Night,* with Shapiro performing alongside Chubby Checker, Del Shannon, Gene Vincent, and others. Lennon and McCartney saw opportunity: they offered her a new song, "Misery," which she turned down. No matter, as George Harrison recalled: "That tour was when we first did the Moss Empire circuit, the biggest gigs that there were in England at the time, other than the Palladium. We were quite happy with that."[14]

The Shapiro tour began in Bradford, Yorkshire, and continued on to Doncaster, with a short break for two Cavern gigs: headlining an all-night "Rhythm and Blues Marathon" on February 3 and their last lunchtime slot the next day. Epstein had interspersed January's live gigs with TV appearances on *People and Places* and the BBC radio's Light Programme's *Here We Go,* and more work on the BBC's *Saturday Club* and *The Talent Spot* and Radio Luxembourg's *Friday Spectacular.* All this activity sharpened their ensemble for the big day: their first album recording session, which came right after finishing the first five-night leg of the Shapiro dates. They briefly dropped out of the tour after the February 9 show in Sunderland, Durham, to make the 275-mile, five-hour drive down to London for a good night's rest.

THEY ARRIVED AT the EMI studios on the morning of February 11 to deliver the "live" album they had discussed with George Martin. He had heard them at the Cavern, knew what they could do, and decided to simply roll tape. "Let's record every song you've got," he told them. "Come down to the studios and we'll just whistle through them in a day." They started around eleven, finished ten hours later, and Martin grabbed his "live" album for EMI.[15] Historians have stressed the mad rush of this session as if it were somehow unusual, but it simply stacked two three-hour sessions into a single day, and the Beatles stretched things out. If absolutely necessary, a producer could bring singers or guitarists back in to redo a part or two, but live-to-tape was the standard.

The goal was simply to record the best parts of their live show, which the Beatles had been doing sometimes twice a day on stages a hundred miles apart. And Lennon, McCartney, and Harrison had been chomping at the bit for this opportunity since forever, from their "That'll Be the Day" demo in Percy Phillips's living room as Quarrymen to their Decca audition on New Year's Day of 1962. Thirteen months later, standing still in a studio suddenly held out new promise, as well as aesthetic appeal—the chance to listen to one another more closely as they played.

Lennon was shaking off a bad cold, nursing tea, milk, cigs, and Zubes cough lozenges throughout the day to soothe his aching throat; you can hear his threadbare vocal cords straining to reach notes, as if a live wire were shorting out his larynx. The long Hamburg nights color the attitude in the sound: tired, yes; game, absolutely. They opened with ten takes of "There's a Place," then nine of "Seventeen" (which became "I Saw Her Standing There").

The first myth to puncture about this session is that it was a slapdash affair. "We told them we were having a break," engineer Richard Langham told Mark Lewisohn, "but they said they would like to stay on and rehearse. So while George, Norman [Smith] and I went round the corner to the Heroes of Alma pub for a pie and pint they stayed, drinking milk. When we came back they'd been playing right through. We couldn't believe it. We had never seen a group work right through their lunch break before."[16]

Dogged persistence yielded effortless spontaneity; this kind of focus made it all sound easy. After lunch came seven takes of "A Taste of Honey," eight of "Do You Want to Know a Secret?," overdubs on "There's a Place" and "Seventeen," and eleven takes of "Misery." After dinner they continued with thirteen takes of "Hold Me Tight," three of "Anna (Go to Him)," one of "Boys," four of "Chains," and three of "Baby It's You." To finish, a group huddle settled on one of their Cavern staples, "Twist and Shout," of which they chose the first of two takes.

These session details unveil previously hidden priorities. They believed in "There's a Place" enough to pour out ten takes of it first thing in the morning, only to return for three more overdubs later that afternoon. Building on the flirtatious silences that dimpled "Love Me Do" and "Ask Me Why," this number began with a tricky stop-time vocal duet at the top of each verse, like a musical double take—an exquisite pirouette that lifted the entire song with a giant wink. This gesture had both daring and fragility, and seeded one of the most beguiling aspects of their music as a whole: those mercurial Lennon-and-McCartney vocal duets, which suspended increasingly quixotic promises, musical flights soaring into emotional koans. The narrative space Lennon and McCartney retreat to is the singer's mind ("and there's no time"), the imaginal realm where romance rides waves of idealism. In song, this riddle spins out as a metaphor for rock 'n' roll's ideal state, where melody transcends its backbeat and joy doubles down. After so much gigging and pressing on despite hard luck, this music chases down smiles toward sweet arrival.

So a one-day session yielded ten of the fourteen tracks for the band's debut with "Hold Me Tight" getting held for the next record. Workmanlike time pressures yielded a well-sequenced set of tracks. Since recording "Please Please Me," they had written "Seventeen"—"I Saw Her Standing There"—which Martin would surely have jumped on as a single if he'd known about it. You can hear them start to purr in this song, as if the songwriting begins to catch up with their vivid, roomy ensemble. The most obvious hook was the flatted-sixth chord on the final word of "I'll never dance with another . . . *Oh!*"—which tickles the title phrase right out of its skin at each repetition. The song quickly got singled out as the perfect album opener, a short fuse triggering an indefatigable originality. This was the song they had been trying to write ever since Martin sent "Love Me Do" back for a rewrite the previous June. Lennon rewrote McCartney's opening lines from "Well she was just seventeen . . . She was no beauty queen" to the infinitely more suggestive and expansive ". . . You know . . . what I mean," injecting a pause like a lump in the throat. To set off your debut album with an original number that nodded knowingly toward Chuck Berry's narrative swagger launched a sequence of thrilling proportions. And by the end of side one, the album introduced the entire band through lead vocals (Paul with "Standing There," John with "Misery," George with the Cookies' "Chains," Ringo with the Shirelles' "Boys," a number he had done with the Hurricanes). The era's typical pop album put hit singles at the top of side one and slid downward from there. The Beatles' unerring confidence withheld their hit single as the opening track for side two, boldly holding back even stronger original material to sustain a long-playing album. Along the way, they handed off "Do You Want to Know a Secret?" to George for a droll dash of inscrutability. The sequence alone on this debut album sent grandiose conceptual signals. As much thought had been put into sequencing as song choice—and they had been stewing about song choice ever since that dreadful first day of 1962 at Decca.

As a closer they might have picked any number of their slew of covers: "Long Tall Sally," "Money," "Rock 'n' Roll Music," "That'll Be the Day" (sentimental favorite), or "Johnny B. Goode," all of which they had learned to close with in Hamburg. Lennon's choice on "Twist and Shout" creates a giant tipping point: with a throat so sore others noticed the blood staining the milk in his bottle, he could easily have handed off closing vocal duties to Paul ("Long Tall Sally" was more dynamite in reserve). But "Twist and Shout" shows just how hard Lennon had fought over material behind the scenes, and how determined he was not to make the Decca mistakes that had held the promise of this session so far in the distance.

"Twist and Shout" is one of those pregnant microcosms of rock 'n' roll; like "Louie Louie" by the Kingsmen or "Wild Thing" by the Troggs, it binds together forces at play in the sound that ridicule simplicity. Bert Berns (aka Bert Russell) and Phil Medley wrote the number for the Top Notes, who recorded it with Phil Spector on an Atlantic session in 1961 and then vanished. Enter Cincinatti's Isley Brothers, looking to tailgate on Chubby Checker's 1960 "Twist" craze, itself a cover of a B-side by the saucy Hank Ballard and his Midnighters ("Work With Me Annie"). Checker never escaped the Twist: after the original hit returned to the number one slot in early 1962, he turned in "Let's Twist Again (Like We Did Last Summer)," "Slow Twistin'," and "Teach Me to Twist" through 1962, the same year he married Miss World Catharina Lodders and starred in *Twist Around the Clock* and *Don't Knock the Twist*.

But Checker himself seemed incidental to the Twist's life force; as a black, his talent was Teflon ("[He] sounded uncannily, on record, like a white man imitating a black man," wrote Jonathan Gould.)[17] His first Twist song had set off an early pop explosion, a portent of Beatlemania that began as a dance, morphed quickly into a metaphor for an attitude less stodgy than swing, and then into a worldview, smirking at the establishment through mainstream coverage in *Esquire* and *Time*. Joey Dee and the Starlighters became the house band at the Peppermint Lounge in Midtown Manhattan on the crest of their "Peppermint Twist," a massive hit in early 1962. Dell comics followed with a comic-book series. If "Camelot" was JFK's official Broadway theme music, "The Twist" cued his "secret" mobster-moll and movie-star trysts.

British listeners never knew the Isleys' number until the summer of 1963—the Beatles copped it from Radio Luxembourg, on the Wand label import. (In one of many reversals, the Beatles' album track launched the Isley Brothers single in Britain.) The Isleys, a gospel trio retooling doo-wop, were following up their modest RCA hit "Shout (Part I)," which reached number forty-seven in September of 1959 and reappeared at number ninety-four in March 1962. A song's reappearance like that means the audience clamors for more. The obvious move was to jump onto that Top Notes song, which had tried to siphon more gas out of the Twist. Since Berns and Medley had simply merged "Twist" with "Shout" using the "La Bamba" template, the Isleys rushed to cover it as a way of tailgating their previous hit: it worked, breaking into the top twenty in June 1962.[18]

The Isleys' arrangement dramatizes how punctual and stylized black acts needed to be in those days. After dumping the original's awkward bridge, the Isleys simply added a cornball horn-and-handclaps arrangement, broken up with a standard-issue rave-up to work the crowd—if you didn't know it was the same band, you'd swear it was a cynical take-off of their own "Shout!" Few listening to the original Top Notes track would have predicted its ultimate success; it was a tightly wound cultural conundrum, a white-penned novelty piggybacking on a rip-off of another novelty, one of those miraculous mistakes that mutates from obscurity into a cultural virus.

Who knows what Lennon heard in Ronnie Isley's lead vocal on "Twist and Shout"—but he must have heard an opening, an idea about freedom that cried out for a tougher, leaner beat. The Beatles' attack alone carried symbolic force: as a garage band, they filtered the Isleys' high-tone horns and handclaps down into guitars and vocals alone, which turned the entire project into an ideal of self-sufficiency, a sound that said, "This thing will cut water if we trim its sails." Where the Isley Brothers kicked Berns and Medley's sketch into a song, the Beatles both compressed it and fleshed it out, turning it into a much larger idea. When you listened to this new band cover the track, the Isley Brothers version suddenly sounded both quaint and pregnant: Ronnie's wriggling lead rang out all the more pronounced for the square frame it had to squirm through. Everybody hearing the Beatles do this song heard faint echoes of the Isley Brothers in their heads, and the marvel lay in how the Beatles conquered the track without patronizing their models. The Isleys' arrangement wore pressed shirts, cuff links, and polished shoes; the Beatles sound wore leather. They also did the Isley Brothers' "Shout!," of course, the gospel sing-along with Lennon hurling expletives into its coda ("We're fookin' shoutin' now!")[19] But in both songs, the racial politics in the music didn't disappear so much as turn metaphorical—the

Brits pouncing on this style escaped cynicism and landed on the far side of beatific. In "Twist and Shout," Lennon made the Isley Brothers' sexual subtext overt, lacing a cynical play on Chubby Checker's "Twist" with irony and subterfuge.

The final layer of Lennon's daring may be his boldest stroke, and yet to most of us it's still nearly invisible. Instead of straining to copy black vocal mannerisms, Lennon dumped them, acted as if they weren't crucial. That whole moptops-in-suits pose may have been coy, but it didn't begin to suggest the carnality Lennon leaned into here, somehow sidestepping the white envy of black virility that spooked most American parents. Compared with Mick Jagger, say, Lennon had no hangups about sounding completely white, even when pitting himself against the black standard. Only a Brit could have pulled the carnal thread from this song's distracting racial knots, revealing it as something beyond a white author piggybacking on a Twist novelty for a black gospel act.

The Beatles' signature, those mounting vocal rave-ups, did something more than intensify the song. By rewinding its spring each time, they coiled up before setting things off just a hair beyond listeners' expectations, and this incomprehensible delay yanked everything up again for another swell of feeling. Those escalating "Oh"s, stacked one by one, piling up Beatle upon Beatle into the final refrains the way they used to leapfrog over one another on the Reeperbahn, held back the energy like a human dam, until it spilled over into Lennon's gusher lead ("Shake it up baby now . . ."). After goading the others steadily for the song's first half, Lennon rode this bronco of a band while lashing it from above for one last victory-lap verse before it lunged to an exhausted finish. On top of all the takes they had given "There's a Place" and "I Saw Her Standing There," Lennon somehow hoisted the entire day's work up beyond euphoria, to a place where greatness winks at every challenge. On this recording of "Twist and Shout," the Beatles lay claim to a defining irony: fearsome originality wrought from somebody else's pile of junk.

THE LP SESSION in the can, the band rejoined the Shapiro tour, mimed "Please Please Me" for *Thank Your Lucky Stars* on February 17, and sat back down to write: "From Me to You" and "She Loves You" popped out of them in the back of a coach. "We weren't taking ourselves seriously," Lennon remembered, "just fooling about on the guitar. . . . I think the first line [of 'From Me to You'] was mine and we took it from there." Only after toying with all those "me"s and "you"s did Lennon pick up a copy of *New Musical Express* to see how they were doing on the charts: "Then I realized—we'd got the inspiration from reading a copy on the coach. Paul and I had been talking about one of the letters in the 'From You to Us' column."[20]

The last night of the tour, March 3 in Stoke-on-Trent, they yielded to public demand that they close the show's first half. All the television and radio exposure had paid off; "Please Please Me" hit number one the next week. The force of its breakthrough quickened the cultural pulse, and the pace of their travels. Oldham had stood at the back of the stalls with Epstein at one of these Shapiro tour shows, nursing some prescient realizations. A "tangible sense of mad hysteria" began rising up through the crowd, he remembered, and when the Beatles appeared, something new opened up, a sound Oldham could only call "the roar of the whole world":

> The noise that night hit me emotionally, like a blow to the chest. The audience that evening expressed something beyond repressed adolescent sexuality. The noise they made was the sound of the future. Even though I hadn't seen the world, I heard the whole world screaming. The power of the Beatles touched and changed minds and bodies all over the world. I didn't *see* it—I heard and felt it.[21]

When Oldham looked over at Epstein, they both had tears in their eyes.

On March 5, in between gigs at St. Helens and Manchester, the Beatles laid down three more songs: "From Me to You," "Thank You Girl," and, finally, "One After 909" (which stayed in the vault). Already, in the spring of 1963, the studio was becoming a refuge where they greeted familiar faces and got some actual work done—collecting themselves to pursue musical ideas.

And they never seemed short of ideas. "From Me to You" sneers confidently at the very conventions it's built upon (the unison vocals that unravel into harmony with each line, those perfectly placed "woo"s that greet each return of the verse). "Thank You Girl" rings out like the mirror image of "Misery," so overwrought in its happy-to-hook-up that it verges on irony—and just where it starts to go overboard, it caves in to pleasure. And "One After 909" is an enduring puzzle; a great throwaway when it was cut, it never came to light until the dismal *Let It Be* sessions in January 1969, when it revived all their best ensemble impulses. (Apparently, Lennon was never happy with its stupid-inspired lyric—"Then I find . . . I got the number wrong!"—its most endearing quality.)

This sudden jolt of new material airlifted the Beatles right out of Liverpool: they had played six Cavern gigs in January, three in February, and exactly none in March. This had the strange effect of increasing the town's visibility on England's map even as its favorite sons outgrew their testing ground. When Bob Wooler announced that "Please Please Me" had hit number one, an awful hush fell over the Cavern audience. The world had suddenly snatched them away from their hometown listeners: a jam-packed final August appearance would be their last. To this day, Liverpool's pride in the band gets tangled up with loss.

EPSTEIN HAD ALWAYS had his eye on the larger scene, and many long-term ambitions. He quickly diversified his holdings. After "Love Me Do," he expanded his NEMS roster with Gerry and the Pacemakers, Billy J. Kramer with the Dakotas, the Fourmost, Cilla Black, and Tommy Quickly. Not all found success, but those that did were often propelled by Lennon/McCartney material, which literally swarmed the British charts in 1963. Even not counting the Beatles, these acts scored a total of forty-five weeks on *Record Retailer*'s top-ten charts. In all, Epstein's office handled eighty-five top-ten records for the year.

On April 14 Lennon met Del Shannon, the Michigan singer with the enormous range who had won a huge British audience with his 1961 debut song, "Runaway." He joined the *Thank Your Lucky Stars* TV taping on a bill with the Dave Clark Five and did a double take when he heard the Beatles' material. He promised Lennon he'd record "From Me to You" when he got back to America. (Shannon's rather subdued version reached the U.S. top one hundred later that summer.) After the show, Lennon headed up to a Richmond club called the Crawdaddy with Andrew Loog Oldham to catch a new band, the Rolling Stones. Like Oldham before him, Lennon did his own double take: "They're like what we used to be before Brian ponced us up," he exclaimed. "I'm in the wrong band!"[22]

On April 8, the day the Beatles performed in Portsmouth, Hampshire, John Charles Julian Lennon was born at Liverpool's Sefton General Hospital. Like his own father, Lennon was away when his son was born, traveling back to London for a radio interview and an evening performance. This was only the most immediate signal that fatherhood had failed to change his priorities. He visited wife and child the next day before dashing off again—this time to Birkenhead, and then a Good Friday return to the Cavern for an eight-hour "Rhythm and Blues Marathon."

In a cruel replay of Julia's own isolation with John, Lennon didn't see Cynthia or Julian again until June. During John's travels, Cyn's mother, Lillian, flew back from Canada to help with the baby. The three of them moved in together with Mimi at Mendips. This spoke well enough of Mimi, but compounded family ironies: the woman who had refused to attend her nephew's wedding now took in his wife and son as he pursued rock 'n' roll stardom. Naturally, Cynthia quickly rediscovered Mimi's "sharp tongue," which she often aimed at Julian, "a screamer." When Cynthia went out, Mimi often stashed the baby in his pram in the garden so as not to bother her paying lodgers.[23]

For all the cultural shifts embedded in Lennon's music, his own personal history repeated itself. His runaway career became one with his callousness toward his new family, which doubled as passive aggression at husband- and fatherhood. Seeing as his own experience was no better, he seems not to have dwelt much on Cynthia's plight. On April

28, Paul, George, and Ringo went off together for a holiday in Santa Cruz, Tenerife, in the Canary Islands. Serenely contemptuous of Lennon's situation, a lusty pop star with a perfect family front, Epstein booked a separate holiday for the two of them—the homosexual manager and the new father—in Spain.

BY SINGLING LENNON out for a private vacation that spring, on the crest of the band's first number-one single, Epstein tensed up a political knot at the band's center. During a BBC profile of Epstein produced in 2003, McCartney said he was convinced Lennon went along to send Eppy the signal that he, John, was the leader of this band, the one with a direct pipeline to their manager.[24] There was enough at stake to force this relationship, which both parties described as "intense," into being a success.

But very few acts talk about their managers in the terms Lennon did: "It was very intense—but it was never consummated." And in retrospect, this trip looks simply bizarre. Consider Epstein's motives: here was a businessman taking his brash young bandleader off to a hotel three weeks after his first son was born and expecting everybody, even Lennon's wife, to look the other way—after all, he had provided lodging for the couple all during her pregnancy (in his Falkner Street "bolthole"). He was just beginning to see the fruits of almost eighteen months of toil: recognition was beginning to pour in, and suddenly his management office was flush with cash. So the invitation has a whiff of manipulative guilt, as if he could depend on whisking John away: "I put you lot up when you got married," he seems to have bargained. "Stash your wife and kid and run off with me on holiday." His staff had doubled, and his menagerie of acts now included Gerry and the Pacemakers, the Remo Four, Cilla Black, and the Big Three—and Lennon was half of the songwriting partnership whose material he was tapping for all of them.

It wasn't just that Epstein knew he had leverage on the young couple; it was that he used it with such selfish disregard. And why was Lennon so compliant? Surely, even at the time, many must have sensed his huge ambivalence about marriage, let alone fatherhood. There are numerous testimonies to his open womanizing in this period, in both England and

Spain. And what did the hyperaware Lennon think when he flew off with Epstein—that people *wouldn't* suspect a personal encounter of some kind? Could his bluster and rising popularity quell such talk?

Young people have been known to make just such miscalculations, and Epstein had a track record for emotional jackpots. For Cynthia, the very shock of the news of John's holiday inhibited protest, which tells you something about her inner, psychological twinset: don't question the men, especially about their business. And her very complacency fueled Lennon's lechery—he would need a much tougher woman to keep him in line. Was this a new mother's trauma, postpartum depression, or simple denial—or all three? Cynthia's demureness reflects the growing tumult around the Beatles' career and how suddenly it altered everybody's daily life. Cynthia barely felt "married" to Lennon as it was, keeping her status secret according to Epstein's rules, giving birth without John there to support her. She nursed her colicky newborn at her in-law's, listening to Lennon's voice overtake pop radio while newspapers chased the Beatles' every move and zealous fans and photographers inhibited her own.

Epstein booked a suite at the Avenida Palace in Barcelona. Lennon seems to have opened up to very few people about the holiday, and Yoko Ono has never answered questions about it. But in 1991, Christopher Munch devoted an entire film script to the incident, called *The Hours and Times,* with a slaphappy performance by Ian Hart that gets at both Lennon's sexual confusion and his blinding faith in the music. *The Hours and Times* catches the spirit of Epstein's loneliness and Lennon's faux worldliness, if not the particulars. When Lennon does broach the subject of their (mutual?) attraction, it only accents the discomfort: "I enjoy hearing about your conquests—this lorry driver, that docker," he says. "Yes, well, that's all very well," Epstein replies, "but it's when it comes closer to home—I just don't know what to say when that happens."[25] Munch has Lennon invite a stewardess back to the hotel, "pulling a bird" to mock Epstein. But Munch throws a curveball: "Their union is consummated not by sex but by dancing to her prized new Little Richard single. It's a delicious denouement," wrote Richard Harrington in the *Washington Post.* The dance scene is the most liberating moment of the film.[26]

Two closer-to-home accounts tell of this trip, one from Lennon's close friend Pete Shotton and the other from Alistair Taylor. The two versions are similar enough to seem plausible. Shotton's account has the sharp pang of honesty to it; Epstein's come-on to Lennon was a mixture of dread and devotion. "Eppy just kept on and on at me," John told Shotton, "until one night I finally just pulled me trousers down and said to him: 'Oh, for Christ's sake, Brian, just stick it up me fucking arse then.'" But Epstein surprised him by saying, "I don't do that kind of thing. That's not what I like to do.'" Instead, Epstein said, he simply wanted to touch John, "and so I let him toss me off."[27] This is more than Lennon told Taylor, who kept whatever confidences Epstein may have told him a secret:

> [Lennon] told me afterwards in one of our frankest heart-to-hearts that Brian never seriously did proposition him. He had teased Brian about the young men he kept gazing at and the odd ones who had found their way to his room. Brian had joked to John about the women who hurled themselves at him. "If he'd asked me, I probably would have done anything he wanted. I was so much in awe of Brian then I'd have tried a night of vice-versa. But he never wanted me like that. Sure, I took the mickey a bit and pretended to lead him on. But we both knew we were joking. He wanted a pal he could have a laugh with and someone he could teach about life. I thought his bum boys were creeps and Brian knew that. Even completely out of my head, I couldn't shag a bloke. And I certainly couldn't lie there and let one shag me. Even a nice guy like Brian. To be honest, the thought of it turns me over."[28]

Both these quotes have the feel of truth to them; this is what Lennon might have told each of these people, at different times, while still guarding other secrets. The full truth of the matter, only Lennon and Epstein knew for sure.

Epstein could be manipulative, but he arranged things in order for Lennon to ridicule him—it gave him a jolt. Between cajoling him about his "nancy boys," Lennon would sneak off for quickies with waitresses and dance-dates with a bravado that seemed to overimpress Epstein—which was likely Lennon's motive. "She was *friendly,*" Lennon would report. From Lennon's side, this is adolescent fiddling; "pulling birds" with Epstein displayed the same kind of gamesmanship as playing "king of the mountain" with the other Beatles. Making Epstein blush had already become gruesome sport, and the sexual humiliation coloring such scenes toys with something more menacing. Lennon looked up to Epstein, but needed to prove himself superior, and rub Epstein's nose in his covert life. Humiliating his manager also spilled over into Freudian revenge. And Epstein's enjoyment of Lennon, even at the cost of his self-respect, reveals something desperate, even debasing, about his own desires—not just obsessing after something he couldn't have, but reveling in its rebuke each time Lennon told of a new conquest. In their codependent dance of mutual manipulation, Lennon rewarded Eppy with shame.

Both Shotton's and Taylor's accounts came after Lennon's death in 1980, and both seem plausible given the quotes each principal gave while he was alive. Where Pauline Sutcliffe suggests that Lennon had been intimate with her brother, she underlines it as speculation. Everybody who knew them together at art school and in Hamburg claims they were unusually close; but doesn't it make sense for the young Lennon to be unusually close to one of his first and best adult friends, somebody who mediated and played out the intimate tension of his relationship with McCartney? By 1970, at least, Lennon had confessed to so many blasphemous secrets in interviews it's hard to imagine he would have felt shy about a homosexual encounter. The Beatles may have called their *Let It Be* director, Michael Lindsay-Hogg, a "fag" behind his back; but by the early 1970s, when he moved to New York City—perhaps with Yoko Ono as his moral guide—Lennon lent his name to all manner of gay rights causes and would have known the power any of his own homosexual experiences might have had in left-wing circles. In his early thirties, he would have had numerous conversations with peers who had experimented with alternative sexualities and been nonetheless manly for it. If there was an encounter, it was probably as Shotton described or as Munch portrays—a fumbling to express affection that was just out of reach.

The more provocative signals Lennon was sending by going away with Eppy were to his wife and his band. Cynthia, shell-shocked from childbirth and hounded by fans, barely registered Eppy's maneuvers; McCartney, Harrison, and Starr were probably suspicious of Lennon's power play, if not feeling outright ditched. Lennon returned with a song, "Bad to Me," not up to Beatle snuff, which he finished with McCartney and dumped on Billy J. Kramer for a left-field hit that summer. After snubbing Epstein on holiday, he snubbed him again with a subpar song.

In May, the Beatles played the Liverpool boxing stadium on a bill with Gene Vincent in between Cavern gigs, and then joined the Roy Orbison tour with Duane Eddy, Ben E. King, and the Four Seasons, who all had dropped out by the end. Orbison had started out in Wink, Texas, recorded "Ooby Dooby" at Sun Records in Memphis back in 1956, and gone on to write "Claudette" in Nashville for the Everly Brothers. But his early 1960s singles on the Monument label were surging operatic melodramas that cast him as a gloriously doomed loner in shades: "Only the Lonely (Know the Way I Feel)," which Orbison originally wrote for Presley, followed by "Running Scared," "Crying," and finally that spring's "In Dreams," an avalanche of self-pity redeemed by his epic resolve. The British embraced Orbison as a demigod the way they had Eddie Cochran and Buddy Holly: as one of their own, as if his heroic insecurity made him a royal subject. But by the end of this tour, even the mighty Orbison bowed to Beatlemania: screams for "Please Please Me" began to win the nightly battle, and by the last week Orbison let the Beatles close the show. With seven years behind him in the business, as both performer and writer, Orbison befriended the inquisitive young Beatles, admiring their ravenous curiosity almost as much as their music. "You can't measure success," Lennon would later say, "but if you could, then the minute I knew we'd been successful was when Roy Orbison asked us if he could record two of our songs."[29]

The Lennon-Epstein trip to Spain remained "quiet" until June, when it surfaced at Paul McCartney's twenty-first birthday party on June 20. With their debut album in the middle of its thirty-week reign at the top, the Beatles held court as musical kingpins at a relative's home in Huyton to slip the fans who already hung around their houses. Billy J. Kramer remembers the liquor flowing, and Lennon getting pissed, literally and figuratively.

"So, Lennon, how was your honeymoon?" Bob Wooler cracked, meaning Spain, publicly humiliating the top dog in the salty Scouse manner. The Cavern compere, whom Lennon once introduced to Epstein as his "father," knew just which Lennon scabs to pick. Beside himself at Wooler's innuendo, Lennon began pelting the smaller man with punches, to the point where Kramer and the Fourmost's Billy Hatton had to pull him off. Wooler lay bruised and bleeding on the lawn as Lennon shouted and glowered. Somebody piled Wooler into a car and took him to a hospital emergency room.

"It wasn't nice," Kramer emphasized many years later. "[John] was, uh, *very* abusive and told me how I was fuck-all," Kramer said. "And I'll tell you the truth, I had a very good relationship with John. . . . I mean, the next time I saw him after that incident there, he came around to shake hands and apologize. And he said, you know, he was fucking pissed."[30]

And Wooler's remark inflamed something far scarier in Lennon than simple homophobia. By this point, chatter about Epstein's designs on John whisked throughout Liverpool, and the strict macho code required a public brawl at any hint of homosexuality. As the leader of this volcanically successful band, this newly married, renowned womanizer feared the damage to his growing reputation more urgently than ever— especially if it came from someone as close as Wooler. If he could pound it down somehow, perhaps he could frighten away the very idea of it. Somewhere inside, Lennon also pummeled at Alf, his own father, who abandoned him and his mother back in 1940.

Wooler got stitched up, and the next day Lennon made amends through Epstein's NEMS office in the form of a £250 payoff and a note of apology. (This was fifty pounds more than what Epstein handed out to the parents of pregnant fans.) The scene, with its echoes of Lennon's lashing out at Sutcliffe in Hamburg, reminded everybody of the terrifying darkness that seeped from Lennon when he drank, complete with memory lapses and remorse. London's *Daily Mirror* ran an item on the scuffle, which included Lennon's public apology. No other Merseysiders commanded such coverage.

This tabloid coverage, and the transaction finessed through Brian Epstein, signaled a new machinery to Lennon's persona, whose blackout violence could not be kept from the world any longer. His only tack was to overcompensate. Even his wedding smells of loss, the shotgun cliché: his compulsion to do right in this situation brooked only narrow choices. To the world, the hell-bent mop top concealed a grief-ridden adolescent, sublimated for years at great emotional cost behind a bipolar muse.

11

Thick of It

BEATLEMANIA BECAME AN ALL-CONSUMING MEDIA FRENZY IN BRIT-
ain over that summer of 1963, reshuffling everybody's long-held assumptions about class, pop, and good manners. Yet the Beatles' appeal
remained oddly provincial even as they ascended to the upper ranks. As
familiar faces in the major music papers, even the London dailies began
running their quotes and noting their habits. Each week, the BBC featured a new program, either *Pop Go the Beatles* (which ran for fifteen
weeks) or *Saturday Club* with Brian Matthew, with a stream of songs that
combined the band's stage show with their enormous Hamburg song
archive. By August, with "She Loves You," it was hard to imagine how
they could get any bigger. And still the giant American market resisted.

Guilelessness typified their manner. At a brief television interview,
McCartney and Lennon sparred gamely to the usual questions about
their upcoming Royal Variety Performance. In the days leading up to
this November show, Conservative politician Edward "Teddy" Heath
had derided the band for their northern accents, saying their speech patterns were "unrecognizable as the Queen's English." This struck Lennon as overt class snobbery, the kind Scousers reveled in exposing, and
he replied by saying he couldn't understand Heath's accent:

Q: John, in this Royal Variety Show when you're appearing
before royalty, your language has got to be pretty good

obviously—this thing about Teddy saying that he couldn't
distinguish your . . . the Queen's English.

JOHN: (mock sophistication) I can't understand Teddy! I can't
understand Teddy saying that at all, really. (He smiled,
paused, and looked seriously into the camera.) I'm not going
to vote for Ted.[1]

Since there was no china shop Lennon wanted to streak through
more, the queen's stage was set for more than music. Now that they were
performing for royalty, they would certainly have to tidy up their act
more than with their mere matching suits. But in Lennon's mind this
was simplistic: they hadn't been invited just to sing, had they?

Earlier in September 1963, after drinking their way through a Variety Club awards luncheon at the swank Savoy Hotel on the Strand, Lennon and McCartney had jumped out of a cab near Ken Colyer's Studio
51 jazz club off Charing Cross Road and spotted Andrew Loog Oldham. Oldham had left Epstein's employ and had been pouring his street
smarts and fashion bravado into the Rolling Stones. He had just walked
out of a club rehearsal in despair at finding the right follow-up to "Come
On," the Chuck Berry number that gave the Stones their first hit—
something better than another American oldie. Oldham juggled several
agendas: pushing journalists to see the band, wrangling studio time,
cajoling engineers, playing at producing, and molding Jagger, Richards,
Jones, Wyman, and Watts into the force he knew they could become. It's
a measure of Oldham's pluck and self-possession that he served as producer of these early Stones singles even though he had never before set
foot in a studio.

Oldham hadn't seen the Beatles since he'd lit out from under Epstein
to launch his Stones crusade. He tried to hide his mood, but Lennon and
McCartney could tell he was fretful. "They smiled at each other," Oldham wrote, and followed him back down toward the basement rehearsal:

Once downstairs, the boys quickly got to work teaching the
Stones "I Wanna Be Your Man." Yeah, they gave us a hit, which
was certainly my oxygen, but more than that they gave us a real

tutorial in the reality they were forging for themselves; lesson of the day from John and Paul. I went from downed to reprieved to exalted as the two Beatles ran through their gift for the open-mouthed Stones.[2]

"The whole procedure took about twenty minutes," recalled Rolling Stones insider James Phelge, "and the result was that the Stones no longer had a problem regarding their next single."[3] To the relatively younger and less experienced Stones, this was an act of creative bravura: "the north and south of musical life," as Oldham described it, both an open lesson in songwriting and an act of generosity from pop royalty to their budding rivals. "At that rehearsal, an inspired Brian Jones added the roar of his slide guitar, John and Paul enjoying as much as the Stones and I the spontaneity of the moment." The "unfinished bridge was finished there and then in front of everybody, proscribing in your face."[4]

The next day, the Beatles turned around and made their own recording of the song, as part of their ongoing sessions for the second album, which had begun in July. On August 3, they had given their last Cavern appearance; later that month, Robert Freeman shot the cover for the new album in Bournemouth, where they settled in for a six-night run at the Gaumont Cinema. In the midst of all this, John and Cynthia finally left Julian with Lillian and took a honeymoon, thirteen months late, to Paris, where they met up with Astrid Kirchherr.

Over in America, England might as well have been another planet. It's difficult to underline the slower pace at which culture traveled in this pre-Beatle era, a time with no Internet, when even international phone calls were saved for dire emergencies. As John and Cynthia decamped to Paris, George Harrison traveled to Benton, Illinois, with his brother Peter to visit their older sister, Louise, who had settled there with an American husband and wrote letters home from Chuck Berry's fabled paradise of hamburgers, drive-ins, and movie stars. They stopped by the local record shop and were disappointed to find no Beatles records and no name recognition. Some Americans have vivid memories of hearing the band for the first time before their Ed Sullivan appearance and wondering when they would hit: budding producer and impresario Kim Fowley heard a stray California deejay play the Beatles singing "From Me to You" on the radio that summer and thought to himself, "That sounds like the Everly Brothers with *three*-part harmony!"[5]

TWO TELEVISION APPEARANCES that fall sealed Lennon's "lovable scoundrel" persona. The first came on the Royal Variety Performance before the queen mother and Princess Margaret at the Prince of Wales Theatre on November 4. Backstage before their appearance, when Epstein asked them for samples of their between-song repartee, Lennon threatened to introduce "Twist and Shout" by instructing the royals, up in their tony boxes, to "rattle their fuckin' jewelry." As if a button had been pushed, Epstein went red. (Screenwriter Alun Owen picked up on the way Lennon ribbed Eppy, toned it down, and desexualized it for an ongoing bit in his script for *A Hard Day's Night.*) Once he stepped to the mike onstage, however, Lennon simply cut the profanity and turned his threat into a beguiling bit of charm, topping even McCartney's remark that Sophie Tucker was their "favorite band." "Would the people in the cheaper seats clap your hands," Lennon began, emboldening himself for the punch, "and the rest of you, if you'd just rattle your jewelry." And then he smirked as if he'd just pulled down the queen mother's knickers.

Lennon's smirk betrayed all innocence, the way the music betrayed any notion of sobriety: the intrigue lay in the barely concealed coarser subtext; the entire act had just enough juice to be beyond description, with enough cheek to glide beneath the establishment's radar. If McCartney was cute and a bit plucky, Lennon came across as caustic, impatient, an impudent comic shredder of pretension and hypocrisy. Lennon didn't have to use any swear words to get his point across. To the younger generation, his arrogance and defiance shone right through; for the staid upper classes, it was easier to pretend he didn't really mean it. Cheek could be tolerated; vulgarity might have sunk the whole enterprise. Anyway, "Twist and Shout" went beyond vulgar; it was more like a previously private pleasure made public—nobody needed a diagram connecting "Twist and Shout" to the birds and bees. Doing the shimmy in suits only gave the whole thing a biting subversive glee.

That sense of duality, of outrage posing as decency, tickled the band's sound, gave the music an irresistible kick. Of course, you could also hear the tension in the band's set list and ensemble, with McCartney carving out the old-school sentimental corner in a way that gave the harder material imaginary historical weight. Epstein had half-framed the Beatles as "all-around" entertainers, but nobody could really make any sense of this in the new context of a rock 'n' roll act, a band that swerved gamely between Meredith Willson and Chuck Berry, laced with originals on parallel planes, from "P.S. I Love You" to "I Saw Her Standing There." Here was something perhaps only Britain could embrace: not kids aping American idols, but something better, retranslating the rebel pose as something beyond John Osborne's angry young men and the new working-class pride. American music done this well, performed by northerners, became something glamorous in and of itself: the simple joy of music shot through notions of class, gender, race, regionality, and even nationality, popping up straight as a youthful phenomenon in a world apart, played out as some waking dream of ambition, possibility, and generational solidarity. "You can rattle your jewelry," Lennon seemed to say, "for all the good it'll do you."

Lennon's second defining TV appearance was taped on December 2 (for broadcast on April 18, 1964), with the beloved comedy team of Morecambe and Wise, who had roughly the same Sunday-night status as Ed Sullivan had in America. The duo started back in 1951 as part of a *Parade of Youth* series when they were both older than the Beatles were now (this bit gets reprised on the Beatles' *Anthology* video). By 1963, Morecambe and Wise ruled British TV comedy as establishment fixtures. The Beatles sang "This Boy," "All My Loving," and "I Want to Hold Your Hand" in front of a small studio crowd, and then closed the show with scripted shenanigans. Eric Morecambe—the tall one with glasses—greeted them as the "Kaye Sisters," a popular British singing group from the 1950s, with Ernie Wise correcting him. "Hello, Bungo!" Morecambe shouted to Ringo back on his drum stand. "No, that's *Ringo!*"

Wise corrected again. Then they went into a stale routine redeemed by Beatle cutups and surrealist body movements.

"Do you like being famous?" Morecambe turned to Lennon and asked. Lennon shifted from goonish to mock serious and retorted, "Oh, it's not like in your day, you know." With this, he gave his taller host a perverse once-over with his eyes, up and down his frame, sizing him up flirtatiously, concluding with disgust. Morecambe barely recovered, and the audience came apart. In a dazzling, transformative moment, Lennon's once-over cemented everything their music hinted at: his manner simply dismissed this tired, silly-straight duo as passé.

"What?" Morecambe said, turning to Wise. Lennon had just written him off, on his own TV show, in ways he didn't quite understand. "Ah, that's an insult," he concluded, waving it off as his partner dissolved into giggles. Then he turned back to Lennon: "What do you mean, 'not like in my day'?" "Oh, my dad used to tell me about you," Lennon replied, his hand indicating, "when I was knee-high." "You've only got a little dad, have you?" Morecambe shot back, cracking Lennon up. "That's a bit strong, init?" Morecambe complained again to Wise.

Suddenly, Lennon had turned Morecambe into an outsider on his own set. "There, that's it I've had enough. I won't be insulted," he told his straight man. Wise suggested they do a song. "Oh, yes!" Morecambe responded, "one that my dad will remember," adding, to Lennon, ". . . that I used to do with *your* dad." Lennon suggested "Moonlight Bay," the 1951 Doris Day hit, and the Beatles went off to get seersucker jackets and boaters and straw hats. Morecambe returned in a Beatle wig. They all launched into barbershop harmony as Morecambe interjected "Twist and shout!," "I like it!" (from Gerry and the Pacemakers' hit) from behind them, getting older every second.

The routine was stock variety-era setup-and-punch-line, anchored by Wise and Morecambe's familiar patter. But Lennon's readings tore holes in his script and brought both random comic sparks and a defiant abruptness to it all, as if to say, "In your day show business went along just so. Now you don't know what we'll do, do you?" Infinitely tamer than Lennon's crack at the Royal Variety Performance, the scene still caught Lennon's slippery absurdity; his attitude made propriety squirm. "The show won't be aired for a couple of months," somebody overheard the TV producer say. "Let's hope they're still popular then."[6] Standing atop these two comic giants, the Beatles—Lennon especially—made them seem infinitely smaller. In Britain, this appearance conferred national stature on the Beatles as inspired clowns; in America, nobody saw it until it was released on the *Anthology* DVD in 1995.

AT THE TOP OF this show-business ladder, the Beatles wound up socializing with some of the same people who had turned them down on the way to Parlophone. One of these was Decca's Tony King, a promotional agent who was tight with Andrew Loog Oldham. In January 1964, the celebrated American producer Phil Spector brought over his "Be My Baby" girl group, the Ronettes, for a UK tour with the Rolling Stones, and King went along to "look after them." This meant steering Spector's girlfriend (and future wife), Veronica ("Ronnie") Bennett; her older sister, Estelle; and their cousin Nedra Talley away from the guile of Brian Jones, Keith Richards, and Mick Jagger.[7]

Never was a producer, the geek at the dials, more lauded and revered, than Phil Spector was in the UK, both before and throughout the British Invasion. "[His] curved sunglasses made him look like the living embodiment of New York nightlife," wrote photographer Robert Freeman.[8] The Beatles, of course, emblemized everything Spector's girl group stood for, and as fanatics themselves, they considered Veronica Bennett the style's queen. Bennett, a twenty-one-year-old who projected sexual wisdom, flaunted a mysterious racial allure: her Native American–black mother had married a white man. Through a mystical haze of dark eyeliner, she unleashed a two-ton voice from beneath a perfectly stacked beehive, as if no man had yet proved worthy of her mythic wiles. Lennon hit on her at a party held by Decca's Tony Hall, after doing *Val Parnell's Sunday Night at the London Palladium* together on January 12. "You were great," she remembered him telling her. "Just fuckin' great."

"It was obvious that these guys listened to a lot of records," Ronnie wrote, "because they knew as much about American music as we did. Or more. The Beatles loved all the girl groups, and they knew every Motown song ever put out. They kept telling us how much they loved our long black hair, and how our whole look blew them away." John, George, and Ringo (Paul hadn't come along) chatted and danced, getting the Ronettes to show them the latest American moves: the Pony, the Jerk, the Nitty Gritty. Harrison took an interest in Estelle as Lennon zeroed in on Ronnie. The two Ronettes compared notes in the ladies' room and decided to enjoy themselves. Bennett's memoirs draw a picture of Lennon the operator (and a rare instance when his moves were politely declined):

> John grabbed my arm and said, "C'mon! Let's go explorin'!" Before I knew what was happening, John dragged me upstairs to this long hallway where the bedrooms were. Then he started walking down the hall, jiggling all the door handles, hoping to find an empty room. . . .
>
> We finally found an empty bedroom at the end of the hall, a huge room with a cozy little window seat that looked out over all the lights of London. It was breathtaking. I walked into the darkened room and sat down, staring out the window at this fairy-tale land of lights and towers that seemed to go on forever. "Oh," I sighed. "It's beautiful."

They talked about how strange it was to be so young and so famous, how much had changed so quickly, and how once you broke through to a certain point, the business let you coast a bit. "I felt pretty close to John right then," Spector writes, "like he understood all the things I wanted to know. I knew he was one of these heavy brain people, just like Phil." She could also tell he was moving in fast.

"When he leaned over and started kissing me, I have to admit he made me forget about Phil for a few seconds. But just a few." But she insists nothing happened, which was either reverence on Lennon's part or sheer modesty on hers.

> We kissed for a couple of minutes on that window seat. And for me, that was a pretty big deal. . . . I hadn't done much more than

kiss a guy on the lips up until then, and that included Phil. Romance was everything, and sex was still a mystery. But the way things were going on that window seat, it didn't look like it was going to stay that way for long.

Ronnie wound up turning Lennon down, gently. "John didn't seem too upset," though, she recalled, "because after we went back downstairs, we danced and had a great time for the rest of the night."[9]

HISTORY HAS GIVEN Epstein a reputation as a small-timer, but his approach to the American market was full of daring and resolve. In negotiations with the *Ed Sullivan Show* producers, who included Sullivan himself, he contracted a groundbreaking three appearances, complete with top billing, all before Capitol had released "I Want to Hold Your Hand" stateside. Sullivan had seen Beatlemania for himself while on a connecting flight at Heathrow the previous October 31. Along with his producer Bob Precht, Sullivan saw the fans screaming as the band returned from a week in Sweden, and decided for himself that this phenomenon, whatever it was, just might translate. If he was wrong, he could boast of exposing Americans to a genuine British spectacle.

Epstein negotiated a forward-thinking deal: in that era, a booking on the Sullivan show garnered a $7,500 fee for a single appearance. In exchange for three appearances—two live and one taped—Epstein lowered the Beatles' overall fee to $10,000. All Epstein wanted on top of that was round-trip airfare and hotel bills in New York City and Miami, which Sullivan covered. To Sullivan this was a bargain, but the bigger bargain came through the priceless exposure of the Beatles' "arrival" in America. It took cunning on Epstein's part to play this hand as an event, even if nobody expected it to supersede everything that led up to it.

Once the arrival itself became a happening, other appearances fell into place. Between the three Sullivan shows, Epstein booked the band at the Coliseum in Washington, D.C., and at Carnegie Hall. Only late in December did "I Want to Hold Your Hand" start lighting up American radio switchboards, and deejays argued over who "broke" the record.

With this, Capitol Records suddenly had to answer customer demand where they had once shooed away George Martin's entreaties. CEO Alan Livingston reluctantly decided "Hand" had hit potential in ways "She Loves You" and "Please Please Me" didn't—his criteria have still gone unexplained. Knowing about Epstein's Sullivan bookings for February, he budgeted $50,000 for a major marketing campaign, which kept Capitol employees working overtime during the Christmas holiday once the top forty sparked. George Harrison had wandered unrecognized into an Illinois record shop just three months before. The campaign included "The Beatles Are Coming" bumper stickers, posters, billboards, and banners. In Hollywood, an item about *Psycho* star Janet Leigh wearing a Beatle wig ran on the celebrity wires.

While Epstein was in New York with Billy J. Kramer in November, finalizing the Sullivan contract, he did an interview in his Regency Hotel room with a *New Yorker* reporter, which ran as a lead "Talk of the Town" piece in the December 28, 1963 issue. (The magazine had tapped very good British sources about the act and its following.) Reports also ran in *Time*, *Newsweek*, and *Life* the week of November 15, 1963. The condescending tone of these reports brushed off this "moptop" craze as peculiarly British.

But Epstein's choice of the *New Yorker* for his interview signaled the same kind of foresight he had shown about *The Ed Sullivan Show*. Certainly, he found it gratifying that America's most prestigious literary weekly took an interest. Did he also suspect his base was broader than teenagers? His other meetings in New York were taken up with Capitol Record executives, planning the promotional campaign. A year ago the Beatles had flown off for a final two-week stint in Hamburg, and now here he was on the precipice of unimaginable exposure, using the Royal Variety Performance as his launchpad for America.

What's curious is just how close to the surface all these things seem in his long *New Yorker* interview, which aligned all the buttons the Beatles soon pushed. Weeks before their national television debut, Epstein told the story of how Ed Sullivan had caved in to British Beatlemania at Heathrow Airport: "At that time, it happened, the Prime Minister was supposed to fly out to Scotland, and the queen mother was supposed to land from a trip to Ireland. But everything was out of whack, because, you see, the Beatles were flying in from a tour of Sweden, and the whole airport was in an uproar because of the crowds that turned up to welcome them. Mr. Sullivan knew a good thing when he saw it." The Beatles, Epstein continued, had broken "every conceivable entertainment record in England. They are the most worshipped, the most idolized boys in the country. They have tremendous style, and a great effervescence, which communicates itself in an extraordinary way." He even ventured a few aesthetic remarks ("Their beat is something like rock 'n' roll but different from it.") and a running leap at how their charisma ruffled show-business-as-usual: "They have none of that mean hardness about them. They are genuine. They have life, humor, and strange, handsome looks."

Finally—and here the average *New Yorker* reader might have taken pause—Epstein suggested the Beatles were something beyond mere entertainment, exotic and unusual even to Britons: "Their accents are Liverpudlian—of the Liverpool area—and they have been called a working-class phenomenon," he said. "But I disagree with the sometimes express notion that their appeal is *merely* to working classes. The Beatles are *classless*." Imagine if Colonel Parker had said Elvis Presley was "raceless" or that race mattered less in his music than his audience's response to it. Knowingly or not, Epstein had stumbled on a juicy conundrum. In America, of course, *everybody* is classless—Epstein spoke to the U.S. market as only a Brit could, unveiling his entrenched class anxiety, boasting about the crossover they had already made as northerners raiding London's show-biz establishment. For Americans to embrace a British act performing American music would be the ultimate hat trick, and for this he drew the parallel between class and race the Beatles had unveiled in the sound.

But Americans, of course, thought of Europe and Britain as cultural dynasties, "where all the history comes from," as comic Eddie Izzard once said, and all the respectable music and art, too. Epstein's remarks got at something more universal and, in retrospect, more knowing about how far the Beatles had already taken rock 'n' roll. "This isn't just a teenage phenomenon," Epstein tried to tell Americans. "Mummies like the

Beatles, too—that's the extraordinary thing. They think they are rather sweet. They approve," he insisted, regaling American parents with how his "boys" outfoxed previous rock 'n' roll creatures like Elvis, Little Richard, Jerry Lee Lewis, and Chuck Berry.[10] Epstein charmed this American outlet the same way he had won over Dick James and George Martin. The Beatles got little old ladies who drank tea humming their songs and tapping their toes—how could the rest of the world possibly resist?

One Sweet Dream

THE BEATLES SO THOROUGHLY REVISED OUR IDEAS ABOUT "AMERI-can" music, its style, roots, and tributaries, that it's hard to imagine how they ever could have remained a British phenomenon. All through 1963, Capitol Records waved off American release of their hits even as Britain, the far more conservative cultural sensibility, succumbed. This was peculiar not least because EMI, Parlophone's umbrella company, was, after all, a global conglomerate, and Capitol Records its subsidiary. Capitol's leverage was sheer numbers: the American music market swamped the UK in terms of sales, and Britain's track record with pop stars was perceived as terminally lagging, although this was more a matter of perception. And the prevailing myths about the Beatles' "American moment" tend to get abstracted by the gust of their arrival.

George Martin's status as a boat rocker within EMI made it hard for him to exert much influence on getting his band marketing support abroad. Once again, the era's extreme cultural xenophobia, in both America and Britain, flattened any arguments about potential popularity until Ed Sullivan hitched his wagon to Beatlemania just as the royals had. At each stage of the game, Beatlemania saw the establishment catching on to a youth-driven yet supremely talented phenomenon, not inflating an artificial hype around a manufactured act. Fleet Street figured out how to sell more newspapers than even Profumo through the Beatles, which was good business practice even before it was sincere cynicism.

For once, America would have a lot to learn from the British charts—and acquiesce to a new cultural trade imbalance.

Epstein's underrated strategy had them in front of the press immediately after landing, and the interviews persisted—in the back of limos, in hotel rooms, over the phone—throughout the visit. "Direct" documentarians Albert and David Maysles, who had just finished shooting *Orson Welles in Spain* (1966), filmed the entire visit with hand-held cameras for a possible TV special, now an indispensable eye-of-the-storm piece called *The Beatles: The First U.S. Visit*. Epstein knew the Beatles were unflappable, and he was playing their second-strongest suit to put them over now that they had their first American hit record: their charm. If they could win over the American press the way they had Fleet Street, he reasoned, the music would do the rest. As America greeted them as newcomers, they leaned on a whole year's experience as gadflies. They held the press the same way they held their audience: through irreverent retorts that skirted vulgarity, and a knowing sense of show-biz politics that made them seem perched on some higher vantage, laughing at the circus erupting all around them. They made the overhyped atmosphere seem ridiculous even as they exploited it. Presley sneered at how easy it was to puncture stale showbiz traditions; the Beatles amplified this with mirthful self-consciousness.

Ringo Starr ultimately had the simplest explanation for how this final stretch of audience was conquered: "Things used to fall right for us as a band. We couldn't stop it. The gods were on our side. We were fabulous musicians, we had great writers; it wasn't like a piece of shit was being helped, and things just fell into place . . . but we were worried about America."[1]

By the end of 1964 the Beatles had become a cultural meteor, a global phenomenon, with hit records from Australia to Ireland, and stars in the runaway movie *A Hard Day's Night,* embraced even by doubting critics. The barrage of Lennon-McCartney songs that poured out this year alone made them ruling titans, and they gave a fair number away to lesser acts (Billy J. Kramer, Cilla Black, Peter and Gordon), showing astute aesthetic judgment about what they recorded with the Beatles and what they handed off to others.

Before they crossed the Pond, though, Lennon and Harrison continued courting Veronica and Estelle Bennett with fancy dinners in London as the Ronettes finished up their tour with the Rolling Stones. Ronnie remembered: " 'Tell us about the Temptations,' George would say. Then John would ask, 'What's Ben E. King really like?' So we'd just go down the list, telling them stories about all the acts we worked with at the Brooklyn Fox. And as we'd talk, John and George would sit there like they were hypnotized."[2]

On January 16, the Beatles began a three-week booking at the Olympia Theatre in Paris, staying at the Hotel George V. Harrison brought along a copy of a new record he was obsessed with, *The Freewheelin' Bob Dylan*. On only his second album, Dylan turned in an all-original breakout with meteors like "Don't Think Twice, It's All Right" and "A Hard Rain's A-Gonna Fall." Lennon and McCartney sponged it up as only two songwriters could while they hammered out sound-track songs for their movie, which would begin filming in March. Photographer Harry Benson also remembers them working on "I Feel Fine," and future biographer Barry Miles recalls McCartney playing a working draft of "Yesterday" for publisher Dick James, whose only response was "Do you have anything that goes 'Yeah Yeah Yeah'?"[3]

In Paris, Epstein got word that "I Want to Hold Your Hand" had shot from its number forty-five debut to number one in America, 1.5 million copies sold in five days. *Meet the Beatles* was rushed into stores to piggyback on the song and became the fastest-selling LP in history. When they sat down to celebrate the news, somebody snapped a picture of the Beatles with pots atop their heads. Later that night, Benson took photos of a celebratory pillow fight Lennon started back in their hotel room.

The Beatles gathered up friends to fly with them to New York. Lennon insisted on bringing Cynthia, refuting Epstein's dictum about pop idols not having wives more firmly than ever.[4] But Phil Spector wouldn't allow the Ronettes to take up Lennon's invitation to join the flight. He sent them home early, perhaps suspecting Lennon's designs. Back in New York, Ronnie was watching on television as Phil Spector got off the plane behind the Beatles at John F. Kennedy International Airport.

"I wanted to strangle him!" she wrote. "*We* couldn't fly back with the Beatles, but there *he* was, standing in front of all the cameras after the Beatles got off their plane. . . . That's when I first realized how badly Phil really wanted to be a star himself."⁵ Spector, whose pop dynasty had influenced the British groups beyond all description, glommed onto the Beatles. He cast himself as a symbolic protector, shepherding them into his own promised land, as if he were engineering the vast changes beginning to pour in from Britain. Spector's moment was ending as a new one began.

THE BEATLES' ARRIVAL in America finds broadcast news flirting with myth. Because of the huge impact of their first visit, though, many still confuse this early American trip with their U.S. concert tour later that August. In fact, this first visit included only three TV appearances (two in New York, one in Miami) and three live shows (two at Carnegie Hall, one in Washington, D.C.).

America, of course, had just walked through one of its darkest holidays in the weeks following the Kennedy assassination. Most of the tired psychobabble on Beatlemania revolves around the cliché about a nation's pent-up anxiety following this national grief. This assumes that had the Beatles not arrived, many of the same teenage girls would have been found weeping in their rooms over the fallen young hero, or that TV ratings in general would have dropped. In fact, it's far more plausible that the outburst of Beatlemania channeled a complicated mixture of forces that sent the country into swooning denial over Kennedy's persona, his recklessness in both his personal life and his rash Cold War Cuban-missile-crisis machismo. In death, America absolves its heroes of all manner of sins.

But putting Kennedy aside, Beatlemania was a far bigger phenomenon than the grief over a presidential assassination and a country's ideas about itself. The trauma drew Hollywood right into its internal debate about its virtues, and how the West's lawless past had suddenly reared into the present as nightclub owner Jack Ruby shot Lee Harvey Oswald on national television. Ever since Elvis Presley had returned from

Germany and resumed his career, for example, Hollywood had been reshaping the King's image with an eye toward how his teen base was settling down into mainstream middle-aged family life. With Kennedy cut down, new cultural totems sprang up to fill this void. Even as Hollywood struggled to figure how to remake Johnson into its new leading man, rock 'n' roll suddenly provided at least two. This Beatles *Ed Sullivan* appearance suddenly made Hollywood seem vaguely irrelevant—as if Tinseltown was losing its touch with youth icons. By extension, the old music order, ruled by Frank Sinatra, Dean Martin, and Perry Como, simply wilted.

"What was truly fresh in 1964 was the post-Kennedy euphoria," writes J. Hoberman in his survey of 1960s cinema, *The Dream Life.* "The apocalypse had happened and we remained. The fever broke. The crisis passed—anything seemed possible. . . . Where *The Manchurian Candidate* anticipated the fearful Kennedy scenario, *Dr. Strangelove* simply dismissed it. . . . Kennedy was dead and we lived on!"[6] For Capitol Records, the holidays were spent in overdrive. Company executives sensed a volcano rumbling and had pressing plants churn out copies of the "I Want to Hold Your Hand" / "This Boy" single and a debut album, *Meet the Beatles,* which plucked numbers from Parlophone's *Please Please Me* and *With the Beatles.* By January, radio had come to a boil, and the marketing campaign took hold. Americans now heard Beatle records daily, if not hourly, and the Christmas push ensured enough product for the deluge. A fierce scramble for advertising dollars erupted between competing stations, like WMCA, WABC, and WINS (Murray the K's third-place top-forty station) in Manhattan, all vying for teen ears. Running a radio contest promising T-shirts for airport visitors was simple and effective, even when demand far outgrew supply after the first thousand shirts ran out. Different numbers get reported, but Capitol's marketing campaign brought at least three thousand teenagers to the airport, and a fierce radio advertising war snowballed their exposure to a state of delirium—it took on a raucous momentum that found deejays staking out hotel lobbies and bribing stagehands.

The hype alone might have smothered less determined and charismatic acts. A lot of the media noise simply confirmed the cynicism then fueling the flimsy Broadway musical *Bye Bye Birdie*. In *Birdie*'s world, Ed Sullivan played pope, laying his hands on young performers and ushering them into a new status as mainstream celebrities. The nation gathered around his communal campfire each week to sanctify its most cherished stories of talent and self-invention. The Beatles upended this fable with an unforeseeable twist: here were British musicians performing previously American archetypes—and reviving the style as if it were somehow worthy of respect. As New York succumbed to Beatlemania, the UK screams got a jolt of American boosterism, with Liverpool cast as the new Bethlehem, and the Brits suddenly mystical, exotic avatars.

THE FLIGHT TO AMERICA was ripe with anticipation, nerves, and some pop-industry heavies catching a ride. The press pool included the *Evening Standard* reporter Maureen Cleave; the *Daily Express* photographer Harry Benson, who booked the exclusive shoot on the flight; and the *Liverpool Echo* reporter who shared a name with Beatle George Harrison.[7] Epstein sat in the economy cabin with the press while the Beatles stayed up front in first class. Beatle Harrison was coming down with the flu, but there were salesmen pitching trinkets, and stewardesses brought a stream of pens, bracelets, pillows, and plastic watches for the Beatles to look at for endorsement. Epstein was flooded with proposals and had set up Seltaeb ("Beatles" spelled backwards), the endorsement company, to handle these petty affairs. Nobody had ever made much money on trinkets.

Lennon sat next to Cynthia, alternately enthused and petrified. "I Want to Hold Your Hand" had changed the game, but there was the immediate, crushing question of whether they could meet sudden American expectation, especially where even Britain's biggest teen idol so far, Cliff Richard, had faltered. Lennon had talked openly with writer Michael Braun about their American jaunt and how slim their chances were. "After all," he had said, "Cliff went there and he died. He was fourteenth on a bill with Frankie Avalon," and George said that Richard's movie *Summer Holiday* was second feature at a drive-in in St. Louis.[8]

But successful British pop crossovers were actually more common than many assumed. The first British act of the modern era to reach *Billboard*'s number one was Vera Lynn, in 1952, with a song called "Forget-Me-Not." Lonnie Donegan, the skiffle king, actually appeared on *The Perry Como Show* with Ronald Reagan. The Tornados had scored a number one with "Telstar," Joe Meek's oddly futuristic junkyard production, in 1962. And as recently as November 1963, Dusty Springfield had had a hit with "I Only Want to Be with You." In Lennon's mind, fear sparred with these breakthroughs. He knew he had a chance; what he couldn't predict was how Beatlemania might translate. Was it merely a British fad? Would their softer material dilute their commitment to Chuck Berry and Little Richard? Or, conversely, would they need to ponce themselves up even more than Epstein already had to get over as big as they hoped?

Approaching Manhattan's intimidating spires, the pilot announced that there was a crowd down below. At first the Beatles thought a dignitary was landing ahead of them. Then the pilot clarified: there was a crowd waiting for them. "It was so exciting," Ringo said, "flying into the airport, I felt as though there was a big octopus with tentacles that were grabbing the plane and dragging us down into New York. America was the best. It was a dream, coming from Liverpool." McCartney distinctly remembered feeling all the worry fall away: "We thought, 'Wow! God, we have really made it.' I remember . . . the great moment of getting into the limo and putting on the radio, and hearing a running commentary on *us:* 'They have just left the airport and are coming towards New York City . . .' It was like a dream. The greatest fantasy ever."[9]

Once they descended from the plane—looking back at Benson for one of the few photographs of the police barricades below—Epstein had them stand on a Pan Am dais for a press conference. Expectations for a British pop band were low; Epstein knew the first flank could be crucial. If he could get stories running ahead of the Sullivan TV appearance that weekend, they'd gain a bigger audience. His hunch became an extraordinary media coup, flooding the airwaves and news programs with Beatle quips and giggling asides—once they were media fodder, the only question was how they might possibly live up to their publicity.

To their huge new audience they seemed natural and fresh and un-flappable, handy with a quip for any situation and with an unerring sense of how to keep the press off guard. But another glance at Michael Braun's *Love Me Do!*, the quickie biography that appeared in British shops in the fall of 1963, reveals how much of the Beatle persona was in place by the time "She Loves You" hit the charts in August 1963, and how much of the Beatles' repartee of February 1964 was well-rehearsed patter. When reporters started in with their inanities, the Beatles simply welcomed them to their ongoing party. "What do you think of Beethoven?" someone cried out, highlighting all the prevailing assumptions about pop music as trendy piffle. "Great—especially his poetry," Ringo responded on cue. In fact as detailed by Braun, this kind of thing had been an inside joke between the Beatles and the British press for several months. Press conferences had become a tired show-biz cliché ("How do you like your costar?"), but nobody expected pop stars to strip the form of its legitimacy. "Can you play us a song?" came another query. "No," Lennon said. "We need money first." These quips, now standard Beatle lore, quickly entered the American lexicon. Low expectations gave them spark; cheeky accents gave them sting. Pop stars one-upping Groucho Marx—now, that's news. And these were *British* pop stars. The American press succumbed to the swoon.

THEY LANDED IN NEW YORK on Friday, February 7, and the news cycle was ready for its upbeat weekend color story; Friday's quotes ran on that evening's news and in the next day's papers. Murray Kaufman—Murray the K—an insecure balding deejay who rang through to interview the Beatles by phone in their room at the Plaza, was obliged with station IDs and chatty quotes he reran for months on end. Kaufman inserted himself into the band's graces, but the Beatles found him perplexingly gauche. At one point during a live broadcast, Lennon called him a "wanker" (Scouser slang for "jerk-off"), daring him to figure out what it might mean.[10] Murray sprinted ahead, ignorantly preening just to have access. In America, such oblique Lennon vulgarities went in sideways, all the more charming for their inscrutability.

On Saturday, they held a rehearsal on the Sullivan TV set. Afterward, Epstein had set up a meeting with Rickenbacker's owner and president, Francis Hall, across Central Park. An astute marketer among musicians, Hall had noticed Lennon's Hamburg Rickenbacker from news clips and figured he could interest the Beatles in some newer models. Hall understood how territorial musicians feel about their instruments, so he brought along Toots Thielemans. Lennon remarked on his work with the George Shearing Quintet. "If it's good enough for George Shearing, it's bloody good enough for me," Lennon said. The scene undermines Lennon's exaggerated contempt for jazz. Lennon doubtless knew Thielemans's "Bluesette," his 1961 solo pop hit, which featured the great harmonica player and guitarist as a whistler. Lennon was so proud of this meeting he went back to Britain and bragged about it to Chris Roberts at the *New Musical Express*: "For the people who say we're not interested in music, we get the chance to meet a lot of great musicians and talk to them. This guy knocked us out."[11]

Sunday morning brought yet another rehearsal, and this time Harrison stayed in bed with the flu to rest up for the performance; Neil Aspinall stood on his stage marks for the cameras. In the afternoon, with George in place, the band taped "Twist and Shout," "Please Please Me," and "I Want to Hold Your Hand" on a new set for their third Sullivan appearance (broadcast on February 23, after their debut, live, later on the ninth and the Miami show on the sixteenth).

Ringo Starr remembered that rehearsal as both crucial and mind-numbingly frustrating: after run-throughs, they visited the control room to make adjustments to the sound board, making sure the balance levels between voices and instruments got flagged with chalk. While they went off to lunch, though, a cleaner came in and wiped all the chalk off the board.[12] These sound deficiencies marred Lennon's vocal mike.

But the overall impression the Beatles made bulldozed any balance problems. By Sunday evening, the momentum that had built up around the Beatles exploded into seventy-three million viewers, besting the Presley record of sixty million eight years before. Brian Epstein deserves credit, but no press agency would dare it: a smash hit, "I Want to Hold

Your Hand"; drawing kids out to the airport for a triumphant arrival on Friday; newspaper quips and adult misgivings throughout the weekend; a watershed first appearance on *The Ed Sullivan Show* that Sunday; and suddenly a huge, larger context loomed up—an all-conquering musical euphoria that swept aside all hesitation. The broadcast trumped even the arrival's hysteria, the press conference, even the hit single's juice, in a thrilling set that connected previously stray dots.

The size of the audience remains inexplicable; the musical galaxies that came into view still glow. At least half the fun was watching the Beatles, performing with preternatural self-confidence, light their sonic firecrackers right in Sullivan's staid living room, his embalmed stare suddenly the look of mummified Tin Pan Alley. "So you think America bounced back after the war, do ya?" their attitude chided, out-maneuvering witless Yanks at their own game. Attempting to smile back, Sullivan revealed a cosmic disconnect, sealing the Beatles' bond with their audience.

Cynicism took a holiday: the Beatles played right into Sullivan's variety-show format while transcending it. Their first number, a jaunty original ("All My Loving"), was followed by McCartney (the bassist!) singing "Till There Was You," from 1957's Broadway hit *The Music Man*. This took cheek—and this McCartney guy had cheeks to spare. How could a band so hip get away with such hokey sentimentality? It had to be a joke, right? (The arrangement, complete with flamenco acoustic guitar, was lifted off Peggy Lee's 1960 *Latin ala Lee!* album, which was not re- motely rock 'n' roll.) On the other hand, where did this joke land? On Sullivan? On parents? Elvis Presley had sung gooey ballads, sure; but that was almost the only rule he didn't break. The Beatles delivered this "girly" stuff with relish, as if scribbling delirious mash notes between tossing imaginary cherry bombs into the surrounding magic and comedy acts.[13] As with a lot of the pap their records sat next to on the pop charts, the Beatles ridiculed prevailing show-biz hackery simply by performing on the same bill; the rock 'n' roll slot made everything else seem hope- lessly dated.

This Sullivan set, combined with the *Meet the Beatles* LP fans were devouring, transformed a genre that was widely considered dead or dying. Critic Richard Meltzer called the Beatles' revival of rock 'n' roll "the biggest long-shot in the history of long-shots."[14] The idea that music by Chuck Berry and Buddy Holly and Little Richard could recapture a younger audience—indeed, find their songwriting royalties tilted upward through Beatles sales—was simply unimaginable, even as "I Want to Hold Your Hand" climbed the American charts in the wee hours of 1964.

By connecting so many dots hidden away in this glorious sound, the Beatles confirmed all the latent possibilities in the style, and promised much more. Cramming all of contemporary pop inside the same musical brackets as Chuck Berry, Carl Perkins, Little Richard, and Buddy Holly had radical, albeit counterintuitive, overtones. Right after "All My Loving," which tumbled out of them like a waterfall, they settled down into McCartney's doe-eyed "Till There Was You," which to the parents said *Music Man* and to the kids said "dreamboat." This one cover, easily the weakest number of the batch, accomplished the unthinkable: it rewrote the way Americans heard their own music history. Suddenly, in the course of an hour-length TV show, ideas that had lain dormant came alive, and connections were made that set off chain reactions in listeners' minds even before they had heard the band transform a novelty like "Twist and Shout," unfurl a peerless doo-wop sail like "This Boy," or spin something altogether original like "From Me to You." This shift was both audacious and comic: free-fall rock 'n' roll in the form of a good-bye song that erased heartache, segued without (much) irony into a soft-core standard from a Broadway musical. The simple contrast between these two numbers was old-fashioned show-business shorthand for "range," only without the pretense. It immediately endeared McCartney to mothers and gave pause to skeptics preparing their "noisy" pans.

To close that opening set, "She Loves You" was a Roman candle that kept on crackling after the final cadence; it told of unspeakable pleasures and dizzying thrills, a wild ride that shot past in a blur, cracking open rock's story along the way. Think of Presley's outrageous metaphors of freedom, the image of the all-American quarterback grabbing a black girl on the dance floor and strutting proudly through white middle-class living rooms. That image had been pressed back at the time of Presley's army stint and Buddy Holly's plane crash. Now the Beatles held out something even more intoxicating: long-haired foreigners interrupting the evening with such high comic spirits that they had the family at "All My Loving" and lit sparkles in everybody's hearts by "She Loves You." This musical punch went down so easy that by the time its spike kicked in you forgot where you were or how you'd gotten there. The impact spun a thousand heady questions on the tip of its "yeah, yeah, yeah" hook, and those delirious, high-harmony "Oooh"s turned everybody's mind to mush. The ratings signaled one kind of marker; these intangible musical effects of *The Ed Sullivan Show* appearance left all parties forever changed.

ROCK 'N' ROLL HAD ALWAYS given off a spirit of inclusion and guile, and the Beatles simply adopted that spirit as their own. Their choice of covers revealed an uncanny connection with everything progressive in pop, from Motown to girl groups. The girl-group material, especially, sent the signal that the Beatles came not just as conquerors, but conversationalists who engaged with the style as if it were some huge, ongoing argument of ideas. The band stormed its stage fully formed, and their "foreignness" hinted at larger, more daring implications.

The Sullivan audience, and fans who ran out to pick up Capitol's *Meet the Beatles,* heard galloping embrace, from swooning doo-wop ("This Boy") to rakish R&B ("I Saw Her Standing There"—an original in the Chuck Berry mold—and Arthur Alexander's "Anna"). Alongside their Little Richard and Carl Perkins covers, they slung Motown (Barrett Strong's "Money," Smokey Robinson's "You've Really Got a Hold on Me"), girl groups (the Marvelettes' "Please Mister Postman," the Shirelles' "Boys"), and soul raves that threw off giddy, intractable sparks. The Beatles were already tinkering with the style—exploiting new cracks in the sound, writing songs that implied even more than they delighted— the crashingly coy understatement of "I Want to Hold Your Hand," for example, or the way Lennon's attack on "You've Really Got a Hold on Me" was as much about love as it was about white regard for black, or British for American, style.

It has taken history to clarify how far the basic idea, the seed of all the mania, was actually borne out in the music itself, a point missed by too many scandal-driven biographers. As early as shows and radio appearances supporting "Love Me Do," listeners heard something new in the Beatles that few other pop groups had. It was far more radical than the simplistic explanations of white British "working-class" youth performing sturdy R&B. (This claim must always be qualified by Lennon's insistence on his grammar-school status—the American equivalent of a prep-school boy.) And while the R&B element in their sound was cued to the seasoned interplay between McCartney's bass and Ringo's teasingly expert offbeats, "Love Me Do" is richer even than this. The vocal harmonies on the word "Plea—ee—ee—ease" not only evoke the Everly Brothers, but raise an intriguing question: What if the country-duo-group tradition got hooked up with the Chicago-electric-blues tradition? What if this new band seemed "exotically" foreign, safe, and accessible enough to make the aesthetic argument seem not just persuasive but inevitable?

Range only began to make sense of how the Beatles were reframing American music. The Chuck Berry chassis that anchored songs like "I Saw Her Standing There," "Please Please Me," "She Loves You," and "I'll Get You" was offset by a softer, less pressing impulse, and some of these soft-pedaled songs even bore Lennon's fingerprints, especially "Ask Me Why," "All I've Got to Do," and "From Me to You." Chuck Berry wouldn't be caught dead singing such romantic pap. But the idea of Berry with a gang of buddies, maybe even a songwriting partner, made a different kind of musical sense, and only made Berry's impulses sound more contemporary.

In other words, the Beatles became symbolic of something much larger than themselves almost as quickly as they became surpassingly famous: toward a unity, a cross-fertilization and commingling of previously distinct musical strands. Almost as quickly as they became stars, they embodied an idea, a new myth about the music itself and how it might grow. Nobody had made these connections before, and now the future was whirring past in a blur of swaggering offbeats and enticing backup harmonies.

So THE CONTEXT OF KENNEDY's memorial to youth gave way to a new exhortation of youth on a grander scale, four-headed and beatific, arty yet giddy, foreign-looking yet somehow familiar-sounding, hilarious on the surface with strong undercurrents of seriousness, lust, and resolve, a sense that enormous shifts had already happened. There is no question that Beatlemania answered the Kennedy assassination, that there are ways in which these two events played off each other, required each other, just as Profumo sought a British antidote to scandal.

Not only was rock 'n' roll a vital, healthy style which many had taken for dead; it was abruptly redeemed—even better, most parents still despised it, making it a revolution in plain sight. From now on, and for at least the next decade, rock 'n' roll carried a subversive force within the mainstream that made it seem like truants were the new power brokers. As world politics grew increasingly complicated and interdependent, it brought the Beatles immense cultural prestige.

That this renewal came as a British import made even less sense, which in turn made it irresistible. It gave the Beatles their halo effect. Rock's second act began on a familiar stage with a transformational new context: these British youths, brash yet enchanting, new yet instantly recognizable, held up an astonishing cultural mirror to Americans. Their command of rock 'n' roll made it seem like they'd always known us, grinning strangers who had cracked our aesthetic DNA and were suddenly, inexplicably, lifelong friends.

AFTER A DAY OFF, as the papers reported the record-breaking *Sullivan Show,* the Beatles got on a train to Washington, D.C., for their first American concert, at the Washington Coliseum. Ringo, the new kid in Beatletown, was suddenly a star alongside the rest of them: "Being cheeky chappies saved our arses on many occasions, especially then, on the train to Washington, because the guys from the press had come to bury us. These reporters, being New Yorkers, would yell at us, but we just yelled back. . . . That's what endeared us to them."[15]

The Coliseum seated eight thousand fans and placed the Beatles on a stage in the center, like a boxing ring. Unaccustomed to their setup, they simply used their Vox amps and the house's public address system. There were no stage monitors and no sound check, so they had to balance their ensemble and vocals as they went along. Ringo had to turn his drum set around after every three songs when stagehands rotated the stage. And despite all this, the set is all conquest and hunkering down for the future—old scores are torn to shreds, and raw potential seeps out of every number. (The Maysles brothers include the set in their film.) If promise was a sound, it was the sound of that scream that Epstein and Oldham first marveled at the year before. They may not have been able to hear themselves, but rock tunesmith Marshall Crenshaw holds this set among his favorite Beatle moments: "They played as if they still had something to prove, which of course they did. . . . but nobody expected how much or how sure of themselves they already were. That sound has such thump to it, such force, it really is a proving ground for the Beatles as live musicians."[16]

Just as the royals had attached themselves to channel some Beatle heat, so, too, did political functionaries as the band passed through Washington. This kind of thing made Lennon feel like a trained seal: "We were supposed to put up with all sorts of shit from Lord Mayors and their wives, and be touched and pawed like in *A Hard Day's Night,* only a million times more. At the American Embassy or the British Embassy in Washington, some bloody animal cut Ringo's hair. I walked out, swearing at all of them, I just left in the middle of it."[17]

In Miami for the second *Sullivan Show,* the band hung out at their beach hotel, waved to the girls from their windows, and got photographed breaking out into song in the swimming pool for a famous *Life* photograph. It was the week before Sonny Liston fought the fast-talking Cassius Clay, and photographer Benson got the Beatles to do a publicity stunt with the young fighter.[18]

Here's an early peek into celebrity one-upmanship: who was rubbing up against more heat? Who would benefit from the publicity more, the Beatles or Clay? And the photos turned out to have a much bigger historical impact than anybody might have guessed at the time: peering back into February of 1964—with Clay not yet Ali, and the Beatles at the symbolic dawn of the 1960s—the civil rights movement, counterculture, and anti–Vietnam War sensibilities come alive in these pictures. It's an image of youth rebels mugging madly at stale institutions like segregation—and the only known photos of Lennon and Ali smiling across the canyon.

They also hit the clubs, one night catching insult comic Don Rickles, who brought the spotlight down on the band and cut loose, which made their awestruck British souls recoil. "If we'd had him on our own terms we could have made mincemeat out of him," Lennon said. Ringo remembered another cherished act they caught, and the gap they began to notice between their view of the style and America's: "We went out to see the Coasters, who were heroes with 'Yakety Yak.' People were *dancing* to them in the club, and I just couldn't understand it. These were rock-'n'-roll gods to me, and people were dancing! I was just so disgusted."[19]

A homecoming crowd swarmed their London arrival, far outnumbering the three thousand Americans who had greeted them in New York. British fans couldn't claim any self-respect if they let American fans out-obsess them simply by dint of population. The BBC filmed it as a news event and broadcast the return to triumphant prose during its Saturday-afternoon sports show *Grandstand*. "What did you think of America?" David Coleman asked. " 'It's bigger,' said Ringo.[20]

The American debut proved a watershed, but the Beatles kept moving. Epstein had them tape a *Big Night Out* performance for broadcast on February 29, and then pointed them back into the studio to finish the sound track for the feature film they would begin shooting in early March.

Their recording schedule registers a slew of new numbers, and a swift new authority in the studio. On the morning of February 25, George Harrison's twenty-first birthday, they laid down vocal and guitar overdubs for McCartney's "Can't Buy Me Love," the next single, which they had started recording in Paris, before nine takes of Lennon's "You Can't

Do That," which was slated for its B side. In the afternoon they recorded McCartney's "And I Love Her" in two takes and "I Should Have Known Better" in three. Martin dressed up "And I Love Her" with a key change for Harrison's flamenco acoustic guitar solo, and it sounded like the virgin offspring of "Till There Was You" and "P.S. I Love You," a choice weave of devotional lyric and worried melody that remains an early peak. Lennon ranked it among his partner's later classics like "Yesterday" and "Michelle." These sessions rang out with new vigor, as if all the hints dropped on their first two records had sprouted full-blown tracks.

Lennon and McCartney felt the pressure, and the songs made the necessary leap; heaps of adulation fueled grand creative gestures. All this new material would support their next venture, the full-length film Epstein had set up with comedy producer Walter Shenson. Shenson had come off two successful British comedies, 1959's *The Mouse That Roared*, with Peter Sellers, and its 1963 sequel, *The Mouse on the Moon*. This was the typical deal for a pop group: shoot a quick movie to cash in on its sound track. To hedge their bets, they hired a Beatles favorite, Wilfrid Brambell, from the hit TV series *Steptoe and Son,* to play McCartney's wayward grandfather.[21] On *Steptoe,* Brambell's son was always chiding his father for being a "dirty old man." Brambell was also Irish, an honorary Liverpudlian to British viewers. This sop to the TV audience meant the movie might at least break even. Epstein and Shenson brought in an American director who had worked in UK commercials, named Richard Lester, who had made a film with Sellers and Spike Milligan called *The Running Jumping & Standing Still Film.* He'd also directed *Mouse on the Moon* and *It's Trad, Dad.* The *Goon* connection won him Lennon's approval: "We didn't even want to make a movie that was going to be bad, and we insisted on having a real writer to write it."[22]

Lester led them to Alun Owen, a Liverpool playwright who wrote scripts for television's *Corrigan Blake* and *Armchair Theatre.* Owen had the aura of a Scouser's John Osborne, a working-class type who had popularized dissent onstage with the West End's *Progress to the Park* and *The Rough and Ready Lot,* and with *No Trams to Lime Street* for TV. Like Michael Braun, the American writer who scribbled down Beatle dialogue to drive his *Love Me Do!* paperback, Owen went on the road with the band in the fall of 1963 to observe the crowd phenomenon and write specifically for the band's situation; since they had never acted before, there was a great effort made to make them comfortable with lines and dealing with other actors on a film set. Casting them as themselves in a familiar situation ("a day in the life"—arriving in a town by train, rehearsing for a TV show, and making an escape) might help them over the most obvious imaginative hurdles.

Owen has never gotten the credit he deserves for capturing Lennon's character, from which the cruelty, womanizing, and homoerotic danger all seep out subtextually. This was the first fictionalization of "Lennon," and it went a long way toward introducing him in ways that still make more sense than not. As the seed to his ongoing persona, he couldn't have asked for better lines. As Braun had, Owen wove key ingredients of Beatles charm into the narrative. Lennon's character spars with Norm (Norman Rossington) cued by the Epstein chemistry, minus the sexuality. But in so many ways this "Lennon" character works as a soft-core version of the real thing, something he could upstage in real life. It's his "rattle your jewelry" line done up cinematically, and it signals his harsh side without indulging it. Owen rubs Lennon's edges down, but only metaphorically.

In the final cut, Lennon's presence is almost manically subdued. He plays "Lennon," the smartest, most impatient band member, while "Ringo" gets corraled by the grandfather's grandstanding. This version of Lennon has no need to break out and go "parading," he's keelhauling the parade from the inside. While Lennon went on record many times denouncing what he read as a watering-down of his sensibility, the movie's reputation rests even more on the script than on its direction. The music alone would have made it a huge hit; the dialogue made it a classic. "Give us a kiss," he tells the stiff old bag whining about his rights in the first-class train cabin. "I hereby declare this bridge . . . *open*," he opines in a campy falsetto, snipping a wardrobe fitter's tape measure. Disparaging the script rang of protest-too-much refusal: "We were a bit infuriated by the glibness of it. It was a good projection of one façade of us—on tour, in London and in Dublin. It was of us in that situation together, having to perform before people. We *were* like that. Alun Owen saw the press conference so he recreated it in the movie—pretty well; but we thought it was pretty phoney, even then."²³

This leap to film made all kinds of career sense, but it made Lennon wary in ways that puzzle most Americans. "The trouble is," Lennon told Braun after reading Owen's draft, ". . . it's only us who can write for us." His first line in the script had him saying, "Uh, who's your friend, Paul?" "I wouldn't say that," Lennon told Braun. "I'd just say, 'Who's the old crip?'"²⁴ This quote came before Lennon met with Lester, who, unlike many other directors, encouraged improvisation on his sets. Just observe Owen's scathing indictment of the nameless TV director in a tacky sweater, whom Victor Spinetti plays with imperious precision.

Owen casts Lennon as the wayward brain lost in a world of puffery. It's all here: the political indignation, the absurdity, the contempt for class distinctions, the offhanded attitude toward all manner of authority. Rock critic Lester Bangs ranted contrarily about the absurdity of Owen's "generation gap," how, in a way, Brambell would make more sense as Lennon's grandfather. "The Beatles were four yobs, or rather three yobs and a librarian named Paul," Bangs wrote. "Fuck the Beatles, fuck the songs, fuck the cute direction and Marx Brothers comparisons: it's BLA-TANTLY OBVIOUS that the most rock 'n' roll human being in the whole movie is the fucking grandfather! That wily old slime of Paul's! He had more energy than the four moptops put together! Plus the *spirit*! He was a true anarchist!"²⁵

But Bangs overlooks how his critique is at odds with Lennon in the rest of the film. Owen has Lennon confront the grandfather for an even better story. This grandfather, teeming with unsolicited candor, teaches our heroes how to sneak into restricted gambling clubs and pick up rich women. ("I'll bet you're a fine swimmer," he says to a heaving cleavage.) Even so, Lennon gets the last word, after they rescue him from the police station with Ringo, the film's climactic chase scene. "But I'm clean," he confides to Lennon, after a thousand retorts about how his hygiene some-how makes him "respectable." His parading over, he looks to Lennon for absolution. "Are ya?" Lennon shoots back, unfazed—he's had the old man's number all along.

And he's mocking every pretension in every scene while slipping straight-faced into poetically charged ballads like "If I Fell," looking on facetiously as McCartney sings "And I Love Her" even as he supports him, and radiating goodwill and infectious high spirits during filler like "I'm Happy Just to Dance with You" and "Tell Me Why," numbers that would be peaks in anybody else's set.

British audiences saw all these characters drawn with utmost scrutiny to class distinctions—how these "working-class" northerners tickle staid entertainment-bizzers to death. Spinetti's director is the kind of arrogant prima donna who's worked his way up to a "respectable" position and can't help dropping his class resentment into every conversation. "I've won awards, you know." "I could listen to him all day," Owen has Lennon say.

Spinetti remembers Lennon and the others as fit, game, and more winning than most through sheer charisma. "Lennon came up to me after our first day on the set together and said, 'When Dick shouts "Action!" the other actors jump up and become different people, but you stay the same. Does that mean you're as terrible as we are?'

"The banter that I heard on my first day never stopped," Spinetti recalls. After catching on to how scenes get wrapped and people hang out, the band became regular players in a floating crap game of conversation. "Soon I found myself sitting with these four young men, talking to them as if we had known each other our whole lives. It was something to do with all of us being provincials. I'd come up from Wales and they'd come down from Liverpool. I've made lots of films, but I've only met two other people like that—Richard Burton and Orson Welles."[26]

This mood fuels the movie's high spirits alongside its musical bounty: Harrison singing "I'm Happy Just to Dance With You" has all the family warmth behind it of older brothers prodding a sibling to take the reins; Lennon's rhythm guitar on this track kicks Harrison along like he's spurring a horse. Lennon's "I Should Have Known Better" sustains one long ripple effect of his careening harmonica; and "If I Fell" balances hesitant devotion on an emotional precipice. With McCartney's upper harmonies, the song gave Lennon's onscreen shell a hard-won vulnerability to make him the movie's most three-dimensional character.

Offstage, Lennon was described as a "hard case." That's what Epstein told his father, Alfred Lennon, when a newspaperman brought him around to meet his son on the movie set. This would be the first time the two had seen each other since that Blackpool scene in 1946 almost eighteen years before. Alfred claims to have been reluctant, in his memoirs, and the encounter appears to have been awkward but not hostile. Epstein reassured Lennon that despite what the papers were saying, he had no interest in "jumping on the band wagon," or asking for money. Alf writes that Lennon "vaguely remembered" being in Blackpool with his dad, but couldn't remember exactly when. They parted politely if ambivalently, but Alfred was soon short on cash, and sold his story for £200 to a publication called *Tit Bits*. On Epstein's advice, Lennon made Alfred a gift of £30, then put him on a weekly stipend of £12 to keep him quiet. This seemed to have worked for a while.[27]

WHILE THE BEATLES FILMED, the American charts played catch-up with all their British releases. The legendary *Billboard* charts dated April 4, 1964, showed Beatles singles monopolizing the top five slots, a first and a lasting record. It's more understandable knowing that American listeners were simply devouring British records made throughout 1963, as the UK recording dates show:

Billboard's Top Five Singles, Week Ending April 4, 1964

1. *"Can't Buy Me Love"* (1964)
2. *"Twist and Shout"* (1963)
3. *"She Loves You"* (1963)
4. *"I Want to Hold Your Hand"* (1963)
5. *"Please Please Me"* (1963)

Somehow this legend obscures the comet's tail: seven more Beatles singles listed throughout the top hundred. Swan cashed in on Capitol's marketing: "She Loves You" bumped "Hand" off the top slot at the end of January; and by March, Vee-Jay scored with "From Me to You," neither of which Capitol had yet released. Even a Vee-Jay subsidiary like Tollie put out "There's a Place" and "P.S. I Love You," and MGM hustled the old Hamburg Tony Sheridan tracks into success by February. Capitol was being punished for its oversight; although every company was simply working overtime to fill a demand that might have gobbled up even more records had there been any.

Finally, there was another Lennon-McCartney on *Billboard*'s top hundred: "World Without Love," from Peter and Gordon (which Billy J. Kramer had rejected as too soft). And as famous as this *Billboard* top five record remains, even that was trumped down under, where the Beatles monopolized the top *six* Australian chart positions. As Americans dealt with this four-headed monster set loose over top forty radio, the British checked front pages for leaks from the movie set.

The group's last day of shooting (April 24) pressed up against a TV special (*Around the Beatles*), Scottish dates in Edinburgh and Glasgow, and BBC radio tapings (*From Us to You*), before a three-week holiday in May, their last break of the year.

John, Cynthia, and young Julian Lennon had been living in a temporary London apartment that spring. John had bought a family home outside London and hired decorators to overhaul its interior. At least outwardly, he seemed to be investing in some fantasy of domesticity. The three of them finally moved into their new house, called Kenwood, in Weybridge, Surrey, but had to live up in the attic as renovations dragged on. It was yet another delayed homecoming. To soften the blow, Lennon took his wife off to Tahiti for a vacation, via Amsterdam and Honolulu, with George Harrison and Pattie Boyd, a model he'd met on the film set. Epstein booked them as Mr. and Mrs. Leslie and Mr. Hargreaves and Miss Bond. During the first days of travel the press caught up with them in Hawaii, but after a first day getting used to their boat ("Cynthia and I were feeling sick and puked everywhere," Harrison remembered), they had some privacy, swimming and snorkeling and sailing from island to island.[28]

June and July saw Australia and New Zealand erupt with echoes of the mania that had visited the Beatles in America (Cynthia had to finish settling into Kenwood alone with Julian). Nobody wanted to carry on without Ringo Starr, sidelined with tonsillitis, but the band was pressured to keep its commitments; Epstein could simply not figure when he could squeeze in rain dates with the year so crowded. A session man named Jimmy Nicol played at being a Beatle for three weeks until Ringo rejoined the tour. Reporters were waiting for the band when they returned to London. Lennon wanted to get the rumors out of the way first: they had *not* been pelted with eggs from "non-diggers."

Unlike their first three albums, their fourth LP (to be called *Beatles for Sale*) competed for studio time with near-constant world touring between May and September. Tracks took shape as a patchwork of sessions scattered across several months between live gigs and TV shows. Two sessions just before their American tour inched them toward an album sequence, with two new songs and two new covers: on August 11, they worked up fourteen takes of "Baby's in Black," and three days later came "I'm a Loser" (eight takes), "Mr. Moonlight" (four takes), and "Leave My Kitten Alone" (five takes), which got held. On their way back to the States, they did a gig at the Opera House in Blackpool with a mod band called the High Numbers, soon to be the Who. The next morning, on August 18, they flew from London to San Francisco (with refueling stops in Winnipeg and Los Angeles), where nine thousand screaming fans greeted them.

In the six months since the *Ed Sullivan Show* appearances, North American audience fever had grown. That first trip had been a tease, and a marketing coup. For the summer, fans waited anxiously to see and hear them in their hometowns. Epstein booked twenty-seven concerts in twenty-five cities over thirty days, including such onetimers as Jacksonville, Florida, and Ontario, Canada, cities that would never see the band again. Booked at $50,000 per show in large municipal arenas, the Beatles grossed more than a million dollars in ticket sales alone. Beatlemania swelled: *A Hard Day's Night* had proved a major summer hit, so they returned as titans, not upstarts. Beatlemania had only one setting: more.

Fan idolatry began to worry people, and not just the inner circle. As the Beatles worked their way through airports and hotels and found themselves even more hemmed in than before, there were fewer daring escapes, and increasingly complicated evasive maneuvers. The Beatles insisted that Epstein hire his own security detail after a shortage of policemen in Toronto put them at serious risk. Most local police forces were overwhelmed, and improvised with overtime detail, but all of them were learning the game as they went along. Everybody agreed: this was a completely new level of crowd numbers and hysteria, which made those chase scenes from *A Hard Day's Night* look tame.

Perhaps Epstein thought the schedule was reasonable, but the sheer press of people proved exhausting, and summoned mixed emotions: this was adulation beyond the band's wildest dreams, but it was also fierce and defensive daily work that involved enormous compromises to everyday dignities. And it put their fantasy America, the wild Chuck Berry world of burgers and shakes, where they had forged their love for the music, into vivid relief.

A young reporter named Larry Kane, from Miami, joined the tour, selected by Epstein as a regular because his business card made him look like the news director for Florida's tiny WFUN. In truth, he was green, and ambivalent about his assignment—a hard-news guy who resented getting sent out on this teenybopper story. His basic decency turned him into a lifelong Lennon friend.

From way back, Lennon had had a coarse habit of insulting whoever approached him, as a way of screening out jerks, poking people to find out where they lived. This approach intensified with fame. Kane remembers the first time Lennon greeted him with scorched earth charm. Kane had flown from Miami to San Francisco on August 19. After a meeting of the press entourage with Derek Taylor, the PR liaison, he dropped by to meet the Beatles in their hotel suite, only to be accosted by Lennon. "Why are you dressed like a fag ass, man? What's with that? How old are you?" Epstein turned red. Kane decided to punch back: "Well, it's better than looking scruffy and messed up like you." Lennon simply stared.

Kane played a hunch and switched subjects: he asked Lennon about Vietnam. This caught Lennon by surprise. Kane watched his face light up, and listened to a "scathing diatribe" against the Gulf of Tonkin Resolution, just passed on August 7. President Johnson had rammed the measure through Congress to begin escalating American troop buildup in Southeast Asia. "I was taken aback by the intensity of his anger and knowledge base," Kane wrote, "and also by the eloquence of his protest." Kane left not knowing what to think, but on his way back to his room he felt a tap on his shoulder: "Hey, really enjoyed the interview," Lennon said, "specially about the war in Asia. Liked the talk. Look forward to more stuff. Sorry about the clothes bullshit."[29]

The combination of Kane's comeback and his challenging political question had won Lennon over. And it told Kane something peculiar about Lennon: he had a fervent political conscience, read the papers, and felt completely at ease discussing American world politics as President Johnson connived his way into the war. It would not be the last time the two discussed Vietnam.

Somewhere the band had mentioned that they liked jelly beans, and suddenly it was hard for them to get through a number without feeling the hard candy shells hitting their bodies onstage. The opening night of the tour, San Francisco's Cow Palace, had to be stopped twice because the band was getting pelted. Police came onstage and pretended to impose order. Even at this early stage, Kane remembers, there was a quality of mania spinning out of control. Afterward, a plane was waiting to take the entourage to Las Vegas. "How did it feel out there?" Kane asked Lennon.

"Not safe," Lennon replied. "Can't sing when you're scared for your life."[30]

The Sahara Hotel was hopping with girls when the Beatles' limousine pulled up in the early morning after their postconcert from San Francisco. Private hotel detectives shepherded the band in and up to the twenty-third floor, where Epstein had booked his typical entire floor for the Beatles and the touring party. Kane had barely fallen asleep before he awoke to a heavy knocking at 5 A.M. He opened his door to Neil Aspinall's new roadie, Malcolm Evans. "We need you. Can you put on a tie and jacket?" Evans, Derek Taylor, and Aspinall asked him a favor: would he go down to the lobby and explain to a worried mother that her twin girls were all right—even though they'd been found unchaperoned in John Lennon's bedroom? They were among a parcel of girls who had penetrated security and threatened to puncture the Beatles' clean image with scorching headlines. Kane took a deep breath and bailed Lennon out, even though he had no idea what the circumstances may have been. This earned him a trusted place in the tour's inner circle.

Another incident told of how Lennon tested even trusted confidants. During the flight from Las Vegas to Seattle, Kane heard the word "kike" leak out of the rear of the plane, where the Beatles and Taylor were seated. He heard it again and couldn't contain himself. He headed straight to the Beatles' small compartment, stuck his head in, and said, "Listen. I just wanted to say that I heard a word that really pisses me off. I'm Jewish, and I won't stand for that crap. I mean, whoever said it, can't you think before you talk?" Everybody blanched. Kane returned to his seat and figured he had just handed in his pass.

After a few minutes, Taylor came forward to put things right, taking the fall even though Kane knew it was not his voice. "Doesn't matter. It was said nonetheless. I'm sorry," Taylor replied. Soon Lennon came up to sit with Kane. "We had a relaxed and compassionate conversation about the roots of prejudice in Liverpool," Kane recalled. Standing up to Jewish slurs was not Epstein's style: he was treated like a brother for the rest of the tour. Even as a hard-core news guy, Kane was astonished at how big the Beatle story was as it kept unfolding. Epstein caved in and hired a private security detail at every concert. In Montreal, 150 people were treated for injuries after the crowd swarmed the band's brief set. "American audiences were not just shrill and manic," Kane remembered, "they seemed to want to devour their idols whole."[31]

On their first trip to New York since doing *The Ed Sullivan Show* six months prior, Ronnie Bennett hooked up again with Lennon at the Warwick Hotel, their base for the area's gigs in Forest Hills and Atlantic City. Murray the K called her to hitch a ride up to the Beatles' suite so he could do interviews: the Ronettes, he knew, were on the band's official guest list. When Ronnie walked into the hotel suite that afternoon, she remembers Lennon turning cynical about the vast array of refreshments. "We're prisoners up here," he said, "so they have to feed us well." After Murray finished his yapping and had his photo taken with the Ronettes and the Beatles, John and George and Ronnie and the others sat down on the floor, spun records, and talked all afternoon.

By evening, Ronnie sensed a change come over the scene. "A lot of the people who'd been hanging around during the afternoon had already left, and as I looked around, I noticed that there seemed to be a lot more young girls in the suite than there were when the press was hanging around earlier. You didn't have to be a genius to figure out that a whole new kind of scene was about to start."[32]

One of the bedrooms seemed to exert a special pull. "C'mon," Lennon said to her. "Don't you want to see what's so interesting?"

By this point, of course, all kinds of rumors swirled around the Beatles' activities. They were well-known partiers, and any kind of date conferred immense status.

But the bedroom scene Ronnie described in her memoir reeks of adolescent exhibitionism. "When people saw that I was with John, they kind of moved aside, and that's how I got my first clear view of the naked girl on the bed," having sex with one of the Beatles' entourage. "I guess it was enough to just be in the same hotel suite as them, as if that gave her something to tell her grandchildren." For Ronnie, then a virgin, the whole spectacle had a surreal air, of deeply forbidden acts suddenly enacted as ritual. "This was 1964," she wrote, "when you couldn't even get films with that stuff in them—and here was an actual girl having naked sex in every different position!"

With Ronnie on his lap, on a "ringside seat," Lennon couldn't hide his arousal. She felt a mix of discomfort and odd curiosity. "I was all ready to leave the hotel, but for some reason I didn't particularly mind staying, either. As strange as that whole situation was, I was never the least bit nervous around John. I felt secure around him." For all his lust, she was moved by something else in him.

Lennon led her into his bedroom to "recapture" the atmosphere they had shared in London. "He stood behind my chair and let his hands fall down on the back of my neck. It felt so good that I had to remind myself that I couldn't be doing stuff like this." With all her might, she gently started telling John about her romance with Phil Spector. He interrupted. "I know all about you and Phil. I just thought you and I might have something, too." Despite his persistence, she left without incident.

Lennon called her up the next day announcing a great escape, asking her advice on where to find some good eats. Ronnie picked John and George up and took them to her favorite barbecue haunt in Harlem, Sherman's, at 151st and Amsterdam, where she and Lennon wordlessly settled into a friendship. She reported no more romantic encounters.[33]

A FIFTY-YEAR VANTAGE makes it hard to appreciate how suddenly everything was happening, and how much pressure Epstein felt about taking advantage of the moment. Martin asked for two albums per annum in addition to quarterly singles. At a time when pop was disposable, in a business sector where every flash of success was fleeting at best, the Beatles were constantly pitched the question "What will you do when the bubble bursts?" as if it were theirs to control, or they had any spare moments for reflection. Answering this question across America became a chore and then a joke and then a tiresome existential broken record.

According to press agent Tony Barrow, Lennon still insisted on humiliating his manager. John walked in on Epstein and Barrow one day, "beaming broadly," shook Tony's hand, and walked over to where Epstein was sitting. "At the last moment John's hand plunged down to Epstein's groin and he grabbed hold of his testicles and held on tightly. Epstein involuntarily gasped in pain and my eyes watered in sympathy. Still grinning broadly and gripping relentless John simply said: 'Whoops!' " Shocked and disgusted, Barrow could barely speak. "This happened in 1964 at a point in time where John and the other Beatles still seemed to have a great deal of respect for Epstein—far too much, I thought, to do something like this to him, especially in front of any third party." Like other staffers who recall such scenes, Barrow concluded that Lennon had deliberately humiliated Epstein in front of an employee. "If I had not been in the room I don't think he would have bothered."[34] Flaunting perversion to both love interests and colleagues seems to have been a Lennon specialty.

Epstein's ham-fisted scheduling led to disjointed recording sessions between bouts of travel. Three final sessions in late September and early October gave them enough tracks (fourteen) for the next album, although by this point it was happening in such a flurry that all sense of continuity evaporated. On the last day of September, they laid down three more originals: "Every Little Thing," "What You're Doing," and "No Reply," which Lennon had originally offered to Billy J. Kramer. October 2 and 3 saw them rehearsing and taping an appearance on the American TV show *Shindig!* On October 6 they whipped off "Eight Days a Week," thirteen takes, during which a stray "I Feel Fine" guitar lick popped up, and two days later, "She's a Woman" sprang out of them.

The next morning, on Lennon's twenty-fourth birthday, they launched a seven-day tour of Britain opening in Bedford and finishing in Hull. October 18 found them back at EMI to work on "Eight Days a Week," "Mr. Moonlight," "Kansas City," and five new numbers, two of which were originals: Lennon's "I Feel Fine," and McCartney's "I'll Follow the Sun." The others were Carl Perkins's "Everybody's Trying to Be My Baby," Chuck Berry's "Rock and Roll Music," and, finally, Buddy Holly's "Words of Love." This streak finished off product for the Christmas market deadline and measured their determination at turning so many bullet points into solid work (even if slightly less pronounced than the *Hard Day's Night* all-original breakthrough). And still they kept moving: the next day they mounted another week-long UK sprint, opening in Edinburgh and landing in Brighton. When they returned, they laid down "Honey Don't," remade "What You're Doing," and tore comic holes in the Christmas-record script that Tony Barrow had prepared for their fan club. Then they hit the stage again for a two-week tour, from Exeter through Dublin and back to Bristol. November eased up a little, but included three TV appearances—on *Thank Your Lucky Stars, Top of the Pops,* and *Ready Steady Go!*—a BBC radio taping, and Lennon's appearances to publicize his now-best-selling book, *In His Own Write.*

IN THE UK, SOME OF THE BIGGEST aftershocks from Beatlemania coursed through the unlikely world of high literary culture. To this crowd, a pop star making girls scream had fairly obvious apocalyptic overtones. But a pop star setting off debate about modern verse—now, that was something so far beyond the establishment's grasp that their embrace seems almost craven. Michael Braun had became intrigued with some pages Lennon passed along to him during 1963 and showed them to his editors. The punning title gathered a sprawling assortment of absurdity through disjointed prose, cartoons, and verse that cleared the low hurdle of a quickie riding on its author's notoriety.

Perhaps because the Beatles commanded enormous space across the country's newspaper real estate, Bob Dylan seemed the far more likely music figure to assume the mantle of bard, or at the very least start issuing volumes of poetry. Already, Dylan attracted British esteem as a "poet," long before this debate started up in America, and allowed skeptics to disdain Lennon as a mere pop star while Dylan still wore his acoustic folkie halo. Many writers gloss over how Dylan's leap to rock 'n' roll during the coming season came as a far greater shock to British sensibilities than it did to American ears. For Lennon to issue verse in book form ahead of Dylan had a kind of weird British advance revenge to it, as though they could not just conquer American music but best them at the word game as well, and who better to do so than the giant pop star whose brains were obviously way too advanced for this rock stuff he would surely grow out of?

Lennon and Dylan began to spar in the British imagination, the antic Scouser who always threatened to go round the bend against the oddly prolific American whose epic abstractions quite nearly absolved him of being Jewish. Since *In His Own Write*'s release on April 7, 1964, reviewers had gone overboard to praise Lennon's unlikely literary success while conservative scribblers—like that old man on *A Hard Day's Night*'s train—lambasted yet another example of youth's ingratitude. *In His Own Write* became another Beatlemania sideshow that gave Lennon's pop stature heft.

As it had in Bill Harry's *Mersey Beat,* Lennon's verse boasts such a loopy, scabrous energy people overlooked how much subversion lay embedded in its cryptic asides. Two quotes followed this first publication around. The first came from a review from London's *Times Literary Supplement:* "It is worth the attention of anyone who fears for the impoverishment of the English language and British imagination." (Not many read the succeeding phrase: "Humorists have done more to preserve and enrich these assets than most serious critics allow.")[35] The other comes from Lennon himself, who arrived hungover to accept the Foyles Literary Prize at a luncheon, unaware that he was expected to give a formal speech. "Thank you, you've got a lucky face" was how the press quoted his mumbled thank-you, and the fiasco, a narrowly fumbled embarrassment, scored as a win.

McCartney wrote the dedication, declaring that absolutely none of it made much sense, and didn't need to. In a blur, the term "Joycean" became attached to Lennon's prose, as if he were somehow the great Irish bard's bastard son, when the truth was Lennon had never so much as read anything by Joyce. When he finally did, his quote was priceless: "It was like finding Daddy." Lennon and Joyce make a pair in how they contort many of the same techniques and treat language as a rubbery material through which they stretch their thoughts. But the Joyce label does a disservice to Lennon precisely because it springs completely unburdened by the influence; and while the means can be similar, the ends are completely different.

Paradoxically, an American Joyce scholar, James Sauceda, turned in the best analysis of Lennon's prose in a book called *The Literary Lennon: A Comedy of Letters* (1983). Sauceda has a good feel for Lennon's tactics and knows how and when to make the more enlightened Joyce comparisons. Lennon's prose has the unusual quality of begging for more attention and threatening to suffer from overpraise. He clearly addressed many of these ideas better through music, even when you wish he'd written a "Dead Dog Walking" song. (The best musical analogy to "Unhappy Frank" might be "I Am the Walrus," which is a good deal more oblique and less cunning.)

Tortured spellings turn into puns, and word mashing creates poetry out of unlikely collisions. Instead of "witty," Lennon writes "writty," mashing "witty" and "writing" or "written" into a single pregnant word. Sauceda notes how a lot of this overlaps with some of Joyce's own wordplay, including some key words like "bored" for "born" in *Finnegans Wake,* so the serendipities can be striking. But they are only serendipities. Similarly, in "All Abord Speeching," "abord" can mean both "about" and "aboard," and "speeching" enfolds both "speaking" and "teaching."

Sauceda notes how many details Lennon gets correct in his gibberish back-cover autobiographical sketch, "About the Awful," like Hitler's single testicle (which Lennon calls a "Heatlump," neatly combining the physical attribute and the reverse reproductive imperative).

Sauceda's keen insights, however, don't plumb the biographical aspects of Lennon's work here; and now that Aunt Mimi's pedantry and John's Oedipal rage become clearer, several themes leap out. The first is Lennon's fondness for dogs, both as a symbol for the Beatles (in the drawing on page II, "Drawing Two") and in morbid tales like "Good Dog Nigel." In "Nigel," he uses the name of his Quarry Bank mate Nigel Walley—the only witness to Judy's death—for a sick verse about a happy dog who's about to be killed, just as Mimi put his dog, Sally, down one weekend while he was away at Julia's. To the Beatles and their circle, these references would have been sharp, piquant to the point of tragic.

Only McCartney would have identified with how bent humor can express the utter futility that follows losing one's mother in adolescence. "Unhappy Frank" also doubles as a screed against "mother," both Mimi and Julia, for overprotection and lack of attention, respectively: "Wart am I but a slave tow look upon with deesekfrebit all the peegle larfing and buzing me in front of all the worled." Injecting pidgin German into this rant only magnifies the regimented enslavement portrayed as boyhood.

Having squeaked through the Foyles luncheon with a deathless misquote, Lennon agreed to appear with Peter Cook and Dudley Moore on their experimental new television show, *Not Only . . . But Also,* at the end of November 1964. They set it up as a twist on the tired cliché of the author making a guest appearance merely to read from his book, and Lennon seemed relieved at not having to wear his Beatle mask. Moore prefaced Lennon's appearance with an anticlimactic apology, as if readying the TV audience for some audacious experiment it couldn't be trusted to enjoy, especially at a phase when rock stars couldn't possibly put two sentences together. "Poetry and music," he intoned drily, "this uneasy marriage of the arts has caused a lot of controversy for a long time; many opinions are for and many against. We leave you to judge for yourselves. . . . What we're going to show you is a visualization and 'musicification' of a poem of a young poet named John Lennon. The poem is called, quite simply, 'Deaf Ted, Danoota, (and me).'" Then Lennon began to read from *In His Own Write,* with the camera crosscutting to several different readers, with awkward pauses and miscued laugh lines going south— none of which distracted from the rhythmic authority of the verse. On the line "Sometimes we bring our friend, Malcolm," actor Norman Rossington appeared with "Malcolm" scrawled across his forehead. Additionally, Rossington and Moore read "Unhappy Frank." Right at the end of the program, as the credits were rolling to Moore's signature tune "Goodbye-ee," John flitted maniacally in front of the camera, as if escaping from his minders.

13

Watching the Wheels

AT THE BEGINNING OF 1965, A NEW BEATLES STATURE SETTLED IN over the rest of pop, and it's worth stepping back to view the larger frame to see how broadly their influence stretched. An onslaught of 1965–66 hits, from both sides of the Atlantic, now form the core of "Classic Rock," that slippery conundrum of a style that was all about the Ongoing Now. While the Beatles set this boom in motion, competing talent created new substreams, many of which quickly expanded into new genres. All of it worked as metaphor for the ideas and attitudes the songs reflected, a social upheaval that seemed to dance.

Ascendants like the Rolling Stones and Bob Dylan turned in defining skyscrapers ("Satisfaction," then "Like a Rolling Stone"); a thriving middle class set up shop in the musical suburbs (the Beach Boys, the Byrds, the Hollies); and a staunch underground yowled of unrest still to come (the Animals, the Kinks, the Who, the Sonics). Week after confounding week, early Beatle promise became manifest in single after dazzling rock single, tracks that would dominate radio playlists for decades. And while reigning over the pop world in 1965 with four singles ("Eight Days a Week," "Ticket to Ride," "Help!," and "We Can Work It Out"/"Day Tripper"), each a powerhouse of a different stripe, the Beatles created ripples that were often as tempting as the hits themselves.

The larger irony of Lennon's creative arc resides in how this emerging middle period—*Rubber Soul* in late 1965, *Revolver* in 1966, and *Sgt. Pepper* in 1967—drew from all this chart activity to harness a new authority: through his ears, and the Beatles' ensemble, the rock album grew more conceptual than a mere sequence of discrete songs. The historical nuances steering this larger story touch on all the extremes the Beatles toyed with in their sound.

Hindsight deprives contemporary listeners of the Pervasive Now that that season's hits encircled, one of those thrillingly rare collisions of artistry with popular taste that ranks with F. Scott Fitzgerald's novels in the 1920s and 1930s, Charlie Chaplin's and Alfred Hitchcock's films, or the rash of subversive TV sitcoms like *Roseanne* and *Seinfeld* throughout the 1990s. Top 40 radio streamed intoxicating musical perfumes. Nearing fifty years later, simply scanning these charts can give you tingles: in December 1964, Phil Spector released his last great micro-epic from the Righteous Brothers, "You've Lost That Lovin' Feeling," a huge international hit, which zipped past the Zombies' "Tell Her No," a refusal so enticing that Lennon approached the band about producing. March brought Motown's lithe, ethereal "My Girl" by the Temptations, which seemed to glide on an idealized plane summoned by the civil rights movement. Listeners got lost in such delirium, but there were too many distractions to linger: "My Girl" got bumped aside by "Eight Days a Week," atop for two weeks, and then by the commanding cry of "Stop! In the Name of Love" by the Supremes. "The Last Time," the Rolling Stones' first Jagger-Richards original Stones hit, came careening around the next corner, a guitar's dagger to the heart of disaffected cool. Come May, Lennon's cunning "Ticket to Ride" held firm atop Ringo's white-hot delayed drum patterns, alongside "Help Me, Rhonda" by the Beach Boys, a Rubik's Cube of vocal harmonies.

This was all foreplay for that summer's avalanche, each hit more tantalizing than the last, variety chasing experiment. June alone brought a lusty "Back in Your Arms Again" by the Supremes, the confessional "I Can't Help Myself" by the fiercely proud Four Tops, and a shimmering, magisterial incantation of Dylan as electric prophet in "Mr. Tambourine Man" from the Byrds. You could have freeze-framed rock history right there and called it a golden era. But July served up two giant set pieces: the Stones' "(I Can't Get No) Satisfaction" (rock as carnal unrest) and Dylan's "Like a Rolling Stone" (rock as bottomless, implacable, leering social unrest).

For Dylan, this electric assault threatened to suck the air out of everything else, only there was too much radio oxygen to suck. "Like a Rolling Stone" was the giant, all-consuming anthem of the new "generation gap" disguised as a dandy's riddle, a dealer's come-on. As a two-sided single, it dwarfed all comers, disarmed and rejuvenated listeners at each hearing, and created vast new imaginative spaces for groups to explore both sonically and conceptually. It came out just after Dylan's final acoustic tour of Britain, where his lyrical profusion made him a bard, whose tabloid accolade took the form of political epithet: "anarchist." As caught on film by D. A. Pennebaker's documentary *Don't Look Back,* the young folkie had already graduated to rock star in everything but instrumentation. "Satisfaction" held Dylan back at number two during its four-week July hold on *Billboard*'s summit, giving way to Herman's Hermits' "I'm Henry the Eighth, I Am" and Sonny and Cher's "I Got You Babe" come August, novelty capstones to Dylan's unending riddle. (In Britain, Dylan stalled at number four.) The ratio of classics to typical pop schlock, like Freddie and the Dreamers' "I'm Telling You Now" or Tom Jones's "It's Not Unusual," suddenly got inverted. For cosmic perspective, yesterday's fireball, Elvis Presley, sang "Do the Clam."

Most critics have noted the Dylan influence on Lennon's narratives. Less space gets devoted to Lennon's effect on Dylan, which was overt: think of how Dylan rewires Chuck Berry ("Subterranean Homesick Blues") or revels in inanity ("Rainy Day Women #12 & 35"). Even more telling, Lennon's keening vocal harmonies in "Nowhere Man," "And Your Bird Can Sing," and "Dr. Robert" owed as much to the Byrds and the Beach Boys, high-production turf Dylan simply abjured. Lennon also had more stylistic stretch, both in his Beatle context and within his own sensibility, as in the pagan balalaikas in "Girl" or the deliberate amplifier feedback tripping "I Feel Fine." Where Dylan skewed R&B to suit his psychological bent, Lennon pursued radical feats of integration wearing a hipster's arty façade, the moptop teaching the quiet con.

Building up toward *Rubber Soul* throughout 1965, Beatle gravity exerted subtle yet inexorable force in all directions. Roger McGuinn of the Byrds spoke ecstatically about leaving *A Hard Day's Night* determined to form a band, and built his sound around Harrison's jangling Rickenbacker electric twelve-string, used in the title song's delirious opening chord and closing arpeggio—which seemed to imply all things to all listeners. Within a year McGuinn had steered his folkie taste into folk-rock, turning Dylan's "Mr. Tambourine Man" into a space-age duet threaded between neon guitars. Everywhere there was inexorable melody; everywhere there was booming, luxurious beat.

REMARKABLY, LENNON AND THE BEATLES surveyed this vast new world of sound and ideas under expert cover as bubblegum pop stars. The previous fall, of 1964, had seen the band turn sideways (with *Beatles for Sale*), but only in the way comets dip from view. In this new climate, they absorbed their surroundings and pushed back with better material, more ideas, and a newly relaxed confidence even as their schedule hastened forward. No matter how relentlessly Epstein packed their calendar, their minds always seemed to be leaping out ahead.

After finishing the group's second annual Christmas Show at the Odeon on January 16, 1965 (capping three weeks of nearly twice-daily performances), John and Cynthia Lennon flew off to Switzerland with George Martin and his soon-to-be second wife, Judy Lockhart-Smith, leaving Julian with their new housekeeper, Dot Jarlett. Only the Alps would do for Lennon to practice skiing for ten days in anticipation of the next movie's Austrian sequences. One night, Lennon broke out for Martin a new song he had been working on to cheer the producer up after an injury. It bore the working title "This Bird Has Flown." The rest of the time he scribbled to meet a publishing deadline for the literary followup to *In His Own Write*. He returned to six weeks of filming and a summer of touring the world's stages. Epstein had mapped out another European tour for July, with a live TV broadcast from Paris, followed by another major American tour in August and at least one concert in Mexico (which was later scrapped).

It's telling that Lennon sat on this song, "This Bird Has Flown," for several months. The band began recording material for its second film as director Dick Lester rewrote the script to accommodate some vacation, with sequences set in the Bahamas as well as in Austria. The plot leapt unevenly from life inside the Beatle bubble to broad James Bond parody. As the Beatles recorded and Lester preproduced, Epstein flew to New York to arrange the August tour schedule, under strict instructions about how their second U.S. tour would scale back from the manic pace of the first. Although amenable, he couldn't resist making trade-offs in the number of dates versus larger venues. One of his earliest bookings came from a Manhattan meeting with Sid Bernstein, who was anxious to follow up 1964's Carnegie Hall dates at a more profitable space. The year before, Bernstein had walked Epstein down to Madison Square Garden for a look-see. Now he suggested an even bigger venue.

These deals went forward as fans read the Beatles' *Playboy* interview (in the February 1965 issue), which hit newsstands over Christmas 1964. This high-profile exchange included a prescient discussion of religion, with distinctions between "atheism" and "agnosticism" from all four. Are any of you churchgoers? *Playboy* asked. "Not particularly," Paul offered. "But we're not antireligious. We probably seem antireligious because of the fact that none of us believe in God."

Lennon assented: "If you say you don't believe in God, everybody assumes you're antireligious, and you probably think that's what we mean by that. We're not quite sure 'what' we are, but I know that we're more agnostic than atheistic. . . . The only thing we've got against religion is the hypocritical side of it, which I can't stand. Like the clergy is always moaning about people being poor, while they themselves are all going around with millions of quid worth of robes on. That's the stuff I can't stand." The only sin worse than piety, Lennon argued, was hypocrisy. When the interviewer asked if Lennon was speaking for himself or for the entire group, he shot back: "For the group." And George added, "John's our official religious spokesman."[1]

Too bad for Hefner's hot tub, these comments went unnoticed—the world was still too enamored of Beatle magic to take umbrage. And with four individuals, the entertainment wires had plenty to report. Ringo

Starr married Maureen Cox in February at the Caxton Hall registry office, with Lennon and Epstein standing beside him, while Paul vacationed in Africa. Starr's marriage echoed Lennon's: Maureen gave birth to Zak Starr eight months later. Epstein still fretted about negative female reaction as a second Beatle gave up bachelorhood, to the point where even Harrison got quoted saying, "This means two married and two unmarried Beatles—two down and two to go."[2] The newlyweds honeymooned in a secluded spot near Brighton; but once again, the location leaked and fans swarmed their honeymoon.

Increasingly, EMI's Abbey Road studios became the Beatles' island of control. Where the schedule pushed down on their time, sessions began lasting longer, and the number of takes per song swelled as needed. Sessions over the week of February 15–20 yielded eleven tracks toward the untitled sound track, beginning with "Ticket to Ride," "Another Girl," and "I Need You." They still needed a title song, but remained productive enough to set aside two strong efforts. Ringo's "If You've Got Trouble" burst forth in a single take (it would have made a dapper theme song for Ringo's lead role in the upcoming film, but got held), before "Tell Me What You See," in four takes. February 19 saw "You're Going to Lose That Girl" in two basic takes plus overdubs, and they finished on the 20th with "That Means a Lot," the second number from these sessions to get held, and handed to P.J. Proby for an overproduced, melodramatic single. This last track, however, had more potential—they returned to it after filming *Help!* in the Bahamas.

THE WORLDWIDE SUCCESS of *A Hard Day's Night* gave their second film a bigger budget, color stock, and more glamorous locations. *Help!* was arranged with some vacation in mind. Apart from easing the daily schedule, the Beatles' accountant, Dr. Walter Strach, advised an offshore tax shelter to protect their earnings. Strach was installed in the Bahamas for a year to make this possible. Lester booked three weeks of shooting there, followed immediately by another three weeks in Austria. They would have to finish the sound track along the way.

Spinetti, their *Hard Day's Night* costar, remembers the Bahamas mainly for falling ill and for Lennon's contretemps with a local British dignitary. He got right back into conversation with the band on the trip over. "You've got to be in all our films," Harrison told him. Otherwise, he said, "me mum won't come and see them, because she fancies you." Each Beatle stopped by Spinetti's room individually: Lennon performed German gibberish; George brought him milk and cookies; Ringo sat down and read him a good-night story; Paul poked his head in the door, asked if he was all right, and fled.[3]

Lester ran a congenial set as the Beatles sneaked off to smoke joints; the cutting-room floor piled up with takes interrupted by rampant giggling. The maiden-voyage charge of making a movie had worn off, and work progressed with typical show-biz contours. Rumors flew about Lennon and costar Eleanor Bron. Ringo got thrown into the water before announcing he couldn't swim. Spinetti noted how nonchalant the Beatles remained even as their world had begun to shrink.

At the tail end of three weeks of shooting with no days off, Spinetti remembered there were location shots at a military camp—a makeshift hospital for the infirm and elderly. "We had been filming in this deserted army shack, a wooden frame with a tin roof, and all the doors and windows were closed, and all these kids inside, old people . . . it was just rotten, filthy. Dining on a royal feast that evening, John says to his host, 'This morning, we were filming in this old deserted house, and we looked through the windows and saw all these sick kids and old people. How do you reconcile that with all this?' And the man said, 'Mr. Lennon, I am the minister of finance, and I have to tell you that I do this job voluntarily, I do *not* get paid for it.' And John took a slow look round. 'Well, you're doing better than I'd have thought.'" BEATLES INSULT GOVERNOR, the headlines ran the next day. But Spinetti recalls the governor barely noticing, even though the other Beatles were nodding in assent to Lennon's remark. "When we eventually left, we were virtually booed off the island."[4]

Lennon later remembered this scene as a drunken rage: "The most humiliating experiences were like sitting with the Mayor [*sic*] of the

Bahamas, when we were making *Help!* And being insulted by these fuckin' junked up middle-class bitches and bastards who would be commenting on our work and commenting on our manners. I was always drunk, insulting them. I couldn't take it. It would hurt me. I would go insane, swearing at them." Spinetti warned Lennon about popping off in public. To the actor, Lennon seemed daft about how seriously everybody took him. "I'm only a songwriter, Vic," Lennon told him, "I'm no fucking martyr."[5]

Harrison remembers celebrating his twenty-second birthday in Nassau (February 25). As he sat on the side of a road, Swami Vishnudevananda approached him. "He was the first Swami I had met and he obviously knew we were there," Harrison remembered. "He told me years later that whilst meditating he had a strong feeling that he should make contact." He gave Harrison a book that he stowed away to read later on. Subsequently, he found it preached the same philosophy espoused by the Maharishi Mahesh Yogi.[6]

ACCORDING TO CYNTHIA LENNON's most recent memoir, Alfred Lennon paid John another surprise visit, this one to Kenwood, after Lennon returned from Austria, just as he had done the previous year on the *Hard Day's Night* set. He introduced himself as "Freddie." Rather than displaying the delight for which his father had been hoping, John flared up, asking, "Where have you been for the last twenty years?" "Freddie" stayed in the Lennon house for three days, until John and Cynthia became convinced that he had contacted his son for financial rather than sentimental reasons. After dismissing him, Lennon fell prey to guilt, and resumed his annual allowance after threatening to cut him off.[7]

Another giant intrusion on Lennon's consciousness took chemical form. In late March, John and Cynthia went out with George Harrison and Pattie Boyd for a dinner with the dentist they shared, one John Riley. They were already daily marijuana smokers, but in public, they preferred Scotch and Coke, and snuck joints in the bathroom. The Beatles made irresistible marks for Swinging London's thrill seekers.

Riley fancied himself a swinger, and dosed his guests with LSD.

Cynthia remembered the room beginning to swim and Riley erupting in laughter. Harrison and Lennon scolded him and took Pattie and Cynthia out to Harrison's Mini Cooper S as the drug was beginning to take effect. Cynthia recalled:

> The trouble was we were in central London, a good hour from home, and George had no idea which way up the world was. God knows how we made it, but after we had gone around in circles for what seemed like hours we eventually arrived at George and Patti's home. . . . The four of us sat up for the rest of the night as the walls moved, the plants talked, other people looked like ghouls and time stood still. It was horrific.[8]

Her account doesn't entirely square with what Pattie Boyd remembered in her memoir *Wonderful Tonight* (2008): "We were really keen to get away and John Lennon said, 'We *must* go now.'" They had planned to catch Epstein's new act Paddy, Klaus and Gibson (with Klaus Voormann, their Hamburg friend). "These friends of ours are going to be on soon," Lennon told Riley. "It's their first night, we've got to go and see them." But Riley tried to keep everybody at the table. When he told them they had just been dosed through the coffee, Lennon erupted. "How dare you fucking do this to us?" he demanded. George and Pattie didn't even know what LSD was, but Lennon had read about it in *Playboy*. "It's a drug," he told them. As its effects grew stronger, they felt even more strongly that they should leave. Pattie thought the doctor must have hoped for an orgy to break out. Somehow, they arrived at London's Ad Lib club. They entered the elevator only to start hallucinating its red light setting it aflame. Inside the club, they bumped into Mick Jagger, Marianne Faithfull, and Ringo, none of whom seemed to quell the increasing inner hysteria and the "elongating" tables. They drove home at a frantic crawl.

Cynthia vowed never to take the drug again, but Lennon and Harrison were intrigued. "It was as if I had never tasted, talked, seen, thought, or heard properly before," Harrison said. "For the first time in my whole life I wasn't conscious of ego."[9]

———

Lysergic acid now began to mix with Lennon's steady intake of alcohol and grass as the Beatles reentered the studio, and a new strain of dislocation slowly seeped into his muse. Back at EMI on the evening of March 30, the Beatles remade McCartney's "That Means a Lot" with five more takes, but were still unhappy with it. As with Ringo's "If You've Got Trouble," this bespoke a pride they took in the rest of *Help!*'s sound track, only they never came back to it. This tells you something of their confidence, or of something more troubling—George Martin's lack of authority, perhaps? How could a producer not hear "That Means a Lot" as anything but masterly?

Crafting richly layered rock narrative under the guise of pop stars was one trick; consigning juggernauts to the vault while pounding out tracks for a movie, another. "That Means a Lot" finally came out on the *Anthology* in 1995, but it remains a stumper, a clue to how out of touch McCartney could be with his own strengths. Surely this was a track Lennon should have urged him to release—its melody alone trumps "The Night Before" or "Another Girl" or even "I've Just Seen a Face." The lyric borrows heavily from ideas spun out first in "From Me to You" and "She Loves You," as a lover measures his inner state against hearsay. Strung on a delicious guitar lick that settles gently down into understated rhythmic offbeats, punctuated by Ringo's discreet snare, the groove itself is disarming. But it's all an echoey bedding for McCartney's rubbery vocal, which grows from purring self-reflection to damn-it-all revelation in one miraculous arc of feeling across two key areas (a ploy he revisits in "Here, There and Everywhere" and "Penny Lane"): "A touch can mean so much/When it's all you've got."

Unlike on most of the other numbers from these sessions, the production is thick but detailed, with each individual line carefully etched. The recording admires "You've Lost That Lovin' Feeling" from a respectful distance; it's an Englishman's version of Phil Spector's Wall of Sound, with heft but no fat. Here's what Spector might have sounded like if he had but an ounce of British reserve. Its note of defeat ("Love can be . . . suicide") gives much of McCartney's preening self-regard, in this and many other songs, some measured respite. The other Beatles' judiciously delayed vocal harmonies don't answer the lead; they simply join it at the ends of phrases, a strategy used on this track alone and never again. And the swells in the middle eight expand in the fadeout as McCartney hints at "Hey Jude" vocal glories: his all-consuming yet restrained affection becomes giddy release into the fadeout. P. J. Proby's rendition discards nuance and uncorks the emotion for a good example of sixties bathos: the melody was enough to make it a hit, but his recording sounds like a Johnnie Ray rerun.

IN ADVANCE OF THE BAND'S spring sessions, Northern Songs Ltd., the publishing company that held the rights to all Lennon and McCartney's material, in February 1965 began its listing on the London Stock Exchange, opening with two out of five million shares at 9p apiece. Opening day was bumpy; the price dropped to below 6p, but shares were soon selling at 14p.

The world grabbed brief glimpses of the band peeking from long hours in the studio, broken up by hastily arranged radio and TV spots. They did overdubbing and miscellaneous shots for Lester at London's Twickenham Studios at the end of March, mimed "Ticket to Ride" and "Yes It Is" for *Top of the Pops* on April 10, and played five songs at the *New Musical Express* Poll Winners Concert at Wembley the next day. More film work took place on April 12 and 13, when Lester approached Lennon with a new title, to replace the film's working title, *Eight Arms to Hold You*.

In Lester's mind, "Help!" suited the mock–James Bond caricature of the script, but it posed a special conundrum for the songwriter. Lennon tilted the lyric inward, which tweaked the movie's burlesque tone with an imperceptible edge, as if the Beatles, looking down on their own project, had reservations. They went into EMI's studios on April 13 to tape the title song, in twelve takes, with multiple overdubs. On the 16th, Lennon and Harrison appeared on the also newly retitled *Ready Steady Goes Live!* for an interview, promoting their "Ticket to Ride" single. The record came out three days later. At the end of that month, Peter Sellers visited the set of *Help!* to present the Beatles with their first Grammy Award, for Best Performance by a Vocal Group, for *A Hard Day's Night*. Sellers called it a "Grandma" award. In America, the Grammy telecast featured a short film of the presentation on May 18.

In advance of their second feature film release, more Beatle product clogged the cross-Atlantic muddle. Capitol Records finally won the rights to release the Swan and Vee-Jay material from 1962 and 1963 and put out *The Early Beatles* for the American market in March 1965, using Robert Freeman's 1964 photo for the UK's *Beatles for Sale*. This was quickly subsumed by April's futuristic "Ticket to Ride" / "Yes It Is" single, a diagram of the gaping aesthetic distance traveled in two impossibly swift years. A backlog of songs quickly crowded the *Billboard* charts, an almost literal echo of the previous year: "Ticket to Ride" went to number one while *The Early Beatles* grazed the top twenty. It wasn't until June that America got to hear the *Beatles for Sale* tracks that Britain had been listening to since the previous November, with a marketing mosaic called *Beatles VI,* which included two tracks they had dashed off at Capitol's request: "Bad Boy," which got filed on a UK title called *The Beatles Oldies* later that year, and "Dizzy Miss Lizzie," which landed on the *Help!* sound track.[10]

The wires noted how all four Beatles attended Bob Dylan's Royal Festival Hall appearance, captured by D. A. Pennebaker's *Don't Look Back* documentary. Dylan's recent *Bringing It All Back Home* featured a side of electric rock, and this would be his last acoustic-only tour. Convulsed over Dylan's identity, his British audience parsed every lyric, mistrusting his flirtation with rock 'n' roll more for its flight from literary pretense than inexplicable lack of explicit social protest. The Beatles' attendance conferred royal approval of Dylan's vexing persona, whichever guise it took.

WITH THE PUBLICATION OF Lennon's second book, *A Spaniard in the Works,* the Dylan rivalry intensified. *Spaniard* was both hastier than its predecessor and more ambitious, with more wordplay by the pound. *In*

His Own Write featured several genre parodies (letters to the editor, school lessons, scripts). *Spaniard* took the genre stuff further, ranging out into mock sagas like the title tale and "The Singularge Experience of Miss Anne Duffield," an account of Harold Wilson's 1964 ascent to prime minister in "We must not forget . . . the General Erection," a gossip-column parody in "Cassandle" (spinning off Cassandra's narcissistic column in the *Daily Mirror*), a "Last Will and Testicle," and several long poems, alongside a flurry of new drawings.

Lennon wrote the poem "Our Dad" during at least two confrontations with Alfred Lennon in this period, but the verse lurches from autobiographical to fantastical. Instead of a seafaring ne'er-do-well, Lennon opens his ode with the verse:

> *It wasn't long before old dad*
> *Was cumbersome—a drag.*
> *He seemed to get the message and*
> *Began to pack his bag.*

"I'm old and crippled," he says on his way out the door. "You're bloody right, it's true," the family responds. It's hard not to read Lennon's own emotional defection from Cynthia and Julian here, seeing as he had long since packed himself off, with nowhere to go. (In another story, "Silly Norman," mother is a "muddle," both a revered elder and a common whore—as much a puzzling over Julia and Mimi as a peculiar intimation of Cynthia.) In "Our Dad," Lennon sustains such brittle enmity through a hectoring, bouncing children's rhyme for eighteen stanzas, only to crash down into a bitingly satiric reversal for the final lines: "But he'll remain in all our hearts/—a buddy friend and pal." This toys with exhausted British notions of the inertia toward "happy endings," to which all such "odes" necessarily conform. Lennon's verbal contortions accent the pathology of "normal," as though anybody could "tidy up" such harsh, consuming hostility. No wonder he preferred venting through rock 'n' roll: reading Lennon's prose can feel halting, as if the energy behind the words suffocates their multiple meanings. Detonating conformity was one of the few themes Lennon's pen mastered, but his drawings convey more emotional mayhem with greater elegance.

DURING THE SCRAMBLE to finish the movie songs before the Beatles hit the road, Epstein got a June call from Buckingham Palace. The Beatles would be listed as recipients of MBE—Member of the British Empire—awards from the queen, he learned. This was as much a matter of economics as it was of status and celebrity fawning: the award was not for culture but for trade. As much as politicians had promised an upswing in Britain's economy, everybody knew it was the pop-music exports that had made Britain flush, that the tourist money fueling Swinging London filled its coffers. In weathering the subsequent storm of protest from retired military types, the royals were nothing if not pragmatic.

Recording had been compressed, but *Help!*'s sound track bested *Beatles for Sale* from six months earlier; they were learning to keep the aesthetic ideas afloat amid torrents of activity. Lennon's title song and "You're Gonna Lose That Girl" posed a new threat with sturdy finesse, but in numbers like "The Night Before," "Another Girl," and Harrison's "I Need You," boy still meets, finds another, or loses girl; the musical wheels spun unattached to substantive gears. Their ensemble, increasingly nimble yet determined, gave this material flair beyond its ambition. Only "You've Got to Hide Your Love Away" fit inside the larger arc of Lennon confessionals, the male anxiety shifting beneath "If I Fell," "I'm a Loser," and "Norwegian Wood" and not as piercing. This resignation signaled a new Lennon mode, a disquiet that would seep into "I'm Only Sleeping" and "I'm So Tired."

Paradoxically, much of the band's work in this dense season was upstaged by McCartney's lone "Yesterday," which echoed inside the idea of a Tin Pan Alley classic. The song was so pure, and so credulous, it sounded as if it had sprung from the Hollywood musical forever looping in McCartney's mind, the imaginary rock 'n' roll past he kept inventing as he went along. He walked around for months with the melody and the dummy words "Scrambled egg," certain he had heard it somewhere before, running it by older London show-biz pros, like *Oliver!*'s Lionel

Bart, to make sure he wasn't unconsciously cribbing it. When he finally sat down and played it for the others, incorporating Lennon's three-syllable "Yesterday" for the title phrase, they threw up their hands: it was simply not a band number.[11] Martin suggested strings, but McCartney blanched. So Martin scored it for the more highfalutin string quartet atop McCartney's solo acoustic guitar. The finished product was placed on *Help!*'s sound track, but it sat outside that box on both stage and album. In America, it became a single and dominated the autumn charts with four weeks at number one, for their biggest seller since "I Want to Hold Your Hand."

Here was a superbly ironic punch line to the season's forward momentum. Was "Yesterday" even a rock 'n' roll number? In Lennon's ongoing quandaries about such McCartney swill, it created new tension in the partnership. Lennon could not help admiring it, or enjoying the profits he would share in its extraordinary publishing returns. But it was never a song Lennon would have written on his own, and if the Beatles had to put it on a record, there was no place for him to so much as harmonize alongside his songwriting partner. For the album, Lennon made sure to follow it up with "Dizzy Miss Lizzie," to conclude *Help!*'s side two, as if reiterating all the arguments about the band's priorities since the Decca audition. This slammed the sound track shut with a reliable Larry Williams number as touring season swallowed them up again.

To top *The Ed Sullivan Show* from the previous year, Epstein took promoter Sid Bernstein's bait, leapfrogged Madison Square Garden, and booked Shea Stadium. Fifty-six thousand fans stilled for the Beatle helicopter as it settled on the New York baseball field on August 15. "A hush fell over the crowd, it was this mind-numbing moment, like watching the Gods descend from the sky," recalls critic Richard Meltzer, who attended both Shea shows, in 1965 and 1966.[12] From there, they went through Toronto, Atlanta, Houston, Chicago, Minneapolis, Portland, San Diego, Los Angeles, and San Francisco by the end of that same month.

Reporter Larry Kane, who rejoined them on this tour, reported that fans crowded onto the runway in Houston while the propellers were still running. "Not only did they swarm the tarmac but when the engines of the planes were finally turned off," Kane says, "some of the older fans managed to climb onto the wings with lit cigarettes in their hands waving to the entourage inside." There were many such close calls.[13]

As *Help!* hit theaters at the end of July, Epstein met with Walt Disney to discuss the possibility of the Beatles performing songs for the upcoming animated film of *The Jungle Book*. Later, John Lennon nixed the idea; Disney wound up using laconic Scouser accents for the film's four shaggy-haired vultures. On August 14, they taped another *Ed Sullivan Show* appearance before a live studio audience at Studio 50 in New York: "I Feel Fine," "I'm Down," "Act Naturally," "Ticket to Ride," "Yesterday," and "Help!" The tour whooshed by in a blur of mad dashes and isolated hotel rooms.

AFTER A SIX-WEEK BREAK beginning September 1, the Beatles hit the EMI studios on October 12, flush with new material, determined to hold their own atop the summer's pop avalanche. Curiously, stronger songs reduced studio takes. They began with five attempts of Lennon's "Run For Your Life" on October 12 and then "This Bird Has Flown," which featured George on sitar. The next day came "Drive My Car," in four takes. October 16 brought three more takes of "Day Tripper" and some vocal overdubs to finish the track; then they started Harrison's "If I Needed Someone." On the 18th, more work followed on "Someone," with lead and backing vocals and Ringo on tambourine. Then came Lennon's "In My Life," in three takes the same session. Few of their songs for *Help!* had emerged so quickly.

And on October 26, the Beatles reported to Buckingham Palace to receive their MBE awards.

At a press conference after the ceremony, reporters crowded around Lennon to ask what he thought of the uproar the awards had caused. A Canadian politician had said he no longer wanted his MBE because it "put him on the same level with vulgar nincompoops." A rash of air force squadron leaders had returned their medals, claiming the MBE had been debased. John replied that most of the complainers had earned their medals "for killing people. I'd say we deserved ours more. Wouldn't you?"[14]

The veterans who returned their awards in protest seemed to miss the point: the Beatles had revived Britain's economy, restored its sense of self-confidence, and turned its postwar socialist experiment into an inarguable success. And in a 1982 interview with Lennon biographer Ray Coleman, former British prime minister Harold Wilson justified the award in similarly practical terms: "I saw the Beatles as having a transforming effect on the minds of youth, mostly for the good. It kept a lot of kids off the streets." Even beyond that, Wilson noted, "They introduced many, many young people to music, which in itself was a good thing."[15]

Posing for the world's cameras, the Beatles put on their best grins, as if oddly touched that the ruling class seemed to care. By this point, they knew the royals were sponging off of their celebrity, but Lennon opted not to rattle anybody's jewelry with his quotes. Rumors swirled that they had snuck off to have a joint in the royal loo. The rumors became enshrouded in the official myth long after the Beatles admitted only to tobacco nerves.

Where the royal honors stirred controversy, history measures them as a blip in the ongoing story—nothing like the blips to come. The Beatles headed back to work, and again the schedule reveals an increasing studio efficiency: fewer basic tracks (for foundation) and more layers onto the crowded four-track equipment. Recording continued with "We Can Work It Out," vocals on October 29, and November began with rhythmic tracks for "Michelle." "What Goes On" got revived for Ringo from March 5, 1963, on November 4, and the evening session tracked a twelve-bar blues with George Martin on harmonium, one of the few takes from these sessions that got held (until 1995's *Anthology*). The following days brought remakes of McCartney's "I'm Looking Through You," Harrison's "Think for Yourself" (called "Won't Be There with You"), the 1965 Christmas message (in which "Yesterday" turned to derision), Lennon's "The Word," a second remake of "I'm Looking Through You" with a new rhythm track, and a final thirteen-hour marathon finish with the vocal splendor of "You Won't See Me," "Girl," more work on "Wait," and vocal overdubs for "I'm Looking Through You." Martin sequenced the album's songs on November 16, and sent *Rubber Soul* off to be mastered and ready in shops by the first week in December.

RECORDED ALMOST ONE YEAR AFTER *Beatles for Sale,* under almost exactly the same conditions, *Rubber Soul* has no hint of the previous record's fatigue. *A Hard Day's Night* was the band's first all-original sequence; *Rubber Soul* came close to this formula, adding two tracks from George Harrison, a Buck Owens knockoff from Ringo, and a startling leap forward in both theme and tone. "We were just getting better, technically, and musically, that's all," Lennon later concluded. "Finally we took over the studio. In the early days, we had to take what we were given, we didn't know how you can get more bass. We were learning the technique on *Rubber Soul*. We were more precise about making the album, that's all, and [we] took over the cover and everything."[16] Having conquered the rock 'n' roll ideal, they leaned back into the beat and delivered an adult record—dance was secondary on this album in a way it had never been before. This was not music you made sense of by making out or moving along with it; it was all shadows and subtext, an experiment in suggestion and elliptical gestures that was at once nervy and guarded, extroverted yet discreet.

In America, the *Help!* sound track appeared in September, followed by *Rubber Soul* barely three months and a creative light-year later. By October, the charts had shifted dramatically toward social protest ("Eve of Destruction" by Barry McGuire), sleek yet hook-laden piffle ("Hang On Sloopy" by the McCoys, cowritten by Bert Berns, who'd written "Twist and Shout"), and romance ("Yesterday"). November brought the Stones' "Get Off My Cloud" and the Supremes' "I Hear a Symphony"; December saw the Byrds' "Turn! Turn! Turn!" and the Dave Clark Five's "Over and Over." The year's commercial blockbusters were Dylan's "Like a Rolling Stone," the Stones' "Satisfaction," and the Beatles' "Yesterday," two incendiary bombs followed by a lullabye, images that defined these acts for years to come. In reality, the Beatles would have had a fifth U.S.

number one that year if "Day Tripper" had been included on Capitol's resequence of *Rubber Soul;* the track swarmed the British Christmas season as the perfect holiday single but had to wait for the new year to dominate American radio. For Americans, the geographic delay wound up dispersing the musical energy away from the band's best work rather than in favor of it.

Dylan's overt influence on *Rubber Soul* skirted imitation. Ever since "You've Got to Hide Your Love Away," a new psychological acuity had risen up in Lennon's love songs, making them at once particular and universal. His romantic insecurities were unique, but of the stripe almost every young couple could identify with. "Norwegian Wood" posed the lover's mind as a maze; it caught the exotic, bohemian mood of an emerging London chic and detailed an off-kilter affair as doubt tipping toward the existential. Boy gets girl in this song, but under the most confounding of emotional circumstances. "What tryst is worth this kind of emotional hangover?" Lennon seemed to ask.

McCartney's standout track was not "Michelle" (a cousin to "And I Love Her" and "Yesterday" with fancier chords and French lyrics), but "You Won't See Me," which was unbearably chipper on the surface and leaked nagging hesitation from every luminous harmony: boy loses girl but wonders if he ever really had her to begin with. The bummer lyric gets joined to incandescent vocals to express the gap between love and great sex, reaching toward a closeness sex alone can't deliver. The production was a marvel: the vocal work hints at breakthroughs like "Paperback Writer," "And Your Bird Can Sing," "Nowhere Man," and *Abbey Road*'s "Because." Brian Wilson and the Byrds had goaded the Beatles into proving that no matter what kind of harmonies were happening elsewhere in pop, they were a peerless, muscular choir, leaning into every nuance, relishing every finely honed detail, competing with their meticulous ensemble for attention. As each verse comes around, the backup vocals increase their intensity, both in mood and in upper descants, until the entire track gains a momentum more emotional than rhythmic. The very idea of singing while playing many of these songs now became daunting—such studio musicianship became impractical, not to say irrelevant, onstage (they never attempted this track live). As early as the elaborate vocal harmonies attached to "You Won't See Me," the argument to stop touring began as an outgrowth of their musical sophistication.

RUBBER SOUL's RESTRAINED MUSICAL confidence brought new momentum to the London scene. The Beatles had long since graduated into cultural symbol, a beast that wasn't nearly big enough to absorb and reflect all the desires its audience projected onto it. Pots of money flowed in and around pop, and Britain, almost in spite of itself, began to seem trendy. Even the Union Jack, long a totem of an empire's oppression, flipped into status symbol. London itself graduated into pop's new center, an international jet-setter's hub, not least because it seemed a source of magic and poetry. "London is the most swinging city in the world at the moment," Diana Vreeland proclaimed in *Vogue;* and to Americans, the weirdest thing about her self-evident proclamation was its utter lack of irony.

As the media glare descended, this larger pop moment embraced music, fashion, design, film, architecture, and all things mod (a term derived from modern-jazz buffs in the late 1950s). Any town that sprouted a brand this fetching must be hip by association—and once again Liverpool got the shirk. Teen desire erupted through Mary Quant's outfits; and once clothing shops flourished all down Carnaby Street, they spread to Mayfair, Chelsea, and Kensington. Models and actresses like Pattie Boyd and Jane Asher turned into Beatle girlfriends and then part of "ideal young couples." Roger Miller followed up "King of the Road" with "England Swings" at the end of 1965 for a giant reversal of cultural salutes: this country crossover act topped UK charts by genuflecting to pop's new center.

A Geoffrey Dickinson cover collage trumpeted *Time* magazine's "Swinging London" issue in April 1966. By this point, Quant's jersey minidresses, with their sleek zipper lines and casual flair, had been distributed stateside by JC Penney since 1963. Quant added PVC (polyvinyl chloride) to her palette of threads, creating go-go outfits that shone like raincoats, bright colors topped by enormous sunglasses. Twiggy (aka Lesley Hornby) became an international supermodel wearing op-art miniskirts, suggesting art worn around town. With her reverse-Beatle bob, a babe who cropped her hair like a boy, Twiggy practically invented Quant instead of the other way around. *Time* had spotted a trend, but it was already cresting: within another year the international pop "scene" torch would pass to San Francisco.

The faded suede jackets the Beatles wore in Robert Freeman's *Rubber Soul* shot fed Swinging London's international elan, and they gazed down from its cover like cool avatars, musicians who were too hip not to set fashion trends. The collarless jackets in which Epstein outfitted them back in 1963 now seemed like portents, the idea that even young men could go spiffy at no cost to their machismo. Characters like the "Norwegian Wood" couple, with her fancy furniture and liberated attitude, became the ideal of hipsters everywhere.

Like 1962's "The Twist," Swinging London became a social metaphor for everything groovy, sexy, and fun. In cultural terms, to swing meant celebrating the tension between modernity and tradition in every facet of life. As Andrew Loog Oldham, now managing the Rolling Stones, had already discovered, fashion had a head start on pop, so as trendy shops opened with irresistible names like I Was Lord Kitchener's Valet, the movement fed on itself. In this new frame, Christine Keeler's 1963 nude portrait looked prophetic. This new cult of British youth paraded through new magazines like *Queen* and *Petticoat*, expressing pleasure in the very idea of getting and spending, consumption itself, which helped turn all things British into desirable exports.

Pop's new relationship between viewer and subject leapt across mediums—*Help!* had whispers of this, especially in its flimsy Bond pretext. Michael Caine's portrayal of Alfie Elkins, the cad who befriends the camera / audience throughout *Alfie*, became a signature piece of self-conscious cinema. Antonioni's *Blow-Up* portrayed a fashion photographer based on David Bailey (played by David Hemmings), with models Veruschka and Peggy Moffitt (and the Yardbirds in a club scene) playing themselves. In an early sequence that doesn't hold up, Hemmings's character has a wan orgasm during a fashion shoot. It's all about the vain, empty obsessions of the beautiful people. Cued off the cynical exhaustion in Fellini's *La Dolce Vita,* the entire charade has the feel of empty-headed sleaze, but everybody looked fabulous. The industry scarecrow Alun Owen had George Harrison slice up in *A Hard Day's Night* was replaced by figures with style and menace. On television, Honor Blackman and then Diana Rigg conveyed a cool, detached and faintly ironic heat for their *Avengers* counterpart, Patrick Macnee, wearing black leather cat-suits and jackboots alongside his bowler hats and tight jackets. (The se-ries neatly overlapped the Beatles career, 1961–69).

As if making up for lost time, broadcast entrepreneurs seized on a loophole in the BBC's media monopoly. Three pirate radio stations be-gan broadcasting from offshore, pumping out fare more closely aligned to the charts: Radio Caroline, Swinging Radio England, and Wonderful Radio London. (Americans would get a taste of Radio London as paro-died on *The Who Sell Out* in 1967.) These "underground" stations dis-rupted everyday British imaginations to stoke the increasingly surreal atmosphere. In July 1966, Britain even won the World Cup. In every aspect—economy, fashion, music, international status—the Beatles headed up a resurgence of British cool that was quite unlike anything its subjects had ever experienced before, or have experienced since.

On that year's Christmas message sent out to the Beatles' fan club, the band ridiculed McCartney about "Yesterday," lifting its sentimental skirt like sailors taunting a streetwalker. To hear these naughty schoolboys turn its melody into a sea shanty was the sound of parody sharpening some manic competitive edge. But by then, "Yesterday" had legitimized the Beatles as a mainstream product, and sent Lennon further into out-sider status within the band he supposedly led. His response was aestheti-cally decisive: if *Beatles for Sale* showed the wear and tear of a schedule few could keep up with, *Rubber Soul* leapt over many of the same hurdles with ease and showed just how attuned Lennon and McCartney were to their audience and peers.

By the end of 1965, *Rubber Soul* had set their previous work in a new context, absorbing the best from Dylan, the Stones, the Byrds, the Lovin' Spoonful, the Animals, and the Hollies. Yet despite its cheeky title (red-olent of the R&B slag-off of white soul, or "plastic soul"), it remains suc-cinct, even modest. Many cite it as the Beatles' best work, and the effect was singular even though Americans got a thinned-out, ten-song version which began with the temperate "I've Just Seen a Face" instead of the sterling "Drive My Car." Nobody else could have produced this work at this point, and it sent shudders through the pop industry—suddenly, the Beatles had outgrown the teen market that once defined them, and reshaped rock as songs with adult characters, situations, and inner lives. Rock 'n' roll, shedding its teen identification, became rock as early as *Rubber Soul*'s track two, with the exquisite discomfort of Lennon's "Norwegian Wood": girl snubs boy, her stylish furniture a symbol of expensive regret.

Another Kind of Mind

WITH THE BEATLES, LENNON BANGED OUT A CAREER OF UNPRECE-dented creative consistency and success. But at home, his marriage to Cynthia flatlined, and his three-year-old son, Julian, took a number as Daddy hid in the attic doing tape experiments, hit the nightly club scene, and descended into an increasingly distant drug haze. In only three dizzying years, the Beatles had changed the world, but like all mythic figures they came due for a whopping backlash. Theirs could only be measured against the previous pitch of adoration.

Working at the height of his creative powers while finishing *Revolver* during the spring of 1966, Lennon sank down into an emotional void that would last two years. He completed this mid-period masterpiece only to walk through a nightmarish world tour and then collapse. For the first time in his career, at age twenty-six, Lennon fled to the Continent, alone, to ponder what life after the Beatles might be like and what could possibly sustain him outside his band, the tightest of musical circles. In the classic addict's slope, Lennon used softer drugs casually at first as a social lubricant and gradually found himself beholden to all manner of intoxicants. The Beatles' status as supreme rock gods, surpassing all others, brought them the highest-quality grass and acid then circulating, and it was a point of pride with him that he could hold the most liquor and ingest the most chemicals. An unspoken studio ethic involved sneaking bathroom joints; but after sessions, hard drugs and clubbing into the wee hours became nightly rituals. Entire weekends got set aside for tripping at country estates.

From the time he awoke in the afternoon until he collapsed early the next morning, Lennon's system processed a jumble of uppers, downers, pot, and booze. The wonder is not just that the band did such solid work in this chemically naïve era, but that they survived some of the compounds passed along to them at all. Many, many other casualties in these circles fared far worse.

The more Lennon attended to his professional life, the more his unfinished emotional business taxed his peace of mind. The loss he had carried around since Blackpool, his uncle's death when he was fourteen, his mother's death three years later, and his best friend's death when he was twenty-one, mocked his outward success, creating a disconnect between his inner and outer worlds. Lennon's subconscious was gripped between his celebrity songwriter status and the loss he armored with so much bluster. His misery often presented itself as cruelty, a bitterness that made no sense given his privileged circumstances.

Ringo Starr provides a clue to some of this in *Postcards from the Boys,* a joyride with curlicue drawings and breezy puns that couch a few secrets: "I can say this now (if he was here John could tell you) but suddenly we'd be in the middle of a track and John would just start crying or screaming—which freaked us out at the beginning. But we were always open to whatever anyone was going through so we just got on with it."[1]

The studio, among his mates, was the only place Lennon felt comfortable enough to cough up his ghosts.

At home, he slept throughout the day, then spent hours secluded in his Weybridge attic, making experimental tapes of his new obsession, Indian ragas George had played for him on his reel-to-reel machines. By the time the band toured to support *Revolver* in the summer of 1966, everything that once had seemed heady and euphoric about Beatlemania had suddenly given way to something more ominous: crowds careened closer to violence, and security intensified. The ravages of Beatlemania began to echo Lennon's anxiety. A simple misunderstanding led to an international diplomatic incident in the Philippines; and in America's Bible Belt the Ku Klux Klan began picketing their shows.

McCartney's old-school work ethic kept a professional check on Lennon's excesses as they continued to write together. But this partnership began to shift: increasingly, they finished off each other's lines or suggested endings or transitions instead of writing head-to-head, as they had in the glass-tiled foyer at Mendips. Epstein and Martin kept Lennon's schedule humming, but he also grew apart from Epstein during this final tour and retreat. Epstein felt slowly edged out of some major band decisions and began a downward spiral of his own.

In the midst of it all, the Beatles could barely hear themselves onstage, and this put a hex on the whole enterprise, made their first love of music-making ring hollow. Once the source of their power and ambition, live performances became a sequence of empty gestures for riotous fans who counted music secondary to the spectacle. Their faith in their ensemble, which had sustained them through so many bleak treks in Aspinall's van, began to falter.

Richard Lester had invited Lennon to Spain to work as a character actor on *How I Won the War*, and Lennon beached himself on this movie set to recover. This represented escape as much as diversion from the Beatle grind. Unlike his week with Epstein in Spain three years earlier, in late 1966 Lennon found himself alone on the island of Majorca.

Lennon's emotional state was no mystery to the other Beatles, and some of his private disorientation leaked into a public profile in the Sunday papers just as the band began work on *Revolver*. Cynthia Lennon's memoirs report how Lennon napped away a lot of downtime early in the year, became increasingly aloof, and went off on eccentric shopping sprees to fill his mansion up with trinkets. This drift came into full view for Maureen Cleave, a journalist with whom Lennon spoke freely. If some earlier comments had made Lennon seem cantankerous and flippant, now he began to sound more and more as though even Beatle projects left him restless. "Christianity will go," he told her. "It will vanish and shrink. . . . I'm right and I will be proved right. We're more popular than Jesus now; I don't know which will go first—rock 'n' roll or Christianity."[2]

Cleave put this infamous quote into an article which ran in London's *Evening Standard* on March 2, 1966, as "How Does a Beatle Live? John

Lennon Lives Like This." She described a tour of Lennon's Weybridge estate and a shopping trip into London at the tail end of John's longest vacation—more than two months—since Beatlemania first swallowed up normalcy three years earlier, when "Please Please Me" reached number one. A lot of Cleave's knowing detail, in the now-transparent guardedly intimate tone of a lover, hinted at Lennon's crumbling inner life. Walking through rooms of model racing cars and electronic gadgets gave Cleave the impression of a bored eccentric. "One feels that his possessions—to which he adds daily—have got the upper hand," she remarked, noting the many tape recorders, television sets, telephones, and cars: a Rolls, a Mini Cooper, a Ferrari, which were in various stages of newly applied décor.

Cleave noted how Lennon's junk had the upper hand on his relationships, too. Julian followed them around the house carrying "a large porcelain Siamese cat." The child would attend the Lycée Française in Kensington, Lennon assumed, since that's simply where "privileged kids" go. To Cleave, Lennon's detachment from his son seemed pronounced. "'I feel sorry for him,'" John told her. And then out came this whopper: "'I couldn't stand ugly people even when I was five. Lots of the ugly ones are foreign, aren't they?'" His wife, Cynthia, barely got a mention. John slept "indefinitely" and was "probably the laziest man in Britain."

Somewhere, Lennon's head swam with the gleaming arrogance of "And Your Bird Can Sing," the alternate reality of "Rain," the shimmering cynicism of "Dr. Robert," and the jagged psychic fault lines of "She Said She Said"—songs that extended the veiled personal metaphors of "Norwegian Wood," "I'm Only Sleeping," and "Nowhere Man." The new numbers paraded a dazzling detachment between singer and song, with a subliminal intimacy that only grew over repeated listenings—they sounded like subtexts to Lennon's epic, heaving subconscious, triumphant statues perched atop personal defeat. He led with the more experimental strain: the obsessively droning "Tomorrow Never Knows" and "Rain," which grew out of his homemade tape collages, became the first two songs he took into the studio for the *Revolver* sessions in the coming weeks. These required more time and more production ingenuity.

By now, Lennon had perfected the role of precocious counterculture mouthpiece. Just another dotty pop star posing as an aristocrat, most Britons thought as they read Cleave's profile, yawned, and turned the page. The "Jesus" comment became a yardstick of how differently the British and the Americans perceived both celebrity and religion—and still do. Lennon's countrymen accepted his offhand spiritual remarks more as an attempt to describe how fame's bubble felt from the inside than a critique of religion. Lennon was simply repeating remarks all four Beatles had made in *Playboy* thirteen months earlier with the same philosophical aplomb. His attitude gave off a luxurious anomie, the rock star padding around his mansion, slinging quotes to ridicule the stale Sunday-celebrity-profile cliché. In England, Cleave's puff piece gave off not the slightest whiff of controversy.

THE MATERIAL LENNON AND McCARTNEY polished off for *Revolver* confronted a radically shifting pop context. The more perplexing aspects of the Beatles' influence had a counterintuitive effect, pivoting the pop scene toward new conundrums. The Beatles' popularity unleashed inspired amateurs as much in love with idea as sound; pop became a high-stakes parlor game where ideology often trumped skill. So much ingenious trash began hitting the charts that being as good as the Beatles hardly mattered; the ambition to make the reach was often enough to put a band over. The attitudes driving hits from deities like the Rolling Stones and Bob Dylan spread to frat boys like the Swingin' Medallions and lowlifes like the Seeds, to obscurities like the 13th Floor Elevators and ? and the Mysterians. Retrospect still blurs how much chance and accident steered rock's new adventurism. We now think of this as a golden period; at the time, the idea that a song like "Dirty Water," a screed about Boston's Charles River sludge by some punk Los Angelenos called the Standells, could become a Fenway Park Red Sox anthem seemed inconceivable.

Coming from the most popular act in show business, the Beatles' records suggested worlds within worlds, and everybody defined themselves against this new standard. Andrew Loog Oldham positioned his scruffy Stones to the left of the Beatles' axis, dramatizing just how expansive rock's center of gravity had grown. Beginning with the early Jagger-Richards songwriting breakthrough, 1965's "The Last Time," the Stones turned a careening guitar hook into one long sneer, a hooting inversion of Beatle charm. "Paint It Black" and "19th Nervous Breakdown" extended this sneer while broaching the "generation gap," diagramming establishment hypocrisy (how could anyone over thirty denounce "drugs" while popping prescription pills?). Brian Jones's sitar work on the former nodded toward "Norwegian Wood" as it pumped up the cynicism. In concert, Mick Jagger wagged his finger and taunted his audience to make Elvis look a prude, and Stones shows became symbolic of all the untidy heat and furor kept in check by the Beatles' suits and bows. As the Beatles progressed, the Stones pushed hard against Lennon and McCartney's formal ingenuity, and a new subgenre, garage rock, disavowed all "respectability" and "sophistication."

Garage rock spun out of surf instrumentals and doo-wop covers as an abbreviated swish of guitars, bass, and drums, and often an organ line leering from on high. A resounding movie image of the ethic gets enacted by John Belushi in *Animal House,* which takes place in 1962, when he smashes Stephen Bishop's acoustic guitar against the wall after some unbearable folkie piffle ("I Gave My Love a Cherry"). If anything, it sounded as if rock 'n' roll had devolved from slavish stylistic imitation down into a food fight; instead of whites "borrowing" black sounds, suburbanites attempted King-sized vocal heroics through Motown's soul pop. That's why Otis Day and the Knights' *Animal House* set at the black club several scenes later, doing "Shama Lama Ding Dong," crashes through like gangbusters: here was the forbidden hooch white ears craved.

Just as technique seemed secondary to young actors like Warren Beatty and Jane Fonda, so, too, the skill behind the Beatles, the Stones, and Dylan counted among the least interesting aspect of their records. Spurning polish, garage-rock players instead paraded accident as inspiration, inanity as triumph, and disorder severed from craft as a peculiar sophistication all its own. How could anybody possibly improve on "Louie Louie"? Who needed "pretension" when untrained teenagers proved so adept at creating noise so disdainful, contemptuous, and convulsive? The new style elevated guitar sounds, indecipherable lyrics, and hazy, uneven beats into a disarming amateurishness; at first whiff, the stuff smelled like rotgut.

Layered on top of these racial crosscurrents came a dialogue between British and American tastes like never before, which took root in the pre-Beatle era through surf rock. A larger stylistic arc connects the Tornados' "Telstar" in 1962 (UK), a tough, grainy instrumental, up to the Trashmen's "Surfin' Bird" (U.S.), a December 1963 patchwork of the Rivingtons' "Papa-Oom-Mow-Mow" (August 1962) and "The Bird's the Word" (March 1963). In between came the Beach Boys, with "Surfin' USA," "Surfer Girl," "Little Deuce Coupe," and "Be True to Your School" (throughout 1963) and "Louie Louie" by the Kingsmen (peaking at *Billboard*'s number two in December 1963). As Beatlemania swept the world, the cross-the-pond dialogue continued, with songs like "Wooly Bully" by America's Sam the Sham and the Pharaohs and "Wild Thing" by Britain's Troggs (June 1966). Souped-up jalopies like "Farmer John" and "Double Shot of My Baby's Love" brought to mind the title of J. D. Salinger's barbed short story "For Esmé—with Love and Squalor." Two years into its heyday, nobody could imagine garage rock lasting beyond next month. Its doomed immediacy still gives the music a mischievous swagger.

If not already inebriated, innocent listeners found themselves dumbfounded by the noise; and given the right combination of chance and opportunity, this raw energy gained momentum to deliver mysterious new realms of thought. Repetition acquired trance-like sophistication: at around the sixteenth repeat of the fuzziest guitar riff, new overtones emerged, sending new layers of sound and idea afloat above everything else. Sometimes, the song itself hung suspended atop the sound that had been set in motion (think of Them's "Gloria" or Captain Beefheart's "Diddy Wah Diddy"). As with jazz, key parts of this style were accidental; musicians came up with "alien" sounds they "made sense of" as they played. The glorious, unending laps players take around refrains in Dylan's "Like a Rolling Stone" release even more energy than they gather up; the more they hug the song's corners to make sense of Dylan's casual threats, the more his disdain hovers over them, tantalizingly out of reach. In such defining moments, a stylistic genie got released from its bottle, and many found new places for themselves just by chasing some of the same riffs atop their own beats. And all these trance-like motifs set up exotic, psychedelic contexts that sounded scripted for hallucinogens. It was a very short leap between Beefheart's bluesy "Diddy Wah Diddy" and his avant-garde mural *Trout Mask Replica* three years later. An even shorter eighteen-month gap links Lennon's minimalistic "Tomorrow Never Knows" with the sprawling "I Am the Walrus," in the same vein. In this paradoxical way, garage rock seeded many an avant-garde impulse. Simply tracing where the music ended and the drugs took over was half the fun.

The garage rock ethic pitted primitive defiance against radical experimentalism, a tension that found an unlikely plainspoken voice. It's the sound of Andy Warhol's blank-faced arrogance, or the bored audacity with which he silkscreened soup-can labels onto canvas. The same snarl fueled "Are You a Boy or Are You a Girl?" by the Barbarians or "Too Many People" by the Leaves. Repeated listenings unveiled layer upon layer of sound, accidental crossbeats of unspeakable fervor, music that couldn't be bothered with self-consciousness; it only turned pretentious long after the fact.

Garage rock followed a traditional rock 'n' roll arc, derided at first and later exalted into a realm that supported entire careers, from Creedence Clearwater Revival and Cheap Trick to the Pretenders, the Replacements, Nirvana, the White Stripes, My Bloody Valentine, the Black Keys, and the genre's Übermensch, Bruce Springsteen. The style dominated rock throughout 1965 and 1966 at least as much as pop ballads, and led directly to a new variant, "psychedelic rock," which shot off in a different, more elaborate direction—the distance between Lennon's "Rain," which cast nature as a rich, abiding metaphor, and "Lucy in the Sky with Diamonds" and "A Day in the Life," which roamed the new spaces the style had opened up.

Punctuated by surprise and innuendo, a rash of hits thrived on vivid transatlantic contradictions. America embraced a mythical British Invasion while British ears caved in to American acts once again. In February 1966, Smokey Robinson and the Miracles had "Going to a Go-Go," which one-upped the Stones; folk held steady with Simon and Garfunkel's "Homeward Bound." UK acts counterbalanced professionalism with R&B smarts: Peter and Gordon scored with a McCartney number, "Woman" (a song idea Lennon would rewrite much later); the Small Faces got stone serious with an R&B ditty called "Sha-La-La-La-Lee." In March, the Kinks sent up scenesters in "Dedicated Follower of Fashion"; and come April, Lennon visited New York's Lovin' Spoonful—who were touring Britain to support "Daydream"—backstage at the Bag O'Nails Club. By the time Otis Redding covered the Stones' "Satisfaction," he revealed a peculiar and cunning soulful template beneath all the hype. It took Americans at least another year to embrace Redding into their rock mainstream; to the Brits, soul coverage like this had no higher authority.

This revelatory conversation between UK and U.S. acts, and UK and U.S. listeners, achieved new force: the Byrds soared "Eight Miles High" on rocket-fueled guitars; the Troggs sliced open "Wild Thing," with a two-note, kindergarten recorder, signifying way beyond its pay grade. Summer rolled in with the Kinks' radiant "Sunny Afternoon" and Simon and Garfunkel's folk-rock fake-out "I Am a Rock," the Four Tops' gritty pop "Loving You Is Sweeter Than Ever," and the Lovin' Spoonful's pop-grit "Summer in the City." You could typify the range and stylistic sweep of charts by the imaginary diagrams linking "Ain't Too Proud to Beg" by Motown's Temptations with "With a Girl Like You" by the Troggs, which was as nothing compared to the gap between "Wild Thing" and "With a Girl Like You," a distance that gave off supernatural Beatle echoes. By August, Otis Redding pumped "I Can't Turn You Loose" and Peter and Gordon turned effete and provincial with "Lady Godiva" (there'll always be an England). Come autumn, the Supremes wagged their fingers while winking all the way through "You Can't Hurry Love."

This inimitable gust of top-forty hits between 1965 and 1966 has long since wallpapered our minds. But at the time, garage rock rebutted the idea that any pop need transcend its moment; each single crystallized a new "now" and raised expectations about what came next. With so much to hear and ferret out of three-and-a-half-minute tracks, this dense activity slowed time down. Ideas upstaged formulas, and garage rock stormed radio to become far more listenable than it had any right to be; most of this stuff made three-chord blues sound complicated. Boosting Lennon's ethic of "fun" became paramount—the "narrator" of "Louie Louie" wandered around lost in his own world, perhaps even a different world than his band's, but the effect simulated a drag-race game of chicken: the players were all responding to some imaginary ideal, with some giant invisible force drawing them forward, cutting them off, and whirring past again.

Like the R&B, doo-wop, and surf novelties it sprang from, this junior-varsity R&B held up far better than suspected, and kept oldies radio formats aloft in millions of advertising dollars for generations to come. Captain Beefheart's "Diddy Wah Diddy" held out a prankster's promise: blues as abstract truth. The raw menace of his voice toyed with all the forbidden buzz in Bo Diddley's encyclopedia of danger, "Who Do You Love?" Beefheart's record tipped over into existential delight, the joy of making noise for noise's sake.

To Lennon's voracious ear, garage rock reeked of potential—all this activity only confirmed the gambles he had made on the music since Hamburg. He helped tweak garage rock into psychedelic rock, where thickened textures wove colorful, elaborate lines of thought—ugly became the new beautiful, and chiming guitars conveyed new technical sophistication (Nazz's "Open My Eyes"), encroaching on Eastern mysticism ("Rain" and the Electric Prunes' "I Had Too Much to Dream Last Night"), a dandy's threads spun out as jangly guitars. In much the same way Muhammad Ali's championship bouts played out as civil-rights sagas, each Beatle hit carried larger meanings for both rock's style and its audience's aptitude. The pop scene resembled a giant extension of the Merseybeat scene, with Beatle musical ingenuity lifting the world's pop boats, confirming everybody's appetite for sacred thrills, shared secrets, and collective mirth.

LENNON AND MCCARTNEY HAD JOINED this garage rock conversation as early as their Beatle covers of the Marvelettes' "Please Mr. Postman" and the Shirelles' "Baby It's You," and were keenly self-conscious about its implications. The tensions they mastered straddled Lennon's experimental-philosophical with McCartney's more traditional-romantic. But as progressive as their writing and productions were, their ethic of utterly simple yet compelling sounds defined and transcended garage rock to give this larger scene a giant forward thrust.

Lennon and McCartney engaged this tension from different vantages: McCartney's formalism supplanted Lennon's experimentalism like a giant frame to rock's momentum. As kingpins, the Beatles were both standard bearers and innovators, pop stars and creative eccentrics. Beatlemania became a larger metaphor for the idea of rock as it secured its hold on the mainstream imagination: each successive single built upon the last in a larger dialogue about the ideal of cool, how much style mattered, and how far the genre might go. A new way of hearing the Beatles rose up through this wider context: rock's middle ground could be defined by the space between McCartney's romance and Lennon's abrasiveness, between the sweet of "Yesterday" (cynical craftsmanship) and the sour of "Run for Your Life" (craftsmanship exploiting cynicism). In the context of his notorious outbursts of "sick" humor, Lennon's murderous threats (the homicidal misogyny of "Catch you with another man, another man, that's the end-UH, *little girl*") revealed more in the inward sighs that followed each utterance of "Girl" than did the deadpan schmaltz of "In My Life." In such numbers, Lennon's reserved sentimentality checked McCartney's glib "sincerity."

By harnessing the larger ideas they heard at play in rock 'n' roll on *Rubber Soul,* the Beatles' tight ensemble ornamented thin writing (George Harrison's "I Need You") the same way compression, and varied repetition, brightened up their rhythmic workouts. The taut repetition on the single "She's a Woman"—vocal calisthenics for McCartney's larynx—became a lesson in withheld intensity, a salute to the delayed backbeats and roiling, understated tension of Stax's Booker T. and the M.G.s on 1962's "Green Onions." Those clipped silences, looming between the offbeats of those opening guitar chords, amplified the illuminating stop-time breaks from the opening phrases of "Love Me Do," "There's a Place," and "She Loves You" (after "with a love like that"). On the other hand, the relaxed confidence of *Rubber Soul* emphasized the band's democratic roots. Many of their ideas went slumming just for kicks: Ringo's charming singing on "What Goes On" flowed from an utterly democratic impulse (and ironically cemented his "lucky" image).

MOST HEALTHY MUSIC SCENES can be measured by their fringes, and one important garage-rock act of the period fused many of these contradictions to become one of the most important acts of all time: the Velvet Underground, former art students who lured a classical violist, John Cale, into concept rock. Warhol hired the act to perform for his "Light Shows," which combined downtown flair with uptown chic. Even Dylan paid respects to the unfazed wizard at his Factory; it was as if a new court of aesthetics emerged whole from an overwrought mainstream. The Velvets produced obscure records that became at least as influential as the Beatles', if nowhere near as popular, without even glancing toward McCartney-style "respectable" melodies. Likewise, there were no "cute" members of the Troggs or the Trashmen—or Sam the Sham and the Pharaohs, who simply turned minority status (Sam was Hispanic) into a costume of comic menace and magic-house intrigue. Sam's "Wooly Bully," which might otherwise have been a novelty number, became a decisive piece of nonsense from April 1965—its silliness skated across Dylan's manic assault on reason. Borrowing a page from Dylan's playbook, garage rock worked a baffle-your-enemies shtick instead of the usual outsmart-or-outplay-the-competition.

Another measure of the scene's health lay in heady regional outbursts. Portland's Kingsmen were followed by the Northwest's more ambitious Paul Revere and the Raiders, a swift-kicking band that scored hits like "Hungry" and "Kicks," an antidrug song that circled back on itself: if kicks were so hard to find, how come these seemingly tossed-off hits kept colliding in the top ten?

Some of this bravura trickled down onto mainstream television. The Beatles' 1965 eponymous Saturday-morning cartoon show, spun off from *A Hard Day's Night,* in turn helped inspire a weekly NBC 1966 sitcom following *Help!,* called *The Monkees,* produced by television's Bert

Schneider and Bob Rafelson, with Don Kirshner overseeing the music. These twin ripoffs pulled at Beatlemania from both ends: on the one hand, they siphoned off the cuddly and cartoonish aspects of the band's popularity for an even younger, preteen audience, and the contrast gave the real-life band more heft. They also smoothed over and whitewashed any political relevance Lennon and the others began to display at increasingly bogus press conferences.

Kirshner gave situationist theorists new grist for "discourse" and postmodernism: the Monkees, conceived and produced in Los Angeles as American-sitcom Beatles, became "authentic" pop product. On their weekly prime-time TV show, they amplified the mainstream impulses behind every teenager's preoccupation with forming guitar chords, perfecting tom-tom swirls, and combing their hair just so to copy their heroes and impress girls. Kirshner backed up his puppets with sharp songwriters (Tommy Boyce and Bobby Hart, Neil Diamond, Harry Nilsson, Gerry Goffin and Carole King) and in the studio, many of Phil Spector's Wrecking Crew: Hal Blaine on drums, Glen Campbell on guitar, Larry Knechtel (the pianist who went on to play "Bridge Over Troubled Water" on keyboards). And yet, where the Beatles could be reduced to cartoons, the Stones and Dylan couldn't be, and it gave both these figures more leftist credibility—even though Lennon had been the earliest to speak out against the Vietnam War, in essence a prophet in 1964. McCartney professed himself a Monkees fan; Michael Nesmith showed up at the *Sgt. Pepper* orchestral party. And yet the Beatles had a lofty perch: they held court far above these commercial spinoffs and made them seem all but irrelevant, if mindless, fun. (This made for antic parlor games: the Monkees enjoyed an inverse curve to the Beatles; the more control they gained over their records, the more their music waned.)

The ultimate test of garage rock came in how it felled a former giant like Phil Spector, who attempted two final production numbers, the first a delirious triumph, the second a sphinxlike masterpiece. The Righteous Brothers' "You've Lost That Lovin' Feeling" stormed top-forty radio like a volcano of dismay and regret, while "River Deep—Mountain High," from Ike and Tina Turner, scored only in Britain. Against all the new inspired amateurism, Spector bombast suddenly rang pompous. Pop's great white whale of romantic desire reared up one last time, then submerged.

INSTEAD OF SPONGING OFF their peers, the Beatles acted as if all the new sounds gave their material momentum. Embracing many of the new trends, they invented a few more. Lennon heard both rock's essential underpinnings and its future in garage rock's premise: that four unskilled boys with the simplest of setups (guitar, bass, drums) could attack the music with more depth and imagination, and make a bigger impact, than any "pros" involved at the same level of hit-making. This tension, between primitivism and sophistication, accident and calculation, mirrored Lennon's emotional quandaries as the Beatles streaked through their middle period.

Rubber Soul outlined how folk rock, and the Beatles' embrace of group dynamics, enhanced their larger sense of pop; *Revolver* advanced this mode and brought in third-person address, and even subtler, more intricate technological solutions to questions few others were even asking (tape loops, multiple overdubbing, and bigger ideas stringing everything together). Bigger questions, political and philosophical, crept in: Harrison's opening number cut the "Taxman" down to size, and concluded with death as a précis to McCartney's ballad about aging and loneliness, "Eleanor Rigby." The album worked in vivid images of privation and alienation ("She Said She Said") among bursts of hubris ("And Your Bird Can Sing") that reached toward some final, defining transcendence ("Tomorrow Never Knows"). Could a unifying force be gathered from all these threads? Could anyone connect the dots between conservative sugar-pop and wild-eyed anarchism to create a larger synthesis? Could Lennon resist such a dare?

As they entered the studio in April 1966, the band's work turned obsessive, the camaraderie uneven. McCartney was photographed about town with his chic girlfriend, the actress Jane Asher, and when she traveled, he played Swinging Londoner almost as if he knew he was in a play. Lennon's closest musical friend led a charmed celebrity life, while

Lennon's wife and child wedged envy into their competitive partnership. The band started the year's studio work with an overdub session for the August 1965 Shea Stadium concert. The final tracks included some composites from the Hollywood Bowl concerts, since Shea's sound didn't work.[3] Then they scattered for time off and work on independent projects, and their first extended breather from three grueling years of non-stop touring and recording. With their MBEs, they had earned enough leverage with Epstein to demand more downtime, and the status to say and mean no to more and more requests for appearances. Beyond spring studio sessions and summer touring, they committed themselves only to keeping fall options open.

In this curiously productive and compelling middle period, Lennon and McCartney kept collaborating as their voices veered apart. The world's most famous songwriting partnership split into distinct halves, the cute one contemplating social isolation ("Eleanor Rigby"), the brute idealizing childhood ("She Said She Said") and chasing relief ("Tomorrow Never Knows"). "We Can Work It Out" framed a lover's argument as Lennon's minor bridges tried to undermine McCartney's major verses. In a larger context, they volleyed song themes back and forth between *Rubber Soul* and *Revolver*. McCartney's "Eleanor Rigby" and "For No One" were not just extensions of "Yesterday" but elaborations on Lennon's "Nowhere Man." And while the vocal ensemble grew and flourished from *Rubber Soul*'s "Nowhere Man," "You Won't See Me," and "Girl," there were no Lennon-McCartney duets on *Revolver* that rivaled "There's a Place" or "If I Fell" or "Ticket to Ride." As an index of their friendship, their vocal duets grew more infrequent. This made their chemistry even more magical when it jelled.

"Yesterday" had been the first McCartney solo track the previous year; these spring 1966 sessions yielded two more McCartney did without the group, one more isolated than the next. Lennon helped compose "Eleanor Rigby," and George Martin scored it for doubled string quartet, or octet, to darken its mood. On "For No One," the basic track sported keyboard and drums, overdubbed with McCartney on clavichord, Ringo on cymbals and maracas, and symphony player Alan Civil on French horn. McCartney's sessions grew more elaborate, his partnership with Martin a natural outgrowth of his formal pretensions; Lennon produced more and more home demos in his Kenwood attic using two-track reel-to-reels, piano, and acoustic guitar. Now they touched up each other's near-finished numbers more than they fed each other lines.

Work on *Revolver* started with "Tomorrow Never Knows," the most experimental track, with major progress made over the first two days of recording, on April 6–7. Norman Smith, Martin's engineer throughout many of the Beatles' early recordings, had been promoted, so the control desk brought a new face, twenty-year-old Geoff Emerick, to the party. His ears and technical curiosities would transform Beatle recordings for the rest of their career, and his memoirs account for much of the band's internal dynamics and work habits.

The *Rubber Soul* sessions had settled into a vaguely regular schedule of afternoons and evenings, while still leaving time for clubbing after signing off between 10 P.M. and the early hours. The *Revolver* sessions grew more intense, lasting well past midnight from early on, and gave Emerick headaches about rides home after the Underground had shut down. Ten- to twelve-hour studio blocks marked the Beatles' work schedule between April and June for six, sometimes seven, days running, from early afternoon into the early morning hours. Typically, they knocked off up to twelve takes for a basic track (rhythm section of bass, drums, and guitar) and then overdubbed lead vocals, harmonies, extra percussion, and the like for several days afterward to build the final mix.

LENNON'S MUSICAL DABBLINGS with Indian ragas came alongside readings in Eastern mysticism, trends influenced by the latent underground scene. McCartney introduced Lennon to his London friends Barry Miles and John Dunbar, who ran the Indica bookstore, a hub to London's counterculture. Dunbar's marriage to Marianne Faithfull (whom Andrew Loog Oldham signed to sing Jagger and Richards's "As Tears Go By") faltered on his heroin addiction and Mick Jagger's designs on his wife. McCartney helped Miles and Dunbar paint their shop, and they passed along to Lennon Timothy Leary's book *The Psychedelic Experience: A Manual Based on The Tibetan Book of the Dead,* then making the rounds as a "trip guide." Tibetan mystics chanted the original text to achieve an intense meditative state; when acid still had "recreational" cachet, Leary, the ex–Harvard psychology professor, proposed his book as a mental gameplan. In these elite London circles, LSD tabs provided a "shortcut" to this ancient, transcendent experience. Why meditate for days or years to reach enlightenment when you could recite from a handbook as you popped a pill? Leary's book gave drug culture a "legitimate" spiritual backdrop.

To Lennon, the book cried out for a soundtrack. He set this road map to the mind with the ultimate garage-rock conceit: a single chord driven furiously from beneath by bass and drums, with only two shifting modal harmonies up top (the I chord alternating with b-VIII). Guitars entered only as backward solo. While McCartney branched out further and further into his harmonic progressions ("Here, There and Everywhere" sports a cunning double-key narrative, the template for "Penny Lane"), Lennon distilled his new song down to a single chord, which flickered against its minor dominant (or Mixolydian V), wavering between this reality and the next. As rhythm subsumed harmony, random noise emerged triumphant. It was as if garage rock had been pointing toward something all along, and "Tomorrow Never Knows" became its ultimate vector and leaping-off point.

On the first day, April 6, they put down the drum and bass in three takes and labeled the tape "Mark I." The next morning, McCartney, enamored of Stockhausen and Varèse compositions he'd heard through Dunbar and Miles, came in with tape loops he'd made on his living room reel-to-reel, which gave the track's opening moments an unearthly sweep. To get these effects, Martin had several Beatles and friends stand holding fingers, pencils, empty reels, and other objects to string through the long, quarter-inch tape loops so they cycled on top of one another simultaneously. "I held up my jam jar for a huge loop to run through, and I felt I was helping create the latest in cutting edge artistic fusion," Barry Miles remembers.[4] Like the defining Mellotron introduction to "Strawberry Fields Forever," or the finely shaded vocal harmonies on "Don't Let Me Down," McCartney's role on this Lennon track tends to go undernoticed.

Later that day they did five early takes of McCartney's soul workout "Got to Get You into My Life." The next day they perfected "Life" with three more takes and began to think about adding horns. The following week brought "Love You To" on Monday, April 11, and their next single popped out over three intense days: "Paperback Writer" and "Rain," songwriting leaps that brought new technical verve to their studio technique. For months, McCartney and the other Beatles had been pestering Martin to deliver sturdier, more punchy bass sounds, the kind they were hearing on labels like Motown (with the indefatigable James Jamerson) and Stax (whose house band, Booker T. and the M.G.s, featured white-knuckler Donald "Duck" Dunn). These complaints arose again during rhythm tracks for "Paperback Writer" and led to an ingenious solution from engineer Ken Townsend.

Before graduating to headphones (or "cans"), the Beatles used unidirectional microphones and sang directly in front of a huge white playback speaker dubbed "the White Elephant." This enormous, oversize wooden box pumped out lively sounds they reacted to while singing, the next best thing to fronting live instruments without having to play as they sang. The microphone placement prevented the instrumental playback from leaking into their vocal tracks; by pointing them directly at the singers, these particular microphones never picked up the "leak." This setup gave much of the early Beatles singing animation and punch. The switch to "cans" can be heard on a lot of the more intimate singing and harmonizing that begins with *Sgt. Pepper.*

The White Elephant had personality. "It's a big playback speaker," Ken Townsend remembered, "and for playback in the studios it had incredible bass." At this "Paperback Writer" session in April, Townsend struck on a weird notion. "You sat in the control room and you heard all the comments from George Martin and the Beatles, and you sort of put two-and-two together. . . . It wasn't because I felt we needed more bass, it was because the artist thought we needed more bass," he went on. Townsend wondered if that White Elephant might absorb as well as it projected.

Simply by plugging the speaker into a different jack (to send rather than receive an electronic signal), Townsend reversed the White Elephant's capacity—the speaker became a microphone. Instead of using it to sing along to, McCartney performed his bass line as usual through his regular amp, placed in front of the White Elephant, which picked up his sound and fed it into the control board. (In place of a microphone picking up the vibrations from his bass amp, a speaker picked up vibrations from another speaker cabinet.) The results were magnificent. On the playback, everybody marveled at the newly rich and booming McCartney bass sound.

But Townsend, a modest gentleman, describes some of the other factors that played tricks on their ears while they were mixing Beatle records. Townsend had been assisting George Martin on Beatle sessions since the early days in 1962; he joined EMI in 1950, and ultimately rose through its ranks to become director: "The Altec loudspeakers that we used in the control room, later on [it was] discovered that these were bass light. So in actual fact . . . the bass response was actually there sometimes, but we couldn't hear it! When we put better speakers in the control room with more bass, we no longer had to fight for bass and the records got better."[5] The settings on Capitol's American equipment, which didn't always correspond to the settings the EMI engineers had mastered Beatle recordings to, complicated this playback situation. For a long time, Capitol engineers thought Beatle recordings sounded terrible, and they added reverb to everything they pressed to help wash over what they perceived as imperfections from EMI's shop. This added still another layer to the tensions between UK and U.S. perceptions of the Beatles' sound.

Over the next two sessions the band laid down the five complete rhythm tracks and overdubs for "Rain," widely regarded as McCartney's bass breakthrough, not just his solo breaks but the soaring melodic lines he traced surfing Ringo's terse, involuted drumming. As part of the Beatles' ethic never to repeat themselves, even when they'd stumbled on an ingenious solution, the White Elephant speaker bass feed did not appear after the B side, "Rain"; each new track demanded its own unique solutions.

Shortly after Maureen Cleave's Lennon profile appeared in Britain,

Capitol contacted Brian Epstein about supplying another album cover, this time for the *Yesterday and Today* compilation, set for June. To maintain its annual three-album schedule, Capitol culled tracks from the British editions of *Help!* and *Rubber Soul* and snagged three numbers from their current sessions ("Dr. Robert," "I'm Only Sleeping," and "And Your Bird Can Sing"). Epstein called Robert Whitaker, the Melbourne photographer he'd retained on staff for just such quick-and-dirty assignments. Whitaker made a habit of posing subjects with props to prompt whimsy: during a previous Beatle photo shoot, they had pointed brooms at one another, a session best known as the series Capitol slapped on *Beatles '65*. This time, Whitaker took things a step further.

Whitaker suggested a pose to explode the tired cliché of the "cuddly moptops," and the Beatles dove in. They grabbed Whitaker's props and sat in white jackets, cackling and jostling, their bodies draped with raw animal flesh and dismembered baby dolls. Those white jackets atop turtlenecks were a nice touch—butchers, doctors, or mental patient stewards? The sick humor of Lennon's cripple jokes and mental spastics suddenly sprang to life, and he pushed hard to make it the official American album shot.[6] Curiously, there are no quotes about Epstein's opinion on this photo, but the gesture reeks of the Beatles' contempt for Capitol's artificially sequenced albums. Implicit in this deal, which stripped *Revolver*'s American edition of three key Lennon tracks, was the controversy-baiting cover photo they forced Capitol to publish. One hundred thousand copies were printed before Capitol panicked and recalled them, leading to a notorious collectible item—for roughly thirty thousand of these, Capitol hastily pasted over the originals with new art, and "steaming off" the outer layer took on overtones of the occult: unveiling the smiling madmen underneath the corporate pose.

The replacement photograph showed the Beatles seated around a giant trunk in casual garb: John, arms folded and sneering in a mod-striped blue jacket with dark slacks and white socks; Paul sitting beneath him, inside the trunk; Ringo in a collarless Nehru shirt and jacket; George standing behind them in an off-tan shirt and billowing white tie. Compared to the body parts it replaced, this looked tame. But their mod clothes and patronizing expressions gave off an unfazed confidence, as if they were still toying with those body parts in their heads. The new cover mocked the very idea of a more "acceptable" pose.

But both the "Butcher cover" and the "more popular than Jesus" quote lay dormant while the band returned to the studio for many late-night sessions from April through June. As they recorded, the Rolling Stones' *Aftermath* quickly ascended the charts, and the group's singles, "19th Nervous Breakdown" and "Paint It Black," saturated the airwaves, alongside Otis Redding's cover of "Satisfaction," the Byrds' "Eight Miles High," the Troggs' "Wild Thing," the Silkie's "You've Got to Hide Your Love Away," and the Kinks' "Sunny Afternoon."

STUDIO INGENUITY and upside-down engineering tricks became hallmarks of most Beatles recordings from here on in, and the band loved raiding the instrument closet underneath the control room stairs in Studio 2 for weird sound effects (as on "Yellow Submarine"). But they also tweaked their guitar sounds through their writing: for "And Your Bird Can Sing," McCartney and Harrison coiled around each other on their Epiphone Casinos for a winding duet, a dual lead that made Lennon's bitterness shimmer; "Dr. Robert" had sunbursts of resentment. No sooner had they finished "Bird" than Harrison's "Taxman" went from basic tracks to final arrangement in two days.

For all his wild-man, wire-the-limousine eccentricities, in practice Lennon resembled a technophobe; threading tape into a reel deck often gave him fits. This lack of skill turned him on one night when he accidentally threaded a reel to play backward: he had brought home a rough mix of "Rain" and in a stupor began running it the wrong way across the magnetic heads. He loved the result. Martin spliced out his opening vocal passage on "Rain" and ran it backward for the fade-outs of that same number, and "I'm Only Sleeping" used backward guitar doodles to convey the invading dreamscape of his afternoon naps. By the end of April, passing the halfway mark, Lennon had brought in "I'm Only Sleeping" (April 27), which included a cheeky yawn over McCartney's bass break (at 2:00). Martin scored and conducted the string parts for "Eleanor Rigby" (April 28). Working side-by-side on separate songs on the 29th, Lennon laid down his vocals for his track and McCartney tracked "Rigby."

Epstein intruded on *Revolver* sessions for a couple of promotional events: at the May appearance at the *New Musical Express* Poll Winners' Concert at Wembley, they reached back to five songs from 1964–65 for what would be their last UK live appearance until 1969: "I Feel Fine," "Nowhere Man," "Day Tripper," "If I Needed Someone," and "I'm Down"; they tracked BBC interviews on May 2 and lip-synced promotional films for "Paperback Writer" and "Rain" on location in Chiswick Gardens on May 20. Back in the studio, the band regained its momentum quickly with "Yellow Submarine," cut in five delirious takes on the evening of May 26.

THE NEXT NIGHT, all four Beatles attended the Bob Dylan show at the Royal Albert Hall, just as they had the previous spring. This year, however, Dylan had morphed from adored folkie bard into rock sage. For his first electric tour, he brought along Johnny Rivers's drummer, Mickey Jones, to play with a Canadian crew, the Hawks (later known as The Band). Several nights earlier, in Manchester, someone in the crowd had yelled "Judas!" as Dylan lit into "Like a Rolling Stone," rock mythology steamrolling over folkie holdouts.

By this point, Lennon and Dylan were circling each other warily, as much friends as friendly competitors in rock's great superstar sweepstakes. Lennon gobbled up everything Dylan put out just as surely as Dylan listened carefully to Beatle albums. *Blonde on Blonde,* Dylan's double-disc masterstroke (with "Just Like a Woman," "I Want You," and "Visions of Johanna"), came out shortly after this, and Lennon had likely heard advance acetates, enough to be intimidated, not least because Dylan had turned the druggy waltz of "Norwegian Wood" into fodder for his own daunting one-night stand, "4th Time Around." In this transatlantic duel between narrative wizards, Lennon felt insecurities he couldn't articulate. Dylan, on the other hand, had way too cool a façade to let on about feeling intimidated, even though the dramatic threat of his rock move had far more Lennon to it than Lennon numbers had Dylan fingerprints ("You've Got to Hide Your Love Away").

They partied on Beatle turf in the clubs after the gig. D. A. Pennebaker caught their car ride to the Mayfair Hotel on Stratton Street for part of his unreleased documentary on Dylan, *Eat the Document* (much of which appeared in Martin Scorsese's *No Direction Home*, in 2006, and was cited in *Keys to the Rain: The Bob Dylan Encyclopedia*, by Oliver Trager, in 2004). This heavily bootlegged car scene captured the two pop stars jabbing each other verbally about pop's lesser royalty, the only footage of the two songwriters conversing. Conducting a mock interview, Lennon accused Dylan of backing the Mamas and the Papas "big-ly." "I knew it would get to that," Dylan shoots back with mock condescension. "You're just interested in the big chick [Mama Cass Elliot], right? She's got hold of you, too. She's got ahold of everybody I know. Everybody asks me the same thing. You're terrible, man." Dylan pushes back by asking Lennon about the band Silkie, the UK group that charted with "You've Got to Hide Your Love Away" (on a session co-produced by Lennon and McCartney).

There's an affection between these two as they fiddle with their superstar masks, but Dylan slurs his words and has to work hard to hold up his head, as though the chemicals compete for control of his body. None of the shtick seems to float, or to amuse them as much as they hope it might. Soon after this, Dylan begs his driver to pull over so he can be sick. Even Lennon, no stranger to hangovers, looks embarrassed to be riffing with Dylan in this condition. On the verge of a huge creative breakthrough, Dylan seemed gutted by drugs, living for his shows but absent for the rest. It's hard to tell how much Lennon identified with him on this level, but he must have taken small comfort to see a fellow rock star so worn down by touring.

The Beatles scurried to finish *Revolver* as the summer's touring season approached, adding elaborate sound effects to "Yellow Submarine" (in a daffy session with Brian Jones, Marianne Faithfull, George and

Pattie Harrison, Neil Aspinall, Mal Evans, and Abbey Road staffers John Skinner and Terry Condon). The next day, Harrison led them through his third track, marked "Laxton's Superb" (which became "I Want to Tell You").

With vocal overdubs remaining for "Eleanor Rigby," "Good Day Sunshine" (just three takes on June 8), and "Here There and Everywhere" the following week, they mimed both "Paperback Writer" and "Rain" for the BBC's *Top of the Pops* and then stopped off at the Waldorf Hotel on the Strand for a *Pet Sounds* listening party. To avoid the anticlimactic response that America had given Brian Wilson's latest album, Bruce Johnston, the Beach Boys' newest member, brought over a tape with Epstein's former assistant, Derek Taylor (now promoting the Byrds in Los Angeles). An avowed Beach Boys fanatic, Taylor knew Lennon and McCartney would want to be among the first to have a listen. Kim Fowley, an L.A. scenester, remembered the two Beatles arriving in their collarless jackets, hanging on every note:

> Everybody sat listening intently as the music played. When it ended, Lennon and McCartney went over to the piano together, noodled about with some chords, and had a private conversation about something, right in front of the rest of us. Then they came up and shook our hands, told Johnston how much they admired it, and just as quickly they were gone.[7]

McCartney let it leak that he prized "God Only Knows" as the "greatest song ever written." Andrew Loog Oldham, now the Rolling Stones' manager, took out a full-page ad in *Melody Maker* to proclaim *Pet Sounds* the "greatest album ever made." In the ongoing debate between the primal and elaborate, and the American vs. British inclinations in rock style, the UK's response to *Pet Sounds* proved clairvoyant. The very idea of Wilson seeking out Lennon and McCartney's blessing would have been unthinkable even three years before, when the favor would most likely have been sought from the other direction. In this way, Wilson's fate linked up to Spector's: cherished abroad, *Pet Sounds,* like "River

Deep—Mountain High," didn't get the Capitol marketing support it deserved and peaked at number ten before a rapid falling off at home.

FROM THERE, LENNON AND McCARTNEY went straight back to EMI for nine more takes of "Here, There and Everywhere." The "She Said She Said" session came on the last day (June 21), after an afternoon of mixing the rest of the tracks into an album sequence. The band recorded four complete takes of Lennon's song between 7 P.M. and 3:45 A.M., while batting around album titles—*Abracadabra, Magic Circles,* and *The Beatles on Safari*—until *Revolver* got the nod. Racing to hit the stages Epstein had booked them the world over, a new commotion devoured the band, leaving scant time for reflection on how the rock star with the sharpest fangs, elsewhere so preening, ambitious, and arrogant, openly envied the state of childhood ("When I was a boy everything was right"), as his partner scored nursery-school sing-alongs ("Yellow Submarine"). Fewer still suspected this tour would be their last.

AGGRAVATING MANY OF THE SAME frustrations Lennon and the Beatles felt during the previous summer's performances, *Revolver* barely changed the rigors of the live game. The sounds they chased in the studio led to all kinds of tricks, edits, tape treatments, and sleight of hand, and along the way, they lost track of how any of it might be reproduced live. The sound checks that have become routine for touring bands ever since were unheard of at this point, and 1966 concert-amplification technology lagged even further behind their material than EMI's equipment. They could barely hear themselves play or sing, and the crowds seemed to scream that much louder. Yet ambition compelled them to attempt the fragile vocal harmonies of "Nowhere Man" despite these enormous handicaps. One night, in exasperation, Lennon vented his frustration with how the Beatles struggled to hear themselves straight to the audience: "Don't listen to our music. We're terrible these days."[8]

As the screams intensified, a new fear crept into the Beatle camp. "I remember when George was in Germany he got a letter saying, 'You won't live beyond the next month,'" George Martin recalled. "And when they went to Japan they had such heavy guards they couldn't move anywhere. The Japanese took those death threats very seriously."⁹ After appearances in Munich and Hamburg, they flew straight into a storm that forced them to lay over for nine hours in Anchorage, Alaska. By the time they landed in Tokyo at three the next morning, the press had labeled the storm "the Beatle Typhoon," the most rain Tokyo had seen in ten years. When asked about it at their press conference, Lennon remained blasé: "There's probably more wind from the press than from us."

The storm had symbolic gust: the media sensed a mania edging toward violence, and editorial pages warned of possible riots all over the world. Reporters pitched surreal, inane questions that seemed out of touch with the scale of events and the pitch of the crowds. The day-to-day meetings with the press turned confrontational. At another press conference in Tokyo, a reporter asked the group: "What are you going to be when you grow up?" Lennon replied: "If you grow up yourself you'd know better than to ask that question."¹⁰

Rigid Japanese security prevented the Beatles from leaving their hotel rooms for their entire three-day stay, although Lennon managed to sneak out for some shopping, spending more than $20,000 to impress an astonished antiques vendor with his range and taste.¹¹ When he was caught, the police threatened to withdraw their "protection" for the band, which felt more like detention. For their first and only performances on Japanese soil, they performed three evenings inside the Nippon Budokan Temple in central Tokyo.¹² Outside the hall, protestors attacked pop music's "desecration" of a sacred Japanese site.

From Japan, the Beatles lurched into their bizarre encounter with Imelda Marcos, the Philippines' first lady. Marcos, the former beauty queen who became the original Iron Butterfly, had enough vanity to match her husband Ferdinand's corruption. They had been in power not quite a year when the Beatles came, and their effrontery could not be quantified.

Ever since their MBEs the previous summer, a Beatle appearance had taken on the stature of a royal visit and conferred international prestige on a country looking for attention. The Epstein operation, however, while efficient in rock terms, lacked diplomatic finesse. The Manila *Sunday Times* greeted the Beatles' arrival with the following story: "President Marcos, the First Lady, and the three young Beatles fans in the family, have been invited as guests of honor at the concerts. The Beatles plan to personally follow up the invitation during a courtesy call on Mrs. Imelda Marcos at Malacañang Palace tomorrow morning at 11 o'clock." Epstein called the local promoter, Ramón Ramos, to wave off this distraction: his boys had a day off after the concert; there would be no scene at the court where some dignitary might clip Ringo's hair. Unwittingly, Epstein slapped the Marcos regime in the face. Ramos had leaked the schedule to the press before confirming with Epstein, who strictly guarded his boys' days off.

Unaware of any problems, the band played two shows before a total of eighty thousand shrieking fans at the Rizal Memorial Football Stadium. There's a finely tuned fictional account of their show from the novelist Eric Gamalinda:

> On the eve of the Beatles' arrival, a young *colegiala* threatened to jump off the roof of the Bank of the Philippine Islands building unless she was granted a private audience with the band. . . . And when the Beatles finally opened with "I Wanna Be Your Man," you could feel the excitement ripping through you, a detonation of such magnitude your entire being seemed to explode. I couldn't hear anything except a long, extended shrill—the whole stadium screaming its lungs out. I looked at Delphi [his younger sister]. She was holding her head between her hands and her eyes were bulging out and her mouth was stretched to an O, and all I could hear was this long, high-pitched scream coming out of her mouth. I had never seen Delphi like that before, and I would never, for the rest of her life, see her as remorselessly young as she was that afternoon.[13]

Epstein and the Beatles awoke the next morning to a TV nightmare: state television broadcast weeping children at the Marcos palace, newspapers blared "Imelda Stood Up," and death threats swamped the hotel and the British Embassy. The Beatles had "rebuffed" the autocratic rulers and were abruptly requested to leave. Almost as soon as they realized their mistake, they worried about how to escape. The government withdrew its heavy security detail and Ramos sat on the gate receipts. Fleeing their hotel, they encountered more hostility at Manila's airport, where a "tax commissioner" insisted on collecting a cash percentage from the show they had yet to be paid for. After tense negotiations, Epstein finally "filed a bond," essentially a bribe, to assure their safe departure.[14] A crowd of angry Filipinos saw them off, chanting: *"Beatles Alis Diyan!"* ("Beatles Go Home!").

They flew to New Delhi, but instead of respite, hundreds of screaming fans greeted their arrival because the media had leaked their whereabouts. Giving up on a couple of days' peace, they flew back to England a day ahead of schedule, where they could at least enjoy fan assault on familiar turf. The BBC met them for quotes at Heathrow, and they lay low for the rest of the month. "We're going to have a couple of weeks to recuperate before we go and get beaten up by the Americans," George Harrison quipped.[15]

INSTEAD OF AMERICANS PREPPING to give them a victory lap around the States, their most popular turf, Beatle record-burnings erupted throughout the South as "Yellow Submarine" hit the charts, and Capitol Records went into crisis management. In late June, the label had released *Yesterday and Today,* bearing Whitaker's "butcher cover," the grinning Beatles looking out from beneath raw meat and limbless dolls. Retailers recoiled, and Capitol had to pull its product and issue a letter from vice president Ron Topper. It's a classic "blame-the-Brits" corporate statement, without apology: "The original cover, created in England, was intended as 'pop art' satire. However, a sampling of public opinion in the United States indicates that the cover design is subject to misinterpretation. For this reason, and to avoid any possible controversy or undeserved harm to the Beatles' image or reputation, Capitol has chosen to withdraw the LP and substitute a more generally acceptable design."[16]

The controversy vaulted the album to the top of the charts, as "Paperback Writer" and "Rain" clobbered radio. *Revolver* came out in early August 1966. Between *Rubber Soul* and *Revolver*, Lennon's "more popular than Jesus" quote got isolated, reframed, and used as a sensationalist headline on the cover of *Datebook*, a teen magazine, beneath THE TEN ADULTS YOU DIG/HATE THE MOST. Combined with the "butcher cover," Lennon's quote gave the Bible Belt conniptions. A deejay in Birmingham, Alabama, read Lennon's quotes on the air while smashing vinyl. Thirty radio stations in eleven states followed suit. Southern pastors thundered for Beatle boycotts from their pulpits. Even the Vatican weighed in, although Lennon's remarks were directed at the Anglican Church: "Some subjects must not be dealt with profanely, even in the world of beatniks," said Pope Paul VI, simultaneously denouncing both Lennon's comment and millions of Beatle fans. Before the band even set foot in America, most Southern radio stations had purged themselves of the demon Beatles.

Concert sellouts had dropped off in 1965 largely because Epstein booked larger houses. This time, promoters were nervous, not just about selling tickets but preventing riots. With his sense of fatherly protectiveness, Epstein flew on ahead to New York to reassure American promoters about refunds should dates be canceled.[17] After many phone calls to an obstinate Lennon, he convinced him that his remark had placed his fellow Beatles in real danger, and Epstein scheduled a press conference in advance of their opening concert.

Arriving in Chicago from London on August 11, Lennon sat with the other Beatles, took questions, and issued an "apology" that wire stories carried around the world. He entered the hotel conference room crammed with reporters itching for a "gotcha" moment and, for the first time, had to spin something out of defeat instead of batting down the usual inanities. His face ashen, the Beatle who had never appeared anything but effortlessly self-confident, seemed beside himself with fear. His statement mixed grudging contrition with a piercing resentment at the malevolence his comments had uncovered: "If I had said television is more popular than Jesus," Lennon sputtered, "I might have got away with it. . . . I just said 'they' are having more influence on kids and things than anything else, including Jesus."

Now the swoon lashed back, grabbed its humbled moment from rock's great quote machine, and reveled in the sight of Lennon groping for words: "I'm not saying that we're better or greater, or comparing us with Jesus Christ as a person or God as a thing or whatever it is. I just said what I said and it was wrong. Or it was taken wrong."[18]

To American parents who had yet to be charmed, this seemed like the Beatles' just comeuppance. Finally, these cheeky Brits would get taken down a notch like some other ne'er-do-well freaks like Jerry Lee Lewis and Chuck Berry. Beatlemania, far more intense and sweeping than the hula hoop or Elvis Presley, had also grown far more threatening to middle-class mores. To be honored by their queen and then remark so casually about how they had assumed the role of Christ in teenage life, well, this simply made Lennon too big for his rock-star britches.

And throughout these political and religious controversies, the press kept inflating the bubble, even while asking about the inevitable burst. Lennon had trouble avoiding sarcasm at such moments. When asked if Lennon and McCartney might someday replace Rodgers and Hammerstein, he quipped, "We don't want to be Rodgers and Hart, either."[19]

Despite Lennon's Chicago "apology," and subsequent press conferences in New York, Seattle, and Los Angeles, the controversy acted like fertilizer to the ignorant. In Alabama, two thousand teenagers tossed their Beatle vinyl into bonfires, drowning out a pro-Beatle protest across the street. The Ku Klux Klan picketed the Washington, D.C., show and threatened the band on television. At the evening show in Memphis later that week, a firecracker went off in the audience, and all the other Beatles instinctively turned their heads toward Lennon, presumed shot.

Then the Beatle "typhoon" that had derailed their Tokyo trip two months before returned, this time to Cincinnati. The downpour forced them to reschedule Saturday's outdoor show at Crosley Field on August 20, for Sunday, August 21, which might have been easy enough. But Epstein kept on schedule by jetting them 341 miles between afternoon and evening sets to make their appearance in St. Louis, where they performed for twenty-three thousand people beneath a giant rain tarp. For McCartney, this was the last straw: he finally capitulated to Lennon, Harrison, and Starr's urging that this be their last tour. "We were having to worry about the rain getting in the amps and this took us right back to the Cavern days—it was worse than those early days. I don't even think the house was full," McCartney remembered:

> After the gig I remember us getting in a big, empty steel-lined wagon, like a removal van. There was no furniture in there—nothing. We were sliding around trying to hold on to something, and at that moment everyone said, "Oh, this bloody touring lark—I've had it up to here, man." I finally agreed. I'd been trying to say, "Ah, touring's good and it keeps us sharp. We need touring, and musicians need to play. Keep music alive." I had held onto that attitude when there were doubts, but finally I agreed with them. . . . We agreed to say nothing, but never to tour again.[20]

They couldn't hear themselves play, their audiences were too busy screaming or protesting to care, and the havoc they had to march through to get on and off the stage had become far more trouble than any pleasure they might still glean from the music. Downpours only made Epstein push them harder, and the stage made Lennon feel like a walking target. *Revolver*, a new creative peak, had heightened the hysteria. But for the moment, they followed Epstein's counsel and kept their decision to themselves.

The Beatles took the stage at Candlestick Park in San Francisco on August 29 with a collective sense of relief and finality. The audience, unaware of this unspoken farewell, embraced them with a deafening pitch, convincing them that Beatlemania had let loose spooks it was best to avoid. There was something in the crowd's mood of careening, almost desperate, adoration that made the Beatles feel like the tail wagging a rabid dog. Harrison remembers putting timed cameras on the amps: "We stopped between tunes, Ringo got down off the drums, and we stood facing the amplifiers with our back to the audience and took photographs. We knew, 'this is it—we're not going to do this again. This is the last concert.' It was a unanimous decision."[21]

In his nonfiction phantasm *The Electric Kool-Aid Acid Test* (1968), Tom Wolfe used this concert to describe the warped, compulsive frenzy in the air. Wolfe built his narrative around novelist Ken Kesey (*One Flew Over the Cuckoo's Nest* and *Sometimes a Great Notion*), who had already led some early acid happenings on the West Coast with the Grateful Dead and Hells Angels. Kesey attended the show with his Merry Pranksters. After watching a thousand California teenagers trip to light shows, Candlestick Park struck Kesey as mania at its final stage of darkness, and echo of the band's *Ed Sullivan Show* debut well into spoilage (he called it a "cancer"). Wolfe's passage doubles as a portent of Altamont, the late 1969 speedway concert where the Hells Angels killed a black man in the front row during the Rolling Stones set.

Just when the noise cannot get any louder, Wolfe writes, "it doubles, his eardrums ring like stamped metal with it and suddenly GHHHHHOOOOOOOWWWWW, it is like the whole thing has snapped, and the whole front section of the arena becomes a writhing, seething mass of little girls waving their arms in the air," which he likens to "a single colonial animal with a thousand waving pink tentacles." Kesey felt a twinge of fear watching the Beatles that night. As he watched them "play the beast," delight in their God-like crowd manipulations, Wolfe describes how he also sensed their futility: "One of the Beatles, John, George, Paul, dips his long electric guitar handle in one direction and the whole teeny horde ripples precisely along the line of energy he set off—and then in the other direction, precisely along that line. It causes them to grin, John and Paul and George and Ringo, rippling the poor huge freaked teeny beast this way and that—"

Here was a "vibrating poison madness," Wolfe writes, that filled the universe with "the teeny agony torn out of them." All around him, girls start to faint, as if the noise suffocates them, and the security staff starts carrying limp bodies to first-aid tents as the crowd surges. To Kesey, the scene resembles a disease, "a state of sheer poison mad cancer. The

Beatles are the creature's head. The teeny freaks are the body. But the head has lost control of the body and the body rebels and goes amok and that is what cancer is."[22]

FLYING BACK TO LONDON, Lennon felt even more release fleeing the United States than he had fleeing the Philippines just a month before. The freakish democratic abandon of America seemed to hold no less peril than Ferdinand Marcos's fascistic state security and media. The same musical forces that found elegance and structure in the studio had somehow turned violent and chaotic in concert. As the objects of late-stage Beatlemania, the Beatles were the first to duck an obsessive, all-consuming adoration. Rock celebrity had turned a perilous corner and gave their public appearances a fervor that was both tempting and hostile, euphoric and self-devouring.

Their creative investment in *Revolver* had been total, but the world preferred to harass them for state dinners, rebellious humor, and religious quotes. At every turn, distractions upstaged the music. Their material, with its layered tape effects and intricate vocal harmonies, had already defied and outgrown live performance. Prompted by their studio work, the decision to stop touring turned from aesthetic breakthrough into survival mechanism.

AFTER THIS LONG BREAK from Cynthia and Julian, which had followed hard upon three months of manic night-and-day recording, Lennon's personal life was unspooling. The other Beatles had long suspected this, given his frequent trysts, which only accelerated on tours. Arriving home at Kenwood, Lennon spent just a few nights with his family before setting off for Spain to film *How I Won the War*. Perhaps he hoped Spain would sober him up, disrupt his routine, and get him back on track. Like any self-respecting Englishman of that era, he packed a good read to help sort it all out: Nikos Kazantzakis's semiautobiographical best seller, *Report to Greco,* since he'd been so taken with that author's popular *The Last Temptation of Christ.* Perhaps he'd figure out something else to do now that the Beatles had decided to stop touring. Perhaps if he could get away from all the noise, he could think clearly.

Instead, his detour from Beatle work bestirred a roiling subconscious. He traveled first to Hanover, Germany, with Neil Aspinall, and got National Health "granny" glasses and an army haircut, which made the international news wires just as Elvis Presley's had back in 1958. In Lennon's mind, perhaps, this marked an improvement on Presley's career—at least he entered a fictional army instead of the real thing. After a short trip to Hamburg, Lennon and Aspinall met up with Mc-Cartney in Paris. Once filming began, Harrison went to India to study sitar with Ravi Shankar; Ringo stayed at home with his son, Zak; and McCartney returned to London to write the score to *The Family Way*. Then he hitched around France in disguise.

After a month of shooting, Lennon felt rested enough to summon first Ringo and Maureen, and then Cynthia and Julian, for visits to Majorca (note how his drummer got the call before his wife and son). With Lennon ingesting nothing harder than grass and wine, his loneliness crept back anyway. He enjoyed the work, but life on the movie set involved a lot of waiting around, shooting the breeze with fellow actors like Michael Crawford, and fiddling about on his guitar. Perhaps he'd caught his breath and found himself ready to reengage. Or perhaps he felt guilty about leaving his son, and resigned himself once more to family life. Still, when the filming finished, husband and wife traveled back to Weybridge separately.

Leonard Gross, *Look* magazine's European editor, visited Lester's set and drew a very different portrait from Maureen Cleave's just six months earlier. Getting off the treadmill had given Lennon a much needed respite and led to the gift of a once-in-a-lifetime song: "Strawberry Fields Forever," which he pursued slowly over six weeks, even though the more he worked on it, the more out of reach it seemed. The working tapes show him going over and over his key phrases, repeating them as if constantly questioning their resilience, and they survived many puzzled exams. Yet no matter how often he returned to the work, its uncertainties only deepened. The most complete compilation of the song's formation comes on a bootleg disc with more than fifteen demos, first embryonic, then gaining in confidence even as its mysteries held firm. In one of the few examples of Lennon's songwriting habits, it's almost as if he converses with the song daily to see how it responds, if it suggests new words or melodic patterns as he nudges it forward. With his personal life disintegrating, and his professional life a quandary, his songwriting provided a distinct yet tremulous answer.

Leonard Gross became smitten by Lennon's poise. "Lennon is not on; he is simply original," he wrote. Lennon talked to Gross about everything, from his frustration with acting to his role as a Beatle to the youth movement gaining momentum around the world: "Everybody can go around in England with long hair a bit, and boys can wear flowered trousers and flowered shirts and things like that, but there's still the same old nonsense going on. It's just that we're all dressed up a bit different."[23] Self-conscious about his influence, he was already vastly skeptical about political change.

In fact, Lennon's remarks in the fall of 1966 foreshadow the combative tone of his famous late-1970 encounter with *Rolling Stone*'s Jann Wenner, which seemed abrupt and callous during the Beatles' breakup. Contrast those 1966 quotes (above) with Lennon's "revelations" to Wenner in 1970: "The people who are in control and in power and the class system and the whole bullshit bourgeois scene is exactly the same, except that there's a lot of fag fuckin' middle-class kids with long hair walking around London in trendy clothes. . . . The same bastards are in control, the same people are running everything. It's EXACTLY the same!"[24]

Like a punctured wound, Lennon's language is more caustic in this later quote, but the sentiment is analogous. Taking a breather from the Beatles, his head was already weighing the cost of the celebrity grind.

When Gross questions Lennon about the "more popular than Jesus" flap, he incites an uncharacteristic defensiveness—about not religion but his public persona: "I'm not a cynic," Lennon insists. "They're getting my character out of some of the things I write or say. They can't do that. . . . I'm slightly cynical, but I'm not a cynic. One can be wry one day and cynical the next and ironic the next." There's a difference between making remarks about politics and society on one day and his overall belief in "life, love, goodness, death," Lennon argues.[25] (It's almost as if he's saying: "Trust the art, not the artist.") His cynicism, he insists, shouldn't be mistaken for a larger worldview.

LENNON CAME HOME to one of London's worst winters, only to slip back into his downward spiral of acid and late-night clubbing. Whatever level of sobriety he'd managed in Spain was quickly erased. At Kenwood, Lennon headed straight up to his attic to make a demo of his new song, which he played for McCartney. McCartney worked out the keyboard introduction on Lennon's latest gadget, a Mellotron keyboard, which sat on his landing (too big for the attic doorway). Although he prepared a rough mix at Kenwood, when he played it for the others at EMI studios, Lennon sat alone with his guitar. His own early attempts to figure how to get the song down on tape had left him even more puzzled. He wanted to hear how his band reacted to it.

Returning to his regular haunts, he poked by the Indica bookshop and gallery, where John Dunbar was mounting an exhibit by a trendy New York Fluxus artist named Yoko Ono. The Fluxus movement grew out of Marcel Duchamp's insouciant Dada style from pre–World War I and stressed performance and audience interaction with highly conceptual art pieces and installations. Yoko Ono's early reputation flowed from her influential free-form concerts in Greenwich Village, attended by the avant-garde's leading composer and theorist, John Cage, and Duchamp himself. She came to London with her second husband, Tony Cox, and their two-year-old daughter, Kyoko, to attend an international conference on modernism.

Ono had already met Paul McCartney. During an early gambit to secure rock-star patronage, she knocked on his Cavendish Avenue front door and asked him if he'd contribute an original manuscript to celebrate Cage's birthday. Ono's strategy combined two purposes: to flatter McCartney with her artistic credentials and introduce herself to a wealthy rocker who might invest in her work. McCartney declined but did refer Ono to his partner, Lennon, as "the artist in the group."[26] (This echoes the way Lennon had once sent Klaus Voormann to Stu Sutcliffe as the band's "artist" back in Hamburg.)

Barry Miles had stocked Ono's private publication, *Grapefruit,* a book of instructions that toyed with perceptions that resembled Zen koans. "She had published it herself," Miles remembered, "so it was a very small press. And I'm sure she saw that I was one of the few shops who carried it."[27] The Indica bookstore had expanded into the space next door for a makeshift gallery, and they offered Ono an exhibition. Dunbar invited Lennon in as a potential sponsor the day before Ono's opening—a millionaire investor who might want in on the ground floor of the next big thing. Lennon remembered meeting Ono there amid her art, and being at once intimidated and amused.

Beneath a mass of long and straight jet-black hair, Ono's tiny frame and passive demeanor suggested a Japanese version of Andy Warhol. She had trouble taking Lennon the rock star seriously, but welcomed his interest in her work and politely led him through her pieces. In one room, he climbed up a ladder to look through a spyglass, where he found the word "Yes." This surprised and tickled Lennon, who had seen his share of art-school pretension. "If it had said 'No' or 'Up yours,' I would have been put out."[28]

He asked if he could pay her five pounds to hammer a nail into a piece of wood. Not before the show, she responded. (In this single gesture, Yoko Ono followed only Veronica Bennett Spector as among the few women in Lennon's life as a Beatle to tell him no.) How about an imaginary payment and an imaginary nail? Lennon countered, and Yoko Ono smiled in recognition. But that first meeting, cordial and mostly professional, passed unnoticed. It has since entered Lennon mythology as a pivotal encounter, one in which Lennon's entire worldview was thrown into question. But it's not clear that the scene held any particular meaning for either of them at the time it happened. In his current frame of mind, wrestling "Strawberry Fields Forever" to the ground and falling back into the home life he had just escaped, Lennon took in Ono's work as a happy blip in a fog. The blurry line between his drugs and Ono's art must have been pronounced. She sent him a copy of *Grapefruit* as a thank-you, and he kept it by his bed.

WHEN THE FOUR BEATLES regrouped for the first time since Candlestick Park for an EMI session in Studio 2 on November 24, 1966, the familiar room became lit with uncertainty. Lennon didn't look like himself. For the first time anyone could remember, he wore spectacles, which he had never done in public. He'd grown accustomed to his character Private Gripweed's "granny" glasses and enjoyed seeing more clearly without the first-generation hard contact lenses he had struggled with. Cigarettes were lit, tea served, and expectancy hung in the air as John Lennon picked up his guitar and announced his new number: "Strawberry Fields Forever."

There is no tape of Lennon's first performance, but it's grown into legend because of George Martin's quote (and the working demos that have leaked since): "When John sang 'Strawberry Fields' for the first time, just with an acoustic guitar accompaniment, it was magic," George Martin remembers. "It was absolutely lovely. I love John's voice anyway, and it was a great privilege listening to it."[29] Sung alone in front of the others, this mélange of surreal fragility must have had a quixotic effect coming from a tough hide like Lennon's. Suddenly, their most reliable cutup had enchanted them with a reverie of youth, which somehow made him sound older—and made the others feel older as well.

Lennon's narrative ("Let me take you down 'cause I'm going to . . .") retreats to a childhood idyll, the grounds of Woolton's Strawberry Field Salvation Army home. Both musically and lyrically, the song surpasses anything Lennon had written before, trumping even "Tomorrow Never Knows" from earlier that year. The lyrics were experimental, figurative, and nonlinear; the music had new color and fluidity, the slow-motion quality of listening to something underwater, and yet simultaneously a clear, visionary presence, as if the most hallucinatory images were tumbling from a subdued narrator waking up inside a dream. For the Beatles, the images evoked the backyard at Mendips, where Lennon had a treehouse, and his infatuation with the child's frame of mind. It must have felt like eavesdropping on a close friend's dream therapy:

No one I think is in my tree
I mean it must be high or low

Although hesitant and uncertain, the music finds a curious inner calm: in real life, the Strawberry Field grounds were one step from an orphanage, and as an abandoned child, Lennon must have felt a strange identification with the children there. At age four, he watched his mother, Julia, give away a daughter he would never know; it would have been completely natural to fear himself just a step away from the same fate.

"I've seen Strawberry Fields described as a dull, grimy place next door to him that John imagined to be a beautiful place, but in the summer it wasn't dull and grimy at all: it was a secret garden," McCartney writes in his memoirs. Raised in a "proper" home by his aunt Mimi, he looked forward every summer to the marching bands that played the fêtes in its yard.

"John's memory of it wasn't to do with the fact that it was a Salvation Army home; that was up at the house," McCartney says. "There was a wall you could bunk over and it was a rather wild garden, it wasn't manicured at all, so it was easy to hide in. The bit he went into was a secret garden like in *The Lion, the Witch and the Wardrobe,* and he thought of it like that, it was a little hide-away for him where he could maybe have a smoke, live in his dreams a little, so it was a get-away. It was an escape for John."[30]

McCartney's sympathetic support followed on this understanding of his partner's personal associations. That first evening they recorded a spare version with electric guitar, two Mellotron tracks (one of which often gets mistaken for a slide guitar), and backing vocals behind Lennon's lead. Four days later they abandoned this version for a second, more band-oriented arrangement, featuring McCartney's now-distinctive Mellotron introduction.

"Strawberry Fields Forever" sounds like a dream reassembled in a bottle, but it required elaborate postproduction work to capture its emotional fragility. The recording process itself resembled the jumbled lyric, with intense sessions followed by days of Lennon's second thoughts. The song was delicate, but it also had grit, and Ringo's lopsided tom-toms loosened it up (another track where Ringo's left-handedness made his fills sound oddly spry). On the other hand, the band aimed for an ineffable tone it couldn't quite hit, and the tempo kept accelerating with each take. Perhaps some outside instruments could shake up the sound and bring the words more color.

At this point in their studio work (late in 1966), remakes were not unusual. They had scrapped early takes of "And I Love Her" and "What

You're Doing," and the feel of "Norwegian Wood" changed dramatically from first take to final mix. Only "That Means a Lot," with its complex arrangement, had been abandoned after reconfiguring. But after a couple of weeks working on McCartney's "When I'm Sixty-four," Lennon asked Martin to draw up a new arrangement for "Strawberry Fields Forever," with cellos and trumpets. That way he might get at the mysterious feel as he'd first imagined it—anyway, McCartney always got the high-class treatment from Martin. "He'd wanted it as a gentle dreaming song, but he said it had come out too raucous," Martin remembers. "He said, could I write him a new lineup with the strings. So I wrote a new score and we recorded that. But he didn't like it."

Working on these new tracks, Lennon got carried away again, adding backward tape loops, a wild percussion section, maracas, odd piano bits, and spoken lines like "Cranberry sauce" and "Calm down, Ringo." Still, the track stumped him. Finally, in late December, Lennon asked Martin to join the two separate tracks, as he liked features from each, and felt that splicing them together might somehow split the difference. Martin sympathized with Lennon's indecision.

"It still wasn't right," he remembers. "What he would now like was the first half from the early recording plus the second half of the new recording. Would I put them together for him? I said it was impossible." Martin pushed back as a musician: the two tracks were in different keys, at different speeds, he said. "You can fix it, then," Lennon chirped on his way out the door.[31]

Martin's solution spliced the two pieces together using the Mellotron's swooping guitar sounds to camouflage two edits (between the words "Let me take you down 'cause I'm" at 1:00 and "going to"). For the remainder of the song, Lennon's voice has the oddly disfigured aura of somebody singing through a mental fog, the result of the slight tape warp to match the two different pitches. The result married an expressive fumbling with ingenious tape manipulation. Refrains limped alongside Starr's wobbly drums; verses suspended percussion to peer myopically through horns and strings. There are two narrative angles in the song which blur together at different points: the first is the child, the aimless, thought-spinning boy whose mind wanders, and the second the adult who's peering through this child's frame, trying to see what the child's eye sees. (This echoes and compresses the tension inside "She Said She Said," where Lennon sings, "When I was a boy/Everything was right," and steers the band right off its regular meter.) This doubling gets played out in the two opposing arrangements, band versus orchestral instruments, and the genius is how Martin engineers the track to travel these parallel planes at the same time. These narrative contortions also marked a profound break from the material Lennon had worked on with McCartney. "Strawberry Fields" may be an early attempt to compensate for this loss by forging a split voice—different angles (verses and refrains) seen through the same lens.

By February 1967, Epstein had caved to pressure from EMI and Capitol for more product, a single to fill the gap between albums: *Revolver* had been released more than six months earlier, and at the rate they were going, this new album could take at least that long again. The band kept trying to slam the brakes on their career: for four years in a row they had churned out two LPs a year—only in 1966 did they get away with the second of these being *A Collection of Beatles Oldies,* a compilation of hits. The band's holing up in the studio didn't give the label much leverage, but they did insist on releasing two of their finished tracks as a single: "Strawberry Fields Forever" and "Penny Lane." This, in turn, shifted the evolving concept of the tracks that followed—from a self-conscious evocation of their childhood into something more universal on the state of their fame.

Because "Penny Lane" made the obvious choice for a single but "Strawberry Fields Forever" had masterstroke woven right through it, they issued the two songs to follow "Day Tripper"/"We Can Work It Out" as a double A-sided single, encouraging radio stations to play both sides. So it became another physical symbol of the increasingly disparate worlds Lennon and McCartney inhabited, with their differing views of childhood filtered through their differing views of songwriting. It was as if the self-contained argument of "We Can Work It Out" now split across two separate sides of the same single. "Penny Lane" sought out a majestic optimism that repeated listenings betrayed—McCartney's buoyancy quickened with ironic verve; "Strawberry Fields" turned even the act of radio listening into an intensely private experience, everybody eavesdropping on somebody else's waking bad dream. (McCartney's song also mirrored Lennon's double narrative: his boyhood view of an "ordinary" bus roundabout gets overlaid by his sly adult's commentary; where the boy thinks, "Very strange," the grown man thinks, "And though she feels as if she's in a play/She is anyway.") That McCartney line forecasts the slippery tension between narrative voices in "A Day in the Life" and how reality haunts illusion throughout *Sgt. Pepper*. In a subtle way, it recalls that ingenious line Buck Ram wrote for the Platters in "The Great Pretender": "Too real is this feeling of make-believe."

Lennon's song has more poetic intrigue: he sings "Strawberry Fields Forever" in the quietly time-frozen voice of John the boy, examining adult anxiety from the mind's eye of his childhood. This new psychological vantage point goes deeper into the fear, grief, and alienation Lennon surveyed in "She Said She Said" and, before that, "If I Fell," "I'm a Loser," "You've Got to Hide Your Love Away," and "Nowhere Man." One of the world's most famous men kept a public musical journal of estrangement.

Writing and recording "Strawberry Fields Forever" transformed Lennon's creative arc: it hinted at the depths of his late-Beatles themes, staked out territory for his early solo career, and transformed the Beatles from performing moptops into studio hermits, from coming-of-age youths into nostalgic adults. Although psychedelic numbers like "Rain," "Dr. Robert," and "And Your Bird Can Sing" were influenced by the keening harmonies and ringing guitars of the Byrds, Lennon never sounded as if he were trading one style for another; as before with Chuck Berry, imitation only delivered him to a new level of originality. "Strawberry Fields Forever" expanded the hallucinogenic drone of "Rain" into layered colors that shifted when lit by his vocal inflections. The lyrical freedom of his free-form verse produced a supernatural calm. Tracks like "A Day in the Life" (his next song), "Lucy in the Sky with Diamonds," and "I Am the Walrus" would soon spring from this same aesthetic impulse as his wordplay blossomed alongside his chord changes.

"Strawberry Fields Forever" became Lennon's first glimpse of life beyond his group, and part of the recording's ironic pull lies in how the Beatles drape a group sensibility around Lennon's abstract psyche, something only the most intimate of musical friends could do. Cued to the music's new reach, they all grew mustaches for the avant-garde video shoot, a prelude to the coming beards and shoulder-length manes. But the song's difficult birth took place in the wake of a global media assault, Ku Klux Klan death threats, and a disintegrating marriage and song-writing partnership. As most of Lennon's primary relationships began to crumble, his muse brought him a song that would redefine his life both aesthetically and personally in a single stroke.

15

In a Play

HISTORICAL VANTAGE TELLS US THAT BY LATE 1966, LENNON'S MEN-tal state plumbed dangerous new levels of concern in every area except his music: with his marriage a sham, only fatherly obligations to his son kept him around, out of guilt and a vague sense of duty. As sessions began in November, Lennon walked around in an increasingly isolated haze, driven from Kenwood to sessions to clubs and back, downing amphetamines to wake up, smoking marijuana casually throughout the day, drinking heavily, and confusing his LSD tabs with all his other bedside pills.

This lifestyle clawed at his insides even as his *Sgt. Pepper* material challenged new technical hurdles. Cynthia Lennon crystallized Lennon's profound dependence on his band with a knowing quote: "They seem to need you less than you need them."[1] This comment hints at an inner resolve, and an understanding of Lennon's character, that rarely gets emphasized; as ironic outsider, Cynthia had the only clear-eyed take on Lennon's group motivations.

Set aside the psychic wiring of childhood abandonment, multiple personal losses, and his battle-ax auntie, and consider Lennon's professional dilemma: What does the world's most famous rock star do after he creates a pop masterpiece like *Revolver*—and nobody notices? Even worse: instead, people target you as a religious criminal?

This melancholy forms the giant subtext to *Pepper*'s peculiar menagerie of sounds and characters. The album's gradual inanition, summarized by "A Day in the Life," has no release valve, such as *Revolver*'s "Yellow Submarine." The Lennon wordplay in "Lucy in the Sky with Diamonds" ("newspaper taxis" and "kaleidoscope eyes") makes for a sophisticated sense of psychedelia as a giant mural painted in uplifting colors, but it has no metaphorical sophistication, no undertow of feeling or layered suggestion. The world grasped on to the song's acronym "LSD" without stopping to consider how even if intentional (which Lennon studiously denied), it featured one of his weaker subtexts. "Lucy" floats as pure fantasy, and although Lennon won the Lennon-McCartney argument on *Sgt. Pepper*'s sequence ("A Day in the Life" his giant trump card), the balance of power within the band had already shifted. Lennon dropped his Beatle reins without a fight. In the ongoing war over the band's identity, Lennon folded his material into McCartney's concept with ease, trouncing him aesthetically while ceding political influence. With McCartney's blistering guitar lead on Lennon's "Good Morning Good Morning," his confidence swelled from cowriter to coproducer, lead conceptualist, and ultimately guitarist and drummer. As Cynthia's quote suggests, Lennon leaned on McCartney even more than he leaned on his wife.

ON THE BUSINESS FRONT, Brian Epstein's five-year management contract, dating from 1962, appeared on the horizon for renewal. His relationship with the band had cooled ever since their decision at Candlestick Park to stop touring. Instead of supporting them aesthetically, Epstein took this turn as a rebuke. NEMS Enterprises had reorganized itself twice over the past two years: in 1965, Epstein had taken over the Vic Lewis Agency, to handle Donovan ("Mellow Yellow") and Petula Clark ("Downtown"), and brought Vic Lewis on board as NEMS director. More recently, he had begun socializing with Robert Stigwood (dubbing him "Stiggie"), who had made an offer on NEMS that tempted Epstein. He turned down Stigwood's buyout the way he had rejected innumerable offers from both sides of the Atlantic. But with Stigwood, inexplicably, Epstein agreed instead to a merger, giving him the title of "co-managing" directorship and the reins for day-to-day business. This made everybody apoplectic, especially the Beatles once they got wind of it. Paul McCartney described their reaction to the critic Greil Marcus in 2000: "We said, 'In fact, if you do, if you somehow manage to pull this off, we can promise you one thing. We will record God Save the Queen for every single record we make from now on and we'll sing it out of tune. That's a promise. So if this guy buys us, that's what he's buying.'"[2]

To placate his boys, Epstein stayed on as manager of the Beatles but handed responsibility for most of his other acts to Stigwood. Alistair Taylor, Epstein's longtime friend, couldn't believe Epstein had sold himself so short. This self-destructive move came long before Epstein slid into paranoia and emotional despair during the recording and release of *Sgt. Pepper.* Like a lover who breaks things off because he fears the partner will do so first, the loss of his precious Beatles sent him into a self-recriminating fog.

It's DIFFICULT TO ACCOUNT for Lennon's productivity during the *Sgt. Pepper* sessions, when his cloistered existence entered new realms of detachment. Show-business buffers gave him the freedom to use drugs in nearly any context. Music became his lifeline—he seems to have stayed "sober" for studio work on his tracks, while almost everything else, including his relationships within the band, became a wash. This created a thin working foundation, and the cost in personal relationships became very high. For the first time in the Beatles' schedule, Lennon disappeared from not just some McCartney tracks but also most of Harrison's. Those who blame Yoko Ono for "breaking up the Beatles" have yet to explain Lennon's withdrawal before the romantic involvement even began.

As casual use of marijuana spread, horror stories attached to cocaine and heroin seemed like so much ranting from elders, one more unendurable lecture. To this innocent, pre-Altamont culture, drugs promised inner growth, an expansion of consciousness, the seeking out of hitherto-untapped worlds, and all the naïve talk that fueled "Tomorrow Never Knows" and even "Got to Get You into My Life" ("Maybe I could see

another kind of mind there"). The slow decline from "soft" hallucinogens to "hard" narcotics, the bottoming out and fatalities of Janis Joplin,
Jimi Hendrix, and Jim Morrison were all yet to come in the rock world;
they have since become hoary show-biz clichés.

But in early 1967, there were no 12-step rehabs or family interven-
tions, and treatment centers were focused on drying out (with methods
like pill-induced "sleep cures") rather than laying the foundation for
long-term recovery. Epstein frequented the Priory Clinic, in Putney, a
glorified country club, which specialized in fat-wallet elites and entertainers. He'd become a regular visitor, using the clinic as a place to escape and get his strength back before more bingeing. But an increasing
paranoia—and a continuing stream of blackmail threats threatening to
expose his homosexuality—made his trips more frequent as his role in
Beatle affairs diminished.

As the counterculture ascended the mainstream during 1967's Summer of Love, rock stars remained defiant: ambitious and corrupt vice
squads began clashing with celebrities over small amounts of cannabis,
which had begun with the celebrity busts of Mick Jagger, Marianne
Faithfull, and art dealer Robert Fraser at the home of Keith Richards—
Redlands in Richmond—in February. To most observers, however, marijuana presented only the mildest of social problems; making examples
out of high-profile cases would do little to sway the behavioral tides. Picking on musicians for grass seemed the height of overdoing it.

In this atmosphere, the politics within the Beatles began to shift. Adolescent gamesmanship persisted in how Lennon and Harrison taunted
McCartney to take LSD (Ringo had already partaken in 1966).[3] This
drug-taking got folded into Lennon's jealousy of his songwriting partner's lingering bachelorhood: McCartney had a long-term girlfriend, Jane
Asher, who he said had an "open" understanding about the "rules of the
road," a bachelor pad close to the studio, and no kids to worry about. Of
course, McCartney's setup had pitfalls Lennon overlooked: Asher traveled frequently for her own international acting career, and McCartney's
entitled celebrity attitude tested the already strained long-distance relationship. Lennon couldn't help but envy his partner's romantic "arrange-

ment," betraying a bad conscience even though he acted like a single man himself.

This rarefied celebrity privilege baffles most mortals: with access to the most beautiful groupies, the best drugs, and exalted status at the trendiest nightclubs, Lennon's inner life roared with emptiness, where adoring looks from his son only made him feel helplessly inadequate. Perhaps this is why Lennon's connection to his muse became all-important, a microscope to his subconscious: "Strawberry Fields Forever" maps his emotional state with Freudian particularity, right down to the Woolton site where he discovered live summer music, the dark well of feeling that he brought to songs like "If I Fell," "I'm a Loser," and "Help!" The other three Beatles knew Lennon's private life toyed with disaster, and they watched as only best friends can. As musicians, the most support they could offer encouraged his gifts and strove to hit the marks set by his songs. The worse Lennon's depression got, the sharper his songwriting skills became, almost as if they were his only reliable connection with his world and peers.

For the first six months of 1967, the Beatles released only one single ("Penny Lane"/"Strawberry Fields Forever" in February, a world in itself), did scant interviews, and secluded themselves in the studio. In the slowed time of the classic rock era, especially considering that the pop norm had been two albums a year surrounded by singles every two or three months, this stretched out into endless weeks and then months. Rumors spread to every teen's bedroom that they were finished, working on a record they might never complete, for an audience that had outgrown them. Withdrawing from their audience this way, the Beatles took a giant leap at great risk: to resign from live performance struck almost everybody in their circle (except perhaps Martin) as decidedly daft, and certainly temporary. Epstein opposed it with all his might and hoped some time off might persuade them otherwise. This insistence probably worked against him. That a rock band as successful as the Beatles could "retire" from the stage posited new realms of pretension. The coincidence of their material demanding more and more studio time only confirmed their decision to stop touring: the more they worked, the more their ensemble rewarded them. The "canned" audience sounds greeting their retreat from the stage heighten this irony.

For Epstein, the former retailer, this seemed unbearable. He saw himself as a promoter and worried frantically if his boys were not touring and charming everybody in public. He had few doubts about their recording skills; he simply fretted selfishly that they might have outgrown him. He carried on making deals: Al Brodax, the executive producer of the popular American ABC Saturday-morning cartoons, solved the problem of fulfilling their feature film contract: why not simply animate Beatle songs for the big screen? Since they had rejected all scripts for a 1966 film project, and were clearly not inclined to rehash any Dick Lester comedies, Brodax got the nod. The *Revolver* song "Yellow Submarine" morphed into a children's cartoon feature.

Also during this period, Epstein began divesting himself of NEMS and transferring control over to Robert Stigwood. Weathering competing streams of guilt, envy, self-pity, and pride, Epstein exiled himself. Another manager might have kept diversifying beyond the trendy new Saville Theatre he opened in London's West End. Having discovered and nourished the world's greatest entertainment, Epstein could afford to sit back, book other acts, and let the tide recede from four years of backbreaking work. But his own drug dependencies worked their corrosive effect: he saw himself as ostracized from the Beatles' ongoing aesthetic progress, and responded like a spurned lover. Lennon sent Epstein a card at the Priory in July 1967, which read: "I love you . . . I really do."[4]

WHILE OMINOUS, Beatle politics served the music, making *Sgt. Pepper* at once a glow-in-the-dark bauble and a message about the messengers. For a lark, the Beatles decisively renounced their teen image once and for all, adopting fictive characters to announce a new phase. The splashy Victorian band costumes, the epitome of "square," only sharpened their hip new looks the way ties and suits had once put quotes around their Hamburg leather expressions. The album's tour through celebrity, its trick mirrors and death curves, became an all-consuming metaphor for life itself: as hippies and psychedelic hard rock entered the scene, the

Beatles had a grip on it all before the Summer of Love party even began. And the music transcends its era well enough to serve as a defining statement. *Sgt. Pepper* recreates its era while commenting on our own. Addressing their audience from the mists of their own fame, the Beatles put quotes around the very idea of their previous "act" as moptops, of all rock acts posing for their fans, of all show-biz acts of all time and all audiences hungry for myth. Like fame, its strategy is seduction, but the punch line is abrupt. Without "A Day in the Life," the whole fantastical world might just float away.

The start of the *Sgt. Pepper* sessions in late November 1966 pulled the Beatles into an evening-to-early-morning schedule that swung between haphazard and obsessive. Most sessions began around 7 P.M. and went well past midnight, some until 3 A.M. Lennon either hit a club or three before arriving home at Kenwood near dawn or brought tapes home to work on, rose after lunch, then held songwriting sessions with McCartney or chilled in his TV patio, playing the "Nowhere Man" off his own kitchen. Here's how Cynthia describes him: "John took LSD regularly. He was hungry for new experiences and never afraid to experiment. . . . [He] threw himself into it with abandon, convinced that this was the way to greater enlightenment, creativity and happiness." Even worse, Lennon began bringing people home with him, a "ragged assortment" from clubs. "He'd pile in with anyone he'd picked up during the evening, whether he knew them or not. They were all high and littered our house for hours, sometimes days on end. . . . John was an essentially private man, but under the influence of drugs he was vulnerable to anyone and everyone who wanted to take advantage of him."5

After the stop-and-start December sessions on "Strawberry Fields Forever," McCartney brought in "Penny Lane," his answer song, in December 1967. In the middle of "Penny Lane," the Beatles taped a wildly improbable jam with avant-garde atmospherics, and submitted the tape to the Carnival of Light Rave, scheduled for the Roundhouse in Kilburn on successive Saturday evenings, January 28 and February 4. The posters plastered around London for the event proclaimed: "Music composed by Paul McCartney and Delta Music Plus."

This day's attempt lasted thirteen minutes and forty-eight seconds—among their longest takes to date—a single-track basic take and various overdubs that included drums and church organ, a wildly distorted lead guitar, gargling into their microphones, and John and Paul screaming random non sequiturs like "Barcelona!" and "Are you all right?" They passed along the tape through contacts at the Indica gallery and bookstore, but not much more is known about the session.

During the Beatles' recording seclusion, former Animals bassist Chas Chandler brought a young black guitarist over from New York, aghast that nobody in America had signed him up as the next big thing. Word among musicians spread quickly. A quiet-spoken figure in person, who seemed modest beyond all reason, Jimi Hendrix had huge hands that stroked and caressed unimaginable sounds out of his Fender Stratocaster. To start with, he played it upside down as a left-hander, reversing its strings so his patterns were hard to follow, even for another leftie like McCartney. His playing had such sheer charisma that his stage garb—headbands, bell-bottoms, a long Afro, and wild, luminous psychedelic scarves—seemed secondary to his guitar heroics. Hendrix began playing around London clubs in late 1966 with a bassist and drummer that Chandler recruited, and quickly demolished all known standards for virtuosity. Some *Ready Steady Go!* and *Top of the Pops* appearances turned heads, and soon his club shows were dotted with rock gods. Even Eric Clapton, who had left the Yardbirds to form a new hard-rock trio, Cream, called him a genius.

All four Beatles heard Hendrix at Epstein's Saville Theatre during the *Sgt. Pepper* sessions. Like everybody else, Hendrix was a huge Beatle fan, and he fiddled with garage-rock yarns like "Wild Thing" and "Hey Joe" until they rang out like phone calls from rock's future. He also specialized in Dylan, both radioactive chariots like "Like a Rolling Stone" and sitcoms like "Can You Please Crawl Out Your Window?" Unlike Lennon, Hendrix invested all his creative energy in his playing—it was as if he cultivated all the pique and turmoil of "Tomorrow Never Knows" down to the amazing variables alive in six amplified strings. And he hadn't even made his first record.

Some 1967 calendar entries punctuate an era as psychedelic pop culture took shape. McCartney attended a Jimi Hendrix show at the Bag O'Nails club on January 11 and went back into the studio the next day to add two trumpets, two oboes, two cors anglais (English horns), and a double bass to "Penny Lane." The next night, McCartney took along Ringo to hear Hendrix again, and the following night at the Royal Albert Hall, a group of underground creatives who launched the alternative *International Times* newspaper with Barry Miles as editor, and the trendy UFO Club, held a "happening" featuring Allen Ginsberg, Adrian Mitchell, and Lawrence Ferlinghetti reading their poetry aloud.[6] Granada Television interviewed McCartney for a film called *It's So Far Out It's Straight Down,* narrated by Michael Parkinson, a sympathetic documentary on the emerging psychedelic scene that won huge TV ratings. The day after that, the Beatles recorded their first four takes of "A Day in the Life."

"Penny Lane" had every appearance of being finished when McCartney came into the studio on January 17 and requested another overdub: a piccolo trumpet, the kind he had recently heard on a BBC broadcast of Bach's Brandenburg Concerto no. 2.[7] McCartney sang the melody; Martin wrote it down on a staff for a B-flat piccolo trumpet; and the English Chamber Orchestra's Dave Mason played the session.

That same morning, Lennon spotted a *Daily Mail* headline: "The Holes in Our Roads," which read, "There are 4,000 holes in the road in Blackburn, Lancashire, or one twenty-sixth of a hole per person, according to a council survey." That last detail didn't make it into the song, but it didn't have to: counting and apportioning potholes by population packed enough punch as a sublime bit of mindless bureaucracy, tedious task work tunneling into its own irrelevance. "If Blackburn is typical there are two million holes in Britain's roads and 300,000 in London," the article continued. Lennon noted:

> I was reading the paper one day and noticed two stories. I was writing "A Day in the Life" with the *Daily Mail* propped in front of me on the piano. One was about the Guinness heir who killed himself in a car. That was the main headline story. He died in

London in a car crash. On the next page was a story about four thousand potholes in the streets of Blackburn, Lancashire, that needed to be filled.[8]

Recalling his uncle George teaching him to read by going through the *Liverpool Echo* headlines, Lennon began drafting another song that gave him almost as much trouble as "Strawberry Fields Forever." This new song's ambition drove him into a sandpit. The verses came together, starting with a tribute to an Irish Swinging London dandy, Tara Browne, son of an Irish peer (Dominick Browne, House of Lords, who married Oonagh Guinness, heiress to the ale fortune). Tara Browne's Lotus Elan sports car zipped through a red light at the intersection of Redcliffe Square and Redcliffe Gardens in South Kensington late on December 18, 1966, only to ram into a parked lorry. His date, a Swinging London model named Suki Potier, walked away unscathed. The coroner's report appeared in the *Daily Mail* on the same day Lennon found the story about Blackburn potholes. McCartney later recanted this connection, saying, "The verse about the politician blowing his mind out in a car we wrote together. It has been attributed to Tara Browne, the Guinness heir, which I don't believe is the case, certainly as we were writing it, I was not attributing it to Tara in my head. In John's head it might have been. . . . The 'blew his mind' was purely a drug reference, nothing to do with a car crash. In actual fact I think I spent more time with Tara than John did."[9]

A vast blank spot in the song, normally the stretch where a "middle eight" or a bridge might be fitted, seemed more than empty, a trailing question mark smack in the center of an otherwise beguiling setup. Ambitious problems sought ambitious solutions. McCartney brought in a fragment from another unfinished number, and they stitched it into Lennon's middle in a completely different voice: a second storyteller. McCartney's internal soliloquy traces the steps of a professional man caught up in the daily grind, unself-consciously marching about his duties, climbing aboard the morning bus without an original thought in his head or any worthwhile feelings in his gut. This internal diary entry parodies what editors routinely slice from even great writers' journals ("Woke up, fell out of bed, dragged a comb across my head").

Two days after the *Daily Mail* news item the Beatles recorded the song's basic track with both these sections, and had their roadie, Mal Evans, count out the twenty-four bars in between, marked by a ringing alarm clock. Fixing one hole had only created another; they would have to figure that out later. Holes in the road became holes in a song as the work progressed. (Pasting up Lennon's song may have given McCartney the idea for another song: "Fixing a Hole.")

On the last two days of January, the band headed down to Knole Park, at Sevenoaks in Kent, twenty miles outside London, for a promotional film shoot to support their next single, "Strawberry Fields Forever" and "Penny Lane." Swedish filmmaker Peter Goldman chose the site for its fifteenth-century house and golf course. Klaus Voormann, who had moved on from Paddy, Klaus and Kim to play bass for Manfred Mann, had recommended Goldman to the Beatles. Tony Bramwell, now Epstein's publicist, produced the venture for Subafilms, one of two Beatle film companies that would eventually get folded into Apple Corps. The set included an old upright piano that the Beatles poured paint into and a tree where they did slow-motion jumps, a colorized echo of the "Can't Buy Me Love" sequence that Dick Lester had shot three years earlier.

The experimental nature of the clip, and all that "paint" getting applied to their "instrument," attempted to do through film what the songs did with narrative. When Dick Clark showed the film to his *American Bandstand* audience, teenage faces fell. Mustaches erased the idea of "cute." Instead of performers bothering to lip-sync to their latest single, the film screened like a sci-fi project gone awry. (Today, it looks like an earnest collegiate experiment.) During a break in the filming, Lennon stopped in at a Sevenoaks antiques shop and bought an 1843 poster describing a traveling circus straight out of Vincent Crummels's theater troupe in Dickens's *Nicholas Nickleby*. The bill described daring feats, complete with waltzing horses.

WORK CONTINUED ON OTHER TRACKS as "A Day in the Life" progressed. After taking in the Cream Saville Theatre show on February 5, the Beatles jumped on horseback for the "Penny Lane" shoot. Final film sequences at Knole Park took place on February 7, and the next day they were back in the studio laying down "Good Morning Good Morning." Next door to the Beatles at EMI, beginning in Studio 3, Pink Floyd, the UFO Club's house band, were recording *The Piper at the Gates of Dawn,* with George Martin's former engineer, Norman Smith, producing. These EMI rooms got scheduled tightly enough that the Beatles wandered to other studios popping up around town, like Regent Sound and the De Lane Lea. Their first session at Regent included the first three takes of "Fixing a Hole," before returning to EMI for the orchestral session on February 10.

McCartney's song fragment wedged into "A Day in the Life," but there were still some blanks to fill in. McCartney came up with the idea of filling the hole preceding his narrative with a "giant orchestral climax," constructed as a twenty-four-bar bridge connecting Lennon's detached narrator with McCartney's everyman. Martin wrote down a score on manuscript paper with parts for individual musicians that included a "squiggly line," indicating a continuous rising swell of sound. For this evening session, forty musicians gathered in the cavernous Studio 1, having been cajoled into evening dress, and Martin and McCartney took turns conducting. Snatches of this filmed event have leaked out over the years: it's a full-fledged "performance" inside a recording studio, for the musicians themselves and invited guests, with the concertmaster wearing a gorilla's paw on his bow hand, another participant sporting a clown nose, and many in funny hats. One bassoonist tied a balloon to his horn.

Friends like Mick Jagger and Marianne Faithfull and the visiting Monkee, Mike Nesmith, were given 16mm cameras to shoot anything they liked, and they stayed after with Keith Richards, and Simon and Marijke of the Dutch design group The Fool, to tape four takes of a giant collective "OMMMMMMMM," the best idea for the song's ending anybody had come up with so far.[10] Now that all the holes were filled, how to bring it all to a close became the song's final paradox.

The "Day in the Life" sessions worked like a talisman on all the other tracks—its tonal departure serving as a counterexample to the rest of the material. Work continued on "Only a Northern Song" (which didn't make *Sgt. Pepper*'s final cut), "Good Morning Good Morning," "Being for the Benefit of Mr. Kite," more "Fixing a Hole" overdubs, an experimental recording called "Anything," eight takes of "Lovely Rita," and rehearsals for "Lucy in the Sky with Diamonds." On February 20, Martin got a reluctant Geoff Emerick to toss calliope tapes of Sousa marches into the air and then edit them back together randomly for Lennon's "Mr. Kite."

Then a new solution to "A Day in the Life" took shape: the original ending, friends humming "OMMMMMMMM," lacked finality and resolve, and they searched for something more dramatic, like a gunshot or a cannon, which would provide the right climax to the song and album. On February 22, John, Paul, Ringo, Mal Evans, and George Martin raised ten hands to simultaneously strike at two pianos for a giant E-major chord, which Martin overdubbed three times, adding harmonium, to extend its length to the forty-three seconds it lasts, but you can still hear a chair squeak at 4:49 as they hold the keys down. It took nine takes to get the chord struck simultaneously to Martin's satisfaction, and he enhanced the sound electronically to bleed every ounce from its decay. Then they repeated the orchestral buildup from the "bridge" as a kind of ear-fake: first this led to a new song; now it drove listeners off the edge.

The preceding week's "Lucy" rehearsals turned the song into *Sgt. Pepper*'s quickest session, recording in seven takes on March 1 with vocal overdubs on March 2. A *Life* magazine reporter visited the studio just after this, only to describe a transitional tedium. "We are light years away from anything tonight," Martin told the reporter. "They know it is awful now, and they're trying to straighten it out. It may be a week before they're pleased, if ever."[11]

The "Lucy" session seemed to set off a new streak; the starts began gaining on all the fits. In short order, a brass section and Harrison's lead guitar were added to the title track; "Getting Better" got seven takes on March 9, and "Within You Without You" began production on March 15, "She's Leaving Home" on the 17th. Lennon told a BBC interviewer on March 20 that there would be "no more 'She Loves You's" before heading back into the studio to record lead and backing vocals onto "She's Leaving Home." Amid all this ensemble work, several important tape edits took shape: the audience sounds for the opening of the record were compiled from the orchestral session on February 10, and the Hollywood Bowl audience from 1965, for the transition between the opening song and "With a Little Help from My Friends."

Too busy to attend the annual Ivor Novello Awards on March 20, Lennon and McCartney granted a BBC radio interview to Brian Matthew about their winning songs, "Yellow Submarine" (best A-side single for 1966) and "Michelle" (most performed song of 1966). This interview contradicted many of McCartney's post-1980 statements about "Yesterday," recorded in 1965, which by this early date was already the runner-up to "Michelle" for most-performed song of 1966. Here McCartney acknowledged that Lennon came up with the title, and the conceptual hook, for "Yesterday." Lennon complained about the string arrangement on the Andy Williams rendition.[12]

A PIVOTAL MOMENT in the *Sgt. Pepper* sessions came as Lennon's personal turmoil bled into his work; he could be so articulate about life's illusions, many failed to see how lost in illusion he was himself most of the time. As they completed work on "Getting Better" and "Lovely Rita," Lennon took ill at the microphone on March 21, and George Martin took him up to the roof for some air. He had mistakenly confused an amphetamine "upper" with an LSD tab and begun tripping in the middle of a take (too bad Matthew hadn't shown up for that). Martin, oblivious to the drugs taking effect, came back down to continue work. Paul took him home that night to his house nearby. Bramwell remembers the incident: "John spent the night perched on the roof of Abbey Road tripping, staring at the frosty stars and waiting for the dawn. Eventually, Paul and George went up to get him down before he fell off. Paul took him home and, to help John out, he also dropped some acid to get on the same plane and stayed up all night, keeping him company."[13] As the critic Ian MacDonald notes in *Revolution in the Head,* this friendly gesture became a coming out for Paul, who had previously refused to take the drug.[14]

Typically, they carried on as though nothing extraordinary had happened. Lennon returned to the studio by March 23 for the backup vocal session on "Getting Better" and lead vocal work for "Good Morning Good Morning," on March 28 for organ, guitar, and harmonica overdubs on "Mr. Kite." In that same session, McCartney tore the face off "Good Morning Good Morning" with a vitriolic Casino guitar solo that leapt up from deep inside the song's withheld fears—another Lennon-McCartney collaboration that showed McCartney's supernatural sympathy for his partner's paranoia.

Ringo still needed a track, so the next day Lennon and McCartney finished off writing "With a Little Help from My Friends" at McCartney's house, as biographer Hunter Davies looked on. His is one of the few descriptions of a songwriting session on record, and it captures the ramshackle, free-association qualities of their songwriting method. Cynthia Lennon even makes some suggestions, which Lennon bats down:

> "How about," said Paul, "*Do you believe in a love at first sight.*"
>
> John sang it over and accepted it. In singing it, he added the next line. "*Yes, I'm certain it happens all the time*"[sic] . . . "What's a rhyme for time," said John. "Yes I'm certain it happens all the time. It's got to rhyme with that line."
>
> "How about I just feel fine," suggested Cyn.
>
> "No," said John. "You never use the word 'just.' It's meaningless. It's a fill-in word."[15]

After a nostalgic visit to "Can't Buy Me Love" and "Tequila," they called Ringo to tell him his song was finished, even though it still needed some fleshing out—they could do the rest as they recorded. The very next day, "With a Little Help from My Friends" got cut in eleven takes with the working title of "Bad Finger Boogie."

There were still tracks to be written, but the *Sgt. Pepper* concept had taken hold, and the album was far enough along that they needed to shoot an album cover. McCartney had drawn a draft of his idea for the pop artist Peter Blake, and Michael Cooper's camera was booked for March 30 at Chelsea Manor studios. The Beatles got into highly stylized, brightly colored Victorian band costumes as Blake posed them in front of a giant mural of celebrities, some wax figures, some photographs, for an elaborate setup that anticipates a Photoshop digital software montage. They took more pictures sitting down together, one of which appeared in the album's gatefold, then returned to the studio to finish "With a Little Help from My Friends," overdubbing bass, tambourine, and backup vocals.

Such lively work led to serendipitous connections, like the way "She's Leaving Home" came about. Retracing Lennon's newspaper grab for "A Day in the Life," McCartney had found a story in the *Daily Mail* on February 27 about a runaway named Melanie Coe, and "She's Leaving Home" sprang out of him. In a weird coincidence, McCartney had voted Melanie Coe a winner at age fourteen, on a 1963 *Ready Steady Go!* show, and awarded her an Elvis Presley album as a prize. He and Lennon remembered the name and fashioned the song around her. As one of the few topical songs the Beatles produced, "She's Leaving Home" nearly treats the parents as the runaway's victims in Lennon's background rejoinders: "What did we do that was wrong?" But even here there's an irony that quickens their resolve, before an odd narcissistic note: "We never thought of ourselves . . . Never a thought for ourselves." Patting yourself on the back for your own selflessness smacks of Aunt Mimi, floating on self-pity and oblivious to the protagonist's reality.

As THE *SGT. PEPPER* sessions wound down, group discussions wandered to future ventures, and rock's generational wars erupted anew. When they weren't in the studio, the Beatles held business meetings with their tax advisor, Dr. Strach, to establish a new company. Strach advised them that their accumulated capital, more than £2 million, exposed them to a hefty tax hit. But if they reinvested this in a business, they could save and build toward a new entity. They rechristened their original company, the Beatles Ltd., as a new partnership, Beatles and Co., a collective that gave each band member

5 percent; and they created a new, as yet unnamed corporation, which would control the remaining 80 percent. Under this new arrangement, individual songwriting royalties would be paid directly to the authors of a particular song, but all money earned by the Beatles as a group would go directly into Beatles and Co., taxed at a less punishing corporate tax rate.

Originally, Brian Epstein had big retail plans for the concern, according to Alistair Taylor: "One big idea was to set up a chain of shops designed only to sell cards; birthday cards, Christmas cards, anniversary cards. When the boys heard about that they all condemned the scheme as the most boring yet. Sure that they could come up with much better brainwaves, they began to get involved themselves."[16] At first, the new company housed itself in Epstein's NEMS office. But while Epstein schemed about how to set up new revenue streams for his boys, he also wriggled out of day-to-day operations. Now a hub of Swinging London, his Saville Theatre shows became the place most rock fans could hope to spot a Beatle in the Epstein box: Lennon and Starr heard Chuck Berry and Del Shannon there on April 19. On April 24, all four Beatles caught Donovan's show.

On a whim, McCartney dashed off on April 5 to the States to surprise Jane Asher for her twenty-first birthday. On his way to Central City, Colorado, where Asher was appearing as Juliet, he visited a Beach Boys studio in L.A. for a session on a song called "Vegetable" (from the doomed *Smile,* the follow-up to *Pet Sounds*). Aboard the plane home, he sketched out ideas for a possible film concept and began writing a title track, "Magical Mystery Tour." In his absence, Lennon "emerged from his fog long enough" to have his Rolls-Royce painted in swirls and flowery cartouches by The Fool, the Dutch design collective, Tony Bramwell reports. "If you really couldn't do without a Rolls," wrote the music scenester Simon Napier-Bell, "you could always have it painted in gaudy psychedelic colours. (A sign of disrespect for its status.)"[17]

Then the Stones scandal resurfaced. Mick Jagger, Richards, and Robert Fraser, the art dealer, were finally hauled into a London court on April 18 and charged with possession of illegal drugs. The arrest had caused a scandal in the press, and the music industry gossiped about how by exempting George and Pattie Harrison (who were quickly ushered out of the crime scene), the ruling class revealed an impeccable grasp of rock's elite. A critical calculation underlay this Stones fracas: even booking a "lesser" Beatle like Harrison would bring about too great a backlash. "We are not old men. We are not worried about your petty morals," sneered Keith Richards to his arraignment judge. The rock world hustled monies and sympathetic editorials as Jagger and Richards spent three weeks in jail. The famous *Times* editorial—entitled "Who Breaks a Butterfly on a Wheel?"—by a noted conservative *Times* editor, William Rees-Mogg, was widely viewed as a turning point in police attitudes toward marijuana. (The U.S. equivalent would have been the *National Review*'s William F. Buckley advocating for Ken Kesey's Merry Pranksters.)

The Beatles recorded straight through the storm, mostly buffing up errors and editing in transitions. The final session, on April 21, inspired a silent joke: the out-groove gibberish and dog's whistle (the high-pitched fifteen-kilocycle tone, inaudible to human ears), brought more than seven hundred hours of work to a close. In sheer studio hours logged, this was an unprecedented amount of time to devote to a pop—or any—album. But Beatle fingers itched. They dove right into McCartney's new "Magical Mystery Tour" track for three more days of recording.

ONLY AFTER *SGT. PEPPER* drew to a close did Lennon encounter Yoko Ono again, and this time even bystanders—and Ono's husband—could read their chemistry. At the end of April, Tony Bramwell saw Lennon take in the 14-Hour Technicolor Dream event at Alexandra Palace. Ono appeared on the bill doing her *Cut Piece,* while her husband, Anthony Cox, roamed in the audience, scouting for patrons. (A May 17 BBC show called *Man Alive: What Is a Happening?* depicted Lennon looking chicly disoriented.)

Bramwell remembers the event and the weird, space-out effect Ono had on Lennon's trip. It was the kind of "happening" where "Suzy Creamcheese doled out yellow banana-skin joints," and Bramwell saw Lennon come in with John Dunbar wearing an "Afghan-embroidered skin coat" and looking "very stoned." Lennon told Bramwell they had been watching the event on TV down in Weybridge and jumped into his Rolls. "As we were chatting," Bramwell writes, "John's attention was caught by Yoko, who was giving a Fluxus performance with stepladders and scissors center stage, beneath the acrobats and jugglers swinging from the soaring cast-iron gothic pillars." Lennon, at first distracted, soon became mesmerized by Ono's performance.

Ono's *Cut Piece* had become a signature: she sat onstage and invited audience members to come up and cut off pieces of her clothing. She did this in a variety of settings for various lengths of time, until most or sometimes all of her clothes had been snipped off. She sat impassively, as if imprisoned, while the audience decided how far to take it. Even in a clinical museum setting, this piece generated great tension, as if Ono were a proxy for women everywhere, feigning indifference while the world tore off layer after layer of her self-respect.

In this psychedelic setting, however, Bramwell remembers a "strangely unpleasant" vibe—with a light show and loud music, the piece became doubly disorienting. The sound of scissors slicing Ono's clothing was amplified through loudspeakers, and some spectators began attacking her. She sat passively, like a specimen exposed for experimentation. When she was left completely naked onstage, some assistants led her away and she got dressed. This all struck Lennon as morbidly fascinating, as if somebody had read his mind and inverted the Beatle "Butcher cover" into a live set piece: the sick humor of dismembered dolls extended into pure theater, anchored by a woman who refused to turn away from the humiliation. The piece only worked if Ono's gaze held steady, and her fortitude impressed him.

As a cynical rock insider, Bramwell couldn't deduce anything more going on than Lennon getting tweaked by Ono's "mild S&M." But he did note how Ono's husband wandered around the club with a handheld movie camera, "urging on the mob." When Cox came upon Lennon, "I saw a very knowing look flicker through Tony's eyes."[18]

ALTHOUGH THEY DELIVERED the *Sgt. Pepper* masters to EMI for postproduction, the Beatles went right on recording. They still needed material for *Magical Mystery Tour*, but they also did something new: they just jammed, as if reluctant to find the *Pepper* sessions coming to an end. On May 9, they laid down sixteen minutes of an instrumental that has never surfaced; and on May 11, they gathered at Olympic Sound Studios in Church Road, Kensington, where George Martin supervised engineers Keith Grant and Eddie Kramer (who went on to produce Jimi Hendrix). The song they recorded, "Baby, You're a Rich Man," had a Lennon verse with a McCartney refrain that sounded thinner than any of their EMI sessions. It fell into the *Yellow Submarine* pile, but got slapped on the back of "All You Need Is Love" once it became the next single.

One day later, they recorded McCartney's "All Together Now" in nine takes with only acoustic guitars. The next week, Lennon and McCartney began work on a number that would lie dormant for two years, "You Know My Name (Look Up the Number)." The master track contained five parts and took over fourteen takes, with Lennon on guitar, McCartney switching off between piano and drums, and Brian Jones dropping in on alto saxophone. Before *Sgt. Pepper* made its radio debut on Chris Denning's *Where It's At,* the Beatles went to Putney to play an acetate for Epstein at the Priory Clinic. (Like a forbidding parent, the BBC turned red at "A Day in the Life" and refused to broadcast the song, banning it even before release. How could anybody hear that hook ["I'd love to turn you on"] as anything but hallucinogenic bedlam? This excision only made the record's finale more tempting.)

During that week of *Sgt. Pepper*'s release in late May, the band cut Harrison's "It's All Too Much," in four takes at the De Lane Lea Studios, Kingsway, and then had another late-night jam session. Epstein came into town to throw a huge release party at his flat on Chapel Street near Buckingham Palace, in the posh Belgravia neighborhood, where the press gathered to hear the new music, and the four Beatles, decked out in psychedelic scarves and jackets, were photographed in front of Epstein's fireplace. Then Epstein scuttled back to the Priory.

It would be easy to dismiss *Sgt. Pepper* as rock's most overrated album if it weren't the Beatles' most underrated group effort. Almost everything you need to know about the band lies in its grooves, and it holds the best and worst of what they're most famous for. Given that the major theme is their own fame and its discontents, there's plenty of good raw material. It's too fanciful for the garage-rock purists, but not nearly progressive enough for the avant-garde crowd—fringe tastes deplore how it passes the something-for-everybody test. *Revolver* strung together songs around a loose concept, a discussion about sex, death, taxes, and stimulants, held together by the idea of four Beatles talking into the night. Lofty ideas about "Taxman" avarice and thrifty spinsters needing "another kind of mind" to "relax and float downstream" engaged with each player like strong personalities in a sporting bull session. The Beatles' own personalities gave *Revolver* cohesion, and it hung together because no other band could have made it. Both of these albums have long since transcended their moment; at the time, they struck many intelligent ears as audacious, impregnable, and too rich to imbibe in one or even several sittings.

Sgt. Pepper's cover shot alone now spars with Duchamp's mustachioed *Mona Lisa*, or Warhol's *Campbell's Soup Cans,* as a defining piece of pop art. And like those counterparts, the album's enormous impact steals attention from its poetry. American radio stations competed with each other to play it in its entirety for days on end. As one of rock's earliest release "events," it created its own unique moment in rock history. But in retrospect, the Beatles seem to be addressing history itself. *Sgt. Pepper* contemplates the emptiness of flower power while posing as its emblem.

Critics dote on *Sgt. Pepper* as rock's great conceptual breakthrough, but *Pepper* created rock criticism. For the first time, a rock record prompted major newspapers like the *New York Times* and the *Times* in London to run formal record reviews of a pop act, and not by classical critics like William Mann. On June 18, the *New York Times* ran a sympathetically youthful voice of dissent from Richard Goldstein (who "was almost lynched," quipped Robert Christgau in *Esquire*[19]): "Like an overattended child, *Sergeant Pepper* is spoiled. It reeks of horns and harps, harmonica quartets, assorted animal noises, and a 41-piece orchestra. . . . An album of special effects, dazzling but ultimately fraudulent. . . . When the Beatles' work as a whole is viewed in retrospect, *Rubber Soul* and *Revolver* will stand as their major contributions."[20] *Pepper*'s reputation expands its appeal; but its popularity is also ironic, an echo of its underrated critical status. The Beatles themselves always downplayed its significance, feigning disinterest in the fascination that bringing back the title track as a reprise could give the sequence "thematic" unity. But the unities persist, even if unintentional—if the Beatles taught us anything, it's how meanings can leap from accidents.

McCartney's album cover design casts the world's most famous celebrities—and a few choice obscurities, like Stu Sutcliffe and occultist Aleister Crowley—gathered around a fictional "Victorian" Beatles brass band, as if posing for an old-fashioned photograph. The frame suggests one of their school pictures, with celebrity classmates past and present gathered in anachronistic reunion. In front of them, the word "Beatles" is spelled out in flowers atop newly toiled dirt, with "moptop" Madame Tussaud wax figures looking on balefully from the left—it's a graveyard for Beatlemania.

This great historical parade of celebrities, presided over by the Beatles at the funeral of their former image, suggests how fame can rob the best work of meaning. A mix of UK and American figures crowd each other out, from Mae West and Karl Marx to writers like Edgar Allan Poe and Oscar Wilde beside classic Hollywood stars Fred Astaire, Laurel and Hardy, and Marlon Brando. (Lennon being Lennon wanted Jesus Christ next to Adolf Hitler, but got voted down.) Klaus Voormann's *Revolver* cover displayed the four Beatles conjoined in a single collective consciousness, spilling out from all that long hair. McCartney's *Sgt. Pepper* design gave the Beatles a fictional identity just like all these others, and the visual statement blended mockery with satire. "If we're so famous," their faces seem to say, "what happened to all these nice folks?"[21] There's an undertone of disbelief and suspicion about these mythic forces that gives the Beatles pause.

In its own scary way, parodying the myth becomes another mythic move. Posing the band members beside this famous lineup compared them to these figures and tied their fate to history. The songs picked up this theme, and others, in the ongoing stylistic discussion between McCartney and Lennon. Their collaboration found its peak, with eccentricities that fed off each other's strengths, for a sequence that would be all but impossible from the same relationship within a year's time (with the "Lady Madonna" single, say, or the tempo argument around "Revolution"). Lennon's word-painting influence on McCartney in "Fixing a Hole" plays out much the same way as McCartney's melodic influence on Lennon in "Lucy in the Sky with Diamonds." And McCartney's contribution to "A Day in the Life" tends toward the avant-garde (postmodernist narrative!), whereas Lennon's influence on "Getting Better" ("It can't get no worse!") takes a decidedly upbeat turn.

Everything that follows *Sgt. Pepper* conveys the sense of each partner going back into his corner and cultivating his core musical beliefs rather than reaching out toward the other's challenge—from here on in, they dabble on each other's turf as a kind of virtuoso display, instead of collaborating: Lennon's lullaby "Good Night" can only get overdone in the McCartney ballad vein, where McCartney's "Why Don't We Do It in the Road?" might as well be John and Yoko's *Liebestod*. The Lennon-McCartney magic still erupts, but more as moments of ensemble and vocal harmonies than the elaborate negotiations that make up a partnership. Turning the worn seams of their teamwork into a subject ("A Day in the Life," like "We Can Work It Out," or "I've Got a Feeling") remains one of their more brilliant strokes. But when Lennon's vocal harmony leaps atop McCartney in that final, expectant verse of "Hey Jude" (on the repeat of the words "Take a sad song and make it better"), it sounds nostalgic—and that's barely fourteen months later (August 1968).

Overly self-conscious as only Lennon could be, the "A Day in the Life" track spelled out the Lennon-McCartney collaboration as inimitable, two halves of the same whole warring against each other: in the verse, Lennon's angry iconoclast gets struck numb with inaction; McCartney's upbeat tradesman awakes to an imprisoning routine. Each imagines the other as a kind of idealized self, and each lets the other down. "Penny Lane" posed itself as an answer song to "Strawberry Fields Forever," pitting McCartney's child's vision of his schoolday bus stop against Lennon's Salvation Army home. Instead of taking up an argument against each other in the same song, as in "We Can Work It Out," the songwriting cell now divides and splits in two; the collaboration once so hard to decipher now wears its template on its sleeve. (That earlier single quickly turns prophetic, and ironic, once *Sgt. Pepper* gets released.)

Does McCartney's first-person bridge work as the dream life to Lennon's news reader from the previous verse, or does the morning bus reefer send the listener back into Lennon's waking nightmare? By dropping his song inside Lennon's frame for another voice within the same head of the narrative consciousness, McCartney's workday stiff acts out one version of Lennon's newsprint estrangement and willful ignorance; as a character in this song, McCartney details an everyman alive yet unmindful to the world around him. What's more horrifying, they seem to ask: being oblivious to everyday reality or sensitive to it?

Sgt. Pepper elaborates on a coy parody of Victorian gazebo bands, and "When I'm Sixty-four" situates the rock tradition as an extension of music-hall shtick, as far from the racially charged contemporary thrust of rock as seems possible. This imaginary past that McCartney summons for rock 'n' roll locates his stylistic approach to the music. Lennon is a rocker by temperament, McCartney a rocker by means; he's happy to express himself in a variety of genres, and rock is simply one part of his palette. *Sgt. Pepper* dwells in a parallel world, with a fictional band serenading a fictional audience in bright colors and popular songs.

For more than thirty minutes, *Sgt. Pepper* avoids *Revolver*'s harsher truths: the sleazy drug doctors, tax collectors, and duplicitous women. *Pepper*'s women are all desirable, romantic prizes like "Lucy," the gentle geriatric romance partner of "When I'm Sixty-four," and the buxom parking attendant of "Lovely Rita" ("Filling in a ticket in her little white *book*"). The exception is the young lady in "She's Leaving Home," who's on a mission to upset her parents—her quest for love is ripped from a soap opera ("Meeting a man from the motor trade" sticks out like a line Lennon didn't work on, or couldn't be bothered with). But as fetching as "Lucy" or "Rita" might be, romance can't save the narrator of "A Day in the Life" from his story. He can barely see the edges of it himself: salvation is out of reach.

McCartney's work balances and enlarges Lennon's, in both subtle and dramatic ways, for a secret subtheme. The song-within-a-song triumph of the album's final track is only its most virtuoso touch; the songs within an album within a persona—within a career—become the larger frame of reference. If you hear the album as one of bright, dapper, psychedelic showmanship, which opens with three lively and irresistible songs ("Sgt. Pepper," "Friends," and "Lucy"), each successive Lennon number traces darker and darker colors, from the disorienting freak show of "Mr. Kite" to the scrambled urban rush of "Good Morning," a dystopian corn-flake jingle. Amid Lennon's increasing unease, McCartney's chipper "Getting Better" and "When I'm Sixty-four" take on a fragility they might not otherwise have had—it's not his lover who needs a pep talk in the first, it's the singer, and "Sixty-four" broaches the intimidating fear of age by tacking hard against celebrity insecurities: will our audience stay with us after we lose our mighty good looks?

All this converges in "A Day in the Life," where Lennon's weariness becomes McCartney's benign neglect—two versions of the same disaffection. *Sgt. Pepper* has too long been written off as a diversion, an "accession to its times," in Greil Marcus's words, when it codifies many of the aesthetic and technical breakthroughs of *Revolver* and gives many of those same freighted intellectual themes mainstream appeal. *Pepper* reaches toward a tragic statement manifested in "A Day in the Life": fame is hollow, corrupts both artist and audience, and remains at best illusory. Yet people still praise that track's technical feat while ignoring its hangover. "Strawberry Fields Forever" plumbed the loneliness of the world's most famous man, the hangover that would sound utterly cliché were it not so unguarded, so inimitably John Lennon: part Beatle, part loner in his own band. "A Day in the Life" lifts *Sgt. Pepper* from its reputation as mere totem of Swinging London: it's the hangover of a million bleary-eyed morning-afters shared among his listeners.

Long before he posed naked with Yoko Ono, Lennon posed naked with the Beatles, in antique Victorian band uniform and mustache. His chillingly understated vocal on "A Day in the Life" ranks with the overt anguish in "Cold Turkey," *Plastic Ono Band,* or the competing voices that crowd the consciousness of "I Am the Walrus." The detachment of "Strawberry Fields Forever" turns sorrowful here, a confessional of not just the elaborate *Sgt. Pepper* charade but also its necessary Beatle counterpart. As the detached yet infinitely sensitive narrator, Lennon sings for everyman, for how technology isolates us from the modern world, how mass-produced newspapers and media can't save dying industrial towns, and how the very technology used to capture his intimate ache ("Oh boy—"), the most elaborate Beatle recording (complete orchestra performing without a score), expresses merely the utter futility of human progress—including Lennon's greatest invention of all, the Beatles.

Knowing that Lennon had willingly trapped himself in this Beatle role, with the compound interest he collected on the loss of the three people he loved most, it's easier in retrospect to hear all this gathered up in his voice. At the time, it simply worked as a sober free fall sealing off a dazzlingly colorful musical trip. Where *Revolver* came cased in black-and-white, *Sgt. Pepper* radiated color in both its cover confection and its rococo production; stretching two four-track recorders toward primitive eight-track recording techniques opened up the Beatles' sound with new clarity and definition. Each instrument occupied its own special place in the sound, giving each incidental touch of tambourine and maracas its own glow, and their famous group harmonies a luminous sheen. On tracks like "With a Little Help from My Friends," *Sgt. Pepper* made the taut, sardonic boys choir in "Dr. Robert" sound even more compressed.

In the larger sequencing story of how the Beatles bookend their album sides, "A Day in the Life" sits at some distant emotional pole to "Within You Without You," George Harrison's deadpan dive into Eastern mysticism. Harrison's ode is a downer prayer, a list of all the connections people miss in life, all the unfulfilled spiritual potential. The laughter he tacks on at the end underlines its dour tone (it only comes to life in the instrumental refrain with Martin's orchestra). "A Day in the Life" is the sentiment that's too costly to utter even as it comes pouring out, as if Lennon had tried to unpack McCartney's "Eleanor Rigby" refrain: "All the lonely people/Where do they all come from?" and came up short. If so many Beatle fans were so hungry for Beatle music, what did that say about the state of their inner lives?

IN ONE COLORFUL FLOURISH, the rock world entered a new era: the psychedelic scene perched on the edge of an unforgettable summer of new sounds, new acts, the Monterey Pop Festival, and the advent of "mass bohemia." The excitement extended and broadened the Beatles' appearances at the Royal Variety Show Performance in November 1963, or *The Ed Sullivan Show* in February 1964. Now they huddled together for an even bigger spotlight: a worldwide satellite TV hookup Epstein had booked for June 25, 1967. The *Sgt. Pepper* launch got a giant booster shot in London from Seattle's Jimi Hendrix, who opened a Saville Theatre show that week with the title song, giving McCartney one of his favorite career moments. McCartney greeted Hendrix at the party afterward with a huge joint, saying, "That was great, man"[22] (The supporting acts were Procol Harum, who did their austere rewrite of a Bach choral prelude, "A Whiter Shade of Pale," a new Lennon obsession; the Chiffons; and future McCartney Wingman Denny Laine.)

Dropping *Sgt. Pepper* on the market, after so many months of rumors and anticipation, might have been enough for some bands. But you don't mess with a hitting streak, and the Beatles kept their heads down. After a rough master of "You Know My Name (Look Up My Number)" got assembled, McCartney went into the studio with his brother, Mike (calling himself Mike McGear), to produce *McGough and McGear.* Already "You Know My Name" had sprung from an early hours wrap party that got goofier with each refrain, suggesting the Marx Brothers on hash. It's also a warm-up for that winding, grandiose fade-out to "All You Need Is Love," which carried listeners off into a netherworld of Glenn Miller ("In the Mood") and an early Beatle signature as out-of-the-blue nostalgia (Lennon's parroting "She loves you yeah yeah yeah . . .").

They talk about "Love" as a whimsical throwaway, but the band worked on the track throughout June in complicated sessions and rehearsals for the live broadcast. The program, called *Our World,* featured performances from eighteen countries around the world in the first global satellite hookup ever mounted. With the entire world basking in *Sgt. Pepper,* the new Lennon track became its sing-along coda, almost as if he had second thoughts about unleashing "A Day in the Life": on June 14, they prepared a foundational rhythm track in ten takes, and on June 19, they put down multiple vocal overdubs with backing drums, piano, and banjo. (That same day, across town, in an attempt to oust their manager, Andrew Loog Oldham, the Rolling Stones recorded "We Love You.")

Then McCartney threw a wrench into the works with an interview that aggravated the recent Rolling Stones marijuana controversy. In his back garden in St. John's Wood, he sat down with an ITV interviewer and revealed that he had "experimented" with LSD several times. "It seemed strange to me," remembered George Harrison in the *Anthology*, "because we'd been trying to get him to take LSD for about eighteen months—and then one day he's on the television talking all about it."[23] Not only was McCartney unapologetic, he proclaimed how LSD had opened his mind and made him a "better person."

Immediately after the revelation, McCartney took a patronizing position with the reporter, scolding him for not only asking such a question but also broadcasting it. "I'm going to get the blame for telling everyone I take drugs," McCartney proclaimed. "But you're the people who are going to distribute the news." This showed a well-heeled propensity for public relations: days before the band performed before its largest audience ever, editorial pages were aflame denouncing McCartney's influence on his audience. Only a year after Lennon pronounced the band "more popular than Jesus," McCartney got roasted for the chemicals Lennon had been sprinkling on his cereal for nigh on a year.

"ALL YOU NEED IS LOVE" completed the musical arc they had started with "Strawberry Fields Forever" back in December 1966, and after Ringo laid on his snare drumroll opening (just before the head-fake French national anthem) for the mono mix, they put it out as a single on July 7. Then they began scheming as to how to shape their post–*Sgt. Pepper* empire, and whether to continue with Epstein as manager. A concept for a new umbrella company took root during the summer of *Sgt. Pepper,* when, for one last season, the Beatles seemed invincible. Woven in through a variety of business and personal escapades, Epstein got the distinct message that he would not be a party to the new venture; whatever his role, he wouldn't be full partner. With the *Our World* live show, he had just booked the Beatles on the biggest stage of their—or any—career, to an audience

of half a billion people linked via satellite. But their plans for the future
maintained an exclusive tone. Even if they were still on friendly terms,
this new "Apple" talk didn't feature Epstein at the helm. If anything,
to him it probably looked more like an end run around renewing his
contract.

To Epstein, the Beatles began hanging out with suspicious flakes.
The Dutch designers The Fool were already a part of the Beatles' plans
for a clothing store, either as graphics wizards or fashion designers or both.
And Lennon became personally attached to an electronics gadget freak
named Alex Mardas, from Greece, who was quickly dubbed "Magic Alex"
and sent off to invent a master mixing board boasting seventy-two tracks,
wireless speakers, and a thousand miraculous eccentricities to dazzle his
new patron. Alex persuaded the band to buy a Greek island where they
could retreat to make music and take as many drugs as they pleased
without the bother of taxes or unfriendly police. "It will be amazing," as
Chet Flippo, one of Paul's biographers, quotes Lennon as saying. "We'll
be able to just lie in the sun."

> It was some indication of the power the Beatles actually pos-
> sessed that they were able to get a special tax dispensation from
> Chancellor of the Exchequer James Callaghan. They bought a
> little cluster of six islands in the Aegean Sea for £100,000. They
> visited it once, tired of it immediately, and the Beatle paradise
> was later sold.[24]

"They returned a couple days later having funneled wads of money
on their way in and back out," Barry Miles recalled. "It was the typical
Beatle story: some real-estate deal where they came back fantastically
rich."[25] Epstein was not consulted. Insiders spotted the Beatles at key
London clubs, catching bands and doing session work. John and Cyn-
thia, keeping up appearances, caught the Marmalade at the Speakeasy
("I See the Rain"); Paul contributed piano and vocals to the Chris Barber
Band's "Catcall," a revision of Paul's song "Catswalk."

The Greek island had been a weekend distraction from their larger
idea: to set up their own company, beyond the Beatle trinkets Epstein

once suggested. Brainstorming continued throughout the summer: surely they had earned the power to publish their own material by this point. And reinvesting their wealth meant they, as ambitious creatives, could pursue all of rock culture's exploding new mediums: films, recordings, and artist development. Here was a chance to reinvent themselves on a variety of levels, not just in Epstein's image. Since they practiced songwriting and recording like championship dabblers, these new possibilities reignited old enthusiasms.

From the Beatles' standpoint, Epstein's business activities had sent conflicting signals, and his anxieties only inspired more suspicion. He didn't respond to all the new possibilities in the air, and he had been spending a lot of time in the Priory Clinic of late. While overseeing the Saville Theatre, Epstein had already transferred his holdings and title to Robert Stigwood. In fact, during the last weeks of summer, he consummated all this by selling his company behind the Beatles' backs almost as if certain they might turn against him at any moment. At contract negotiations that fall, he may well have simply announced his retirement to hand the whole business over to Stigwood.

Stigwood had bounced around London's management circles for years and finally come up swinging with the Bee Gees, the tuneful and fey Australian outfit that had turned his fortunes around. Compared to Epstein, "Stiggie" was hard to fathom as any kind of threat.[26] But between the enchantments set off by the music, and the drugs that had become second nature, that summer was lousy with diversions. Many business details went unattended. The band's engrained trust in Epstein, and the resounding success of *Sgt. Pepper,* held sway. Even as they sought greater control over their interest, none of them seemed overly worried that this Stigwood deal might clog up their other plans. And Epstein had grown wary with how easily his boys could be distracted.

The biggest distraction yet took the stage at the end of August, when Pattie Harrison, a convert to meditation, invited George and the other Beatles to hear the Maharishi Mahesh Yogi speak at the London Hilton on Park Lane. The Maharishi had gained notoriety by watering down Hindu principles into a generic practice known as "Transcendental Meditation." Its appeal was broad-based: you didn't have to believe in any type of god or deity; the simple practice of meditation calmed the mind and made modern life's anxieties easier to manage. At workshops and retreats, his lectures were punctuated with delirious, high-pitched giggles, lest anybody take him too seriously. In that manner that now seems almost like a parody of New Age good intentions, he linked the best of Buddhism's here and now to the respectability of ancient Indian teachings.

As a successor to Epstein, this Maharishi won over Lennon with a ticklish sense of humor and the promise of inner peace. On another level, as a hounded celebrity, Lennon found that the idea of peace and quiet, and of the untapped healing qualities of the human mind, provided an appealing contrast to his drug burnout. Even if they sensed some of the weightlessness in the Maharishi's teachings, the other Beatles may have urged Lennon in this direction for chemical reasons alone.

The band was impressed enough with the Maharishi's gentle calm to sign on for a retreat at University College in Bangor, North Wales, over that last weekend in August. They invited Epstein to follow them when he could. But the Maharishi's naïveté was somehow contagious: they set off for the train to Wales as their training entourage floundered. As they clambered aboard the train at Paddington Station with their wives, Cynthia Lennon got held back with the mob by a policeman as the train pulled out from the station. Like Pete Best missing the bus home from Birmingham in 1962, the moment registered in her mind with a dull thud of recognition. She caught up with them on a later train. The day after arriving in Bangor, they announced to the world's press that they had quit drugs to adopt the Maharishi's principles of Transcendental Meditation.

For a brief moment, Lennon seems to have been auditioning the Maharishi for Epstein's role of father protector. As the Beatles left for Bangor, Epstein planned a big party at his country house in Richmond while still holding out promise of joining the Beatles in Wales. Another up-and-coming manager, Simon Napier-Bell, entered the picture at this point, just as Epstein suspected the worst in Lennon's new mentor. Napier-Bell ran a band called John's Children and cowrote Dusty Springfield's "You Don't Have to Say You Love Me," which served as the title to his 1983 memoirs. He remembers that Epstein was bored and depressed by running NEMS and made the deal with Stigwood to get rid of the day-to-day headaches of managing his own company. If Napier-Bell wrote himself into the saga immodestly, he's too entertaining a figure to leave out.

His memoirs recount a sexual demo derby of London pop management, the petty one-upmanship and street scams that made rock's backstage at least as beguiling as any of its superstars. Napier-Bell's distinctly British gloss on the Beatles' relationship with Epstein, though, betrays too much sympathy with Epstein's point of view:

> It was impossible to meet Brian Epstein for the first time without puzzling over the Beatles' success. So much of it had depended on that fantastic intimacy they projected in their stage act which made all the kids in the audience long to know what they were saying to each other, what secrets were behind those intimately exchanged glances. But the main secret The Beatles shared was how four tough working-class lads had come to accept the benefits of acting coquettishly for a wealthy middle-class homosexual.[27]

Unintentionally, this "British" viewpoint gets lost in the particulars of class distinctions; everyone sees what they want to see. "Brian was playing games all the time, with himself as much as anyone else," Napier-Bell writes. It was during this season of dabbling in retail clothing and surfing on psychedelic philosophies that Epstein began chasing Napier-Bell. When asked by Napier-Bell about his relationship with the Beatles, Epstein replied: "There's real love between the five of us." What about the "giggling guru"? Brian professed acceptance, with giant exception clauses: "I never minded other people being around. I'm not jealous. Not of girlfriends, wives, even other boyfriends, but the Maharishi seems to want to kill their affection, not for anyone specific, but affection in general." Epstein seemed most disturbed by the guru's effect on Lennon. "At the moment I feel I've completely lost him."[28] Epstein had no illusions when it came to Lennon's rapture over this new older man. One week he was the Beatles' manager; the next week Lennon took on a new confidant, threatening Epstein's power, feeding his paranoia.

If Napier-Bell can be trusted, they shared confidences about Beatlemania's sexual thrills, how overwhelming and seductive the crowds were. Epstein told him a story:

> "One night I pushed my way into the middle of ten thousand screaming kids, right into the middle of the chaos, and let myself go in a falsetto voice. I went absolutely berserk and it was the most erotic thing I ever did in my life. Like the first time I got to kiss John after I'd been crazy about him for ages, but afterwards I was incredibly ashamed of myself. I felt really guilty, as if someone might find out."

Epstein took Napier-Bell back to his Belgravia home that evening after their dinner talk, but Napier-Bell refused his physical advances and left him alone, "lost in a private sadness, his lips slightly pursed, his eyes unfocused," trailing off into a "gloomy trance."[29]

ON THE SUNDAY MORNING of that same weekend late in August 1967, Alistair Taylor took a call from Epstein's secretary, Joanne Newfield. Epstein's servants couldn't get him to respond to knocks on his locked bedroom door. By the time Taylor arrived, Joanne had called a doctor, who forced his way in, to find Epstein's body sprawled across his bed, eight different pill bottles on his table. "All the bottles had their caps properly in place and all of them were still quite full of pills," Taylor remembers. He insisted to anyone he talked to for many years that Epstein would never have committed suicide. "There was no empty bottle that I could see. By the side of the bed there was a pile of correspondence that he had obviously been going through. . . . There was no sign of a note or a message, no blood, no disturbance of the bedclothes. Brian just seemed to be asleep with the bedclothes over him."[30] The coroner ruled Epstein's death an "accidental homicide" from the cumulative effect of bromide in Carbatrol. He was thirty-two.

Napier-Bell got the call on Sunday afternoon while in Scotland with journalist Nik Cohn, and made connections only insiders seemed privy to. Back at home, his answering machine was stuffed with messages from Brian. "And in North Wales," Napier-Bell writes, "the giggling guru was stealing the last vestiges of his influence over the person who'd meant most in [Epstein's] life. I wasn't the only one who'd gone away that weekend. . . . Perhaps it was just that I had an answer-phone and the Maharishi's holiday camp didn't."[31]

It fell to another NEMS staffer, Peter Brown, to call the Beatles in Wales with the terrible news. Jane Asher picked up the phone, and called for Paul. They left at once, as the other three Beatles convened a press conference. Marianne Faithfull writes how "the Maharishi instantly exploited Brian's death. . . . The Beatles were shattered. I can hardly bear to remember it." And according to Faithfull, the Maharishi saw the situation suiting his own interests. She says that he told them: "Brian Epstein is dead. He was taking care of you. He was like your father. I will be your father now."[32]

It's easy to patronize all the flaky spiritual types who moved through sixties culture. But Lennon responded to the Maharishi's methods sincerely, as a way of confronting his drug intake and repairing his marriage with Cynthia. On his very first retreat, not only was Cynthia left behind at Paddington Station but news arrived of Brian Epstein's death by overdose. Knowing now of the personal nightmares this conjured, we can surmise that a crushing sense of anguished recognition must have rushed through him. All of his intimate relationships seemed to end in sudden, irretrievable death.

Epstein had been Lennon's first great conquest. They beguiled each other in the darkest ways possible: Lennon enjoyed humiliating Epstein in front of peers and staff, and Epstein's low self-regard and homosexual shame kept him coming back for more. He adored Lennon as much as he felt deserving of Lennon's emotional abuse. As *Sgt. Pepper* progressed and the Beatles pushed Epstein aside to take greater control over their career, he responded by trying to cut them out of his own fortunes, resentful that everything he had done for them now somehow seemed like a mere backdrop to their untouchable star status. The Liverpool shop-keeper who had delivered Lennon from his provincial upbringing and helped him conquer the world had failed to keep up with the band's transformative powers. A new Beatle company on the horizon promised even greater creative frontiers; but Epstein's reluctance, and his own inexplicable restructuring of NEMS, steered their professional relationship into a ditch.

Finally, Epstein's descent into prescription drugs and alcohol, and frequent "sleep cures," may have served as a cautionary tale to Lennon: despite their invitations, Epstein preferred to stay in London for another party as his boys went off to sit with the new mentor. With so many business and personal issues unresolved—perhaps irresolvable—Lennon's loss must have felt inexplicable, damned, and soured by something beyond fatalism. No matter how rich or successful he got, no matter how much revenge he took on the world for his troubles, or how many riches poured down on his accomplishments, life always had a cruel retort.

Journalists swarmed around Lennon and Harrison (Ringo kept to himself), both of whom gave quotes with spiritual happy talk about passing over and sending feelings to the departed. Lennon's ashen expression in news footage belies his words: his face recalls the "more popular than Jesus" apology in Chicago, grief mixed with fierce anger, weary at how even in private moments like this people shoved microphones in his face to ask what he thought. Even making statements to reporters shows how completely at a loss Lennon felt in the hours after Epstein's death: for all his bluster and arrogance, he didn't have the wherewithal to simply ask for privacy, which would have been a perfectly reasonable request. The Maharishi had counseled the Beatles about death. "He told us . . . uhh . . . not to get overwhelmed by grief," Lennon stammered to reporters. "And whatever thoughts we have of Brian to keep them happy, because any thoughts we have of him will travel to him wherever he is."

Did the Maharishi offer any words of comfort? "Meditation gives you confidence enough to withstand something like this, even the short amount we've had," John replied, his eyes suddenly hoping something could make it so as he mouthed the words. "There's no real such thing as death anyway," Harrison ventured. "I mean, it's death on a physical level, but life goes on everywhere . . . and you just keep going, really. The thing about the comfort is to know that he's OK."[33]

It took a long time for the world to guess precisely how complicated Lennon's feelings were that day. It's another point where Lennon's cocksure composer rubbed against a frightening artlessness. Perhaps he felt it might help take the sting out of Epstein's death if he made some public statement; perhaps he simply needed public validation about the sudden turn of events to help him through this new trauma. "Making sense of it all," and trying to set it all within the Maharishi's framework, shows just how lost and abandoned he felt. There were worlds of unfinished business with Epstein, even as they plotted new business without him. It remains one of the central ironies of Lennon's career that as his music enchanted millions, he lurched from one wrenching loss to another.

THE BAND SPENT THAT FALL of 1967 creating *Magical Mystery Tour,* which would prove to be their first major flop, partially redeemed by the queasy, indelible Lennon oil spill of "I Am the Walrus." Threads from "Tomorrow Never Knows" and "Being for the Benefit of Mr. Kite" returned as frayed strands in this music: the group harmonies had all but disappeared, there were no Lennon-McCartney duets, and all of Lennon's verbal twists felt overgrown, with too many targets, a thousand private jokes colliding in song. "Walrus" slowed a bad acid trip down for bilious humor.

The motives behind *Magical Mystery Tour* combined everything that was impulsive and whimsical about the sixties with the tired conceit of pop stars dabbling in film. Since they had successfully skirted this pothole in their first two movies, which operate as parodies of rock stars on the big screen, the prime motivation for the *Mystery Tour* project feels misguided. The larger career arc they rejoined after the initial television broadcast of the film testifies to the redemptive power of the Beatles' ambition—and their comeback became a defining component of what made them great.

The group left Bangor promising the Maharishi they'd meet up with him soon in India for lengthier study. But once home, Lennon's mood worsened. "I thought, 'we've had it,'" Lennon later remembered.[34] A group meeting early in September determined that any trip to India would need to be postponed. Riven with insecurity, they resolved to keep working, manage themselves, and get through the next project, putting off spiritual advancement until the New Year. McCartney gave an interview to the *New Musical Express* on September 9 that outlined plans for a new TV project and sound track, but little else. He didn't mention Epstein. All four Beatles attended Epstein's memorial service on October 19, down the road from EMI, at the New London Synagogue on Abbey Road.

Ideas about film itself were undergoing radical flux in this period, and the edgiest "modern" cinema found documentaries and experimental improvisation cornerstones of the new sensibilities. Ken Kesey's Merry Pranksters, and their bus of psychedelic enlightenment, served as the Beatles' role model. McCartney convinced the others how stories would spring out spontaneously from all the serendipitous situations most travelers encounter, and their sound track would rescue any weak moments. Perhaps it was the concept that tripped them up: tripsters roaming America in a psychedelic bus, with Jack Kerouac's sidekick, the mythical Neal Cassady, at the wheel, blasting rock music and "turning on" the youthful tribes to expanded consciousness and delirious carnality, just didn't translate well to Brits plunked down in the Midlands for a mystery tour. No sooner had they plotted the general outline of the shoot than they found themselves on a bus getting into trouble with routine details like food, lodging, schedules, setups, and scatterbrained plots. Tony Bramwell describes the world's biggest rock stars learning dreary tasks of management with forty extras inside a traffic jam of fans and press.

Luckily, enough goodwill and joie de vivre rescued some moments, and several sequences took shape between trips to the recording studio: "The Fool on the Hill" got the star treatment with the only professionally shot video of the project. (McCartney filmed this on his own in France. And it's not hard to guess who put it way up front, right after the bus leaves, a sop to leading with more sentimental material.) One of

Lennon's bits involved a scene he wrote straight out of a dream: with his hair slicked back, in waiter's tuxedo, he shovels spaghetti into an enormous woman, as if reenacting all the garbage of politesse he had to feed Aunt Mimi as a child. But it doesn't have enough bite to strike much of a Lennon singularity; it's anybody's childhood resentment ballooned into a nasty comeuppance (and a rough premonition of a scene near the end of Monty Python's *The Meaning of Life*). "Jimmy Johnson," the giddy host, seems like an unctuous version of McCartney himself ("You are *all* my friends," he announces). Johnson introduces the bus driver as "Alf," but he gets no lines and no interactions throughout the film. You half expect Sigmund Freud himself to join the frolic and connect all these symbolic dots.

As Lennon's emotional slump began to infect his muse, his brilliance took on a brittle pedantry. The recently closed West Maling Air Station, near Maidstone in Kent, a huge expanse of concrete blocks built to absorb the impact of Nazi bombs, served as a giant outdoor set for "I Am the Walrus," the sole music video from the film with any spark or guile (a touch of lust might have rescued some other sequences). Clumsily staged policemen held hands atop the concrete, swaying to the music, and a string of white-jacketed figures waved to the audience before trailing along behind the bus as the bobbies stepped into line at the back during the fade-out.

The song's recording, however, fares much better. George Martin's frame blurs into the material for a beguiling mix of form and content; "Walrus" could be one of the few Beatle tracks that's even more imaginatively produced than conceived. It descends into a long, disorienting fade-out, the tail wagging the song even more frantically than the false ending of "Strawberry Fields Forever" or the musical gags bookending "All You Need Is Love." As sheer idea, "Walrus" trudges through its hairy arrangement toward a conventional, identity-crisis ego-fragmentation lyric, announcing its Lewis Carroll and Edgar Allan Poe idolatry rather too cravenly. Lennon had already earned these comparisons, and "Glass Onion" went so far as to suggest he'd outpaced them. (Lennon later regretted confusing Carroll's "Walrus and the Carpenter" character as hero instead of villain, which makes his point in a backhanded, circuitous way—as in "Strawberry Fields Forever," he's not in control of his message.) Where "Strawberry Fields" has humility, and some gentleness, "Walrus" turns on all the faucets for a flood of imagery; it could be his least humorous stab at surrealism. He sings from the other side of some enormous creative chasm, the voice of LSD devouring a once-virile personality, the drug slowly curdling its host.

In some ways, the bottoming out of "Walrus" also works as a dark psychedelic prophecy of the escalating violence, protest, and assassinations to come in 1968. The track stands as a mockery, the only song to upstage *Magical Mystery Tour*'s governing concept—more material on this level might have rescued more of the film. By contrast, McCartney toys with sentimental clichés like "Your Mother Should Know" and piffle like "Hello, Goodbye," the same impulses that steered some of *Sgt. Pepper* into fanciful sitcom ("Getting Better," "Lovely Rita").

Epstein's managerial finesse became tangible by his absence. *Magical Mystery Tour* arrived stillborn. It premiered on Boxing Day, on BBC One, a black-and-white network at the time even though the entire shoot had been conceived in psychedelic color. The reviews were savage, and pundits argued over how, or whether, the Beatles could earn back their prestige. Another broadcast in color on BBC Two several days later only confirmed the first impression. Just six months earlier, *Sgt. Pepper* had turned on the world. Now the Beatles stared failure in the eye.

I Should Have Known Better

Tₕₑ SHEER DENSITY OF EVENTS BETWEEN 1968 AND 1970, THE LATE-Beatle period that produced *The White Album, Let It Be,* and *Abbey Road,* can still detract from their accomplishments on these albums. Perched as they were atop twin ideals of hope and unity, the band began to splinter. World events synced up uncannily with Lennon's personal upheavals, triggered by a gaping career disconnect at the end of 1967: where unwieldy Beatlemania led to a defining essay on fame and their persona with *Sgt. Pepper's* "A Day in the Life," the amateurish unraveling of *Magical Mystery Tour* telegraphed Lennon's larger detachment. As they descended an old-fashioned Hollywood staircase in white tuxedos to sing its finale, "Your Mother Should Know," they couldn't have been more out of touch.

This Beatle career crisis shrank against the larger historical canvas: instead of bounding out ahead (as they had with *Rubber Soul* and *Revolver*), the band began to play catch-up with its audience. The battles between students and their parents, soldiers and the fathers who cynically sent them to Vietnam while denying them the right to vote, between patriotic hard-hat construction workers and the college-deferred sons (and daughters) of the ruling class, reached a contentious pitch in America rarely seen since. The great "Classic Rock" explosion during the Beatles' middle period (1965–67) had slowed time down, even made it stand completely still. In the early months of 1968, world events tumbled ahead at a frightening pace, and the cultural shifts took manic swerves. In this late phase, the Beatles cultivated their own disintegration as a late theme, as if rock celebrity had become so all-consuming that they could only reinvent themselves as individuals.

It's worth remembering, however, that for one sunny season, 1967's fabled Summer of Love, Lennon's "All You Need Is Love" revived all the hope and possibility Beatle music had pointed toward since "She Loves You" and "I Feel Fine" and "The Word." While it lasted, "All You Need Is Love" emblemized the dreamy potential on parade at the Monterey Pop Festival, where McCartney muscled Hendrix onto the bill for his American "debut." By pouring lighter fluid on his Stratocaster and setting it on fire, Hendrix lit the psychedelic desires Lennon first glimpsed in "Rain" and "Tomorrow Never Knows."

It's hard to say exactly when, but the simplistic chorus to "All You Need Is Love" began to ring cheery, and throughout 1968, world headlines drowned out its idealism. Compared to the cascading harmonies of Brian Wilson's "Good Vibrations" (1966), or the choral waterfalls in "Nowhere Man" and "Good Day Sunshine," the unison reiterations in "All You Need Is Love" rang wide but not deep. It's a measure of that era's shift in consciousness that you can't hear Lennon's song anymore without a twinge of foreboding, the sound of hope overreaching its grasp.[1]

Sgt. Pepper, that great melodic symbol of psychedelic utopia, somehow intimidated rock's mood off its axis; as the era unraveled into protest and violence, Lennon's "All You Need Is Love" grew fragile, and less durable (unlike most of their work up to this point). Even Lennon's winning self-mockery—the French national anthem fanfare, or the Tin Pan Alley fade-out—can't quite redeem the number's cheeky nostalgia. Within a year of its debut, events made the refrain seem not just gullible but outmaneuvered. The song stayed the same, but its meanings had trouble transcending new realities.

A TICKER TAPE of that season's headlines, as 1967 gave way to 1968, plowed under every optimistic impulse. In October 1967, as Lennon and McCartney wrapped up filming and began compiling *Magical*

Mystery Tour footage in separate editing sessions, one hundred thousand protestors marched on Washington's Lincoln Memorial and later held an all-night vigil at the Pentagon. Two antiwar activists, Abbie Hoffman and Jerry Rubin, dubbed themselves "Yippies" and, in a defining stroke of media theater, announced that their collective spiritual energy would levitate the Defense Department. Norman Mailer turned the spectacle into a scathing interior drunkalogue in his nonfiction "novel," *Armies of the Night,* which dramatized the tangle of hypocrisies at play between youth and entrenched power. Mailer's seething epic spared no one, including old-guard leftists like himself who self-consciously exploited the students' flair.

The North Vietnamese army's Tet Offensive at the end of January 1968 stalled out as a military action but turned into a psychological coup, convincing millions of Americans that the Vietnam War was intractable. As the American presidential primaries started up, antiwar demonstrators hoped to exploit these contradictions. Students began to see American university campuses as potent symbols of the military-industrial complex. Most major universities, they argued, depended on Pentagon spending to keep scientific research afloat, so these connections had direct relevance to the war. To the antiwar activists, tuition stoked the war machine. This all made perfect sense to students, and many of their professors, who had held teach-ins on Vietnam as early as 1965. Leftist professors found themselves pitted against their own administrators. Campus marches, sit-ins, and rallies became symbolic of this larger confrontation.

As Democrats tussled over war policy, and the Beatles' new single "Lady Madonna" ascended the charts, the presidential race suddenly caved. Minnesota senator Eugene McCarthy, the antiwar candidate, stunned political circles on March 12 by losing the New Hampshire primary by a mere 7 points behind President Johnson. This primary reshuffled the deck: Senator Robert F. Kennedy officially entered the race, and Johnson morphed from presumptive incumbent into lame duck. At the end of the month, Lyndon Johnson announced to a stunned nation that he would not seek reelection (just as the "Lady Madonna" refrain, "See how they run . . . ," taunted him from the top forty). In *At*

Canaan's Edge, the third volume of his monumental history of the "King Years," Taylor Branch defines Johnson's motives as noble, even patriotic: all his high-flown strategies had failed, and now even his most trusted advisors were telling him that defeat in Vietnam seemed likely no matter how much armor and human life he committed to the cause. Admitting failure and stepping down became the most honorable move left to him. The war's frustrations, and the surging antiwar movement, had shamed Johnson from office; the man who had won more votes than any candidate in American history in 1964 could no longer defend his own foreign policy.

But what should have been a huge victory for the antiwar effort turned into a renewed struggle for America's soul—a struggle that has adopted various metaphors ever since. Every step toward peace brought a new wave of violence. Pro-war factions argued that dissent, as in Jane Fonda's visit to Hanoi, meant sympathy for the Communist North Vietcong. Numerous American cities had suffered three successive summers of urban riots, shaking civil rights optimism to its core: as far back as early 1967, the Reverend Martin Luther King Jr. had expanded his antiviolence rhetoric to include war resistance and economic justice, to widespread disdain. The Black Panthers, an Oakland splinter group determined to arm itself in self-defense, suffered a brutal FBI raid on April 6, 1968, which left one member, Bobby Hutton, dead. On April 15, the Spring Mobilization against the Vietnam War began across major universities, and the following week, the Students for a Democratic Society (SDS), formed eight years earlier at the University of Michigan, occupied five buildings at Columbia University, including the president's office, for a week. All this tumult turned the Beatles into political figures by fiat.

MOST SIXTIES CLICHÉS ABOUT flower power and long hair distort the many internal conflicts within leftist youth culture. In America, inner-city uprisings had become an annual nightmare. Fueled by the kerosene of prejudice and poverty, the race riots that burned through Watts in Los Angeles, in 1965, also visited Cleveland (Ohio), Waukegan (Illinois), Benton Harbor (Michigan), and Atlanta (Georgia), among other places, in 1966. The 1967 Summer of Love, a privileged catchphrase that blacks regarded with contempt, added Roxbury (Massachusetts), Tampa (Florida), Buffalo (New York), Newark and Plainfield (New Jersey), Cairo (Illinois), Durham (North Carolina), Memphis (Tennessee), Cambridge (Maryland), Milwaukee (Wisconsin), and Minneapolis (Minnesota) to the list. Then, just when people thought fear had reached its pitch, Martin Luther King Jr. fell to an assassin's bullets on April 4, 1968 in Memphis, Tennessee, where he was organizing striking garbage workers. Two months later, after winning the California presidential primary, the left's most promising antiwar candidate, Robert Kennedy, fell to bullets that seemed anything but random.

The antiwar movement that later gathered in Chicago to protest the Democratic National Convention, in August 1968, hoped to turn these traumas into peaceful planks. Mayor Richard J. Daley's police clubbed down even such modest aspirations. And in the perverted logic of the times, peace-loving, nonviolent defiance to a cynical war fueled support for Republican candidate Richard Nixon's slim victory that fall. Once Johnson stepped aside, Nixon's vague centrism, aimed at a "silent majority," rallied battered Republicans, who feared a long season in the wilderness after Barry Goldwater's 1964 meltdown. The Democratic candidate, Johnson's vice president, Hubert Humphrey, refused to take an antiwar stand, forfeiting votes from younger McCarthy and Kennedy supporters— and you still had to be twenty-one to vote.

The Beatles' meditational retreat to the pilgrimage center of Rishikesh in Uttarakhand, at the foothills of the Himalayas, in February and March coincided with McCarthy's primary surge and Johnson's withdrawal, and posed new challenges for rock music's relevance. Just as the Black Panthers tilted more toward violent positions after Dr. King died, so, too, did radical voices begin dominating antiwar movement debates once Nixon got elected and the Vietnam saga stretched out indefinitely. Well before the Kent State killings of four students in May 1970, the tipping point for sixties protest came when peaceful demonstrations, no matter how principled and popular, proved less and less effective as political dissent.

SELF-INVOLVED AMERICANS still view these ruptures in civic law and order as symptoms of a cultural breakdown, which, at the time, made rock the music of transgression. Long hair signaled contempt for the system that waged war so brutally and systematically punished dissent. Authorities successfully patronized campus peace rallies as longhairs running wild. (Some "hippies" actually cut their hair to campaign for McCarthy so they couldn't be so easily disparaged.) These student rebellions, largely confined to America between 1964 and 1967, then mushroomed into a global phenomenon. In Europe, student protests in Paris unraveled into general worker strikes, freezing France's economy with unprecedented force. "What had started as protests against the Vietnam War expanded to something far wider," remembered the activist and author Tariq Ali. "The talk was of revolution. Everything about modern capitalist society was suddenly called into question."[2] Even in Czechoslovakia, a presumed Kremlin puppet state, President Alexander Dubček encouraged a free press, and for one surreal summer, anti-Soviet sentiment seemed as if it might actually defy Moscow's grip. This would have been unthinkable just months before. "Be realistic—demand the impossible," went the cry from the Paris streets that May.

Demonstrations broke out everywhere, even in Mick Jagger's "sleepy London town." Citing Her Majesty's support for America's war policies, actress Vanessa Redgrave joined ten thousand anti-Vietnam demonstrators in Trafalgar Square on March 17, which turned into a riot when some broke off and headed toward the U.S. Embassy in Grosvenor Square to deliver a protest letter. Redgrave joined in chants of "Ho, Ho, Ho Chi Minh, we will fight and we will win!" The protestors met with armed police barricading the embassy, and trouble broke out: two hundred people were arrested, eighty-six injured. The Foreign Office reported that one hundred members of the German SDS (Sozialistischer Deutscher Studentenbund), "experts in methods of riot against the police," had instigated the violence in London. Such propaganda had already reached the level of establishment cant, which blamed the violence on the demonstrators instead of the police, who were usually the only armed people in the area. Jagger attended this march, and spun from it the Rolling Stones' next single, "Street Fighting Man," which appeared in August.

Hey! Think the time is right for a palace revolution
But where I live the game to play is compromise solution

Leftists, however, were already skeptical about Jagger's commitment to sweeping radical change, and with Rolling Stones' branded credit cards and a knighthood (in 2003), he would earn their skepticism in bulk. But at the time, antiwar activists favored his "Street Fighting Man" stance even though its ambivalence rivaled Lennon's "Revolution," as we'll see. (The following year, in "You Can't Always Get What You Want," Jagger sang: "I went down to the Chelsea drugstore/To get my fair share of abuse," as if he had been victimized by the cops as much as anybody and had foreseen the futility of protest, which was disingenuous at best.) When the BBC banned "Street Fighting Man," Jagger submitted his handwritten lyrics to Tariq Ali to publish in *Black Dwarf,* one of the many new leftish broadsheets.

Had the Beatles released Lennon's "All You Need Is Love" in the summer of 1968, they would have been laughed offstage. And there's no possibility of Lennon's rabidly noncommittal "Revolution" coming at any moment before May 1968, when he wrote it. Mass media's radio, TV, film, newspapers, and magazines, which had largely been brought to life by the Beatles' intense early fame, morphed into a daily swish of information, and a new layer of tension grew between how skillfully the Beatles tickled this new media beast and how their music reacted to world events. When "All You Need Is Love" assumed the finale of the *Yellow Submarine* film, which premiered that agonizing summer of 1968, it cozied right into that cartoon's alternative world, a children's project that traded in cultural relevance for fanciful colors. When they left for Rishikesh, the Beatles' biggest problem was fixing their career after *Magical Mystery Tour.* The world they would return to had slipped a few gears. So had Lennon's home life.

AS A MEASURE OF THEIR RESOLVE, they had come back to the studio in the new year after a barrage of bad notices. Critics from all quarters had savaged the film from the Christmas 1967 holidays: London's *Daily Express* called it "blatant rubbish," the *Los Angeles Times* announced the

"Beatles bomb," and the American NBC network even canceled its option—Americans had to wait to see *Magical Mystery Tour* on the art-house and campus circuit. BBC radio, convinced of its own authority despite the ineptitude of "censoring" "A Day in the Life," struck "I Am the Walrus" from its airwaves for "indecent lyrics"—the term "knickers" being roughly analogous to American "panties." The band's reputation plummeted. Originally, they had moved forward with *Magical Mystery Tour* to stave off creative inertia by keeping themselves busy in the wake of Epstein's death. But in retrospect, this can be seen to have only forestalled the larger questions left by his absence.

Now, in early 1968, they dashed off a few songs, and filmed a brief cameo for *Yellow Submarine,* before heading off to India, the trip they had delayed from the previous autumn. They acted as if these *Magical Mystery Tour* critics were simply balmy. In fact, they settled right back into a productive mode that produced both their next single ("Lady Madonna") and three more tracks: Harrison's "The Inner Light" (started at Bombay sessions during his work on the *Wonderwall* film sound track), and Lennon's "Hey Bulldog" and "Across the Universe," which he donated to the World Wildlife Fund.

"Madonna" had a curling McCartney piano lick that tipped its hat to trumpeter Humphrey Lyttelton's jazz instrumental "Bad Penny Blues," from 1956 (an early Joe Meek production). McCartney's groove crossed the dapper Lyttelton with the more ribald Fats Domino, and the oblique lyric sidestepped the music-hall mannerisms of "When I'm Sixty-four." At the last of these sessions, on February 11, the promo shoot for a "Lady Madonna" film got sidetracked when Lennon showed up with a new number: "Hey Bulldog." Of these four tracks, Lennon thought the least of "Bulldog," and it quickly joined the *Yellow Submarine* slush pile (and eventually got cut from the final edit, although not the sound track). This last February session also marked the first time Lennon brought a new Japanese girlfriend, Yoko Ono, to the studio.

AT FIRST, the short, meekish Japanese woman seemed like just another eccentric Lennon dalliance. George Harrison remembers that Lennon "had just started his relationship with Yoko before we went out to India."[3] And Lennon later admitted his mind was a jumble once he started his new fling: "Yoko and me, we met around then. I was going to take her [to India]. I lost my nerve because I was going to take my ex-wife *and* Yoko, and I didn't know how to work it. So I didn't quite do it."[4] Indecision prevailed, so he took Cynthia, hopping back on the marital seesaw to try to make things work. He also sprang a seat for Alex Mardas, the eccentric electronics wizard John Dunbar had introduced him to.

Ambivalent about his future and the Beatles', increasingly uncomfortable at home, Lennon felt his rock-star lifestyle spiraling downward. There were signs that he'd wearied of this treadmill, and saw Rishikesh as a respite, similar to his trip to Spain in 1966. Like an alcoholic begging for one more chance, he promised Cynthia to reform his bad habits and become a better husband and father, and together they looked to meditation as a marital retreat. But he had trouble sustaining these pledges. Cynthia's memoirs detail a detached, distant husband and father, who swung from optimistic devotion to testy reproach. At the beginning of the year, the *Daily Mail* ran a small item about Lennon's father, Alfred Lennon, who had been inexplicably invited into the Lennons' home for a stay. But it didn't last long.[5]

Lennon's mood swings find testimony in several contemporary reports. Shortly before the trip to India, he spent the weekend with Derek Taylor, former Epstein press agent and Apple publicist, and his family at their country house. There were five children—"They seemed incredibly happy and contented," Cynthia remembered. Lennon returned and put his arms around his wife: "Let's have loads more kids, Cyn, and be really happy."[6] At this, Cynthia broke down, as if some part of her knew Lennon was all talk. "What the hell's the matter with you, Cyn, what you crying for?" he asked. She could only "blurt out" that she couldn't bring herself to see a bright future for the family, no matter how badly she wished for it: "I was so disturbed by John's outburst that I even suggested that Yoko Ono was the woman for him."[7]

Insight like that caught Cynthia between dread and hope, but she steadied herself amid the countervailing storms, revealing why Lennon was attracted to her in the first place. "I always felt that he expected a great deal more of me," she wrote. "I really wasn't on his wavelength as much as he would have liked. He needed more encouragements and support for his way-out ideas."[8] Dot, their housekeeper, reported that Ono had been to the house "on numerous occasions" asking for Lennon when he was away. After a time, Cynthia calmed herself, and tried to think of the trip to India as a chance to repair the marriage, get some quiet romantic time alone away from Julian, and work on their fading intimacy. Cynthia's mother, Lil, moved back into Kenwood to look after Julian. John and Cynthia joined George and Pattie, Pattie's sister Jenny, and Magic Alex at the Maharishi's ashram. "We would be meditating for many hours each day, there was no place for a child," Cynthia reasoned.[9]

BUT WITH LENNON, the only thing worse than delving into drugs was sobering up enough to pin his hopes on Transcendental Meditation, as if that might save his marriage. "We can make it work, Cyn," he told his wife. "When we're in India we'll have time for us and everything will be fine."[10] Others who were close to him recognized his sudden attachment to the Maharishi as a transparent substitution father figure he sought while grieving Epstein's loss.

In one galling, signature move, Ono had turned up at a Beatles travel meeting in London, afterward hopping right into Lennon's limo behind his wife. After they dropped Ono off, Lennon waved off Cynthia's protests. It's doubtful that he and Yoko were still platonic "friends" by this point, but Lennon stuck to his story. Mysterious postcards began arriving at Kenwood, with Yoko Ono slogans on the back, beseeching Lennon to "Watch for me, I'm a cloud in the sky," phrases that resembled the instructional koans in *Grapefruit*.

These postcards followed Lennon to India, where he plunged into meditation, received private tutorials from the master, and moved out of his bedroom with Cynthia for private quarters after two weeks. Cynthia later learned that he was stealing off to the local post office each morning, or getting Magic Alex to go, to snare those missives in advance of the regular mail. Soon after, Cynthia discovered a typewritten letter

Yoko had sent John that hinted at more. But Lennon kept brushing her suspicions off, even as he admitted that Ono had been sending him many letters and postcards: "She's crackers, just a weirdo artist who wants me to sponsor her. Another nutter wanting money for all that avant-garde bullshit. It's not important."[11] Cynthia wanted desperately to believe him.

As LENNON PROMISED to keep his marriage intact while sneaking around with his new lover, an American journalist, Lewis Lapham, prepared for a trip to India to cover the Beatles for the *Saturday Evening Post*. Eastern mysticism had ballooned into a trend, and the Maharishi became one of its figureheads. The same magazine editors who had covered Swinging London now sent young reporters like Lapham after this story as a lifestyle feature.

Lapham began by visiting the Beach Boys in California, who all spoke fondly of the Maharishi and his recent presentation at the Felt Forum. Brian Wilson's mother was about to undergo her "initiation," while his control freak of a father, Murry, considered following lead singer Mike Love to the Maharishi's ashram. "If my dad goes to India," Wilson told Lapham, "I'll know that the Maharishi has done his job."[12]

Arriving in Rishikesh, Lapham met John O'Shea outside the Maharishi's ashram. O'Shea was AWOL from Norwalk, Connecticut, "recently mustered out of the United States Marine Corps. . . . Together with other Americans, he was living in the farmyard with a peep of chickens." Like other locals who watched as celebrities flocked to the compound, O'Shea told Lapham that the Maharishi was in fact a "mountebank," pushing a commercial product, "like learning to play the piano in six easy weeks."[13]

For a spiritual teacher, the Maharishi had a knack for manipulating journalists. At first, minions told Lapham the holy guru was far too busy for interviews. The very next day, the Maharishi welcomed the young reporter as if he were a "plenipotentiary sent by the American State Department." Lapham found the kindly old man small and frail. Unlike the sweet, giggly troll portrayed by the media, he spotted "a vaguely troubled expression in his eyes." Lapham noted another aspect to the Maharishi's Beatle appeal: "His voice had a musical resonance in it, and it was his way of ending his sentences on a rising note of near hysteria that suggested the twittering of birds."[14]

Along with other musicians, like Donovan, and Mike Love of the Beach Boys, the retreat attracted Hollywood glamour in Mia Farrow and her sister, Prudence. Mia, at twenty-three, had just extracted herself from a whirlwind marriage to Frank Sinatra. "We were a reverent, drab group of fifty or so men and women of various nationalities, ages, and professions," she writes in her memoirs. "Maharishi suggested that we meditate for twelve hours of the day, taking short breaks as we needed. . . . When we encountered one another along the gravel paths or beneath the trees, we exchanged other-worldly smiles and the Sanskrit salutation 'Jai Guru dev.' " (Lennon had already used this mantra as the refrain for "Across the Universe.")

Farrow remembers Lennon expressing the typical frustrations with long exposure to quietude: "Whenever I meditate," he told her, "there's a big brass band in me head."[15] The overall mood was serene, but Farrow describes "several frightening, emotional eruptions," enough to prompt the Maharishi to assign "team buddies" to help them look out for one another. It's not hard to imagine Lennon among other heavy drug users, all detoxing simultaneously. Prudence Farrow's buddies were George and John, and "they took their responsibility seriously. Every morning and most afternoons they met in Prudy's room, where they discussed their respective lives, the meaning of existence, and who Maharishi really was."[16] "Dear Prudence" grew out of this friendship.

The Beatles' accommodations, Lapham noted, were more spacious than those for "meditators of lesser stature," with indoor plumbing and comfortable furniture. The talk was all about how the band would stay for a full three-month term and then travel with the Maharishi to his lake houseboats in Kashmir, where they would take written and oral exams. Cynthia Lennon was dressed in "vivid and tailing silk," Lapham remembered, and was very beautiful, but had an air of sadness about her.[17]

As Lennon unwound, he suffered the classic symptoms of LSD withdrawal: "I was in a room for five days meditating. I wrote hundreds of songs. I couldn't sleep and I was hallucinating like crazy, having dreams where you could smell. I'd do a few hours and then you'd trip off; three- or four-hour stretches. It was just a way of getting there, and you could go on amazing trips."[18]

Ringo arrived with Paul four days after Lennon, with one case each of baked beans and eggs. Magic Alex smuggled in some hooch from the village across the river, which tasted like petrol, Cynthia remembered. A scene from the *Anthology* relates their first gathering with the swami, the group sitting cross-legged on the floor in a circle with the bearded old man. Lennon got up, walked around behind, and patted him on the head, saying, "There's a good little guru."[19] Everybody dissolved into giggles, including the Maharishi. The ashram's social politics swelled with adolescent gamesmanship. Most residents were American or British, but a few of the Swedish students had already won a reputation for meditating beyond all reason: one of them sat for twenty-one hours straight, as if endurance equaled enlightenment.

John became increasingly aloof: he rose early and left the room without speaking to Cynthia. Once he took his own room, he withdrew from her completely. "From then on he virtually ignored me, both in private and in public." When she approached him about his distance, he pushed back defensively: "I just can't feel normal doing all this stuff, I'm trying to get myself together. It's nothing to do with you. Give me a break."[20]

In the *Anthology,* McCartney tells of a revealing interaction between Lennon and the guru, who shared Lennon's obsession with technology. One day, a helicopter came to take the Maharishi to an appearance in New Delhi, and the students all traipsed down to the river to see him off. Before departing, he offered one of them a quick ride alone with him in the chopper. "Of course, it was John," McCartney remarks. "I asked him later, 'Why were you so keen to get up with Maharishi?'—'To tell you the truth,' he said, 'I thought he might slip me the Answer.' That was very John!"[21] Only later did Cynthia figure out what preoccupied Lennon. Early morning posts brought letters from Yoko almost daily. "There was I," Cynthia reflects, "trying to give John the space and un-

December 18, 1963. BBC Paris Studio, London. The "From Us to You" recording session, broadcast the following week on the Beatles' own two-hour radio special.

February 9, 1964. Phil Spector makes sure to get his photo taken with Cynthia and John in first class as the Beatles fly to America.

December 18, 1965. Alfred Lennon reclines with a cigarette for a photo shoot to publicize his single, "That's My Life."

July 8, 1966. Heathrow Airport, London. The Beatles, with their manager, Brian Epstein, greeted by two hundred fans after arriving in London.

March 30, 1967. EMI Studios. John listens to a playback in the control room during the *Sgt. Pepper* sessions, with producer George Martin and technical engineer Ken Townsend (right).

![photograph]

"When two great Saints meet it is a humbling experience. The long battles to prove he was a Saint."—Paul McCartney

Unfinished Music No. 1: Two Virgins: Yoko Ono/John Lennon

Summer 1968. EMI Studios. John and Paul enjoy a light moment during the *White Album* sessions.

opposite: Summer 1968. "When two great Saints meet, it is a humbling experience. The long battles to prove he was a Saint." McCartney's dedication adorns Lennon's nude self-portrait with Yoko on the cover of *Unfinished Music No.1 Two Virgins.*

March 20, 1969. ". . . You can get married in Gibraltar near Spain." John and Yoko pose with their marriage certificate.

April 22, 1969. Apple rooftop. John changing his name to John Ono Lennon on the site of the concert that closes the movie *Let It Be*.

December 15, 1969. Times Square, Manhattan. One of eleven billboards John and Yoko purchased in major cities to deliver their Christmas message for peace. *below:* February 11, 1970. Studio Eight, BBC Television Centre, London. Taping a performance of "Instant Karma!" for *Top of the Pops.* Yoko sits blindfolded as Klaus Voormann (with beard) plays bass in the background behind her.

July 23, 1971. Ascot, England. Posing with an exit sign in the "spare room" at Tittenhurst, readying for a move to Manhattan.

November 8, 1972. New York. John bows at Yoko's feet the morning after Nixon's re-election landslide. At the party the previous evening, Lennon had openly cheated on her in the next room.

derstanding he asked for, with no idea that Yoko was drawing him away from me and further into her orbit."²²

Although Ringo left early, complaining about the food, the other three Beatles stayed on, and most remembered the atmosphere as friendly and calm. When Lennon grew disillusioned with the Maharishi, Cynthia watched in disbelief at the intensity of his anger toward someone she found a perfectly serene, inoffensive leader. She suspected Alex Mardas of planting ideas in Lennon's head, like some devious Iago. "A couple of weeks before we were due to leave, Mardas accused the Maharishi of behaving improperly with a young American girl, a fellow student."²³

Lennon later remembered how leaving the Maharishi meant a confrontation, something he usually avoided like disease. So he bore into the mystic, funneling all his leftover grief around Alf, Julia, and Brian, and one episode seemed to confirm Lennon's suspicions. The Maharishi asked why Lennon insisted on leaving, and Lennon shot back, "Well, if you're so cosmic, you'll know why." I don't know why, the old man answered, you must tell me. And Lennon kept on at him, saying, "You ought to know." Lennon reports: "He gave me *such* a look. And I knew then when he looked at me, because I'd called his bluff. I was a bit rough to him. I always expect too much," before adding this whopper: "I'm always expecting my mother and I don't get her, that's what it is."²⁴

Some accounts have Harrison joining in Lennon's indignation; others have Lennon acting alone, seeking confirmation from George but otherwise not involving him. Lennon later told Cynthia he had been having his own doubts about the Maharishi's "interest in public recognition, celebrities and money." Both Cynthia and Harrison went on record as being vaguely miffed at Lennon's outburst—they considered the Maharishi a sweet old man whose greatest crime, perhaps, was in enjoying the spotlight a bit too much.

The Maharishi made a convenient proxy for Lennon's suspicions about Cynthia: Mardas produced a letter another camper named Tom Simcox had written to her, which inflamed Lennon's jealousies even though he had spent the whole time sneaking in letters from Ono. On the way out of the camp, Lennon wrote a new song about being made a fool of by an Indian mystic. George diplomatically urged Lennon to rewrite "Maharishi" (it became "Sexy Sadie").

ONCE BACK AT HOME, Lennon's routine failed to revive his dashed hopes for an improved family life. Cynthia remembers them returning to the same bed, "but the warmth, and passion we had shared for so long were absent." And the marital discord seeped into the way Lennon treated Julian. Paradoxically, Lennon's confessions to Cynthia about his infidelities led to a "moment of real warmth," Cynthia writes. "We were in the kitchen when he said, out of the blue, 'There have been other women, you know, Cyn.'" She was taken aback, but also touched by this sudden bout of honesty from her distant, distracted husband. "That's okay," she told him. At her most naïve, she seemed at times the perfect match for Lennon's overindulged savvy. "He came over to where I was standing beside the sink and put his arms round me. 'You're the only one I've ever loved, Cyn,' he said, and kissed me. 'I still love you and I always will.'"[25]

But this confession didn't clear his conscience the way he must have hoped, and Lennon's aloofness returned. At one point, Cynthia even suggested he get back in touch with Yoko Ono. "She seems to be more on your wavelength." Lennon suggested that Cynthia go off to Greece for a holiday. Lennon had to finish some songs for the imminent Beatles recording sessions, and band meetings became more and more involved in launching a new company, and that was eating up everybody's home time. Cynthia was reluctant at first, hoping to spend more time with John and to get him to spend more time with Julian. But he persuaded her, and Julian went off to stay with Dot the housekeeper's family nearby. As Cynthia packed to leave, John didn't even get out of bed, waving to his wife "in a trance-like state I'd seen many times before. . . . [He] barely turned his head to say good-bye."[26]

DURING CYNTHIA'S TRIP to Greece, Lennon and McCartney traveled to New York to publicize the Apple company's launch. They gabbed with reporters on a tugboat circling Manhattan, and Lennon got testy at a hotel press conference. On *The Tonight Show,* Lennon seemed unaware that he was sitting next to his old Hollywood free spirit twin, Tallulah Bankhead, then appearing as *Batman*'s Black Widow on television. Lennon and McCartney pronounced their time with the Maharishi as a fling, a mere eccentric phase. Now that they were launching a business, everything would be different.

When he returned to Kenwood, Lennon busied himself with his attic reel-to-reel tape recorders and invited his boyhood friend Pete Shotton for a stay to keep him company. Shotton had invested some of Lennon's money in a supermarket chain and now became involved at the earliest stages with Apple as a manager. In his memoirs, he describes how Lennon lit on a new idea and decided to call together all the company principals the next morning. Shotton was hoping he'd forget overnight, but the next day, Lennon was anxious to ride into London.

His inner circle—all three Beatles, Derek Taylor, Neil Aspinall, and Shotton—were summoned into a secret Apple board meeting. They took their seats keen to hear what Lennon was so excited to tell them. "Right," John began from behind his desk. "I've something very important to tell you all. I am . . . Jesus Christ come back again. This is my thing." Stunned, Paul, George, and Ringo stared back at Lennon, perhaps calculating the effects of chemistry at play in his head. The scene was "utterly surreal," Shotton remembers, unguardedly arrogant and yet somehow delivered with perfect aplomb.

After some awkward silence, the meeting dissolved, and the Beatles made excuses for their partner: he tended to be a bit bonkers sometimes, you know, wouldn't hurt a fly, but working with the man got you used to this type of circus. Not to worry. Lennon and Shotton went out for drinks. John told the waiter he was Christ. "Oh, really?" said the man blandly. "Well, I loved your last record. Thought it was great."[27] That seemed to break the spell.

According to many timelines, this Jesus Christ episode occurred on or around May 18. On May 19, Lennon made a call to London and sent his driver to collect Yoko Ono to come spend the night at Kenwood. Shotton remembers him telephoning "out of sheer boredom." "There's *something* about her," Lennon told him. "I'd just like to get to know her a bit better . . . and now's a good time to do it . . . with the wife away and all." The next morning, Pete arose to find John sitting at the table in his favorite little morning room off the kitchen. Wrapped in the kimono robe he preferred round the house, Lennon was chasing down one of his beloved boiled eggs with gulps of hot tea. "I haven't been to sleep," he told Shotton. "Yeah, I was up all night with Yoko." But as Shotton began to leer mischievously, Lennon cut him off with dead sincerity. "Yeah, Pete, it was great," he said quietly.

Then Lennon asked Shotton to find him a new house to live in. This struck his friend as "no less incredible" than declaring himself Jesus Christ only twenty-four hours before. "I want to go live in it with Yoko," John told him. Just like that? Shotton asked. "Yeah, just like that. JUST LIKE THAT. This is IT, Pete. This is what I've been waiting for all me life. Fuck everything else. Fuck the Beatles, fuck me money, fuck all the rest of it. I'll go and live with her in a fucking TENT if I have to."

John and Pete both jumped to their feet. "This is incredible," said Pete. "It IS incredible," Lennon responded. "Just incredible. It's just like how we used to fall in love when we were kids. Remember when you'd meet a girl and you'd think about her and want to be with her all the time, how your mind was just FILLED with her? Well, Yoko's upstairs now and I can't WAIT to get back to her. I felt so hungry that I had to run down here and get meself an egg—but I can hardly bear to be away from her for a SINGLE MOMENT."[28]

So messianic intimations of greatness may simply have signaled a looming sense of upheaval in search of a trigger. If Lennon couldn't be the Savior, then perhaps he should trust these same restless impulses struggling for control of his life and jump ship. Shotton remembers Lennon as "euphoric" that morning, even as they both spoke about the new difficulties this would bring down on everybody. Cynthia's name was not so much as mentioned, never mind Julian's. Such were the preoccupations of the free-love ethic: beyond the hypocrisies of men wanting frequent noncommittal sex with many partners, the children simply got lumped in with the baggage of an unwanted wife.

But it's also a sign of Lennon's provincialism and something more: he barely knew Yoko, except that she had a reputation as a trippy artist, felt perfectly comfortable telling him no at her exhibition back in 1966, and seemed perfectly comfortable getting scooped up by Lennon's driver and leaving her own husband and child, to stay up all night playing with sound effects.

A couple of days later, Cynthia returned to Kenwood from holiday full of high spirits. She strode toward the morning room to see if Lennon fancied dinner out, only to find the curtains drawn, and an unfamiliar presence in the house. "There was no Dot to greet me, no Julian bounding through the door, shouting with delight, for a hug." When she caught her breath, she realized she was looking at Lennon and Yoko Ono, sitting on the floor, cross-legged, facing each other in robes, next to a table of dirty dishes.

"Oh, hi," Lennon said matter-of-factly.

Cynthia blurted out the only thing she could think of: "We were all looking forward to dinner in London after lunch in Rome and breakfast in Greece. Would you like to come?"

"No, thanks," Lennon replied. Greeting his long-suffering wife with a new lover, wearing her own robe, Lennon had set things up just so he could get caught, treating Cynthia as if she was "an intruder" in her own home.

"In my worst nightmares about Yoko I had not imagined anything like this," Cynthia writes.[29] She turned and raced out of the house.

ONO'S HEADSTRONG CAMPAIGN to win Lennon's affections had finally worked out. Her life up to that point had been a series of just such brash moves. Although born, before World War II, into a prominent family of Japanese bankers, the young Yoko Ono was scarred by much of the same emotional neglect and class anxiety that Lennon suffered in Liverpool. Her artistic personality combined Eastern detachment and Western passion, Buddhist play and Christian self-consciousness. Long before she met Lennon, her high-art ambition had mixed with pop-art candor to make her a significant draw for progressive galleries.

Born on February 18, 1933, in Tokyo, Yoko had a prestigious Japanese

pedigree.[30] Her mother, Isoko, was the granddaughter of Yasuda Zenjiro, one of Japan's most famous "merchant princes." Zenjiro founded
the Yasuda Bank and built one of the largest *zaibatsù,* or corporations,
in early modern Japan. The son of a poor samurai, Zenjiro retired from
business to become an elderly philanthropist, a cultural icon who gifted
Yasuda Hall and Yasuda Kōdō to the University of Tokyo. He held
a sacred place in family lore even before he was assassinated—as if
sounding early a family theme—at the age of eighty-two by a right-
wing ultranationalist, in 1921. His son Zenzaburo, Yoko's grandfather,
had already joined the House of Peers (or aristocrats) when he took
over his father's business. But unlike his hardworking father, Zenzaburo retired early to enjoy his wealth. His daughter Isoko, Yoko's mother,
struck the forward pose of a *moga* (literally, "modern girl"), a 1920s
term that connoted social chic and worldliness. By 1945, the Yasuda
Bank ranked as the fourth-largest *zaibatsù,* after Mitsui, Mitsubishi,
and Sumitomo.

On the paternal side, Yoko's ancestry was no less illustrious. Her
great-grandfather, Saisho Atsushi, was a viscount with the Tokugawa
shogunate, the warriors overthrown by the Meiji Restoration of 1868.
Tsuruko, Yoko's grandmother, had actually studied English and music
at a Protestant college and converted to Christianity. She married Ono
Eijiro, the intellectual son of an impoverished yet respected samurai. To
win over his new in-laws, Eijiro gave up academia to become president of
the Japan Industrial Bank. His son, Yeisuke, who married Isoko, earned
degrees in Economics and Math from Tokyo's Imperial University. Ono
Yeisuke had aspirations to be a concert pianist but followed his father's
path and gave up a promising aesthetic career to conform to the family's
banking interests.

Just before Yoko came along, Yeisuke, as a high-ranking official at
the Yokohama Specie Bank, specializing in foreign exchange, was transferred to San Francisco. With Yoko, Isoko soon followed her husband to
America, where they lived until 1937, when they returned to Japan. At
age four, Yoko entered Keimei Gakuen, a Christian academy founded
by the Mitsui family, for children who had lived abroad. Yoko's family

returned to America, for a banking assignment Yeisuke had been given in New York City, just before war broke out.

Perhaps because of these relocations (transience imprinted itself on Yoko's childhood much as it did on John's), the Ono family sprouted intense personalities, and Yeisuke encouraged his children in music as a way of compensating for his own dashed ambitions. As a result, Yoko Ono's blended lineage created a unique family environment for a war child: she received a half-Buddhist, half-Protestant upbringing in a worldly, aristocratic family that marked her as a modern child of Japan's upper class. Reading, education, and aesthetics were stressed daily in the home, which would always color the little girl's lively independent streak.

As war came, Ono Yeisuke found himself stationed without his family in Hanoi, Vietnam, running Tokyo's wartime bank. At the height of the American air raids on Japan, in March 1945, Isoko returned to Japan with her three children and took shelter in a bunker in Tokyo's Azábu district. Soon after, they fled to the Karuizáwa mountain resort to hide alongside the imperial family. Some of Yoko's memories of being twelve include huddling in that bomb shelter with her mother and being teased by the rural children for "smelling like butter" (*bata kusai*), a racist taunt that marked her outside, "city-girl" status. Here, Yoko remembers learning to flex an iron will. She and her brother Keisuke lay on their backs: "Looking up at the sky through an opening in the roof, we exchanged menus in the air and used our powers of visualization to survive."[31] You can imagine John and Yoko sharing earliest memories of bombs, craters, and lost relatives.

When the family returned to Tokyo after V-J Day, they found the city completely destroyed. Later, they learned that their father had been imprisoned in a French-Indochinese concentration camp in Saigon. Like the rest of the country, they started life over again, while hearing of the horrors of the atomic bomb dropped first on Hiroshima, then Nagasaki. The Americans who had dropped those bombs now occupied their country.

THE GENERATION THAT GREW UP in the shadow of that devastation learned to act as if the war had never existed, as if they could jump-start life after such gaping atrocities and bury its phantoms without a trace. After the war, Yoko attended Gakushuin, or Peers' School, her family maintaining the artistocratic and intellectual profile its members had held for centuries. This secondary institution was exclusive to members and relatives of the imperial family and the Japanese parliament, until the peerage was dissolved under General MacArthur's occupation. When Yoko Ono entered classes there in 1946, her classmates included Emperor Hirohito's eldest son, Akohíto (who would assume his father's title upon the emperor's death in 1989). Another classmate was Yukio Mishima, the almost mythic novelist and nationalist martyr; he committed ritual *seppuku* (suicide) in 1970 to protest "aberrant Westernization."

Unlike her third husband, Yoko excelled at academics. In 1952, she became the first female student accepted into the Philosophy program. The postwar intellectual mode at Gakushuin focused on the economic radicalism of Karl Marx, and existentialists like Kierkegaard and Sartre, as seen through the Zen Buddhist ideal of pure being. In this collegiate postwar setting, "People were acutely conscious of the need to reinvent their own lives," notes historian John W. Dower.[32] Although she dropped out after two semesters, this Gakushuin curriculum influenced Ono's austere style in whatever medium she adopted, to project a sense of "wonderment," or the pure Zen state of "emptiness."

When her father became director of the Bank of Tokyo's U.S. operations, the Ono family moved again, this time to the affluent suburb of Scarsdale, New York, in 1952. Yoko enrolled at Sarah Lawrence College, the renowned liberal-arts college in Bronxville, New York, that often attracted artistic daughters of well-to-do-families. She dropped out again, in 1955, this time to elope with Ichiyanagi Toshi, a Juilliard pianist and composer, to Manhattan. Drawn to highly creative, innovative men at a young age, Ono married Toshi in 1956, and together they pursued the most contemporary ideas in music and art. It was in New York that Yoko connected with the downtown scene, where musicians like jazz pioneer La Monte Young and composer John Cage were questioning the foundations of modernism and the nature of music itself.

The New York avant-garde that attracted a young Yoko Ono was in the throes of a modernist exuberance that reached its high point in the fifties; among its leaders was a musician and pedagogue, Shinichi Suzuki, who gave lectures on Zen philosophy at Columbia University, and became an intellectual lightning rod. Pieces like John Cage's *4'33"* (of silence) were directly inspired by Suzuki's instruction in the Dao and Zen principles. Like the Beat writers Ginsberg and Kerouac, these contemporary composers were inspired by Suzuki's emphasis on everyday existence as ultimate enlightenment, and the Zen ideal of unself-conscious experience trumping the mind's propensity to overcomplicate the simplest sensations. In his generationally influential book *Silence,* John Cage aimed to reorient the classical audience to the here and now, particularly the mundane "noise" of a typical concert hall: the sounds of bodies shifting in their chairs, ventilators humming, the creak of furniture, and the awkwardness of enforced "silence." This quietude, of course, was never really pure silence at all, but simply a heightened awareness of any hall's random underlying sounds. Yoko Ono took this idea further, declaring: "The only sound that exists . . . is the sound of the mind."[33]

Cage adopted these Eastern concepts into his own work. "Theirs was a cry to give art back to a social, rather than merely aesthetic, realm of meaning," says art historian Alexandra Munroe of the new avant-garde. "Just as earlier manifestations of Dada and anti-art arose in Zurich [in the 1920s] in response to the cultural and moral blight wrought by World War I, when all that modernist progress had promised went severely wrong, so too the postwar avant-garde, emerging from the horrors of World War II renounced the abstractions of high art for the poetry of quotidian existence."[34] This concept of art roughly mirrored the dual pretensions of rock 'n' roll, which employed crude sounds to express big ideas, and many of these New York figures admired the emerging pop art work of Europeans like Peter Blake, Eduardo Paolozzi, and Richard Hamilton. Soon, a young advertising designer from Pittsburgh with a reverse charisma, Andy Warhol, would emerge from this ferment to become the art world's negative Elvis.

Yoko Ono's background in both Zen Buddhism and grade-school Christianity, as well as her international upbringing, provided her with a hybridized sensibility and gave her direct access to the ideas fueling these new crosscurrents. Above all, she noted, "the essence of Zen that connected with Cage and all of us was a sense of laughter. Laughter is God's language."³⁵ Perhaps she saw the innate Orientalism in Warhol's face, and in his work.

So many fans assume that Ono had little previous work of her own and merely grafted herself onto Lennon's empty celebrity. The truth suggests something quite different. In fact, in 1960, after being befriended by Cage and his circle, Ono rented a cold-water loft at 112 Chambers Street and staged a series of concerts that became legendary in the avant-garde world. This "Chambers Street series" featured a cross-section of artists, from poets and dancers to composers and musicians. As later cataloged by the downtown Reuben and Judson galleries, Ono provided a new frame of reference for these experiments across mediums, and the series became a touchstone for the rest of 1960s art. All of which seemed, in fact, like a preamble to what she would later do with Lennon.

Art luminaries like Peggy Guggenheim and Marcel Duchamp attended some events, which became the talk of the underground. George Maciunas invited Ono into his Fluxus collective, a new society of modern artists who rejected abstract expressionism and embraced "conceptual art," a term coined by Henry Flynt. The Fluxus spin on modernism focused on "happenings"—events where audience participation with the art and artist was inseparable from the art itself. As in the exploding rock music scene, the very point of seeing a Fluxus piece was in creating, or completing, the art with the artist. The democratic ideal literally invited the audience to step onstage, which brought new dynamics to how the art functioned. Participants got a very different charge from the one mere observers got. Instead of being formalized in a fancy frame, Fluxus ideas thrived in nontraditional settings—anywhere but a musty museum.

Comfortable in many disparate worlds, Ono returned to Tokyo in the spring of 1962 for her exhibition at the Sogetsu Art Center, where she won critical accolades as a leading Japanese artist. But like most foreign occupations, the Americanization of Japan led to a resentful aftertaste, as "gratitude" for the occupation faded. With the Cold War metastasizing in Southeast Asia, a growing anti-Americanism prevailed, among both religious conservatives and cultural progressives. John Lennon and the Beatles felt the brunt of this traditionalism when protestors demonstrated against their appearance at the Nippon Budokan Temple in 1966, originally built for Tokyo's judo Olympics competition of 1964. Because judo and martial arts have a spiritual dimension in Japanese culture, many thought the site too "sacred" for popular concerts. A similar political purism, of course, had led to the assassination of Yoko Ono's great-grandfather back in 1921.

Despite her role in the New York art scene of the early sixties, Ono remained wary of American influences. In October 1962, her husband, Ichiyanagi, invited John Cage and David Tudor to Tokyo to perform at the Sogetsu Art Center. But even at this early stage, Ono felt as though there was too much hero worship of these American figures. In addition, she felt patronized, as if being her husband's wife overshadowed her own art. Add to this Cage's nickname, "Jesus Christ," which Ono perceived as evidence of a degenerative bourgeois streak in avant-garde culture. Her dual persona, as successful artist versus wifely appendage of a pianist, further strained the marriage and led her into a debilitating depression. A failed suicide attempt prompted her family to institutionalize her for several months. While she was in the hospital, a young American jazz musician and filmmaker, Anthony Cox, tracked her down out of admiration for her work. They were soon involved, his admiration hastening her recovery and release from the mental ward. In June 1963, they married and Yoko gave birth to her first child, Kyoko Chan Cox, that August.

Fully recovered, Yoko Ono returned to Manhattan with her new husband in the fall of 1964, and the Fluxus group embraced her as a person with her own agenda. She appeared at Carnegie Hall, and her work was shown at the Judson Gallery and at the East End Theater in 1965. The following year, Ono and Cox traveled to London with Kyoko to attend the Destruction in Art Symposium (DIAS), which gathered artists from around the world to investigate many of the same radical ideas the Fluxus group espoused. Her influence in avant-garde circles was already pronounced. By this point, Ono had developed her *Cut*

Piece—part art, part theater—which combined violence with anti-art and won her a provocative reputation for acting out feminist themes before there was such a term.

The Indica bookstore looked to Ono to kick off its gallery opening (simply an extension of the bookstore) with some major artistic noise. Outrage and controversy would sell tickets, and this far-out Japanese artist, who came with John Cage plaudits, sold tickets. The show that John Lennon saw in November 1966 constituted the largest collection of Yoko Ono's work to date. Aside from the hammer-and-nail and climb-the-ladder pieces prominent in most descriptions of this show, it also included Ono's shrewdly comic *White Chess Set,* where all of the pieces were white. Players would begin moving pieces to play an oversize match but quickly get mixed up as to whose pieces were whose, to the point where any game of capturing the queen and entrapping the king became increasingly pointless.

Intellectually, Cynthia proved no match for someone of this background. As she remembers in both memoirs, she returned home within a couple of days after the initial "confrontation" to find her husband acting as though nothing had happened, a front he insisted on throughout that week. The couple had a long talk, during which John explained Yoko's presence as just another fling. They even made love afterward, and Cynthia began to feel better, although she sensed John was "dabbling" in drugs again. It was her last chance: if she had kicked him out, or laid down a new gauntlet about his behavior, Cynthia might have found some self-respect—and earned some respect from Lennon. But the grooves of cheating and denial were too deeply engrained in him by this point.

In fact, the old pattern reasserted itself so quickly it became a fait accompli: Cynthia would always be Lennon's doormat, and he couldn't stand himself for having such a wife. Yoko's zealous pursuit seemed almost Greek in its intensity and focus. The contrast between these two women prompted less a decision than a tumble into a new world: Yoko had a professional identity all her own, yet seemed willing to engage in a creative partnership; Cynthia had always been, and would always be, identified *through* Lennon. And Lennon must have hated himself as much for how he treated his wife as for her unyielding compliance.

TIM RILEY | 395

That he fell back into drugs at this point jibes with the overarching pattern. Cynthia's mother had discovered a stash of LSD while they were away in India and flushed it down the toilet. This infuriated Lennon, but "he couldn't confront her without admitting that he used it, so he had to keep quiet." Cynthia's timeline seems confused, however, as she remembers John's affection running up to his trip to New York. She actually wanted to go with him, but he waved her off, calling it a business trip with little time for relaxing. She sensed him freezing her out again.

In the tradition of running off for a holiday instead of working everything through, Cynthia installed her mother in Ringo Starr's flat in Montagu Street and went off, this time to Italy. She came back one night to find Magic Alex "hovering outside the hotel," and it began to dawn on her that Alex had always been doing errands for Lennon, even by chaperoning her in Greece. "We went inside and found Mum sitting in the lobby, looking distressed," Cynthia writes. "I asked Alex what was going on. He said, 'I've come with a message from John. He is going to divorce you, take Julian away from you and send you back to Hoylake,'" her hometown outside Liverpool.[36]

Shell-shocked, Cynthia suddenly fell ill. Her mother flew back to England as their Italian hosts pampered Cynthia with hot drinks and cold flannels. In an Italian newspaper, she saw photos of John and Yoko attending the opening night of *In His Own Write,* which dates this Italian trip to mid-June.[37] When she recovered, she went straight to Montagu Street, where her mother was staying. There she found flowers her husband had sent to mock her mum. "Beat you to it, Lil," John's card read, meaning he had beat her to the apartment. "Hours after I arrived an envelope was delivered by hand," Cynthia says. "The letter inside it informed me that John was suing me for divorce on the grounds of my adultery with Robert Bassanini. Presumably Alex had told John I had been out with him [in Italy]."[38]

There are plenty of ways in which Cynthia and John were incompatible, many of which their own friends in art school spoke of quite openly when they first started going out. But for Lennon to accuse Cynthia of adultery at this point reeks of emotional abuse larded on top of years of physical and psychological selfishness. Through Peter Brown at the Apple offices, Cynthia tried to reach John for weeks after she returned, but he refused to take her calls. Then Brown gave Cynthia the message that with Lennon engrossed in recording sessions, they should swap living quarters: John and Yoko moved back into the London flat, and Cynthia, Julian, and his grandmother returned to Kenwood. It was no small irony that Lennon—without even speaking to his wife—sought to sail through a season of international turmoil by escaping into a new relationship, a future symbol of rock romance, that in personal terms cost him at least as much self-respect as he had already spent. For his dual duties as loyal emissary, Lennon began to imitate Elvis, presenting Magic Alex with a brand-new white Mercedes.[39]

Cynthia's role in John Lennon's life tends to get short shrift. She was upstaged and outflanked in so many ways that our media-filtered understanding of her is necessarily warped, even after she wrote two books. Removing her successor from the equation, she comes across much differently. Cynthia anchored Lennon with consistent affection and understanding, bore him a son, and stayed committed through all of Beatlemania's many personal indignities. To toss her aside with such contempt only meant that his Beatle fame, which Lennon had unveiled as transparently hollow on *Sgt. Pepper,* had a corrupting effect on the way he treated those closest to him. In this rarefied and pampered sphere, his focus narrowed to one of exclusive self-interest, to the point where even fatherhood, where one might have expected some sensitivity, crumbled. Had Cynthia done anything remotely like this to him, Lennon could have added such cruelty to his roster of victimhood. As it was, the emotional inertia of his own hurt and misguided urges was all that he seemed to care about.

How?

From May 1968, when they first began living together, until September 1973, when they publicly split up for eighteen months, John and Yoko were inseparable. Lennon positioned them as two intense artists who needed each other so badly that all other concerns became secondary, and they projected a hyped-up mixture of mutual obsession, creative reciprocity, and narcissistic oblivion. His public face read romantic delirium, but the overlapping political agendas Lennon pursued as the Beatles worked on *Let It Be* and *Abbey Road* were unguardedly selfish, and Ono became a clever, not to say cynical, decoy to his withdrawal from the band. History ladles irony on this moment: the band that had once literally slept on top of one another in Neil Aspinall's van now sought to pool all their collective business interests just as their two most productive songwriters formed new families. For added curiosity, both new Beatle wives had non-British upbringings.

After leaving her first husband in Tucson, Arizona, Linda Eastman returned to the East Coast with her daughter, Heather, and became a rock photographer with a colorful reputation in the scene's elite boys' club. Like Ono, she came from a well-to-do background that bespoke education and worldliness. Her mother, Louise Sara Lindner Eastman, was heir to the Lindner Department Store fortune; her father, born Lee Epstein, practiced entertainment law at his own firm in Manhattan while collecting modern art. They raised four children in Scarsdale, New York, and, like many other Russian Jewish emigrant offspring, had gradually assimilated into mainstream New York life.

McCartney's on-again, off-again engagement to Jane Asher, which had greased tabloid sales for months, finally crashed when Asher returned early from a theatrical job to find McCartney cavorting with another American, Francie Schwartz ("Frannie"), that summer of 1968. (While staying at McCartney's during that same period, John and Yoko watched TV in the evenings with her. One day they returned to find a card on the mantelpiece in Paul's familiar handwriting, which read: "You and your Jap tart think you're hot shit." When Lennon confronted McCartney, his partner laughed it off, saying he'd done it "on a lark." Within a few days, John and Yoko moved on.)[1] McCartney had already met Eastman at the Bag O' Nails club in 1967 when she was on assignment photographing "Swinging London," and again at a Procol Harum concert at the Speakeasy.

When he spoke with Linda next, at Epstein's *Sgt. Pepper* party in May 1967, Linda took some famous photographs of the band in full psychedelic regalia, standing at Epstein's fireplace. McCartney began pursuing her seriously during the summer of 1968, soon after Lennon became obsessed with Ono—both Beatles were drawn to women whose intellectual pursuits in the past differentiated them from an endless bevy of groupies. These romances have enough of a tit-for-tat quality to suggest how much Lennon and McCartney's intimate pursuits were entangled with their musical one-upmanship.

Lennon and McCartney expressed these tensions throughout the band's final eighteen months together with varying degrees of sincerity and prevarication. The received line on this period is how everything worked to pull Lennon and McCartney—and the Beatles—apart. But the music conveys a different story: despite their differing personalities and writing sensibilities, the band became their rallying point, and every ensemble impulse held them together even as they composed from separate orbits. Nightfall and bemused introspection mark Lennon's "Good Night," "Cry Baby Cry," and McCartney's "Blackbird," as well as twilight duets like "Don't Let Me Down," "I've Got a Feeling," and "Because," where romantic themes double as songs about male bonding and reluctant farewells. In these songs, the Beatles pushed rock into a new maturity, where teenage-identity themes became larger metaphors for fraught intimacy ("Two of Us," "Don't Let Me Down," "You Never Give Me Your Money," "Carry That Weight"). If their financial disputes created havoc, the music always pulled them back together even when they were at loggerheads. Divergent interests only quickened their ensemble. Creating alliances amid all the tension turned into an imposing late theme, as they proved themselves their own biggest fans: nobody had more trouble putting this career to bed than the Beatles themselves.

LENNON LOST HIMSELF in a flurry of new projects with Ono. For their first several weeks together, John and Yoko mooched beds off London friends, first at McCartney's house in St. John's Wood, then at Apple A&R man Peter Asher's place, then Neil Aspinall's before settling into Ringo's empty Montagu Street apartment in late July, where they stayed through the end of 1968. Their intense rapport manifested itself immediately; a new creative chemistry infused a series of side projects as Lennon recorded his Beatle material. Before they even moved out of Kenwood, Lennon and Ono shot an experimental movie, *Film No. 5 (Smile)*, a long, sustained take of Lennon smiling on his back porch, as if one of those indelible facial frames from *A Hard Day's Night* got elongated into a Warhol feature. They also made the film *Two Virgins,* which debuted at the Chicago Film Festival later that fall. And paralleling the Beatles sessions throughout the summer of 1968, Lennon mounted his first art show and visited rehearsals for Victor Spinetti's staging of *In His Own Write*, a one-act production of the National Theatre at the Old Vic (produced by Sir Laurence Olivier). He may not have dealt with his drug habit, but he certainly rousted himself from boredom.

A casual afternoon song-demo session at George Harrison's Esher home has been widely bootlegged as "the Esher Demos," the most complete record of the band's familiar preproduction routine: like a script's first table read, or a newsroom's first editorial meeting of the day, song run-throughs preceded discussion of a general outline for an album as material got sketched out for the first time. As with the Hamburg Star-Club tapes from New Year's Eve, 1962, this tape reveals how thoroughly conceived and arranged most of this *White Album* material already was even at this early "demonstration" phase. Each songwriter prepared his own demo tape to sing along to, to suggest vocal harmonies, rhythmic figures, and guitar breaks. There were at least two tape recorders in the room, since whoever taped this session (most likely Aspinall) caught Lennon, McCartney, and Harrison singing along with themselves, with Ringo chiming in on congas for a sound unlike any other. This uncanny setup displays the band's elaborate shorthand, where even early drafts graduate from lyrics and melodies to band music as it would ultimately be produced for tape. Far from sketchy, early drafts of most Beatles songs arrive fully conceived, with imaginative spaces mapped out for the others. Production blueprints were inseparable from song arrangements. Even unfinished songs like "Happiness Is a Warm Gun" or "Sexy Sadie" give off an underlying ensemble energy, grooves so suggestive you can almost feel the others eager to add their as-yet-invisible parts. The distance between the Esher Demos and *The White Album* is largely technical; the raw material is all there.

Perhaps, in Lennon's mind, his harried schedule provided an excuse to avoid his wife and son. Apple aide Peter Brown turned into Lennon's royal go-between, fending off Cynthia's frequent phone calls. Finally, after many, many queries, Brown confirmed a time for Lennon to discuss matters in person with his wife at Kenwood. When Cynthia opened the front door, she found Yoko standing beside him, both of them dressed in black.

"I barely recognized John," Cynthia noted, and she worried about his drug use; although the remote air of her husband's new companion must have slighted her. "It had been only a few weeks since we'd last met, but he was thinner, almost gaunt. His face was deadly serious. There was no hint of a smile, even when Julian ran up to him. He was, quite simply, not the John I knew. It was as if he'd taken on a different persona. . . . What power did she have over him? The thought of her looking after my son was ghastly."[2]

The couple sat awkwardly in Lennon's former living room as Julian hovered about them, staring wide-eyed at his father's new partner. Such a scene is unsettling for any child, but it must have been particularly traumatic for Julian, who saw his father so rarely in the first place. "What did you want to see me for?" Lennon began impatiently. In the past, he had avoided confrontation with women at all costs, and he had gone to great lengths to avoid this one. But when finally forced to meet with his wife and child, he came out blasting, no matter how hypocritically. Cynthia sent Julian to her mother in the kitchen, tracing the very same steps Lennon had taken at the same age of five when Julia confronted Alfred in Blackpool. Here, the roles reversed: instead of the mother unwittingly rescuing the boy from abduction to New Zealand, Lennon came to threaten Cynthia and virtually ignored Julian.

Once the boy had left the room, Lennon threw a curveball, with Ono sitting calmly at his side. He accused Cynthia of cheating on *him*, with "that yankee cowboy," he hissed, the actor Tom Simcox, her Rishikesh friend whose note Mardas had purloined. This betrays a deeply cynical streak: as a tactical matter, Lennon may have reasoned the angle worth a try even if false, since he could afford more expensive lawyers and massage his story later through Apple's publicity machine. After all, he was a championship talker, and commanded fairly reverential treatment from the press when he so desired. Putting Cynthia on the defensive constituted his best strategy for that, given that he would soon be negotiating a settlement. This maneuver backfired.

The other cynical motive behind Lennon's accusation played to the issue of public identity: no matter how this situation unraveled, Cynthia and Julian stood to be big losers. Cynthia's status greatly depended on her being Mrs. Lennon. As the mother of his only child, this got tied up with the only reason she would have tolerated all his infidelities for so long, or roped her mother into the many indignities of his celebrity lifestyle. To sit still for his accusations in her own home created a new low for Cynthia to contemplate from the marriage that she had hoped to salvage just weeks before. If anything could have upstaged her arriving home from Greece to find Yoko Ono padding around in her robe, this would be it. His attack, both humiliating and unexpected, shocked

Cynthia to her chair. It's easy to imagine a weaker character cracking up on the spot. John and Ono left quickly after that first encounter, without John so much as hugging Julian. After a few days, Cynthia collected herself and countersued, giving London divorce lawyers a taste of Beatle litigation yet to come.

With John finessing his silent treatment, the other Beatles retreated where they would have otherwise been in touch with Cynthia on at least a weekly basis—Ringo, after all, was still a neighbor. But Paul, reflecting a deep sense of personal honor, was the only one to pay Cynthia and Julian a visit. After his fallout with Jane, he found himself single, and full of regrets. He knew Cynthia well enough to pay his personal respects. He brought small comfort, and a big song:

> The only person who came to see me was Paul. He arrived one sunny afternoon, bearing a red rose, and said, "I'm so sorry, Cyn, I don't know what's come over him. This isn't right." On the way down to see us he had written a song for Julian. It began as "Hey Jules" and later became "Hey Jude," which sounded better. . . . Paul stayed for a while. He told me that John was bringing Yoko to recording sessions, which he, George and Ringo hated.[3]

Beyond the echoes of Alfred and Julia, this romantic impasse parallels the crossroads Lennon and McCartney encountered five years earlier, when Lennon married Cynthia with the quaintest of old-fashioned motives: to put a respectable face on his indiscretions.[4] In McCartney's mind, Lennon's first marriage appeared rash and unwise. Still, everybody liked Cynthia: knowing Lennon's unpredictability, everybody benefited from her reliable emotional anchor and unswerving devotion. Suddenly, for Lennon, these qualities counted for far less than creative stimulation.

Visiting her in the midst of John's new fling, which would hopefully blow over any week now, Paul sang Cynthia an early draft of a new song, inspired by the child Lennon couldn't bear to confront ("Hey Jules, don't make it bad/Take a sad song and make it better"). After all, McCartney had known the boy's namesake, Lennon's mother (Julia,

Julian, Jude), and the melody swelled with redemption to all who heard it. The romantic fallout at the heart of the band—between two song-writers who had no zipper control—became the subject of the song that revived the Beatles' bond with their audience, beating out even "I Want to Hold Your Hand," "She Loves You," and "Yesterday" to become their best-selling single. In the days they spent working out the song before recording, Lennon heard his own situation in early McCartney drafts ("You have found her, now go and get her") and pronounced it finished by barely touching it. Depending on your vantage point, keeping his fingerprints off McCartney's lyric was either the most selfish, or the most generous, response Lennon could have had.

WITH SO MUCH FRESH MATERIAL, *White Album* sessions began in promise before splaying every which way as personality conflicts flared. The week after the songs were demo'd at the Esher meeting, the band gath-ered at EMI to give "Revolution" eighteen takes, adding overdubs to cre-ate Lennon's lead vocal takes (sung lying on his back) through takes 19 to 20. But the track ran to over ten minutes, trailing off into a fascinating distention of sound effects, pillow talk, and garbled radio. Lennon sim-ply cut the final four minutes and began piecing together an entirely new track, which became "Revolution 9."

Yoko kept a revealing audio journal of this early "Revolution" ses-sion, which still circulates among bootleggers for rare insight into her state of mind. "You mustn't do anything without me!" she tells John. She praises Paul for communicating with her as an equal and even professes that she has grown to like him as "a younger brother." When John goes up to the control booth, however, Yoko claims to be "the most insecure person in the world right now," clearly terrified that John will abandon her and return to his family at any moment.[5]

By now, Yoko had graduated from "flavor of the month"—her early Apple nickname—to an appendage, and Lennon's grace period with the press quietly lapsed. The couple made their first public appearance together at the National Sculpture Exhibition in Coventry, where they planted acorns for peace at Coventry Cathedral on June 15. After that, reporters pounced. On June 18, Lennon brought Yoko Ono to the opening night of *In His Own Write* at the Old Vic.

The confidence he displayed in his music rang smug as he paraded his new lover on his arm in public. Lennon had no patience for how long it took the rest of the world to catch up with his personal life; he simply behaved as though people should get accustomed to his new flame and pay attention to his work. Throughout the spring, he had brainstormed with Victor Spinetti to shape his verse for the stage, and Spinetti remembers this collaboration more than the media commotion. The two rarely discussed the personal upheaval Lennon was traveling through. "Backstage after the first night, he came up to me beaming, and said, 'Victor you *cunt*! [a Scouser endearment]. You reminded me of all the things that got me started in this stuff before rock 'n' roll came along.'"[6] The press, however, blared the bigger story. Reporters yelled, "Where's your wife, John?" as John and Yoko ran into the theater. The next morning, infidelity headlines upstaged his leap to theater. Still in shock, Cynthia and Julian watched the paparazzi hound him from where they had fled in Italy.

RUMORS HIT THE STREET that the Beatles were recording again, and Apple projects quickly competed with one another for attention and studio time. McCartney produced and promoted Mary Hopkin, Apple signed a new group called Grapefruit, and life around the 95 Wigmore Street offices took on a surreal air of playing at the music business. The Beatles came and went, dashing off ideas and plunking themselves down into studios for consults. While creative in intent, most Apple endeavors now swirled with chaos.[7]

Peter Asher, Jane's older brother, had come aboard as an A&R man and soon brought in a young singer-songwriter named James Taylor. When Starr and Harrison flew to California, where Harrison was to appear in a Ravi Shankar documentary, McCartney hung back to tape "Blackbird," and Lennon and Ono collected EMI sound effects for "Revolution 9." When Harrison and Starr returned, McCartney took off to promote Mary Hopkin in Los Angeles and Harrison helped Lennon with "Revolution 9." Harrison skipped the brass session for "Revolution 1," though, to produce and play his underrated "Sour Milk Sea" for Jackie Lomax, his own Apple signing.

In Lennon's mind, no theatrical premiere impeded work on his tracks. Sessions forged ahead with Martin's new twenty-year-old assistant, Chris Thomas, as Lennon led his band through an obstacle course called "Everybody's Got Something to Hide Except Me and My Monkey." With its trapdoor transitions and pointed counterrhythms, the number tested every facet of the Beatles' ensemble, and they spent a whole session leaping its hurdles in rehearsal before devoting another full recording day to seven takes. The final six-count guitar break held back a flood of energy before opening the spigot into the fade-out, cowbells flailing. Other tracks ambled off into multiple takes that never found traction. The sheer number of songs they pounded out created an exhausting schedule; and unlike previous years, when the sessions had rewarded concentration with ingenuity, these sessions began to drag. Band members routinely avoided one another's songs, and engineers dodged Lennon numbers instead of jockeying for the chance to work with him.

Some weeks the schedule scans as though Lennon simply hadn't the time to notice, or care, what others thought, never mind sleep. On July 1, John and Yoko launched a joint gallery exhibition, titled You Are Here, at the Robert Fraser Gallery near the British Museum. From there, they released 365 white helium balloons with messages encouraging people to send return notes on where the balloons were found. The next day they jumped right back into work on Lennon's "Good Night," which he had tracked alone on guitar for Martin to score for strings, and then "Ob-La-Di, Ob-La-Da," the first sketch of which included only Ringo and Paul in seven takes. Saxes were overdubbed onto that sketch before the whole thing was wiped and restarted, with twelve takes at Lennon's new tempo on July 8.

Fed up with McCartney's endless fussing over this ditty, Lennon, lead engineer Geoff Emerick remembers, cracked after endless takes chasing McCartney's precise instructions. "I am fucking stoned!" Lennon declared, "and this is how the fucking song should go!"[8] With that, he hammered out a quicker intro on the piano that gave the sing-songy tune some sardonic bite. That evening, the band minus Lennon and Ono attended the press screening for *Yellow Submarine*. They returned the next day to remake "Revolution" at a quicker tempo, after vetoing Lennon's desire to make their first attempt the next Beatles single. It's too slow, came the band's response. Lennon's new arrangement roared off a blast of overloaded lead guitar that quotes Pee Wee Gayton's "Do Unto Others," a 1954 Imperial side.

Two weeks after the gallery exhibition, on July 15, as the Beatles started work on "Cry Baby Cry," Apple moved from Wigmore Street to 3 Savile Row, the address seen in the movie *Let It Be*. The next day, after ten more takes on "Cry Baby Cry," in which the Beatles barely seemed to cooperate with one another, never mind the technicians, Geoff Emerick walked out, calling the atmosphere "poisonous": "If anybody of the band members had done anything that an overly defensive John viewed as a potential slight to his new girlfriend—who sat by his side impassively the entire time they were making the album—he would be lashing out at them all with his acid tongue."[9]

Lennon was so happy with the "Revolution" remake, he pitched that as their next single. The song Cynthia heard when McCartney came to console her, however, quickly bumped Lennon's headline. (While Lennon and McCartney worked on this new number, Harrison went into Studio 2 and laid down an acoustic take of "While My Guitar Gently Weeps.") The finished song, "Hey Jude," became famous as a collaboration story: McCartney introduced Lennon to the melody with a "dummy" (or placeholder) lyric, hoping Lennon could punch it up. Lennon, disappointed about redoing "Revolution," was nonplussed at what his partner had come up with. According to myth, Lennon signed off on McCartney's "dummy" lyrics at first pass.

"We're both going through the same bit," Lennon announced, after taking the line "You have found her, now go and get her" literally.[10] However, we now know they spent at least one entire day on "Hey Jude" alone together at McCartney's house before a week's worth of sessions at two different studios, so they probably worked this lyric harder than they let on. Like "Yesterday," or "In My Life," each of which went through many drafts, "Hey Jude" sounds too cleanly born to be free of effort. It's the highest kind of art: that which conceals its craft.

The track's effortless feel belies its bumpy recording. They rehearsed "Hey Jude" assiduously before tracking six takes of it at the first EMI session and adding another twenty-three takes the next day. But slower grooves can be demanding in curious ways, and capturing this one proved elusive. A documentary film crew attended one of these sessions, filming McCartney at the piano, Ringo on drums, and Lennon playing acoustic guitar, with Harrison up in the booth alongside Martin and engineer Ken Scott. This session ended with a terrible row about Harrison's lead guitar line, which McCartney vetoed. They weren't in a rush, but EMI was inexplicably booked, and they still wanted to improve the basic track.

To keep the musical momentum rolling, they booked more sessions, plus an orchestra, at a new Soho shop across town called Trident, which boasted London's first operational eight-track recorder. Tony Bramwell remembers EMI treating new technology "like the Enigma decoding machine that they cracked at Bletchley and drove off in an olive-green camouflaged truck with an armed guard to be returned—sometimes months later—like a new rocket installation, under conditions of great secrecy."[11] This put the Beatles in the awkward position of "inventing" eight-track recording procedure—by linking two four-track machines for eight-track simulation on *Sgt. Pepper*—but unable to use it for their follow-up. The fourteen-hour Trident session remade the basic rhythmic track and received new bass, lead and backing vocals, and Martin's orchestration the second day. More overdubs and mixing took place on a third.

Sure enough, this Trident eight-track tape they brought back to EMI sounded funky. The EMI playback equipment gave Ken Scott fits. Scott had actually snuck into Trident to help with the session (even though the EMI headmasters considered such "sneaking around" scandalous) and remembers being satisfied with what he had heard.[12] But when he played back the master tape at Abbey Road the next day, he couldn't explain the murky sound to George Martin. "Just at that moment, John Lennon walked in," Emerick writes. "George Martin, in his inimitable manner, turned to John and said bluntly, 'Ken thinks the mix sounds like shit' "[13] Luckily, Emerick happened to be picking up some personal effects, and Martin grabbed him to help fix the Trident sound. When Emerick reappeared to help Scott, Lennon cried, "Ah, the prodigal son returns!"

"Paul hit a clunker on the piano and said a naughty word," Lennon gleefully crowed, "but I insisted we leave it in, buried just low enough so that it can barely be heard. Most people won't ever spot it . . . but WE'LL know it's there."[14] The group voted to put "Hey Jude" out as the next single, with the new, rockier version of "Revolution" as its B side. The "Penny Lane" single pattern reasserted itself: Lennon had fussed over "Revolution" just as he had over "Strawberry Fields Forever" the previous year, but the McCartney track got far more airplay. In the battle for hits, McCartney's star presence began to upstage Lennon's.

As if this weren't plenty to keep track of, the band pulled the plug on their Baker Street retail-clothing store, which had devolved from its previous year's headlines, and sponsored an open raid on the final stock, which turned into a near riot. Despite their first business division collapse amid the constant onslaught of tabloid coverage, the Beatles' ability to focus on music reveals how far their ensemble groove carried them from one crisis to the next—where the business, relationships, and outside activities caused friction, the music held them together.

With "Hey Jude" reviving that ensemble, and the Apple label's first single appearing to dizzying triumph, the band went straight back to work on two more numbers that didn't even make the final cut. Once Emerick had helped equalize the Trident sound, Harrison led the band through "Not Guilty" over two nights, staying until 5:45 A.M. on August 8 to go through over one hundred takes. On August 14, Lennon laid down a zany track called "What's the New Mary Jane," which had the frazzled, ditzy air of a pothead rounding some cosmic bend, credited to Lennon-McCartney even though Lennon more likely wrote it with Alex Mardas.

Also in August, they finished "Yer Blues" and added horns to McCartney's solo "Mother Nature's Son," before Harrison brought in Eric Clapton for "While My Guitar Gently Weeps," which Harrison suggested to him out of the blue as they pulled up to the studio. "I was quite taken aback by this and considered it a funny thing to ask, since he was the Beatles' guitar player," Clapton writes. "I was also quite flattered, thinking that not many people get asked to play on a Beatles record. I hadn't even brought my guitar with me, so I had to borrow his." It would not be the last time Harrison would revive sessions by inviting a surprise guest.

Clapton's read of this session portrays Lennon and McCartney as critical of both Harrison and Starr, wisely interpreting Harrison's invitation as more about group politics than virtuosity. (One of Harrison's finer musical traits was to steer clear of the whole "guitar hero" playbook.) "George would put songs forward on every project only to find them pushed into the background," Clapton remembered. "I think that he felt our friendship would give him some support, and that having me there to play might stabilize his position and maybe even earn him some respect. . . . We did just one take, and I thought it sounded fantastic." John and Paul, however, were "noncommittal." But their behavior slowly relaxed. Together, the band listened to the track over and over in the control room. After adding some effects and assembling a rough mix, the group then played some of the other songs they were sitting on—an event rare enough that Clapton felt as though he'd "been brought into their inner sanctum."[15] Here was a band confident enough in its work to turn a guest spot into a small listening party with an acknowledged rival, and they knew word would spread about what Clapton heard.

Clapton's perceptions reflect Lennon and McCartney's attitude toward both Harrison and Starr, and anticipate the next wallop. One day, Emerick recalls, John and Ringo happened upon McCartney's brass overdub to "Mother Nature's Son" and "shattered" the good vibe; but after they left, the bassist laid down two more songs: "Etcetera," which has never appeared, and "Wild Honey Pie," a wacky throwaway (as if responding to Lennon's "Mary Jane"; there was more than one pothead in this band). Finally, at the end of a long, grinding summer when song takes stretched out indefinitely and wait times lasted even longer, Ringo Starr simply walked out.

It's hard to emphasize how dramatic a move this must have been, coming from its most insecure member, the last to join, and its most

politically adept. To drum on Lennon and McCartney songs his whole
career would have been more than enough to keep any player with less
self-respect groveling until the act hit Vegas. But Ringo had always been
the perfect fit for the band precisely because of his humility, which many
still mistake for dumb luck. With two of the biggest egos in the business
running sessions, and a third figuring out how to gain a foothold with
his original material, Ringo's sturdy presence on the stool in back anchored the band's dual monarchy as nothing else could. So far, disputes
had tended to be between Lennon and everybody *except* Ringo; these
sessions are a first, where McCartney's veto of Harrison's "Hey Jude"
lines signaled greater political tension.

Ringo's abrupt walkout measures the band's deteriorating purpose.
Far more than in any previous sessions, group interactions had turned
into political quicksand; his peers treated him like a hired hand and
made him play a waiting game on a daily basis. You might think Harrison would have joined Ringo's protest for moral support, but the other
three simply forged ahead: McCartney's "Back in the USSR" spilled out
with its author on drums, Harrison on guitar, and Lennon on bass (for
the first time). That same day in August, Cynthia served Lennon with
divorce papers. McCartney laid down two more drum tracks the next
day, and then put down his own bass track and lead vocal, and Lennon
and Harrison sang along with handclaps. They all felt quite sure Ringo
would return in a day or two, and they kept the whole incident quiet
from the press (which shows just how much control they exercised around
their image).

Then they tackled Lennon's "Dear Prudence" all over again at Trident studios, with McCartney impersonating Ringo on drums (he may
imitate Ringo even better than he imitates Little Richard). The next day
brought overdubs and lead vocals. They mixed "Prudence" at the end
of August as the "Hey Jude" / "Revolution" single hit stores, their first
record with the new, frankly enigmatic green Apple label, designed by
Gene Mahon.

Through gallery owner Robert Fraser and Barry Miles, McCartney
had begun collecting paintings by the surrealist René Magritte, one of
which was an oversize apple sitting inside a typical morning room (*The*

Listening Room, 1958). As the new logo for their company, it sat inside the 45-rpm grooves as a photographic still life, with a hole in the middle suggesting a donut, as if the subtext read, "This is not an apple." Along with their string of witty album covers and packages, it was another design coup.

AFTER A BAND MEETING where egos were massaged, Ringo returned to EMI on September 3, and the group prepared for a David Frost (*Frost on Sunday*) TV appearance. McCartney smothered his drums with flowers. Ringo's walkout got resolved just before George Martin left for a long-planned vacation in September.

Martin's departure became an index of the indecision and miscommunication among principals—he was clearly as much a part of the band's dysfunction as their own superstar preoccupations. Martin, who had sat by for all manner of madness, including a Lennon acid trip in the middle of *Sgt. Pepper,* was stumped by the band's current quandary. The sessions dragged on far beyond what anybody had planned, and they already had more than enough material for a very strong album. They had simply failed to tell their producer that they were intent on creating a double record to complete a contractual matter with EMI and move ahead with Apple. Martin's departure (or escape) was his way of throwing up his hands; he had always been against a double album. McCartney was so self-involved he didn't seem to realize Martin would take a break. Chris Thomas was absolutely petrified. Martin had simply left him a note saying, "Feel free to attend Beatles sessions." "But Paul walked in and he was obviously a bit knocked about the whole thing," Thomas remembers. "'Well, if you want to produce us, then produce us. But if not, then you can just fuck off!' And I just went 'What?! Nobody said anything about *producing*.'"[16]

Thomas, at just twenty-one, had to prove himself very quickly to appease the four-headed monster. "It was more like, 'Well we'll give you a try, and if you don't measure up, you're out.'" A storied producer now, with a thousand credits, Thomas can laugh about it.[17] Over the first several days remaking "Helter Skelter," he proved his musical smarts and quickly won the band's trust. He got producer credits on session logs, and Lennon insisted his name get listed on the album credits. In a small way, the band's sealed perimeters opened up to include a new engineer, which may have helped convince them that Martin was not the "essential" man he made himself out to be. Another side benefit to Martin's absence came as the Beatles liberated the new 3M eight-track machine from EMI technical engineer Dave Harries for the remaining work, doubtless using the competing Trident machine as leverage.

"Hey Jude" sounds like a benediction, and it gave the Beatles' relationship with their audience the jolt of recognition everybody had been waiting for. Finally, the summer of turmoil and loss took refuge in a perfect single from the band that had always reflected the audience's best hopes back to itself. But the song also trumpeted the Beatles' new company, Apple, and everyone agreed it needed a proper televised launch, especially after the retail-clothing fiasco on Baker Street. It had been more than a year since their last formal album (*Sgt. Pepper*), and with the world reeling from war, revolution, and student protest, the band's spring oldies romp, "Lady Madonna," began to sound like cheery tokenism (and couldn't quite atone for *Magical Mystery Tour*).

The *Frost on Sunday* appearance on September 8 kicked "Hey Jude" into the stratosphere. Already, radio had made the song inexorable; it soared beyond everything else it followed that summer, including Otis Redding's aching, posthumous "Sittin' on the Dock of the Bay" and Archie Bell and the Drells' "Tighten Up," as well as strong work from Simon and Garfunkel ("Mrs. Robinson") and The Doors ("Hello, I Love You"). The stiffest aesthetic competition to "Hey Jude" came from Lennon's old sparring partner, now a mumbling god: Bob Dylan had put out a quiet, commanding acoustic album, *John Wesley Harding,* back in December 1967. As 1968 wore on, its fiercely obscure tone seeped through rock's heavier textures. These were the competing sounds that soundtracked Chicago's days of rage.

For both "Hey Jude" and "Revolution" on TV, the instrumental background came from the master track, and the vocals were done live. This gave McCartney's close-up shots immediacy and freshness, with Lennon, newly hippified, harmonizing beneath. "Revolution" added

McCartney and Harrison doing their doo-wop "bow-ohm, shoo-be-do-wah, bow-ohm, shoo-be-do-wah" rejoinders to the faster tempo, an instant collectible, the irresistible new groove giving leftists fits: the song was a tour de force of rock classicism, but they chafed at Lennon's seemingly deliberate irony. "There is freedom and movement in the music, even as there is sterility and repression in the lyrics," Greil Marcus wrote. "The music doesn't say 'cool it' or 'don't fight the cops'. . . . The music dodges the message and comes out in front."[18]

Again, the debate over this song brings a case where all sides make valid points. Taped on September 4, Lennon reiterates his "count me out—in" hedge, which got criticized as fence-sitting, but could just as easily be construed as emphasizing awareness of the left's setbacks in Paris, Chicago, and Prague since Lennon's first take on the same lyric in early June. In interviews, Lennon insisted on the equivocation. For all the controversy surrounding "Revolution," and how it disappointed radicals, close attention to Lennon's comments reveals ambivalence vying with principle. To Lennon, revolution for the sake of revolution seemed as wrong-headed as the politics that had steered the system wrong in the first place. Wiping out the existing order would only create a vacuum, he argued. Just where had any modern, all-inclusive "revolution" succeeded—Communist China? Lennon's Mao reference puts the onus on "revolutionaries" to come up with something better—"We'd all love to see the plan":

> But if you go carrying pictures of Chairman Mao
> You ain't gonna make it with anyone any-how . . .

Why should any social "revolution" necessarily refer to Communism? Lennon asked. Mao may have found Marx useful, but he was clearly a cautionary counterexample: in Lennon's view, backing China's Communist tyrant equaled enforced abstinence. Paradoxically, Lennon's "Revolution" makes Winston Churchill's famous argument about democracy: that it's the most oppressive system tried "except all those other forms."

The song became a flash point, and Lennon did his best to answer for it in interviews with the leftist press. On September 17, Robert

Fraser brought journalist Jonathan Cott to Lennon's apartment for his first lengthy interview for *Rolling Stone,* the San Francisco bimonthly that had debuted with Lennon (as Private Gripweed) on its cover the previous year. Like the faster "out/in" version of "Revolution" he sang on *Frost on Sunday,* this interview took place just weeks after the Democratic National Convention in Chicago, somehow an American rejoinder to Russian tanks that had rolled into Prague, wiping out Prague Spring hopes. Lennon's attitude shifted markedly from when he wrote and recorded either version of the song, and yet his candor remains decisively nonviolent and antimilitant. "There's no point in dropping out because it's the same there and it's got to change," Lennon told Cott. "But I think it all comes down to changing your head and, sure, I know that's a cliché." What would Lennon say to a black power guy, for example?

"Well, I can't tell him anything 'cause he's got to do it himself," Lennon replied. "If destruction's the only way he can do it, there's nothing I can say that could influence him 'cause that's where he's at, really. We've all got that in us, too, and that's why I did the 'Out and in' bit on a few takes and in the TV version of 'Revolution'—'Destruction, well, you know, you can count me out, and in,' like yin and yang. I prefer 'out.' But we've got the other bit in us. I don't know what I'd be doing if I was in his position. I don't think I'd be so meek and mild. I just don't know."[19]

While the *White Album* sessions had already produced more than the usual walkouts and musical standoffs, the wonder is how many gratifying rhythmic waves the Beatles still shaped. "Birthday" turned into an all-night affair: the bassist, first to arrive, at 5 P.M., reworked yet another Bobby Parker "Watch Your Step" circular riff, and the Beatles laid down twenty takes of the track, until eight-thirty, and then broke to watch *The Girl Can't Help It* at McCartney's house with Chris Thomas and Pattie Harrison. Revived by the energy from Gene Vincent, Eddie Cochran, Fats Domino, Little Richard—and a bodacious Jayne Mansfield—they returned to the studio to finish nine more takes and overdubs (with Pattie Harrison and Yoko Ono singing backup, Yoko's first) for a final mono mix at five-thirty in the morning.

In October, they finished off "Honey Pie," "Savoy Truffle" (without Lennon), "Martha My Dear" (without Lennon), Harrison's "Long Long

Long" (without Lennon), "I'm So Tired," "Bungalow Bill," and "Why Don't We Do It in the Road?" (featuring McCartney and Ringo alone). If "I'm Only Sleeping" was one long slow leak of a song, "I'm So Tired" was the flat tire of celebrity tedium flopping around in Lennon's head. Singing "curse Sir Walter Raleigh" while dragging on a cigarette, Lennon exhales with an addict's anguish over the physical compulsion, the inability to quit, and the profiteer's trickery that got him hooked in the first place. "I'm So Tired" also became a song that expressed everything about the sessions that made them both unbearable and worthwhile, exhausting and yet meaningful, Lennon turning fame's fatigue into an exercise in redeemed contempt. If "Birthday" celebrated the heights the band could still plunge into, "I'm So Tired" conveyed the weariness that was setting in.

Finally, on October 13, four months and a lifetime after starting, Lennon recorded the last song, the open-wound ballad named for his mother, "Julia," by himself. It still captures the isolated dread, confounding fear, and free-fall grief his mother's death summoned in him, and it's hard to imagine he would have found this same emotional pitch in front of the others. Alongside "Look at Me" (written in India), "Julia" hints at the amplified anguish to come on 1970's *Plastic Ono Band*.

THE TRACKS COMPLETED, Harrison and Starr fled, and Lennon and McCartney put *The White Album* to bed with Chris Thomas over one final, grueling session where they mixed, sequenced, and mastered all thirty numbers in twenty-four hours to meet EMI's November 22 release date for the Christmas market. "Not many people realize, sequencing comes at the end and it can be tricky," Thomas remembers. "You think certain tracks go together and then you try it and they don't, so you go back and try it again . . . and you go round for a bit like that. It can be a brain-boxer."[20] At one point, Thomas came upon McCartney sprawled across a mixing board, completely conked.

After Lennon agreed to let "Hey Jude" win the A side of the band's summer single, backed with the revised, faster version of "Revolution," the battles over sequencing during this marathon twenty-four-hour session included Lennon's snarky title to "Yer Blues," despite McCartney's arguments that the track deserved better. But there was no doubt in Lennon's mind about commanding three studios at once and every engineer who was available to help him mix and master "Revolution 9," and staring down McCartney to insist on its inclusion against everybody else's wishes. This last one proved him not just right but prescient in ways McCartney still doesn't seem to understand. It's possible Lennon used "What's the New Mary Jane" as a negotiating chip to keep "Revolution 9" in track sequence—he'd give McCartney "Wild Honey Pie," but insisted on concluding with "Revolution 9." (Did McCartney answer this by placing Lennon's "Good Night" afterward as a hushed coda? Or was that Lennon's insecurity, leaping into the void and then pulling back?)

Emerick's memory of how "Revolution 9" made the final cut has the sting of resignation: "I heard through the grapevine that John and Paul ultimately had a huge row over 'Revolution No. 9,' Paul absolutely did not want it on the album, and John was just as adamant that it would be on there. In the end, of course, he got his way."[21] McCartney can still give reporters quotes about wanting credit as the "true" avant-garde Beatle when he's never talked about "Revolution 9," or defended it alongside his vaunted affection for John Cage and Edgard Varèse.

Perhaps "Revolution 9" makes the most "sense" as an audio collage in the same way Richard Hamilton's *Just What Is It That Makes Today's Homes So Different, So Appealing?* (1956) worked as a visual collage of American magazine advertisements. Since his splash at the Independent Group's 1956 This Is Tomorrow show, Hamilton had inspired many pop art imitators. He went on to become an influential instructor at Newcastle-upon-Tyne, with students who included Roxy Music's Bryan Ferry. Robert Fraser suggested Hamilton for the *White Album* design, and the choice extended the Beatles' identification with the pop-art movement and its principles.

As Eduardo Paolozzi did in *I Was a Rich Man's Plaything* from 1947, Hamilton's "Just What Is It . . ." compiles all the hoarier aspects of consumer culture into an "idealized" living room haunted by Al Jolson from the window, trying to "make sense" of all the competing modernist images of perfection, unity, and art. What kind of "art" hangs on the wall of the future? A cartoon-book cover next to an old-fashioned portrait of a dignitary above a woman (wife? mother?) sitting on the couch dressed as a stripper, touching her left breast, with "pasties" on her nipples. The dad, "Mr. Universe," flexes for the camera with a huge Tootsie Pop obscuring his undies.

For the Beatles, Hamilton aimed to create something as iconic as *Sgt. Pepper,* only completely different, and he sold them the sheer white sleeve by saying it would "stick out" in crowded record shops. In Hamilton's hands, however, this simple gesture transformed a "high"-art device with a Dada conceit: the cover "photo" was a blank white space, with the words "The BEATLES" stenciled at an angle off-center above a serial number. The idea merged the "limited edition" lithograph or etching category with the mass-produced pop album, the blank projection screen of a band so famous they needn't appear on their own album with the pretense of printing a limited number of copies for collectors.

It's not clear whether Hamilton heard "Revolution 9" before conceiving his poster design, but the collage and pop-art conceits play off Lennon's extended sound quilt—the parallels are striking enough that Hamilton's fold-out print probably made "Revolution 9" more accessible to more listeners. In the poster, Hamilton mirrors Lennon's aural ideas through visual imagery. Like a good art student, Lennon uses appropriation, ironic quotation, and commodity fetishism, editing together the chaos of Beatlemania (wild screams) with found sound (from radio, TV, and crowd noise) and transforming them into a larger, fully realized theater of the mind. If "Revolution 9" was a dreamscape, Hamilton's collage suggests a formalized, static snapshot of its images in motion. As an experiment in the same line as "Tomorrow Never Knows" and "Strawberry Fields Forever" and "I Am the Walrus," "Revolution 9" is a pure exploration of how Lennon's bugged subconscious sounds, or at least how he imagined it might.

FINISHING OFF THIS GIANT ALBUM, the single biggest project in the Beatles' career, might have felt like relief to Lennon and Ono. But their increasingly active public profile hid some explosive secrets. Already, they faced a harsh British conservatism for the way they snubbed marital convention and parenthood. Kyoko, Ono's daughter, had stayed with her father for the interim, but Ono was preparing for a custody battle. Beyond this, Lennon grew his hair down to his shoulders, and Ono confronted far more prejudice and hate mail for being a rock star's Japanese girlfriend than she had ever confronted as an avant-garde artist. On top of all this, John and Yoko broke two more giant taboos that only aggravated everything else.

Ono had become pregnant as early as May 1968, and must have known her condition by June, or July at the latest. This means Lennon accused Cynthia of adultery at Kenwood in June while fathering a new child with Yoko—a child they desperately wanted. It makes his confrontation both more abusive and glaringly hypocritical. Second, Cynthia's remarks about John looking thin and "gaunt" hint at heroin abuse as early as June, and the Beatles knew of his new proclivity even sooner, and probably swapped junkie readings of "Happiness Is a Warm Gun" behind his back when they recorded it in July ("I need a fix 'cause I'm goin' down"). So beyond upsetting his divorce settlement, Ono's pregnancy threatened their recreational heroin sniffing. And only a deeply addictive and disorienting narcotic like this explains why they still portrayed themselves as victims of both Lennon's band and his larger circle even as McCartney and Starr gave them shelter.

Other forces allowed Lennon to present a much more sympathetic picture to the world. On Friday afternoon, October 18, barely twenty-four hours after John got home from his epic *White Album* mixing session, he and Yoko awoke to a loud banging on their front door. The London Drug Squad, led by Sergeant Norman Pilcher, ordered them to allow police dogs in for a drug raid. Ono answered the door, but seeing police, and dressed only in a vest, she bolted it shut again and returned to bed with Lennon, who called his solicitors. Sergeant Pilcher later reported that "An attempt was made to enter the premises by way of a rear ground floor window but this was prevented by Lennon who held the window closed." The detective sergeant claimed Lennon had said: "I don't care who you are, you're not bloody coming in here." A struggle ensued for eight minutes as they tried to force open the front door. Lennon finally relented and let them in.[22]

He had known he was in Pilcher's sights. His friend Don Short from the *Daily Mirror* had tipped him off. But coming off that final *White Album* marathon, Lennon was caught off guard. Once the police established that the twenty-eight-year-old Beatle and thirty-five-year-old Ono were alone, they all waited half an hour for two search dogs, Yogi and Boo-Boo, to sniff out the four large rooms. By that point two lawyers and several press photographers had also arrived, as word spread of Lennon's troubles. Although the dogs discovered only 219 grams of cannabis resin, about two ounces, hidden in a leather binoculars case, they hauled John and Yoko into custody amid a squall of paparazzi. (Starr had taken over the flat from Jimi Hendrix, who had a ghastly dope reputation even then, so Lennon had scoured the place for drugs when he and Yoko moved in after their awkward stay as guests of McCartney's in St. John's Wood.)

No account of London's upper tier of law enforcement would be complete without Norman Pilcher, who climbed to the rank of detective sergeant by arresting Donovan in 1966 and the Rolling Stones in 1967. Mick Jagger and Keith Richards actually did time in jail, a miscalculation that brought enough notoriety to earn Pilcher a veiled sneer in Lennon's "I Am the Walrus" ("Semolina Pilchard . . . climbing up the Eiffel Tower"). Busting Lennon suggested that Pilcher understood rock's rough pecking order—nobody brought bigger headlines. John and Yoko were taken to Paddington Green police station and charged with possession and "obstructing the police in the execution of a search warrant." The next day at Marylebone Magistrates' Court, the couple was remanded on bail and their case was scheduled for November 28.[23] A picture snapped outside the courtroom showed Lennon sheltering a distraught Yoko from baying paparazzi. (They used this shot on the back of *Unfinished Music No. 2: Life with the Lions*.)

Lennon's arrest renewed the war of public relations between the fading cultural values of those in power and the new ethic of subversive pleasure from the young. Jagger and Richards had been sprung from

jail the previous summer. But tabloids like the *News of the World* still fueled negative opinion by reporting on elaborate rock parties, even tipping off officials in exchange for headlines. In this heated atmosphere,
John and Yoko were engulfed in a press frenzy.

The next week, they stirred more outrage by announcing that Ono
was carrying Lennon's child, due in February 1969. Suddenly, it was
clear that Yoko had become pregnant before Lennon left Cynthia the
previous May, and this trumped even his marijuana bust. History con-
demns them further, now that we know of Ono's heroin use during this
period.[24] To the public of that era, though, the event underscored how
even as the Beatles soared back into favor with a hit single and pending
album, they were no longer untouchable. In the establishment mind,
Lennon deserved scorn for abandoning his first wife and Julian, who
had turned five. As the court papers put it, Lennon's was an "offense of
moral turpitude."

Within a fortnight, Ono was admitted to Queen Charlotte's Hospital
in Mayfair. Between five and six months pregnant, she showed symptoms she might miscarry, and doctors urged hospital bed rest to save her
baby. With the timeline of Lennon's extramarital love affair now a public matter, his first wife was granted a swift divorce, and sole custody of
Julian, on November 8. At month's end, Apple Records released John
and Yoko's first album, *Unfinished Music No. 1: Two Virgins,* a series of
tape experiments recorded the previous May in Lennon's attic, packaged
between full frontal (and rear) naked photos of the couple holding hands,
eyeing the camera with bemused indifference. Even as the musical *Hair*
shocked Broadway audiences with its nude cast, for the prudish Brits
("No sex, please"), this image was roughly ten times as mortifying.

"Originally, I was going to record Yoko," John said, "and I thought
the best picture of her for an album would be naked. So after that, when
we got together, it just seemed natural for us both to be naked. Of course,
I've never seen my prick out on an album before."[25] EMI's CEO, Sir
Joseph Lockwood, refused to distribute the record, saying both parties
looked "ugly." In some ways, because neither John nor Yoko possessed
"conventional" Hollywood beauty, their celebration of their natural bodies was a revolution in itself. Track Records, an independent label,

stepped in to handle the product in the UK. In America, Tetragrammaton handled distribution by papering over the nudity with a brown paper sleeve, with only John and Yoko's heads peering from behind an oval cutout. Officials in New Jersey weren't having any of it: they seized the product as "pornographic." "When two great Saints meet it is a humbling experience," McCartney wrote in his understated yet revealing dedication. "The long battles to prove he was a saint."[26]

Public outrage was sudden and irreversible: the sharp-witted Lennon, the "engine room of the Beatles," who had presided over the English music scene for the past five years, honored guest in 1965 at Buckingham Palace for his MBE, had suddenly morphed into a busted hippie and faithless husband. This was a fate far worse even than *Magical Mystery Tour*. At least that was simply daft—a pretentious home movie posing as a Christmas TV special. Lennon had not only abandoned his child and wife but—worse still—begun dabbling in wacky art projects with an Oriental consort, a Japanese hippie turned concubine with strange first and last names. All this counted against Ono even before her outspoken (then radical) feminism.

To the older generation, Lennon's crime lay in taking a lover and abandoning his family. Add to this the token racism of Anglo-American society, which viewed Yoko as a foreigner, an Asian seductress. And to Lennon's fans, it was hard to figure which offense was greater: setting up shop outside the Beatles, or this strange new companion, a far-out "conceptual artist," a New York "intellectual," who in addition to being foreign was downright alien. Wasn't Yoko Ono another one of those arty, pretentious sophisticates Lennon enjoyed mocking? In the wake of 1967's *Sgt. Pepper* and "All You Need Is Love," it almost seemed as if he were flushing all the Beatle goodwill down the toilet. In America, a novelty song by an unknown nineteen-year-old singer named "Rainbo" voiced what many fans were thinking: "John, You've Gone Too Far This Time." "Rainbo" was a pseudonym for future Oscar nominee Sissy Spacek.

HOUNDED BY THE PRESS, separated from Julian, and finished with his latest Beatle epic, Lennon moved into Ono's hospital room, preferring the confines of a healing chamber to the Beatle bubble. He slept at her bedside for two weeks, on the floor first and then, when the hospital relented, an adjacent cot. The two of them filled time by making tapes on a portable cassette recorder, writing poems, reading the papers aloud, and singing songs ("No bed for Beatle John," Yoko ad-libbed). With the drug hearing still ahead of him, Lennon distracted himself with a cartoon called "A Short Essay on Macrobiotics," for the underground magazine *Harmony*.

As Yoko's condition worsened, they placed a microphone on her womb and recorded the child's heartbeat. Having weathered their first eight months together, they desperately hoped a child might bring them the comfort the rest of the world withheld, and sanction their affection with the promise only babies bring. Here, something inside Lennon found its voice: insisting on staying with his lover instead of fleeing toward his manager or his band, he fought the hospital authorities to sleep on a cot if that's what it took. He didn't seem to care if his label rejected his experimental noise or the law hassled him for drugs or nudity; his goal was to comfort Yoko and secure her strength for a healthy baby. Cynthia could only wonder how such a forbiddingly small and intense woman brought about such a gallingly decent reversal in Lennon's behavior, although you could analyze this gesture as compensating for the child he had abandoned.

No heroic measure, by Ono, Lennon, or medical authorities, could ultimately prevent what increasingly appeared as inevitable. Yoko, who had already suffered miscarriages with Anthony Cox, finally lost Lennon's child on November 21. The child was buried quietly at a secret location; no paperwork has ever surfaced.

Given no time to recover, Lennon appeared the next week in court on drug charges. His solicitor told the judge that Yoko had miscarried as a result of the arrest and surrounding press storm. Beyond their loss, there were fears about how a conviction might affect Yoko's visiting visa status, as well as her custody of Kyoko. All charges against Yoko were dropped; Lennon pled guilty only to cannabis possession.[27] In exchange, the court waived the obstruction charge. Lennon paid a fine of £150 plus 20 guineas in court costs. It seemed like a good deal at the time.

That fall, as Lennon lunged from crisis to metaphysical trauma, *The White Album* flew out of record shops, its all-white cover an instant talisman that mixed hip nonchalance with austere craftsmanship. *Two Virgins* followed and flopped, but not because of any outrage its cover inspired. Those who picked it up bought it for its cover, and treated the record's experimental sounds as a mild curiosity, something to be listened to once and filed away.

By the end of the year, political obsessions loomed so large that they distorted the personal tragedies of John and Yoko. Jonathan Cott's landmark *Rolling Stone* interview ran in the issue dated November 28, 1968, with John and Yoko's naked bums on the cover (anticipating *Two Virgins*), and a series of letters appeared in the *Black Dwarf* about listeners' lost faith in the "Revolution" single: "An Open Letter to John Lennon," signed by columnist John Hoyland, criticized the Beatle of naïveté, and denounced his dabbling in political themes without understanding the street's-eye view of the organizer: "Recently your music has lost its bite. At a time when the music of the Stones has been getting stronger and stronger. . . . The Stones have understood that the life and authenticity of their music—quite apart from their personal integrity—demanded that they take part in this drama—that they refuse to accept the system that's fucking up our lives. . . . There is no such thing as a polite revolution." The letter reflected a political intensity so profound that only those alive at the time can understand Hoyland's criticism and his recognition that the political violence of this period had now made the Beatles seem staid.

Such criticism understandably had an effect on Lennon. His printed response touched on themes he would stick to even through his most radical phase in the early 1970s, when he joined up with politicos Hoffman and Rubin in Greenwich Village. He was adamant about nonviolence, and how the concept of any "revolution" rang hollow without a clear plan for what new society might replace the old:

Dear John,

Your letter didn't sound patronizing—it was. Who do you think you are? What do you think you know? . . . I know what I'm

up against—narrow minds—rich/poor. . . . I don't remember say-
ing that "Revolution" was revolutionary. . . .

Lennon zeros in on the key point about destroying what's wrong with
the existing political systems. Of course there's something wrong with a
system that inspires such a destructive response, Lennon argues, since it
would only reinforce the existing violent pathologies.

What are the alternatives? Lennon demands. What new system of
government will replace the old? And if the Beatles vs. the Stones inspires
the same kinds of arguments, then such analogies provide weak frames
of reference, and listeners can't be paying very close attention. Rock 'n'
roll had already been a powerful force for changing people's worldview;
ambivalence about political upheaval would seem to be a relatively sane
response to 1968's dilemmas.[28]

It's curious that leftists like Hoyland weren't more incensed by *Magi-*
cal Mystery Tour, which overplayed the psychedelic conceits just as the
antiwar movement surged. With the billowing success of the "Hey Jude" /
"Revolution" single, and the thirty songs that came tumbling after on
The White Album, the Beatles erased *Magical Mystery Tour* from pop
consciousness. In any other context this would have done more than simply revive their career. But an audience once enthralled by the Beatles
now seemed immune—Lennon's engagement wasn't enough, or didn't
measure up to radical hopes, or sent the wrong signals when he could be
doing so much more.

The battle in the United States between youth and the establishment
had reached one impasse after another, and the Beatles had regained
their footing only to find they had lost some relevance. The punch line
came just as Yoko entered Queen Charlotte's Hospital the week after the
arrest: Nixon's "law and order" campaign, and cynical "Southern strategy," elected him president of the United States in November 1968,
dashing what was left of antiwar hopes.

Ever since, the sixties rock mythos has been oversimplified beyond all
reason: to the left, it represents a ferment of change and possibility; the
right still uses it as shorthand for all manner of cultural ailments, from
sexual and women's liberation to religious freedom, abortion rights, and

civil dissent. Ronald Reagan, governor of California from 1967 to 1975, went on to become president in 1980 by leveraging these same cultural divides, and George W. Bush, a boomer himself, ran his entire presidency on these themes. As the Vietnam War dragged on, American campus dread of Nixon between 1968 and 1974 reached fever pitch, rivaled only by progressives' distaste for George W. Bush two generations later.

As 1968 BEGAN TO RECEDE into the holidays and New Year, Lennon and Ono grieved the loss of their first child by diving back into public appearances. The times called for activist rock stars, and no *Two Virgins* nudity scandal or miscarriage would get in the way of their promoting their romance as performance art. Their most notable performance came at Stonebridge House in Wembley, on December 11, where the Rolling Stones were filming *Rock and Roll Circus.* The prospective TV special featured the Who doing "A Quick One, While He's Away," Taj Mahal, and the debut of a band Jagger had discovered, Jethro Tull.

Lennon sang a shaky version of "Yer Blues" with Keith Richards on bass, Eric Clapton on lead guitar, and Hendrix's Mitch Mitchell on drums, billed as the Dirty Mac. Lennon and Jagger taped a halfhearted introduction, but the entire project got shelved due to the Stones' misgivings about their own tired performance. It was Brian Jones's last appearance. Between Lennon's vocal and some admiring support, "Yer Blues" achieves a sloppy grace that lives on in the ABKCO DVD which finally appeared in 1996. But the comedy bit with Jagger flops.

Over Christmas, John and Yoko took the stage at the Royal Albert Hall for a "Celebration in December" art benefit, billed as an "Alchemical Wedding," in which they squirmed inside a white bag on the stage, shades of stunts still to come. The following week they dressed up as Mr. and Mrs. Santa Claus for the Apple Christmas party.

To get his comments into the British press alongside Cott's *Rolling Stone* interview in America, Lennon greeted two students, Maurice Hindle and Daniel Wiles, for a long talk that expanded on leftist discontent with "Revolution." Lennon, fast becoming an authority on political revolution, stuck to his ambivalence, insisting that "ruthless destruction" would only lead to having "ruthless destroyers" in power. The Soviets were just as ambitious as any Capitalist country when it came to competing in the Olympics or the Space Race, he continued. Lennon added that the petty bickering on the far left about being "extremer than thou" revealed them as "exclusionary snobs," incapable of leading, never mind organizing, a united movement. "But I tell you what," he continued, "if those people start a revolution, me and the Stones'll probably be the first ones they'll shoot. Y'know, I mean that. . . . And it's him—it's the guy that wrote the letter that'll do it, y'know. [Gestures around to his stockbroker mansion] They'd shoot me just for living here, y'know."[29]

Ono's miscarriage may have pricked Lennon's conscience, and prompted some meager attempts at civility. He in fact asked Cynthia for visitation rights with Julian. She in turn asked their longtime chauffeur, Les Anthony, about the scene at the Montagu Street flat and he described it for her over a cup of tea:

> He told me it was just as well that Julian hadn't gone to the . . . flat while John and Yoko were there. "It was a complete tip," he said. "They were doing heroin and other drugs and neither of them knew whether it was day or night. The floor was littered with rubbish. Couldn't have had a little one there."[30]

Cynthia duly moved out to find her own place with Julian, and John and Yoko returned to Kenwood for a month near the end of the year to get the property sold. Then they took over Ringo and Maureen Starr's neighboring house as the Starrs moved into Peter Sellers's home. Only a year earlier, Lennon had been marching down glitzy stairs in a white tuxedo, snapping his fingers to "Your Mother Should Know" for the finale of *Magical Mystery Tour* as protestors marched on the Pentagon. Now, as he moved into Ringo's house with a new lover, the Lennon who sang "I Am the Walrus" seemed like a character from some distant past.

Thank You Girl

G RIEF-STRICKEN BY THE LOSS OF THEIR CHILD AND BACK ON HEROIN, Lennon and Ono showed up exhausted and aloof for the shoot of *Let It Be* in January 1969. The project hung on a loose McCartney theme, a wide-open rehearsal for a television special that would build to a climactic live show on some exotic stage: a cruise ship, an Egyptian pyramid, or the Royal Albert Hall as a fallback. Starr (having previously walked out after being humiliated) and Harrison wanted nothing to do with Beatlemania logistics and refused to commit to anything more than a single live gig. The shoot's daily hassles reflected underlying fissures. The continuing debates about the finale, whether to continue or simply abandon the project, and the band itself became a running commentary throughout the month; the show within this show veered between grudging compliance and open disintegration.

The schedule turned into its own punch line: Starr had contracted to appear as Peter Sellers's adopted son in the movie adaptation of Terry Southern's absurdist novel *The Magic Christian,* set to begin shooting in early February 1969. Whatever the Beatles decided, they had only one month to work up new material. Lennon's arrest, Yoko's miscarriage, Apple's first-year stumbles, the grueling finish to their last sessions, the film crew union rules which dictated a ten-to-five schedule, and the drafty cold of the Twickenham soundstage—all compounded the band's weakening bonds. By this point, McCartney had assumed the leadership role Lennon once took for granted: without Epstein to tell them what came next, McCartney simply rallied the others to keep everything from spinning too far off course. But poisonous months had passed since McCartney's last cinematic brainstorm, *Magical Mystery Tour,* and now his enthusiasms met blank stares.

Michael Lindsay-Hogg, who had filmed the "Hey Jude" and "Revolution" promotional films for *Frost on Sunday,* hired on to shoot the loose, cinema-vérité format. Almost immediately, the band scaled back the idea of a foreign jaunt and booked for January 18 the old Roundhouse venue, the place where Barry Miles launched his *International Times* alternative newspaper in 1966 (with Soft Machine and Pink Floyd). As the Beatles sleepwalked through rehearsals, auditions for *The Magic Christian* progressed on the same lot. More than twenty-nine hours of film were shot at Twickenham during that first week of January 2–10, before Harrison, doing a Ringo, abruptly quit. "See you 'round the clubs," he said on his way out.[1] The transcripts from all these bootlegs, the most complete recorded documentation of any Beatles sessions (compiled in *Get Back* by Doug Sulpy and Ray Schweighardt), provide sobering insight to the band's interpersonal toxins.

Listening to these tapes, it's hard to reconcile the unfocused drift of the music with the Beatles' status: all through the holidays and into January, the double *White Album* dominated the album charts (without a hit single), on its way to outselling every other album they had ever released. *The White Album*'s oblique anti-conceptual format, and its free-ranging thirty tracks, made it more challenging to absorb than *Sgt. Pepper* or *Magical Mystery Tour;* a reinvention on this scale presented looming contradictions framed with formal rigor—swinging from "Glass Onion" to "Ob-La-Di, Ob-La-Da" sounded like familiar tropes stretched to extremes. How could such different sensibilities coexist in the same band, never mind between songwriting partners like Lennon and McCartney? To their audience, the Beatles' continuous reinvention of rock 'n' roll meant inventing new ways to be popular, transforming themselves into new versions of the core idea. Between themselves, however, they grasped at new reasons to stay together.

Assenting to McCartney's rehearsal-to-stage concept, they agreed on one guiding musical principle: they wanted a spare ensemble without any of the tape manipulation or studio trickery they had mastered on their five preceding projects. This home-baked ethic rode psychedelia's backlash, the "roots" impulse behind "Lady Madonna" and the "Revolution" single taken one step further: overdubs were shunned, although heavy editing ultimately concealed an abundance of flaky takes. Where *The White Album* inverted *Sgt. Pepper*'s conceptual conceit (no metaphor, no theme, no cover, no band, no pretense at "otherness"), their new venture chased yet another new ideal: ensemble interplay as bedrock. Rock's studio wizards revived their garage band origins as grown-ups.

This "back-to-basics" idea, eventually dubbed *Get Back* after a McCartney number, answered two influential records from 1968: Bob Dylan's hushed *John Wesley Harding* and the Band's backwoods *Music from Big Pink*. Intrigued by these projects, George Harrison jammed with these musicians in upstate New York over Thanksgiving 1968 and brought back song demos to pass around (material that wound up on *The Basement Tapes*). On the hundreds of bootlegs from these January 1969 sessions, Harrison can be heard launching into "Please Mrs. Henry," "I Shall Be Released," and the Band's "To Kingdom Come"; at one point the Beatles considered recording "Million Dollar Bash." (Some of these Dylan songs had already leaked: producer Joe Boyd, who comanaged the UFO club where John watched Yoko's *Cut Piece* in 1967, soon showed up with "Million Dollar Bash" at Fairport Convention's *Unhalfbricking* sessions.) To Beatle ears, a new challenge hung in the air: could they produce music this intimate, this lived in, without fussing over its production? What would a new "live" Beatles album, without embroidering, sound like at this point? As a motivating idea, all four Beatles seemed as curious about this as anybody.

In its final released form, the locations for *Let It Be* split the footage up into three distinct sections: early rehearsals on a huge soundstage with no recording equipment at Twickenham Studios (where they had worked on *A Hard Day's Night* and *Help!*); the new Savile Row basement of Apple Corps headquarters, where George Martin booked an eight-track recorder (but didn't really "produce"); and the compromise finale, an unannounced rooftop set where the band played for an impromptu audience overlooking London's foggy skyline. Each venue held its own quirks and complications, but John and Yoko's withdrawn expressions and distracted air spooked the final cut; surely a Lennon this reserved, this withdrawn, didn't typify Beatle sessions.

In the movie, Yoko Ono's blank passivity became the public face of Lennon's force field. His seeming indifference made it convenient for the Beatles—and then the world—to blame her for his withdrawal from group work. Unlike when she contributed singing to "Birthday," and lent her uncredited hand in "What's the New Mary Jane" and "Revolution 9," during previous months, Ono sat like a question mark as the Beatles trotted out their new songs for one another in *Let It Be*. A smile squeaked through, but only when Lennon twirled her around for an oblivious waltz during Harrison's "I Me Mine." McCartney's comments verged on schoolmarmish at some rehearsals, which only made Lennon seem more remote, as if prowling around the edges of the band, working up the nerve to quit. His passive-aggressive campaign, imposing Ono on the others as a putative fifth Beatle at both musical and business sessions, dared each of them to quit before he did—first Ringo, the previous summer, and in this month, Harrison. Cynthia's observation from the previous spring circled back again ("They seem to need you less than you need them"), only this time Lennon's withdrawal carried a subliminal threat. Just a year before, he barked throughout the zany fade-out to "Hey Bulldog" with his new flame; now he seemed completely, defiantly submerged. We know today that Lennon was drowning grief in heroin; in the movie, the couple's attitude scans as benign contempt.

To open the sessions, Lennon greeted the band with a promising new song, "Don't Let Me Down," a gently swaying blues that shouldered greater meaning as the month progressed. As they had done in so many previous opening sessions ("Tomorrow Never Knows" for *Revolver*, "Strawberry Fields Forever" for *Sgt. Pepper*), the Beatles spent this first session arranging a new Lennon track into three distinct sections: verse, refrain, and bridge ("I'm in love for the first time"). By the time "Don't Let Me Down" premiered on Apple's roof, its open-ended address became an involuted farewell to the band, its audience, and Lennon and McCartney's songwriting partnership.

———

DESPITE THIS PROMISING LENNON NUMBER, that first week of shooting in early January nearly derailed the entire project. McCartney had plenty of songs to share, but he uttered open disappointment that Lennon had only one. Time was when Lennon would partner up with McCartney to get songs ready in advance of recording sessions. Now the band wondered if Lennon would even show up and, if he did, have enough energy to interact. The final cut of *Let It Be* features a famous contretemps between McCartney and Harrison on camera, but George's walkout actually followed a row with Lennon on January 10, in the middle of Chuck Berry's "I'm Talking 'Bout You." He simply put down his guitar and announced he was "quitting the Beatles *immediately*." Just as they had when Ringo left the previous August, the other three carried on, either assuming that cooler heads would prevail or that a private meeting would patch up the spat. This time, the press got wind of it, and Harrison gave a quote to the *Daily Mail* on January 16 confirming the "tiff," adding, "There was no punch-up. We just fell out."[2]

Within a couple of days, the band held a private meeting at Ringo's home. Apparently, both Yoko and Linda Eastman attended, but Yoko persisted in "speaking for" Lennon, who remained silent, as the others despaired at how to get through to him. Predictably, the meeting went nowhere: in fact, Harrison's beef with Lennon boiled down to how he hid behind Yoko. Her performance at this meeting only fixed Harrison's resolve. On set the next day, McCartney referred to Harrison still being "on strike," and a discussion ensued between McCartney, Linda Eastman, Neil Aspinall, Lindsay-Hogg, and Ringo, about the band's fragile situation. McCartney defended John and Yoko, standing up for their "sincerity," even as he complained about how Yoko intruded on the pair's already dwindling songwriting sessions. Eastman, Aspinall, and Starr all contributed more cutting appraisals. McCartney outlined two options: either "oppose Yoko and get The Beatles back to four or . . . put up with her."[3] As for the stalled film project, McCartney suggested they pay the crew, see out the week, and check if the situation improved. If not, the Beatles might just fold. Later that afternoon, when Lennon and Ono finally arrived, Lennon tried out a new song,

"Dig a Pony" (which had a winding, circular riff resembling "Day Trip-per" and "Birthday," sliced into half time for the verse). Perhaps they had turned a corner.

The next day, Peter Sellers dropped in for a visit and wondered why cameras were rolling on a huge set with no action. *Get Back* recounts a barbed back-and-forth between Sellers and Lennon as the movie star poses with the band for a photo. Peter apologizes for arriving without drugs, since he knows Lennon is fond of them. John mockingly proclaims that they've "given up" drugs, having whitewashed that matter for Hunter Davies's authorized biography. Then Lennon warns Sellers not to leave needles in the men's lavatory, citing his own drug arrest—but hastens to add how he "understands that people in show business need to take drugs to relax." The other Beatles cover their faces with embarrassment, as if they've just given Lennon the same lecture (not to leave his works in the bathroom), but Lennon plows forward. Sulpy and Schweighart report that Lennon "flatly states that drug-taking is better than exercise," while Yoko jokes that "shooting up heroin *is* exercise."[4] This *Let It Be* outtake screens a lot funnier than it reads, even if it stumbles on John and Yoko's heroin use, another source of the stalled sessions and Lennon's productivity. It also hints how they may have graduated from sniffing to syringes.

That second week at Twickenham became a wash: the Beatles joked acidly about the end of the band, or how Clapton might replace Harrison; McCartney needled Lennon about his lack of material; and Lindsay-Hogg watched a lot of footage go down the toilet. A second group meeting with Harrison that weekend hatched a temporary peace. (It's not clear whether Ono attended this meeting.) Perhaps a change of space would tilt the sessions in a new direction. They canceled the Roundhouse date, and decided to ditch the drafty Twickenham set for the basement room of their Apple offices, where they could get more comfortable.

Among many other unfinished projects, "Magic Alex" Mardas had been sent off to build a seventy-two-track console, which was either unusable or unworkable (EMI blocked Mardas at every turn). EMI itself was just making the leap from eight-track to sixteen-track; seventy-two sounded fantastical. So George Martin installed a portable eight-track machine in Apple's basement for on-the-fly recording so that filming could continue. A couple of days later, the *Disc and Music Echo* ran Lennon's quote from a Ray Coleman interview that steered Apple's ship straight into its iceberg: "Apple is losing money every week. . . . If it carries on like this, all of us will be broke in the next six months."[5] Naturally, Apple's bankers and tax lawyers frowned on this kind of talk, even if Lennon had a reputation for overstatement. Shareholders were unaccustomed to rockstar loose cannons of Lennon's stripe, and McCartney could not enforce discretion. Lennon openly repeated his financial dread every time a reporter brought it up. This rant caught the eye of a notorious industry fixer named Allen Klein in New York. Imagine the other Beatles' frustration: defiantly mute in rehearsals, Lennon could not resist yapping to the press daily, as if determined to sabotage their joint venture.

LUCKILY, CHANGING THE REHEARSAL space, and the appearance of an old Hamburg friend, reversed the band's lethargy. One of the beguiling twists to the late Beatle story arc is how George Harrison's songwriting star rises just as Lennon and McCartney's collaboration declines. Harrison had been friendly with Billy Preston ever since they met in October 1962, when they shared a bill as openers for Little Richard's act at the New Tower Ballroom in New Brighton, Wallasey. Preston played keyboards for Little Richard's band, and the show came around to Liverpool's Empire Theatre later that same month. Both bands also appeared together in Hamburg during the Beatles' fifth and last visit to the Star-Club, at the end of 1962. Preston had bounced around during the sixties, playing for Sam Cooke (notably on 1963's urbane yet soulful *Night Beat*) and the house band on ABC-TV's *Shindig!* His latest gig had him touring with Ray Charles, passing through the Royal Albert Hall early in 1969. Harrison caught the show after a *Let It Be* session, greeted Preston backstage and invited him to sit in with the Beatles.[6]

Harrison's visit to Dylan's Woodstock sessions and his invitation to Eric Clapton to solo on "While My Guitar Gently Weeps" convinced him that an outsider could revive stalled sessions. Dylan and the Band treated Harrison as an equal, while in his own band, Lennon and McCartney persistently patronized his material, even as it began to peak. (Lennon, in fact, sat out most of Harrison's Beatle recordings from here on out.) Taking in an ally could only ease Harrison's reentry into the contentious Beatle orbit. Along with lobbying for Ringo Starr to replace Pete Best, bringing Preston into the *Get Back* project stands as a defining move for Harrison: he single-handedly rescued *Let It Be,* and pushed his material throughout 1969, until *Abbey Road* featured his best work yet.

When they greeted Preston at Apple on the afternoon of January 22, the group's emotional tone changed drastically: Preston's keyboard figures gave the Beatles new lines to listen and react to; he also freed them up to focus on arrangements. With an old friend in their midst, tensions eased, and work progressed more smoothly. Harrison's resignation had slammed the door on desultory group workouts; now, with less than ten days on the clock, work lurched forward.[7]

On January 25 these five did takes of "Let it Be," Harrison's "For You Blue" and "Isn't It a Pity?" and their discussions about how to bring it all to a close led to a rough notion of a concert on the roof. With spirits flagging, and sessions dominated by endless oldies jams (some of them sprightly, and underrated), they sought the simplest solution. On the 27th, they rehearsed "Oh! Darling," then let it drop as they assembled a track list for the live show: the following day, parts for "Get Back" and "Don't Let Me Down" took more shape, with Lennon taking lead guitar on the former and McCartney figuring out a contrapuntal bass line on the latter. On the 29th, instead of running through the set list, they lapsed into oldies again: "Besame Mucho," the first number they had played for George Martin back in 1962; an early stab at Lennon's "I Want You (She's So Heavy)"; then Buddy Holly's "Not Fade Away," and a slow burn on "Mailman Bring Me No More Blues," the Holly favorite released on *Anthology 3*, with a bleak Lennon vocal that made for an oddball cousin to "Please Mr. Postman."

ON THE AFTERNOON of January 30, the four Beatles climbed up to the roof of 3 Savile Row to see how Mal Evans and Neil Aspinall had set up their equipment. Director Lindsay-Hogg stationed four cameras on the roof, another at Apple's reception desk, and one more roaming around the street to catch listener reactions. In the basement, engineer Glyn Johns manned a mixing board from audio feeds winding down four flights of stairs. The unlikely setting sparked a burst of inspiration: ambivalent and wary, the Beatles were about to cancel when Lennon simply pitched forward, saying, "Fuck it, let's play." The situation proved too tempting: to act out a cinematic pun on that old Drifters' song by Gerry Goffin and Carole King, "Up on the Roof." This set, their last live performance together, has the piquant double quality of a band rediscovering itself while bidding a fond farewell.

The whole charade has a larkish tone, scaled down from the New Year's hopes of a Royal Albert Hall or Roundabout finale, and nobody seemed to anticipate the cold: January breezes, somehow symbolic, whipped off the surrounding buildings with only the music to warm the band's fingers. McCartney wore a formal black jacket and white shirt; Lennon put on Yoko's fur coat; Ringo had a cheesy red plastic mac; and Harrison stood off to stage right with green sneakers beneath his furry overcoat. To the left and behind McCartney, Billy Preston, in a leather jacket, crouched over a Fender Rhodes electric piano.

As they started their first take of "Get Back," the conservative tailoring district of Central London peered upward at the noise wafting from above. Slowly, and then very quickly, the band began to surf wave after redemptive wave of ensemble fellowship, as if warming up against the cold air strengthened their resolve against an entire month's tiresome indecision. Ringo's inimitable shuffle, tidy yet propulsive, made "Get Back" both roomy and concise, tickling the band's ensemble in ways that brought mystery and surprise to every cadence. Lennon plays a tart lead lick behind McCartney's vocals, and turns in lower vocal harmonies by the second refrain. (Between takes, Lennon hits the mike with deejay patter: "We've had a request from Martin and Luther . . .") They struggle at first, the balance is off, but by the second take they're hitting kicks with verve, the song puts on some flesh, and McCartney spurs the momentum with some jubilant screams on top, gunning for home. When

Ringo interrupts the second fake ending for a coda, he trips things up with a stumbling yet perfectly controlled tom-tom roll, spilling the song into a victory lap for McCartney to scat over.

If they had any doubts about how their unproduced sound might fare against Dylan and the Band, this rooftop set quickly gave back far more than what Lindsay-Hogg's cameras had caught so far. "I've Got a Feeling" opens humbly: a ringing guitar lick that hits a deceptively simple stride with a Lennon-McCartney duet during the verse; it drops into a gentle rolling groove. The climax comes as McCartney starts wailing, as if he can shout down the song's paradoxes: "All I've been looking for is somebody who looked like you!" And then a wiry guitar line uncoils with a nudge from Ringo, and the groove settles back into the familiar opening cadence. The song glides on a riddle, another side-by-side Lennon-McCartney patchwork that inverts the typical "We Can Work It Out" and "A Day in the Life" format: McCartney burrows down into raw feeling in the verse and tail, and then Lennon pans back for an innocent bystander counter-section ("Everybody had a hard year . . ."). These distinctive fragments circle each other like cats, counterparts snugly joined. The understated irony nearly overwhelms the performance: it's a tapestry of Lennon and McCartney's songwriting themes and formulas describing their dissolution. After a final verse where Lennon's out-of-body slant descants McCartney's uplift, the band coils the song back up into one last dangling question mark.

There's a scene in the film during a break when McCartney talks to Lindsay-Hogg about writing "One After 909," which he and Lennon never finished—the words were too corny, he remembers. But they light into the song on the roof like a forgotten truce, a long-withheld hope fulfilled, and it catches gusts of feeling from their earliest heights. The band has a full gait now, they can do anything, so they hold back and dig into this slight adolescent novelty, a teenage breakthrough, to project something more layered than simple nostalgia. Now the song converts simplicity into valediction, a token of triumphs whooshing past, and in their adulthood, it sounds like the best ambitions have all come true: between themselves, their audience, and their songwriting muse. Lennon and McCartney plant their vocal harmonies like banners rippling in the breeze: if you didn't know any better, they might be brothers, spiritual twins pitching headfirst into gale winds. "Move over once [pause], move over twice [pause] . . . *Come on baby don't be cold as ice!*" The music unfurls around their voices like too-familiar jokes reaping peals of laughter. This "One After 909" take transfers virtually uncorrected from rooftop to disc, and toots along atop Ringo's lively yet laid-back verve. (On its tail, Lennon starts singing "Danny Boy," as if it belongs to the same canon.)

McCartney harmonizes on top of Lennon on "I Dig a Pony" for yet another vocal color that masks his supple control. Ringo misses the first count-off for a false start, but then the groove hits a steady gait, lean yet muscular, and the track resembles "Hey Bulldog" or "I Feel Fine," another sturdy guitar workout based on the same arpeggios that drove "Day Tripper" and "Birthday." Lennon garners this familiar setup with sly sincerity: the closing cadence ("All I want is you/Everything has got to be just like you want it to") so closely resembles a devotional outcry that it buoys the surrounding verbal flotsam.

After a second take of "I've Got a Feeling," featuring even more harmonies from Lennon, and more risky Harrison guitar work atop his verse, some defining questions hover over the music: How could such wan rehearsals yield such onstage magic? How did this much confident simplicity spring from three weeks of desultory deadlock? Following Lennon's "Don't Let Me Down," the expectations game suddenly veers into relaxed, bluesy ambition: the band renews itself with every phrase; they lean into breaks without knowing where they'll land, and they land with such assurance and comfort that every downbeat redoubles release and forward motion. When Lennon flubs his "Don't Let Me Down" lyric on the second verse, inserting gobbledygook, their laughter warms the sound anew.

In "Don't Let Me Down," irony toyed with intimate conundrum: here was Lennon, the putative tough, who had done his best to piss off both audience and band by posing naked and positioning his new lover in the band's crosshairs, singing about how brash and desperate love made him feel, earning back no small measure of respect and self-assurance from his band as he does. This number, a paean to Yoko and never-ending romance as pop staple, swells into a farewell pledge to Lennon's band, with overtones of all they've been through, and winds up glimpsing Lennon's solo insecurities. As he did in "If I Fell," Lennon pledges devotion to his new partner by reiterating how risky love feels and the high cost of emotional commitments.

As if concurring in Lennon's conceit, McCartney shadows with an exquisite upper harmony for the refrains and writes a beguiling lower melodic bass guitar lead beneath the bridge ("I'm in love for the first time"). Descending in steps, this McCartney descant traces the song's emotional puzzle from below, a new strand of competitive counterpoint. The second take features a fearsome Lennon lead vocal: even though he flubs the lyric, the band shakes loose a steady-rolling vibe from its unprepossessing frame. Like the baroque piano that interrupts "In My Life," the instrumentation becomes a waking symbol of the song's lyrical puzzle: true love as quiet panic.

A lark turns into a modest set for the ages, an argument about how middle-aged paunches can rock just as steadily as anybody, thank you, and Lennon pulls off sincerity, running off with a Japanese-American homewrecker, even muttonchops, without seeming anything less than a Beatle. During the second and closing "Get Back," the cops push past Mal Evans behind Ringo and Lennon and Harrison's guitar amps fail. This causes momentary confusion, and then, as Evans convinces the bobbies this will be the last song, the band gallops the number home, with McCartney ad-libbing over the coda ("You been playing on the roof again . . . and that's no good!").

"I always feel let down about the police," Ringo said later. "Someone in the neighbourhood called the police, and when they came up I was playing away and I thought, 'Oh great! I hope they drag me off.' I *wanted* the cops to drag me off—'Get off those drums!'—because we were being filmed and it would have looked really great, kicking the cymbals and everything. Well, they didn't, of course, they just came bumbling in: 'You've got to turn that sound down.' It could have been fabulous."[8]

When they finish, Lennon steps forward to say good-bye, apologizing for the abruptness and unfinished edges with feigned modesty: "I'd like to say thanks on behalf of the group. For ourselves, I hope we passed the audition." On that roof, for about forty minutes, they made the troubled Apple offices beneath their feet seem incidental. It was exhilarating, for both the band and its listeners, but ephemeral.

ON HIS WAY INTO APPLE the next day, McCartney posted a card to Ringo that read simply: "You are the greatest drummer in the world. Really."[9] Lindsay-Hogg posed them in front of his cameras for formal sequences of quieter material they couldn't do on the roof: somber takes of "The Long and Winding Road," "Let It Be," and "Two of Us," with McCartney in a dark suit, lit with a spotlight, singing lead. All these numbers now sounded like weak metaphors for everything these sessions had wrought, a love affair creeping toward some unknowable yet inevitable finale. Lennon played sloppy bass and contributed sympathetic backup vocals to McCartney's gospel move, and eventual title song, "Let It Be." The material had its strengths, but this last session felt like a wake, as if returning to their offices had given them all an emotional hangover.

When this session was finished, nobody could bear to listen to the tapes, let alone prepare them for mixing and release. The combination of material and overhang from the previous day's surge gave this footage a mournful feel. They wrapped the shoot, called it something besides success, and put it on the shelf until they could figure out what to do with it. *Let It Be*'s dour mood—and ironic-uplift finale—makes a lot more sense in retrospect. "Behind the scenes, everything was falling apart": if only the Beatles had copyrighted that phrase for the future VH1 series *Behind the Music.* As with so many other rock clichés, this one started with the Beatles reluctantly circling one another, avoiding the inevitable clash.

Three days before the rooftop concert, Allen Klein had flown in from New York to meet with John and Yoko at the Dorchester Hotel to make his pitch, and he had done his homework. The fact that other sharks hadn't connived their way to such a meeting sooner measures the bluster of Lennon's stormy evasions. Lennon had met Klein backstage at the Rolling Stones' *Rock and Roll Circus* shoot the previous December, but only informally. Something savvy and manipulative in Klein told him that if he could get Lennon to identify with him, he could win him over. With fourteen years in the business, Klein dropped names like Sam Cooke, Chubby Checker, and Mick Jagger, presenting himself as a tough New Jersey street kid, as if he knew Lennon would be comparing him to Epstein the retailer.

Klein's Hungarian father had been a butcher, and he made sure to mention how his parents had split in his childhood, and his auntie raised him, just like John. Lennon admired Klein's candor, the curses that spiced his vernacular, and his compact, pit-bull demeanor; to Lennon's mind, perhaps, Klein resembled a New Jersey Scouser. Where suits like Dick James patronized the Beatles ("Do you have anything else that goes 'Yeah Yeah Yeah'?"),[10] Klein made sure to recite Lennon lyrics to him from memory. Klein knew rock 'n' roll history, and had already invested emotionally in Lennon's work in a way James never had.

Klein's specialty, learned as a label accountant in the late fifties, leveraged a keen understanding of how record companies systematically cook their books. He proved himself in the early 1960s by approaching Bobby Darin with a plan to win him back royalties. Once his negotiations allowed him access, he audited Darin's account and sent him a check for $100,000. Klein used this gambit repeatedly. Sam Cooke hired Klein as his business manager in 1963 to negotiate a favorable deal as he launched his own record label, SAR Records. Klein won Cooke an unprecedented package deal from RCA, which included gate receipts, back royalties, and a hefty percentage of records sold in an era when even managers typically left such particulars unattended.

Because British law lagged on copyright issues compared with America, Andrew Loog Oldham sought out Klein in 1965 to consult on better contracts for the Rolling Stones. Oldham had been winging it, and Klein took their business game up a notch; Lennon would have heard about this on the grapevine and in club chatter with Jagger. In 1967, Klein bought out Cameo Records, which included lucrative catalogs by the Animals, Herman's Hermits, Bobby Rydell, ? and the Mysterians ("96 Tears"), and the Twist's Chubby Checker. This track record convinced Lennon that Klein could turn Apple around.

In meeting with Klein, Lennon answered an emerging McCartney threat. McCartney had recently taken up with photographer Linda Eastman and met with her father's legal firm in New York. In addition to falling in love, he began to see solutions to many of Apple's business tangles through the extensive experience of Eastman and Sons, who had pioneered intellectual copyright and entertainment law. Clearly, Mc-Cartney angled to hook up the Beatles' business interests with his new relations. Lennon's head was clouded both by grief and smack, but he knew how McCartney's melodic lilt could conceal bald aggression, and historians tend to let his foresight on this matter go uncredited. With many variables yet to crumble, Lennon acted impulsively to counter Mc-Cartney's tack, in what he perceived as his own self-interest.

Another strand of Lennon's cross-Atlantic thinking came into play here, right at the moment when the band's sessions seemed shakiest and their company clearly needed a grown-up at the helm. Both Lennon and McCartney, in their inimitable ways, chose representatives who extended the more extreme aspects of their characters: each chose American wives and lawyers. Lennon took more heat for his choices, especially since his American wife had Japanese origins, and Klein outblustered even the man who declared himself "more popular than Jesus." But McCartney came to some of the same conclusions as his songwriting partner: the British accountants who had handled their affairs until now were unimpressive, and these Americans expressed more confidence and spoke of far greater potential in their publishing catalog. Even as far back as 1969, it was clear to many that Lennon-McCartney songs would generate cash for generations to come.

At this first meeting with Allen Klein, Lennon barely knew what he might be up against, but he knew what he didn't want: any more suits from Denmark Street like Dick James.[11] Nobody could have predicted that within weeks, James would pit Lennon and McCartney against some of the heaviest London financiers going for control of their catalog. Perhaps, as these latest sessions drew to a close, Lennon could sense the vultures gathering. Perhaps Ono convinced him that the Eastmans, who had a distinguished reputation for representing leading contemporary painters like Willem de Kooning and Jasper Johns, required heavy armaments. In any case, the Beatles had outgrown Epstein, hadn't they? Apple had at least taught them what they didn't like and had no interest in learning: the complicated attentions required by a huge production company. Perhaps Lennon also reasoned that Klein's shark reputation might intimidate British shareholders.

Klein closed his pitch to Lennon by dangling a generous offer: instead of taking a percentage off the top, he would take a commission based only on increased Apple business, meaning he would reap only what he sowed. To Lennon, this seemed more than fair. He scrawled out a note to EMI's chair, Sir Joseph Lockwood: "Dear Sir Joe—I've asked Allen Klein to look after my things. Please give him any information he wants and full cooperation."[12] Like the guilty plea Lennon had entered for his drug arrest three months earlier, it seemed the strongest position to take at the time.

As EMI ENGINEER GLYN JOHNS listened to all the January tapes, marking up the best ones for edits, and Starr filmed *The Magic Christian,* the Beatles squeezed in the odd session while this legal battle loomed. On February 22, they completed thirty-five takes for a new Lennon track, "I Want You (She's So Heavy)," and John overlaid a guide vocal. On Harrison's twenty-sixth birthday (February 25, 1969), he went into the EMI studios with engineer Ken Scott to lay down some new song demos: "Old Brown Shoe," "Something," and "All Things Must Pass." McCartney worked on producing the follow-up to Mary Hopkin's "Those Were the Days," and a new original, "Good-bye." The next week the band gathered again for the two new Harrison songs: "Old Brown Shoe" and the first thirteen takes of a rough draft for "Something." They filed this material toward some new project that might redeem January's project, without concept or producer.

As far as Lennon was concerned, he was free to dabble with his new partner as his band's sessions inched fitfully forward. John and Yoko's schedule conveys a persistence and daring that defies both heroin use and Lennon's vaunted insecurities: in early March, he played guitar for Ono's appearance at a Cambridge avant-garde music festival, which he released as "Cambridge 1969" on *Unfinished Music No. 2: Life with the Lions* in May. Lennon joked that the avant-garde crowd looked down on him almost as much as the rock crowd looked down on her. The album's cover shot showed him slouched next to Ono's hospital bed from the previous November; the black-and-white back picture caught him shielding Yoko from paparazzi as they left the police station after their drug arrest. Unlike the sweetly confrontational *Two Virgins* fracas, these images projected an intimate victimhood, with a strong subtext of how Sergeant Pilcher's celebrity arrest—not drugs—had caused Ono's miscarriage.

PAUL MCCARTNEY HAD BEEN LIVING with Linda Eastman at his Cavendish Avenue home since the previous fall. On March 12, he married his four-months-pregnant bride at the Marylebone Registry Office in Central London, with his brother Michael and Mal Evans as witnesses. Assuming Harrison would attend McCartney's ceremony, Sergeant Pilcher's Drug Squad chose that morning to raid his Esher house, only to come upon Pattie having breakfast alone (she immediately rang George, who raced home from his London Apple office). After being booked, they made their late arrival at McCartney's reception at the Ritz Hotel, which Princess Margaret attended (the overzealous Pilcher would have loved to bust the queen's sister as well, if he could have). Later that day, instead of whisking his bride off for a honeymoon, McCartney returned to EMI for more work on Jackie Lomax's Coasters cover ("Thumbin' a Ride"). Lennon and Ono were in another EMI studio mixing a "peace song."

The Harrison drug bust stole attention away from how none of the other Beatles was invited to Paul and Linda's quickie nuptials. Here was a tabloid item that gave the Beatles new doubts about their status all over again: their music harnessed the cultural tensions of the day, but newspaper stock surged with news of the last Beatle—England's longest-running, most eligible millionaire—taking his bride. British fans lamented an American interloper, and heckled Linda dearly, both by mail and through personal affronts at their London home, for usurping their most cherished bachelor. American fans simply mourned from afar. Most picked up an item that Eastman was heir to the Eastman Kodak concern, which was false.

Splashed across newspapers above the fold, McCartney's wedding pricked Lennon's competitive nerve. Like a brother jockeying for more attention, he determined to marry Ono as quickly as possible. Aides scrambled to find the perfect publicity venue. First they flew off to the august Plaza Athénée in Paris on March 16 for a spur-of-the-moment ceremony, only to discover that they couldn't marry in France unless they stayed in residence longer. Disappointed, they returned to London. Four days later, they tried to get married on the cross-channel ferry but were refused permission to board *The Dragon* at Southampton because of "inconsistencies in their passports." Peter Brown, under Lennon's directive to find the most amenable spot, discovered they could get married on the British-governed island of Gibraltar off Spain. They booked a private jet and flew down with Brown and photographer David Nutter. The British consulate opened at 9 A.M., and there, registrar Cecil Wheeler married them with Brown and Nutter as witnesses. After an hour in Gibraltar, they flew back to a luxury Paris hotel suite.

"We chose Gibraltar because it is quiet, British, and friendly," Lennon told the press, spinning hasty coincidence into myth. "We tried everywhere else first. I set out to get married on the car ferry and we would have arrived in France married, but they wouldn't do it. We were no more successful with cruise ships. We tried embassies, but three weeks' residence in Germany or two weeks' in France were required."[13] In Paris they lunched with Salvador Dalí and then drove up to Amsterdam to stage their honeymoon.

OF ALL THE PUBLICITY STUNTS JOHN AND YOKO PULLED, their two "bed-ins" stick out as defiant *Goon Show* exercises in media manipulation, the closest any Brits came to Yippie media theater. This first affair came via their Amsterdam Hilton suite, billed as a "Bed-In for Peace" that last week in March. They simply booked a room, tacked some homemade posters on the wall, and summoned reporters. Propped up on their pillows, John and Yoko baited the press as nudist wacky artists holding forth on politics. Reporters seemed as stunned by the couple's giggling hubris as their hosts were to be attended so fawningly—they sat angelically, acting miffed when reporters expected something more than sloganeering. Half the giggles stemmed from how many journalists actually fell for the bait; the other half came from watching how vexed the press became at what a "happening" might mean in news terms. The situation quickly morphed into one of those sixties scenes that stopped reporters cold, and turned tabloid scribblers into a press conference on the subject of the West's war-mongering. It was uncanny: John and Yoko had suddenly put the lightest comic touch on the street theater that had seen antiwar protestors gassed and beaten in the Chicago streets the previous summer. Tricking the world into a public honeymoon turned into an even better gag than putting out a naked album cover.

Lennon, a marathon talker, performed wall-to-wall interviews in his bathrobe with anyone and everyone, with a new glint in his eye after so many years answering to "what-will-you-do-when-the-bubble-bursts?" absurdities. Here was celebrity completely reimagined as comic flourish in the service of the antiwar movement, deflating pretention and privilege with an utter lack of sobriety. All through the Beatles' tours, Epstein had set the band up in hotel meeting rooms with a table and microphones. Now Lennon recast reporters like the BBC's David Wigg as mere conduits for his mishmash of profundities and throwaways. The circus atmosphere made the "Jesus" fracas seem hopelessly old-fashioned: "It doesn't help murderers to hang them, it doesn't help violent people to be violent to them. Violence begets violence. You can't kill off all the violent people or all the murderers or you'd have to kill off the government." Fans familiar with Lennon's 1965 *Playboy* quotes on religion recognized this patter: "I don't need to go to church, I think people who need a church should go, the others who know the church is in your own head should visit that temple 'cus that's where the source is." In the same breath, Lennon defended drug use, saying, "I don't regret drugs because they helped me—I don't advocate them for everybody because I don't think I should, you know, but for me it was good." And he reflected on his retreat in India without the hostility he had first vented through

"Sexy Sadie": "I met Yoko just before I went to India, and had a lot of time to think things out there, three months just meditating and thinking, and I came home and fell in love with Yoko, and that was the end of it and it's beautiful."[14]

"We're staying in bed for a week, to register our protest against all the suffering and violence in the world," Lennon told them. "Can you think of a better way to spend seven days? It's the best idea we've had." He conveyed this seemingly irrefutable vantage with the gentlest authority. The coverage, especially in Britain, reeled back in horror, but effrontery only scanned as easy cynicism—Lennon had finally trumped the media at its own game by turning a roomful of press into a giant antiwar noise machine.

Even when pressed to defend his motivations, Lennon seemed giddy:

QUESTION: You see this whole roomful of reporters, photographers, and filmers . . .

JOHN: I think there's something beautiful about it because on all the Beatles tours there's always people who had laughs! The field reporters had a good time when they got the right photograph or the right or wrong picture, or something. It's a happening.

YOKO ONO: And there's plenty people in the world who are sensitive enough. When you report, they will see what we're doing and it's good.

JOHN: But it means this is a madhouse. Everything's too serious.

Both the setting and the absurdity of the "honeymoon" as a happening allowed Lennon to confront the perception of his cynicism, especially when it came to love. He even made his treatment of Cynthia and Julian, and Ono's walkout on Tony Cox and Kyoko, seem whimsical:

QUESTION: What do you see in a conformist institution such as marriage?

JOHN: Intellectually, we know marriage is nowhere. That a man should just say, "Here, you're married," when we're living together a year before it. Romantically and emotionally, it's somewhere else. When our divorce papers came through, it was a great relief. We didn't realize how much of a relief it was going to be until Peter Brown came up and said, "It's over." It was only a bit of paper. . . . It was very emotional, the actual marriage ceremony. We both got very emotional about it and we're both quite cynical, hard people, but very soft as well. Everyone's a bit both ways. And it was very romantic.[15]

A NEWSPAPER HEADLINE DASHED JOHN AND YOKO'S fanciful mood when Lennon came across an item about Dick James, his Northern Songs publisher. James had sold his majority of company stock to a company called Associated Television Ventures (ATV) without consulting either Lennon or McCartney. Incensed at suddenly losing control of his songs, Lennon immediately used his bed as a megaphone to answer the duplicitous move from a man to whom he had entrusted his publishing fortune: "I won't sell. They are my shares and my songs and I want to keep a bit of the end product. I don't have to ring Paul. I know damn well he feels the same as I do."[16]

Dick James never did have a sense of humor. Apparently, he didn't have much sense of loyalty, either: he cut his deal just after both songwriters had wed, and while Lennon was out of the country. James had been the first to express interest in Brian Epstein's Beatles, and he signed up the Lennon-McCartney songwriting team with publishing contracts just as EMI's George Martin signed them. That company, Northern Songs, had traded publicly on the London Stock Exchange since 1965, which now seems absurd—anyone with any confidence in this material would have held the company privately from the start. Once Lennon and McCartney conferred, they wrote a letter to EMI on behalf of the Beatles demanding the company pay their banker, Ansbacher, all royalties, rather than assent to the deal. Instead, EMI froze their assets until the legal complications could be sorted out. At the same time, Triumph Investment Trust, a city merchant bank, began buying up 70 percent of NEMS (and its subsidiary, Nemperor) holdings. Both Northern Songs and Epstein's NEMS Enterprises had been blindsided by corporate take-overs, bringing the Lennon-McCartney songwriting catalog into play.

The bed-in had been a lark, but the public had trouble digesting all these events as a single entity—Lennon seemed to be straying from his minders. How to reconcile the pictures of these daffy hippies in bed with the premiere of Ono's ominous new film, *Rape,* which they attended on their way home at the Vienna Film Festival? For this April Fools' Eve appearance, John and Yoko took the stage inside a large white bag, telling the assembled press that this way there could be no "prejudice" in their communication. When they returned to London, the *Financial Times* on April 5 followed up on the Northern Songs story, reporting, "It appears that Dick James, managing director of Northern Songs, has failed to persuade Beatles Lennon and McCartney to accept the £9 million bid for Northern from ATV."[17]

Preoccupied with matrimony and peace, Lennon and McCartney began to lose control of Northern Songs. And yet their lawyers agreed: there were still more deals to be cut, more legal options to pursue. For all outward appearances, they were still in the middle of the most successful careers in show business history, with a documentary film and its all-original soundtrack in the can. None of the Beatles could stomach sifting through all the footage, but if they couldn't get a TV special or a film out of January's work, they might as well try for an album. Since Glyn Johns had attended most of the sessions while George Martin puzzled over the band's mixed signals (did this project even have a producer?), his ears were probably the best choice to broach the mass of takes for a projected album, and he had been working on the tapes already. McCartney had Johns spend the spring cleaning and editing all those unfinished tracks into a rough approximation of a full-length recording. The tapes forced Johns to fudge the original "back-to-basics" concept: a lot of this material sounded too shaggy, and the first step involved logging numerous takes into their most workable moments, then assembling it all into a huge editing project. Both the album and the movie filtered out oceans of meandering and halfhearted run-throughs that typified this month's work.

McCartney jumped back into the weeds to remix "Get Back" for the single, backed with "Don't Let Me Down." He wrote up über-coy press copy after its radio debut on April 6:

> "Get Back" is The Beatles' new single. It's the first Beatles record which is as live as live can be, in this electronic age. There's no electronic whatchamacallit. "Get Back" is a pure spring-time rock number. On the other side there's an equally live number called "Don't Let Me Down." . . .

> P.S. John adds, it's John playing the fab live guitar solo. And now John on "Don't Let Me Down": "John says don't let me down about 'Don't Let Me Down.'"[18]

On one level, this single reaffirmed everybody's best hopes about the band and its productivity; on another level, it became a crucial argument about the golden Lennon-McCartney touch, and the band's stake in these negotiations with new financiers.

ALMOST AS IF January hadn't happened, and expressing faith in their continuing partnership, when he returned from Amsterdam Lennon telephoned McCartney to collaborate on a new song that narrated the previous month like a teletype: "The Ballad of John and Yoko." Sometimes, it was like riding a bike with these two: in one long afternoon-evening session on April 14, at EMI's smaller Studio 3, they laid down basic tracks, with Lennon on guitars and McCartney backing him up on bass, drums, and harmonies. McCartney helped give Lennon's buoyant self-parody just the right bounce—a musical echo of McCartney's *Two Virgins* dedication.

The material, however familiar, struck at some imaginary genre in the gap between Woody Guthrie's talking blues and Richie Valens's "La Bamba," with a faint air of mid-tempo Tex-Mex at once familiar and ingeniously original. Lennon's song reworked a Chuck Berry melody from "You Never Can Tell," about a "teenage wedding" where the "old folks wished them well," with a deliciously knowing refrain: "'C'est la vie,' say the old folks/it goes to show *you never can tell* . . ."[19] (McCartney answered its guitar lick on his first solo album with an instrumental called "Hot As Sun / Glasses.")

McCartney's upper duet on the last verse ("Caught the early plane back to London") unveiled the first of several twilight vocal duets they had already taped ("Two of Us," "Don't Let Me Down," and "I've Got a Feeling") and the *Abbey Road* series yet to come. Although Lennon and McCartney had long since veered apart aesthetically, the gravitational pull of their partnership exerted an embracing symbolic power. The session was so serendipitously productive it inspired them to grab Harrison's "Old Brown Shoe" from the vault and make the two songs their next Beatles single: a hop-along, hard-luck narrative about Lennon's marriage, supported by his band mate and songwriting partner, which hit number one in the UK (number eight in the U.S.) at the end of May. (The label credited the Beatles, but Harrison and Starr were not on "Ballad." The song served as the third layer of Lennon's campaign to upstage McCartney's nuptials that began with his own Gibraltar elopement and the bed-in.) This time, most of the world yawned at Lennon's Christ analogy, and the number made a feisty opening blast as the partnership prepared to fight for control of their song catalog. Conceived as a wedding jingle, it became ironic prelude to the impending Lennon-McCartney legal feud. The audience latched on to it as a talisman against all other indications—and wildfire rumors—that the Beatles might never record again. Nobody wanted to consider such a thing.

An initial confrontation between Allen Klein and John Eastman (then twenty-nine), Linda's older brother, resulted in a short-term compromise: Klein had convinced Lennon, Harrrison, and Starr to sign a management agreement, while McCartney refused. Klein was installed as the band's manager, and the Eastman father-and-son firm was designated as the legal counsel. As both sides returned to their corners to plan future moves, an unsteady truce steered Apple affairs. Breakup rumors came and went as "Get Back" and "The Ballad of John and Yoko" bounded up the charts; but Lennon kept right on behaving as though he had bigger plans. In between these scattered spring sessions, he sold Kenwood and scouted out a new home with Yoko. Lennon, Harrison, and Starr kept shoving Klein's contract in front of McCartney, who kept pushing it back unsigned, saying, "We're massive, we're the biggest act in the world, he'll take fifteen percent."[20] The rift seemed insoluble. And more and more, Lennon's shenanigans with Yoko seemed geared to turn the band's seismic chapter in music history into a mere footnote.

For starters, Lennon began formalizing his post-Beatle identity. On the overcast, windswept day of April 22, 1969, a month after they married, John and Yoko dressed in black leather and climbed back up to Apple's rooftop, site of the last Beatles concert. Señor Bueno de Mesquita, the bald, bespectacled local commissioner for oaths, oversaw a simple ceremony (called a "deeds poll") and presented the paperwork for Lennon's signature. Henceforth, Beatle John, christened John Winston Lennon by his mother Julia back during the blitz, assumed the name "John Ono Lennon." (He dropped the Winston informally; legally, it stayed attached.)

"Yoko changed hers for me, I've changed mine for her. One for both, both for each other," he said. "She has a ring. I have a ring. It gives us nine 'O's' between us, which is good luck. Ten would not be good luck. Three names is enough for anyone. Four would be greedy."[21] They posed for some photos before running down into the basement for an emotional all-night recording session.

The result has grown more poignant over time. Over a tape of their own heartbeats and that of their miscarried baby, John called "Yoko" and Yoko answered "John" for the entire first side of their *Wedding Album* (released on November 2, 1969). The elaborate packaging made it a commercial failure, and it received scant critical attention, but today those twenty-two minutes ("John and Yoko") project a searing intimacy. Instead of predictably dull and remorseless, this track gradually becomes oddly mesmerizing, their call-and-response touching in a lighthearted, almost fanatical way, a requiem and a goof, a broadside of shifting emotions mysteriously carried by two names echoing in the blank space of their dead child's heartbeat.

Lennon's name-change goes unmentioned in the Beatles' own oral history, *The Beatles Anthology* (2000). At the time, changing his middle name from the dowdy, patriotic Winston to Ono stripped Lennon of much British history and tradition—and the very idea of class "respectability" he held in such scorn. Americans still discount how vexed the British were by the audacity of this gesture. To willfully alter your Christian name was itself a kind of scandal, and to drop Britain's great World War II prime minister in favor of a Japanese who represented, in the minds of many, cruel aggressors in that same war, smacked of insolence. The act crystallized a keen sense of cultural betrayal: in marrying Ono, Lennon became a traitor to his fans and his countrymen, an idea that lay just below the surface of all the ink spilled on the Beatles' breakup and his marriage from that point forward. The only way he could have ruffled more staid British feathers would have been to take the middle name Adolf.

To his fans, taking Yoko's middle name became just another piece of his wacky multimedia romance and increasingly eccentric behavior. With one of his feet still in the band and several other feet dabbling in political whimsy, solo recordings, gallery openings, and avant-garde tape reels, the ceremony that altered Lennon's identity for the last eleven years of his life flickered past, another in a dizzy series of public acts. It was quickly overtaken by a second bed-in in Montreal, an obscenity suit for erotic lithographs, bag-ins, and looming Beatle feuds.

In hindsight, though, this rooftop ceremony stands out as a defining moment in the evolution not just of John Lennon the man but of John Lennon the persona, symbol, and bearer of rock 'n' roll values. Beatle business affairs had deteriorated into arguments and hostile standoffs since Ono attached herself to Lennon and he insisted on her constant presence—in the studio and in the boardrooms and bathrooms of Apple headquarters. By marrying Yoko and changing his name, Lennon signaled his nascent feminism and formalized a year's worth of defiance toward McCartney and the other Beatles.

Also that day, Lennon and Yoko announced the formation of their new company-within-a-company, Bag Productions Ltd., to handle financing and publicity for their various art projects. Ono now assumed the combined roles of the other three Beatles: primary business partner, de facto family, best friend, and musical collaborator. Months before he recorded *Abbey Road* with the band, Lennon stepped over a line that separated his Beatle years from everything that came after.

THROUGHOUT APRIL AND MAY 1969, recording sessions advanced on "Oh! Darling," "Octopus's Garden," a new guitar solo for "Let It Be," and the revival of "You Know My Name (Look Up the Number)," first tracked in 1967, now edited down, omitting a charming ska section, for a possible B side. On May 2, "Something" received a makeover with thirty-six new takes. This new track included McCartney's exuberant bass line, which Harrison would duet against when he cut his guitar lead during the orchestral overlay in August. A long medley also began to take shape with a song called "You Never Give Me Your Money," in another thirty-six takes at Olympic Studios. Glyn Johns invited the band to listen to a mixing session for the *Let It Be* material, and they were pleased enough with his work to book a photo session at EMI, replicating their *Please Please Me* cover leaning over the balcony for the proposed new album, *Get Back*. But with so many new songs taking shape, and so many other balls in the air, they stopped short of putting it out.

In early May, Lennon and Ono finally bought a property called Tittenhurst, seventy-two acres of land surrounding a Georgian mansion in Sunningdale, near Ascot in Berkshire, once owned by tycoon Peter Cadbury, for £145,000. Ironically, Lennon had once considered buying the house with Cynthia. Cynthia wrote that she knew it "because John and I had been to look at it with the other Beatles couples a year or two earlier. It was beautiful, with extensive grounds including its own market garden. For a crazy moment we'd considered buying it and all moving in together, in a kind of Beatles commune."[22]

Not that moving into a new home slowed them down. Besotted with their first honeymoon's media triumph, John and Yoko couldn't wait to get back at it, and they set their sights on America. But immigration authorities refused their visitation request because of the previous year's marijuana arrest and their subversive peacenik reputation. Instead, they headed for Montreal, took a suite at the Hôtel Reine Elizabeth, and were granted a ten-day stay from the Canadian government. They snuck out on the third day to apply for a U.S. visa, which never came through. But the strategy worked: from Montreal, they captured a lot of U.S. broadcast attention. This time, Lennon came armed with another new song, "Give Peace a Chance," to record right in the hotel room with their guests, who now comprised both journalists and various celebrities: LSD guru Timothy Leary, comedians Dick Gregory and Tom Smothers, even "Downtown" singer Petula Clark (making some publicist's day). They all crowded around the bed among photographers, news cameramen, and overhanging radio microphones as Lennon led them through the helplessly catchy refrain, encouraging people first to clap on the off-beats, and then the on-beats, which worked better (this being Canada). The debt to Chuck Berry's run-on lines in "Too Much Monkey Business" rang out palpably; as a result, Lennon sang (and faked) the wordy verses while everyone else joined in on the chorus.

Radio calls came in from all over. One from San Francisco's KYA-AM survives, inviting Lennon to hold a bed-in in the "city of love." Another station, WNEW, asked:

> QUESTION: Do you condemn civil rights demonstrations?
> JOHN: I don't condemn them; I'm with them. I'm just saying: Isn't it about time they thought of something else? There have been marches for sixty years. It's ineffective. Someone asked us what would you suggest we do? I said you've got women, use sex. Every day in the popular papers, they have bikini-clad girls. Use sex for peace![23]

In June 1969, *Rolling Stone* magazine ran a report from Ritchie Yorke, who was organizing the Toronto Rock 'n' Roll Festival and hoped to mount another free rock festival there the next summer. Yorke emphasized Lennon's commitment to nonviolence as a way of papering over his surface takes on Russian and European history:

"We're trying to interest young people in doing something for peace," Lennon said, toying with a white carnation. "But it must be done by nonviolent means—otherwise there can be only chaos. We're saying to the young people—and they have always been the hippest ones—we're telling them to get the message across to the squares."

No matter how far out he wandered, Lennon had a gift for following up piffle like that with disarming logic:

What about talking to the people who make the decisions, the power brokers? suggested a cynical reporter. Lennon laughed. "Shit, talk? Talk about what? It doesn't happen like that. In the U.S., the government is too busy talking about how to keep me out. If I'm a joke, as they say, why don't they just let me in?"[24]

By this point, Lennon and Ono were taking heat from leftist papers that criticized the flippancy of sitting in bed as meaningful protest. They answered this charge directly to *Rolling Stone,* and while many remain unconvinced, their argument didn't lack for logic. "We worked for three months thinking out the most functional approach to boosting peace before we got married," Ono told Yorke, "and spent our honeymoon talking to the press in bed in Amsterdam. For us it was the only way. We can't lead a parade or a march because of all the autograph hunters. . . . Bed-ins are something that everybody can do and they're so simple. We're willing to be the world's clowns to make people realize it."[25] By admitting to their clownishness, they trimmed off critiques from all sides.

And they were not just interested in preaching to the converted. For years the Beatles had been forced to meet with town mayors and their daughters for autographs and phony chitchat before or after concerts, part of the duty they paid on their fame. Lennon had always hated being led through such charades. This time, determined to shed his Beatle reputation, he gleefully confronted some of the bigwigs who dropped by to ride his publicity coattails. Cartoonist Al Capp, hardly a conformist himself, entered the suite for an on-camera chat, and he brought along his copy of *Two Virgins* (this sequence appears in the John & Yoko's *Year of Peace* DVD).

"Only the shyest people in the world would take pictures like this," Capp said, holding up the cover as if it proved his point conclusively. When John and Yoko started talking back to him, he looked as if he'd been caught unawares. "What, you don't think shy people ever get naked?" Lennon asked.

"If that isn't a picture of two shy people I'd like to know what 'shyness' is," came Capp's feeble reply. While contending that he "denounced" people who called the picture "filth," Capp clearly viewed it as poor taste at the very least, somewhere out there beyond decency. "I think everybody owes it to the world to prove that they have pubic hair, and you've done it! And I applaud you for it."

Then Capp tried to confront Lennon with his latest Christ quote, from "The Ballad of John and Yoko," but he misquoted the lyric. "Rubbish, I didn't say that," Lennon shot back, correcting him. "The way things are going they're gonna crucify me—and you, baby (laughs)," Lennon scolds him. "And all of us."

At another point, Capp winced at Yoko and let loose a misogynist slap: "You've got to live with that? I can see why you want peace, God knows you can't have much." In the end, Capp walked away grinning to himself, and Lennon's press agent, Derek Taylor, looked appalled. Lennon seemed elated. Finally, after years of politely shaking hands with the locals as a Beatle, he talked back to these "elders" and controlled the conversation. What was it about his music that made people expect him to be "polite" while they insulted his wife, anyway?[26] "I think John behaved very well there," Paul McCartney commented many years later, "because the guy is actually slagging off Yoko—and that's one thing you don't do. You don't slag off someone's missus—that's tribal time, isn't it? I think John was very good. It was: 'Let's not sink to his level.'"[27]

As the latest chapter in John and Yoko's press charade aired around the globe, six-year-old Julian happened to catch his father on television. "What's Dad doing in bed on the telly?" he asked his mother. "Telling everyone it's very important to have peace," Cynthia answered between "gritted teeth, . . . all too aware that John had found it impossible to allow for peace between us and that the small boy asking the question was paying the price."[28]

LENNON'S PRIVATE INTERACTIONS with Cynthia and Julian posed a sharp dissonance to his buffoonish peace theater. Soon after John and Yoko settled at Tittenhurst, Peter Brown relayed an invitation through Cynthia for Julian to join them in their new house for the weekend. Warily, Cynthia consented, and heard mixed feedback from Julian. Her son reported his fear of the dark house at night, as he slept in a separate wing from his father, and that "John sometimes had angry outbursts toward him, shouting at him for the way he ate or being too slow, which had made Julian nervous. He was afraid of provoking John, who switched very quickly from playful to furious." But Cynthia delighted in Julian's new nickname for Yoko: "Hokey-Cokey."[29]

On his next overnight, Lennon, Ono, Kyoko, and Julian all went up to Scotland to visit John's aunt "Mater" Stanley in Golspie (Julia's sister Elizabeth), to romp around his favorite summer vacation haunts and introduce his new family, including Kyoko, now five, to his older cousin Stanley. This was the same Stanley who rode the bus with young John up to Scotland on holidays as a child. Unfortunately, on July 1, while driving with both kids in the car, Lennon veered off the road, overturning the car and landing him and Yoko in the hospital for stitches. Cynthia found out about it from the television—she didn't even know Julian had left Tittenhurst. In the confusion about how to get Julian back to his mother, Peter Brown accidentally booked Cynthia a flight to Belfast, so it took her an extra day to return to Edinburgh, and the hospital informed her that the family had already picked up the children. But she remembers Aunt Mater's reaction to Yoko, and the whole sorry business of Julian and Kyoko.

"Mater regaled me with hilarious tales of Yoko's refusing the roast dinner she had prepared and taking over the kitchen to steam bean sprouts for herself and John. 'She looked like a witch hanging over a cauldron with all that hair,' Mater said." Each instance of Yoko's defiance—to

McCartney, Harrison, his aunt Mater, Cynthia—seems only to have endeared her more to Lennon. She did not fit into any mold of British woman he had ever known. According to Cynthia, John told his aunt of his intentions to take Julian away from Cynthia, which provoked a stern lecture from Mater. And again, just as she had sized up Lennon's mercurial role within the group, Cynthia pinpointed Lennon's wayward behavior with his subliminal goals: "Ultimately, of course, it was John who broke up the Beatles, just as he had formed them in the first place. He had moved on in his life, not just from me but from Paul, the other person who was closest to him throughout the sixties."[30]

DURING THE FIRST WEEKEND in July, on the fifth, the Rolling Stones held a free concert for 250,000 fans in Hyde Park, their first with the new guitarist Mick Taylor, just two days after Brian Jones died in his swimming pool. Paul McCartney watched Jagger read Percy Shelley's "Adonäis" and release thousands of butterflies into the air in Jones's name. Introduced with a fair amount of cheek as "The greatest rock 'n' roll band in the world," the band debuted their new single, "Honky Tonk Women." The Beatles were finishing a new album, and yet the Stones suddenly seemed ascendant.

The other Beatles received word about Lennon's accident while recording at EMI, as the skeleton for the medley with "Golden Slumbers" and "Carry That Weight" took shape in one continuous track on July 7. They had finally determined to mount a new recording project, promising George Martin to behave themselves and turn in work "like before." Harrison's "Here Comes the Sun" followed on July 4. When Lennon returned the following week, he elatedly told his bandmates that Yoko was carrying a new baby. This makes the case for how serious he was about starting a new family with her. Her previous miscarriage, conveniently blamed on the drug bust (not on the heroin), and surviving the Scottish car accident could only indicate that this child was meant to be. She joined them in Studio 2 in a large rented bed, with a microphone hanging over her for comments, as they worked on twenty-one takes of "Maxwell's Silver Hammer" (rehearsed but not recorded in both *The*

White Album and *Let It Be* sessions) and overdubs for "Something" and "You Never Give Me Your Money."

The latest twist on Yoko's studio presence was more awkward than ever, but at least it gave Lennon an excuse to skip the following week's sessions for "Here Comes the Sun," "Something," "Octopus's Garden," and "Oh! Darling." He returned on July 21 to start "Come Together," which began with eight takes for a basic track, overdubbed with lead vocal and other instruments the following day. After that, all four Beatles gathered to make "The End" in seven different takes, with drum solos of varying lengths from Ringo for each take, and do more work on "Oh! Darling" and "Come Together." After McCartney laid down his demo for "Come and Get It," Apple's new Scottish signing, Badfinger, jumped on it as a potential hit single for the *Magic Christian* soundtrack. Lennon listened to McCartney from the control booth, before the band launched into "Sun King" and "Mean Mr. Mustard," recorded as a single track. The next day came overdubs to "Sun King" and "Mean Mr. Mustard," and then "Polythene Pam" segued into "She Came in Through the Bathroom Window" as another continuous track, in thirty-nine takes.

WHILE LENNON SAT OUT many *Abbey Road* sessions, the album was shaping up nicely. And there were even sparks flying in some of the Lennon and McCartney collaborations, now in the form of fitting song fragments together. By the end of July, a rough draft of the song medley emerged: "You Never Give Me Your Money," "Sun King"/"Mean Mr. Mustard," "Her Majesty," "Polythene Pam"/"She Came In Through The Bathroom Window," "Golden Slumbers"/"Carry That Weight," and "The End."

In August, they started work on Lennon's "Because," with George Martin sitting in on an electric Baldwin spinet harpsichord, and tracked the first of three elaborate vocal trios (mixed as nine separate voices) onto take sixteen. With all these basic tracks finished, the Beatles assembled early in the day outside the front gates of EMI Studios on August 8 for a cover shot. Photographer Iain Macmillan stood atop a stepladder with his camera in the middle of Abbey Road to snap the band crossing the zebra crosswalk, back and forth, because they couldn't be bothered to fly to Mount Everest, their grandiose first choice. This fallback shot, four longhairs walking in step with one another across a tree-lined London avenue, became more emblematic than the *Sgt. Pepper* cover itself.

Overdubs and orchestral sessions continued until August 20, when the songs were sequenced and some final edits stitched in. This *Abbey Road* sequencing had a peculiar back twist: the jolting cold finish of "I Want You" had been conceived as the *finale* to the album, with the two sides reversed (the medley being the centerpiece of side one) and the running order of side two as follows: "Come Together," "Something," "Oh! Darling," "Octopus's Garden," "I Want You (She's So Heavy)." The sides were flipped, and the order of side one adjusted—only in the final mastering stages. What sounds like a perfect layout to history's ears came about by inverting the two sides.

The band gathered on Lennon's new Tittenhurst grounds on August 22, wandering around by the former servants' quarters. Everyone had a beard except McCartney; Lennon wore a wide-brimmed hat, and a solemn-faced Ringo had a garish scarf flaring out of his jacket. These became the cover shots to the synthetic American 1970 album, a haphazard singles compilation, called *Hey Jude* (to which there is no remote British counterpart). *Abbey Road* came out the last week of September, and that fall, "Something"/"Come Together" turned into a smash international hit. With the album all but finished, the Beatles took a break and read newspaper reports of a huge rock festival in upstate New York in the middle of that August. In painful contrast to Ono's two miscarriages, Linda McCartney gave birth to Mary, the first of three children with McCartney.

In the weeks before *Abbey Road* appeared, Lennon and Ono worked at their Apple office fielding interviews, signing paperwork, and hatching new schemes. On September 12, the phone rang with a call from someone named John Brower in Toronto. Brower told Lennon's assistant, Anthony Fawcett, about a rock 'n' roll festival happening that weekend featuring Chuck Berry, Little Richard, Jerry Lee Lewis, and Bo Diddley. Lennon grabbed the phone when he saw Fawcett's notes: he agreed to appear for a set if Brower could clear his immigration and visa documents and send him round-trip first-class tickets. Brower blanched: he had simply wanted Lennon to endorse the show, grab a quote for publicity. But his lineup had pushed a button for Lennon.

Alan White, later the drummer for Yes, remembers getting Lennon's phone call about the trip: "I'd like you to play on stage with me," Lennon told him, "I need a drummer. I saw you playing and I really would like you to play with me." White thought someone was playing a prank. Then the phone rang again. "It's John," he said. "I would really like you to come and play. Really, it's me." White had just turned twenty; he gladly obliged.

The next day, a car took him to London Airport, where he met up with John, Yoko, Klaus Voormann, and Eric Clapton in the VIP lounge. "We rehearsed on the airplane," White remembers. "I was playing on the back of the seat and we just played some standards, a couple of Beatles songs. It was put together very quickly."[31]

In addition to rehearsing "Blue Suede Shoes" and "Dizzy Miss Lizzie," Clapton also remembers rehearsing "Be-Bop-A-Lula," Lennon's treasured Gene Vincent song, which didn't make the set. They also worked up "Yer Blues" and a skeletal new number about heroin withdrawal, "Cold Turkey," still shy of its signature guitar lick. "Give Peace a Chance" would close. Lennon famously took ill before the set, which Clapton remembers as sheer rock 'n' roll intimidation: "We found out we were going on between Chuck Berry and Little Richard," he writes, "and John was terrified, overwhelmed I think by the fact that he was going onstage with all his heroes." Backstage, they did "so much blow" that Lennon vomited and Clapton had to lie down.[32]

Energized by the sudden triumph of the Toronto gig, and nonplussed that the Beatles turned the song down, Lennon recorded "Cold Turkey" over two sessions with his new band (with Ringo Starr sitting in for Alan White). The same band laid tracks for Yoko Ono's "Don't Worry Kyoko" at Lansdowne Studios on October 3.

Between Toronto and the studio, Lennon attached a roaring guitar lick to the frame of "Cold Turkey"—a clipped, melodic taunt that bent the classic Chuck Berry gesture into gnarled curves. Somehow, this lick gathered up the song's self-loathing into a single gesture, binding feverish tension into a vortex of assault. (The guitar hook sprouted from similar figures in "Yer Blues," and "I Want You [She's So Heavy].") Hearing the Toronto version back again, you can hardly believe the lick doesn't yet exist—it's as if they're circling around it, chasing it down, fighting hard to figure out where the song wants to land. There are those who steadfastly refuse to believe Lennon ever sniffed or injected heroin, to whom this recording stands as the ultimate reproof. Its unrelenting yawp also takes the measure of Lennon's Beatle withdrawal. The Beatles' refusal to record "Cold Turkey" gave the track a final, unforgiving sting.

This fall also saw John and Yoko return to film, churning out *Honeymoon* and *Rape Part II,* among others. The most famous of these became *Self-Portrait,* an homage to Warhol that froze for forty-two minutes on Lennon's penis. "The critics wouldn't touch it," Lennon boasted. That November, on an apparent whim, Lennon sent his chauffeur to pick up his MBE award from Mimi Smith's mantelpiece in Poole and made headlines anew with his letter to the queen:

> *Your Majesty,*
>   *I am returning my MBE as a protest against Britain's involvement in the Nigeria-Biafra thing, against our support of America in Vietnam and against "Cold Turkey" slipping down the charts.*
>   *With Love,*
>   *John Lennon*[33]

This caused a commotion in the press, especially among those who had originally protested the Beatles award. That flippant "Cold Turkey" remark proved particularly small-minded to some. People who took offense at that kind of thing, however, were just the sort Lennon targeted.

LENNON CONTINUED TO BEHAVE AS IF THE BEATLES were a sideshow to all his new projects, as Apple's priorities finally collided. After *Abbey*

Road appeared, the world soaked up the new music as a gift, happy to deny the evidence of their ears since at least *The White Album:* the four corners of this quartet had stretched its frame beyond the breaking point. This was enough to send Lennon over the edge: on September 20, 1969, as McCartney led off a group meeting by talking about how the Beatles should get back to "little gigs," find their way back to the rooftop heights of "Get Back" and "One After 909," Lennon suddenly summoned the nerve he had been lacking for at least nine months. As McCartney puts it, "John looked at me in the eye and said, 'Well, I think you're daft. I wasn't going to tell you till we signed the Capitol deal but I'm leaving the group.' We paled visibly and our jaws slackened a bit."[34] Later, Lennon admitted:

> I knew before we went to Toronto. I told Allen [Klein] I was leaving, I told Eric Clapton and Klaus that I was leaving and that I'd like to probably use them as a group. I hadn't decided how to do it—to have a permanent new group or what? And then later on I thought, "Fuck, I'm not going to get stuck with another set of people, Whoever they are." So I announced it to myself and to the people around me on the way to Toronto. Allen came with me, and I told Allen it was over. When I got back there were a few meetings and Allen had said, "Cool it," 'cause there was a lot to do [with the Beatles] business-wise, and it would not have been suitable at the time.[35]

Kim Fowley, rock scenester and announcer at the Toronto show, remembers talking to Lennon backstage about how the Beatles had "failed": "We stopped making records we wanted to hear ourselves, where every track was better than the last," Lennon told him.[36]

Poring over these dates, a vague lineage to Lennon's outrage emerges: *Abbey Road* mixed, sequenced, released; jumping off the ledge at the Toronto Rock 'n' Roll Revival with a new band; returning to offer "Cold Turkey" to the Beatles; sensing a finality to their rebuff; heading into the studio anyway with Ringo and cutting his first great solo rock 'n' roll track . . . no wonder Lennon finally had what it took to make his announcement: if Paul had offered "Come and Get It" to the Beatles and been turned down, he might well have behaved in kind. Instead, McCartney saved his working drafts ("Teddy Boy" from the *Get Back* sessions, and soon "Every Night" and "Maybe I'm Amazed") for his solo album the following spring.

Lennon promised not to go public with his announcement, however, since Klein had started delicate negotiations with EMI to extend the Beatles' contract. With the Beatles' assets frozen since the Northern Songs takeover, everybody understood the need for new revenue—they all had lawyers to pay. Klein's new terms with EMI proved winning: he boosted the Beatles' royalty rate from 17.5 percent to 25 percent on U.S. sales and committed the band to two albums per year, either as a group or individually (this provided a significant loophole). And their new royalty terms jumped to $0.58 per album until 1972, when the number leapt to $0.72. Reissues were assigned the rate of $0.55, increasing to $0.72.[37] These rates were the highest in the industry up to that point, so in Lennon's eyes, Klein had proved effective.

But Klein had also promised to get Northern Songs "for nothing," and negotiations with ATV had disintegrated. Klein's plan involved taking out several loans against Apple Corps to buy back Northern Songs. But McCartney's father-in-law, Lee Eastman, sent ATV a letter saying Klein had no authorization to act on Apple's behalf (McCartney had never signed with Klein, although he had given Klein the verbal go-ahead for the deal). Understandably, ATV backed out.

Both ATV and Apple then launched campaigns directly to a small block of investors, for control of Northern Songs' shares. During this lobbying, a Lennon quote hit the papers that shattered his own shareholders' faith: "I'm not going to be fucked around by men in suits sitting on their fat arses in the City!"[38] This tipped wary investors over to ATV's side. The existing Lennon-McCartney publishing contract obligated them to continue writing songs for the company through 1973. But with no control over the company's direction, they decided to sell their shares and simply collect royalties on songs they'd already written, divesting themselves of any future attachments to ATV. Lennon and McCartney sold their stock in October 1969 for £3.5 million. Harrison and Starr chose to keep their shares.[39]

As this transaction went forward, Lennon learned that McCartney owned more stock than he did: his songwriter partner had been instructing their mutual Apple aide, Peter Brown, to buy up shares in secret. When the paperwork revealed this, Lennon's take was 644,000 shares (worth £1.25 million) and McCartney's added up to 751,000 shares (£1.4 million). The discrepancy meant far less to Lennon than his partner's deception. A verbal agreement had been broken: they had set up Northern Songs with equal shares in their songwriting concern. As far as Lennon could tell, if they had not been forced to sell at this point, McCartney might have gone on scavenging shares indefinitely. Northern Songs carved up ownership as follows: the principal songwriters, Lennon and McCartney, each held 15 percent; Brian Epstein's NEMS received 7.5 percent; Dick James and his partner Charles Silver nabbed 37.5 percent each; Harrison and Starr a mere 1.6 percent each. Lennon could not have been more shocked: not only had Epstein sold them out for a pittance, but his own songwriting partner, an intimate since age seventeen, had gone behind his back to gain more influence in their publishing. Lennon spoke of McCartney's betrayal until he died; McCartney rarely mentions it. It's hard to fathom that *Abbey Road* would have been made if Lennon had learned of this even three months sooner.

Then, on October 12, Yoko miscarried again. By current standards, nobody paid much attention to the baseline chain-smoking and drinking that wallpapered their daily lives. But of course neither of them had come to grips with drugs, and with the suggestion of heroin in her system as recently as January (when they joshed about shooting up with Peter Sellers), it's a wonder she conceived and carried the child as long as she did. This time, however, events plowed under whatever grief John and Yoko endured over the loss. Lennon, glad for the distractions, hurtled ever forward. Surely, nature wouldn't keep on robbing him, not after everything he had suffered to get this far to find his creative new life partner and begin a new direction. Given the scanty evidence of a plunge, he seems to have recovered much sooner than he did from Ono's first miscarriage just seven months previously.

Lennon kept his promise not to let the band's fallout leak to the press, but more and more he behaved like a free man, just as he had done increasingly since he latched on to Yoko Ono. *Abbey Road* sailed onto the charts, and George Harrison enjoyed a deliriously sunny hit single with "Something," his first Beatle A side (the B side, Lennon's "Come Together," commanded a lot of radio as well). And most hard-core fans stayed in denial about the farewell gestures encoded in the album's layout. At Christmas 1969, John and Yoko punctuated their bed-in year with an ambitious billboard campaign, featuring enormous white spaces in Times Square, New York; London; and eight other major cities. The signs read:

WAR IS OVER!
IF YOU WANT IT
Happy Christmas from John & Yoko

At the press conference held announcing the campaign, a reporter shouted out, "How much does all of this cost?" "We don't know," Lennon answered. "But we're accepting donations, and we've already had some, and anyway however much it costs it's less than a single human life."[40]

An expanded defense of his peace campaigns came in an early 1971 interview with Richard Robinson: "Yes, they sell war beautifully. I mean they've really got it sewn up you know. TV and everything. They've conned a lot of our people into . . . They're busy shaking their fist at the *Daily Express* saying what they wanted in any disguise they like, either topless or paper bag or whatever publicity gimmick you're using."[41]

Almost as if they had to squeeze in more activity before the decade slammed shut, John and Yoko made appearances and returned to Canada before spending their last Christmas in England. They joined George Harrison for some gigs with the Delaney and Bonnie band at the Lyceum Ballroom, billed as "Peace for Christmas." Apparently, Eric Clapton, who invited Harrison, enjoyed blending into the rest of the group instead of shouldering superstar expectations, and alongside Klaus Voormann, Bobby Keys, Billy Preston, and drummers Keith Moon, Alan White, and Jim Gordon, Lennon appeared as first among equals.

Together, they piled on for a seven-minute version of "Cold Turkey" and then Ono's "Don't Worry Kyoko (Mummy's Only Looking for Her Hand in the Snow)" stretched to over half an hour. Also on the bill: the Hot Chocolate Band, the Pioneers, the Rascals, Jimmy Cliff, Black Velvet, and disc-jockey "Emperor Rosko." John and Yoko capped off the 1960s by returning to Canada, where Prime Minister Pierre Trudeau, known as a jet-setter, agreed to meet with them. They spent forty-five minutes in his office, and Lennon left with promises of Canadian government assistance for the peace festival he hoped to mount the following summer. Afterward, they met with the critic and futurist Marshall McCluhan, author of *The Medium Is the Massage* and among the first to recognize the Beatles' intuitive grasp of multimedia mythology. He had just set up a new department at Toronto University, where he taught a radical new field, Media Studies.

RELAXING IN HIS NEW HOME over the holidays, Lennon submitted to several days of interviews with zoologist and surreal artist Desmond Morris, best known for his book *The Naked Ape* (1967). Morris had selected Lennon for his portion of a TV show devoted to the sixties, called *Men of the Decade*. The program aired on the BBC on December 30, and a lot of this footage shot on Tittenhurst's grounds can be seen in the 1998 documentary *Imagine: John Lennon*. For his portion, Lennon joined portraits of Ho Chi Minh, chosen by Mary McCarthy, and John F. Kennedy, chosen by Alistair Cooke.

Morris had progressive ideas in mind, and his interview quoted Lennon roaming his estate on December 2, intercut with clips from the Beatles' career, his songs, his bed-ins, and drug arrest, reflecting on the counterculture, peace, and how quickly the cultural ground had shifted during his seven years of fame. Lennon seemed particularly taken with Woodstock as a cultural symbol: "The biggest mass of people ever gathered together for anything other than war," he enthused. "Nobody had that big an army that didn't kill somebody or have some kind of violent scene like the Romans or whatever, even a Beatle concert was more violent than that and that was just 50,000. And so the good things that came out were all this vast peaceful movement."[42]

Morris tried to smooth Lennon's radicalism for the mainstream by interpreting his sensibility as forward-thinking: "This eccentricity of his is more than a mere anti-establishment device, it also represents a plea for fantasy—if you like—in an unromantic age, a plea for the unofficial and the inconsequential in an age of officialment over organisation, a plea for unsophisticated fun in an age of sophisticated weapons. Above all—it's a plea for optimism."

Lennon himself continues:

This is only the beginning—this sixties bit was just a sniff, the sixties were just waking up in the morning and we haven't even got to dinner time yet and I can't wait, I just can't wait I'm so glad to be around and it's just going to be great and there's going to be more and more of us, and whatever you're thinking there Mrs. Grundy of South Birmingham on toast, you don't stand a chance. (A) You're not going to be there when we're running it and (B) you're gonna like it when you get less frightened of it.

At the end of the show, Morris told the audience how their poll for the decade's greatest figures had turned out, with Lennon the only pop star:

> President Kennedy
> Sir Winston Churchill
> Dr. Barnard
> Mr. Harold Wilson
> Prince Charles
> Prince Philip
> H.M. the Queen
> President Ho Chi Minh
> John Lennon

Ranking up there with Churchill must have given Lennon a jolt— the name he had just shed alongside the name that was too controversial to be listed in full (note the omission of "Ono" in Lennon's listing). And that list planted a seed in Lennon's mind. Soon he plucked the name "Kennedy," but not Churchill, out for use in a new song. (The Beatles had already skewered Wilson in Harrison's "Taxman.")

There was plenty to cherish as Lennon walked the grounds at Tittenhurst with Desmond Morris: in the previous eighteen months, he had extricated himself from a static marriage and completely revamped his public image outside his band, and he was settled in his new mansion with his brainy Japanese wife who had almost as many crazy ideas as he did on a daily basis.

Lennon's curious humility sparred with hubris as he pored over the decade and how the next one stretched out in front of them. He had left the Beatles but agreed to keep that under his hat as Klein negotiated with EMI to keep Apple afloat. Yoko had transformed his life and given him ideas about how to step outside his Beatle identity, but they had already suffered two miscarriages together, and such trials are not for sissies. As at many different junctures with the Beatles, Lennon turned his transition away from the band into a theme; the questions of identity, and solo careers in the immense shadow of the Beatles, now began to hang over all of them. Once this new riddle grabbed hold of Lennon, his typical impertinence wrung it for all the material he could. He had started by redefining himself through Yoko, but he underplayed how traumatic leaving the Beatles was to his pride. In the months to come, Lennon's muse kept insisting that despite all his losses, including Yoko's two miscarriages across eleven months in 1968–69, he had not yet begun to grieve.

BEYOND BEATLES

1970–1980

Just We Two

L ENNON'S SOLO YEARS TRACE A RADICALLY DIFFERENT CREATIVE ARC from his Beatle career. By adopting a Scouser's lower-class resentment to sneer his way into show business and conquer the world ("just rattle your jewelry"), his songwriting guile as a Beatle veered between musical fox and spiritual jape; hit movie songs and romantic ballads underwrote experimental rock concepts and lurching self-expression. In the sixties, Lennon had increasingly defined himself against McCartney to stretch standard songs toward impudent forms: the love triangles in "She Loves You," "If I Fell," and "You're Gonna Lose That Girl" sprint forward into coy first-personisms, like "Norwegian Wood" and "Nowhere Man," and on through single-chord tape fantasias like "Tomorrow Never Knows," even more personal statements like "Strawberry Fields Forever," and toward the outer reaches of "I Am the Walrus," "Glass Onion," "Happiness Is a Warm Gun," and his kitchen-sink manifesto "Revolution 9."

Lennon's radical threads dovetailed into early experimental solo efforts with Yoko Ono. Then, just as he set out on his own from the safest show-business harbor anybody had ever conceived, he redirected these stylistic extremes back into conservative frames. "Come Together" wedged hallucinatory doggerel into a tightly knit blues. And where "Hey Bulldog" and "I Dig a Pony" suspended nonsense atop blues forms, the daring on *Plastic Ono Band,* his first post-Beatle solo effort, is all thematic—here, even his lyrics trace a new minimalism. As if he couldn't simply release something on his own, Yoko Ono's *Plastic Ono Band* album is the experimental mirror piece, and it still holds up extremely well, given that her strong suit was more visual and conceptual than musical. (Nobody would mistake these albums except for the title they share.) Anyone still underrating Lennon's guitar flair needs to account for his yammering squalls on Ono's "Why" or his slide work on "Why Not."

The Beatles' career now assumes such a familiar shape in rock mythology that it's easy to forget their pioneering stature at the time. In late 1987, critic Mark Moses summed up the band's influence back when reviewing an installment of their CD reissues for the *Boston Phoenix:* "Somewhere in our subconscious, we expect sufficiently ambitious bands to have life spans that mimic the contours and even the tempo of the Beatles'. In its grossest form, their trajectory could be described as frenzied pop mastery / unstuffy elegance / conceptual coup / renunciation of conceptual coup / end in pieces."[1] One way of looking at Lennon's solo work is as Beatle John in reverse: blazing string of hit singles ("Give Peace a Chance," "Cold Turkey," "Instant Karma," "Power to the People") / kiss-of-death critical breakthrough (*Plastic Ono Band*) / utopian popular surge (*Imagine*) / political animus (*Some Time in New York City*) / midlife crisis as cautionary tale (the Los Angeles Troubadour incidents) / mid-period lull (*Mind Games, Walls and Bridges, Pussy Cats*) / celebrity collaborations (Elton John, David Bowie) / roots move (*Rock 'n' Roll*) / greatest hits (*Shaved Fish*) / retire early: grand pause. Then: comeback.

Compared to his Beatle period, Lennon's emotional life became ever more bound up with his work: during the sixties, his creative work collided with reality at irregular intervals; he wrote his most revealing song, "Strawberry Fields Forever," while alone in Spain in October 1966. *Rubber Soul, Revolver,* and *Sgt. Pepper* countered an emotional black hole, which boomeranged back into so-called "reality" through more sobering material typified on *The White Album* and in later blues forms. In the early seventies, Lennon's mediocre work channeled his emotional ennui more directly—his solo period contains weak records, but they tend to be weak in interesting ways. And his vocal audacity rescued him from many a wrong move. The hinge between these two periods comes with *Plastic Ono Band*, a thematic extension of "Cold Turkey," which equated heroin withdrawal with pulling out of the Beatles.

Reducing Lennon's end-game to pithy quips dramatizes just how far outside typical pop norms the new John Lennon brand reached. Insiders seesawed between delight and bewilderment at his uneven muse; the larger audience adopted him as another wacky eccentric who showed up on Dick Cavett or Mike Douglas or the Jerry Lewis telethon, paraded through wire stories and pulp magazines, presented at the Grammys or duetted with Elton John. Once again, the Atlantic Ocean barely explained the huge gap in Lennon's persona: his British homeland never forgave him for relocating to America, while American fans cherished his presence and joined his battle for residency. He willingly traded his musical integrity to support radical causes: aesthetics became less important than protesting injustice ("John Sinclair," "Attica State") and feminism ("Woman Is the Nigger of the World," "Woman").

The Beatles and the 1960s defined each other, but for such a political decade, most of their music aimed somewhere beyond politics. Toward the end, Lennon pushed his peers to comment more directly on their era. Similarly, Lennon's solo persona took shape as the sixties unraveled: his individual voice developed as America suffered a malignant presidency and constitutional crisis, and his marital squalls paralleled his legal battles, both over residency and intellectual property rights. He joined Woody Guthrie, Martin Luther King Jr., Charlie Chaplin, and many, many others in J. Edgar Hoover's impressive string of intimate enemies. To British ears, a Japanese wife, cultural resentment, and radical politics made this post-Beatle Lennon seem vaguely ungrateful; to Americans, flashing a peace sign for photographer Bob Gruen in front of the Statue of Liberty, there were few greater symbolic Americans.

Paradoxically, the theme that grew increasingly more intense during Lennon's solo career was his ongoing competition with Paul McCartney for a hit single, career reversal, or defining moment—the song, album, or tour when either might confidently step outside the other's shadow. Lennon began breaking away from the band long before McCartney accepted the end, and the two wrote coded telegrams to each other across the pond as though volleying tennis balls of resentment and reproof as only sibling rivals could. McCartney's high point during Lennon's lifetime was *Band on the Run* from 1973, which contained "Let Me Roll It," a guitar hook clawed from the death grip of "Cold Turkey." Lennon slammed the door on the band by boldfacing his self-confidence, screaming, "I don't believe in Beatles," only to lob "How Do You Sleep?" to emphasize how defensive he remained. Without the Beatles to frame his braggadocio, each Lennon outburst sheathed insecurity. Lennon and McCartney each had more than enough talent to sustain himself with original material, but looking over their shoulders noticeably distracted both.

To THE BEATLES AS INDIVIDUALS, the band's dissolution had wrenching emotional effects. Typically, McCartney hid his grief by retreating up to rural Scotland; Lennon lashed out at anyone and everything for his first two solo albums. In symbolic terms, the end of the group took on vast cultural ripples, to the point where the messy legal battles became symbolic of how hard it was to let go of the larger Beatle ideal and the cultural authority their albums conferred.

To start with, the Beatle catalog retained such vitality on radio that it seemed cheap to watch this band dissolve in a blizzard of lawsuits. Courtroom haggling demeaned their aesthetic significance and corroded a lot of the charm they had traded on for so long. For the Lennon-McCartney songwriting team, so long a symbol of individualism within a larger partnership, crashing on the banal rocks of a showbiz publishing feud reflected an era's coming-of-age anxiety. Well into the seventies, the 1960s still refused to die.

Every Beatle year between 1962 and 1969 brought convulsive changes in both persona and musical development, rippling outward into the way everybody absorbed and interpreted the band's influence; how people thought and behaved, the ideas they carried around about themselves and their world, had forever changed. Now came the biggest change of all: the fallout and aftermath of show business's biggest brand. Because the Beatles were as much pure symbol as they were musicians, the whole collapse-of-empire story became a tussle all by itself: who would control this narrative? In these mythological terms, John, Paul, George, and Ringo were already ancient, so it took years for everybody—these solo artists and an audience reluctant to let go of any possibility of reunion—to accept the new reality.

Lennon did his best to nudge things along. But dropping his Beatle persona meant confronting why he had erected such a beguiling façade in the first place. The end of the Beatles meant peeling back skin, exposing old wounds. When his defining band began to topple around him, all Lennon knew how to do was grab on tight to the woman who seemed to understand him best and lurch forward into parts unknown. Yoko Ono helped persuade him to aim at rock star fame beyond even Beatle fame: his solo status comprised a multimedia performance artist who dabbled in politics and whose marriage constituted a new writing partnership, voicing new utopian ideals nestled in a romantic frame. And whatever else everybody made of their romantic hype, all arrows pointed toward a true partnership. Until 1973, John and Yoko spent few nights apart— and Lennon liked to brag about bringing her into the men's room. Now, as the press began publishing his quotes about feeling frustrated inside the band that had carried him for so long, Lennon adopted an even fiercer tough-guy cheek while one-upping every celebrity couple since Taylor and Burton.

Lennon left the band quite literally kicking and screaming. McCartney, outmaneuvered and outnumbered by Lennon, Harrison, Starr, and Klein, retreated with his new young family and gathered up his spirits for the coming fight. Linda, who already had a daughter, Heather, from her first marriage, gave birth to Mary at the end of August 1969. In those days, Linda took as much grief from McCartney fans loitering around his Cavendish Avenue home as Yoko did from racist hate mail, usually postmarked UK. Lennon carried on with Ono in public as though nothing much had changed: the Beatles had just released an album and spun off a huge international hit with George Harrison's old-fashioned romance, "Something." But the B side, Lennon's hushed, inviolable "Come Together," received lots of airplay, reminding pop how many leagues ahead of the game the Beatles remained.

To Lennon's mind, however, another hit record played straight into Beatle myth. Wasn't new product just another way of fulfilling everybody's overhyped expectations? They had now released two complete albums built from fragments, and everybody on the inside could see they worked more and more independently. The ensemble peaks of *The White Album* and *Abbey Road* happened in spite of their faltering friendships, not because of them. (This ironic tension between the band's musical fluidity and their interpersonal squabbling rivals even Harrison's late songwriting surge.) And the four musicians had still not reconciled what to do with the *Get Back* tapes, which they feared might ruin their reputation.

Beatle news was old news; new windmills called Lennon's name daily. He used his ground-floor Apple office to hold court with the press, sent acorns to politicians to plant for peace, worked on lithographs, and carried on in general like the madman he hoped the world still adored. There had always been a certain flexibility about the band and its aura; Lennon simply carried a bigger megaphone than the others—McCartney and Harrison had each worked independently on movie soundtracks, and Ringo dreamt of an acting career. As long as they took care of musical business together, Lennon felt free to carry on with whatever else caught his fancy. In this post-Woodstock autumn, as *Abbey Road* graced the airwaves, EMI—and the Beatles' worldwide audience—resisted rumors of the band's imminent breakup simply by wishing that the music had once again won out over the band's conflicts.

As far as the public knew, *Abbey Road* sounded like another conquest, complete with iconic album cover and imaginative musical expanse. When pressed, even fans might admit to two side one clunkers, Ringo's "Octopus's Garden," which sounded like a mere "Yellow Submarine" sequel, and McCartney's overbaked trifle "Maxwell's Silver Hammer," which Lennon loathed (calling it "granny music"). Without the churlish undercurrents of "Ob-La-Di, Ob-La-Da," the synthesizer sheen in

"Maxwell" quickly wore thin. If only McCartney had let Lennon take a run at the lead vocal of "Oh! Darling."

As he turned his sights on his new life with Yoko Ono, Lennon expected a reprieve, or at least a whiff of relief. But the Beatles were not something anybody, even of Lennon's outsize eccentricities, could simply set to one side. He had put it best himself back in 1963, to Michael Braun: "This isn't show business. It's something else."[2]

DEALING WITH THIS CONFOUNDING BEATLE SYMBOLISM became Lennon's next great subject: the Beatle cataclysm cried out for a soundtrack; perhaps he could use his parents as some kind of allegory. The biggest band in the world would necessarily throw the longest, most excruciating wrap party, right? And whatever "Cold Turkey" had represented (withdrawal projected outward, a bomb tossed at royalty and its subscribers by returning his MBE, among other metaphors), its anguished concision left a lot of ideas on the table. Even as Harrison and Starr joined up with Lennon and Klein, Lennon must have blanched at how the Beatles could actually turn "Cold Turkey" down—now there was a starting point. Time to dream up the next big thing.

Naturally, telescoping his new partnership into the end of his band complicated the new, improved John and Yoko romantic image, too: perhaps if the Beatles survived as fiction, he might fall back on them still. That way, Lennon could project fearlessness beyond what he felt capable of. If the Beatles were really over, that meant free fall, and none of his most intimate friends to bounce off of. And so, in his inimitable, discursive manner, he simply plowed forward.

In many ways, Lennon and the others had already faced this new struggle squarely, even sung it with lust, in "Carry That Weight," which was impossible not to hear as intimidating yet collapsing faith in their own legacy. All of the ex-Beatles would spend the rest of their careers trapped in this defining conundrum: how to create new music for themselves that didn't depend on the Beatles. In many ways, Ringo Starr was best positioned for this mission, and his first two solo albums rival *McCartney* and *Plastic Ono Band* for sheer pluck. *Sentimental Journey,* which commissioned big-band arrangements from leading orchestrators (like the pre–Michael Jackson Quincy Jones) for the songs of Ringo's Tin Pan Alley childhood, makes for a respectable farce: Ringo as crooner, who invests material like "Stardust" and "Love Is a Many-Splendored Thing" with a goofy grin, whimsy of inimitable understatement. Doing Tin Pan Alley, Ringo was still far preferable to, say, Jack Jones or John Davidson. On the other hand, Ringo never got to host his own game show.

Starr's *Beaucoups of Blues,* a Nashville session, brought the same flair to country songs, chiefly by Charlie Howard ("Love Don't Last Long" and "I Wouldn't Have You Any Other Way") and Sorrells Pickard ("Without Her" and "Silent Homecoming"). Ringo, a "shit-kicker" from the Dingle, sounded like a Nashville hick. And with hands like Pete Drake on steel and D. J. Fontana on drums (Presley's Sun Studios drummer), he could relax and let the band carry him. Most British critics abhor these sides, while Americans tend to ignore them. Unlike the other three, you get the distinct impression Ringo would have killed to play Vegas.

Harrison, on the other hand, flooded the engine with a double album, *All Things Must Pass,* overproduced by girl group svengali Phil Spector and supplanted by a third disc of ungainly jams (warm-ups that are more fun to participate in than to listen to). For a while there in 1970, Lennon had to read headlines like MAYBE GEORGE WAS ALWAYS THE MOST TALENTED AFTER ALL, which only fueled his revenge fantasies.

As the most overtly and expressively self-conscious of the four, Lennon knew full well that listeners would always compare anything he did to his immensely popular work with his former band, which made him timid in ways he hadn't bargained for, and wasn't used to. He compensated by reverting to his earliest pleasures, his wackiest instincts and most subversive impulses. In early 1970, this meant flailing about and grasping at chances as songs took shape. And in addition to Yoko, he turned to another musical partner to guide his voice and material for tape: Phil Spector, the titan he'd always wanted to work with.

"Allen [Klein], Yoko and I had been talking about him [Spector]," Lennon told Spector's early biographer Richard Williams. "He'd had some kind of relationship with Allen, not a business one . . . or maybe it was. Anyway, they knew each other, and Klein really put us together. That's one of Allen's arts, bringing people together. It's like a patron in the Arts. I mean, patrons used to get their percentages as well. . . . It's the same kind of thing."[3]

Paradoxically, his insecurity fed Lennon's enormous ambition: his first several solo records (the singles "Cold Turkey," "Instant Karma," "Power to the People," and "Happy Xmas [War Is Over]" and the *Plastic Ono Band* and *Imagine* albums) count as his best, made at the most precarious time for his emerging new identity, at many of the same studios he had worked at as a Beatle. For *Plastic Ono Band* and "Cold Turkey," he deliberately chose Ringo Starr as his drummer, which conveyed both aesthetic insecurity and bold self-possession. (His choice of Manfred Mann's Klaus Voormann on bass doubled as a cold, hard slap in the face to McCartney. No scene-stealing from the lower staves, thank you.)

One theme that emerged from this early solo period was just how chaotic and restless Lennon's sense of self always had been—it was there underneath all those different Beatle guises, and it cropped up again in solo forms: towering pop romantic ("Instant Karma"), moon-howling ex-lover as wounded narcissist (*Plastic Ono Band*), New Age sage ("Imagine"), protest-song pamphleteer (*Some Time in New York City*), middle-aged cage-rattler and nostalgist (*Mind Games, Walls and Bridges*), hopeless and defiant romantic ("Stand by Me" and *Rock 'n' Roll*), and finally, aging hippie house-husband on extended leave and father-redeemed-by-son in *Double Fantasy*. Each of these personas required steady maintenance, and Lennon was at his most revealing when caught contradicting his own billboards, either singing with others or trying to fit an outsize ideal into a half-assed concept. In retrospect, it's clear just how hard he fought to get out from under the Beatle curse. In the end, though, he lived up to his sign-off line on the defining solo debut: "I just believe in me . . . Yoko and me . . . and that's reality," the corny, self-deflating myth of the giant who foreswore his kingdom for truth and beauty, only to lose everything so he could fight for it on adult terms all over again.

THE FOUR SOLO CAREERS unveiled previously hidden internal politics as each man packed and moved out from the cozy Beatle mansion. Lennon seemed closest to Ringo, and then George; neither Harrison nor Lennon ever appeared on a McCartney solo album or vice-versa, whereas Ringo played for all three. Of course, Lennon's solo "career" had begun as early as 1968 with numbers like "What's the New Mary Jane" and "Revolution 9" during the *White Album* sessions, and then his avant-garde projects with Ono. Casual jams reflected these affinities as well: John and Yoko appeared onstage with George Harrison, Eric Clapton, and the Bonnie and Delaney band in London in December of 1969. Harrison was slumming with the band after sitting in for a night and having rather too much fun; he appeared onstage anonymously until it got reported in the music press. Mostly they got away with two weeks of touring, with Clapton and Harrison sharing lead guitars almost before most audiences figured this out.

Only two semi–Beatle reunions reached the press in the early seventies, both offstage. McCartney joined Starr, Clapton, and others at Mick and Bianca Jagger's wedding in Saint-Tropez in 1971; and Lennon, Harrison, and Starr did a session for Ringo's *Ringo* album early in 1973 in Los Angeles. Harrison and Lennon often sat in on each other's solo tracks, and drummer Alan White remembers Lennon anonymously adding acoustic guitar to *All Things Must Pass*. Harrison appeared on *Imagine* (1971), *Mind Games* (1973), and *Walls and Bridges* (1974). Ringo appeared on all three others' solo records, most notably Lennon's first, *Plastic Ono Band*, where he set down a new visceral authority in rock drumming and teased a new riddle from the band's interpersonal chemistry: here Lennon and Starr's musical intimacies rival Lennon and McCartney's.

McCartney contributed material and played and sang on Ringo albums (most notably on 1973's *Ringo*, with a standout track, "Six O'Clock"), but never on a Lennon or Harrison solo record. Lennon also contributed to Ringo's projects (1973's "I Am the Greatest," which rivals

"With a Little Help from My Friends" as a Ringo signature, plus a guide vocal of the Platters' "Only You" and the writing of "Goodnight Vienna" the following year). On Harrison's work, Lennon chose anonymity. Lennon and McCartney never played on each other's solo sessions, save for one informal Los Angeles jam from 1974, bootlegged as *A Toot and a Snore,* named for a snowy-oldies session with Lennon, McCartney (on drums), and Stevie Wonder; the dates coincide with reports about McCartney's visit to Lennon's Malibu hangout with Starr, Keith Moon, and Harry Nilsson. However, to prevent runaway rumors and preserve their hard-fought integrity as solo figures, Lennon and McCartney visited far more often and warmly throughout the seventies than they let on to the press.

But in the beginning, the spat had an epic stature, and when Lennon used the term "divorce," few considered it an exaggeration. Never one to acknowledge grief, let alone submit to it, Lennon seems to have been so convinced of his choices that grieving came as a surprise, if it came consciously at all. The pop world at large may have lost its center, but Lennon seemed to feel everything more keenly, and in more complicated fashion, than the other three. As usual, he wanted his future to happen yesterday, the way some songs just tumbled out. But his divorce from the Beatles made his divorce from Cynthia look like child's play, since these early conflicts defined the legacy of the Lennon-McCartney publishing catalog indefinitely.

THE BEATLES MADE IT THROUGH 1969 intact, if only in spirit. Part of the problem came from the façade they felt forced to construct around Apple. Some cite reports of Lennon's decision to quit the band as early as November 1968, when the others probably greeted it with the same bemused alarm with which they took in his announcement that he was Jesus Christ six months earlier.

This fiction, of an ongoing band with a future, came apart in a series of events over which they quickly lost control, and of which Lennon typically considered himself the victim. The *Two Virgins* controversy resurfaced as police raided Lennon's erotic lithographs from the London

Arts Gallery on New Bond Street on January 16, 1970. The gallery reopened that afternoon, but a summons entered Lennon's legal file, and the underground reveled in how eagerly the authorities leapt for the bait.

Combined with John and Yoko's peace campaigns, these tired obscenity charges stoked an increasing cynicism in the expanding boomer electorate. In Britain, this culminated in the *International Times* obscenity case, which sent its editor, John Hopkins, to jail. To British youth, this seemed unfathomable: the American student protests had grown far bigger in number, and the black power movement raised the ominous specter of radicals with automatic rifles terrorizing the post-riot world. That the UK government had succeeded in sending student leftists to jail for pictures of nipples seemed the height of absurdity, especially given the volatile, progressive fumes rock 'n' roll had been spewing for years. A feeling of defeat hung over the counterculture as the new decade crept into view.

After a trip to Denmark to visit Ono's daughter Kyoko, who was living there with her father, Lennon tooled around in a snowmobile, and the couple shaved their heads to auction off their locks "for peace." The new Tittenhurst mansion they planned to move into underwent renovations for a new studio, so they stayed with friends and moved in slowly as work progressed. Part of Anthony Cox's divorce agreement with Yoko allowed him to film the couple for several days, granting him exclusive rights to the content.[4]

Approximately one hundred twenty minutes of this cinema verité circulates in bootleg circles. The footage features a single handheld camera for an extended look at John and Yoko, roaming around a kitchen area and some bedrooms, listening to the radio, rolling joints, and watching TV with their new political cause, Michael X, a British Malcolm X wannabe who latched onto rock star patronage. The only dramatic moments come at the end, when Lennon appears on *Top of the Pops* to sing "Instant Karma," with Yoko behind him, knitting blindfolded.

The song's uplift rebuffed any cultural malaise. Lennon had woken up on January 27 with a new song exploding in his head, music that felt like the antithesis of "Cold Turkey" and all its careening exhaustion. He ordered a piano delivered to his Apple office and jumped in his car to lunge at one of his long-held pop ideals: to record and mix a single in one day. Everybody who heard it knew it was a hit, and EMI could barely get it out fast enough for Lennon: it appeared on February 9.

"I'm fascinated by commercials and promotion as an art form," Lennon said later, "I enjoy them. So the idea of 'Instant Karma' was like the idea of instant coffee, presenting something in a new form. I wrote it in the morning on the piano, and went into the office and I sang it many times. And I said 'Hell, let's do it,' and we booked the studio, and Phil came in and he said: 'How do you want it?' And I said 'fifties,' and he said, 'Right,' and boom, I did it, in about three goes. He played it back and there it was."[5]

Richard Williams also talked later on about that day with Lennon:

It was a surprise session, typical of those days. Alan White remembers getting a phone call, saying that John wanted to do a session at EMI, and White "just turned up." According to John, Spector was absent as the evening began. "We were playing, and we weren't getting very far," he remembered. "I knew I had a hit record. I'd written it that morning, and I knew I had it, but it would've taken me a couple of days to make, building up and building up and running between the two rooms. That way, it might have turned out very heavy and funky, like 'Cold Turkey,' but then Spector walked in."[6]

Alan White, the Toronto Plastic Ono Band drummer, tried out a wayward drum fill in the middle of the second verse that Lennon adored—after the line "Why in the world are we here?" White tilted the whole track sideways for a few bars and then jumped right back into the groove, as if some alternate reality tore a brief hole in the song. (This linked the material with other deliberate Beatle mistakes, like the extra beat in "Revolution," or the sideways 6/4 bar that launches the coda to "Everybody's Got Something to Hide Except for Me and My Monkey.") With Harrison on guitar and leading the chorus, it all jelled spontaneously: "Suddenly when we went in the room and heard what [Spector had] done to it . . . it was fantastic. It sounded like there was fifty people playing." Some hangers-on got in a car, "drove into central London to a discothèque," noted Williams, "and dragged people out to the studio to sing the infectious chorus, 'All shine on . . . like the moon and the stars and the sun,' behind John."[7]

One of these people happened to be Beryl Marsden, the young Liverpool singer Lennon had admired at the Cavern. Lennon was thrilled with the original rough mix that came out in Britain. But Spector snuck back to the States and kept working on it, and Capitol put out a remixed version of the song for the U.S. market later in the month. "It's the only time anyone's done *that,*" Lennon told Williams, sarcastically berating both Spector's pretension and Capitol's history of fiddling with Beatle tracks, a practice he took care to avoid as a solo artist.

As EARLY AS MAY 1969, WHILE LENNON, Harrison, and Spector worked on "Instant Karma," Allen Klein had trimmed Apple company fat by littering the place with pink slips. ("At one point, the company was losing money faster than the British government," went Eric Idle's joke in his TV parody, the Rutles). Apple offices kept functioning, but mostly as a façade. Even Brian Epstein's assistant from the old NEMS shop on Charlotte Street in Liverpool, Alistair Taylor, had sought a Beatle override unsuccessfully. Film, electronics, and avant-garde divisions got the ax, except for Geoff Emerick, who was kept on to build his dream studio in Apple's basement (and deliver the ultimate humiliation to Alex Mardas). Once built, this studio served as an elite facility for a brief period and was then closed. Demonized as both an American and a ruthless capitalist, Klein watched as Peter Asher stole off to California to launch James Taylor's huge career. Only Derek Taylor, the colorful press chief, still held court most days in his second-floor office. But this now seems like another Klein calculation: Taylor simply kept feeding the band's activities to his extensive contacts in an adoring press; why mend an unbroken myth machine?

For a time, Lennon and Ono enjoyed driving into London, holding forth to the press, and hatching new plans for festivals, events, art exhibitions, and future projects. Thrilled by Woodstock, and unshaken by the

Rolling Stones' Altamont fiasco (documented in the film *Gimme Shelter*), Lennon worked with Canadian promoters Ritchie Yorke and John Brower, who planned a huge outdoor music festival in Toronto the following summer. Yorke wrote dispatches about the utopian event in *Rolling Stone,* but Lennon could not hold on to his wish that it be free and finally abandoned it in early spring.

With all the band's earnings from previous releases funneled into a frozen escrow account, Klein lobbied for a new release for quick cash: Couldn't they cobble together something from that album and film made back in early 1969? Bootleg activity had turned *Get Back* into both a headache and a giant sunken cost. Now Lennon brought Phil Spector back in to see if he could sidestep the rough mixes that Glyn Johns had prepared from the previous spring. It's a measure of the band's low regard for these sessions that they not only sat on these tapes for a year but stopped doing so only under threat of bankruptcy. Lennon, Harrison, and Starr concurred that a revival of *Get Back* material could give them some wiggle room to sort out Apple's mess; but McCartney, who loathed Klein, left countless messages unanswered from his Scottish hideaway. His absence, and complete unwillingness to communicate with the others, became silent assent.

Riding the brash stylistic coup of "Instant Karma," which neatly stitched Lennon's futurism with a booming girl group echo (with an opening piano quote from Richie Barrett's "Some Other Guy"), Spector set up shop with fourteen-month-old Beatle tapes from January 1969. All four Beatles had pronounced the project hopeless. Within a couple of weeks, Lennon came away dazzled: "When I heard it, I didn't puke," he said. "I was so relieved after hearing six months of this like black cloud hanging over, that this was going to go out. I thought it would be good to go out, the shitty version, because it would break The Beatles, you know, it would break the myth. 'That's us, with no trousers on.' We were going to let it out in a really shitty condition, and I didn't care. I thought it was good to let it [the Glyn Johns mix] out and show people what had happened to us, 'This is where we're at now. We can't get it together. We don't play together anymore, you know, leave us alone.'"[8]

Had it worked, they might have pulled off a major PR reversal—but the other three Beatles hadn't counted on McCartney's plan: he had been recording his own material and booked some London studios with engineers Alan Parsons and Chris Thomas to finish a solo project. Even more brazenly, he intended to release it within weeks of Spector's *Let It Be;* the feature film was slated for late spring release. As the first Beatles record produced without George Martin, Spector's *Let It Be* incensed both Martin and McCartney. When he finally emerged from Scotland to give Spector's package a listen, McCartney spat nails in a letter to Klein, reprinted in the *Anthology:*

He addresses Allen Klein with deeply sarcastic formality and tears apart Spector's arrangement: "In future no one will be allowed to add to or subtract from . . . one of my songs without my permission . . ." He then gives Klein explicit instructions on how to fix the overwrought production. McCartney insists he had considered orchestrating the track, but decided against it. As for the new version, he gives explicit instructions: reduce volume for strings, horns, voices, and all added noises; bring up lead vocal and Beatle instrumentation; completely remove the harp and reinsert piano statement at the end.

He signed it bluntly: "Don't ever do it again."[9]

Because McCartney steadfastly refused to answer his messages or attend Apple meetings, Ringo was sent to his Cavendish Avenue home to discuss putting off Paul's solo debut. After all, McCartney had an interest in the *Let It Be* project: it would give them all solvency and options, and for the good of Apple, they hoped the genial Ringo could persuade McCartney to be reasonable and follow Lennon's lead from the previous fall: put off talk about a breakup until the band's new record had a chance to perform.

They all underestimated McCartney's determination. In one of the biggest confrontations yet, with Ringo as proxy, McCartney let loose all his rage at Spector's mixing "Long and Winding Road" without his input, and Klein's bulldozer style, by many accounts shouting Ringo from his front door. Starr returned to the others and suggested they simply gulp hard and go along with both albums coming out during the same season. In some ways, this accidental decision worked in everybody's favor.

In some UK promo copies of *McCartney,* Paul conducted a coy self-interview where he blandly let slip he would probably never work with the others again. If this wasn't intended as a bombshell, McCartney made sure its effect got felt. On April 10, the press materials for *McCartney* spurred the *Daily Mail* headline: PAUL IS QUITTING THE BEATLES. Quoting the "self-interview," Apple's Derek Taylor dealt with a new deluge of phone calls. "They do not want to split up," said Taylor's official statement, "but the present rift seems to be part of their growing up. . . . At the moment they seem to cramp each other's styles. Paul has called a halt to The Beatles' activities. They could be dormant for years."[10]

Lennon couldn't believe McCartney's gall, and how the press ate it up. After all, McCartney hadn't put on his own gallery shows and made private art films and concocted zany media events from his honeymoon suite or appeared with an impromptu band at a Canadian festival with new solo material. Lennon had already jumped off the deck in public not once but innumerable times without his bandmates—they had even refused to record "Cold Turkey"—and yet here came Paul, announcing, "the Beatles are over." McCartney even took journalist Ray Connolly out to lunch and tried to backpedal the whole thing, which created more furor. All of Lennon's attempts to upstage McCartney were reversed in a single day.

"I wasn't angry, I was just—'shit!'" Lennon told Jann Wenner later:

> He's a good PR man, Paul. I mean he's about the best in the world, probably. He really does a job. I wasn't angry. We were all hurt that he didn't tell us what he was going to do. I think he claims that he didn't mean that to happen, but that's bullshit. He called me in the afternoon of that day and said, "I'm doing what you and Yoko were doing." . . . And I said, "Good." Because that time last year, they were all looking at us as if it was strange trying to make a life together and doing all the things and being fab, fat myths. So he rang me up on that day and said, "I'm doing what you and Yoko are doing and putting out an album. And I'm leaving the group too," he said. I said, "Good." I was feeling a little strange, because he was saying it this time—a year later.[11]

From Lennon's point of view, McCartney's maneuvers seemed hypo-critical and self-serving. How could anybody buy the idea that McCartney was breaking up the group when it was Lennon who had been actively releasing independent work ever since the spring of 1968? Did McCartney's perpetual good cheer, even when twisting the knife, detract attention from his guile?

When reporters went around the horn compiling quotes from the others, Lennon simply said, "You can say I said jokingly, 'He didn't quit, he was fired.'" John and Yoko issued a hoax press release announcing: "They have both entered the London clinic for a dual sex-change operation." As usual, Ringo Starr uttered the best break-up quote: "This is all news to me."[12]

"I remember Lennon being very upset when McCartney made the papers with his announcement of the breakup," columnist Ray Connolly recalls:

> He had told me months before that he was leaving the Beatles, and I wrestled with that private confession terribly, wondering whether I should print it or not, knowing it was a huge story. But Lennon had asked me not to because of his contractual obligations. Now he tore me down for sitting on it, and I was stupefied. "But John," I said, "you told me not to break that story . . ." He had no hesitation: "You're the journalist," he said derisively. Of course he would have been upset no matter what I did, but he took a certain pleasure in blaming me for McCartney's ingenious PR play.[13]

McCartney's guile wasn't all public relations. Instead of cowering in the shadow of the great Beatle monuments, McCartney simply acted as if the Beatles were a Saturday-morning cartoon, and as if leaving the band and making a little solo record were of no consequence. This is what Scousers refer to as "cheek," a giant flip-off couched in a smile, the sort of brutal reduction Lennon most admired in McCartney's ego. He had already handed off a hit record to Badfinger ("Come and Get It"), Apple's Scottish protégés, and *McCartney* contained a potential monster hit, "Maybe I'm Amazed"—a Beatle track from top to bottom, even though his bass playing paled compared to his fluid work on *Abbey Road*. It was as if McCartney hadn't just quit the Beatles, he had quit the bass, which betrayed far humbler musical ambitions. McCartney seemed to orchestrate the whole charade—a soft-core solo tour de force, a press eruption, a looming legal standoff—with a churlish virtuosity, which gave John and Yoko pause: Lennon's former partner had played a hand that would be very tough to beat.

In the midst of McCartney's end-of-Beatles campaign, the gap between leftist activism in America and Britain widened. In Britain, this took shape around an underground newspaper, *Oz*, which invited schoolkids to help edit one issue. The May 1970 issue included an article which parodied Rupert Bear, created by one Vivian Berger, who pasted the head of the cartoon character onto an X-rated cartoon by Robert Crumb. (Coincidentally, Paul McCartney had just bought the rights to Rupert the Bear to develop as a children's project.) Unfortunately, like a lot of censors before and since, the Obscene Publications Squad lacked humor, and since the *Oz* editorial offices had already been raided several times (mostly for photos of shirtless females), this time they made their case.

Oz had just been through a debilitating Australian trial around similar issues; now its British publication became the counterculture cause of 1970, accused of "conspiracy to corrupt public morals" and fined out of operational costs. Alongside Barry Miles's *International Times* being hauled into court for carrying a classified ad with "homosexual content," this defeat dragged antiestablishment morale to new lows. (In 1971, Lennon took a look at the situation and coughed up one of his better political songs, "Do the Oz," to help the paper defray its legal costs.)

While British authorities derailed youth culture's momentum by chasing obscenities, American protests had long since darkened. The Vietnam War entered a prolonged stalemate as President Nixon played a cynic's game of outmaneuvering his critics: "Peace with honor" became double-talk for bombing Laos and Cambodia, stretching Cold War "domino theory" beyond all reason. In this netherworld of war logic, one had to "destroy villages to save them." It took a Pentagon insider, Daniel Ellsberg, to leak the military's history as the Pentagon Papers, which pulled the thread from the official narrative. Ellsberg emerged as a counterculture hero, an insider willing to stand up to corruption. Student unrest became a weekly headline, to the point where Governor Reagan of California proclaimed, "If it takes a bloodbath, let's get it over with."[14] He got his bloodbath. Later that month, a radical leftist SDS faction formed the Weather Underground and plotted a bombing campaign on government buildings in New York, California, Washington, Maryland, and Michigan.

The courts finally acquitted the Chicago Seven (including Tom Hayden, the author of the Port Huron Statement, and Yippies Abbie Hoffman and Jerry Rubin) in February 1970, but the charges of "crossing state lines" were upheld until overturned on yet another appeal. At the end of April, the Vietnam War intensified. On the advice of Henry Kissinger, Nixon began bombing Cambodia to stop the supply lines and safe harbor of the Vietcong, a war crime that would render Henry Kissinger's 1973 Nobel Peace Prize a moral affront. On May 4, four college students were killed and nine others wounded by the Ohio National Guard, ordered to push back against protestors at Kent State University. The cruel thud of police clubs at 1968's Democratic National Convention had turned fatal: America's own soldiers were now gunning down peaceful, unarmed civilians on a state campus. Two more students were killed at Jackson State University in Mississippi on May 14. 1968's political assassinations still haunted the American mind. How many more nonviolent marches would it take to end this immoral war? How many more students would be killed expressing their constitutionally protected right to peaceful dissent?

A new protest song appeared that summer: Crosby, Stills, Nash and Young's "Ohio"—snarling guitars driving a plodding, mournful groove that owed a lot to the barren outrage on Lennon's "Cold Turkey": "Tin soldiers and Nixon coming / We're finally on our own . . ." By May 9, when one hundred thousand antiwar protestors marched on Washington, the mood had turned bitter and antagonistic. Only now they had a new song to sing: Lennon's "Give Peace a Chance," still credited to Lennon and McCartney. Lennon counted it among his most cherished accomplishments and hoped to write more songs in the same vein; perhaps he began to realize how unforgiving the verse was for large crowds, with prolix, run-on stanzas that vexed even solo singers.

WHEN *LET IT BE* SHOWED UP IN MOVIE THEATERS over the summer of 1970, it captured this frayed cultural hangover like a bookend to *A Hard Day's Night*'s Beatlemania only six years before. In the public's mind, early distinctions took shape between the album and its feature-length film, which did poor business up against *Woodstock* (which ultimately grossed more than $50 million). The same figures who once snubbed the grim businessman in the opening sequence of *A Hard Day's Night* now invited their audience into rehearsal dysfunction. What kind of insolence was this, inverting showbiz tradition by allowing their huge worldwide audience to eavesdrop on these dreary, end-of-the-line scrimmages? Only those in the know deciphered the January 1969 filming date; this out-of-order anomaly made an awkward appendage to the *Abbey Road* songs that were still on the radio. *Let It Be* slumped in theaters like the first countercultural dinosaur.

Lennon saw the movie in San Francisco with *Rolling Stone* publisher Jann Wenner: "There were a couple of jam sessions in *Let It Be,* with Yoko and The Beatles playing, but they never got in the movie, of course. I understand it all now. . . . That film was set up by Paul for Paul. That's one of the main reasons The Beatles ended. I can't speak for George, but I pretty damn well know, we got fed up of being sidemen for Paul." Lennon's voice collapses as he spills these secrets, knowing how vengeful they'll sound: "After Brian died, that's what began to happen. . . . The camera work was set up to show Paul and not to show anybody else. That's how I felt about it. And on top of that, the people that cut it, cut it as 'Paul is God' and we're just lying around there. And that's what I felt. . . . There were some shots of Yoko and me that had been just chopped out of the film for no other reason than the people were orientated toward Engelbert Humperdinck."[15]

There are two comic shots of Ringo peeping from behind his limousine in front of Apple and feigning shock when Heather, Linda's daughter, hits one of his drums. But Ringo's balefully detached expression, especially during the Twickenham sequence, rivals Lennon's quietude.

The closing rooftop set was almost too successful—it didn't make any sense coming after all the stops and starts and a wearied McCartney looking up at the camera on "Let It Be" and "The Long and Winding Road." By the time fans screened the movie, the breakup was public knowledge, and it looked like a leftover diary of defeat. Here were the Beatles falling apart, and the whole myth of sixties utopianism seemed to crumble with them. That final sequence on the roof, the briefest reprise of past glories, closed the movie with an ironic freeze-frame, as if trying to stop the inevitable.

Here was another chance to argue about cultural identity and how Americans had done the most to bring down Britain's pride and joy. British critics in particular lashed Phil Spector for the applied histrionics on the *Let It Be* album. But Spector had no trouble pushing back: "Most of the reviews were written by English people, picked up by the American Press, and the English were a bit resentful of an American, I don't care who it was, an American coming in, taking over. They don't know that it was no favor to me to give me George Martin's job, because I don't consider myself in the same situation or league." As far as Spector was concerned, the band's regular producer, George Martin, had failed (even though the Beatles deliberately kept him out of this loop). Seen from his point of view, Spector did everybody a favor with a rescue job. Besides, Spector didn't consider Martin, or anybody else, in his league at all: "I don't consider him with me. He's somewhere else. He's an arranger, that's all. As for *Let It Be,* he had left it in deplorable condition, and it was not satisfactory to any of them, they did not want it out as it was. . . . If my name hadn't been on the album, there wouldn't have been all that."[16] (That's like a composer calling a piano player a mere "instrumentalist." From Spector's imperious vantage, an "arranger" is a lowly hired hand.)

The Glyn Johns version of *Let It Be* (which included Lennon's "Don't Let Me Down" and McCartney's "Teddy Boy") circulated widely among fans who preferred the material without the commercial gloss. But the noise around Spector's work is a red herring: all he did was buff up rough tracks—another producer might have made different choices, but Spector's are perfectly respectable as far as it goes. *Let It Be* became a Rorschach test. Most of the British sharks felt Spector never deserved to get his hands on Beatle tapes in the first place. Glyn Johns's mix has achieved the status of "lost classic," although its dashed-off brilliance lacks sonic definition. Spector has the dubious distinction of overseeing the one album not produced by George Martin, the one that elevates all Martin's other Beatle achievements.

Unlike *Abbey Road,* which sported Harrison's hit single "Something" and the cathartic finale of "Carry That Weight" ("Boy . . . you're gonna carry that weight a long time . . .") and "The End," *Let It Be* sounded unfinished and underwhelming, even though Spector dressed up songs where he could, roping in "Across the Universe" from early 1968. Most famously, he added strings, harp, and female chorus to "The Long and Winding Road," forever alienating McCartney. McCartney seemed not as upset about the actual arrangement as the simple fact that he was not given veto power before its release. His lifelong gripes to rework the record would culminate with his release of *Let It Be . . . Naked* in 2003.

McCartney's obsession with this track seems misplaced: the strings on "Across the Universe" brought no Lennon complaints, and Spector's lush arrangement had plenty of precedent; George Martin added orchestra and chorus wash to Lennon's "Good Night," and McCartney's "Hey Jude" had strings, brass, and choir. If any Beatle song deserved to be smothered in glucose, it would be "The Long and Winding Road." McCartney complaining about Spector's arrangement is a bit like Cher complaining about the tabloids—at a certain level, this material begs to be exploited.

Spector didn't sit by for McCartney's abuse, either: "Paul took the

Grammy for it, though," Spector says. "He went and picked the Grammy up, for the album that he didn't want out, supposedly that we used to ruin him artistically. . . . What did he pick the Grammy up for? Silly."[17]

Like *The White Album, Let It Be* grouped together songs that stressed individuality. Understated ensemble fireworks punched everything up a level, especially on "Dig a Pony," "Get Back," and the quickened pulse of "One After 909," the 1963 song they revived for a nostalgic romp, which bathed the live set in youthful afterglow. Watching the rehearsal sequences during the first two-thirds of the film, there's no predicting the emotional rush "One After 909" gave the band on the rooftop, and in many ways it said as much about their shared history and commitment to the music as even "Don't Let Me Down," which had already been sliced off the album for the B side to the "Get Back" single. *Let It Be* follows *The White Album* by three months chronologically and several eons perceptually. To have dumped thirty songs on the market in November, only to regroup with a new chest of material for January's cameras, argues for the Beatles' intense work ethic. On songs like "Let It Be," "I've Got a Feeling," and "Two of Us," *Abbey Road*'s twilight emotional colors come into view.

This material also sits outside their catalog in ways that make its frame not just anachronistic but anomalous. *Let It Be*'s ensemble and attitude situates it decisively between *The White Album* and *Abbey Road*. But by dumping it on the market in 1970, Klein gave *Let It Be* an after-the-fact brilliance that worked in its favor. A throwaway like Harrison's "For You Blue" or Lennon's "Dig It" (cut down from its original nine minutes) sounded like lost treasure, Beatles filler that would count as inspired moves from lesser groups. That they were so determined to film themselves at this chaotic point in their collapse only underlined their musical bonds. Only a world-class act could get away with that, and the footage told a Sisyphean story of how songs take shape from the ground up. Even the best band in the world starts with song fragments and loose arrangements. Bringing the music in for a landing on the roof restored both their musicianship and their collective self-respect.

The world heard *Let It Be* as a contemporaneous experience, but the sixteen months between its filming and release seemed like a trek across an emotional Siberia to each Beatle. As Lennon retreated into private superstar therapy, more Beatle fumes enlarged the myth. *McCartney* projected an imperious whimsy on the band's close that hinted at extreme form of denial.

In aesthetic terms, none of this fazed Lennon. Except for "Instant Karma," Lennon remained secluded for the first half of 1970, in direct contrast to his nonstop posturing on the world's stage throughout the previous year. As the band's magnificence drew to a close, the end became as hard for its members to accept as for its audience. In the quiet zone before he came out with his divorce record to proclaim his independence, Lennon set new standards that he himself, and the others, would never quite live up to again.

AT THE END OF APRIL 1970, Lennon and Harrison flew to Los Angeles for business meetings at Capitol Records, and then back to New York. The Immigration and Naturalization Service issued Lennon waivers for such short visits, but the trip shows up in J. Edgar Hoover's FBI file. Hoover had already collected letters about Lennon's "pornographic" *Two Virgins* album cover and begun tracing his cross-continental trips as a matter of routine government business. A known "narcotics user" and "radical," Lennon inspired more fear from the establishment than he knew: the FBI files for the April trip open with an entry detailing Lennon and Harrison's visit, visa status, and business locations.

A book had arrived in Ascot's mail that spring. The title caught Lennon's eye: *The Primal Scream,* by a California therapist named Arthur Janov—and then he couldn't put it down. The opening passages described patients who quickly and permanently purged their neuroses by revisiting their most traumatic childhood separations. These intense personal stories pushed all Lennon's emotional buttons, as though all the experimenting he had done onstage with Yoko suddenly had therapeutic potential—wouldn't trying make it so?

That sex-change ruse had a code meaning: John and Yoko enrolled in a four-week course of primal therapy with Dr. Janov, first in Ascot, then in London. Lennon gave it a serious effort throughout much of 1970, as his multiple anxieties proved too cumbersome to cope with.

He committed to a series of private sessions, and a further four months of group sessions in California. Yoko Ono agreed to the same regimen. While Janov visited, they stayed in separate wings of the Tittenhurst mansion. Janov insisted on separating John and Yoko as a key aspect of his treatment:

> I mean, Yoko's been screaming for a long time. Just the words, the title, made my heart flutter. Then I read the testimonials, "I am Charlie so-and-so, I went in and this is what happened to me." I thought, "That's me. That's me." We were living in Ascot and there was a lot of shit coming down on us. And these people say they get to this thing and they scream and they feel better, so I thought, let's try it. They do this thing where they mess around with you until you reach a point where you hit this scream thing. You go with it, they encourage you to go with it, and you kind of make a psychical, mental, cosmic breakthrough with the scream itself.[18]

Lennon had to persuade Janov to accept him as a patient after several rebuttals. Janov recalled that he "initially refused to go to England to treat Lennon, but later when my kids found out that I had refused to go they just went nuts and made me call back and agree."

The Lennons' personal assistant, Anthony Fawcett, describes these visits in his book *One Day at a Time*. Janov came to Ascot and laid down a strict protocol: "They were to be separated from each other twenty-four hours before the first session, completely alone in a room with no TV, radio or phone, only pencil and paper. Yoko stayed in the bedroom and John went to the other end of the house and took over the half-completed studio. This was the first time they had been apart from each other for well over two years, since perhaps May of 1968."[19]

Fawcett describes John and Yoko being surprised by Janov's warmth and youthful appearance, how, like a lot of other California psychiatrists emerging in this era, he exuded Hollywood charisma. Lennon became the star-struck patient. Janov's early phase of private treatments took up three weeks, with separate daily sessions. "We did a lot of it in the recording studio," Janov told *Mojo* magazine in 2000. "While they were building it. That was kind of difficult. But it went very, very well. John had about as much pain as I've ever seen in my life. And he was a very dedicated patient. Very serious about it."[20]

Soon, Lennon and Janov took a suite at the Inn on the Park Hotel in London, and Yoko went to the Londonderry Hotel. After another three weeks, Janov praised Lennon's progress and urged them both to continue at his Primal Institute in California. This would take another four to six months, Janov explained, and he would combine private sessions with group therapy. Only if they finished this round properly, he insisted, would they see the results they were looking for. In private, Janov thought Lennon would need at least another year. While the Primal Institute stressed group sessions, Lennon apparently did not receive rock-star treatment as a group member. "The thing in a nutshell," said John, "is that Primal Therapy allowed us to feel feeling continually, and those feelings usually make you cry. That's all. Because before I wasn't feeling things. I was blocking the feeling."[21] There was only so much Lennon could block, however.

The sudden dash to America overlooked his immigration status: his visa allowed a limited three-month stay. Attending to this matter became all-important: Yoko had been granted custody of Kyoko, but Tony Cox had gone into hiding with her. Upsetting his visa status meant Lennon might complicate reuniting Yoko with her daughter. They had already suffered non-entry dictums from the U.S. government when they tried to mount an American bed-in the previous spring.

Although he never finished treatment, Janov's ideas went straight to Lennon's head, feeding a musical impulse that sent him back to pre-Hamburg guitar rock to express triumphant anger and redemptive ardor. Approaching thirty, he never got closer to the dual passions of childhood. As he returned to Tittenhurst, songs started pouring out of him.

LIKE THE RISHIKESH MEDITATION trip two years earlier, Lennon's California retreat fed him a surfeit of material. He quickly booked EMI's London studios with Phil Spector, and staff engineers Phil MacDonald and Richard Lush, for four weeks of sessions that led to the *Plastic Ono Band*. Lush remembers the sessions as agreeable, even pleasant: "Those were really good sessions, I remember. I always got along with Phil, he was good fun to work with. And we did it all very quickly, because Phil MacDonald did the first two weeks, and I came in for the last two, so it was about four weeks work total. And everything went very smoothly."[22]

Ringo Starr spoke even more fondly than Lush about these sessions: "It was fantastic! It was such a heavy album for me. I was on it so maybe I was just getting off on it because of that, but the songs were so great and there were three guys and the cuts are really terrific."[23] If the sessions were as giddy and professional as everybody remembers, the angst in Lennon's voice came as release. Even to this day, the album makes for acid listening and scopes out a defiantly primitive sound that would make fiercest punk sound thin. In a perversely professional way, this also signals how well EMI had trained engineers like Lush, who separated pure sound from meaning as a matter of technical expertise.

Lennon's vocal attack vents the emotional spoilage motivating these songs. On tape, this material sounded as if it had been marinating far beyond what a healthy person might carry around. In person, somehow, it sounded less agonized than triumphant.

This dual quality hints at Lennon's preoccupations: the seductive yet hollow Beatle myth, and the awful relief made possible by rock 'n' roll. At the time, *Plastic Ono Band* was the kind of early seventies work that gave people the shivers—like the movies *Last Tango in Paris* or *The Godfather,* its confrontational tone gave listeners plenty to think about for the first hundred listenings or so: so this is what it felt like to lead the world's mightiest band. Its contours have grown familiar, but the album's opening church bells still toll for the band and its era, the farewell of an obsessively distracted eccentric, emphatically dismissing years of great work just to clear his palate. Even for Lennon's career, already studded with hyperbole, *Plastic Ono Band* remains one of the great self-deflating gestures in the history of pop culture. Its emotional glare defies everybody's fondest illusions about Lennon. "The Beatles were an act," he says with a glower: "now I get to be John Lennon."

Yoko Ono's indefatigable presence in the sound is palpable, even though she's nowhere to be heard. Everywhere and in every way, the music binds the intensely inward with the defiantly exhibitionist, as the awkward in Lennon stares down the brash. "Mother," the opening track, peels the submerged motivations of "Strawberry Fields Forever" away as primal anxiety. The agony of "Mother" gives way to the *Sesame Street* yelp of "Cookie!" shortly into track two, "Hold On." Chastened yet monomaniacal, the authority in Lennon's Beatle persona shrinks inside these two tracks. New tensions define new poles of Lennon's sensibility: the sheer ambition of the sound, the dry-ice rockabilly of "I Found Out," cuts loose all kinds of fiction with irrefutable force. Lennon doesn't expect anybody to buy the line "They didn't want me so they made me a star" except as the crudest possible metaphor for abandonment—how the world's adoration can't compete with childhood loss.

Like eavesdropping on a hero's therapy session, the scalding anxiety in these grooves cues off Lennon's private yet direct vocals. Lennon's confessional mode transforms his platitudes and ranks with anything he's ever done, from "Cold Turkey" back to "This Boy" and all the compressed fury tamped down into the *Please Please Me* Shirelles' cover, "Baby, It's You," where male anxiety took a shower. But there is no Beatle precedent, no brilliant pop trigger lying in wait behind these tracks the way there is throughout a lot of *McCartney* and *Ram*. The whole thing might sound like a parody of Primal Scream pretensions if Lennon's stabbing attacks didn't slice with such emotional precision. These performances eliminate the distance between singer and song to wed form with content. McCartney has great vocal moments, but here Lennon makes

McCartney sound like a performer who'd invest himself in almost anything—it's an album McCartney could never make.

THE OPENING FUNEREAL CHURCH BELLS at the top of "Mother" descend straight into Freudian reverie. Those somber, quiescent chimes bear down with irrepressible force. Lennon's emotional tone is immediately raw and explosive; his voice threatens and then cracks with each chord change. The frame, an agonizingly slow nursery rhyme, becomes an avant-garde rant, as if "Yer Blues" and "I Want You" and "Cold Turkey" had sprouted an album of harrowing footnotes. Just as Lennon's starkly roiling delivery breaks the spell, a fearsome, tightly coiled ensemble steps in beneath him, chasing his outbursts warily, scared of what they might yield.

The standard nursery rhyme slows to an ancient blues pattern, its harmonies tracing circles through each verse toward a massive, repetitive wheel of a coda ("Momma don't go/Daddy come home!"), which turns of its own sluggish momentum. Somehow, this airtight piano-bass-and-drum trio yields vast orchestral effects; the solo vocals, often doubled in unison, convey a keening intimacy, as if struggling to keep up with the voice in his head.

"Working Class Hero," a ruthless Dylan parody that also works as a scathing smack-down of the luckless Scouser mystique, has the same bitter, stony-faced irony of "You've Got to Hide Your Love Away" or "Happiness Is a Warm Gun." It walks a frightening line, and too many people still hear it literally. This attack is anything but first-person revelation—the first thing Liverpudlians still resent about Lennon's persona is his solid middle-class upbringing and schooling; any talk of his "working-class" background connotes sheer ignorance. And yet the more you understand about Lennon's boyhood, the more poetry leaps out of this lyric: the orphaned father, Alfred, who orphaned Lennon; the wrenching Blackpool choice between his two parents; the ongoing betrayal of living with an auntie just two miles from his mother's home without ever knowing her proximity; and the irony of growing up in poncy Woolton while taking in student lodgers to make ends meet, squeezing two students in a house with only two bedrooms. How can such an economically and emotionally perplexing upbringing in Woolton be reduced to "middle-class"? Just where does such abandoned penny-pinching in a "posh" British golf course neighborhood fit in that culture's scrupulous class distinctions? On another level, Lennon defines showbiz as the new escape hatch for "working-class" strivers. Like art college, pop music became one of the few release valves Lennon devised for outsiders in a closed system.

Tracks like "Mother," "I Found Out," "Working Class Hero," and "Well Well Well" scan like excerpts from your best friend's private diary; you hang on every word while squirming through their revelations. When he surfaces for a romantic sketch like "Love," the mood shifts like a dropping breeze. *The Times* classical critic, William Mann, made pedantic comparisons to Lennon-McCartney "Aeolian" cadences in "Not a Second Time," which always gave Lennon fits. It seemed supercilious that the highbrow snobs deigned to give Beatle popularity some sham intellectual respect. If anything, Lennon's command of musical irony in a song like "Love" resembles the way Schubert brings back a minor theme in the major mode. Like Schubert, the contrast alive in Lennon's fragile hope lurches toward the tragic, as if the minor statement mocks the major mode from below. "Love" subsumes its bleak surroundings to catch sunbeams.

Throughout the record, consolation vies with desperation, the way "Hold On" mops up after "Mother," for example, or the way "Look at Me" seeps from the tormented cracks of "Well Well Well." Side one ends with the simple piano-ballad reassurance of "Isolation" as balm to the wounds inflicted in "Working Class Hero"; side two rears back into the frantic, odd-meter "Remember," which dissolves into the eerie calm of "Love." By the end, Lennon's vocal tour de force redeems the hoariest of seventies "inner self" clichés and surges toward the divine on the concluding "God." The Beatles had perfected the album closer as "big statement" with "Tomorrow Never Knows," "A Day in the Life," and the black hole of "Revolution 9" and "Good Night." Now Lennon ushers in the pop apocalypse: everything you think you know is wrong, Beatle people. Stay tuned for the Great Revelation.

"God" quickly veers toward vengeful parody of the lopsided coda to "Hey Jude," placing both the band and its rock mystique up there with Gandhi and Buddha and Hitler and the inexplicably missing Churchill—smashing busts in the pantheon of twentieth-century culture's museum of heroes and antiheroes with an implicit ellipsis near the end to extend the notion of heroes itself on toward futility. When Lennon lands on the jugular, "I don't believe in Beatles," spitting out the name with rancor, the whole tirade doubles as a pretty good shaggy-dog joke, despite its pretensions. Having shot down his own Beatles alongside class hypocrisy and religious fraud, Lennon's final swipe topples the *Sgt. Pepper* celebrity parade.

And "I don't believe in Beatles" had the weird effect of confirming everything Lennon was pushing up against—just another celebrity inflating his stock by railing against the system. But like "Nowhere Man," or "Revolution," or the longer-form works—*Tommy* and "We Won't Get Fooled Again"—that used rock to denounce rock pretensions, the energy behind the naïveté replenished a lot of Lennon's "pronouncements" and made the reach admirable while magnifying the problem. With this kind of passion, Lennon could have made the phone book sound defiantly enchanting; his delivery here made his most extreme vocal leads ("Yer Blues," "Hey Bulldog," or "I Want You [She's So Heavy]") sound like auditions, a humbled rock original fighting for his sanity.

Perversely, "My Mummy's Dead," a homemade demo tagged on after "God" like an afterthought, detracts attention from Lennon's bigger subject—his disfigurement at the demise of his band ("bigger than Elvis!") has the tug of an unfathomable dilemma, the one beast he might never slay. By this point, Elvis himself was famous for shooting out TV sets in his Las Vegas hotel room. Lennon put television to better use: he stole from it shamelessly and bragged about working with the set on. Instead, he takes aim at the cultural mirror, and indicts everybody who holds on to inflated Beatle hopes that lie somewhere beyond human understanding or, in sixties parlance, confusing hero worship with "faith in the human condition." Such expectations—from rock 'n' roll, never mind its performers—can be even harder on romantics than on natural-born cynics.

THE REVIEWS TENDED to be uninformed raves, but Robert Christgau's "Consumer Guide" capsule in the *Village Voice* spelled out some of the larger aesthetic feats everybody sensed in the sound: "Of course the lyrics are often crude psychotherapeutic clichés," he noted. "That's just the point, because they're also true, and John wants to make clear that right now truth is far more important than subtlety, taste, art, or anything else." Even in its reductionism, Christgau heard expressive technological metaphors: "John is such a media artist that even when he's fervently shedding personas and eschewing metaphor he knows, perhaps instinctively, that he communicates most effectively through technological masks and prisms."[24]

In retrospect, it's difficult to emphasize the shattering effect this renunciation had on Beatle listeners. After two years of nonstop defiance with this new avant-garde wife, Lennon pissed on everybody's fondest hopes. As he slammed the door on his own cage, he denounced the idea that he was shattering any larger symbolic ideal, and in this way only insured that he did so. That the Beatles survived the slam suggests both the band's indomitability and Lennon's parochialism. Only rock's most famous man could renounce his fame while insisting such moves didn't make him even more mythical.

Lennon remained sympathetic and almost heroic even as the swelling tide of "God" swept his Beatle persona, perhaps because Ringo was right behind him on drums and the gentle doo-wop cadence that brought the song home (I-vi-IV-V) had a jaunty, rakish self-deprecation. The chord progression that scaled a junkie's self-ridiculing torment in "Happiness Is a Warm Gun" now connoted reassurance, even redemption, of the type only Lennon's cherished fifties records could.

EXCEPT FOR "AOS," YOKO ONO's *PLASTIC ONO BAND* album was recorded at the same sessions, and comprises some animated Lennon guitar work to cross avant-garde ideas with rock 'n' roll forms. On "Why" and "Why Not" this same ensemble inverts the Lennon hard-core formula for an unconscious descent, a wordless trip built on Ono's virtuosity disguised as vocal chatter. Think of "Revolution 9" as a straight "performance piece"—something musicians might attempt onstage—and Ono's fingernail-across-chalkboard glottal attacks take root as noise for noise's sake. It takes repeated listening, and a forgetting that reverses most pop listening habits, but the payoff reaches a parallel emotional intensity to Lennon's confessional barbs.

In a little-known but probing *Creem* review several months after both these records came out, Dave Marsh dubbed Ono "the first rock scat singer" and favored her record even above Lennon's. "And she's done it without a backbeat," Marsh marveled.

> A major portion of her increased validity must be credited to the fact that she works on one cut ("AOS") with the Ornette Coleman group. Coupled with the fact that this cut was recorded several years ago, long before it became "hip" in the youth community to be involved with avant-jazz figures, one begins to get a real feeling that it is Yoko who was brought artistically downward by her Beatles' involvement rather than vice-versa. . . . She uses her voice here much as John Coltrane used his horn; that is, in order to explore every possible nuance of the word-sound (chord) she scats about, using the word as a base for all but never quite saying it simply.[25]

Lennon's absolute faith in his new partner's aesthetics struck most people as balmy at the time. "Yoko's album complements mine for people who are interested in that kind of thing," he told Howard Smith of WPLJ in New York. "Hers is a kind of, er, well, I call mine like a literate version of what we went through in the last year or so and Yoko's is a sort of a sound picture, rather than a word picture. . . . I was dancing around with the guitar in front of her, sort of catching her eye and she was screaming back at me. It was a fantastic scene. There was just the four of us there, Klaus Voormann on the bass and Ringo on the drums, me on the guitar and Yoko on voice and we just knocked it off you know."²⁶

By contrast, the British press, predictably, mostly dismissed Ono's material, as if avant-garde devices and strategies were still beyond the realm of most rock critics there: "John's material is predictably mysterious and way-out, with him singing in the persuasive suggestive style, and appearing to enjoy every moment. . . . But, it's senseless to try and define Yoko's efforts. They are simply a wicked waste of wax! Lennon—four stars. Yoko—no rating," complained one unsigned *Disc and Music Echo* review.²⁷

John and Yoko's creative largesse lay at some distant pole from Janov's traumatic therapy. Long before there was rock 'n' roll or a group to belong to, there was a father who had abandoned his son, who kept popping up at odd intervals, asking for money. Shortly before Lennon put *Plastic Ono Band* to bed, his Apple office passed along another note from his father. Alf's timing could not have been worse.

They had not seen each other since early in 1968, when Alf stayed for a couple of days at Kenwood. Since then, Alf had remarried and settled in Brighton. His young wife, Pauline, had given birth to a son, David, and they wanted to wish Lennon a happy thirtieth birthday. Lennon invited Alfred and Pauline to come down for a visit to Tittenhurst on Friday, October 9. They brought David along to meet his famous stepbrother.

Lennon seems to have had a long speech planned. And the force of this tirade carried all of the anxieties he had been channeling in therapy and song throughout the year. When Alf and his new family arrived, they were shown by an aide into the back kitchen, where they waited in silence. Then a grim-faced Lennon appeared, followed by Yoko, and they suddenly realized this was not going to be a happy reunion. Pauline describes Lennon's flaming red beard, which made him look "like a fierce and primitive warrior" and rendered their birthday gift of aftershave "laughably inappropriate." Once he began ranting, they got the impression he was stoned.

This may have been true. Or cutting his Janov treatment short may simply have left Lennon's wounds too tender to enter such a confrontation with any semblance of balance or purpose. "I'm cutting off your money and kicking you out of the house," Lennon snapped for his opening. He quickly took a seat and launched his harangue. Turning to Ono for support, Pauline was struck both by her beauty—"flawless skin"—and her air of detachment. Alf tried to speak calmly in answering Lennon's accusations: "I've never asked you for money—it was your choice to give me an allowance." This time, Lennon had no patience for his father's excuses. Yoko remained poised but completely silent, supporting her husband by simply sitting at his side.

Engaging with Lennon only made him angrier: "Have you any idea of what I've been through because of you?" Lennon continued. "Day after day in therapy, screaming for my Daddy, sobbing for you to come home. What did you care, away at sea all those years." "You can't put all the blame on your Dad," Pauline interjected. "Your mother was just as much to blame for your problems." This stirred a vehement rant against Julia, which struck Alf and Pauline as even more alarming. Lennon told them Julia was someone "he reviled in the most obscene language I had ever heard, referring to her repeatedly as a 'whore.'" In this storm, no character could be safe. But Lennon certainly never wrote a song called "Alfred."

John scolded Alf. "Do you know what it does to a child to be asked to choose between his parents? Do you know how it tears him apart, blows his bloody mind?"

Finally, Lennon felt the need to threaten Alfred should he ever try to make money off his famous son: "As for your life story, you're never to write *anything* without my approval," he insisted. "And if you tell anyone about what happened here today. . . . I'll have you killed." Pauline describes the look on Lennon's face as one of "sheer evil" as he went on to explain "in extraordinary detail the procedure by which he would arrange for his father to be shot."[28]

Pauline tried to intervene to defend her husband, but Lennon controlled the scene. When he finished, he simply left the kitchen with Yoko. Freddie, Pauline, and their little son went back to their car and drove home to Brighton. Father and son would never see each other again.

According to Alf's book, Lennon was more agreeable in dealing with the sale of their home than they'd expected, but he was true to his threat about cutting them off. It's hard to tell if *Plastic Ono Band* gave him the courage for this scene, or if Lennon had imagined such a confrontation for so long that it had formed the subtext and secret script for those songs. Alfred raised two boys with Pauline and seems to have had a happy, settled second family much the way his son would. They would speak again, but only by phone, some six years later.

ON DECEMBER 8, 1970, at the ripe old age of thirty, Lennon sat down with Jann Wenner of *Rolling Stone* magazine for one of the great performances of his life, a sprawling interview later published as *Lennon Remembers*.[29] His muscular talk counterpoints *Plastic Ono Band*, offhanded brutality as rock star candor. After this rant was published over the 1970 Christmas/New Year's holidays, nothing about Beatlemania would ever be the same. With too much of the *Let It Be* film and album still hanging in the air, feeding the Beatle beast, Lennon had to get literal on his audience. Despite its frequent exaggerations, false claims, misremembered history, and prickly outbursts, this Lennon sit, brilliantly orchestrated by Wenner, became a central part of rock lore, the venting every rock star would later claim for granted, even though nobody can hold forth like Lennon. It almost made you wonder why in the world McCartney provoked him.

Many listeners picked up the album before they read the interview (release date: December 11, 1970). Like leaked testimony from a bitter custody battle for the soul of a group's mystique, Lennon's use of the word "divorce" suddenly took on added weight: feelings this fierce could only stem from an intimacy that rivaled marriage. Early on, Wenner asks, "Would you take it all back?"

"If I could be a fuckin' fisherman, I would, you know," Lennon responded. "If I had the capabilities of being something other than I am, I would. It's no fun being an artist. You know what it's like, writing, it isn't fun, it's torture. . . . I resent performing for fucking idiots who don't know anything. They can't feel; I'm the one that's feeling because I'm the one expressing. They live vicariously through me and other artists. One of my big things is that I wish I was a fisherman."[30]

That kicked off a windy yet absorbing descent into Lennon's deconstruction of his own fame, how the Beatles had lost control of their story, and how complicated popular success became when it stemmed from—and often blurred—aesthetics. Wenner ran the interview over two separate issues, and each paragraph held more outrage than the last. The insecurities Lennon sang about seemed as nothing compared to the supersize ego they came packaged in: "People like me are aware of their so-called genius at ten, eight, nine. I always wondered, why has nobody discovered me? In school, didn't they see that I was cleverer than anybody in the school? That the teachers were stupid, too? That all they had was information I didn't need? I got fuckin' lost being in high school. I used to say to me auntie, 'You throw my fuckin' poetry out and you'll regret it when I'm famous.' And she threw the bastard stuff out." The resentment in Lennon's voice as he says these things (recently more widely circulated once *Rolling Stone* made the tape available as a podcast in 2006) has a bitterness that can only be explained as carryover from his therapy. In fact, one of the reasons this interview proved so explosive was the way it exposed Lennon's confusion between confessional interview and therapeutic gush. He goes to such pains to denigrate his audience, and the many petty humiliations of celebrity, that half the time it's not clear who Lennon thought he was talking to—Wenner, Janov, his readers, the Beatles, or rock history itself:

It just built up; the bigger we got, the more unreality we had to face and the more we were expected to do. They were always threatening what they would tell the press about us, to make bad publicity if we didn't see their bloody daughter with the braces on her teeth. And it was always the police chief's daughter or the lord mayor's daughter—all the most obnoxious kids, because they had the most obnoxious parents. . . . One has to completely humiliate oneself to be what the Beatles were, and that's what I resent. It just happens bit by bit, until this complete craziness surrounds you and you're doing exactly what you don't want to do with people you can't stand—the people you hated when you were ten.

But he saves his biggest resentment for the Beatles themselves, who set off daggers of invective, mostly against McCartney: "After Brian [Epstein] died, we collapsed. Paul took over and supposedly led us. But what is leading us when we went round in circles? We broke up then. That was the disintegration."

Lennon's talkathon suddenly gave shape to years of withheld tension and made twisted sense of his *Let It Be* passivity. At the end of 1970, this historic interview appeared as blowback to McCartney's own passive resistance during his Scottish retreat. If his ex-partner persisted in his charm offensive, Lennon retaliated with a barrage of self-righteous umbrage. Here was the Lennon-McCartney songwriting partnership reduced to verbal one-upmanship. Lennon had the smarts, the wit, the guile, and a fearless urge to pontificate, but the subtext of all his posturing leaked through the bravado: How could any band contain the likes of Lennon? How had the Beatles possibly stayed together for so long? It made McCartney's patience and forbearance seem Herculean.

And in the other corner, Lennon made this interview style so garishly primal, he opened himself up for vicious parody. Tony Hendra's hooting *National Lampoon* satire ("Magical Misery Tour") came at the end of side one on 1972's *Radio Dinner*. The comedy troupe cynically predicted Nixon's demo-derby landslide as all but inevitable and wove Beatle mythology through bowling-alley stoner talk and game show farce. "Genius is pain!" Hendra howls into the fade-out, as if a thousand spikes had been driven through his privileged rock-star senses. With every line a direct quote from Lennon's *Rolling Stone* interview, Hendra commits the great Lennon deflation of the Lennon deflation, affectionately ripping every *Plastic Ono Band* pretension to shreds.

CRITICS LAUDED *LENNON's PLASTIC ONO BAND* as genius, but his brash interview stole some of its thunder. A lot of Beatle reactions coupled regret with affection: "It was so far out that I enjoyed it actually," McCartney told *Life* magazine when promoting his new single, "Another Day," in early 1971. That would have to be the attitude of the man who had stuck with Lennon through tirade after tirade, and knew how to filter obnoxiousness through a keen understanding of Lennon's insecurities: "I ignored John's interview in *Rolling Stone.* I looked at it and dug him for saying what he thought, but to me, short of getting it off his chest, I think he blows it with that kind of thing. . . . I know there are elements of truth in what he said and this open hostility, that didn't hurt me. That's cool. That's John."[31]

In London, McCartney filed suit against the other three Beatles in the High Court of London on the symbolic date of December 31, 1970. John and Lee Eastman had demonstrated to him that with Klein in charge of Apple, the only way to deal with Epstein's final contract from 1967, which bound the Beatles' fortunes together through 1977, was to dissolve the partnership. McCartney reasoned he couldn't pursue his solo career while still operating as a collective with the other three. The sixties, a splatter-painting era prone to oversimplifications, needed several curtain-closers for its outsize ideals. The *McCartney* album, Lennon's *Plastic Ono Band,* his revenge interview, and a stream of legal headlines became successive fake endings as the uncertain post-Beatle era finally took hold.

I'll Cry Instead

Mᶜ CARTNEY'S SUIT AGAINST APPLE, DURING THE LAST TWO DAYS OF 1970, neatly bookended the Beatle era as Fleet Street's biggest story since the Profumo scandal in 1963. The writ, issued in the Chancery Division of the High Court, sought to dissolve The Beatles and Co.[1] John and Yoko saw the headlines at Tittenhurst and became newly wary. This legal expedition smelled like one more savvy public-relations move from cheery Paul. McCartney's press quotes waved off the intricacies of taxes, publishing, and royalties with panache: "If the three of them want, they could sit down today and write a little bit of paper saying I'll be released . . . that's all I want!"[2] The partnership's one-upmanship had simply moved venues, from competitive collaboration to high command of the great Beatle myth.

Unbowed by Klein's Apple housecleaning and back royalties negotiations, McCartney's suit requested appointment of a receiver for Apple until the settlement and charged Klein with mismanagement of Apple funds. The numbers attached to the case were sobering: credit to the four individual Beatles stood at £738,000, of which £678,000 was due in taxes, leaving £60,000. When the news hit the papers that first day of 1971, the whole "end-of-era" hook proved irresistible for too many gadflies, even though they had already worn it out the previous New Year's. But they needn't have worried: the Beatle mystique was built for the ages, and the era of reissues had not yet dawned.

Because the Beatles had dominated the center of cultural life for so long, their unraveling was traumatic for everybody except newspaper accountants. If the band held the keys to British cultural identity, what did it mean once they went at one another's throat? Was the promise of the band's magic mixture of beat and melody too good to last? Or had the audience simply invested too many hopes in rock musicians who came of age only to be as perplexed as anybody else about moving on from the delirious sixties? All of the Beatles' cultural triumphs gave way to new questions in Lennon's mind: how best to transform sexual liberation, creative triumph expressed in popular terms, and a global peace movement into meaningful political change? As top forty radio put George Harrison's smash single, "My Sweet Lord," on a relentless tape loop, John and Yoko read the newspapers aloud to each other, as they had done in their Amsterdam and Montreal honeymoon beds, and tried to laugh about it. Maybe this year they would get lucky and have a child. Lennon was a big boy, he could outtalk McCartney any day, and he still had plenty in his arsenal for the ongoing PR war.

Within days of the new legal battle, both ex-Beatles fled the country. McCartney flew to New York to hire musicians for his next recording— *Ram*. The Lennons hopped into their limo and headed to Liverpool, where John gave Yoko a tour of childhood landmarks and the Cavern, before they boarded a boat to Miami. From there, they flew to Toronto for interviews with the CBC, and then returned to Miami for a flight to Japan.

From Tokyo's Hilton Hotel, they rang up Yoko's parents to arrange a surprise visit. Ono's mother remembered the meeting with affection, remarking on the rock star's good manners and "quiet" disposition. To Lennon, it was not just important to make a good impression on the Ono family—it felt like he had married into Japanese royalty. And in some ways, he had. Ono's mother remembers a perfectly compliant young man, eager to please, who had no trouble adapting to a class system so similar to his own: "John made his own concession to our custom by taking off his white tennis shoes and leaving them at the door. We offered them tea at a table with chairs but John said it would be more appropriate to behave in the Japanese style. I thought that was very charming."[3]

They talked about Yoko's family, her brother and two sisters, and the Lennons' home in England. But they ultimately couldn't escape the court case that had hounded them from Britain. When Mr. Justice Stamp brought the case to order in London's High Court on January 19, he heard David Hurst QC, representing McCartney, argue that the Beatles' affairs were in a "grave state," estimating there were not enough funds even to pay taxes. A London solicitor tracked Lennon down in Japan, though Lennon tried hard to avoid the call: "I got to Japan and I didn't tell anybody I'd arrived," Lennon complained. "Then suddenly I got these calls from the lawyer. Fucking idiot! I didn't like his upper class Irish-English voice as soon as I heard it. He insisted that I come home. I could have done it all on the fucking phone!"[4] This prompted the couple's early return to England on January 21, to disappointing chart news: John's *Plastic Ono Band* was the kind of hit record that didn't sell very well. It peaked first in America, at number three, over Christmas week, for a thirty-week run. But even the Christmas season couldn't nudge it past number eleven in Britain, where it took only ten weeks to stall out. To cap it off, BBC-TV broadcast *A Hard Day's Night* after Christmas, which sent its soundtrack back into the UK top forty. In the public mind, no mere court case could kill the idea of this almighty band.

THE POLITICAL IMPULSE THAT HAD BEEN BUGGING Lennon since the "Revolution" controversy tugged him in opposing directions: one half yearned to join with fringe radical causes; the other half still idealized music with broad, Beatle-size appeal. When they returned from Japan, Lennon sat down with Tariq Ali, editor of the *Red Mole,* for his most political British interview to date. Ali had run Lennon's letter back in 1968 defending "Revolution" and pursued Lennon as a prominent leftist ever since. Now Lennon determined to backtrack and clarify his earlier positions, as well as deal with some of the fallout from his *Rolling Stone* tirade.

And McCartney's suit likely pricked Lennon's political conscience—surely there were more important things to talk about than how all the bean counters were getting on. Yoko Ono had obviously been chatting with him about art and her storied past as a downtown artist who ran with like-minded freethinkers in the early 1960s. Marcel Duchamp had attended one of her loft concerts even before the Beatles played *The Ed Sullivan Show,* and modernism's great provocateur intrigued Lennon. His remarks to Wenner in the *Rolling Stone* interview revived his inner art student, especially when he said:

> All I ever learned in art school was about fuckin' Van Gogh and stuff! They didn't teach me anything about anybody that was alive now! They never taught me about Marcel Duchamp, which I despise them for, and Yoko has taught me about Duchamp and what he did, which is just out of his—fantastic! He got a fuckin' bike wheel and said, "This is art, you cunts!" He wasn't Dali. Dali's alright, but he's like *Mick*.[5]

All modernists are poseurs . . . like *Jagger.* To Lennon, these art movements resembled nothing so much as another version of rock history. Dada, after all, had been a bohemian response to Europe's descent into World War I, and its strategies overlapped with rock 'n' roll's: self-published magazines, a fascination with typography, advertising, and humor, subtle plays on gender identity, and a constant fluidity between form and content. Most of all, rock music resembled Dada as *anti*-art, the impulse to kick sand in the official version of reality and invest minimalism with ideas that couldn't be ignored. Think of Duchamp's signature acts: placing a toilet in a museum exhibition (signed "R. Mutt"), complete with female pseudonym ("Rrose Sélavy"), or painting a mustache on da Vinci's *Mona Lisa.* Richard Hamilton, who designed the *White Album*'s "limited edition" bare cover, had worked with Duchamp reconstructing some of his major pieces, including *The Bride Stripped Bare* . . . ; and art schools, once an outpost, now teemed with students who admired the Beatles' sophisticated sense of design.

Under Ono's influence, Lennon began making connections between rock's popular breakthroughs and Dada, surrealism, and pop art. He became intrigued by how rock 'n' roll played into every aspect of modernism's mission—to disrupt the "petty morality" of middle-class mores and challenge everybody's assumptions about oppressive political systems, especially during wartime, when third world civilians were bombed and gassed in the name of "honor." The connections Lennon had been trying to make in his music since "Revolution" now steered him toward more radical gestures. Promoting his most personal record, he shifted gears again back toward the political.

Much of his *Red Mole* interview reframes a lot of his embittered *Rolling Stone* quotes, and maps out issues that would concern Lennon for the rest of his life. But since it ran in a political fringe publication, not many Americans are widely familiar with his extended ruminations on these topics. He began by trying to clarify the "Revolution" contradictions: "On the version released as a single I said 'when you talk about destruction you can count me out.' I didn't want to get killed. I didn't really know that much about the Maoists, but I just knew that they seemed to be so few and yet they painted themselves green and stood in front of the police waiting to get picked off. I just thought it was unsubtle, you know."

This may be another case of trusting the art—the song makes Lennon's verbal explanation seem clunky. The quote is delightful if only for his use of the word "unsubtle," which is rich coming from Lennon; it would get attached to his own political songs. And he could have gone further: Mao had become a fashionable radical-chic totem in Europe long before Tom Wolfe branded Leonard Bernstein with the epithet at his Dakota apartment party for the Black Panthers. New Wave French director Jean-Luc Godard had spoken highly of Mao, even after the Chinese leader's crimes against humanity were public knowledge. In leftist terms, Mao had already become the new Stalin, the crowbar figure in defining your attitudes toward socialism.

"I've never not been political, though religion tended to overshadow it in my acid days; that would be around '65 or '66," Lennon continued, "and that religion was directly the result of all that superstar shit— religion was an outlet for my repression. I thought, 'Well, there's something else to life, isn't there? This isn't it, surely?'" Lennon credited psychologist Janov with the notion of "religion as a form of madness," and the therapy itself as a way for Lennon to dissolve "the God trip or father-figure trip. Facing up to reality instead of always looking for some kind of heaven." The discussion continued into practical concerns of how to empower the working class, how the Communists failed to take advantage of the 1968 strikes in France, and how corporate entities still controlled everybody's access to information. "We tried to change that with Apple but in the end we were defeated," Lennon argued. "They still control everything. EMI killed our album *Two Virgins* because they didn't like it. With the last record they've censored the words of the songs printed on the record sleeve. Fucking ridiculous and hypocritical—they have to let me sing it but they don't dare let you read it. Insanity."

And then a new theme emerged from all this rhetoric, the veiled class shame Lennon hid behind. As Aunt Mimi's proper middle-class schoolboy, he identified so strongly with "working-class" music that he bent over backward so it might define him, even if he had to fudge the fact that he was the only Beatle with indoor plumbing. And a new feminism lurched out as the key hypocrisy behind many competing revolutionary notions. Lennon praised Yoko for calling his bluff early on over this, when he thought he was simply behaving normally. He mentioned the Ono phrase "Woman is the nigger of the world" for the first time. "If you have a slave around the house," Yoko asked, "how can you expect to make a revolution outside it?"

Tying his new direct song language in to his interest in Japanese haiku, Lennon closed by articulating an artistic motive behind his political ideals: "The idea is not to comfort people, not to make them feel better but to make them feel worse, to constantly put before them the degradations and humiliations they go through to get what they call a living wage."[6] This formed the exact opposite musical tack he would take on his follow-up to *Plastic Ono Band*.

THE VERY NEXT DAY Lennon called Tariq Ali to play him a new song over the phone: the interview had fermented overnight into "Power to the People." It stuffed all the "in-out-in" ambivalence from "Revolution" back in its hat, quoting his original lyric and declaring, "You say you want a revolution/We better get it on right away . . ." Almost as quickly as Lennon wrote it, he tracked it with his usual crew (Alan White and Klaus Voormann) and had it ready as a single (backed with Ono's "Open

Your Box") on March 12. This single marked an end to running into London to record at EMI: with major work on the Tittenhurst home studio nearing completion, Lennon was eager to record his entire next album there.

After he finished off a few more songs, he called on Phil Spector to produce again and began inviting musicians over to rehearse as "Power to the People" stalled out at number ten. Klaus Voormann returned on bass, with Nicky Hopkins on keyboards, and Alan White instead of Ringo Starr on drums (with Jim Gordon drumming for "It's So Hard" and Jim Keltner doing "I Don't Wanna Be a Soldier Mama"). George Harrison was invited in for slide guitar work (notably on "How Do You Sleep?" "Crippled Inside," and "I Don't Wanna Be a Soldier Mama").

As Lennon recorded and filmed these *Imagine* sessions, the McCartneys snuggled up on the cover of *Life* magazine for a Richard Merryman profile to promote their new single, "Another Day," which competed for radio time with Ringo's "It Don't Come Easy." McCartney held to his PR campaign of being blameless in the Beatles' bust-up. He singled out the Epstein contract the four of them signed in 1967, talking around and through all the Klein-Eastman wrangling. "You see, there was a partnership contract put together years ago to hold us together as a group for 10 years," McCartney explained. "Anything anybody wanted to do—put out a record, anything—he had to get the others' permission. Because of what we were then, none of us ever looked at it when we signed it. We signed it in '67 and discovered it last year. . . . But the trouble is, the other three have been advised not to tear it up."

In his view, the other Beatles forced him to play fate's reluctant emissary, as he hid out in the Scottish Highlands: "My lawyer [and brother-in-law], John Eastman, he's a nice guy and he saw the position we were in, and he sympathized. We'd have these meetings on top of hills in Scotland, we'd go for long walks. I remember when we actually decided we had to go and file suit. We were standing on this big hill which overlooked a loch—it was quite a nice day, a bit chilly—and we'd been searching our souls." The only alternative, as McCartney and Eastman could see it, was seven more years of phony partnership.[7]

Nobody to this day talks about the glaring conflict of interest

McCartney pricked by choosing his brother-in-law for representation. Given the tangle of alliances and sensibilities that made the Beatles so magical, how could the other three possibly side with McCartney when he'd been buying up shares of Northern Songs behind Lennon's back and then balked at Klein for a manager with Eastman as his only alternative? Once his band mates got a whiff of the legal empire McCartney had hitched his wagon to, Klein seemed just the streetwise tough they might need to clean house and fight for their interests. Innumerable takes of "Ob-La-Di, Ob-La-Da" and "Maxwell's Silver Hammer" for the sake of Beatle cheer, perhaps; an army of lawyers attached to the cute one's wife meant long-term trouble.

Journalists never asked McCartney how he might have reacted if Yoko Ono's banking family were pitched to manage their finances. And the press never asked why he felt so strongly about bringing out his first solo album, *McCartney,* right alongside *Let It Be,* creating a retail bottleneck and snubbing the others' efforts to bail Apple out. From Lennon, Harrison, and Starr's viewpoint, they had a renegade in their midst who would stop at nothing to sabotage the company they had formed together. But McCartney's PR charm ran on irresistible hooks: family values and an irrepressible nonchalance that said, "How can you possibly take anybody else's side in this?"

Unlike Lennon's confessionals, "Another Day" resembled McCartney in the "life-passing-him-by" voice of the character from "A Day in the Life," minus the tragic frame. The B side, on the other hand, featured a chilling rock vocal on a throwaway called "Oh Woman, Oh Why," told by a man who's just been shot by his lover ("What have you done?!?"); McCartney sang it like he was bleeding from his gut. In the great back-and-forth between former songwriters, McCartney condensed all his post-Beatle anxiety into a mini–*Plastic Ono Band,* a novelty with a vocal passion that rivaled "Hey Jude"; but as an obscure B side, it never made it onto an album.

THE ROYAL COURTS OF JUSTICE handed down their opinion in McCartney's Apple suit on March 12, 1971. The official forty-five-page opinion by Mr. Justice Stamp furthered McCartney's narrative and began a public demonization of Allen Klein and his company, ABKCO.[8] Every Beatle except for Paul McCartney had signed with ABKCO, and the Apple board had approved a broad arrangement giving Klein discretion over numerous scattered Beatle accounts. Since McCartney had never consented to this arrangement, he asked the court to nullify it. His lawyers presented paperwork supporting McCartney's claim that Klein was unfit to supervise the band's affairs and had mishandled the Apple accounts for the year he had been at the helm.

The judge was quick to find fault with Klein's bookkeeping, especially given the "generous" terms with which he lured Lennon into his initial signing. "On the figures before me what has been charged is not less than three times the amount chargeable under the old agreement, and the excess is at least something over half a million pounds. ABKCO has also charged commission at the rate of ten percent on the royalties still payable under the EMI agreement; that is to say, in respect of the records sold otherwise than in North America. The amount of this charge, according to a schedule produced by Mr. Klein, is £123,871, of which 114,000 has been paid." In other words, Klein not only overcharged, he cost the band three times the amount they would have been charged under the existing agreement with Brian Epstein.

Furthermore, the judge noted, Klein's stewardship of Apple had been anything but professional: "Messrs Arthur Young & Co. [the court-appointed accounting firm] found a state of confusion, papers missing or in confusion, and necessary information lacking. As between the Plaintiff [McCartney] and Apple, the managers of the partnership business, Apple had, for one reason or another, fallen down and failed in its duty."[9] To settle matters, the judge appointed a receiver to "receive the assets and manage the business." This part of the decision froze all of the Beatles' publishing, royalty, and earnings accounts until a new settlement could be reached. "It will be many months before the parties are ready for trial, more before the action can be heard," the judge concluded.

In order to stay afloat, and live to fight another day for monies rightfully theirs, McCartney had forced the others' hand. Now the best they could do was to keep releasing solo albums, and perhaps tour under their own steam, to refill their coffers to pay more lawyers to settle these matters at some future date. It would take another four years of wrangling to finally reach settlement and close the Beatle books.

In the PR sweepstakes over who controlled the Beatle narrative, this decision scored in McCartney's favor. The previous year, his aw-shucks *McCartney* debut and prodding attitude in *Let It Be* vied with Lennon's howling finale to "God" ("I don't believe in Beatles") and venomous quotes in *Rolling Stone*. Now he had taken his band mates to court and proven their alliance with Klein something of a disaster. McCartney made sure to show up in court himself, as plaintiff, which impressed the judge; the other three never set foot in the door. By way of response, Lennon started writing a new batch of songs.

Alan White remembers Yoko Ono being very influential during the *Imagine* sessions—her experience reading and writing music facilitated Lennon's concepts with his players. This new partnership gave John his head and helped his musical fluency. But even though their house and grounds had been upgraded, the Lennons complained about the continuing stream of hate mail they opened. The more Ono talked to him about her downtown art scene in New York, the more Lennon wondered what daily life would be like there. They planned a trip in early June 1971, and seemed smitten by the city's pace the minute they arrived.

According to the Zappa biography by Barry Miles (the same figure who had carried Ono's *Grapefruit* at his Indica bookshop and went on to cowrite McCartney's *Many Years from Now*), the two rock stars met courtesy of the *Village Voice* columnist and radio personality Howard Smith. Smith, who mentioned a forthcoming interview with Zappa, was surprised to hear of Lennon's enthusiasm for the California rock experimentalist: "Wow, I always wanted to meet him. I really, really admire him. . . . He's at least trying to do something different with the form. It's incredible how he has his band as tight as a real orchestra. I'm very impressed by the kind of discipline he can bring to rock that nobody else can seem to bring to it."

Smith took Lennon to Zappa's hotel room; the latter seemed slow to realize Lennon was not putting him on. His band "leapt up," anxious to be introduced, and Lennon spoke deferentially, as if Zappa were the real artist and Lennon simply a pop star. Yoko, on the other hand, "acted like Frank Zappa had stolen everything he had ever done or even thought from her," Smith says. Zappa ignored her. Howard proposed to Zappa that John and Yoko take the stage that night at the Fillmore East in the East Village.[10]

When they walked out onstage for Zappa's encore, the New York audience gasped. Like the Toronto Rock 'n' Roll Revival, Lennon preferred these hastily arranged, unannounced gigs; they gave him less time to get nervous. "For those of you in the band who don't know what's happening," Zappa said, "we're playing in A minor." Lennon had to wrestle with a twitchy amp, and he read his guitar chords off Zappa's half the time. One of the singers from the Turtles put a bag on Yoko's head, and she kept on wailing into her microphone. John and Yoko remained onstage, tweaking the feedback, after everybody else had left. It was an event, but nobody knew quite what to make of it, or whether it pointed more toward Zappa or John Lennon.

"We went down there and I did an old Olympics number," Lennon said, "the B side of 'Young Blood.' . . . It was a 12-bar kind of thing I used to do at the Cavern. . . . It was pretty good with Zappa because he's pretty far out, as they say, so we blended quite well. . . . We did a three- or four-hour gig and it was beautiful. There was no rehearsal. It's much better like that. I'm sick of going on stage and being judged, you know."[11] Before the second show, Zappa, Lennon, and Yoko jammed in the second-level dressing room to an overflow crowd of Fillmore cognoscenti and hangers-on.

Compared to the relative isolation of Lennon's British country mansion, New York's Village scene swarmed with antiwar activists and countercultural creatives of all stripes. And John and Yoko's timing had a certain clairvoyance, given the kind of material Lennon wanted to start writing: the week after they played the Fillmore, the *New York Times* began publishing the Pentagon Papers, Secretary of Defense Robert McNamara's top-secret government report on U.S. involvement in Vietnam between 1967 and 1969. Daniel Ellsberg, a RAND Corporation military analyst, leaked the file as an act of conscience. Government war lies dominated headlines, slowly curdling the Pentagon's official Vietnam narrative. The Nixon administration filed suit to block further publication, but in a celebrated First Amendment case, the Supreme Court ultimately intervened (this all happened during the month of June 1971). This scandal gave the lie to both Johnson's and Nixon's reckless military pursuits, and undermined a sitting president's powers. Lennon's live appearances in New York created new hope among peaceniks: after all, the war machine had started rotting from within. To Lennon, the energy surrounding the antiwar effort felt irresistible; three years after he put out "Revolution," this cause didn't know the meaning of ambivalence.

JOHN AND YOKO RETURNED to Britain briefly that summer of 1971 to promote the new edition of Ono's *Grapefruit,* and to invite the media to an "open house" at Tittenhurst on July 20. They blabbed quotes like buckshot, but the hate mail persisted. "Being misunderstood," John explained to Steve Turner in *Hit Parader* magazine, "is being treated as if I'd won the pools and married a Hawaiian dancer. In any other country we're treated with respect as artists, which we are. If I hadn't bought a house in Ascot I'd leave because I'm sick of it. It's only because it's such a nice house that I'm staying. I'm a fantastic patriot for Britain. Ask Yoko—I never stop selling it! But she finds it hard to love England when they never stop shitting on her."[12]

They flew back to New York in August, only to get pulled into Beatle reunion rumors. George Harrison's mentor, Ravi Shankar, appealed to his rock-star student to mount a large charity event for the struggling nation of Bangladesh. The young country, which broke off from India and fought a civil war in 1970, had created a human rights crisis largely unreported by the Western media. Harrison, whose *All Things Must Pass* late in 1970 yielded a huge radio hit with "My Sweet Lord," planned an all-star rock concert to donate ticket receipts and film and record royalties to the relief effort.

The Bangladesh conflict came after the massive Bhola cyclone hit the coast of East Pakistan in November 1970, killing five hundred thousand people. The government responded ineptly. To aggravate the humanitarian crisis, President Yahya Khan blocked Sheikh Mujibur Rahman from taking office, even though his Awami League won a majority in Parliament in the 1970 elections. Khan arrested Mujibur in March 1971 and launched a bloody assault on the Awami League separatists. This war aggravated the humanitarian crisis, leading to hundreds of thousands of civilian deaths as Khan targeted intellectuals and Hindus. Ten million refugees flooded into India.

Harrison's concert took shape with great urgency throughout July. He invited all three of the other Beatles to appear, and Lennon seemed open to the idea, at least for a time. Rumors lit up fan networks and radio shows. Only after Lennon showed up for a rehearsal did things fall apart: Yoko assumed Lennon would perform with her, since they were now a duo and had been performing together for three years. She felt even more strongly about this in her adopted artistic home of New York City. Lennon either didn't anticipate this or failed to get it straightened out beforehand. A huge row erupted, and Lennon walked.

In fact, Harrison and Klein insisted that the Lennon invitation never included Yoko; Lennon couldn't persuade Yoko that the fans would be expecting him without her. Differing stories circulate around McCartney's invitation, but it's likely Lennon also walked out over his fear of a "surprise" reunion. He didn't want to hit the stage only to get blindsided by a prank, or simply a well-meaning surge of feeling from colleagues who couldn't help themselves. Perhaps some Beatle rumors filtered among the musicians themselves. Either way, this open conflict with Yoko, in front of Harrison and other players, overwhelmed Lennon, who felt doubly embarrassed by his wife before other rock stars, and rarely entered into confrontations where he wasn't the aggressor. Humiliated, he fled straight back to Tittenhurst without Ono.

The concerts went off as Concert for Bangladesh on August 1 (afternoon and evening shows), with Ringo Starr double-drumming next to Jim Keltner and an all-star band, including Billy Preston, Leon Russell, Klaus Voormann, Badfinger, and Eric Clapton. Reunion rumors evaporated the minute Harrison introduced Bob Dylan, who hadn't performed widely in America since his motorcycle accident in 1966. Except for the

Woody Guthrie memorial concert with the Band in 1968, Dylan hadn't appeared on a New York stage since 1966, and he quickly upstaged everybody by reworking five songs that signaled a larger return to form. Once again, Harrison trumped expectations by bringing in a ringer.

British journalist Ray Connolly met up with a distressed Yoko Ono in New York days before the show, just after Lennon had left the country. Ono gave him the rundown, and he confirms how the rift between John and Yoko had more to do with billing than any tiff between Lennon and Harrison. Yoko told Connolly how Lennon tried to persuade her that his appearance onstage with his former Beatles would be what the audience expected, and that spotlighting the John and Yoko act would detract attention from the larger humanitarian cause. Ono's younger sister Setsuko had flown in specifically for the occasion, and now Yoko wanted to follow John back to England and skip the concert entirely.

"Yoko left me the keys to her car and told me to wear John's clothes, and it was a pretty strange weekend," Connolly remembers. "Setsuko got mistaken for Yoko all over town as we wandered around in the days around the big concert."[13]

Even though this Bangladesh concert led to a falling out, the idea of living in New York, where he routinely walked around and ate in public without incident, as is the custom for celebrities in the city, had already seduced Lennon. After he and Ono were reunited back at Tittenhurst, they decided to decamp to New York for a longer stay, and they spent August packing up their belongings. Alan Smith of the *New Musical Express* interviewed Lennon this month about his new album, *Imagine,* and the way McCartney always dodged the issue of taxes when summarizing Beatle business affairs. Curiously, Lennon makes known his abundant affection for the Beatles by telling Smith that while he disagreed with McCartney's methods, he agreed that the band had reached its end. "Look at us today," Lennon argued. "I'd sooner have *Ram, Plastic Ono Band,* George's album and Ringo's single and his movies than *Let It Be* or *Abbey Road.*"

Asked if he'd listened to McCartney's *Ram,* Lennon said: "Of course I did. A couple of times. The first time I heard it I thought, fucking hell, it was awful. And then, ahem, the second time I fixed the record player a bit, and it sounded better. In general I think the other album he did [*McCartney*] was better. At least there was some songs on it. I don't like this dribblin' pop opera jazz, y'know. I like pop records that are *pop records*. I know you yourself didn't like it. I was really surprised when I saw that bit." Then Smith talked to him about the differences between Glyn Johns's *Get Back* and Phil Spector's *Let It Be,* which Lennon defended. "I'm glad the bootleg [*Get Back*] is going about," he said, "because it shows that Paul was wrong when he was putting down Spector."[14]

By the end of August, John and Yoko had packed up all their belongings and posed in Tittenhurst's "Imagine" living room, surrounded by memorabilia and trinkets, as if about to hold a garage sale. But in the ongoing PR show of their marriage, John and Yoko did more than relocate—they hunkered down on American network television.

THE MINUTE THEY HIT MANHATTAN'S ST. REGIS HOTEL, they started calling friends and watching TV and making arty little movies, just as they had done in Britain. Talk-show host Dick Cavett, ABC's hip late-night alternative to NBC's Johnny Carson, took a phone call from Lennon one morning and visited their room, where they put him in a quickie conceptual film. Within a week of their arrival, this conversation spilled onto Cavett's show.

Cavett, of course, was delighted with the booking. He was carving out a position to the left of Carson and had already welcomed Jimi Hendrix and Janis Joplin to his couch. With the famous ex-Beatle about to release a major new album, his second solo effort, featuring John and Yoko as guests boosted Cavett's countercultural cachet.

Lennon walked on chewing gum, wearing an ironic green army shirt, white pants, and black boots; Yoko strutted behind him in an orange velour minidress, black choker, beret, and black stockings. After a bumpy start, the couple came across as animated, curious, lively, and innately funny. Together they unveiled a new agenda, beyond marketing Lennon's new record and talking back to Beatle rumors. Lennon spoke openly of the Beatles in the past tense, confronted Yoko's image as a shrew, and extended his argument about all the great solo work the band was doing. Lennon sometimes fought back his inclination to interrupt Yoko to proclaim his newfound feminism. But the tape reveals him in very good humor, apologetic whenever he steps on Ono's sentences, and generally disarming Cavett's awe at his presence with mock hostility.

To Beatle questions, Lennon replied with tart but polite dismissals, and steered most queries back toward his and Yoko's avant-garde films and recordings. Yoko mentioned how John learned the term "chain-smoking" while reading an article about her. Lennon chimed in, "Smoking kills. . . . It didn't work, Janov. . . . It didn't work, Arthur," insinuating that Janov's therapy promised to "cure" them of cigarettes.[15] They both smoked nonstop.

When Cavett brought up Yoko's image as a witch and dragon lady, they chuckled. Lennon said, "If she took them apart, can we please thank her for all the nice music that George made and Ringo made and Paul made and I've made since we broke up?" which got spontaneous applause. "She didn't really know about us," Lennon says. "The only name she knew was Ringo, 'cause it means 'apple' in Japanese."

To finish their appearance, they opened things up for audience questions. Lennon answered one question about the "out" versus "in" versions of "Revolution," explaining how there were three versions of the song, how he made up the Chairman Mao lyric in the studio, how he regretted that line since it might prevent him from traveling to China, and he wished he played Ping-Pong so he could go over there. Now he believed that courthouse theater (like the Chicago Seven) and the bed-ins for peace had a larger effect on the opposition. "The 'establishment' doesn't understand them, so they can't kill them off," he said.

Then, a question about the recent *Village Voice* letter to the editor set Lennon off on a particularly revealing tirade from the man who twisted "Working Class Hero" into something far more poetic than literal: "I'm not an intellectual, I'm not articulate," Lennon argued sternly. "I'm working class and I use few words, I use words that the people around me used when I was a child. So when somebody comes at me with a bunch of [bullshit], I just give them [bullshit] back, and there it is." There's an illuminating distinction: in Lennon's mind, intellectuals by definition can't be working class.

They closed with some snarky comments on the runaway catch-phrase of the day:

> CAVETT: "My definition of love is not having to read *Love Story* . . ."
>
> LENNON: "Love is having to say you're sorry every five minutes . . ."

Cavett made the era's best possible choice to keep pace with rock's great quote machine, but throughout the interview, he looked torn between reaching for his next question and paddling fast just to stay afloat. Lennon went from zero to caustic in no time, and it was all Cavett and his late-night format could do to keep up with him. Compared to Britain, where the press treated John and Yoko more like a cartoon, the American media embraced their political talk and treated the couple like substantive artists. The U.S. government, however, reacted quite differently.

You Can't Do That

E VERY SUCCESSFUL SONGWRITER WRITES A NUMBER THAT BECOMES his or her signature, and "Imagine" became Lennon's musical autograph upon its release in the fall of 1971, for good and ill. This makes it a cousin to McCartney's "Yesterday," projecting only a slice of Lennon's irascible calm, arguably the least revealing slice. Like "Yesterday," "Imagine" comprises a blatant sop to commercial taste, although it avoids the romantic cliché. As Lennon admitted, it sponges off some "instructions" from Ono's *Grapefruit,* although he wasn't so far into the feminist camp yet as to actually put her name on the song (he gave lip service to this idea later on). Ironically, it was McCartney who made the first move, with *Ram,* putting "Paul and Linda McCartney" onto the songwriting credits, which caused consternation and disbelief from his publishing company when he began asking for separate royalty checks. Both these former partners had not only chosen American wives but insisted on dragging them onstage and having them coauthoring songs as part of their "solo" personas. This suggests how reliant Lennon and McCartney each were on collaborators, how each viewed the creative process as a form of intimacy, and how a wife replaced the other Beatle once the group sundered.

Whether it charms you or strikes you as philosophical cotton candy, "Imagine" could be Lennon's most widely misunderstood song. A hushed vocal atop piano framing a stridently antireligious lyric, it's "Hey Jude" and "Let It Be" distilled into his own image. Instead of listing everything he doesn't believe in, Lennon gift-wraps his tirade at the end of "God" as a hymn to the most benign brand of secular pacifist humanism. In this respect, this gentle sleight-of-hand has a beguiling appeal: Lennon might as well be singing, "I don't believe in God, I don't believe in nationalism, I don't believe in capitalism," as if sixties utopianism had not disappeared but gone mainstream, like the gentle lullaby of a baby-bath-soap commercial. Five years earlier, the Bible Belt had burned his records and sent death threats for such sentiments; by 1971, it was a measure of Lennon's enormous effect on culture that such spiritual doubt seemed largely a matter of individual freedom—the song is sugarcoated agnosticism for the masses.

As the title track to the *Imagine* album, it traced a sea change in Lennon's tone and production approach, airbrushing *Plastic Ono Band*'s anguish for a much larger hit. However, *Imagine* acquired a sunny reputation without soft-pedaling its thematic conflicts; the title track is the only song to "counterbalance" *Plastic Ono Band*'s ordeal. The emotional tone of *Imagine* lurches back and forth between *Plastic Ono Band*'s trauma ("Mother") and heady utopian sentiment ("Love"). Given its scabrous opinions ("Gimme Some Truth") and paranoid insomnia ("I Don't Want to Be a Soldier Mama"), *Imagine* boasts a broader poetic reach—for a full two acts (these first two solo albums), Lennon sings convincingly as though the Beatles are behind him. And songs like "How?" "Oh My Love," and "How Do You Sleep?" wouldn't have sounded out of place on *Plastic Ono Band*.

"Imagine" also has an inimitable touch of Beatle magic to it, a clue that Lennon missed his band mates after heaping two years of constant scorn on them. The album and hit single returned "All You Need Is Love" gallantry to the top ten, convincing many critics Lennon might just be warming up for the great solo career of the four that everybody had fully expected. Even the throwaway tracks had evidence of the salty Scouser stirring up trouble. "Crippled Inside" straddled both skiffle music and ragtime while sidestepping both styles, a rewrite of "Ob-La-Di,

Ob-La-Da" that juggled knives. Jim Keltner's lumbering beat built up a slow-swelling fear in "Soldier," as Lennon voiced what boys pray to themselves alone at night, flummoxed by the Vietnam era's blurred conceptions of "manhood," "bravery," and "patriotism." In an unnervingly stilted and hazy tone, a superstar inverted his culture's prevailing machismo to voice a universal fear of death.

As a post-Beatle landmark, parts of *Imagine* resemble a Lennon album in McCartney clothing, until "How Do You Sleep?" brings such fancies to a full stop. Lines like "The only thing you done was 'Yesterday' / And since you've gone you're just 'Another Day' " unleash a veiled, damningly faint praise of McCartney's spring single.[1] That line gives you pause: does Lennon really mean to compare "Another Day" with "Yesterday"? More likely, it's a cheap shot that belies how closely Lennon watched his ex-partner's work. Lennon lynched McCartney with unrepentant smugness, the same blunt edge that suggested the mock book title "Queer Jew" for Brian Epstein. George Harrison ladled "How Do You Sleep?" with acidic slide guitar to make it the great anti-McCartney diatribe. (McCartney limped back with "Dear Friend," which he wrote after Lennon's *Rolling Stone* interview, on December's *Wild Life*.) Most of the world may have hoped a song titled "How Do You Sleep?" might be about warmongers like Nixon or Kissinger; Lennon sounded somewhat less heroic singing, "The sound you make is mu-zak to my ears / You must have learned something in all those years . . ." The contradiction seems to have eluded him: if he truly no longer "believe[d] in Beatles," why devote his epic, two-part interview to snarling personal attacks and whole songs picking apart his former partner's output?

For all his charisma, Lennon couldn't see the contradictions inherent in preaching peace from one side of his album and spitting vitriol from the other: "I wasn't really feeling that vicious at the time, but I was using my resentment toward Paul to create a song. Let's put it that way. It was just a mood. Paul took it the way he did because it, obviously, pointedly refers to him, and people just hounded him about it, asking, 'How do ya feel about it?' But there were a few little digs on his album, which he kept so obscure that other people didn't notice 'em, you know, but I heard them."[2]

"How Do You Sleep?" gets answered by the disarmingly timid "How?," where Lennon extends his doubts to the larger culture he speaks for. After questioning his own confidence and self-image in the first two verses, he leaps to the universal in the last verse: "How can we go forward when we don't know which way we're facing?" is the more honest and forthright question submerged in the vagaries of "Revolution," drawing on all the emotional privation from his last record to raise bigger questions: how could personal neglect evoke such eloquence? The links between "How Do You Sleep?" and "How?" go beyond the combined word and question-mark alliteration. Lennon's artistic gift—his raging compassion, his epic insecurities—binds up the personal with the political in a feat of understated vocal control. It's enough to steal attention from those "invisible" strings.

In the end, however, no amount of religious, political, or friendship betrayals can upstage Lennon's romantic subversion. Among great songwriting tricks, the most dazzling may be making an unsympathetic subject sympathetic. Throughout *Imagine,* Lennon hitches the Beatles' communal dream to his romance with Yoko Ono. The closing "Oh Yoko!" portrays Yoko as lovable even if her voice grated on every Lennon ideal; if this is what this woman meant to this singer, how could the world possibly resist? "Oh Yoko!" starts where *Grapefruit* leaves off, copping Ono's strategy of taking everyday imagery to weave Zen-like riddles with warm, rippling embrace. "In the middle of a shave" becomes "In the middle of a dream" by the last verse, which harks back to "A Day in the Life" and "I'm Only Sleeping" as a metaphor for the imaginative possibilities couched in the ordinary. "My love will turn you on," picks up on that "I'd love to turn you on" "Day in the Life" catchphrase for a flirtation aimed somewhere on the far side of romantic. Instead of being boastful, Lennon's delivery steers this line toward coyly adorable. The refrain holds frighteningly innocent pleasures, and when Lennon holds out notes on repetitions—"My love . . . will . . . turn . . . you . . . on"—he pulls off a cornball sentimentality to make McCartney blush. Fading away by itself for the album's curtain, Lennon's harmonica sounds almost as joyous and carefree as it had in 1963's "Little Child" or 1964's "I Should Have Known Better." Even to those who still found Ono unsympathetic, Lennon canonized her name for an irresistible track.

IMAGINE CAME OUT WITH HEAVY PROMOTIONAL SUPPORT alongside Yoko Ono's *Fly*, on October 8, 1971, and critics on both sides of the Atlantic lauded Lennon's return and the former Beatle's pop gumption. Within weeks the title single dominated American radio and held firm at number three (stalled by Rod Stewart's "Maggie May" and Cher's "Gypsys, Tramps & Thieves"), his first top-five hit since "Instant Karma" (also number three) eighteen months previously. (No single came out in Britain.) The album quickly went gold in both Britain and America, combining what UK critic Jon Savage called "the best and worst of the man—the idealist and the ranter, the righteous and the vindictive anger."[3]

After he'd finished mixing and mastering the album, and sent the recording off for packaging, John and Yoko leapt into New York's slipstream of activism and radical street theater. That *Dick Cavett Show* appearance in September, where they made late-night's hippest host play catch-up, was just a prelude. As "Imagine" climbed the charts, they hunted for an apartment in the Village and spent every waking hour doing interviews, hitting sessions, catching bands, ducking into art shows, and giving celebrity gadflies fits keeping up with them.

They watched in dismay as the Attica State Prison riot unraveled. Back on August 21, guards had killed an armed Black Panther and author, George Jackson, as he attempted to escape three days before his murder trial; two guards and two more inmates also died in the incident. On September 9, nearly a thousand of Attica's 2,200 prisoners rioted, seized control of the grounds, and took forty-two corrections officers and civilians hostage. Tense negotiations huddled state law-enforcement officials in Governor Nelson Rockefeller's office, where they agreed to twenty-eight of the prisoners' thirty demands—reforms that included religious freedom for Black Muslims, competent medical treatment, and a framework for airing future grievances. Rockefeller responded by ordering the National Guard to storm the prison with tear gas on September 13, leaving thirty-nine people killed: twenty-nine prisoners and ten guards. The coverage blamed prisoners for slashing throats, but the medical examiner discovered that, in fact, the National Guard's raid had slaughtered all ten hostages.

This event galvanized political views, with leftists defending the mistreated prisoners, whose list of demands included more than one shower a week, and right-wingers becoming incensed at the lack of respect for law and order. Like the Kent State killings, and the overarching agony of the Vietnam War, the event underlined class and political fault lines. Now that Lennon and Ono had settled in Manhattan, they joined other New Yorkers in their outrage. And the riot completely reoriented Lennon's political muse as his most popular album rose up the charts.

The first indications of explicit political themes came as Lennon celebrated his thirty-first birthday on October 9, 1971, in Syracuse, where Yoko Ono had mounted an art show with John as "guest artist." Footage from the opening party in a hotel room, by filmmaker and friend Jonas Mekas, shows friends milling about, a tape recording running, and a bunch of songs sung halfheartedly by denizens like Ringo Starr, Phil Spector, Allen Ginsberg, and Jerry Rubin. In *There's a Riot Goin' On*, Peter Doggett describes the scene where Lennon unveils a new song:

> Amidst the musical chaos, Lennon toyed with a new composition. "It was conceived on my birthday," he confirmed later. "We ad libbed it, then we finished it off." In its semi-complete state, the song sounded banal; it gained little in stature when Lennon and Ono completed the lyrics in subsequent weeks. But this coruscating revolutionary protest song sported a timely title: "Attica State."[4]

At the same time, Lennon worked on a holiday jingle. Richard Williams booked a Lennon interview at their St. Regis Hotel suite in Manhattan later that month, where they chatted about future projects while sorting through Lennon's collection of Presley singles to be installed on his jukebox in his new Greenwich Village loft. Lennon talked of a Plastic Ono Band tour with Nicky Hopkins, Klaus Voormann, and Jim Keltner. Yippie Jerry Rubin would play advance man, laying the groundwork for all kinds of music and political theater. And he spoke about doing more sessions with Spector.

"I've got a lot to learn," Lennon told Williams. "It's been seven years, you know . . . but it's important to get the band on the road, to get tight. It's been fun just turning up at odd gigs like Toronto and the Lyceum and the Fillmore, but I'm sick of having to sing 'Blue Suede Shoes' because we haven't rehearsed anything else."[5]

Perhaps Spector talked about the work he and Harrison had done on the *Concert for Bangladesh* tapes; perhaps Lennon had ambitions to carve out his own charity cause. That evening, Williams took notes on the "Happy Christmas (War Is Over)" session at the Record Plant on 44th Street between Eighth and Ninth Avenues. "The 'War Is Over' bit's in brackets, like the old American records," Lennon announced proudly. When he first played the song for Spector, it reminded the producer of an old Paris Sisters song he'd made back in 1961: "I Love How You Love Me," for Leiber and Stoller's Red Bird label. The session musicians that evening included the young Hugh McCracken on guitar. When Lennon learned that McCracken had just played for McCartney's *Ram,* he quipped, "Oh, so you were just auditioning on *Ram,* were you? Yeah, 'e said you were all right."

"Just pretend it's Christmas," John exhorted the musicians in rehearsal. "I'm Jewish," Spector shot back over the intercom. "Well, pretend it's your birthday, then."[6]

As the engineers got the equipment set up right for all the guitars, Spector came out to the studio floor and danced around the room with Lennon. Voormann's flight from Germany was delayed, so one of the guitarists sat in on bass; they were too restless to wait. They kept going over the changes, with Spector running playbacks so the musicians could hear what they sounded like.

The next night, John and Yoko invited the Harlem Children's Choir down to sing the chorus of "Happy Christmas," and tracked Yoko Ono's

"Listen, the Snow Is Falling." Alongside Spector's wide-screen rhythmic track, the sound of a boys' choir on a Lennon record had a counterintuitive effect: it revived their billboard peace slogan with a gently rolling holiday message that has been a seasonal radio staple ever since. Here was a clue that Lennon and Yoko were actually writing together: she sang a marginal bridge lyric ("A very merry Christmas and a Happy New Year/Let's hope it's a good one without any fear"), and they claimed coauthorship of the song. But the overall effect was of a return to the "Give Peace a Chance" template, a "standard" but in a new rock idiom, not a chestnut like "White Christmas," but a seasonal record that put their billboard campaign to a sing-along refrain. Before the vastly inferior Live Aid anthem "Feed the World," the fledgling rock catalog knew few such classics. To his peace anthem ("All You Need Is Love"), antiwar hymn ("Give Peace a Chance"), and fist-thumper ("Power to the People"), Lennon now added a cathartic rock Christmas jingle (without mentioning Christ) as a coda to his defining agnosticism ("Imagine"). Largely through Lennon, rock began to define its audience's rituals.

By early November 1971, John and Yoko moved into former Lovin' Spoonful drummer Joe Butler's 105 Bank Street apartment in the West Village. The couple befriended neighbors, attended local concerts and parties, and developed political plans with activists who had their sights on the summer's coming political conventions. Jerry Rubin and Abbie Hoffman hung out with them regularly. Both men had learned a lot from the 1968 Democratic Convention in Chicago and the trial of the Chicago Seven. Now they set their sights on Republicans.

These authority figures were so clueless, and so easily provoked, Rubin argued, that with a rock star like Lennon at the helm, they could mount a far more meaningful protest. John and Yoko expressed admiration for how the Yippies had cast the itinerant Chicago judge, Julius Hoffman, as the disintegrating establishment's fuddy-duddy, garnering headlines for the movement and advancing the antiwar cause. Judge Hoffman proved his own worst enemy: he had Black Panther Bobby Seale bound and gagged in the courtroom rather than have him removed, and finally sentenced him to four years in prison for "contempt." (Graham Nash referred to this outrage in his 1971 hit single "Chicago," from *Songs for Beginners*.) In short, John and Yoko already admired the Yippies as creatives; the Yippies in turn had long seen Lennon as a nascent politico.

With a name attraction like Lennon on their side, Hoffman and Rubin hoped to enlarge these Chicago courtroom pranks and spring them on Nixon's 1972 reelection campaign. Since Lennon had already talked radical politics quite comfortably on late-night network talk shows, he made a charged symbol for the left's antiwar efforts. Lennon gave generous contributions to Rubin and Hoffman's Rock Liberation Front and took part in street rallies and spontaneous songfests in Washington Square Park. This loose-knit alliance of lefties carried off "media theater" just the way John and Yoko had hoped their bed-ins might inspire people to do. They never imagined that the only figure more paranoid than a rock star like Lennon was the president himself.

Gradually, New York's counterculture music world gathered around Lennon. Through some political friends, Jerry Rubin knew of a group, the Elephant's Memory Band, who had just booked a residency at Max's Kansas City. "Lennon heard about us, and came to hear us at the club," guitarist Wayne "Tex" Gabriel remembers. "And he asked us if he could come play with us sometime. So we said, sure, you know, of course. And that first night he came in and we must have played seven hours together."[7]

The Elephant's Memory Band gets a bad rap from most critics, but Lennon made strong commitments to the group and its work, signed the act to Apple, and helped members with their songs. Yoko Ono used the players for her *Approximately Infinite Universe* project, some of her best rock 'n' roll after *Plastic Ono Band*. The Elephant's Memory Band had an early breakthrough working on the rock score to *Midnight Cowboy*, and when Lennon found them they sported "Tex" Gabriel, a dandy new lead guitarist who had just landed in New York from Detroit.

For this first jam session, they launched into the classics, "rock numbers, all the old Beatle songs and Beatle covers, anything we could think of," bassist Gary Van Scyoc remembers. "And he was singing and sweating and working out, it was quite a session, I wish we had tapes of that evening."

A Village apartment, a Village band: now Lennon could get to work on a new record in his new home and push back against all those oppressive Beatle reunion rumors. Whatever the public perception, Lennon's attitude with these musicians conveyed the utmost respect. Naturally, at first the musicians were intimidated to play with the former Beatle. But they quickly found the rock star quite personable. "It was pretty much like he joined the band," Scyoc says. "It wasn't like he had hired us to back him, he chose us to work with, and we just started working together. He sought out our input constantly, and had a very collaborative approach to rehearsing and getting tracks down on tape."[8]

To Lennon, the idea of joining a band meant acting like a band member. "I've worked with a lot of celebrities since then," Gabriel confirms, "and Lennon had the least attitude by far of anybody I've ever worked with. It was all about getting it right, best idea wins, and he always wanted to hear what we thought of anything he brought in."

For these sessions, Yoko's presence was a given. Gabriel remembers her having more of a sobering effect on her husband, while Van Scyoc has only praise for Ono, her material, and her working relationship with the band. "When John wasn't around Yoko, that's when you'd get the more jovial John, the joking guy," Gabriel says. "When Yoko showed up, he'd be more reserved, less likely to be a cut-up. I never got a good feeling off of her; I'm not sure I trusted her, and she kept her distance more from us, much more than he did." Van Scyoc remembers it differently: "John was simply attentive to Yoko and her material, I wouldn't say he was being 'obedient' or anything like that. I never noticed any difference in his behavior whether she was there or not. . . . I mean, when you were off getting pissed with Lennon, he was not holding anything back, even when Yoko was there."

Half the ease of this new situation stemmed from how John and Yoko came in as partners, without interrupting any previous relationships. "That whole Yoko Ono thing gets blown way out of proportion," Van Scyoc points out. And contact with McCartney actually continued, even though the two stars maintained a very distant public façade. "The

McCartney thing, too," Van Scyoc says. "It was nothing for John to take a call from Paul right in the middle of a session and talk to him for ninety minutes while we took a break. And they were not fighting or arguing. They talked about family, about the search for Kyoko, Yoko's daughter, about McCartney's kids, trips they were taking. It was family stuff. And you would swear they were best friends."

THE *DICK CAVETT SHOW* APPEARANCES that September set off a ripple effect. Living and working in New York made John and Yoko a constant media presence, and Cavett had given them the TV bug. So, in addition to rehearsing new material with his new players, Lennon accepted some of the chat-show invitations that flooded in. On a brief trip to Philadelphia that fall, he and Yoko met an enterprising young TV producer named Michael Krauss.

Krauss had taken over *The Mike Douglas Show* that year with an impossible mandate: to reframe his forty-seven-year-old star, an antiquated big-band singer, for a younger audience. A former Chicago jazz drummer, Krauss had just turned thirty. To get Douglas across to youth culture, he booked guests like Karen Valentine, the actress who played a schoolteacher on the prime-time drama *Room 222;* James Brolin, *Marcus Welby, M.D.*'s sidekick; and singer Bobby Goldsboro. These special guests typically spent the entire week on Douglas's daily show, to build continuity and show off various aspects of their talent. Because of his music background, Krauss quickly became known in industry circles as somebody who booked jazz titans like Bill Evans and Oscar Peterson.

Douglas, a washed-up lounge singer in search of a lounge, got his singing out of the way at the top of each show and then chatted up celebrities and did the odd cooking segment. He was hopelessly square but, like Ed Sullivan, willing to gamble on what rock audience ratings might do for his career. "Douglas just read off cue cards the whole time," Krauss remembered. "He had no idea who many of these people were." Meanwhile, the show's syndication was dropping as Merv Griffin made inroads with the celebrity set from Los Angeles and Las Vegas. When Krauss learned that John and Yoko were staying at the Bellevue Hotel, right down the street from where the show taped, he grabbed an assistant and went straight for his target.

"I was hip to what Lennon was up to at this point," Krauss says. "I had lived in Chicago during the 1968 Democratic National Convention . . . and there was a definite impulse to push back against Nixon's war and the entire establishment, which was beating up peaceful demonstrators and all that." Krauss knew simply booking the Lennons would send a signal to middle America, Nixon's "silent majority," and help his host's ailing ratings ailing host's ratings.

Lennon answered his hotel-room door, welcomed Krauss in, and they jumped into a lengthy discussion about current events: Nixon, Vietnam, the antiwar movement, and all kinds of music. Krauss invited them to be on the show with Mike Douglas, explaining that their ideas needed to reach this larger middle-class audience. He offered to pay them scale, which got a laugh, and then aimed his pitch even higher. "I told them I didn't just want one show, I wanted them for a whole week. 'Here in this room,' I said, 'you're preaching to the choir, but I have a mission: *The Mike Douglas Show* goes into people's living rooms, and there's this whole other audience that needs talking to.' "

Krauss threw his weight behind making the show happen, even if it meant battling his network bosses at Westinghouse every step of the way. He knew there would be fights, but he could barely imagine the scale of the venture. Mostly, he remembered a very warm feeling as John and Yoko agreed to the challenge together: "They were very excited about it all, they asked if they could spend a week putting together each of the five shows, so I said sure."

They agreed to tape in Philadelphia on Thursday nights, and Lennon asked "very politely" if he could have a few minutes to talk it over with Yoko in private. Krauss agreed, and when they came back into the room they all hugged, and Krauss recalled a thrilling feeling at what he had just accomplished: booking the world's most famous rock star on daytime TV in the era before Oprah. "I mean, this is why I got into the business," Krauss says now, "for the big stuff, you know, change the world, expose the older audience to the great things these people were doing. . . . And we all just kept hugging each other, and it was very trippy for a few minutes there, like something very special was going to come out of this meeting."⁹ Krauss could not have fathomed how his producing skills were about to get tested.

Throughout November and December, John and Yoko commuted between New York and Philadelphia by limo to tape their shows. As hosts, they listed the radicals they wanted as guests, including Jerry Rubin and other members of the Chicago Seven. Krauss made every effort to balance this radical agenda with his host's base audience. Rubin showed up, only to explode into expletives ("Fuck the president! Fuck the president!" in a sequence that never aired). When he wasn't massaging his nervous Westinghouse executives, Krauss took daily, hour-long phone calls from Yoko Ono, who wanted to know every detail about each and every guest. Rubin flamed out, but Krauss successfully booked Tom Hayden and Black Panther Bobby Seale. Lennon brought down the Elephant's Memory Band to perform songs from both *Imagine* and his forthcoming *Some Time in New York City*. Yoko smashed a teacup and put it back together over the course of the week to symbolize world peace.

Once Mike Douglas's wife learned of the booking, she started complaining to Krauss regularly, and his superiors urged him to cancel Lennon because of all the noise coming from Douglas's chief protector. From the other side, Yoko Ono's daily calls ultimately drove him even crazier than the network. When he booked a regular comic, Louis Nye, Ono called him to ask, "Who is this Louis Nye?" Krauss explained how Nye's routines gave the show variety and helped with pacing, but Ono complained, "Well, we've never heard of him, we don't think we should be on with him." Krauss had to smooth over her constant harping while keeping everything on track. He wound up dreading her calls. "This went on day after day; Yoko was relentless," he says. "There is no question in my mind she broke up the Beatles. It was awful. . . . You'd take Yoko's call and it always meant a long, drawn-out debate, and she didn't appreciate the different political interests I was juggling just to make it happen."

The other show tradition Krauss engaged in with John and Yoko was to pull off a surprise guest, somebody John hadn't dared ask for,

1973. New York. Producer Phil Spector lounges in front of John and Yoko Ono with the Plastic Ono Elephant's Memory Band, standing. From left to right: John Ward (bass), Gary Van Scyoc (bass), Wayne "Tex" Gabriel (guitar), Jim Keltner (drums), Rick Frank (drums), Adam Ippolito (keyboard), and Stan Bronstein (saxophone).

March 1, 1974. Los Angeles. Julian, John, May Pang, and an unidentified friend at a California poolside.

March 12, 1974. West Hollywood. Lennon gets hustled out of the Troubadour club (Harry Nilsson is behind John).

1974. Liberty Island, New York. Bob Gruen's idea of posing Lennon in front of the Statue of Liberty, America's welcoming monument, became a potent symbol of Lennon's struggle against the Immigration and Naturalization Service.

July 1974. The Record Plant East, New York City. With Elton John during the
Walls and Bridges recording sessions.

Late 1975. New York. John with baby Sean at the Dakota.

opposite: February 28, 1975. The Uris Theatre,
New York. Backstage at the 17th annual
Grammy Awards. Left to right: David Bowie,
Art Garfunkel, Paul Simon, Yoko, and John.

Summer 1980. The Hit Factory studio, New York. During recording sessions for *Double Fantasy,* Yoko knits while John has a smoke at the mixing board.

December 9, 1980.
David Geffen and
Yoko Ono leave
Roosevelt Hospital,
after John has been
pronounced dead.

December 9, 1980.
Elliot Mintz escorts
Barbara Bach and
Ringo Starr out of the
Dakota after their visit
with Yoko and Sean.

Summer 1980. John wearing his Quarry Bank school tie.

who would turn him into a driveling fan. "I always liked to surprise the guest hosts, like when we had Mama Cass on, she was a *General Hospital* fanatic, so I got the entire cast of *General Hospital* to surprise her on the set one day and she was just flabbergasted," Krauss recalls. "I'd always ask, 'If you'd like to meet anybody in the world, who would it be?' I knew Lennon would want to meet Chuck Berry, so I worked very hard to get him on and kept it a big secret until the day of the taping."

When Berry appeared, Lennon gaped at the man backstage, then sang two numbers with him: "Memphis, Tennessee," which he hadn't sung since his BBC radio days with the Beatles, and "Johnny B. Goode," Berry's discrete history of the style, the Presley epic in miniature. It would be the only time these two harmonized.

THEY TAPED ONE SHOW PER WEEK FOR FOUR WEEKS, and Krauss remembers juggling a very eager and conciliatory Lennon against Ono's constant phone calls. Things went relatively smoothly until the final taping, when everything unraveled, and the early camaraderie Krauss felt with John and Yoko nearly exploded just before the last show. By this point, however, the couple's phones were being tapped, and FBI agents followed them around everywhere, which gave their already hounded lives a surreal aspect, especially since nobody believed them when they complained about government harassment.

"We got into a real hassle in my office," Krauss remembers. "Here I was busting my ass to accommodate them; I stuck my neck way out, and yet it wasn't enough for them." Suddenly, John and Yoko accused Krauss of working with the FBI, which he found simply preposterous. "They were paranoid," he remembers thinking. "And John was agreeing with her. . . . She said to me, 'In fact we know you've tapped our phone. We know you're trying to kill John.' And I looked at them in shock and all I could say was 'No, I'm not.' And then I stood up, and John stood up, and we started to go at it: it was 'Fuck you!' and 'Fuck you!'" A show assistant ran back to Mike Douglas's office, so Douglas came running down the hall, followed by security and several executives. Somehow the backstage scene settled down, and everybody walked out onstage to do the last show.

This incident shows just how nervous Lennon got before performing, and how intimidated he was at this early stage of his immigration fiasco. In addition to coping with his cars being followed and hearing phone taps, nobody could believe that what John and Yoko were experiencing had anything to do with reality. The flare-up also shows considerable marital strain. Krauss tried to forget the whole thing, but once the final taping wrapped, John and Yoko acted like nothing had happened:

> After the show I stayed away from them, I had *had* it. At the end of the show, John comes up to me, and it was like nothing had happened, he gives me a hug and shakes my hand and he doesn't let go. And he says, "Michael, I think they went off great, what do you think, were they good for you?" And I just said, "John, they were just great." Yoko was still seated, and she turned to me and said, "Michael, they were terrific, and you're terrific." And just an hour before Lennon was ready to kill me.

These programs aired the following February, 1972, and turned Mike Douglas into a ratings champ because of his counterculture booking. Before the week was out, salespeople called Krauss to tell him, "We just want to thank you: our rate card has increased ten percent, you're making us all money." The viewership jumped to an all-time high, and because Krauss ran the Lennon shows during sweeps week, when Nielsen collected viewer data, they "picked up close to one hundred more stations, and that meant a lot . . . because the show was starting to wither on the vine; now it was this whole new thing." But with all of Lennon's antiwar talk on *The Mike Douglas Show,* the FBI suddenly felt vindicated in stepping up its surveillance against this influential peacenik.

THIS DAYTIME TALK-SHOW success fed the long, late-night bull sessions at the Lennons' apartment, and sent Hoffman and Rubin off scheming for more exposure. The perfect event seemed to drop in their laps even before the *Douglas* episodes aired: Ann Arbor, Michigan, home to the state's leading university, harbored a fervent political scene headed by the radical band the MC5. Its manager, John Sinclair, had been thrown in jail in 1969 for passing along two marijuana joints to an undercover cop.

Ann Arbor rockers championed Sinclair's cause at concerts and through alternative newspaper ads, which caught Jerry Rubin's attention that fall. He networked to get John and Yoko on a benefit bill December 10 in the Crisler Arena at the University of Michigan. Lennon wrote a bluesy slide number called "John Sinclair," which told the man's story and landed on a hiccupping "Gotta gotta gotta gotta gotta . . . set him free!" refrain that coaxed whoops and hollers from fifteen thousand fans who heard its inaugural voyage. Those hiccups, puffing atop a steam engine of injustice and resentment, refashioned Buddy Holly's glottal barbs into political frustration. Also at this event, Lennon debuted "Attica State," the gorgeous and underrated "Luck of the Irish," and Ono's "Sisters, O Sisters," which was backed by Jerry Rubin and a pothead evangelist named David Peel with his troupe, the Lower East Side.

The audience had to wait more than eight hours for Lennon to appear, but the bookings showed good taste: Stevie Wonder, Phil Ochs, and a young Bob Seger (formerly with the System); jazzers Archie Shepp and Roswell Rudd were broken up by leftist speeches and poetry from Allen Ginsberg, Rennie Davis, David Dellinger, Jerry Rubin, and Bobby Seale. Lawyer William Kunstler, who defended the Chicago Seven, sent a taped message which told the audience that Sinclair's "harsh sentence dramatizes the absurdity of our marijuana laws, which are irrational, unjust and indefensible."[10] The event was televised locally by Detroit's WTVS, even though Lennon didn't go on until after 1 A.M. on Sunday morning.

Like turning a key, the concert sprang Sinclair from jail. The Monday after the Saturday-night concert, the Michigan Supreme Court ruled that the state's marijuana statutes were unconstitutional. The TV news footage that evening showed Sinclair coming out of prison to greet his wife and kid. Lennon had finally resolved the ambivalence of "Revolution" and appeared at a political rally with topical protest songs, the way leftists had always hoped he might. And while the songs weren't top shelf for Lennon, they showed lots of promise, binding leftist outrage with rock journalism. In Sinclair's case, it marked a heady victory. If only all revolutions could be this simple.

Reviewers, however, singled out Ono—reviving some of the sting that had driven them out of Britain. "One major factor nearly spoiled the whole thing," wrote Bill Gray in the *Detroit News* on December 13. Lennon "brought Yoko Ono. . . . Mrs. Lennon may be the genius that John keeps insisting she is. Possibly, if he keeps heavily hyping her, someone might believe it. But before a singer can be judged, she must first be able to carry a tune. Yoko can't even remain on key." And the new songs Lennon offered up were "interesting, but lacking in Lennon's usual standards."[11]

The following week, on December 17, the Apollo Theater staged a benefit for the Attica State Prison victims' families, and John and Yoko showed up to play three songs: "Attica State," Ono's "Sisters, O Sisters," and "Imagine." Afterward, Lennon quietly contributed a large check to the Attica Defense Fund.

Backstage, a young photographer named Bob Gruen snapped some photos. He met John and Yoko waiting for their limo and posing for photographs with some other musicians. Lennon told him, "We never see any of these pictures, where do they all end up?" And Gruen replied, "Well, I live right around the corner from you, I'll show 'em to you." A few days later, Gruen brought over some prints, knocked on Lennon's door, and Jerry Rubin answered. Rubin said, "Who are you?" and Gruen told him he was simply dropping off some photos. Gruen's discretion may have made his reputation: "Yoko later told me that nobody ever visited them without wanting to meet them."[12] The next week, they rang him up to take more photos.

ANOTHER JOHN AND YOKO DAYTIME TV APPEARANCE featured a heated political argument, but most Americans never saw it. To promote "Happy Xmas (War Is Over)," which came out on December 1, the couple appeared on a David Frost talk show taped in New York on December 16. Hunched over his skiffle tea-chest bass, Lennon performed with Yoko as a member of the Lower East Side backing David Peel for "The Ballad of

New York," before Peel's group gathered at the lip of the stage for Lennon's "Attica State," "Luck of the Irish" (a shorter version), Yoko's "Sisters, O Sisters," and "John Sinclair." Two middle-aged audience members spoke back after "Attica State" and accused Lennon of sympathizing exclusively with the prisoners. "You make it sound like the only worthwhile people in this world are the ones who committed crimes and were put away," a woman said.

This direct confrontation seemed to take Lennon aback. "When we say 'poor widowed wives,'" he responded, "we're not just talking about prisoners' wives, we're talking about policemen's wives, anyone that was there—" The idea that someone might defend the state's actions at the prison simply baffled him. "They must have done something wrong in the first place, or they wouldn't have been there!" another man shouted, interrupting Lennon. The crowd divided, and the class and cultural lines became clear: the bohemians fielded accusations of glorifying terrorism, and the hard-hat conservative crowd condemned Lennon's response. "We're not glorifying them," Lennon contended, visibly upset. "This song will come and go. But there will be another Attica tomorrow."[13]

Frost seemed intrigued that such a discussion had broken out after the music. But while Lennon argued that he lamented every single Attica death, the audience exchanges veered toward hostile. After the commercial break, Lennon stayed backstage while Yoko handled Frost's remaining questions; the anomaly went unexplained. As when he fled the Concert for Bangladesh rehearsal, such open confrontation spooked Lennon beyond words.

AS A POLITICO, LENNON'S SONGWRITING DIPPED, but not nearly as much as he took heat for. He seasoned his vitriol with humor in many scattered editorials from this period. In early December 1971, he signed a rather flat defense of Bob Dylan, who had suffered months of harassment from a "fan" named A. J. Weberman: "A.J. claims everything Dylan writes is either about Weberman or about heroin. What bullshit," the letter read. "It is time we defended and loved each other—and saved our anger for the true enemy, whose ignorance and greed destroys our planet." The letter was signed: "The Rock Liberation Front, David Peel, Jerry Rubin, Yoko Ono, John Lennon."[14]

The Elephant's Memory musicians remember chatty phone calls with McCartney, but in public, Lennon still stoked the showbiz feud, ridiculing his former partner in print. In a piece he wrote for *Crawdaddy* magazine, he said he heard things on McCartney's *Ram* that struck people as bent. Even if you credited "Too Many People" with some off-handed swipes ("Too many people preaching practices / Don't let 'em tell you what you want to be!"), "Back Seat of My Car" was a make-out anthem that Lennon persisted in pointing in the wrong direction: "Too many people going where? Missed our lucky what? What was our first mistake? Can't be wrong? Huh! I mean Yoko, me, and other friends can't all be hearing things." Defending "How Do You Sleep?" Lennon admitted, "So to have some fun, I must thank Allen Klein publicly for the line 'just another day.' A real poet! Some people don't see the funny side of it. Too bad, what am I supposed to do, make you laugh? It's what you might call an 'angry letter,' sung—get it?"[15]

He got more specific when the UK's *Melody Maker* ran a year-end McCartney interview, repeating a lot of the comments he gave *Life* magazine, with some potshots at John and Yoko's political escapades and slap-happy concertizing. Lennon dashed off a hilarious response, which *Melody Maker* printed on December 4, 1971, capping off a year of exchanges both overt and opaque:

> It's all very well playing 'simple honest ole human Paul' in the *Melody Maker,* but you know damn well we can't just sign a bit of paper. . . . You say, 'John won't do it.' I will if you'll indemnify us against the taxman! Anyway, you know that after we had our meeting, the fucking lawyers will have to implement whatever we agree on—right?

Lennon mentioned a phone conversation where they combed over all the legal issues once more, still getting stuck on Apple issues: "As I've said before—have you ever thought that you might possibly be wrong about something?" And Lennon got defensive when McCartney criticized his playing live, which sent him ranting about all the concerts he'd done even before he'd left the Beatles:

"Half a dozen live shows—with no big fuss—in fact we've been doing what you've been talking about for three years! (I said it was daft for the Beatles to do it, I still think it's daft.) So go on and do it! Do it! Do it!" Lennon listed all his live appearances: "Eg Cambridge (1969 completely unadvertised! A very small hall), Lyceum Ballroom (1969 no fuss, great show—30 piece rock band! "Live Jam" out soon!), Fillmore East (1971 unannounced. Another good time had by all—out soon!!) with the great David Peel!!! We were moved on by the cops, even!!! It's best just to DO IT, I know you'll dig it, and they don't expect The Beatles now anyway!"

Lennon probably projected a lot of himself into many innocuous stretches of *Ram,* but he knew exactly what he was on about with *Imagine:* "It's 'Working Class Hero' with sugar on it for conservatives like yourself!! You obviously didn't dig the words. Imagine! You took 'How Do You Sleep' so literally." He signed off with "No hard feelings to you either."[16] Later that month, Lennon roared from the op-ed page of the *New York Times* about how Nixon made "an Audie Murphy–like hero out of Lieut. Calley [of the My Lai massacre]. People aren't born bloody-minded."[17]

EARLY IN 1972, White House counsel John Dean began subscribing to underground newspapers to keep tabs on radical activities that might threaten the coming Republican National Convention in San Diego. One quote jumped out: "For the past five months in New York City people have been feeling that the worst is over and that people are creating again and coming together again and something new is in the air. Somehow the arrival of John and Yoko in New York has had a mystical and practical effect that is bringing people together again."[18] Shortly after Dean came across this story, John and Yoko's *Mike Douglas Show* appearance aired, staggered across media markets for maximum effect (because it was a syndicated show, local stations could run it according to their own schedules).

Dean didn't work in a vacuum; the White House responded to a February memo passed through the Justice Department, from Republican congressman Strom Thurmond of South Carolina: "This appears to me to be an important matter, and I think it would be well to be considered at the highest level . . . as I can see many headaches might be avoided if appropriate action be taken in time."[19]

In his expansive history of leftist activism and rock music, *There's a Riot Goin' On,* Peter Doggett details how the Nixon administration placed Lennon within its sights: "Lennon was added to the list of dangerous radicals who required constant surveillance by FBI agents. As a British citizen with a conviction for drug possession, he was vulnerable to the whims of the U.S. Immigration Service, who had allowed him into the country on a series of temporary visas." Hoover's FBI sought to deport Lennon and defuse the "plot" against the Republican National Convention. "Ironically," Doggett writes, "in another classic piece of White House miscalculation, the struggle to throw Lennon out of the country generated more publicity for his political sympathies than he could have mustered himself, and added to the impression that the Nixon administration was losing its senses."[20] But the wiretapping and harassment of the Lennons took its toll on their marriage.

Their cherished status as New York City residents was already apparent as early as 1972. On January 8, 1971, the *New Yorker* welcomed them with a "Talk of the Town" piece by Hendrick Hertzberg. With a spacious West Village apartment, Lennon sounded like a Big Apple booster. Hertzberg spoke to him about the apparent contradiction of living like a rock star while singing about "no possessions" in "Imagine": "I don't *want* that big house we [re-]built for ourselves [sic] in England," Lennon told him.

I don't want the bother of owning all these big houses and big cars, even though our company, Apple, pays for it all. All structures and buildings and everything I own will be dissolved and got rid of. I'll cash in my chips, and anything that's left I'll make the best use of. . . . It's *clogging my mind* just to *think* about what amount of gear I have in England. All my books and possessions.

Walls full of books I've collected all my life. I have a list this thick
of the things I have in Ascot, and I'm going to tick off the things
I really want, really need. The rest goes to libraries or prisons—
the whole damn lot. I might keep my rock-n-roll collection, but
even *that* I'm thinking about.[21]

Over in the UK, the Irish "troubles" boiled over enough to turn Mc-
Cartney himself into a politico. He took to the stage on a college tour
with Wings, and put out his own protest single, "Give Ireland Back to
the Irish," at the end of February. March brought Ringo's "Back off Boogaloo," and in May, John and Yoko returned to *The Dick Cavett Show* for
a second run, this time sitting opposite Shirley MacLaine, and performing "Woman Is the Nigger of the World" and "We're All Water." Cavett
had to fight his network bosses, too, to keep the incendiary Lennon lyric.
The week Lennon sang "Woman Is the Nigger of the World" on *Dick
Cavett,* McCartney put politics back on the shelf with his new Wings
single, "Mary Had a Little Lamb."

The more paranoid the Lennons became, the more the FBI gave them
reason to be paranoid. Bob Gruen told Lennon about a strange encounter in the dead of night, which was clearly meant to intimidate him.
One evening Gruen emerged from his photography studio on Twenty-
ninth Street with a friend, and caught a glimpse of someone across the
street taking his picture. A second look confirmed two men in a car
wearing "real old-school fedoras . . . and suits; they looked like G-men
out of the movies, and one of them had a camera." Then the car sped off.
At first, Gruen was simply puzzled. "It became like just another New York
moment, you know, where something happens for some weird reason. It
was only later that we put together that it was the FBI that had been spy-
ing on Lennon and his known associates," he says now.

At another point, Gruen pulled his car out from its parking place
outside the Record Plant on 44th between Eighth and Ninth Avenues
and spotted a tail. "To get to my place in the Village," he says, "you
would have to turn a few times to hit Ninth going downtown, and then
turn a few more times on 14th Street and Washington to get to Bethune
Street." This seemed curious to him at first, until he got downtown.

"Once we got downtown, it was like 3 A.M. in the dead of night, there were no other cars, and it was really weird to get followed all the way home on this circuitous route I took. So when I pulled up to my apartment, I jumped out of the car to watch them make the last turn, and I'm standing there looking at 'em, and the men ducked in the car as they drove by and again I was left thinking 'What was that? Who would want to follow me home?' This really made absolutely no sense until much later, when we learned."[22] Naturally, the FBI wanted Gruen to spot the tail and tell Lennon about it, to intimidate him into leaving the country.

Of course, this kind of thing only made Lennon more determined—if he left America, the country might not let him back in. He settled into work toward a new album with the Elephant's Memory Band and pointed his new songs directly at the repressive forces harassing his every move. Phil Spector came in to produce, and Gruen and some of the band members fault the flow of tequila and harder drugs for creating the tracks' self-righteous tone.

One band member in particular picked up on some previously hidden Lennon ambitions. "He was like a mentor to me," recalled guitarist "Tex" Gabriel, the Detroit native who had just turned twenty. "We used to sit for hours and trade licks, like guitarists do. Lennon always wanted to be a better guitar player, but he knew he never would be. He would ask me how I did stuff, and I would pick his brain about his rhythm chops, which were absolutely great." Many other rock stars might have treated their players as hired guns; Lennon just seemed to be looking for companionship. "There was absolutely no rock star stuff going on there," Gabriel remembered, "it was just two guitarists, working out parts the way they do in every band."

"What Gabriel won't mention is that his mother had died recently before he got the Lennon gig," Van Scyoc says now. "That was a big bond for those two, since Lennon had lost his mother when he was a teenager." The two musicians spent hours together, using guitars as a metaphor. "They sat cross-legged together for a couple hours while the rest of us went off to eat," Van Scyoc remembers, "they had a special thing." Gabriel continues, "He had this basic insecurity, you know, he really didn't walk around with this 'I'm John Lennon' attitude, he really worked hard at his music and it came from a place of 'What's the best way to pull this off?' "23

Like most musicians, even once they got a gig with Lennon, the Elephants held on to their day jobs to support their music, doing TV jingles and studio sessions. They came together in the evenings to work on their tracks. The *Some Time in New York City* sessions started most evenings around seven. "He'd write the song the night before," Van Scyoc remembers, "come in at seven, work up a feel for it, figure out a tempo, we'd have dinner, talk about the track, then go back and get the balance figured out, bang on the drums, then start doing takes. And by seven the next morning we'd have a track—mixed. He liked to work fast. And when it came time to do Yoko's album (*Approximately Infinite Universe*)," Van Scyoc continues, "he gave just as much, to every song, every part for three full weeks. He helped us with our material, our lyrics, too, and we could never convince him to take any credit for that. He was humble like that. Yoko Ono deserves far more credit than she'll ever get."24

A RADICAL BROADSHEET disguised as a rock album, *Some Time in New York City* was released in the summer of 1972 to mostly negative reviews. Its cover laid out the song lyrics as newspaper articles under a *New York Times* headline font. "Sisters, O Sisters" showed a photo of the band with Lennon on *The Mike Douglas Show* set, above a photo of Black Panther activist Angela Davis. John and Yoko appeared over the headline "Woman Is the Nigger of the World"; above Yoko Ono's "We're All Water," a doctored photo appeared of Nixon dancing naked with Chairman Mao.

For some, the imagery alone distracted from the music; for others, the music never lived up to its packaging. Critics tended to undervalue the material based on loftier expectations, but its sturdy, driving lead track, "New York City," a fetching Chuck Berry tribute, and several standout numbers ("John Sinclair," "Woman Is the Nigger of the World") rebuff its weak reputation. A bonus album included some music from the Frank Zappa Fillmore East jams from 1971.

Even when they agreed with the politics, many critics couldn't defend the writing. In the August issue of *Creem,* Dave Marsh took apart the Irish message songs: "'Sunday Bloody Sunday' cuts McCartney's 'Give Ireland Back to the Irish' and it don't even matter much that [Ringo's] 'Back Off Boogaloo' is a better statement on the subject than either." Marsh went on to note how Yoko Ono's bridge muddied a potential marvel of a song, "Luck of the Irish":

Let's walk over rainbows like leprechauns
The world would be one big Blarney stone

Without this intrusion, marred by Ono's off-pitch delivery, Lennon could have released a classic rebellious statement in a beguiling, sentimental mode. But his indulgence of his wife's pretensions compromised both his politics and one of the better songs in this sequence.

"That isn't just false, it's racist," Marsh notes, "in the same way that the insistence of John's Yoko-hype is inadvertently sexist."[25] (Yoko Ono: she's a lot of things, but she's no Sinead O'Connor.) The British press, of course, had a harder time watching Lennon side with the Irish Republican Army. A beloved Brit who had settled in a former colony accusing the English ("the bastards") of "genocide" had a bit too much condescension in it even for rock lefties. Ian MacDonald later reported in *Uncut,* "as FBI papers released in 1997 show, [Lennon] got involved with Irish Republicans in New York early in 1972, having toted a placard proclaiming 'Victory for the IRA Against British Imperialism' at an anti-internment rally in London the previous August. How did Lennon reconcile his pacifism with his support for the IRA? 'It's a very delicate line,' he feigned, soon thereafter quietly discontinuing his romance with terrorism."[26] Being stalked by the FBI sorely tested Lennon's commitment to nonviolence, although this appears to be his only brush with Irish revolutionaries.

As critics wrung their hands, radio recoiled at the word "nigger," and a potential single, "New York City," didn't get the chance it deserved. Out in California, a young deejay at KABC named Elliot Mintz had interviewed Yoko Ono, and he stayed friendly with her on the phone. They discovered they were both telephone freaks. Ono had ideas about the "purity" of the human voice removing prejudice, and Mintz suffered from chronic insomnia—they loved to gab through the night. Pretty soon, Lennon joined in. For kicks, Mintz played *Some Time in New York City* all the way through on the air the week before its release. It got him fired. Lennon found this hilarious. They invited him up to San Francisco, where they could continue their phone conversations in person, and Mintz became a lifelong friend. "Pack a bag and join the circus," said Lennon.[27]

As MORE AND MORE POLITICAL RALLIES and charity events came along, John and Yoko developed a deepening attachment to New York and American society at large. Geraldo Rivera, then a young reporter for WABC-TV's *Eyewitness News,* took on Lennon's immigration case for frequent updates on the evening news, regularly catching him outside the courthouse for quotes. Another Rivera story followed up on a public television exposé of the Willowbrook facility for special needs children on Staten Island, which documented the neglect and dismal living conditions of its patients. Rivera dubbed the facility "the Big Town's leper colony" and stirred up outrage over the lack of care for the mentally ill. Since part of the inequity stemmed from up to fifty patients being supervised by a single staffer, Rivera launched a charity crusade called "One to One," advocating for bigger staff budgets and better hygiene.

In response, the Rockefeller administration restored a $20 million budget cut. Rivera persuaded John and Yoko to stage a charity concert at Madison Square Garden modeled on Harrison's Concert for Bangladesh, filmed for television, dubbed the One to One concert. The bill featured Sha Na Na, Stevie Wonder, Roberta Flack, and Lennon and Ono doing *Some Time* material with the Elephant's Memory Band. Ticket demand added a second matinee show before the evening concert. Ono later repackaged this concert as *John Lennon: Live in New York City,* an uneven set bound together by his continuously inspired singing.

For the show, Lennon boosted the Elephant lineup to thicken the sound for the huge Madison Square Garden venue. "Lennon wanted to hire Hendrix drummer Noel Redding for the gig," Van Scyoc says, "but he wasn't available." So he hired Jim Keltner to double on drums ("Jim was his rock," Gruen confirms), and Van Scyoc suggested the former Elephant bass player, John Ward, for the low end. "He hadn't performed in a while, so he was a little nervous, and he had a sore throat that day," Van Scyoc remembers. "But you'd never know it. It went very smoothly, we might have muffed one arrangement, but he muffed it with everybody else and we just kept going." The band pushed Lennon to sing at least one Beatle number, and they settled on "Come Together," which turned from delicate production piece to virulent antiwar blues.

"Sitting next to him while he sang 'Imagine' has to be one of my all-time biggest moments as a rock fan," remembers Bob Gruen. "It was one of those untouchable moments that sent shivers down everybody's spine." For the encore, they were having such a good time, Lennon pulled out "Hound Dog," which they had never rehearsed. "He was really a huge Elvis fan," Van Scyoc says.

The concert has an uneven reputation, and made a better live experience than recording or film, at least according to those who were there. "That One to One concert was supposed to be the beginning of a world tour," Tex remembers. "But the critics were so sour on that record, and it really took Lennon aback. We were all having such a good time and fighting the good fight."[28] It didn't occur to them that the rest of the world might not hear it the way they did.

The next week, as if affirming they wanted to become mainstream American celebrities, John and Yoko showed up on the annual Jerry Lewis telethon, the all-day charity event to raise money for muscular dystrophy. Lennon sang "Imagine," Ono did "Now or Never," and together they did a reggae version of "Give Peace a Chance."

But the negative reviews and the generalized hostility that greeted Yoko sent Lennon back spiraling into insecurity about his solo career, and the musical value of political activism. In November 1972, the left watched with dismay as George McGovern lost to Nixon in a landslide, the second biggest electoral thumping in modern history to that point (Nixon carried every state except Massachusetts).

This had a devastating effect on what remained of the antiwar left.

For Lennon, it meant that on some level all his activism had backfired, and that once again everybody had lauded his music without listening to his message. At Jerry Rubin's party on election night, Lennon monopolized the tequila and out came the self-loathing and abandonment issues: All the funny sounds on his phone and the blatant tails he spotted from his limo made him suspect Rubin was a CIA agent who had double-crossed him. After all, Rubin had induced the Lennons into the revolutionary fray, and now all their worst fears about leaving Britain were coming true.

Unfortunately, no matter how far Lennon had grown as a musician, the bottle always dragged him right back down into his angry paranoid shtick. He berated his hosts and accused the activists of ruining his career. He blamed the legal process and the shadowy FBI characters who followed him everywhere for hampering his creativity. Meanwhile, Yoko Ono's current songs were indictments of the male chauvinism with which Lennon was treating her.

The party disintegrated, with one humiliation piled on another. Nixon won with bigger numbers than when Johnson defeated Goldwater back in 1964, and now here was the partygoers' own leftist icon, the leader of the Beatles, shaming himself and his wife even further. He began flirting aggressively with one of Rubin's roommates, and Hoffman's sometime romantic partner, right in front of Yoko. Then he took the woman's hand and led her into the next room, playing the rock star with no scruples. The remaining guests were obliged to begin talking more loudly so as not to hear Lennon and his pickup going at it. When he reemerged, he simply took Ono's hand and left.

"That was the only time I remember Yoko breaking down and showing any of us what she was feeling," Tex Gabriel says. "I gave her my sunglasses so she could leave with some self-respect. Everybody in the room knew what was going on, it was extremely humiliating. And we were all just sort of humiliated along with her, having watched Nixon's landslide."[29]

THE FOLLOWING MORNING, John and Yoko took a walk on the pier by the Hudson with Bob Gruen, who photographed Lennon down on his knees to Yoko begging for forgiveness. "He had been drunk, he was sorry, it was the same old story," Gruen remembers. A new wariness emerged in Yoko—how long could this kind of public humiliation continue? At that afternoon's session, Ono sang "What a *bastard* the world is," a searing rebuke of male chauvinism. What kind of justice was this? Ono must have wondered: What did Lennon's romantic idealization count for if not simple monogamy? As much as she adored her husband, Ono had more self-respect than Cynthia—this behavior was not the sort of thing she could build a marriage on.

Lennon had moved to his wife's artistic home and reworked his political identity by bonding with America's most theatrical radicals. But in doing so, he became the target of U.S. authority in ways few could fathom, just as his marriage, already another outsize myth, foundered on his own self-destructiveness.

I'm a Loser

J OHN AND YOKO MOVED UPTOWN—FROM THE WEST VILLAGE TO THE
fortresslike Dakota on Central Park West—during the spring 1973
Record Plant sessions that produced *Mind Games*. The building's notoriously selective co-op board granted them access to actor Robert Ryan's
recently vacated seventh-floor apartment.[1] Leon Wildes, Lennon's attorney, added this as another endorsement of citizenship to the bulging
immigration file.

The building's gothic presence was already famous, mostly for the
gruesome portent of Mia Farrow's horror hit, *Rosemary's Baby* (1968).
John and Yoko's new neighbors included Leonard Bernstein, Lauren
Bacall, and Roberta Flack, then a pop fixture with "The First Time Ever
I Saw Your Face." For some reason, some Britons still look down on the
Dakota, as if Lennon deserved better, apparently unaware of the build-
ing's prestige as a Manhattan address.[2]

Several concurrent legal problems arose as they settled into their new
quarters. The Immigration and Naturalization Services (INS) suddenly
stepped up deportation proceedings based on Lennon's long-lapsed visitation visa, which dated back to 1971. The FBI harassment continued,
and Leon Wildes began to notice strange noises on his phone line. And
the ongoing dissolution of the Beatles took a new turn as Lennon, Harrison, and Starr disentangled themselves from Allen Klein, whose contract expired in April 1973. From Klein's point of view, he had performed

well: even McCartney acknowledged he'd won £5 million for the band in back royalties from EMI/Capitol. But his stewardship of Apple had only exacerbated the rift between him, McCartney, and Eastman, and with every Apple deal it became clearer that the only way the band could settle their long-standing dispute was without Klein.

For his part, Klein remained resolute: "Paul rejected a £1 million offer by the other Beatles to buy him out of their partnership," Klein said of this 1973 decision. "But Paul turned it down. He wouldn't take it. . . . He doesn't want to get out, and that's really the problem. Now you have a company with four partners, each of whom has a different interest, and to get each one to agree to something, like whether Ringo should make a film, becomes almost impossible. How do they stay partners? It's very hard." Klein insisted he had tried to arrange a takeover of Apple and all the other Beatles' interests, in a merger with his own ABKCO company, but that McCartney blocked any such ambitions.[3]

From the McCartney-Eastman side, the only thing Klein excelled at was back royalties—few could run Apple's gridlocked board, and Klein's jackhammer style worked against him. Conveniently forgetting his earlier pledge to Lennon, Klein began collecting commissions on contracts covering catalog material predating 1970. The Beatles found themselves cash-poor and anxious to table the entire conflict. Some sources claim Lennon still resented Klein having sided with Harrison against Yoko in the Bangladesh concert fiasco. What had first seemed frank and honest business strategy had become part of a much larger dispute on how to allocate all the Beatles' resources—for every solo album released under the current agreement, all royalties funneled straight into escrow. Lennon, Harrison, and Starr ultimately took Klein to court to sever their relationship, which resulted in a $3 million payoff and the final Beatles settlement of Apple's finances in early 1975.

Oblivious to such financial arrangements and the tensions they caused, the pop market still clamored for new Beatle product, and the press ran reunion rumors weekly. During their early tours, "What will you do when the bubble bursts?" hounded them everywhere they went. Gamely, they dodged and mocked such nonsense through their recordings, which kept raising the stakes until the question itself rang hollow. Now, barely three years into their solo careers, none of them could promote an individual album without getting asked about playing with the others, to the point where they wondered aloud whether breaking up had been worthwhile. It was like getting pressed about honeymoon details during divorce affidavits. *Rolling Stone,* reporting on the new market for Beatle collectibles at fan conventions, interviewed four rock promoters about how they would handle a hypothetical Beatle reunion tour. They settled on a round figure of $50 million. The noisy, ideas-driven rock critic Lester Bangs—portrayed by Philip Seymour Hoffman in 2000 in Cameron Crowe's *Almost Famous*—declared that any Beatle reunion would amount to "the biggest anti-climax of all time."[4] A conundrum hung in this expectant, early-seventies-rock atmosphere: a yearning for the Beatles pressed up against not wanting to invest in almost certain disappointment.

AFTER *IMAGINE,* LENNON'S MID-PERIOD solo career swung between lacerating self-examination and groping intellectualism, with three albums that proved *Plastic Ono Band* his most emotionally direct yet layered work: in 1973, *Mind Games* followed him out to Los Angeles as his weakest effort yet; *Walls and Bridges* (1974) and *Rock 'n' Roll* (1975) tilted him right back to New York, as if climbing his way out of a mistake. *Pussy Cats,* Lennon's production of Harry Nilsson, also in 1974, straddled the line between greatness averted and desperation absolved. As new acts like the Eagles, Lou Reed, and Led Zeppelin ascended to pop royalty, Lennon's work in this period reveled in the mood of an era still hungover from its glory days: you can hear the difference between a hangover at age twenty-six ("A Day in the Life") and one at thirty-three or thirty-four (the false uplift of "One Day (at a Time)," the dread pulsing through "Scared" and "Nobody Loves You When You're Down and Out"). Such signposts mark the difference between the possibilities left in rock 'n' roll and enforced rock 'n' roll cheer that sank of its own fatigue. "A Day In the Life" remains the more mature statement.

Rock careers travel fragmented paths, mocking and disrupting the linear showbiz narratives of hit records, schlock movie tie-ins, and sprawling end-games. In a lot of rock careers, weak sideshows illuminate core greatness. Dylan's *Self-Portrait* (1970), for example, threw the elusively comic triumph of *Blonde on Blonde* (1966) or the elusively metaphysical *John Wesley Harding* (1968) into high relief, and the Rolling Stones' *Goats Head Soup* (1973), with the hit "Angie," splashed cold commercial water on the band's master stroke, *Exile on Main Street* (1972), which sported not just "Tumbling Dice" and "Happy," but "Sweet Virginia," "Rocks Off," and "All Down the Line," and their second defining cover of a revered Robert Johnson song, "Stop Breaking Down," which rivaled "Love in Vain" (on 1969's *Let It Bleed).* If rock style had been invented by and for teenagers, these acts now walked an anxious middle-aged line: since most of these figures came of listening age to the young Elvis, Buddy Holly, and Little Richard, the very idea of a rock career galloping into middle age carried ironic kick. And like Francis Ford Coppola, determined to reenergize the gangster genre with *The Godfather,* extending adolescent thrills into adulthood became rock's new puzzler.

Like the rock stars it spawned, the sixties rock audience, too, had grown up, and sought out more mature themes. A lot of material from this phase dealt either with outgrowing adolescence or succumbing to it all over again. The Beatles had played out the central coming-of-age story for the medium; now rock stars persisted in chasing youthful kicks. Hitmeister Elton John, for example, never seemed more like a Pillsbury Doughboy than when attempting social commentary ("Ticking," off 1974's *Caribou*). Mick Jagger responded by splitting his persona in two: offstage, he played the celebrity bad boy, but the narrative voice of his songs had already wizened through his immersion in the blues. McCartney's persona reversed Jagger's template: at home, he seemed the model father and family man; onstage, his act persisted with boyish charm. Lennon had already proven such a master of pop forms that his path seemed oddly simple: just fashion a career based on his direct experience, and he'd be fine.

But the real-life hurdles of this career strategy proved daunting. Lennon had already turned in his big statement (with *Plastic Ono Band*); now he backpedaled. Nothing smacked more of passé than a sixties figurehead like Lennon going nostalgic. Worse than that, nostalgia became Lennon's key selling point. With the "Mind Games" single, the author of both "The Word" and "All You Need Is Love"—who had renounced the Beatles, the sixties, and all those adolescent notions about heroic, utopian redemption in "God"—now wallowed in clichés about flower power and positive thinking: "Yes is the answer . . . And you know that for sure." All of a sudden, even "Imagine," released only two years earlier, sounded like the Sanskrit of sixties uplift. On "God," Lennon's brute insights had a bracing, clear-the-air candor; here, he reflected wistfulness as mere audience expectation—a yearning to be played to rather than exposed as cant.

Lennon's vocal, however, had inimitable overtones and kept you straining to hear more layers through his considerable craft: "Mind Games" wafted across radio with sweeping strings doubling guitar lines, surrounding Lennon's voice like a cloud moving across a great horizon of feeling. But the album as a whole lacked a core emotion, or any recurring themes to hang on to; it had all the earmarks of a professionally designed logo. (Most of this material had trouble living up to Lennon's epigram: "Madness is the first sign of dandruff.") The exception proved the rule: "Bring On the Lucie (Freda Peeple)," a rolling protest anthem, with steel guitar atop Jim Keltner's swirling drums, stood out like a great lost classic (and would make a soaring finale to *The U.S. vs. John Lennon* documentary in 2006).

The musical clues all over *Mind Games* diagram a man in an aesthetic rut, a public metaphor for his unspooling marriage. It's one of the few Lennon albums that sounds like "product," where his vocals generally lack inspiration. This music didn't illuminate or qualify much of anything else in his catalog, and the biggest criticism he exposed himself to was disregard for his audience's best hopes. "One Day (at a Time)," an ambitious, multilayered song, sounds like Lennon getting ensnared in McCartney's coy frippery while trying to mock him (with irredeemable lyrics like "'Cause I'm the fish and you're the sea"). In *Melody Maker,* Chris Charlesworth called it "very twee," which to Lennon ranked as anathema.[5] When Elton John put his version on the B side of his "Lucy in the Sky with Diamonds" single, many fans mistook it for an original.

"Intuition" was barely a song at all. Critic Neil Splinter noted: "At one time, I would have said that *Mind Games* is a terrible album because it in no way reflects Lennon's capabilities. But after four solo albums, each one lousier than the last, I'm no longer sure that Lennon is capable of anything other than leading a friendly corner superstar existence."[6] Many other reviewers were kinder, out of sheer sympathy for the amount of stifled talent.

FAR FROM WANING IN THE WAKE OF THE BREAKUP, the market for Beatle product only expanded. In March 1973, the Grammys awarded George Harrison and Phil Spector the 1972 Album of the Year for the *Concert for Bangladesh* set. A bootleg outfit assembled a compilation called *Beatles: Alpha/Omega* and bought late-night TV advertising. It was boldly illegal but flew just under EMI's radar, and began selling briskly.

One of Allen Klein's last acts as Apple administrator was to rush the Apple "Red" (*The Beatles 1963–1966*) and "Blue" (*The Beatles 1967–1970*) double albums to stores in April 1973, to meet soaring demand for an official "greatest hits" package to stem their losses. Both sets signaled a new era of sixties reissues that far outlasted the band's original seven-year run, and they both raced to the top of the charts, becoming two of pop's strongest "catalog" items. Each revived Lennon's original idea for the *Get Back* cover, with all four long-haired Beatles grinning down at the camera from the same EMI balcony they had posed on, six years and several pop lifetimes earlier, for *Please Please Me*. Bootleggers had forced the new product, but the situation only fed reunion frenzy, and reminded pop listeners of rock's black hole. The post-Beatle pop climate comprised the popular (like Three Dog Night or Led Zeppelin) and substantive (Fairport Convention and Randy Newman), but seldom both at once. Acts like Roxy Music, Steely Dan, and Joni Mitchell pulled this feat off, but without anywhere near the same massive cultural success as the Beatles. Not until Fleetwood Mac turned from blues to pop in 1975 did pop gain a new sense of melodic verve, and by then most Beatle rumors had grown wistful.

As the *Alpha/Omega* bootleg rattled the Apple bean counters, Ringo

Starr, in Los Angeles with producer Richard Perry, tackled a Lennon song written especially for him called "I Am the Greatest." Lennon and Ono flew out to take part in the track on March 13, 1973, joining Starr and, ultimately, Harrison. Perry swooned at his good fortune: "We all sort of gathered around the piano and chipped in our ideas and helped complete it. Then the phone rang and it was George, who said, 'I hear there's a track going on. Is it okay if I come down?'" Perry turned to John, who shot back, "'Well, yes, of course. Tell him to get down here and help me finish this bridge.'"[7]

In the UK, this constituted a major story: the *New Musical Express* ran a feature touting a reunion exclusive, despite the tart Lennon reply. "With or without the present situation," Lennon told a reporter, "the chances are practically nil! . . . If any of you actually remember when we were together, everybody was talking about it as though it was wonderful all the time." He hated the disingenuousness of all the Beatle talk almost as much as he feared its seductiveness: "All the press and all the people, all saying how great and how wonderful . . . but it wasn't like that at all! And imagine *if* they did get together, what kind of scrutiny would they be under? Nothing could fit the dream people had of them. So forget it, you know, it's ludicrous!"[8] This sounded as if Lennon had read Lester Bangs's admonition.

Near the end of March 1973, New York judge Ira Fieldsteel ruled on Lennon's temporary visa status, ordering him to leave the country (again) within sixty days or face deportation. Outside the courtroom, Lennon told reporters: "Having just celebrated our fourth wedding anniversary, we are not prepared to sleep in separate beds. Peace and love, John and Yoko." Ono already had a green card, which granted her alien resident status, through her marriage to Tony Cox; Cox had disappeared with Kyoko. While the press wrote reams of sympathetic copy supporting the Lennon case, the FBI had already logged hundreds of surveillance hours to intimidate them out of the country. This only emboldened Lennon's resolve to stay and fight.

On April 1, John and Yoko held a press conference in New York with Leon Wildes to announce the formation of a new conceptual country: Nutopia. "Citizenship of the country can be obtained by declaration of your awareness of Nutopia." To Lennon, this seemed no less ridiculous than the constant runaround his immigration status had been subjected to. "Nutopia has no land, no boundaries, no passports, only people. Nutopia has no laws other than cosmic. All people of Nutopia are ambassadors of the country. As two ambassadors of NUTOPIA, we ask for diplomatic immunity and recognition in the United Nations of our country and our people."[9] As a publicity stunt, it won points for comic flair, but it lacked the froth of the bed-ins, or Lennon's returning the MBE to the queen. Lennon was in the moral right, but these were times that crushed spirits—the antiwar movement lay in tatters after Nixon's reelection, and Lennon's latest campaign seemed tilted against an all-consuming government bureaucracy bent on taking him down. For a rock star who had gone to great lengths to redefine himself as the singer of "Woman Is the Nigger of the World," the epic proportions of Nixon's paranoia made such sardonics seem frail.

WITHIN WEEKS AFTER KLEIN'S CONTRACT EXPIRED, he announced plans to buy Apple outright, sending lawyers off to new galaxies of bickering and paperwork. Around this period, personal relations among the Beatles themselves softened considerably, with reports of informal visits and recording collaborations studding their schedules. Now that Klein was on his way out, they all started getting along better.

The press, however, chewed reunion talk to a pulp. Lennon finally wrote up a statement making hay of it, called "Newswecanalldowithout," a press release ridiculing every legal position, including some of his own:

> Although John and Yoko and George, and George and Ringo have played together often, it was the first time the three ex-Beauties have played together since, well, since they last played together. As usual, an awful lot of rumours, if not downright lies, were going on, including the possibility of impresair allen De Klein of GrABKCo playing bass for the other three in an "as-yet-untitled" album called I Was Teenage Fat . . . The extreme humility that existed between John and Paul seems to have evap-

orated. "They've spoken to each other on the telephone, and in English, that's a change," said a McCartney associated. "If only everything were as simple and unaffected as McCartney's new single 'My Love.' Then maybe Dean Martin and Jerry Lewish would be reunited with the Marx Brothers, and NEWSWEAK could get a job," said an East African official—Yours up to the teeth—John Lennon and Yoko Ono.[10]

For a time, John and Yoko's Upper West Side nightlife fed the tabloids. And they were photographed at an antiwar demonstration outside the South Vietnamese Embassy in Washington, D.C., on June 28, and at Senate Watergate hearings the next day. As part of a complicated loan agreement where Lennon borrowed against future earnings with Klein, Ringo Starr bought his Tittenhurst mansion, with its home studio setup. Then, as if on cue, Lennon's hard living began to catch up with him: the American papers, which generally adored his manic quotability, strayed from the unwritten British rules of celebrity denial. Lennon drank a lot in public, took side girlfriends, and snuck around, and John and Yoko came to the studio more apart than together anymore. Producer Jack Douglas, who had worked with Lennon since *Imagine,* remembers how this talk started: "John was in the control room at a Yoko session I was doing, maybe it was *Approximately Infinite Universe.* Anyway, he cracked up at something he heard, and just then Yoko walked in. He was busted. From that moment on, Lennon was not allowed at Yoko sessions."[11] Those who knew him well knew Lennon to be famously generous and well mannered except when drunk, but lately he seemed to be getting drunk a lot. Old stories about his dark, violent side roared back from Liverpool and Hamburg. "He was a drunk," Bob Gruen maintains, "and Yoko finally kicked him out. It was very abrupt, and had grown into one of those tired clichés, you know: you always say you're sorry, but you always get drunk and screw things up again. Enough! You're out!"[12] Yoko Ono had slammed the brakes on becoming the new Cynthia Lennon.

One night late that summer, as Gruen drove Lennon home from a *Mind Games* session at the Record Plant, Lennon told him to take him up to East 91st Street. "I'm staying with May," he told Gruen, referring to May Pang, who had joined Lennon and Ono as an assistant during Ono's *Fly* shoot back in October 1970, and walked onstage in a bag during *The Dick Cavett Show.*

Yoko made a gamble widely misunderstood in American culture. One day she took Pang aside and gave her a new task: to be Lennon's lover. At first, Pang was horrified—she had no interest in this arrangement. But when Lennon began flirting with her openly, she slowly succumbed. The separation had intriguing complications, with daily phone calls back and forth between Lennon and Ono, a symbolic short leash that Pang toughed out as if she were a late-twentieth-century concubine.

Such arrangements are not rare in certain upscale Japanese circles, where a wife's knowledge of an affair can override concerns about a husband's indiscretions; most Americans, however, have little understanding of the nuances of aristocratic Japanese culture. For some Japanese, the competing value of the family structure holds sway; the wife maintains her status and keeps tabs on her husband. In certain cases, by the wife choosing her husband's lover for him and overseeing an affair, adolescent impulses get resolved without an unruly and costly disruption. This was simply one step away from a gentleman keeping a geisha, that distinctly ruling-class Japanese arrangement that had all the trimmings of refined discretion except for how sex was exchanged for money.

May Pang's memoir, *Loving John,* tells of a young, conflicted woman who realized too late her role as pawn in Yoko's game. Much of the book reflects Pang's revenge fantasy against Ono, and it's easy to imagine a young aide in this position falling hard for Lennon. Pang was all of twenty-two, and since she was an employee, Ono engaged in manipulative sexual harassment just as much as Lennon. As with too many Lennon tell-alls, though, Pang's motive itself is suspiciously personal, and the dirt outweighs the substance. Her tone is matter-of-fact, even as she describes more a complicated married couple working out a private issue than a marriage gone sour. Yoko Ono calls Lennon nearly every day for hour-long details about his life and career, almost as if Aunt Mimi herself were keeping track of her nephew. The most curious aspect of this was how all parties submitted to the setup: Lennon made few efforts to push back against Ono's constant inquisitions, and Pang felt like a kitten sparring with tigers. To make Ono out the lone culprit in this scheme ignores the many subtle allowances and emotional trade-offs each protagonist consented to.

In his larger story, this eighteen-month "separation," often called Lennon's "lost weekend," was merely physical. Lennon looked forward to many of Ono's calls, and Pang accepted Lennon's "legacy issues" while he professed love to his new consort. Like his implicit deals with McCartney, Epstein, and the Beatles, it's another situation where Lennon willingly participated in an elaborate passive-aggressive scheme. Echoes of his Woolton childhood couldn't be more obvious: Lennon had engineered the same dynamic between his mother, Julia, and her overprotective sister, Aunt Mimi. In this latest scenario, Yoko let him run wild to get his zipper problem out of his system. Perhaps she gambled that he would find his new young flame wanting in the conversation department, and perhaps after that scene at Jerry Rubin's apartment on election night 1972, where he publicly humiliated her in front of their band, she doubted whether Lennon was worth staying with for the long run anyway. After years of struggling for recognition behind her more famous spouse, Ono had finally landed herself in a prestigious apartment uptown, and promoters were entreating her to tour Japan—without Lennon. In her home country, she had emerged as a cultural hero, and there was her own career to consider. Neither of them, however, was ready or willing to let go completely, so they simply separated for a while.

But everybody who knew them in this period recalls many more affairs woven in between Pang and Ono. "I've always been surprised that no more girlfriends have come forward," Gruen says now. "There were many, many different women Lennon slept around with, although Pang was with him the whole time. Some she knew about, others she didn't. But she's the only one who's stepped forward to write a book."[13]

Once Lennon hit Los Angeles in September and the split became public, he sloped downward into an all-too familiar type: that of the middle-aged celebrity, fleeing his "romance of the century" for some hard partying with the old-boy network. (In rock terms, thirty-three used to qualify as "middle-aged.") The bed-ins and wacky art happenings had devolved like so many other similar events into a typical clash of egos and appetites. The anti-Yoko crowd could take comfort only to the extent that Lennon reconvened with other rock legends (Keith Moon, Ringo Starr, Harry Nilsson) as an aimless, dissolute has-been coasting on his sixties reputation. For some, this self-destructive route was as idealistic as rock 'n' roll would ever get.

THE ARTWORK FOR *MIND GAMES* featured Lennon walking toward the viewer in a field, overwhelmed from behind by a huge screen of Yoko's profile. Pang reports that Lennon told her, "Look, I'm walking away from Yoko" as if he had constructed a cosmic accident and couldn't quite believe he had it in him. It's one of those crude yet illuminating visual symbols that reveals far more in retrospect: Yoko isn't the other half of the sky, she *is* the sky; figuratively, Lennon can no more "walk away" from her mythic comfort than he can stop breathing. His new antics in L.A. recalled his adolescent binges in Hamburg, but back then he always had Mendips to come home to. The Dakota became this all-protective symbol in the back of his mind, and his deal with May Pang always had this implicit retreat position, although Pang seems to have been too young to detect it.

Lennon, of course, had seen so many celebrity scenes before, he walked through Los Angeles with a vague sense of déjà vu. Somewhere, deep down, he knew he didn't want to end up like Brian Epstein, one too many lost weekends away from a stable home life he had never succeeded at. In Los Angeles, Phil Spector became his new counter example—the fellow genius who was busy screwing up his life even more than Lennon. In the middle of September, Lennon and Pang jetted off together to California, giddy with "freedom" and full of high-stepping schemes. He had been chatting up Spector about making an oldies album, which Spector was wary about, until Lennon convinced him he wanted to be treated as a mere singer (as if there had ever been anything "mere" about Lennon's singing). Coming after the tepid *Mind Games,* this could only be seen as a fallback move. Instead of leading, Lennon followed.

He left Manhattan after contributing a nostalgic book review to the

New York Times, with a verbal alacrity largely missing from *Mind Games.* WBAI public radio had been broadcasting old *Goon Show* episodes, and Spike Milligan had just published *The Goon Show Scripts.*

An unsigned introduction explaining the Goons to Americans read in part: "There was a plot of sorts which was somewhere between a Chinese opera and World War II in comprehensibility. . . . Goonery was not so much a show, more a way of life, and if you have to ask what it was, we'll be here all day explaining the joke. *The Goon Show* expired, to eternal regrets in Britain, on Jan. 28, 1960."[14] Lennon's review ran under the headline, YOU HAD TO BE THERE, AND HE WAS, and he began by saying he was twelve when the Goons first hit, and sixteen "when they finished with me," a "conspiracy against reality" that shaped Lennon's young sensibility. The review bulges with references and side-swipes that recall his best verse:

> Before becoming the Beatles' producer, George Martin, who had never recorded rock 'n' roll, had previously recorded with Milligan and Sellers, which made him all the more acceptable—our studio sessions were full of the cries of Neddie Seagoon, etc., etc., as were most places in Britain. There are records of some of the original radio shows, some of which I have, but when I play them to Yoko I find myself explaining that in those days there was no "monty-pythons flyin' circus," no "laugh-in," in fact, the same rigmarole I go through with my "fifties records," "before rock it was just Perry Como," etc. What I'm trying to say is, one has to have been there! The Goon Show was long before and more revolutionary than "look back in anger" (it appealed to "eggheads" and "the people"). . . . A "coup d'etat" of the mind! The evidence, for and against, is in this book. A copy of which should be sent to Mr. Nixon and Mr. Sam J. Ervin.

While openly adoring all the Goons, Lennon singles out Spike in particular: "His appearances on TV as 'himself' were something to behold," Lennon wrote. ". . . He would run off camera and DARE them to follow him. I think they did, once or twice, but it kept him off more shows than it helped get him on. There was always the attitude that, he was 'wonderful, you know . . . [indicating head].' I think it's 'cause he's Irish. (The same attitude prevails toward all non-English British.)"[15] Note the adoring reference to his wife, Yoko, even as he's headed to Los Angeles with the help.

As if to keep some semblance of a personal life afloat, Lennon moved about Los Angeles briskly—keeping busy as if scared to sit still. Just as *Mind Games* and *Ringo* hit the stores, Lennon showed up with May Pang for the first Phil Spector oldies sessions, where *Rock 'n' Roll* was tracking at A&M Studios and Gold Star in Hollywood. Lennon and Spector had compiled a list of songs, and Spector handled arrangements and booked players like it was 1963. Biographer Mark Ribowsky recalled the producer's point of view: "I just wanna be like Ronnie Spector," Lennon told Phil.

Lennon putting himself in Spector's hands might have been preferable as a musical tactic, but as a matter of day-to-day professionalism, it quickly sprang leaks. "An excessively avaricious Spector immediately paid for the sessions himself," Ribowsky writes in his well-reported account, "thus wresting official control from John, Apple Records, and his American label, Capitol. While *Mind Games* was the name of his last album, it soon came to characterize Phil's design for this one. John could not get through the A&M studio gate unless he told the guard he was there for the Phil Spector sessions."[16] Lennon had begged to be treated like a singer; Spector obliged, turning the *Mind Games* title into a ruse. "You want mind games," Spector seemed to chuckle, "I'll give you mind games."

Dan Kessel, a guitarist and drummer, and son of jazz guitarist Barney Kessel, was part of a coterie who observed many Spector sessions, and he lapsed into conversation with Lennon about old records. "Throughout the *Rock 'n' Roll* recording sessions, we'd talk to John often, especially during breaks between takes and playbacks," Kessel says. "I remember he fell in love with my customized Gibson Everly Brothers guitar while we were recording 'Angel Baby.' He loved playing it so much I let him use it during the sessions. And even though there was no shortage in the Kessel Brothers guitar arsenal, John let me use his guitar, a modified, German hollow-body electric (that he called 'Roger') made in the fifties. Despite some repair work on the neck, it stayed in tune and sounded great." After the session, Lennon pressed his guitar on Kessel as a gift. "I was flabbergasted and gladly accepted his guitar," Kessel says.

Lennon's jaw dropped to hear Kessel talk about catching a Rosie and the Originals show in the late fifties. "John, and my brother David, and I agreed adamantly that 'Angel Baby' by Rosie and the Originals was one of the greatest records of all time, for many different reasons, which we discussed at length. And, after drinking quite a bit, we got all excited and emotional, even crying tears about it and the genius of the B side, 'Give Me Love,' too, and about how we all wished we could have been in the Originals." Lennon hung on every word as Kessel described catching Little Caesar and the Romans, and shared details about the Rosie and the Originals show he heard at the El Monte Legion Stadium.[17] According to Kessel, Lennon would have traded several Beatle guitars for such stories.

Kicked off with high ambitions, the Spector sessions quickly unraveled into bad boys gone wild: liquor, the key culprit, worked as lubricant for a dazzling array of chemicals, chiefly cocaine, then openly abused in Hollywood. One evening, Lennon veered so violently out of control that Spector and a staffer hustled him into his car and took him to the producer's house. Having wrestled the rock star to the bedroom, they bound his wrists and ankles with neckties so he could simply yell off some steam. "They left him like that, tied up like a steer," Ribowsky writes, "with John yelling 'Jew bastard!' at Phil as he left."[18] The old Liverpool anti-Semitism first used on Epstein returned to mock Spector, whom Lennon openly deified when sober.

"Phil had to handcuff John because John would have killed himself," Dan Kessel said. "Yoko really blew John's mind when she threw him out, and he was raging out of his head and threatening suicide. John would sleep at Phil's house and Phil would have to lock the door on him when he'd get too crazy. But when he woke up and it was all over, it was kinda like, you know, 'Thanks a lot for doing that.'"[19]

When Starr's *Ringo* jumped two spaces above *Mind Games* to number four on the Billboard charts, Lennon wrote Starr a postcard: "Congratulations. How dare you. Write me a hit song."[20]

Dropping in on these Lennon-Spector sessions quickly turned into celebrity sport. Harry Nilsson poked his head in the door one evening and revived the friendship from the *White Album* sessions. They tore off to the races. Lennon, of course, had admired Nilsson since discovering *Pandemonium Shadow Show*, enough to mention his name in a 1968 interview. Nilsson enjoyed a huge international hit in 1971 with a Badfinger song, "Without You," followed by "Coconut," from *Nilsson Schmilsson* (1971) hitting number eight; 1972 brought three more hits from the follow-up album, *Son of Schmilsson*. Derek Taylor, the former Apple publicist, produced Nilsson's next project, *A Little Touch of Schmilsson in the Night,* which set the singer's rubbery voice loose on orchestrated Tin Pan Alley standards like "As Time Goes By" and "It Had To Be You," long before such projects became vogue (with Linda Ronstadt's unlikely *What's New* in 1983, which used Nelson Riddle arrangements). Hitting clubs and baiting the paparazzi, Nilsson became Lennon's royal sidekick, and they racked up humiliation upon outrage as the Spector project slowly collapsed around them.

LENNON CUT GREAT MATERIAL with great musicians at legendary studios with the finest engineers, songs like the Ronettes' "Be My Baby," Chuck Berry's "You Can't Catch Me" and "Sweet Little Sixteen," and Spector's own "To Know Her Is to Love Her." But even in his foggy yet maniacal state, Lennon grew wary of Spector's antics, especially when he started waving guns: "Not getting what he wanted during a stormy session, [Spector] drew his gun, pointed it over his head, and fired a shot into the ceiling. John—who had assumed that Spector kept his gun unloaded and on his hip only for effect—was startled. His ears ringing from the shot, he said, 'Phil, if you're gonna kill me, kill me. But don't fuck with me ears. I need 'em.' "[21]

This got the mighty Phil Spector kicked out of A&M Studios. Not one for elegance in his private life, Spector could already make Lennon's legal status look breezy. Ronnie Spector, whom Lennon had chatted up before he ever came to America, had filed for divorce from Phil in 1972, and they now fought for custody of their adopted child, Donte. At first, Lennon agreed to speak as a character witness for his producer. When the time came for him to testify at the custody hearing, Spector couldn't stop hurling obscenities at Ronnie in the courtroom, earning him numerous contempt citations. During one outburst, Spector didn't even notice Lennon slip out of the courtroom. That would be the last time they saw each other.

Spector became Lennon's latest bad example. He may have been lost, unsure in his personal life, and groping toward his next career move, but Spector acted out the next stage of Lennon's downward spiral, so Lennon veered sideways. Sessions unspooled, and since Spector had had the foresight to pay for studio time, he simply sat on the tapes as if they were his. Now Lennon confronted yet another phase of wasted time and studio work, while Spector, whom he had *begged* to work with, held his next record hostage. Lennon's calls went unreturned. Then Spector crashed through the windshield of his Rolls in early February 1974 and suffered multiple head and body contusions. With this final act of bizarre self-destruction, Lennon's dream of singing on a Spector recording fell into indefinite limbo.

As HE SANG out his revived teenage fantasies in Los Angeles, the government ground away at Lennon's immigration status. Separating from his wife at this point complicated his case, and Leon Wildes counseled them both to stay in the country even as the INS kept sending them thirty-day notices. If either of them traveled abroad, the chances of getting back inside the country were dubious. This crimped Yoko's plans to tour Japan, which she weighed not just against her marriage and Lennon's immigration status but her ongoing custody battle for Kyoko.

This bicoastal separation required delicate press management more for these immigration and custody matters than Lennon's career. If anything, his "lost" L.A. weekend only fueled his cocky image as a hard-living rock star. Since he knew he had a strong case against the government, Wildes simply filed for rolling visa extensions to the Immigration Appeals Board. By this point, it was also becoming clear that the U.S. government's deportation threats were empty—harassing John and Yoko had become an end in itself.

Wildes could scarcely believe the level of intimidation John and Yoko described to him. He could only see a cut-and-dried case that amounted to nothing more than a targeted Department of Immigration vendetta against a long-haired rock 'n' roller. The idea that the whole weight of U.S. government bureaucracy was being put into force simply because Lennon was an outspoken peacenik didn't make any sense, either.

By the spring of 1973, Nixon's Watergrate troubles had started heating up, and the press had started reporting on Lennon's legal purgatory. In the *Los Angeles Times*, Phil Spector let loose to music writer Robert Hilburn: "Where is Lennon's own generation? Where are all the rock stars who owe so much to Lennon's influence? Where are all the people whose lives were so enriched by the Beatles' music? Why aren't they demanding that this outrage be stopped?"[22] Prolonging the case only earned Nixon more bad press.

THE LOS ANGELES ROCK SCENE embraced Lennon as one of its own: this "single" former Beatle fit the perfect template of a celebrity—one who's famous for being famous. And this period in Lennon's life recalled his Hamburg exploits, only now his anxieties threatened his marriage, and any musical goals beyond his break from his famous band. The stress began to eat at him. For over a year, Lennon the rock star eclipsed plenty of movie stars for sheer celebrity heat, and he made the rounds making a fool of himself with too much time to kill. "We stayed good friends," remembers Jack Douglas, a Spector engineer, who saw a lot of Lennon in this period. "We hung out, we drank together. I produced that Alice Cooper album, there, *Muscle of Love* [1973]. There was this whole scene at Lou Adler's house in Bel-Air, and I used to drive a getaway car, me and [Jim] Keltner were the usual criminals for that particular job."[23]

A little of this went a long way, even for a titanic drinker like Lennon. So, early in 1974, he announced to Nilsson, "I'm going to produce you." They set up camp at another rented house in Malibu where they could rehearse, and quickly descended into more profligate drinking. *Rock 'n' Roll* had been a fallback project; now Lennon dabbled while waiting for Spector to release the tapes, and took on the Nilsson project just to stay distracted.

Legend has it that one night, catching Ann Peebles singing "I Can't Stand the Rain" at the Troubadour, Lennon returned from the men's room with some Kotex taped to his head. *Rolling Stone* reported that "there were about eleven people in the party; he didn't leave the waitress a tip, and in response to her scowl he said, 'Do you know who I am?' 'Yes,' she said. 'You're some asshole with Kotex on your head.' " *Rolling Stone* ran the quote, but it has since been disproved.[24]

The Smothers Brothers incident, unfortunately, boasts numerous witnesses. The comedy act had booked the Troubadour for a comeback show and invited a roomful of luminaries for a new set of material. Seated at a table near Peter Lawford and Smothers Brothers manager Ken Fritz, Lennon downed brandy snifters and broadcast his inebriated comments to the room. Being a Hollywood crowd, most people recognized Lennon and tried to give him a pass—on any given night, at least a dozen drunken celebrities disrupt L.A. clubs, and Lennon was just the latest. But this elaborately staged evening packed in the press and a stream of notables for maximum exposure, including Paul Newman and Joanne Woodward, Flip Wilson, Helen Reddy, Lily Tomlin, and Pam Grier.

Oblivious to the room's mood, Lennon and Nilsson began heckling the headliners. Lawford complained to the management, and a waitress politely asked them to quiet down. This only nudged them further. Their conduct apparently became so obnoxious that Tommy Smothers stopped the show and got quoted as saying, "There's a narrow line between bad taste and vulgarity, and you've managed to cross it," the type of line Lennon probably heard as a dare.

Then the trouble began. Fritz allegedly rushed over to Lennon's table, grabbed him by the lapels of his Scotch plaid jacket, and told him he'd better be quiet. Some reports have Lennon punching Fritz in the face. When Fritz returned the blow, Lawford tried to pull a waitress out of the way, but not before Lennon's second punch accidentally hit her in the ribs.[25]

Outside in the parking lot, photographers framed Nilsson piling Lennon into his car. On a roll, Lennon heckled the car attendant with more of his moldy celebrity routine: "Don't you know who I am? I'm Ed Sullivan!" The next day, new catchwords glommed onto Lennon's descent: the greatest rock star in the world, the idealist who'd written "Imagine" and "All You Need Is Love," was now just "some asshole with Kotex on his head," kicked from clubs yelling, "Do you know who I am?!"

When he answered to the incident in 1975 on the *Old Grey Whistle Test* show in Britain, Lennon played the Irish lout, blamed the alcohol, and chastised Nilsson for not playing the McCartney role of smoothing over his violent outburst: "I was with Harry Nilsson, who didn't quite get as much coverage as me, the bum! He really encouraged me, you know. I usually have somebody there who says, 'Okay Lennon. Shut up.' And I take it. But I didn't have anybody round me to say 'Shut up,' and I just went on and on. . . . I didn't hit a reporter. She got one thousand dollars or some crap, because I had to pay her off. That's what it was. She wasn't a reporter, in fact."[26] According to Lennon's morning-after rationalization, it's okay to blame your absent minders for accidentally hitting a waitress as long as she's not a reporter.

Even for a cocaine-fueled Hollywood, this incident reeked of washed-up celebrity. It was as if Lennon was morphing into the jaded has-been he most despised. For a towering symbol of rock's vanguard, leaning on Errol Flynn to excuse his behavior barely papered over the washed-up status he lamented so often as a Beatle. And all the self-loathing and animal bravado only induced tirades, more rowdiness of the sort he hadn't known since Hamburg—which to his middle-aged body must have felt desperately innocent, like degenerate salad days.

Work on *Pussy Cats* began at the end of March in Burbank Studios, with all Lennon's favorite boozers gathered at his Malibu rental, where they could "rehearse" for the Nilsson project. On a parallel track, Lennon had begun working on songs for a new solo project, hoping

Spector might come around and his *Rock 'n' Roll* tapes could be salvaged.

ONE DAY, LENNON, Harry Nilsson, Ringo Starr, Keith Moon, and assorted Malibu houseguests got surprise visitors: Paul and Linda McCartney. McCartney had come from London, where Yoko Ono had tracked him down for romantic advice. To Paul, this reminded him of Yoko's approach to him in 1966 as an obscure wacky modernist collecting manuscripts for John Cage's birthday present. And there's a lingering sense of resentment to his quotes about this incident, as though he helped Lennon figure out his way back home without getting the credit he deserved.

"Nobody knows how much I helped John," McCartney said later. "Yoko came through London while he was in LA with Harry Nilsson having a crazy time. . . . And she was nice and confided in us that they had broken up. She was strong about it and she said, 'He's got to work his way back to me. He's got to work at it.'" McCartney asked Ono if he should speak with John and deliver a message. "'Would that be okay? I might see him around and I'd like to be a mediator in this, because the two of you have obviously got something really strong.' And she said, 'I don't mind.' So Linda and I went to California when they were doing *Pussy Cats*."

To McCartney, Lennon's hideout with all these overgrown adolescents had a familiar ring, from Hamburg amphetamines to the weekend acid parties they'd attended at country estates with Epstein. Without quite putting himself above the scene, McCartney recognized Lennon slowly submerging into a familiar dead end. He described the beach house as "a crazed house" and "pretty wild," but he made good on his promise to deliver Ono's message. "I took him in the back room and I sat him down and said, 'I feel like a matchmaker here, but this girl of yours still loves you. Do you still love her?' And he said, 'Yeah, I do but I don't know what to do.' So I said, 'Well, I've talked to her and she still does love you but you've got to work your arse off, man. You've got to get back to New York. You have to have a separate flat; you have to send her roses every fucking day. You've got to work at it like a bitch, and you might just get her back.'"27

Here, in a back room of a rented Malibu mansion, the songwriting partners who had rescued rock 'n' roll from the likes of Chubby Checker and Frankie Avalon, who had split in the most public way over their marital partners and then dragged both of their spouses onstage with them, concocted a John and Yoko reunion. McCartney may have been more anti-Klein than anti-Yoko, but he certainly understood the business complications of putting these two back together again. Behind all the McCartney-Ono business spats still to come lay strands of respect and sympathy for John and Yoko's partnership.

In the midst of McCartney's grown-up reenactment of "She Loves You" matchmaking, some of Lennon's paternal guilt reared up. He finally took May Pang's suggestion to fly his son Julian, now ten, over for a visit. (Both Pang and Cynthia Lennon take credit for persuading him to do this.) The divorce-happy seventies witnessed a surreal visit to Anaheim's Disneyland, with John and May acting like a steady couple to Julian, and Cynthia tagging along awkwardly at her son's insistence, as Yoko Ono called John for updates. Cynthia stayed with Jim and Cyn Keltner, who spoke fondly of Pang and begrudgingly of Yoko. They told her Lennon "seemed to have a love-hate relationship with her, unable to tear himself away, yet constantly angry and resentful."28

EMERGING FROM THIS blur of celebrity pool chat and hootch, Nilsson's *Pussy Cats* feels like a dodged bullet. The album occupies a netherland in Lennon's career: it's neither a failure nor a triumph, with just enough swagger to keep you interested, and exactly zero production pretensions. The material, easily the album's most compelling aspect, spans Dylan's "Subterranean Homesick Blues" to Jimmy Cliff's "Many Rivers to Cross" and the Drifters' "Save the Last Dance For Me," a portal into how much Lennon admired Nilsson's pipes. The lone Lennon song, "Mucho Mongo/ Mt. Elga," has a harmless Caribbean feel and not much else. Lennon's abject lack of pretension as producer becomes the strongest thing about the album: it's a lesser cousin to the *Rock 'n' Roll* project, but Lennon comes on like the anti-Spector, hiding behind all the terrific material and casual stakes.

Lennon fled Los Angeles in June 1974 to finish *Pussy Cats* in New York (it came out in August). Over the next several months, he followed the reviews in the trades of Bob Dylan's tour with the Band to support 1973's *Planet Waves*. These celebrated 1974 shows, captured on a roiling double live album, *Before the Flood*, led to a mid-career aesthetic triumph, 1975's *Blood on the Tracks*, a surge of musical inspiration following Dylan's divorce from his first wife, Sara. Suddenly, the rock colleague Lennon felt most competitive with outside Paul McCartney surged to new career heights using themes Lennon himself had been chasing for almost three years. He must have longed for the same kind of critical embrace.

Back in New York with May Pang, over that summer, some new songs took shape, and Lennon planned some studio sessions toward another solo album. One day a package arrived at Pang's apartment: Capitol Records had finally settled the tussle with Phil Spector and paid him $94,000 for the master tapes to the abandoned *Rock 'n' Roll* project. Lennon could barely stand to open them, never mind listen to what was there. He put them aside while he developed his new project, which became *Walls and Bridges*.

It was an epic season of political dismay. Liberals had finally found justice in all their anti–Vietnam War demonstrations and pursuit of a criminal president. But by this point, the drama of a president hounded from office in constitutional disgrace seemed anticlimactic, given the endless antiwar crusade, the size of Nixon's 1972 mandate, and the high cost in human life and political capital. At the end of July, Congress recommended the first of three articles of impeachment against President Nixon. He resigned the first week in August. And his successor, Gerald Ford, not only pardoned him but rolled forward in Vietnam. To the left, it seemed that even shaming a president from office couldn't disrupt the war machine.

BEFORE THE WORLD ever heard *Rock 'n' Roll*, it was an out-of-reach legend, a project between two masters that couldn't possibly live up to the treasured idea it occupied in the rock 'n' roll imagination. For now, even the hardest-bitten fans had to settle for *Mind Games* and *Pussy Cats* as mid-career signposts, the way Lennon would sound when passionate but without much to say, treading water, which was somehow more depressing even than going backward—at least an oldies album might have some spark of ideas from the Liverpudlian who had reinvented the form as a universal language. *Pussy Cats* didn't sell well, or bode well for Lennon's next release. Here was greatness frozen in place, stuck between purpose and commercial viability. But Capitol heard possibilities in the tapes Lennon submitted for *Walls and Bridges* in New York, especially the surefire hit with pop's biggest radio product, Elton John. The label scheduled the new Lennon album for a late September release.

Bob Gruen happened to drop by the Record Plant the night Lennon tracked "Whatever Gets You Thru the Night." "I came upon Lennon and Elton John doing this song," Gruen remembers. "I knew John well enough to drop in to the studio spontaneously; he would just buzz me up. Sometimes I would hang out, sometimes I would get some pictures. Depended on the scene. This time, I walk in, and Lennon starts chiding me, 'Where you been? Elton's here and we're making a record!' And I said, 'Well, nobody called me, so I didn't know . . .'" Gruen shot them from behind, with Lennon leaning down next to Elton at the piano, talking to him intently about the next take. "I remember Elton asking John if he'd join him onstage to play the song at Madison Square Garden that fall," Gruen says. "John came back with a reluctant 'Well, if it hits number one I'll go onstage,' like he would *never* expect it to hit number one."[29]

When it finally appeared in November 1974, *Walls and Bridges* went a long way toward restoring Lennon's reputation, especially given the lowered expectations he'd been sowing in the tabloids. This record had the feel of hard-fought stability staring down certain doom, and turned ambivalence, loss, insecurity, and emotional foundering into humbled themes: "#9 Dream," the second single, improved on the sweep and desire of "Mind Games" for a cinescopic expanse of sound, and "Surprise Surprise (Sweet Bird of Paradox)" returned to Bobby Parker's "Watch Your Step" riff for steady-rolling payback; it resembled "I Feel Fine,"

"Day Tripper," "Birthday," and "I Dig a Pony" cut up and reconfigured as yet another puzzle in a larger mosaic. Alongside "Whatever Gets You Thru the Night," and a juicy instrumental called "Beef Jerky," it gave the record a rocker's pulse that *Mind Games* lacked. "Bless You" balanced ache and adoration, undermining every line in May Pang's book. Pang always took great comfort from "Sweet Bird of Paradox," claiming it as Lennon's song for her; it's harder to tell how she reacted to "Bless You." This narrator points himself straight back to his wife, if the song itself didn't send her running back for him.

"Steel and Glass," a seething *Walls and Bridges* character study, usually gets heard as a portrait of Allen Klein, but Lennon never spoke of it that way. Its third person could just as easily apply to Lennon himself. Perhaps it's a collage of everything he hated about himself that he responded to in Klein:

> *Your mother left you when you were small*
> *But you're gonna wish you wasn't born at all*

The orchestration that wells up behind these lines shoulders a drama and fatigue Lennon doesn't quite crack with his words. The density of strings and saxes transcends the wallowing tone, the defeated sound of a famous person expressing withering self-pity. This was harder to lament in "Nobody Loves You (When You're Down and Out)," which betrayed a hard-core romantic caving in to cynicism: "Everybody's hollering 'bout their own birthday/Everybody loves you when you're six feet in the ground." The album's weakest track, the only one cowritten with Harry Nilsson, "Old Dirt Road," marks time more by setting a mood than by pruning a theme.

"Scared" splits the Lennon solo conundrum down the middle: on the one hand, the track pulses with a slow panic, and the first two verses thump the tone home something fierce. Even two wolf cries at the top sound less portentous than meek. Changing "Scared" to "scarred" for the second verse condenses Lennon's antic wordplay down to formal ingenuity, and hints that future songs might profit from the same concisions. But as the track progresses, it suffers from production creep, to the point where even the mournful slide guitar solo drowns in a wash of self-righteousness. Lennon smartly elides the third verse within the end of the solo, and "tired" enters as the weak concluding verse: here's yet another rock star, still suffering through adolescence in a middle-aged body, bemoaning the fact that life is hard when he knows better than most not to entreat his audience to feel sorry for him. The lyric turns hackneyed, and instead of the slow-burning grief of "I Don't Wanna Be a Soldier Mama" or "Nobody Loves You (When You're Down and Out)," he settles for a production number that lessens everything else. Perhaps Lennon just needed to prove to himself how morosely self-absorbed he could be, even though he regarded self-seriousness as the ultimate sin.

On the flip side, his love lyrics here have the same gut resolve they did on *Plastic Ono Band*, and betray a much more generous sensibility: "Bless You" imagines his wife in the arms of somebody else and whispers a gentle forbearance against love's betrayals. Both "Surprise Surprise" and "Whatever Gets You Thru the Night" have sass and thump, and the latter practically begs for McCartney's bass.

The cover art sported an eleven-year-old John Lennon's watercolors of cowboys and Indians, curiously undistinguished given the scathing political comedy he was already capable of. And a long disquisition on the surname "Lennon" graced the inner pamphlet, by one Grady O'Spenster, to which Lennon jots, "oh yeah?" But by this point, no amount of self-deprecation and no number of hokey nicknames (Dr. Winston O'Boogie) can veil just how unmoored the Lennon persona has become: in the public's mind, May Pang was a transitional figure, and even when his material had aesthetic heft, Lennon couldn't squeeze his studio players toward the charismatic ensemble his voice once ignited. There are stale records by great artists that just sit there, daring you to unshelve them and listen, remaining mostly records of struggle that strain to shed light on better work. Calling *Walls and Bridges* an improvement on *Mind Games* smacks of faint praise.

In *Rolling Stone,* Ben Gerson teased out the magnificence in Lennon's newfound modesty: "On *POB* the tearing away of veils only revealed another face to Lennon's utopianism. Then (keeping in mind his crucial inconsistency in idealizing his relationship with Yoko) illusionlessness seemed the ultimate liberation. Today Lennon knows that neither dreams nor their puncturing is the answer. There is no neat answer. When one accepts one's childhood, one's parenthood and the impermanence of what lies between, one can begin to slog along. When John slogs, he makes progress."[30] From the rocker who had confounded any kind of slog throughout his career, a Lennon slog was still like a weak Dylan song— better and more revealing than most of its competition. Thematically, it's curious that Lennon delayed taking on this tension as a theme: how to create compelling rock 'n' roll as a middle-aged divorcé, making sense of his life anew after wearing out all his familiar masks. Albums like this rested far more in the shadow of Beatles greatness than Lennon ever wanted them to, and weakened his own pronouncement that "I don't believe in Beatles."

ONCE *WALLS AND BRIDGES* APPEARED in early October 1974, Lennon reluctantly unpacked Spector's *Rock 'n' Roll* tapes, dreading what he might hear. After some listening sessions at the Record Plant, he decided he could call back his *Walls and Bridges* players and take a stab at finishing it off. This aesthetic decision merged with a new business pinch. The head of Roulette Records, Morris Levy, owned the copyright to Chuck Berry's "You Can't Catch Me." Levy had filed suit against Lennon for copyright infringement on the Berry line "Here come old flat-top he come/Groovin' up slowly . . . ," the opening phrase for his 1969 Beatle song "Come Together." Compared to a lot of the sampling permissions suits brought by the digital revolution, this case resembled legal blackmail, and Lennon agreed to settle by putting two Levy-owned numbers on his Spector project. When that project stalled, Levy kept pressing for Lennon to make good on his agreement.

Walls and Bridges strengthened Levy's leverage. Far from fulfilling the terms of his settlement, Lennon's brief, unfinished snippet of Lee Dorsey's "Ya Ya," with Julian on snare drum, raised a red flag. Levy was not amused. He smelled delay tactics and immediately slapped a new lawsuit on the table, for $43 million. Lennon could either revive the *Rock 'n' Roll* project or cave to Levy's demands.

In October 1974, Levy invited Lennon and some players to rehearse at his upstate New York ranch, and after recording was completed in November, Lennon gave Levy a tape of the resulting material as a show of good faith. He argued that he would rework the material for a new release soon. At one point in October, in passing, Lennon even mentioned an interest in Levy's Adam VIII company, which sold records over late-night television ads.

Levy took Lennon's remark as a tacit approval to market the record, which he titled *Roots,* and began soliciting mail orders. *Rock 'n' Roll* was already scheduled for release by EMI in March 1975, but was quickly bumped up to mid-February after Levy's TV commercials began airing. This forced Lennon to round up players again to finish the album properly in New York with eight new numbers: "Be-Bop-a-Lula," "Stand By Me," "Rip It Up / Ready Teddy," "Sweet Little Sixteen," "Slippin' and Slidin'," "Peggy Sue," "Ain't That a Shame," and "Bring It On Home to Me." These tracks didn't blend with the Spector material so much as redeem it, but Lennon's voice made the meaningful connections, and in many other hands the entire project might have collapsed. In the meantime, Lennon had to return to court to block the Levy product until his record could be mastered and distributed.

This time, justice tipped in his favor. In the resulting flurry of lawsuits, a judge awarded Lennon damages of $140,000 for Levy's illegal release of the *Rock 'n' Roll* tracks. Its cover, taken by Klaus Voormann and Astrid Kirchherr's mutual photographer friend Jürgen Vollmer, reclaimed a Lennon photo from 1960, taken on his first trip to Hamburg. As he stands in the doorway, Lennon's greased pompadour and steely gaze epitomize teenage hip, too young to care about anything but music. If he held on to his oldies ideal, marketing this album with a strong single might just redeem all the scrapes he had gone through to get it made.

THE CAMARADERIE AND MUTUAL respect Lennon enjoyed on his Elton John session in September 1974 inspired John to invite Lennon out to the Caribou Ranch studios in Nederland, Colorado, west of Boulder, for a remake of "Lucy in the Sky with Diamonds." Lennon suggested a taut reggae break. As they recorded, Elton enjoyed a huge international hit while *Caribou* topped *Billboard*'s charts, with its iridescent guitar single, "The Bitch Is Back," comic outrage as ear candy. And yet, for Lennon to sit in with Elton at this point seemed less like sponging off pop's new royalty than royalty itself genuflecting to greatness. Lennon must have been the only person in the world who didn't expect their duet to be a smash. Many couldn't help but wonder: could Elton John be a better version of Paul McCartney than even Harry Nilsson, Lennon's new perfect foil?

The "Night" single broke into the number one slot in November, and Lennon had to admit he had agreed to perform it. The Madison Square Garden show on November 28, 1974, marked Lennon's first New York stage appearance since 1972 with the Elephant's Memory Band, and his first crack at lead vocal on "I Saw Her Standing There" (and guitarist Davey Johnston can't resist throwing in a slick "Day Tripper" reference). They also did "Whatever Gets You Thru the Night," and "Lucy in the Sky with Diamonds."

Aside from the huge wail of recognition, and the delight at catching a Beatle performing two Beatle songs, the appearance radiated symbolism. "That concert was a complete surprise, I didn't even know about it," Bob Gruen says. "I was in Connecticut having Thanksgiving dinner with my family, and I got a call that afternoon, drove back into the city, and picked up my tickets at the window. I didn't even have a backstage pass. I had to work my way up to the front to get those pictures. There was only one other photographer there."[31] For many, the concert spontaneously recaptured some of Beatlemania's swoon, however briefly.

On a whim, Yoko Ono went with a friend, a "very weird thing for her to do," Gruen says, and sent flowers to Lennon backstage, thinking that would be the end of it. But as she stood in the audience and watched him perform, she remembered feeling the crowd's overwhelming embrace entwine with something of her own, something she couldn't ignore.

"So I went there," Yoko explains, "and I was watching him from the audience and everybody was applauding like crazy—the house *shook* when he came on—and he was there bowing, but that's not what I saw.

Somehow he looked very lonely to me and I began crying." Another public moment held very private meanings that were slow to emerge.

Lennon didn't know Yoko was in the audience. But they each spoke about this scene afterward, even though it took them several months to sort it all out. "Somehow it hit me that he was a very lonely person up on stage there," Yoko said later. "And he needed me. It was like my soul suddenly saw his soul. So I went backstage. I said hello and he said hello."[32] In a very mysterious yet compelling way, this backstage greeting, the kind you can't predict or choreograph, registered to John and Yoko as part of some larger momentum. But at the time, even the couple seemed bewildered by its implications.

Get Back

Lennon's late solo career, between 1975 and 1980, represents an anomaly not just in his personal life but in the larger story of rock 'n' roll. His withdrawal from the stage at thirty-five, so completely at odds with every myth Lennon ever created about himself, stirred a sense of potential around what he might be doing. After all, even detractors had to admit his solo career boasted deeply inspired work. Perhaps he had ransacked the Beatle castle so ferociously with *Plastic Ono Band* that he never quite regained his footing; *Imagine* settled in as a quiet rock classic, but it had more polish than reach: "Gimme Some Truth" evened out the ranting he attempted in "Give Peace a Chance" for a smooth-ride contempt, but "How Do You Sleep?" sank of its own small-minded rancor. For his last two years with the Beatles (1968–69), Lennon veered toward elaborate conceptual sideshows prodded by Ono's art, branching out into film, gallery, and performance pieces. Ceding his rock 'n' roll stage to her squalls in Toronto took both nerve and a new kind of pretense.

But critics rarely note that once he played rock's doo-wop Nietzsche in "God," Lennon did, in fact, retreat from the musical avant-garde. Although John and Yoko shared the stage with Frank Zappa on their early visit to New York, and again at the One to One concert supporting *Some Time in New York City,* Lennon's formal songwriting experiments receded. In the press he was outspoken and radical, but on record his pop sensibility never wandered. His conservatism dramatized itself best through a curious reversal: Yoko Ono made her best album, *Approximately Infinite Universe,* in 1973, with Lennon's weakest support, the Elephant's Memory Band.

From *Plastic Ono Band* onward, Lennon increasingly moved toward safe, conventional, and overproduced pop, spiked by raunchy outbursts like "Do the Oz," "Tight A$," "Beef Jerky," and "Bring on the Lucie (Freda Peeple)," all B sides and album tracks. His talent for ripe inference, as well as his uncanny bond with listeners, and his increasing silence after *Rock 'n' Roll* and the *Shaved Fish* compilation (both 1975), signaled more unfinished business than irrevocable retreat. His best work plunged into adult rock themes: "Mother," at once a Freudian cry at ripping himself from the Beatle womb, and "Working Class Hero," which absorbed and reflected his parochial Scouser resentment—sarcasm draped in sophistry, his great misunderstood Dylan impersonation.

The uneven mid-period work had held up through piercing songs about midlife stasis—"Nobody Loves You (When You're Down and Out)," "Steel and Glass"—and love songs that grew wary of romanticism— "Look at Me," "Oh My Love," "Jealous Guy," and "How?" right on through "Bless You." By contrast, Lennon's late themes were suffused with deeply felt quietude, as challenging a mood for rock 'n' roll as compliance. Capitol Records underlined Lennon's pop conservatism by releasing "#9 Dream," side two's lead-off track from *Walls and Bridges,* as a follow-up single to his first solo American number one, "Whatever Gets You Thru the Night." "#9 Dream" angled the nostalgia of "Mind Games" off straightforward Beatle romanticism that kept fans in thrall to a reunion, even if it was just a fantasy. Over the holiday season between 1974 and 1975, it hit number nine in the U.S., to become his second best-selling single, behind "Whatever Gets You Thru The Night" and "Instant Karma" and "Imagine" (which both peaked at number three). In Britain, he often scored in the top ten but had to wait until 1980, after he was dead, for "Starting Over" to reach number one. This conservatism, Lennon's hewing to the public favor, reversed his Beatle path, especially considering how *Double Fantasy* (1980) would radicalize rock themes far beyond the agnosticism of "Imagine." For Lennon, casting fatherhood as redemption counts as an exceptional, all-consuming irony.[1]

Given his frequent betrayals of Ono, whom he idealized beyond all romantic proportion, this redemption came with great cost in both personal and mythic terms. While writing songs like "Oh My Love" and "Oh Yoko!" his zipper problem begged for comeuppance. Ono had finally kicked him out, as any self-respecting wife would. In the last interviews, both he and Yoko portrayed his years in the L.A. wilderness, followed by a humbling return in early 1975, as salvation lost and found, the prodigal husband reclaiming an epic lost affair. The bond persuaded even cynics of its monumental stature, the kind of Tristan-and-Isolde love that knew the outer realms of betrayal and forgiveness.

As much as people protested, Lennon's withdrawal from recording after 1975 did the whole Beatle mystique far more good than ill: better he turn in one final decent record and leave behind tempting outtakes than continue ramming his head against the wall of insurmountable expectations. Lennon's weakest solo record, *Mind Games,* held its head above almost any weak McCartney effort and most of Harrison's solo output; even when the material lacked depth, nearly everything Lennon sang rang out with mythos reflected, or just beyond reach.[2]

And to those who lamented Lennon's reuniting with Ono, his entrenched battle with Nixon's cronies turned him into a liberal saint, redeeming all his radical outbursts and misguided agitprop through the quest to remain in America. Among journalists and cultural critics, led by *Rolling Stone*'s Ralph Gleason and the *New Yorker*'s Jonathan Schell, Lennon's INS case shouldered considerable historical weight. Column after column lamented the specter of Lennon as rock 'n' roll's Charlie Chaplin, yet another victim of Cold War furies, hounded out of the country by small, paranoid minds. Lennon's victory compounded the left's sense of relief after Nixon resigned—on a purely political level, Lennon's triumph meant that everybody had won more rights to push back against imperious governments run amuck. (Culturally, of course, Lennon knew he had long since defeated Nixon and his ilk—that's one of the more persuasive explanations for Nixon's paranoia.)

In the days before his death, Lennon portrayed himself as proud, happy father, bread-baking househusband, off the sauce and out of rock's loop, and better for it. The reality was messier, of course, with the radical twist that Lennon kept his indiscretions private and made sure his comeback conveyed a resolve toward stability and composure. He also dodged a central contradiction, the false choice he had created for himself by positioning Ono as the imagined sky on *Mind Games,* an indomitable force of nature. For some reason, having moved back from Malibu to New York with May Pang in June 1974, alternating nights with her and his room at the Pierre Hotel, Lennon felt his choices to be stark: either remain untethered on a celebrity-party circuit between New York and Los Angeles, and risk bottoming out like Phil Spector, or Janis Joplin, or Jim Morrison, or return to Ono and build a stable family. Somehow, he was humbled, or desperate, enough to choose the healthier of these two options. But many listeners mistook the public Lennon persona, the man who wrote "If I Fell" and "Dr. Robert" and "A Day in the Life," for the private person. This public Lennon would have had no trouble pointing out the false dichotomy he imposed on himself. The archest rock 'n' roller sold this choice to his listeners through yet another public-relations flourish, accomplished with the help of one final *Rolling Stone* cover, published in the weeks after his death.

For all the complicated, contradictory, and distressing associations fatherhood summoned in Lennon, he turned his relationship with his third son, Sean, into a mythic bond. The idea of John as the doting father seemed to take everyone by surprise, especially Julian, who had to settle for Paul's sympathy and the dubious distinction of having inspired "Hey Jude." Lennon marked his love affair with Yoko by writing songs like "Julia," and "Don't Let Me Down," and "Oh Yoko!" and his filial attachment to Sean with "Beautiful Boy." A handful of unsurpassed late songs, including "Woman," "Beautiful Boy," "Grow Old with Me," and "Nobody Told Me," reached beyond atonement to seal Lennon's new life-begins-at-forty persona despite all the stray details they conveniently overlooked.

Then, as quickly as he returned, Lennon became spectral, in the most traumatic reversal of all: the rock star shot by a delusional fan. In death, Lennon surpassed the hoariest of clichés: the violent yet accidental deaths of heroes like James Dean, Eddie Cochran, Buddy Holly, Otis Redding; or the cautionary drug abuse tales like Jim Morrison, Janis Joplin, and Jimi Hendrix. Lennon's death recast all of these—and many since—as that of a rock star whose lambent flame expires in the midst of a triumphant comeback.

LENNON'S PERSONAL BATTLES between 1970 and 1975 paralleled his immigration struggles. Many interviews in this period voice his resolve to return to Britain and do more serious traveling. But if he left the United States, he might never get back, and so where once he had used the Beatles as his fallback position while branching out with Yoko, he now stayed in America as a way of falling back in with his wife. This cat-and-mouse game resembled Lennon's passive-aggressive late-Beatle maneuvers: the INS kept threatening to kick him out, but Lennon's legal team kept filing appeals and extending his temporary visas as his case bounced around, in semipermanent limbo, in appeals. Being hounded by Nixon strangely was no match for the pressures of being an ex-Beatle.

Early in January 1975, U. S. district court judge Richard Owen ruled that Lennon and his attorneys, led by Leon Wildes, could access Immigration and Naturalization Services files dealing with his deportation case. Wildes was also granted permission to question INS officials. This gave Wildes leverage to determine whether the whole deportation order was based on his client's 1968 drug conviction, or whether the files would show Lennon was being hounded for political reasons, which eventually proved to be the case. It was a major victory, and Lennon eventually went on the record with Lisa Robinson for *Hit Parader* magazine. His quotes revealed a thorough knowledge of the law, of the U. S. government's overt hypocrisy, and how his British record had been twisted against him.

Robinson asked him how many other lawsuits he was juggling at the time, and Lennon gave the immigration matter top priority. He seemed confounded that the government kept falling back on his 1968 marijuana misdemeanor: "My lawyer has a list of people . . . ," Lennon told her, "hundreds of people in here who got around the law for murder, rape, double murder, heroin, every crime you can imagine. People who are just living here. I want it to end, but I can go on as long as they go on. It'll probably go on until it gets to the Supreme Court."

Lennon also faced legal action from the man he had entrusted with his break from the Beatles, Allen Klein. Klein, the one who won Lennon over by doing his childhood-trauma homework, now appeared as a foe. As Lennon told Robinson: "He's suing me, and Yoko, and all the ex-Beatles, and everybody that ever knew them! And he's suing me individually, me collectively, any version of me you can get hold of is being sued. But immigration is the important one—the others are all just money, somehow a deal will be made. Immigration, that's the one. I mean, if they can take Helen Reddy, they can take me." What Lennon really wanted to do was travel. "That's the thing I really miss most. I miss England, Scotland, Wales, all that sentimental stuff . . . but I also miss France, Holland . . . Germany I haven't been to for years. I'd like to go to South America. I've never been. I'd like to be based here, and just travel."

Robinson's interview plants another clue to Lennon's evolving state of mind. Even before moving back into the Dakota with Yoko, he looked on his Los Angeles period as a nightmare. He describes waking up in the middle of another drunken bender and realizing he had to "straighten out." And the lawsuits required as much attention as he could muster. "I don't know how they happen—one minute you're talking to someone, the next minute they're suing you."

Perhaps he was wooing Yoko through the press the way he had once jilted McCartney. Only this time, when Robinson pressed him about gay rumors, she only got more candor. "I was trying to put it 'round that I was gay, you know—I thought that would throw them off . . . dancing at all the gay clubs in Los Angeles, flirting with the boys . . . but it never got off the ground." Robinson goaded him, saying she'd heard that "lately about Paul."

"Oh, I've had him, he's no good," Lennon shot back.[3]

Then, on January 9, 1975, the London High Court finally ruled on the dissolution of The Beatles and Co. partnership, four years after McCartney originally filed his suit against Klein and Apple. These two court breakthroughs accompanied some phone calls with Mc-Cartney, who invited Lennon down to New Orleans for Wings sessions that would lead to the *Venus and Mars* album. According to Pang, Lennon agreed to go and was even considering writing songs again with McCartney.

One month later, in early February, Lennon paid a visit to Yoko at the Dakota. Pang describes Yoko luring him back with a new hypnotist's smoking cure—an addiction Yoko knew Lennon was eager to break. Pang portrays Yoko as wielding a powerful psychic sway over Lennon. But ever since that backstage reunion at the Thanksgiving concert with Elton John, they had been visiting cordially and continued to speak on the phone daily. Later, Lennon said of this visit, "I was just going over for a visit and it just fell in place again. It was like I'd never left. I realized that this was where I belonged. I think we both knew we'd get back together again sooner or later, even if it was five years, and that's why we never bothered with divorce. I'm just glad she let me back in again. It was like going out for a drink, but it took me a year to get it!"[4]

One early Ono biographer, Jerry Hopkins, speculates that Ono welcomed Lennon back to the Dakota under three strict conditions: that he clean up his drug intake, flush his body of poisons, and adopt a macrobiotic diet; that he "repair the holes in his aura" and submit to her counsel on matters spiritual and astrological; and finally, that she take over his day-to-day business affairs.[5] Tired of endless legal meetings that made the *Get Back* sessions in early 1969 seem like a lovefest, and worn down from months of hard living, Lennon enthusiastically agreed. It didn't hurt that the Beatles court case had just closed. Now he needn't bother Ono with that anymore, either. This time, instead of seeking out a new business manager to handle his affairs, he simply decided to appoint Yoko as heir to what he once expected from Epstein, McCartney, and Klein, and be done with it. He also resolved to clear his desk of all the lawsuits that had dragged on his career, both his immigration status and the Morris Levy lawsuit over *Rock 'n' Roll, Roots,* and settling publishing accounts.

John and Yoko's overriding concern, however, was far from legal. They recast their reunion in glowing romantic terms to the press and privately pursued an even more intimate goal: to have a child. Yoko Ono, as we have seen, had suffered at least three miscarriages with Lennon. Once Lennon moved back into the Dakota in early February 1975, Ono became pregnant almost immediately, as if the fates were once again smiling. Counting back from Sean Lennon's birth date, October 9, puts his conception around February 9. That same week, *Rock 'n' Roll* hit stores, and Lennon went on the Scott Muni show on WNEW-FM, to sync the music up with his rejuvenated marriage: "The separation didn't work out," he said, in a widely quoted interview.[6]

WITH A NEW HIT ALBUM suddenly a reflection of his redeemed personal life, Lennon capped a middle-period trifecta: *Mind Games* entered a tunnel, *Walls and Bridges* groped toward the light, and *Rock 'n' Roll* delivered a huge payoff for rock history—if not on par with early Beatles, then the next best thing. A towering record without the fierce complexity of Lennon's original material, *Rock 'n' Roll* became a great work ardent followers disagreed about. As a vocal performance, it ranks with *Plastic Ono Band* as some of Lennon's most passionately compressed singing. Hearing "Stand By Me" seduce FM radio throughout early 1975 was all the argument you needed that Lennon's solo songwriting career had fallen off: he vented much more through other people's songs on this newly minted classic than he had on either *Mind Games* or *Walls and Bridges*.

Chuck Berry, Gene Vincent, and Buddy Holly all helped shape Lennon's early Beatle persona, and by revisiting these writers, Lennon revived his career with reverse daring—backshifting into oldies mode seemed, paradoxically, both conservative and radical. Whether you take to its thicker arrangements or find them gaudy, the Spector tracks sound like a slow-motion train wreck averted by Lennon's vocals, schlock snatched back from oblivion: numbers like Chuck Berry's "You Can't Catch Me" toot along with colossal jive, and Gene Vincent's "Be-Bop-

A-Lula" bulldozes forward with sheer ebullience. Typically, for Lennon, this wasn't just an aesthetic argument: in 1975, alongside George Lucas's *American Graffiti* (1973) and its TV spinoff, *Happy Days* (1974), this release helped ignite oldies format for FM radio. And it earned Lennon some of his most bipolar reviews.

Like pop stars falling back on country material (and loyal audience) when their careers hit the skids, the "oldies move" can work like a hymn to the gods that ward off doom. The Beatles themselves fell back on early rock 'n' roll during the stalled *Get Back* sessions in 1969, and John Fogerty surfaced with a country-rock pearl, *The Blue Ridge Rangers*, in 1973, after losing control of his Creedence Clearwater Revival catalog. The flip side of this myth succumbs to nostalgia, the symbolic tide writers wade into when their muse dries up. With originality and versatility performed through other people's material as the ideal, the Band's bravura *Moondog Matinee* from 1973 towers over this subgenre, eclipsing efforts like David Bowie's *Pinups* or Bryan Ferry's *These Foolish Things* (which included "You Won't See Me").

HISTORY INSERTED ANOTHER WRINKLE to Lennon's *Rock 'n' Roll* album even long before Spector was convicted of murder in 2009: before *Anthology* came out in 1995, a two-disc compilation of early Beatles BBC broadcasts called *The Beatles at the BBC* appeared, and bootleggers quickly dug deeper for the totality of that work, most notably on a ten-CD box, *The Complete BBC Sessions* (Great Dane, 1994). Eleven CDs of material have since surfaced from these vaults, comprising a huge tapestry of their live set list, encompassing the periods gigging throughout the north of England and Hamburg, before they finally recorded "Love Me Do." The repackaging of this bold new rock 'n' roll frame, the one featured on *The Ed Sullivan Show* in early 1964, rescued the work from American neglect. In 1975, Lennon landed nearby some of the same songs the Beatles had once used to craft their cherished young ensemble.

Their overlapping song selections provide commentary on Lennon and McCartney's shared view of rock history, and where they differed.

For the BBC audience, of course, a lot of this early Beatle material survived in British cultural memory as an oral prehistory to the band's recorded legacy; for Americans, the BBC material trickled out slowly at first. Finally, two years after Lennon's death, in 1982, a syndicated radio special commemorated the twentieth anniversary of the band's first appearance on the BBC, and Americans became familiar with how the Beatles sounded before "Love Me Do." This new substratum of Beatle tracks held implacable charms. The *Rock 'n' Roll* catalog Lennon siphoned off Radio Luxembourg and his mother Julia's banjo chords recontextualized rock 'n' roll anew; play it alongside McCartney's workouts in this vein—1988's *Choba b CCCP* (Russian for *Back in the USSR*) and 1999's *Run Devil Run*—for a diagram of how Lennon and McCartney's early repertoire echoed into middle age.

Lennon's list features several gaping omissions: Eddie Cochran, Jerry Lee Lewis, and the looming invisibility of a singer Lennon shrank from competing with, Elvis Presley. "Blue Suede Shoes" from the 1969 Toronto show and "Hound Dog" at 1971's One to One set remain Lennon's only published Presley takes, one-offs he never returned to. By comparison, McCartney does Cochran's "Twenty Flight Rock" (and superbly), but tackles Presley only twice, with "It's Now Or Never" on a 1988 tribute to Presley film songs (*The Last Temptation of Elvis*) and "All Shook Up" on *Run Devil Run* (1999).

As if to diagram their distinct yet complementary tastes, both Lennon and McCartney's oldies albums are, by any measure, vocal triumphs. On his second effort, *Run Devil Run,* McCartney's virtuoso touch added two imposing originals ("Try Not to Cry" and the title track), which were so attuned to early rock style that many simply assumed they were more obscure throwaways. His wiggling firehose on Larry Williams's "She Said Yeah" spewed especially boyish wrath, a long-awaited answer to Lennon's treatment of Williams's "Bad Boy" and "Dizzy Miss Lizzie." (Like "Twenty Flight Rock," "She Said Yeah" had been a Rolling Stones staple.)

Among the American songwriters Lennon and McCartney both covered, a different conversation took shape: with Chuck Berry, Lennon juiced up "You Can't Catch Me" like a rebuilt Cadillac, and slowed down "Sweet Little Sixteen" to a purr, while McCartney shrink-wrapped "Brown Eyed Handsome Man" into tidy zydeco. McCartney paid tribute to Lennon via Lloyd Price ("Lawdy Miss Clawdy" and "Just Because"), Sam Cooke ("Bring It On Home to Me"), and a Gene Vincent number he heard his partner do numerous times ("Blue Jean Bop"). Lennon alone chose a girl-group standard ("Be My Baby," by the Ronettes, without its signature opening drum calls, a dandy trick) and took on Buddy Holly ("Peggy Sue"), where McCartney backed off both. Instead, McCartney produced an entire Buddy Holly album for his Wings cohort, Denny Laine, called *Holly Days* (1977). This set featured McCartney overdubbing backup parts to Laine's cardboard lead vocals, which is a bit like Prince backing up Cat Stevens. McCartney still has a Buddy Holly tribute record burning inside of him, if he ever takes the leap.

Most tellingly, neither Beatle ever revisited any of the Beatles' own defining covers, such as Smokey Robinson's "You've Really Got a Hold On Me" or Little Richard's "Long Tall Sally," which cemented both their good taste and respect for their own catalog. In 1976, when Capitol reissued Beatle covers and originals for a trumped-up package called *Rock 'n' Roll Music,* it inexplicably excluded defining pieces, such as Lennon singing not only "You've Really Got a Hold On Me" but Arthur Alexander's "Anna (Go to Him)" and the Shirelles' "Baby It's You." To add insult to irony, two of Lennon's *Rock 'n' Roll* tracks lined the coffers of Lennon's rivals: for Buddy Holly's "Peggy Sue," he paid royalties to McCartney, who owned the rights to Holly's catalog; and for "Bring It On Home to Me," he paid rights to Allen Klein, who owned Sam Cooke's material.

In the years since Lennon's death, the cutting-room floor has coughed up a magnanimous Lennon take of Rosie and the Originals' "Angel Baby" and Phil Spector's 1958 number one with the Teddy Bears, "To Know Her Is to Love Her," on the four-CD *Anthology* box Yoko Ono assembled in 2001. But only a plebe would prefer Spector's treatment to the Beatles' earlier renditions of that song for the BBC.

Listening to Lennon's updates, it's important to remember the engines of desire motivating these early Beatle covers: more than many other groups, they performed this material as a living tradition. They paid no mind if Chuck Berry's "Sweet Little Sixteen," a hit in 1958, was already "old" in pop terms by 1963, when they played it on the BBC. For them, these songs had nothing to do with looking back: it was always about how much energy Chuck Berry had set in motion, and how much potential they heard coursing through his pregnant guitar licks. In the strongest Beatle covers, it's almost as if you can sense their original material in the background, pushing its way forward: "You've Really Got a Hold On Me" inspired Lennon's "No Reply" and "Help!" and "I'm a Loser" as surely as "Long Tall Sally" yielded McCartney's "I'm Down."

Returning to "You Can't Catch Me" with Spector for *Rock 'n' Roll*, Lennon tackled the song with similar fervor from a new vantage: if it had saved his life once as a teenager, perhaps it could rescue him again— from celebrity ennui, choppy marital waters, and the quandary of staring down Beatle ghosts while constructing a new persona. For some critics, like Jon Landau in *Rolling Stone*, Lennon sounded tired, incapable of harnessing his lightning-in-a-bottle personality. "In making an album about his past," Landau wrote in May 1975, "he has wound up sounding like a man without a past. If I didn't know better, I would have guessed that this was the work of just another talented rocker who's stumbled onto a mysterious body of great American music that he truly loves but doesn't really understand. There was a time when he did."[7]

Dismissing this music, however, didn't account for the peculiarly lopsided embrace it received, on both the radio and the charts. In the Britain of early 1975, *Rock 'n' Roll* spent twenty-eight weeks on the charts, peaking at number six, outperforming every previous Lennon solo album except *Imagine*. In America, the album tied with *Plastic Ono Band* at number six, but spent only fifteen weeks on the charts, Lennon's weakest performing title since his first three albums with Yoko Ono (the two *Unfinished Music* titles and the *Wedding Album*). After everything the Beatles had done, this early rock 'n' roll material burnished Lennon's reputation more than his coffers. (It also made him the most exotic of UK "exports": an ex-pat Scouser retooling American engines for British drivers.) Furthermore, it made hash of the UK's supposed blackballing of Phil Spector's work after *Let It Be*. Even critics tend to forget that Lennon employed Spector for four out of seven solo albums.

Lennon's oldies set leapt into the top ten on his soaring cover of Ben E. King's "Stand By Me." King had used the song as his second solo flight from the Drifters, back in 1961 (after 1960's "Spanish Harlem" and "First Taste of Love"). He cowrote the number with Jerry Leiber and Mike Stoller, working off a 1960 Soul Stirrers' number, "Stand By Me Father," making it one of Lennon's few gospel-sourced tracks (his other gospel move sets the underrated "Woman Is the Nigger of the World" swaying). Lennon also remade Sam Cooke's "Bring It On Home to Me," but only stitched up with "Send Me Some Lovin'," the weaker of two medleys. The stylistic reach mattered less than the way Lennon twisted nostalgia into a vital contemporary gesture. Where the typical oldies move serves as a stall tactic, a retreat or fallback position, Lennon's immersion in this material suggested enough untapped richness and innuendo to tip the music (originally for and about teenagers) toward adult metaphors. The finale, "Just Because," forges a truce between sentimental nostalgia and rearview regret: how faded teenage romance needn't be patronized.[8]

As "STAND BY ME" became an FM rock radio staple, reviving Lennon's presence after its agonizing delays, Capitol asked him to assemble a solo greatest hits package, called *Shaved Fish,* which got scheduled for Christmas 1975. Returning to the charts in top form sparked a new cross-Atlantic volley with his ex-partner: Paul McCartney had thrown down a sassy guitar slam called "Junior's Farm," which reached number three in November 1974, in between Lennon's hits "Whatever Gets You Thru the Night" and "#9 Dream." "Stand By Me," Lennon's spring 1975 single, bumped into "Listen to What the Man Said," McCartney's *Venus and Mars* hit. (These song volleys across albums between ex-collaborators went back to "How Do You Sleep?" and McCartney's "Dear Friend," and continued on McCartney's *Band on the Run* [1973].)

In Lennon's mind, this jockeying for popular attention must have felt like par—only this time, when he picked up the phone, David Bowie came on the line. "David rang and told me he was going to do a version of 'Across the Universe,'" Lennon recalled, "and I thought 'great' because I'd never done a good version of that song myself. . . . It's one of my favourite songs, but I didn't like my version of it. So I went down and played rhythm on the track. Then he got this lick, so me and him put this together in another song called 'Fame' . . . I had fun!"⁹

Lennon made a series of appearances that spring of 1975 to demonstrate his belief in *Rock 'n' Roll* and reform his "lost weekend" reputation. For the Los Angeles–based music industry, it was as if he'd finally chosen to play the game. In early March, he walked out onto the Grammy Awards as a presenter alongside Paul Simon, wearing a long tuxedo jacket, beige beret, and scarf. Lennon announced the winner, Olivia Newton-John's "I Honestly Love You," only to spy Art Garfunkel bounding up the stage steps, which sent Lennon and Simon off into a string of reunion gags.

JOHN LENNON: (introduces Art to Paul): Which one of you is Ringo?

PAUL SIMON: (to Garfunkel): I thought I told you to wait in the car . . .

JL: Are you ever getting back together again?

PS (motioning to Garfunkel and Lennon): Are *you guys* getting back together again?

JL: It's terrible isn't it?

ART GARFUNKEL (deadpans to Paul): Still writing, Paul? (huge laughs)

PS: I'm trying my hand at a little acting, Art.

JL: Where's Linda? (delayed tittering) . . . Oh well, too subtle that one.

At this same event, McCartney was a no-show for two awards: Best Pop Vocal Performance by a Group and Best Produced Non-Classical Recording, for *Band on the Run*. The Beatles also received a Grammy Hall of Fame Award. Lennon made some of the parties with Yoko Ono on his arm, which ran on the entertainment wires, just like a regular celeb.[10]

As HIS PUBLIC PERSONA restored itself, and he approached his final public performance, Lennon's immigration status turned a decisive corner. In March, Leon Wildes began reporting his findings in the INS files he'd been poring over, saying he now had "information that shows that the Government deliberately ignored [Lennon's] application, actually locking the relevant document away in a safe." One memorandum stated that John and Yoko were "to be kept under physical observance" because of their political activism. This became the first substantiation of wiretapping that the FBI had engaged in, beginning back in 1971. Wildes added that once he found the source for this document, it would "break the case wide open and prove that there has been a miscarriage of justice."

The next month, April 1975, Lennon filmed a TV tribute to Sir Lew Grade, chairman of ATV Publishing (which controlled Lennon and McCartney's Northern Songs publishing concern), at the Hilton Hotel in New York, the result of another court settlement. Lennon and his band members wore face masks attached to the back of their heads, which Lennon called "a sardonic reference to my feelings on Lew Grade's personality!" (two-faced). For "Slippin' and Slidin'" and "Stand By Me," Lennon sang in front of a band called BOMF (Brothers of Mother Fuckers), and for "Imagine," he sang alone with his guitar, his hair pulled back across the top of his head into a ponytail, chewing gum and somehow lending the song a cynical undertone. Honored to be a featured performer at a gala event, he couldn't let the 1969 Northern Songs takeover go unremarked. It marked the last time Lennon sang in public.

By all appearances, Lennon enjoyed his new comeback status and had no intention of retiring. He sat down with Tom Snyder, NBC's smug late-night talk-show host, for a full hour on *Tomorrow* at the end of April. To continue his public-relations campaign for his legal residence status, he brought Leon Wildes out for the final segment. Snyder asked Lennon why he wanted to stay in America when he could live anywhere he wanted. Lennon replied, "I like to be here, because this is where the music came from; this is what influenced my whole life and got me where I am today, as it were."[11]

The following month, Lennon accepted Larry Kane's invitation to participate in WFIL's Helping Hand Radio Marathon, an annual Philadelphia charity event for multiple sclerosis. Kane had traveled with the Beatles on some of their first tours of America, as a radio reporter from Florida. Since then he'd served in Vietnam, bounced around broadcast journalism, and landed as the local news anchor for WFIL.

Surprised and delighted by Lennon's assent, Kane now hosted the biggest draw the event had ever seen. Lennon "spent the entire weekend, every waking moment, pitching for the cause and signing autographs for thousands and thousands of people," Kane remembers. Fans waited in line for hours to shake his hand and say hello, and Lennon patiently signed autographs for every single one. "You can't imagine what an effort he made. He came down on the train and basically said, 'Put me to work.' He told me he always wanted to do the weather, so we did a little gag with him on the evening news. He had a blast."

Frank Rizzo, Philadelphia's mayor and former police chief, made a remark that Kane didn't seize upon until much later. Rizzo shuddered at the idea of such a big star roaming unprotected through the outdoor crowds gathered at the TV station. He assigned extra police units throughout the weekend, which passed without incident. "That guy needs to pay more attention to his security," Kane remembers Rizzo saying.[12]

In June, John and Yoko headed for a summer on Long Beach, Long Island. From here on in, interviews slackened, and Lennon went into retreat from public life. To jerk an impervious system into action, Wildes decided to shift tactics and filed suit against former U. S. Attorney General John N. Mitchell on June 16, 1975, charging "improper selective prosecution." Wildes's gambit worked: if the government wouldn't take Lennon's steel-cased legal defense seriously, perhaps they'd respond differently to an offensive tack. It paid off much better than anyone might have hoped.

THAT FALL of 1975, two happy events found Lennon back in the headlines. On October 7, a three-judge U. S. Court of Appeals overturned his deportation order. Wildes had called the government's bluff, and backed up against a new suit that would have opened more files, the INS finally folded. The government decided any more revelations from such a high-profile case could only damage their eroded reputation. Calling his 1968 UK drug conviction "contrary" to the "U.S. understanding of due process," the ruling spelled out a sweeping reversal of the government's "excludable alien" pursuit: "Lennon's four-year-battle to remain in our country is a testimony to his faith in the American dream," the ruling stated. Instead of being an enemy of the United States, the government now declared him a hero.

Yoko Ono stayed home, due to deliver at any moment. Lennon made his own best narrator for this story later, in the 1980 *Playboy* interview. He talked about a Chinese acupuncturist in San Francisco who listened to their fertility troubles and scoffed at the British doctors: "Heck, you have a child," Lennon quoted the healer as telling them. "Just behave yourself. No drugs, no drink, eat well. You have a child in eighteen months." When Western doctors told the couple they *couldn't* conceive, Lennon realized "that I did want a child, and how badly." And it wasn't just any baby Lennon wanted: "I wanted Yoko's baby, not *a* baby."[13]

Having endured the miscarriages, and an infant who died only days old after the drug arrest back in November 1968, avoiding the public glare for the last two trimesters of Yoko's pregnancy finally left them blessed. It was a lesson they promised to honor. After a long, difficult labor, forty-two-year-old Ono gave birth to Sean Taro Ono Lennon on Lennon's thirty-fifth birthday: October 9, 1975. "I feel higher than the Empire State Building," Lennon told reporters. He also announced Sean's godfather: Elton John. "Ah, we worked hard for that child. We went through all hell together—through many miscarriages and terrible, terrible times. So this is what they call a love child in truth. We were told by many doctors in England that we could never have a child."[14] Relief collided with elation. Apparently, Ono's age was less of a concern during the delivery than her bad reaction to a blood transfer. Lennon, the anxious husband, had to literally force the physician's attention. "Somebody had made a tranfusion of the wrong blood type," Lennon later told *Rolling Stone,* and Ono began convulsing.

"I was there when it happened," Lennon recalled, "and she starts to go rigid, and then shake from the pain and trauma. I run up to this nurse and say, 'Go get the doctor!' I'm holding on tight to Yoko while this guy gets to the hospital room. He walks in, hardly notices that Yoko is going through fucking CONVULSIONS, goes straight for me, smiles, shakes my hand, and says, 'I've always wanted to meet you, Mr. Lennon, I always enjoyed your music.' I start screaming: *'My wife's dying and you want to talk about music!'* Christ! A miracle that everything was okay."[15]

THE LENNON HOUSEHUSBAND MYTH that emerged from his five-year seclusion (1975–80) proved largely true, if oversimplified: after breakfast, Ono descended to the ground-floor Dakota offices to run Lennon's estate, intimidating financiers by pulling out Tarot cards in the middle of negotiations and deploying her reputation as a wacky artist, the high priestess of Lennon's fortune, to outmaneuver opponents. Lennon stayed in to look after Sean. There was help, of course, so between personal assistants and nannies, unlike the many househusbands he inspired, Lennon could afford plenty of time to himself.

Fatherhood became Lennon's new career, and his great late theme. He spent long stretches completely disengaged from the music business. Too many competing yet unreliable testimonies among personal assistants, numerologists, acupuncturists, and other service providers create this period's patchy narrative. The better sources—producers, engineers, musicians, and interviewers—help confirm the contours of Lennon's own accounts. As usual, Lennon exaggerates things. In contrast to his first years with Yoko Ono outside the Beatles, when he courted publicity for his heady romance, for once in his life he shut down his public persona and focused on home life.

Occasionally, Lennon would peep out from behind his curtain to blurb an article he took an interest in. The September 1975 issue of *Modern Hi-Fi & Music* magazine featured an interview with Hal Fein, who mentioned Bert Kaempfert. Lennon responded, banging out familiar absurdist cadences on his typewriter, worth quoting for his inimitable voice.

He begins with vivid memories of his first producer and the record's circuitous path to Epstein's ears:

> *He Fein must have been one of the people working with [Kaemfert]*
> *[sic] . . . but he no rings da bell (too much). Brian (Epstein) didn't*
> *hear the record over the air . . . one of the kids went to his shop to see*
> *if he had our record . . . he didn't . . . so he checked it/us out . . .*

Lennon recalls cutting a few tracks behind "Tony Sheriden" (sic), including "My Bonnie," but that Kaemfert thought the Beatles too bluesy. He signs off with "Those were the days mein friend! Very corduroy, j.l."

He finishes by mentioning the book about the bands first manager, Allan Williams, "The Man Who Gave the Beatles Away," and apologizes for his sloppy typing. It's a hastily dashed-off note that looks toward the epic stories he recounts in late 1980.[16]

As the tumultuous year of 1975 wound down to the happiest of endings, Lennon felt a strong tug to stay in and help mind his child, even as rock stars kept knocking on his door. Over the holidays, John and Yoko invited Bob Gruen to the Dakota to take some family pictures. His hair tied back in a tight ponytail, "Lennon never looked happier to me," Gruen says now.[17] During that Christmas week, Gruen happened to be visiting when carolers came to the door, which initially caused alarm—nobody made it up to that level without getting buzzed through first. Gruen went to see what the noise was about, and the singers turned out to be Paul and Linda McCartney. The scene became a warm reunion, with the McCartneys taking turns holding Sean. Gruen resisted the urge to take photos. The two couples shared Christmas together, ordering out pizza, and watching the sun go down on the Manhattan skyline from John and Yoko's living room. Elliot Mintz, the California deejay, who was also there, remembers the scene, and took vivid mental notes.

"The conversation became less rhythmic, the words more sparse," Mintz wrote later. "I was paying close attention to John and Paul and the way they looked at each other . . . during this Christmas sunset, it was obvious to me that the two of them had run out of things to say." In wry conclusion, Mintz describes a fond farewell between John and Paul, and then adds with withering understatement: "Yoko and Paul have yet to reach comfort level with each other."[18]

CHILDREN'S REDEMPTION OF WAYWARD PARENTS became Lennon's great late theme. He talked about it throughout all his later interviews, retelling the story of Sean's hard-fought journey and how it seemed to link up with his own. Ever since he buried his first child with Yoko back in November 1968, the miscarriages and separations only seemed part of some bigger narrative. "In the way we think," Lennon said in 1980, "Sean chose us as parents. The gift of that responsibility doesn't end. I don't know if it ends when we die. It's an ongoing process. It's a tremendous gift and a tremendous responsibility. And I think responsibility was something I never wanted—of *any* description. . . . It was a three-hundred-and-sixty-degree turnaround." He made it sound as if he'd renounced drugs, even though there's plenty of evidence that he hadn't. Still, it was hard to argue with a quote like this: "More than taking a tab of acid in 1965, you know, that kind of thing, which I thought was the biggest thing that ever hit the world at that time, you know. But this is *more than*."[19]

To many fans, hearing this former acidhead and loose cannon talk about "the gift of that responsibility" was like Little Richard extolling abstinence. And John and Yoko centered their new romantic persona more around parenthood than romance. The young Lennon had created his first family from his band mates, surrounding himself with his best friends making music, presenting a collective front to the world as a way of masking the free-fall isolation. Now, at the age of thirty-five, after years of hard living that had brought him little pleasure and less security, Lennon settled into a daily routine. For the first time in his life, he stepped off the pop treadmill for an extended break.

Three of Us

W ESTERNERS—AND NOT JUST THE BRITISH—PROJECT A BUNDLE of Asian stereotypes onto Yoko Ono, but her detractors discount Lennon's attachment and devotion. His last five years with her only seem, at least on the surface, to provide more fodder for the anti-Yoko school that brands Lennon a caged beast. Ono's reputation as a savvy negotiator and protector of Lennon's estate steals attention from her intellectual whimsy, her delight in upending people's assumptions about art and where it lies in wait. Her severity masks an implacable creativity that has only grown in stature—the work across several mediums bends conventional notions about art, music, and performance. With a furious playfulness, she dazzled Lennon right up through their final collaboration; he adored her pop orgasm on "Kiss Kiss Kiss," from *Double Fantasy.*

All this gives Cynthia Lennon's famous remark a new twist. Cynthia describes a vivid parallel she saw when Yoko Ono took Lennon back in after first kicking him out. "When I read comments from Yoko comparing herself to Aunt Mimi," she says in *John,* "I had to smile. She'd got it dead right."[1] Ono represents more a fusing of Aunt Mimi with her younger sibling, Julia, those feuding Stanley sisters who turned his teenage years into a rigged game of musical chairs. Lennon looked out at them both as he stood with the Quarrymen at St. Peter's Church in July 1957, the day he met Paul McCartney, singing the Del Vikings' "Come

Go With Me": Mimi scowled, Julia beamed. Perhaps as an emergent father, Lennon grew closer to the carefree Julia in Yoko than to the militant Mimi. There's much more evidence that Lennon was happiest in the last five years of his life than not; tearing down Yoko ignores this vital truth.

With the birth of Sean in October 1975, life at the Dakota quieted down, and Gruen's pictures of Lennon holding Sean show a smile breaking his face. There's a fairy-tale aspect to Lennon's Dakota years that bathes his second fatherhood period in a halo of goodness and light. Compared to his lifestyle as a Beatle, and his "lost weekend," this period seems relatively calm: and while the lack of incident sends some biographers off on tangents, it's just as plausible to believe that Lennon enjoyed serious downtime and took care of personal matters.

Gruen stayed close, and now talks openly about how nurturing the John and Yoko myth meant finagling a more practical marital arrangement. "They were friends, they were married, and they figured out a way to make it work," Gruen says. "They had decided to be friends rather than jealous lovers. . . . But he always emphasized: JohnandYoko is one word—they were a team."[2] And Gruen stresses this had as much to do with aesthetics as it did with parenthood. As with many other bohemian couples throughout the ages, the arrangement figured in intimate compromise that snubbed middle-class convention.

LENNON HADN'T SEEN OR HEARD from his father since the confrontation at Tittenhurst in 1970, after which Lennon revoked his allowance and lost touch again. But early in 1976, Alfred's young wife, Pauline, contacted Lennon again through the Apple offices to let him know that Alfred had been diagnosed with stomach cancer. Lennon immediately put a call through to the local hospital in March and had one last conversation with "that Alf." According to Alfred's autobiography, published by Pauline in 1991, John was full of cheer and apologies, saying, "How you doing, whacker? I've been very worried about you."

"Fifteen two," Freddie responded, using one of his favorite non sequiturs. Lennon told his father about his new grandson, Sean, and promised they would meet one day. What must have passed through Lennon's mind now as he spoke with his estranged father? "I'm sorry I treated you the way I did, Dad," Pauline Lennon reports his saying. "I should never have gone to the head shrink. It was a big mistake."

"Forget it, John," Alf replied. "It's just bloody marvelous to talk to you again." The next day, a huge bouquet of flowers arrived at the hospital with a note: "To Dad—Get well soon—With much love from John, Yoko and Sean."[3] Alfred Lennon died on April Fools' Day, 1976, at the age of sixty-three, a month after their final talk. Lennon never spoke of this reconciliation to reporters.

BY 1976, RUMORS OF A BEATLE REUNION SPARKED a bidding war between promoters, a renowned comedy gag, and a colossal opportunity missed. From Los Angeles, promoter Bill Sargent offered the Beatles a guarantee of $50 million to reunite for a single concert, which would fan out via closed-circuit television around the world. None of the Beatles responded. After a month, Sargent doubled his offer, promising payment upon signing. He proposed the Fourth of July as the date, the American Bicentennial. A British promoter, Mike Mathews, responded with an offer of £3 million and proceeds from the closed-circuit revenues, which he estimated at around £30 million.

This gulf between the scale of American and British figures triggered a famous *Saturday Night Live* routine that aired on April 24, 1976, with producer Lorne Michaels offering them $3,000 to sing three songs. "If you want to give Ringo less, that's up to you," he quipped.[4] Lennon happened to catch the show live at the Dakota with Paul and Linda McCartney, who were eager to see that evening's *SNL* guests, former Lovin' Spoonful singer-songwriter John Sebastian (enjoying a revival as the author of the theme song to the *Welcome Back, Kotter* sitcom) and Raquel Welch.

It must have given John and Paul a boost, since they both talked admiringly about *SNL*'s spoof afterward as something they would have scrambled to be a part of. Only they were spent. "He [Paul] and I were watching it," Lennon remembered, "and we went ha-ha, wouldn't it be funny if we went down and we almost went down to the studio, just as a gag. We nearly got into the cab, but we were actually too tired."[5]

Staying at home must have felt right—Lennon started turning down all public appearances. Eager to keep the good vibe going, perhaps even do some writing, McCartney came back the next day with a guitar, but Lennon was stressed out and told him, "'Please call before you come over. It's not 1956, and turning up at the door isn't the same anymore. You know, just give me a ring.' That upset him, but I didn't mean it badly. I just meant that I was taking care of a baby all day, and some guy turns up at the door with a guitar."[6] McCartney headed to Dallas, for more rehearsals with Wings for the forthcoming tour supporting *Wings at the Speed of Sound*.

Michaels's *Saturday Night Live* bit also goes down as the rock fates mocking parental fatigue. It would be the last time Lennon ever saw Paul McCartney.[7]

DESPITE LENNON'S CALMER HOME life, legal problems continued. He appeared in court in New York in the months following Sean's birth to see through his defense of the Morris Levy suit surrounding opening lines borrowed from Chuck Berry and the *Roots* album Levy had hijacked to sell on late-night television. "The reason I fought this," Lennon said, "was to discourage ridiculous suits like this. They didn't think I'd show or that I'd fight it. They thought I'd just settle, but I WON'T."[8]

Judge Thomas Griesa found in Lennon's favor for the majority of this case after hearing lots of testimony, including Lennon's, on the music business and the creative process. In late February 1976, part one of Judge Griesa's three-part decision stated that Levy's publishing concern, Big Seven, was not entitled to damages from Lennon, Capitol, or Apple, for his original claim. Finally, that July, the last two parts were handed down: Big Seven was awarded $6,795 for breach of contract (the original agreement whereby Lennon would pay for quoting the opening lines of Chuck Berry's "You Can't Catch Me" in "Come Together" by recording two songs from Big Seven's catalog). Lennon, however, was awarded $107,700 for his counterclaim that Levy's actions cost him lost royalties on the *Rock 'n' Roll* album, and another $3,500 in compensatory damages for "hurt to his reputation."

Greisa delivered an unusual personal summation from the bench, which touched on the peculiar crossover nature of Lennon's persona. "I am convinced of the fact that Lennon perhaps has a career whose balance is somewhat more delicate than the career of other artists. Lennon has attempted a variety of ventures both in popular music and avant-garde music," he wrote. "Any unlawful interference with Lennon in the way that Levy and the *Roots* album accomplished must be taken seriously."[9]

That July also saw Lennon's long-drawn-out immigration case come to a close, with the official award ceremony for his green card. The event was a simple legal formality held in a small hearing room on the fourteenth floor of the INS Building on July 27. Since the previous October, when the Court of Appeals overturned all previous attempts to deport him, the U. S. government had gone silent on the matter. But the public-relations game drove Leon Wildes to summon several prominent character witnesses on Lennon's behalf to read their endorsements into the record. TV reporter Geraldo Rivera talked about John and Yoko as great humanitarians for the charity work they did on behalf of the children at Willowbrook. Isamu Noguchi, the Japanese sculptor, offered similar remarks. And Norman Mailer reminisced about how American literature still regretted the loss of T. S. Eliot to England, and hoped that America would not also lose Lennon. Even Gloria Swanson, now a physical-fitness freak, testified about what a good influence Lennon could be on the young.

"It's great to be legal again," Lennon said as he held up his green card (actually blue). "And I want to thank the Immigration Service for finally seeing the light of day. I just feel overwhelmed."[10]

ONCE FREE OF HIS VISA problems, Lennon traveled widely, to places as disparate as Egypt, South Africa, and the Middle and Far East, as often alone as with Ono and Sean. *Rolling Stone*'s Chet Flippo reports that in the midst of settling his court cases, John and Yoko made a swift trip to

Egypt to spend the night at the Great Pyramid. Yoko soon "confounded record-company attorneys at legal meetings by showing up as John's only representative (a non-attorney Japanese feminist artist). Now, she turned up for legal conferences garbed in ancient Egyptian robe and headdress."[11]

These furtive jaunts were steered by Ono's coterie of astrologers, psychics, and numerologists. At this point, British observers like to point out that for all his heavy travel during his professional sabbatical, Lennon never landed on British soil. No longer worried about getting let back into the United States, he staved off any ideas of a homecoming or family visits to Liverpool, Dorset (where Aunt Mimi lived), or London.

Their most frequent trips as a family were to Japan, where they stayed for five months during 1978. Lennon also started learning Japanese, and drew constantly during his sabbatical, both brief cartoons and more elaborate character sketches in lithograph. (Today Ono places much of this work in revolving circulation in a traveling exhibition.) A disarming "dictionary" of Japanese words and characters appeared in the museum catalog for "*The Art of John Lennon: Drawings, Performances, Films*," a 1995 exhibition at the Kunsthalle, in Bremen.[12] It begins with *Nippon go o narau*, or "It takes time to learn Japanese": a sober man with Japanese characters on his breast lifts an index finger. The next picture shows *Jibun*, or "Myself," one of those uncanny Lennon self-portraits with spectacles that capture his whimsically essential disguise. Very quickly Lennon elaborates phrase-by-phrase, drawing-by-drawing, to a wild-haired man at the piano, and brief Asian facial expressions for "Sweet, sour, salty, hot and bitter," as a balloon coming out of a man's head.

At the same time, Lennon also wrote some autobiographical sketches in plain verse that appeared later as *Skywriting by Word of Mouth*, and which, like some of his later songs, assume the voice of a parent explaining things to a child.

"John was moving about and sometimes he moved on his own," Ringo Starr remembers. "Yoko used to send him away on his own so he'd grow up. I don't know if he grew up but he certainly went places without her. And I think he had a very strange time in Macao if my memory serves me well." From Nippon, Lennon sent Starr a postcard which read: "back by

9 Oct. love," signed with another drawing of John, Yoko, and Sean, with a sun and a flower, and two stars popping out around Ringo's Monaco address.[13]

ONE DAY IN NOVEMBER 1976, Lennon came home from his Japanese language course to find a note from his Woolton friend Pete Shotton, who was visiting his elder brother in New Jersey.[14] Shotton had been roaming around Central Park with a friend and asked directions to the notorious Dakota, which he recognized from *Rosemary's Baby*. Lennon rang him up later that same afternoon and sent a car to New Jersey to pick him up for dinner.

Within the hour, the Dakota doorman ushered Shotton into the elevator. When its doors reopened, he saw John beaming from the doorway with his infant son Sean cradled in his arms. Shotton was struck both by the baby's gorgeous features (combining the best features from his parents, he thought) and Lennon's fit physical stature.

Following the Japanese custom, Lennon had Shotton take off his shoes, and he remarked how serendipitous Shotton's appearance seemed. He told Pete about taking language lessons, and learning the new word *shoton,* which had made him wonder how his old friend was doing. John and Yoko's numerologist cleared Shotton for a visit once Lennon came home to his note.

Shotton writes about how composed Yoko looked compared with when he had last seen her, and Lennon announced he had made dinner reservations at his favorite Japanese restaurant. What impressed Shotton the most, though, was how cavalierly Lennon refused the offer of his cigarette. He claimed to have quit smoking altogether, which struck his Merseyside visitor as nothing short of miraculous.

Lennon tucked Sean into bed, and the three set out on foot for the restaurant. Having been beside John during the height of Beatlemania, Shotton was nonplussed at how casually Lennon took this early evening public stroll—and how nonchalant New Yorkers were about the rock star in their midst. Lennon clearly enjoyed the relative anonymity of New York's streets. He never got hassled, he said, and people only approached him to tell him how much they loved his music, or perhaps pass along a furtive joint. One thing Lennon had never enjoyed on the streets of London, Shotton reflected, was the respectful distance of strangers.

Shotton describes Lennon's temperament that evening as warm and humorous, as if he had finally reconciled himself to his ex-Beatles status. To top it off, Lennon insisted on paying for the meal and calculating the tip—something his friend had never seen him do as a Beatle. Back at the Dakota, they sat up with Yoko watching Sally Field in the TV movie *Sibyl,* with the sound turned way down low so as not to disturb the sleeping baby. As John proclaimed he had quit alcohol (again), they chatted over several pots of tea, and then he recounted a recent solo adventure to Hong Kong following Yoko's mysterious calculations to reset John's clock with the planet's rotations.

Like many Lennon friends who reported of constant astrological consultants and vague, New Age–y trips to adjust his karma, Shotton simply nodded appreciatively. Whatever he might be doing, Shotton thought, Lennon seemed happy, and looked better than Shotton could have hoped. Lennon pressed a copy of William Duffy's *Sugar Blues* into Shotton's hand as he left, which he did with countless other visitors as well. This became another late Lennon signature: adopting an anti-sugar regimen while sneaking Hershey bars and Gitane cigarettes. That first night sent Shotton home with a warm afterglow.

They dined again two nights later, only this time Shotton described a phone call where Lennon argued with Yoko over the invitation, and described him as pale and stuck in a darker mood than before. As usual, Yoko remained quiet as they chatted and never tried to connect with Lennon's Woolton chum.[15]

THE FOLLOWING SUMMER, 1977, the Lennon family took a trip to an upscale mountain resort called Karuizawa, outside Tokyo. On Lennon's instructions, Elliot Mintz followed once they sent him a plane ticket. The day before Mintz left for Japan, however, some epic news came over the wires: Elvis Presley had died of what appeared to be a prescription drug overdose in his bathroom at Graceland, at age forty-two. It was August 16,

1977. The rock press went into overdrive. Millions of fans around the world began to grieve the King; Graceland became glutted with mourners.

Mintz called Lennon in Japan to give him the news. He remembers Lennon's outré reaction: "Elvis died in the army. . . . The difference between him and us is that, with us, our manager died and we lived. With Elvis, he dies and his manager lives. Come to Japan." Apparently, Lennon couldn't have been less interested in talking to Mintz about Presley's life or musical legacy. Mintz made his way to the hotel, where he was greeted with a mineral bath, a room filled with incense, and a note saying, "We are all together now, just like a family. We'll see you in the morning. John, Yoko and Sean."

Mintz tucked himself in without waking his hosts. The next morning, Lennon opened a screen, looking "high and wonderful."[16] A typical day began with a shiatsu massage, and an ice bath for Ono. Then they would all do yoga, take Sean for a walk, and stop off somewhere for noodles. Yoko wrote about Karuizawa in her notes to her production of Lennon's *Anthology* box set, describing it as a cross between the Hamptons and Vail, Colorado. They cycled to a coffeehouse in a pine forest every day with Sean, and spent afternoons in a huge family hammock in its backyard, giggling and watching the sky. During the rainy seasons, Lennon worked on collages in their hotel room.[17]

Collage filtered into Lennon's personal correspondence as well. A Claes Oldenburg cartoon-gun postcard stamped in New York, overlaid with a headline reading: ADOLF HITLER ARRIVED IN LIVERPOOL IN NOVEMBER OF 1912 FOR A FIVE-MONTH VISIT, came to Ringo Starr's Monaco address in early May 1979: "Dear Ringo . . . Thought you'd like to know." Several days later, another card arrived, this time a plain white ruled index card sent to Ringo's Los Angeles address: "How Hi the Moon (with female vocal harmony) DISCO—NATCH! i know, THIS AIN'T SIMPLE I KNOW" "This is John telling me what sort of things to record," Ringo later wrote. "He used to say, 'Do this sort of track.' 'Do it in a disco style!' He'd obviously just heard Blondie's 'Heart of Glass' which we all loved—that was a really cool record."[18]

IN TOKYO, JOHN, YOKO, AND SEAN stayed in the presidential suite at the Hotel Okura. Mintz describes an intimate informal concert Lennon gave to a Japanese couple there one evening in the sprawling set of rooms accessible only by elevator direct from the lobby:

> Around ten o'clock that night, I was sitting on the couch and John was strumming his acoustic guitar. . . . Suddenly, the elevator door opened. I presumed Yoko had returned, but instead a middle-aged Japanese couple who neither of us had seen before walked down the hallway and entered the dimly lit room. They noticed that there was a man playing guitar and another man seated near a table. . . . They spoke softly in Japanese, and seemed to want to listen to the solo music for a few minutes.

Like Nick Carraway stumbling upon Jay Gatsby as an anonymous guest at one of his own Long Island mansion parties, these tourists didn't recognize the world-famous Lennon. They started to get fidgety, looking around for a server to bring them cocktails. John gave them "Jealous Guy" in English, and after another few minutes, the couple arose and left. When the elevator door closed, Lennon and Mintz collapsed in laughter.[19]

AFTER MCCARTNEY TOURED AMERICA with Wings in support of his 1976 single, the adamantly flaky "Silly Love Songs," Lennon's absence from the scene became a new rock theme. Critics began remarking on how much expectation had built up around any future moves. In the gap between disco and punk, when the Ramones, Talking Heads, the Sex Pistols, the Clash, and Bruce Springsteen were gathering momentum on the sidelines, the mainstream disco pop of *Saturday Night Fever*'s Bee Gees gave rock fans fits. The unmet expectations of Lennon's solo career pressed up against everybody's wavering sense of dislocation, and pop music's overall lack of spine. (For some, it echoed the ghost of Buddy Holly, memorialized in Don McLean's "American Pie": "the day the music died.") There was a lingering sense that had Lennon kept on writing, he would have made the breakthrough a lot of this early seventies material aimed toward.

Dave Marsh of *Rolling Stone* wrote "An Open Letter to John Lennon" that season in his "American Grandstand" column, in late 1977. Hearing rumors of Lennon traveling in Japan, his once ubiquitous presence seemed inexplicable. "Why, the new Ringo album just came out and you're not even on that," Marsh began.

George Harrison had toured America in the fall of 1974, and Gerald Ford's son, Steven, invited him to the White House. Wires carried photos of Harrison with Billy Preston greeting Ford. McCartney's tour made a much bigger noise, and also made Lennon look deliberate in his silence, since he had never really let an opportunity pass before. Even the new president, Jimmy Carter, invoked Bob Dylan lyrics during his inauguration speech in early 1977. Surely Lennon would want a piece of rock culture's new legitimacy.

"Elvis is gone, the Sex Pistols have arrived," Marsh continued, "and instead of trying to get rockers deported, the White House lets them sit around the Oval Office waiting room, looking for an audience with the Peanut King. . . . I think the notion of overt anarchists in the British Top Ten should pique your curiosity." Since Lennon had such a claim on the public imagination, Marsh thought nothing of laying all this on his doorstep, as if none of Lennon's renunciations had registered. "Somehow, without any comment from John Lennon, there's a hole left in our understanding of what's going on."[20] Maybe the unflattering cartoon Jann Wenner chose of Yoko that ran alongside Marsh's piece persuaded Lennon to remain quiet.

SOME OF THE THINGS LENNON left behind provide more clues as to why he needed so much time to himself. Amid demo tapes, private home videos made for Yoko and Sean from hotel rooms, and home movies made in Japan, there's a notorious audio diary Lennon made in 1979 that circulates among collectors. The Los Angeles DJ Elliot Mintz, who later became a celebrity publicist for Paris Hilton, questions the authenticity of many of these audio leaks. But John and Yoko were as lax about interior security as they were when out in public; several personal assistants testify to the vast range of files they had easy access to, and many couldn't resist the temptation to purloin a letter or picture that had never been cataloged. This material still crops up at record shows, auctions, and online.

But on this 1979 tape, Lennon's unmistakable voice begins by noting the date, and he stops and starts several times to collect his thoughts. As one of the only such tapes yet to emerge, it seems like a halting start to a larger oral autobiography, and Lennon's thoughts pursue a rash of associations, smells, and subconscious leaps. Listening to this monologue, it's easy to feel yourself cast as Lennon's therapist, miffed yet fascinated. Did Lennon imagine his wife or son(s) might listen in someday? Or did he plan to listen back to his thoughts later on when he wrote up his Stanley sisters epic? ("A kind of *Forsyte Saga,*" which Lennon mentioned to Wenner.) History frets at all the unfinished business. But to ignore this evidence leaves out a revealing page in the story of Lennon's self-awareness.

He begins on the fifth of September 1979, announcing the ongoing life story of John Winston Ono Lennon, and veers immediately into the only first-person description he left of that early Stanley apartment at 9 Newcastle Road. It's the first place he remembers, he tells the tape, so that's a good place to start. He describes the red brick house with some detail, its front-room curtains always drawn, and a picture of a horse and carriage on the wall, before veering straight into an early nightmare. But just as quickly, he tires of all the description and shuts off the machine, complaining that he can't be bothered.

That earliest memory of a nightmare jibes with the blitz that continued on through Lennon's first year of life. It's hard not to notice how he drops this detail just before a description of the apartment's layout, and then protests he's bored, even though he's described the picture on the wall and the aunt's Cheshire home where it wound up in precise detail. Any shrink would tell you: there's gold in that nightmare.

Then Lennon meanders off into catty talk about Dylan's new single, "Gotta Serve Somebody," accusing him of wanting to be a waiter for Christ. Lennon eviscerates Jerry Wexler's whole *Slow Train Coming* production that the single conjures: Dylan's singing is pathetic, he says, the lyrics embarrassing. Surveying the 1979 rock scene, Lennon remarks how the Mighty Dylan, McCartney, and Jagger seem to be sliding down a mountain, blood with mud in their nails. This leads to a reflection on how competitive he used to feel with fellow rock stars, and how silly it all seems from his new vantage. Even a couple of years back he remembers the anxious panic such competition induced. Now there doesn't seem to be much use to listen to their albums. He still sends out for them, but they all sound pointless.

Lennon has enough wary self-consciousness to realize that even asking after his colleagues' records indicates he's not completely detached, that the ultimate detachment would mean not even knowing when they had new releases. But now, he says, he gets more pleasure than panic from reading the trades. It's all a load of shit, he says to the recorder. Later on in the same sequence, he adds that they're all company men in various masks.

This is what we assume all rock stars do: keep tabs on one another, make assessments, compare their own moves to their peers' in the never-ending game of rock 'n' roll high school, as if they're all perpetual seniors vying for attention, pulling off practical jokes, pairing off with various cheerleaders. In interviews, Lennon was more open than most about this horse race, but this audio diary lets us eavesdrop on the real thing, humanizing the titans of classic rock with mock horror, and a palpable sense of relief.

Then his talk turns to neuroses, their roots, as Lennon chuckles at his young ambition ("I couldn't walk so I tried to run," he sang in "Mother"). In 1954, Lennon was thirteen going on fourteen years old. It was the year before Lonnie Donegan's "Rock Island Line" and his skiffle craze. Long before the Elvis boom confirmed all these new sensations and thrust him into music that affirmed every sexual impulse he could ever imagine, Lennon pressed his face up against the glass of formative sexual desires.

Then some bagpipes come over the radio in the tape's background, and the music sends him reeling back further, to a distant horizon of boyhood summers with his aunt Mater (Elizabeth), where he attended an Edinburgh festival and heard marching bands. His favorites were the Americans, because they knew how to swing. And the summer ceremonies closed with one lone bagpiper, hit by a spotlight, for an emotional finale. Lennon describes the experience in great detail, the memory frozen in boyhood time. He describes always feeling free in Scotland, the same feeling he gets in Japan. You don't feel as though you belong, he says, so you don't have to deal with the social mores as much. It's easier to be yourself in a foreign country, he says. Then he wonders out loud about taking Sean to see Liverpool. Nineteen eighty-one looks like a good year to go, he thinks. Then he shuts off the recorder again.

When he clicks the recorder back on during the same sequence, he drops a bombshell for all the future biographers sitting on his shoulder. He remembers sitting on the bed with Julia, his hand on her bosom, in the apartment at 1 Blomfield Road, off Mather Avenue, near Garston. He had taken a day off school to hang out at her house, and they were lying about together; he wonders aloud if he should have done anything else. It was a strange moment, he says, because he had the hots for another female who lived across the road, but he always thought he should have done something more, and whether Julia would have allowed it. And then the tape cuts off again.

These associations summon more sensory associations, right down to Julia's angora sweater, her yellow mottled skirt, and the adolescent envy he felt toward his stepfather, Bobby Dykins. It's as if Lennon could still smell his mother lying next to him, and the primitive, unwieldy tension between teenage son and his flirtatious, mysterious, musical-mentor and out-of-reach mother. He remembers catching Judy going down on Twitchy, but can't remember exactly what he felt—and then proceeds to describe the envy and confusion with as much articulacy as any shrink has ever hoped for. For Lennon, it was the idea of her going down on *him,* that sleazy little waiter, with his nervous cough and slicked-back hair. Dykins always used to push his hand in margarine or butter and grease his hair back before leaving the house, Lennon pointedly says. He was already feeling up girls, and his own sexual discoveries mingled with a teenager's desire to provoke and dare Julia to favor him over anybody else.

A passionate ambivalence about his status in her house with her daughters welled up like a flood of desire that took shape as a forbidden incestuous impulse.

He used to steal the tips Dykins kept in a big tin on top of a kitchen cupboard, and Julia would get blamed. That was the least those two could do for him, Lennon says bitterly. Already, as an adolescent, manipulating resentments between his elders to poke and prod his mother into noticing his cunning, filching from Dykins's tip jar as revenge, the invisible houseguest thief with an adolescent boy's imperious agenda. And here he sits, a father now himself, shuttled out to Long Island to look for a summer house, like a boy led along by an auntie, or a dilettante who can't be bothered to choose his own vacation spot, an endless search for a new Scotland within driving distance of Manhattan.

TAKEN OUT OF CONTEXT, this matter-of-fact free association about Julia and boyhood feeds intense speculation about Lennon's psychic health. But as he continues, Lennon lays out a context: his self-revelation about middle-age testosterone anxiety, where it's taken him, and where he sits with it on Long Island, nearing forty. He describes reading in a magazine recently about someone's sexual fantasies and urges that continued throughout life. How when this person was twenty and then thirty he thought they'd cool down a bit, and then when he got in his forties he thought they'd stop and they didn't, not when he was sixty, seventy, and he was still dribbling on about it.

Lennon's response is wild-eyed identification. He himself kept hoping that his sexual impulses might lessen over the years, but now resigns himself to the idea that they'll go on forever. Even an amateur psychologist (or a pop audience, or a critic) can trace the larger themes in this monologue, the way Lennon connects superstar gamesmanship, his flirtatious mother, his stepfather's grooming habits, and the primal sexual scene most children grapple with: catching his mother having sex. For Lennon, each strand tugs at complex sources: to start, the superstar gamesmanship takes place without rules, where rock 'n' roll has already torn down so many phony show business benchmarks, redressing empty conventions, only to wind up yet another version of the same old game: grown men trying to outdo one another.

His utterance about his mother leaps from the tape as one of the very few instances where Lennon actually describes her in detail. "Julia," the song he baked alone at EMI after all the other twenty-nine *White Album* tracks were cooked, remains notable for its dreamy particularities ("seashell eyes") and doubles as a love song to Yoko Ono ("ocean child"). But nowhere else in the vast catalog of Lennon interviews does he go into a scene from childhood, the way Julia dressed, the memory of how she smelled, the way it made him feel, and the way his libido was ultimately entwined with grievance and loss. Consider how long it took him to retrieve this memory at all, never mind link it up with a contemporary quandary.

Aside from confirming Lennon's adolescent disdain for Dykins, this audio journal provides a peephole into Lennon's young mind, as he always took pains to speak respectfully of Dykins in many other contexts. Clearly, he felt for the man as they both lost Julia that night in 1958 when she was struck and killed on Menlove Avenue right outside Mendips. It's almost as if Lennon left this tape behind for future biographers to delve into the nature of his sexual dysfunction. Like a time bomb, or forbidden Rosebud, hidden among the artifacts of his life.

Students of psychology may have a different interpretation. Lennon's testimony (to himself? to his child? to his audience, eavesdropping long after his death?) has the air of a person doing his own therapy work in middle age—sifting through dreams, memories, and associations to make sense of a vast subconscious beset by uncertainty. Those incestuous impulses seem like rather ordinary Freudian fodder, especially considering Julia's once-removed status in Lennon's life, her well-known physical and personal charms, and a future rock star's raging teen hormones. This all floods back through intimate details and a shared awkward moment on the same bed where he'd come upon her giving Dykins a blowjob. Is it possible to expect Lennon to long for his abandoning mother without a hint of sexuality?

Given everything he's already spilled in song and interview, it's impossible not to imagine a whiff of sexual magnetism between Julia and John. How could Lennon, the exhibitionist's exhibitionist, not leave a trace of this somewhere for somebody to find? Alone in a car or a hotel room with a tape recorder, did he toy with history? Did he imagine some future ambulance-chasing biographers uncovering this moment? Or is this a MacGuffin, a Lennon prank planted to titillate, throw people off? Revealing to a cassette journal that he let his young teenage hand brush across his mother's chest, just to gauge her response, seems like one of Lennon's more innocent outrages.

LENNON'S RESPONSE TO MARSH and others calling for some kind of "statement" was steadfast silence, and stories began to appear about Ono managing his fortune, buying properties (in Florida and Long Island), and conducting Beatle business in lieu of a new manager. Instead of signing on with a new father figure to replace Allen Klein, Lennon let Ono steer the ship.

When the couple started to peek out of their shell, they began with a full-page ad in the Sunday *New York Times* of May 27, 1979, signed by both of them. They described their retreat and referred to parenting, new philosophies, and the power of wishing. "The past 10 years we noticed everything we wished came true in its own time," the ad started,

> good or bad, one way or the other. We kept telling each other that one of these days we would have to get organized and wish for only good things. Then our baby arrived! We were overjoyed and at the same time felt very responsible. Now our wishes would also affect *him*. . . . Many people are sending us vibes every day in letters, telegrams, taps on the gate, or just flowers and nice thoughts. We thank them all and appreciate them for respecting our quiet space, which we need. . . . If you think of us next time, remember, our silence is a silence of love and not of indifference. . . . PS We noticed that three angels were looking over our shoulders when we wrote this![21]

This prompted Dave Marsh to write another open letter in *Rolling Stone*, apologizing for the first: "If the past two years have taught me anything, it's that every rock fan is on his own. And that this is a Good Thing. No more leaders, which you [i.e., Lennon] said first." Marsh couldn't stand Lennon's precious tone in his ad, which only set off more rumors. Marsh warned against whatever expectancy was in the air, bemoaning comeback records long before they became standard rock career moves, and declaring Lennon a genius for picking the perfect moment to clam up. The statement, Marsh wrote, "actually accomplished . . . the undoing of everything your silence has worked toward; already there has been an avalanche of reunion rumors. Only you, John Lennon, can put an end to them."[22]

LENNON OFTEN STAYED AT A GETAWAY house in Glen Cove on weekends. Sometimes he went with Sean, sometimes the three of them went as a family. There, he made home videos with song demos, always lovingly dedicated to Yoko and Sean, singing songs ("Dear Yoko") that were just as frankly private as the tapes. He introduced himself with the same loopy malapropisms and corny self-aggrandizements, but they were family barbs done purely for pleasure, not to impress a pop audience. He also recorded a Yoko Ono song that became the title track to *Every Man Has a Woman Who Loves Him,* a tribute album for her fiftieth birthday, compiled after his death. Elvis Costello recorded a brittle "Walking on Thin Ice" for the project, alongside turns from Rosanne Cash and Harry Nilsson. Lennon left behind a whispery version of the song himself, a posthumous valentine.

That last year, 1980, Yoko sent John and Sean to Glen Cove for a stretch while she stayed at a friend's house on Fire Island. According to her own admissions to British biographer Philip Norman, she had become addicted to heroin again—a habit she concealed from John through their fragmented relationship and frequent travel. When considering the fairy-tale "happy ending" to the romance, Ono's heroin relapse should factor in: how she waded in deep enough to spend months hiding it from her once-junkie husband and then kicked it cold turkey without his ever finding out.

For her forty-seventh birthday in February 1980, she told Philip

Norman that she woke up in their Palm Beach mansion, El Solano, to find gardenias strewn from her bed all the way down the stairs and into the hallway. "He did that for me because he knew gardenias were my favorite flower. . . . And I felt so guilty because I'd gone back onto heroin and he didn't know."[23] Later that year, Ono determined to kick the drug for good. She claimed to be suffering from a terrible flu, and forbade her husband and son from seeing her until she recovered. This puts Lennon's audio diary into perspective: such frequent and extensive separations from his wife, whom he clearly adored, would rouse understandable sexual anxiety in men with one-tenth of his libido.

Lennon did stints sailing on Long Island Sound off Glen Cove, which gave him an appetite for a more ambitious venture. When he met up with David Scheff, the *Playboy* interviewer, in the fall of 1980, he told him about his sailing trip to Bermuda. With Yoko's encouragement, he chartered a Rhode Island yacht out of Newport, called the *Megan Jaye*, and planned to meet up with Sean in Bermuda.

His first time at sea was typically overambitious—three thousand miles, from Rhode Island to Bermuda, in seven days. "I'd always talked about sailing but my excuse was that I never had lessons," Lennon said. "Yoko's attitude was: 'Put up or shut up.' So she sent me on this trip and I went." So instead of getting sailing lessons, he simply hired a boat with crew and pointed himself toward Bermuda. He already had a sense that Ono had an ulterior motive: "We had talked about making music again," he said later, "but she knew I would fight creating again, even though I said that I wanted to. . . . She sent me specifically to open up my creativity, though she didn't tell me that. She knew I'd have fought it."

After a couple of days at sea, Lennon and the two skippers hit a huge storm, which lasted three harrowing days and made the crew so ill that Lennon had to take over the wheel. "They were sick and throwing up and the captain says to me, 'There's a storm coming up. Do you want to take over the wheel?' I said, 'Do you think I can?' I was supposed to be the cabin boy learning the trade, but he said, 'Well, you have to. There's no one else who can do it.' I said, 'Well, you had better keep an eye on me.' He said he would."

Five minutes afterward the captain went below to sleep, saying, "See you later." So there was Lennon, steering the boat for six solid hours. "You can't change your mind. It's like being on stage—once you're on, there's no getting off." Once they arrived safely in Bermuda, Lennon became convinced that the trial had rejuvenated his muse. "I was so centered after the experience at sea that I was tuned in, or whatever, to the cosmos. And all these songs came!"[24]

ALMOST AS SOON AS THERE WERE SONGS that summer of 1980, Lennon got back in touch with Jack Douglas, the Spector engineer turned producer who had worked on most Lennon projects, beginning as second engineer on *Imagine*. Douglas, now in demand as a celebrated orchestrator of albums from Aerosmith and Alice Cooper, had worked on classic material like the Who's *Who's Next* and introduced Wisconsin's Cheap Trick to the world. He eagerly took Lennon's call and swore on to a secret project.

"He flew me in a seaplane out to Glen Cove," Douglas says. "I picked up all these cassettes from John. He narrated every number, like for 'Nobody Told Me There'd Be Days Like These,' he said, 'I'm gonna give this one to Ringo.' And like on others he'd say, 'This is sort of a calypso number,' or whatever. He just wasn't sure whether he had anything going on that people might be interested in. So he wanted to keep it all under wraps until he knew it was going to reach a certain level."[25]

Under stern orders to keep things quiet, Douglas began rehearsing musicians in Manhattan. "The whole project was shrouded in secrecy," he remembers. "Everything was clamped down, even the studio staffers didn't know what I was working on. For two months during rehearsal and preproduction, I was rehearsing musicians on this material and nobody knew whose project this was. I'd play [rehearsal] tapes back for John in his bedroom, and he made suggestions, and I'd go back and we'd try different things. Some of the musicians guessed, but even then they kept their mouths shut.

"Then, only on the last day of rehearsal, that evening I told the players to meet me at the corner of 72nd and Central Park West, then some of them figured it out. It wasn't until John was sure that this record was really good, and that he could do it, that he turned to Yoko and said, 'Mother, tell the world we're making a record.'"

Much as with the surviving song demos for *The White Album* (the "Esher Demos"), Douglas pondered how to arrange numbers that seemed born complete. "And you know," he continues, "this material, I'd sit and listen to these cassettes, and think, 'What can I do with this?' It was all there. I mean, I did some arrangements, orchestrated things slightly, but it was all there, it didn't really need a producer."

Shortly after Lennon handed Douglas his homemade cassettes, Ono wedged Douglas into one of their marital contests, almost as if she saw herself as the new Paul McCartney. "Then another time I'm out in Glen Cove," Douglas recalls, "Yoko hands me this huge stack of five-inch reel-to-reel tapes, and she says, 'This is *my* stuff. Now *don't tell John,* but *I'm* gonna have some stuff on this record . . .' So now there's already this very complicated situation, with the studio and the players all learning this stuff in secret, there's all this intrigue, John's making a comeback record, and I'm supposed to keep Yoko's involvement from her own husband! It was ridiculous."

Some of this material came together quickly; other stuff needed work. "When I hired the musicians," Douglas says, "John would say, 'Make sure they're contemporaries of mine,' because he would use an oldies jam to get them in a mood for a certain song. This was part of how he got himself comfortable in the studio, singing old songs, but it was also how he cued his players to the groove he wanted on a track."

Douglas decided on Cheap Trick drummer Bun E. Carlos and guitarist Rick Nielsen to flesh out "Losing You." To reach them, he called George Martin, who was now producing Cheap Trick's fifth record, *All Shook Up,* at his AIR Studios in Montserrat. "I had to call Martin at his island studio to book my players," Douglas remembers. "I called him and said, 'Can I borrow some of my guys to play with your guy?'"

After three tart, ambitious power-pop records, Cheap Trick's *Dream Police* reached *Billboard*'s top five album chart during the summer of 1979. This followed up a huge radio hit, Fats Domino's "Ain't That a Shame," that sprang from *Cheap Trick at Budokan.* During release season, the band worked the road constantly that summer to boost its numbers. Coincidentally, Cheap Trick's whopping live cover of "Day Tripper" had been slapped onto a 1980 EP, *Found All the Parts,* and they began hearing about airplay of the Beatles song in Phoenix. Bun E. Carlos remembered getting the call that June: "Jack Douglas called, and they had a song they were having trouble getting a version of, and did I want to play on this thing, and I said sure, you know, like *yeah* . . ." Carlos continues:

> Then we went in and he introduced us to John Lennon, and he said, "Oh you're the guys from Cheap Trick, they told me your name but they didn't tell me what band you're in," so we thought that was kinda neat. . . . We told him, "You know we wanted you to produce our first record," and Lennon said, "I woulda done that no one told me!" We sat around the control booth and Jack played us the acoustic version of "Losing You," and Lennon turned to us and said, you know, "You got any ideas?" In Cheap Trick we did "Cold Turkey," and "It's So Hard," and we did some other Beatles tunes, "Day Tripper," stuff like that. In the band, we're all big *Plastic Ono Band* fans, we're always saying, "Well, how would *Plastic Ono Band* have done this?" Or like, "If this were the next song after 'Cold Turkey,' how would it go?"[26]

Lennon's collaborative approach impressed Nielsen and Carlos, just as it had Tex Gabriel back with the Elephant's Memory Band. When they asked him what tempo he wanted, Lennon simply said, "Whatever you think it should be." They cut the track live with Lennon on rhythm guitar to Nielsen's lead, and then Nielsen overdubbed a second guitar track as they gathered in the booth. "It kind of happened so quickly you didn't have time to really pinch yourself," Carlos says.

Cheap Trick had a hit record on the charts, so hustling between gigs to keep sales going and banging out sessions for John Lennon's secret project were all a part of the new status the band enjoyed. "And John was like, hey you wanna smoke a joint? And we were like 'Sure!' 'Cause we'd been in Canada all week, Cheap Trick, they didn't have pot up there back then," Carlos says. "Lennon got out his guitar and he said, 'This is my "Day Tripper" guitar,' and he had had it refinished and stuff, and we made some wisecrack like 'Oh that's number ten in Phoenix this week.'" Lennon shot them a look. No, Carlos and Nielsen insisted, "we have an EP and it's on there." And then, Carlos remembers, "Lennon's eyebrows kinda went up at that a little, like he hadn't heard, and wasn't sure whether to believe us or not."

After Nielsen's second guitar part, Lennon invited them along for dinner, but Carlos had to beg off: "I told him, 'I gotta go home to Chicago, we're going to Japan tomorrow for three shows and then coming back next week to do another track,' and he goes 'Ah! I married one of the emperor's daughters!'"

Like a lot of touring musicians, Carlos did a good deal of this invisible work, banging out tracks only to be replaced by studio players down the line. He certainly never expected to make the final cut on a Lennon comeback album. "We came in to find a version for the song the other guys couldn't get a version for," he says simply. "We weren't surprised when it wasn't on the record, they just used us as a demo version." Even though Douglas had thought of his Cheap Trick players as perfect for Lennon's tracks, Ono intervened. "Yoko decided Cheap Trick would be riding on Lennon's coattails. Her attitude was 'Who are these people, I've never heard of them! We're not gonna give these guys a free ride,'" Douglas says.

Yoko's own track, "I'm Movin' On," took shape with the same musicians. Douglas had them revive a drum part from their first album that they hadn't used, and Yoko provided some sheet music with words and chords, which Nielsen wrote some riffs around. Then, Carlos says, "John got on the mike and said, 'Mother, dear, why don't you do Tony's first verse and then do the boys' arrangement,' 'cause he was calling me and Rick 'the boys.'" And Yoko shot back: "Fuck you very much, John," and everyone dissolved with laughter. "We just cracked up with that, 'cause it was pretty obvious, you know, they were a team."

Carlos admits that "Our playing wasn't great on Yoko's track, the feel never quite coalesced. But there were things like, Yoko'd be in the booth and say, 'Does anyone want some granola?' or whatever she had, and it looked like animal feed. And John would be like down the hall with the roadies, you know, sneaking a slice of pizza."

JACK DOUGLAS FLEW CARLOS and Nielsen back for another session some weeks later, but Lennon had decided to start mixing what he had (they originally laid out enough material for a double set), thanked them for their help, and signed autographs. Once the tracks were finished, Douglas set about sequencing and mastering, and John and Yoko took meetings with record labels. David Geffen, who had wooed Dylan away from Columbia earlier in the seventies and then lost him, was busy starting up a new label: Geffen Records. Donna Summer and Elton John signed on as his first artists. But the label hadn't released any records yet. He sent Yoko Ono a telegram when he heard there might be a Lennon record, and took a meeting with Ono in her ground-floor Dakota office.

"Well, why should we go with you?" Yoko asked him. "Because I will be very sensitive to who you are and deal with you straight and do a good job," Geffen shot back. Ono pressed him to find out what he knew about her music, and Geffen admitted he didn't know her work, and was even spotty on Lennon's solo career. And Ono reminded him that he hadn't even launched his label yet. But Geffen assured her he would treat them right.

Geffen walked out of the Dakota thinking that he had just sat through the strangest meeting ever. "She had a poker face, very aloof," he remembers. After she ran "his numbers" (a combination of his birthday, address, phone number, and "who knows what"), Ono invited Geffen over to meet John. Without ever hearing the record, Geffen agreed to her terms:

> "Don't you want to want to hear the music first?" I said, "No, I'll wait until whenever you want to play it for me." And she said, "Well, if you wanted to hear the music before you made the deal, we wouldn't have gone with you."[27]

When Geffen met up with John in the studio, they reminisced about the L.A. scene where they had crossed paths in the mid-seventies. Lennon told him how excited he was for Yoko's career, how the earlier hostility toward her seemed to be dropping away.

Like many of the musicians who worked with John and Yoko, Geffen came away with a telling insight as to how they leaned on each other's strengths. "When Yoko's alone, she's Yoko Ono and she takes care of everything. But when she was with John, she deferred to him. She had an incredible respect for what he thought and what he wanted and what he aspired to. She influenced him a great deal and he influenced her a great deal."[28] This adds a new level to our understanding of the creative partnership: Lennon depended on Yoko to handle business negotiations; Yoko relied on Lennon for the personal leverage and mass appeal. Their professional stature depended on a mutual need, much the way the Beatles had developed their ensemble politics.

Jack Douglas had different memories of how they interacted. "I don't mean to sound anti-Yoko because I'm not," he says now, "but there was always some kind of minor war going on. In the end, Lennon would always fold to 'Mother,' he just didn't want the grief. Like when it came time to do the song sequence for *Double Fantasy,* John said, 'Okay, boys, let's make an order. You guys make your order and put it in this hat, and I'll make an order and put it in the hat.' So we drew up our song lists, and my order and John's were fairly similar, they all had John songs on side A and Yoko's songs on side B. And then Yoko looked at these layouts and said, 'No way! If you want to hear John, you've got to hear Yoko, too!' And so we laced them together, first John and then Yoko, throughout the record. But with her, it wasn't really a negotiation, it was like, 'This is how it's going to be.'"

DOUBLE FANTASY WENT INTO PRODUCTION for release on November 17, 1980. Once they put the record to bed, John and Yoko booked press for the first time since 1975. The publicity appeared slowly at first, with articles in *Newsweek* and the *New York Times,* for exchanges with reporters that turned out to be far more enjoyable than Lennon remembered from the past. These expanded to several lengthier interviews as *Double Fantasy* turned into a hit, transforming Lennon's comeback into a major event. The long, compelling *Playboy* interview with David Scheff, taped in September for release in the January issue, hit newsstands in mid-November. Long-form sessions booked with *Rolling Stone,* the *New York Times* Sunday magazine, and several British radio outlets found slots in early December.

In all of these quotes, Lennon held forth with a new confidence, proud of his new songs and unabashedly sentimental about his new home life. For Robert Palmer's *New York Times* profile, which ran on November 9, Lennon went on about his time off and fatherhood, recasting his late career as a salvation narrative. "I was a machine that was supposed to produce so much creative *something* and give it out periodically for approval or to justify my existence on earth. But I don't think I would have been able to just withdraw from the whole music business if it hadn't been for Sean. . . . When I look at the relative importance of what life is about, I can't quite convince myself that making a record or having a career is more important or even as important as my child, or any child."

Another Lennon quote that Palmer used finally came clean about some of the "working class" myths Lennon often fudged:

Going back to the beginnings of rock and roll, Elvis and Jerry Lee Lewis and so on were working-class entertainment; *they* were working class. The Beatles were slightly less working class; for Paul McCartney and me at least, going to university was a possibility. I had all this artsy stuff in me anyway, so we put a little more intellect into our music, just because of what we were. And gradually, expectations for the Beatles became educated, middle-class expectations. And I tended to get too intellectual about pop music, I had this sort of critic John Lennon sitting over me saying, "You did that already, you can't do it again. You can't say it that simply." Now the music's coming *through* me again.[29]

That's a bracing clarification of Lennon's own symbolic stature, broken down for two cultural audiences: in Britain, being working class at the time meant the impossibility of a higher education. In America, such distinctions get lost amid foreign accents and zany humor.

Douglas remembers Lennon feeling recharged by the album's sales and media interest: "He was so proud of *Double Fantasy* turning into a hit, he was going to take the material on a huge world tour. He had already done sketches of the production, hired the musicians, like drummer Andy Newmark, bassist Tony Levin, and guitarist Hugh Mc-Cracken."

With "(Just Like) Starting Over" as its parodic lead single, *Double Fantasy* found traction on the charts, goading big plans. Douglas remembers a lot of conversation about Lennon's old partners, about Lennon returning to Britain, where he hadn't been since 1971, and even beyond the tour, reaching out toward other projects. "There was a Ringo album coming down the pike, and a reunion, at least by the three of them (Harrison, Lennon, and Starr), that was all planned out. That was going to be Lennon's next move after the world tour," Douglas continues. "He talked fondly about McCartney every night, and he always wanted to redo certain Beatles songs, but he really spoke more like he really loved those guys. The only person that he was pissed at was George, because George put out this memoir [*I Me Mine*] and John was really, *really* pissed about that. I remember him saying, 'How do you write about your life and not talk about the guy whose band you were in?'"

THE REVIEWS OF *DOUBLE FANTASY* were positive, but a tricky five-year expectations game tipped against Lennon, especially from the old guard. American critics were disappointed; but British critics seemed crestfallen. Geoffrey Stokes wrote an essay for the the *Village Voice* titled "The Infantilization of John Lennon" and called the music "basically misogynist." To Stokes, the whole househusband pretext stank of public relations, and he characterized the album's concept as "vampire-woman-sucks-life-out-of-man-who-enjoys-every-minute-of-his-destruction." Stokes especially hated Ono's "Hard Times Are Over"—a finale "so all-fired powerful it exists without (present) pain, without conflict."[30] In England, Charles Shaar Murray, a longtime reviewer for *NME,* sounded downright insulted: "Everything's peachy for the Lennons and nothing else matters, so everything's peachy QED. How wonderful, man. One is thrilled to hear of so much happiness. . . . It sounds like a great life, but unfortunately it makes a lousy record."[31]

THAT FIRST WEEK IN DECEMBER, as Reagan assembled his new cabinet, pundits began taking stock of the season. It was the year Solidarity began organizing in Poland, the year America boycotted Moscow's Summer Olympics with sixty-three other countries to protest the Soviet invasion of Afghanistan, and the year before MTV launched. The *Star Wars* sequel *The Empire Strikes Back* topped the box-office receipts. Paul McCartney released *McCartney II*, a milquetoast commemoration of his first solo album's ten-year anniversary, which included "Coming Up," a track Lennon felt obliged to praise, and "Temporary Secretary." It reached number one in the UK, but peaked at number three in America.

Lennon was busier than he had been in almost five years. He sat for three major interviews: Jonathan Cott of *Rolling Stone* taped on December 5; the BBC's Andy Peebles on Saturday, December 6; and RKO Radio on Monday afternoon, December 8. Peebles remembers Ono's strict advance negotiations: how at least half of the questions needed to be pitched directly to her. Slotted for half an hour, before Peebles could blink two hours had gone by and Lennon had taken off, soaring high above his career, looking down, pointing out details nobody had noticed before, remembering names, dates, and songs people had long forgotten, ticking off hit records by other acts nobody knew he paid any attention to, and generally charming this young British radio crew.

"Are you kidding me?" Peebles said many years later. "I remember the very day I saw *Please Please Me* in the record shop, buying it and racing home to put it on. To be interviewing John Lennon that day, I was *dead chuffed*."

When Peebles took a break with his producers, Doreen Davis and Paul Williams, he ran into Yoko after hitting the bathroom. He took her aside to reassure her: "I said I know what we negotiated, I have questions for you, I just need to get a word in, I promise we mean to get your side of the story here." And Yoko, clearly astonished at what was happening, said, "It's okay, it's okay! I had no idea he was going to talk so much."[32] So much talk over so many weeks, and so little overlap. Lennon was just getting warmed up.

As Lennon talked to the BBC, a young man in his mid-twenties began hanging around the Dakota, on Saturday, December 6. Like so many before him, he talked with other autograph hounds and hoped to get a glimpse of his hero. This anonymous figure barely stood out. He had been born in Fort Worth, Texas, in 1955, an air force kid who graduated from Columbia High School in Decatur, Georgia, in 1973. There, he played guitar in a rock band, took Christ as his "personal savior," and carried around a "Jesus notebook."

In October 1980, this young man, at twenty-five, applied for a pistol permit from his home in Honolulu, claiming an attempted burglary at his apartment necessitated self-protection. Later that month, he plunked down $169 in cash for a five-shot Charter Arm revolver with a two-inch barrel at J&S Enterprises-Gun in Honolulu. According to police records, he traveled to New York on Saturday, December 6, spent the night at the West Side YMCA on 63rd Street and Central Park West, and then went over to the Sheraton Center at 52nd Street and Seventh to book a room, number 2730, at $82 a night, for the week.

The afternoon of Monday, December 8 was sunny and promising. Lennon had a number-one hit single with "(Just Like) Starting Over," and plans were progressing for Ono's techno-pop "Walking on Thin Ice" to be its follow-up. The *Playboy* interview, with its detailed deconstruction of Lennon-McCartney authorship, proved newsstand bounty. If insecurities had found voice during the production of *Double Fantasy,* they evaporated in the public's embrace of Lennon's new music. Now that the couple sat atop certain success, they could be selective about his exposure, and finally book some British press.

Annie Leibovitz, who had taken Lennon's handsome portrait for the *Rolling Stone* cover in 1970, returned to the Dakota apartment to follow through on a session from the previous week. She lived upstairs in the same building. Ono recalled the shoot later for *Rolling Stone:* "We were feeling comfortable because it was Annie, whom we respected and trusted, so John seemed not to have any problem taking off his clothes. John and I were hugging each other, feeling a bit giggly and up."

"I was thinking that they had never been embarrassed to take their clothes off, that they could do a nude embrace," says Leibovitz. John immediately assented and took off his clothes; Yoko was reluctant. She agreed to take her shirt off but not her pants; Liebovitz said, "Just leave everything on." She took a Polaroid shot for a test, and all three of them knew they were on to something—that the pose alone would create a stir.

"When I was with John and Yoko, they seemed like gods to me," Leibovitz remembers now. "It's hard to think about that time, but I remember being impressed with the simple kiss they did on the cover of *Double Fantasy.* The eighties were not a romantic era, and the kiss was just so beautiful."33

After putting his clothes back on, Lennon sat down with the UK's syndicated RKO Radio that afternoon and talked his head off. "When I was writing this [album]," he said, "I was visualizing all the people of my own age group . . . being in their thirties and forties now, just like me, and having wives and children and having gone through everything together. I'm singing for them. I'm saying, 'Here I am now. How are you? How's your relationship going? Did you get through it all? Wasn't the seventies a drag, you know? . . . Well, let's try to make the eighties good, because it's still up to us to make what we can of it.'" As the interview ends and the crew breaks up the equipment, you can hear everyone's elation on the tape. Especially Lennon's.

That evening, John and Yoko came out of the front gate to take their limo to the Hit Factory on West 44th Street, to work on Ono's "Walking on Thin Ice," which they were both convinced would break Ono through to the pop charts. Lennon had raved to her about her obvious influence on the B-52's single "Rock Lobster." He seemed certain that once she found the right material, Ono could take her place as the rightful influence on the cutting sounds coming from punk and new wave.

On his way to the car, Lennon signed some autographs on the cover of *Double Fantasy*. Somebody flashed a picture. The person holding the album had unkempt hair and wire-rimmed glasses, and wore a dark raincoat and scarf.

David Geffen, now the doting, friendly record executive, visited the couple at the Record Plant that evening, to listen to the final mix. He remembers Lennon smiling and dancing around, filled with anticipation about Yoko's single. "Wait'll you hear Yoko's record. It's a smash! This is better than *anything* we did on *Double Fantasy*," Lennon said. Yoko remained skeptical, although she seemed to be enjoying John's enthusiasm. "Oh, John, it's not that great," she said. "Oh yes it is," Lennon insisted. "It's better than anything the B-52's ever did. And we want you to put it out before Christmas." Geffen said, "Well, let's put it out *after* Christmas and really do the thing right. Take out an ad." Lennon said, "An ad! Listen to this, Mother, you're gonna get an *ad*!"

Then Geffen gave Lennon some news: *Double Fantasy* would be the number one album the next week in England. "Yoko gave me this real funny look," Geffen remembers, "like it *better* be number one in England. That was the thing she was interested in, not for herself but because John wanted it so badly."[34]

John and Yoko spent the evening at the studio, mixing Ono's track, and decided to pop back home instead of heading out somewhere for dinner. At around 10:50 P.M. that evening, their limo pulled up to the Dakota and the couple hopped out at the curb. As they walked up to the gate, a young autograph hound called, "Mr. Lennon," pulled out his handgun, dropped to a "combat stance," and pulled the trigger five times into the singer's back before he could turn around. Four of the shots ripped through Lennon's flesh—two on the left side of his back and two in his left shoulder.

Two witnesses saw the shooting: the Dakota elevator operator at the door and a cabdriver who had just dropped off another passenger. Somebody called 911. From their nearby patrol car at 72nd and Broadway, about three blocks away, Officers Steve Spiro and Peter Cullen heard a report of shots fired. When they arrived, they found the killer standing "very calmly," reading his book, J. D. Salinger's *The Catcher in the Rye*.

Bleeding profusely, Lennon had somehow stumbled all the way through the courtyard of the Dakota into the lobby, where he lay bleeding in front of Jay Hastings, the doorman. A second patrol car arrived with Officers Bill Gamble and James Moran, and they loaded Lennon into the backseat of their squad car rather than wait for an ambulance. Moran reported Lennon "moaning" from the back. Officer Moran asked him, "Are you John Lennon?" and Lennon moaned, "Yeah."

When they arrived at Roosevelt Hospital, Dr. Stephan Lynn could tell Lennon was beyond hope as the gurney whooshed past, but a team set about trying to revive him anyway. He had lost too much blood, and all attempts to get his heart beating again failed. Dr. Lynn pronounced Lennon dead at 11:15 P.M. The autopsy by Dr. Elliott M. Gross, chief medical examiner, said Lennon had died of "shock and loss of blood" and that "no one could have lived more than a few minutes with such injuries." The lack of gunpowder burns on Lennon's skin indicated the shots must have been fired from farther than eighteen inches.

DAVID GEFFEN HAD GONE STRAIGHT from the Record Plant to his apartment and turned his phone off. After a few minutes, he noticed the light flashing, so he picked up and heard a strange woman's voice tell him, "I'm a friend of Yoko's, John's just been shot. They're at Roosevelt Hospital. Run right over." Geffen thought it was a crank call. Just to make sure, he called the Record Plant, "and they said, no, it's impossible, he just left here ten minutes ago." Then Geffen's phone rang again, and the same woman asked him, "Why haven't you left? He's shot!" Geffen called her back to verify, and then took a call from his partner, Eddi Rosenblatt, who'd seen the news bulletin on television. They met to grab a cab downtown.

Security was tight at the hospital, and Geffen had to yell his way past guards to find Ono:

> It was such a scene. There were cops everywhere, big cops, you know. You feel so intimidated, and all I could think was that I had to get to Yoko. . . . Finally, someone opened the door and

I ran in. Yoko was in this little room, hysterical, and I just picked her up in my arms. She said, "Someone's shot John. Can you believe it? Someone shot him." I was in shock.

Then a policeman called me outside and said, "He's dead. He died on arrival at the hospital." It was like an explosion in my mind.[35]

Ono was led away when doctors told her of her husband's death. "Tell me it's not true!" she was quoted as crying. Later, Geffen issued this statement on her behalf: "John loved and prayed for the human race. Please do the same for him."[36]

As mayhem rapidly descended on the Upper West Side, the most common feeling was one of disbelief, the stillness of a December evening violently sundered, as if the sixties had finally and irrevocably ended, only ten years too late. Many heard about Lennon's death from ABC-TV, when Howard Cosell came back from a commercial break with an inexplicably sobering tone that shrank the Dolphins-Patriots *Monday Night Football* game to a pinpoint. Cosell had hosted a rare appearance by Lennon in his booth as a guest celebrity six years earlier, in December 1974, when Lennon raved about hearing "Yesterday" come over the PA system.

On this night, Cosell's supernatural egotism went limp: "This, we have to say it, remember this is just a football game, no matter who wins or loses. An unspeakable tragedy, confirmed to us by ABC News in New York City: John Lennon, outside of his apartment building on the West Side of New York City, the most famous, perhaps, of all the Beatles, shot twice in the back, rushed to the Roosevelt Hospital, dead on arrival."

In New York City that night, spectacle engulfed the Dakota. News cameras and policemen swarmed the scene; flowers and photographs began piling up against the great Victorian façade. Pedestrians, caught unaware, stopped dead in their tracks as word spread. They turned direction, as if in mid-step, and began striding toward Central Park West, pulled by an invisible force, eventually the pull of the music. Beatle songs and spontaneous sing-alongs started up, faded away, and returned. Candles illuminating tearful faces contested the city's great darkness. Extinguished either by wind or use, they were quietly relit.

Jay Hastings sat at his post in the Dakota lobby, his shirt still flecked with Lennon's blood, and talked to reporters in a daze. He recognized the gunman. "He seemed like a nice guy," Hastings told *Rolling Stone.* "Some bum came up and asked him for money, and the guy gave him a ten-dollar bill. The bum was ecstatic and kissed him and everything. He didn't bother anyone here; I hardly noticed him."[37]

The crowd seemed to speak in a hush, as if participating in somebody else's bad dream, mortified to be part of the scene yet unable to turn away. "I keep thinking about all those years when the government tried to deport him," said Joe Pecorino, who played the John Lennon character in *Beatlemania,* then running at the Winter Garden Theater. "Now it's too damn bad they didn't."[38] Sentiments like this echoed throughout much of the British press.

In shock, and increasing futility, American fans watched TV late into the night; still others awoke to Beatle tracks blanketing morning radio, and shock jocks quietly humbled. Five hours ahead of New York time, Britons awoke to the grim news, which disturbed the patter of their morning chat shows.

Epilogue

THE DAYS FOLLOWING LENNON'S DEATH PASSED IN A HAZE OF PUBLIC mourning. Elliot Mintz remembers being in the front office of the Dakota the morning of December 9 when Ringo Starr rang in. "He was calling from a pay phone, he told me. He said, 'I'm here, I want to come over, do what I can to help. How do I get past all the stuff?'" Mintz told him to meet him on 73rd Street and sneak in a back door. Half an hour later, Starr's car pulled up and Mintz walked him very slowly toward a Dakota service entrance. "We got about halfway there without anybody recognizing him, and then photographers started running after us," Mintz says. Ringo just kept walking, and told Mintz, "Don't run from them, it will just make it more difficult." By the time they got to the entrance, photographers surrounded them.

Mintz took Ringo and his fiancée, Barbara Bach, up in the elevator to the Lennon suite. "The meeting was short but somehow got quoted accurately," Mintz reports. "Ringo told Yoko, 'I know exactly how you feel,' and Yoko said, 'No, you don't.' He was one of the few people who came in to see her and just talk with her. And then I remember taking him downstairs, but by then the building was completely surrounded, and we had to walk through the crowd to get back to his car."[1]

An AP photographer caught Starr, Bach, and Mintz as they stepped back out from the rear entrance. After Ringo left, seventeen-year-old Julian Lennon arrived from North Wales. The surging crowd in front of the Dakota spilled over into Central Park West, with many people, men and women, openly weeping, holding signs, playing Beatle songs on boom boxes, and singing along with impromptu guitars. Many had stayed through the night; many more joined the throng in the morning hours. On television, the three networks regularly interrupted programming, in a scene that would be repeated with Princess Di's funeral in 1997, with footage of the multimedia vigil unfolding around the world. Crowds gathered at Liverpool's Cavern on Mathew Street, outside the former Apple offices on Savile Row in London, and beneath the rooftop concert location from *Let It Be*.

John Eastman called his sister's house and woke his brother-in-law, Paul McCartney, with the news. McCartney hung up and called Yoko Ono. He went into the London studio later that day just to keep working as the enormity sank in. Reporters caught him on his way inside AIR Studios on Oxford Street, and badgered him for a quote. "Bit of a drag, isn't it?" he blurted out, obviously reeling from the news (the video of this exchange shows a man in a barely suppressed rage). But the phrase looked so bad in print he had to come back and explain himself. In doing so, he let loose with some enticing candor on his partner's persona:

> If I had known John was going to die, I would not have been as stand-offish as I was. When John started slagging me off, I was not prepared to say "you're quite right," I am human. Nobody would sit there and be called an Engelbert Humperdinck as I was and say, "Oh, fine, I think you're right." I just turned round and said, "piss off." Had I known it was going to be that final— and quick—I wouldn't have said it.
>
> John was not the big working-class hero he liked to make out. He was the least working-class of the Beatles. He was the poshest, but he did have rather a tough upbringing.[2]

George Harrison issued a statement that read, "After all we went through together, I had—and still have—great love and respect for John. I'm stunned. To rob life is the ultimate robbery."[3]

The day also brought a quote from Lennon's aunt Mimi, from Dorset.

Her first thought at hearing his name had simply been "What's he done now?" Reflexively, she began by reiterating her primacy in his life: "John looked upon me as his mum. . . . There was never the possibility that he would be just an ordinary person. He'd have been successful in anything he did. He was as happy as the day was long."[4]

NOT SINCE THE ASSASSINATIONS of Martin Luther King Jr. and Senator Robert Kennedy in 1968 had Americans gathered in such numbers to share this shock and dismay, but the event precipitated similar outpourings throughout the world. It was as if all the turmoil from Lennon's era rushed back to fill the countercultural void created by November's election of Ronald Reagan as president. By the evening of December 9, the network newscasts had gathered up reports from around the globe and channeled the grief on display at symbolic locations like Mendips in Woolton and Hamburg's Reeperbahn. Radio stations played "Imagine" nonstop, and for the first time, the music rang nostalgic in preposterous ways—at once comforting, reassuring, and utterly absurd. Every familiar gesture seemed portentous, prophetic yet unimaginable, especially in "The Ballad of John and Yoko," when Lennon sang: "The way things are going they're gonna crucify me!" It could never be true, and it was too true to take in all at once.

Late-night TV tributes interviewed Beatles authors and rock scribes; few found anything worth saying. At the Philadelphia Spectrum, two months into his tour supporting *The River,* Bruce Springsteen argued with his E Street Band about whether to go onstage at all. When he did come out, he told the audience: "The first record that I ever learned was a record called 'Twist and Shout' [cheers], and if it wasn't for John Lennon, we'd all be in some place very different tonight [cheers]. It's . . . it's an unreasonable world and you have to live with a lot of things that are just unlivable, and it's a hard thing to come out and play. But there's just nothing else you can do." And with that Springsteen kicked off "Born to Run," turning his breakout anthem into a volatile mixture of rage, regret, and canceled hope. On bootlegs, you can hear a riotous conviction buried in the sound that somehow the music might reverse history, or lunge toward some kind of meaning where there didn't seem to be any.

In the first of many new ironies, Yoko Ono now found herself sympathetic. A wave of feeling went out to her, and to Sean, combined with a peculiar celebrity worship hitting a new pitch. In Toronto, thirty-five thousand people gathered in the freezing snow for a candlelight vigil on Tuesday night. By Thursday, wire services from Florida and Utah reported two suicides related to Lennon's killing. Ono responded in a quote to the *New York Daily News:* "People are sending me telegrams saying 'This is the end of an era and everything.' I'm really so concerned. This is not the end of an era. 'Starting Over' still goes. The Eighties are still going to be a beautiful time. . . . It's hard. I wish I could tell you how hard it is. I've told Sean and he's crying. I'm afraid he'll be crying more. . . . But when something like this happens, each one of us must go on."5

She announced that Lennon's body was being cremated according to his express instructions, and the ashes would be scattered in the Atlantic. As a memorial, she asked for ten minutes of silent prayer in his honor at 2 P.M. on Sunday, December 14. "John loved and prayed for the human race," she said. "Please pray the same of him. Please remember that he had deep faith and concern for life and, though he has now joined the greater force, he is still with us here."

On Friday, Yoko issued a longer statement in block capital letters, unveiling as a mother consoling her son a very different picture from her persona up to this point:

I TOLD SEAN WHAT HAPPENED. I SHOWED HIM THE PIC-
TURE OF HIS FATHER ON THE COVER OF THE PAPER AND
EXPLAINED THE SITUATION. I TOOK SEAN TO THE SPOT
WHERE JOHN LAY AFTER HE WAS SHOT. SEAN WANTED
TO KNOW WHY THE PERSON SHOT JOHN IF HE LIKED
JOHN. I EXPLAINED THAT HE WAS PROBABLY A CONFUSED
PERSON.

SEAN SAID WE SHOULD FIND OUT IF HE WAS CONFUSED
OR IF HE REALLY HAD MEANT TO KILL JOHN. I SAID THAT

WAS UP TO THE COURT. HE ASKED WHAT COURT—A
TENNIS COURT OR A BASKETBALL COURT? THAT'S HOW
SEAN USED TO TALK WITH HIS FATHER. THEY WERE BUD-
DIES. JOHN WOULD HAVE BEEN PROUD OF SEAN IF HE HAD
HEARD THIS. SEAN CRIED LATER. HE ALSO SAID "NOW
DADDY IS PART OF GOD. I GUESS WHEN YOU DIE YOU
BECOME MUCH MORE BIGGER BECAUSE YOU'RE PART OF
EVERYTHING."

"I don't have much more to add," Ono concluded, requesting a ten-
minute worldwide vigil on December 14 at 2 P.M. (EST). She signed it,
"Love, Yoko and Sean"[6]

THAT SUNDAY, December 14, in front of St. George's Hall on Lime
Street, more than thirty thousand Liverpudlians gathered and joined in
singing "Give Peace a Chance," just up the block from Charlotte Street,
where Lennon once cadged 45-rpm singles from Brian Epstein's NEMS
store. More than five thousand people had waited throughout the night in
the rain. A bandstand featured local groups and Beatles records, which
caused a fracas when the soundtrack was inexplicably switched to another
channel, with one hundred people reportedly injured. But by evening the
crowd went quiet for the vigil at 7 P.M. (2 P.M. New York time). In Melbourne, Australia, crowds began gathering at 6 A.M. Like the crowds in
Hyde Park and Trafalgar Square, as well as in Seattle, Boston, Chicago,
Los Angeles, Philadelphia, and, indeed, around the world, those in Central
Park fell quiet to honor Ono's wishes. At the end of ten minutes, "Imagine"
began playing on the public-address system, and the crowd slowly dispersed
over the next hour as a light snow started to fall.

In dozens of countries, people made pilgrimages to gather with
friends, families, former band mates, lovers, and music industry colleagues.
Sheryl Lester, twenty-eight, brought Shelly, her six-year-old daughter, to
Central Park. "We lost more than John Lennon," she told the *New York
Times*. "We lost our adolescence. So everybody is here more or less to
mourn."[7]

Lennon's death carried pointedly different meanings from the political losses of the past, or the celebrity deaths yet to come (Princess Diana, George Harrison, Michael Jackson). In part, this deranged fan's bullets made everybody feel both guilty and culpable, as if those Ku Klux Klan threats from 1966 had somehow wafted their way across time to Lennon's doorway. Another layer of feeling drew from the noblest sentiments he expressed (in songs like "The Word," "All You Need Is Love," and "Give Peace a Chance"), about how the audience that the Beatles had created and challenged—once a beacon of hope in the midst of generational upheaval—had fallen prey to the same chaotic forces it once resisted.

The whole scene made the Beatles and the sixties feel both closer and much farther away than a mere ten years; as music blared from bandstand speakers in New York, reporters noted the gathering's resemblance to a peace march: "Mostly they heard Beatles' songs, including a few that had been rallying calls a decade ago. When the crowd realized that a number called 'All You Need Is Love' was beginning, it surged with a charge almost electric in its intensity," Clyde Haberman reported in the *New York Times*. "It was as though an anthem had been played. Suddenly, thousands of hands flailed the air, forming a sea of 'V's' with their fingers—the familiar peace symbol that many had not flashed in a long time. And they sang."[8]

In the next issue of the *New Yorker,* Jonathan Schell pursued another irony:

The one activity of the mourners—prayer for Lennon's soul, suggested by his widow, Yoko Ono—was both silent and invisible. The silence seemed to create a space into which the strong emotion felt by Lennon's generation—and by many who were not of his generation—could rush. In fact, in that quiet interval the generation itself, with its old message of "Peace" and "Love" held aloft again on placards, magically reappeared in public for the first time in years, after losing itself in the general population for a while. In a noisy and distracted age, a silence had proved more eloquent than any number of words could have been.[9]

This moment of silence, Yoko Ono's inspired request, worked as a balm in a frenzied atmosphere.

After her initial statement to the press, Ono fell silent. Reports soon emerged that she had donated a million dollars to the city of New York to maintain a Strawberry Fields memorial garden in Central Park, across the street from the Dakota, where fans now gather every year on October 9, Lennon and Sean's birthday, and December 8.

ROLLING STONE's tribute hit newsstands like an existential punch line just before New Year's 1981. Annie Leibovitz's cover photograph, at once spontaneous and conceptual, captured a naked and reverent Lennon, eyes closed, curling up to kiss Yoko, who wore a chic black turtleneck atop blue jeans, her gaze fixed just beyond the frame. This visual eulogy, with Lennon's bare knees hugging Ono's womb, froze his image in humbled salute. Taken just hours before his death, it seemed as if Lennon were apologizing from the afterlife for every man who had ever acted like a jerk to a woman. ("Oh, it was really great," Lennon told David Geffen, "I got undressed and wrapped myself around Yoko.")[10] With this photograph, the explosions at the end of "A Day in the Life," or "Remember," turned startlingly visual. Lennon heaved a silent but conclusive exclamation point from the hereafter.

At first gradually, and then very quickly, death smoothed over the annoying contradictions and prickly outbursts in Lennon's persona. It was almost as if he hadn't really died until that picture showed up, and then his death was far too real, too immediate, too out of reach to fully comprehend. There was nothing casual, or cynical, about this pose—it was at once lighthearted and deadly earnest, honest and yet disarmingly unself-conscious, revealing far more about Lennon, John and Yoko's relationship, and their ideas about themselves, than anything on *Double Fantasy*. After the requisite double takes, it sponged up the viewer's grief and made Lennon's life, death, and music seem both vivid and enticingly remote.

This celebrated picture became Lennon's farewell—the kind of stark, unapologetic image he and Yoko excelled at as early as their naked cover to 1968's *Two Virgins*. As Ronald Reagan took the oath of office in January 1981, the image began to echo down into rock history. All the quandaries gathered up in Lennon's music filtered through this last, exhibitionist pose, revealing all his dysfunctional upbringing more dramatically than any audio journal, or hit song, possibly could. Now Lennon kissed his wife good-bye from the cover of a magazine he'd helped to launch, as "Woman" and "Imagine" overtook "(Just Like) Starting Over" as radio elegies.

This final Freudian diagram of Lennon's dependence, and reverence, for his wife also works as a cunning visual pun. Although routinely cited as one of the most famous magazine covers ever, Leibovitz's photograph remains widely misunderstood. "That famous pose, that was John's idea," Bob Gruen says. "Naked and curled up against a fully-clothed Yoko, that was his play on the guy who always gets photographed in his clothes with some naked girl crawling all over him, the *Playboy* routine, you know. He wanted to do the reverse, he wanted to turn that macho idea on its head, he wanted to be *her* prize."[11] Above all, the photo pulled a sly punch: mere mortals could have posthumous hits, only a legend could choke a pose like that from death itself.

"(Just Like) Starting Over" had held the number one position on *Billboard*'s charts since early November and was still there the day Lennon was murdered. But mixed *Double Fantasy* reviews now gave way to a rash of testimonials, critical tributes, and celebrity quotes. Unlike the earlier *Village Voice* review by Geoffrey Stokes, music editor Robert Christgau defended the album in his obituary, articulating the complicated goodwill greeting the record now that it began selling fifty thousand copies a day: "John Lennon learned not merely to make do with his compulsions but to make something fairly miraculous out of them." Any Lennon fan, Christgau insisted, needed to deal with Yoko Ono, if not on aesthetic terms, then political terms at the very least. "The marriage itself, first of all—neurotic, but also, as we used to say, liberated, with male and female roles confounded, not just reversed."

In today's culture, the idea of a rock star devoting himself to fatherhood

seems downright normal. Back in 1980, however, in the wake of the defeat of the Equal Rights Amendment, Lennon's stance had a radical influence, and snubbed clouds of macho rock-star mythology. "Stay-at-home
fathers who can afford live-in help rarely attend to parenting with John's
care and intense devotion," Christgau argued. It's hard to emphasize how
progressive Lennon's fatherhood was, even after all the liberal positions
he had taken in letter and song: to be a self-declared "househusband"
in 1980 was to be that rarest of men, the kind who not only advocated
but lived a new feminism. Being Lennon, he couldn't stop bragging about
it, of course. But in Lennon's case, the impulse had humble origins, a
desire to make good with this son where he had failed with Julian, and
perhaps as well a response to the abandonment he himself had suffered
as a child.

Like a lot of critics, Christgau pointed out how many of the late interviews featured a talkaholic Lennon, who both "credits Yoko with saving
his life and finds it difficult to let her get a paragraph in edgewise." In
death, Ono's presence acquired genuine public sympathy for the very
first time. Whether you cared for her art or not, her pain was palpable
that first week. "Anyone who wants to dismiss Yoko," Christgau continued, "with her astrology, her peace-is-here-if-you-want-it—as a paramys-
tical crackpot should find me somebody else who can manage fortune
like she was playing chess, learn to sing rock and roll, and make a genius
happy all at the same time."[12] In a twisted way, the culture's neuroses
around death raised the art of marriage between two such fierce people
into something sacred. They had been loud, obsessive, wacky, offensive,
flaky, even tiresome; but now one final photograph fixed them in history,
as much avatars for their era as reflections of it.

As YOKO AND SEAN GRIEVED, staffers old and new emerged from the
seventh-floor apartment, taking journals, cassettes, letters, files, many,
many private artifacts and keepsakes, in the hopes of selling them on the
black market. Robbed of a husband, and a father to her son, Ono was
painfully betrayed again by the loss of many precious personal emblems
in the chaos after the killing. One of Lennon's last personal assistants

tried to protect the late Beatle's journal by sneaking back into the Dakota and retrieving it, claiming Lennon had made him promise as much. "Fred Seaman was an opportunist: he kept the journal," Jack Douglas says of this last assistant, who wrote a book. "Seaman knew a shitload of stuff, he was right there at the center of their lives for a long time. But all that stuff they said he stole, it wasn't like that at all. John used to get so much stuff, people would send him appliances, gadgets, pots, everything you can imagine. John would simply say to his assistants, 'Hey, you want this?' John used to just give it to him. Then, after he died, Yoko started asking for receipts and written confirmation of John's gifts, and that's just not how it worked."[13]

Douglas speaks with great sympathy and forgiveness about these events, even though he claims to have suffered lengthy harassment, mostly as a result of other staffers' behavior. "Of course, after he [Lennon] died it all went very weird," he goes on, understating the cosmic funk that descended on the Hit Factory. "Yoko got really paranoid and thought I knew too much shit, and anybody who knew a lot of stuff, she wanted destroyed, or at least made sure that when their book came out no one would believe it. [Yoko] kept fucking with me about six months after Lennon's death. I mean listen: I forgive her, she was upset, she was grieving, and she paid, more than anybody else, Yoko *paid*. I always respected her music, and enjoyed working with her immensely, especially sessions like the *Approximately Infinite Universe*. But she surrounds herself with the worst of the worst, and she's so ready to believe the stupidest rumors about people she's trusted, it's just insane."

LENNON LORE SAT ATOP BEATLE lore as the myth ballooned into veritable fiction and intrigue over the years.

After the enormous outpouring of feeling generated by the memorial gatherings, tribute records soon followed, including "All Those Years Ago," George Harrison's maudlin 1981 single that marked the first recording with Harrison, Starr, and McCartney harmonizing since 1969.[14] There were plenty of buried tracks to raid: Bryan Ferry shed all his ironic detachment for blatant hero worship with "Jealous Guy";

Sean's godfather Elton John plucked imagery from "Dear Prudence" to write "Empty Garden." In Liverpool, Adrian Henri, a Merseyside scribe made famous by 1967's best-selling *The Mersey Poets,* turned in a fragile tribute that offered a fan's exhausted remorse in the wake of the summer 1980 race riots in Toxteth. Henri's words caught the lingering grief many Britons felt at how Lennon had "crossed the road" (the Atlantic Ocean). The poem closed with an image of "the inevitable stranger" dangling in the air, a question mark puncturing any sense of consolation: "You do not cross the road to step into immortality / At the dark end of the street waits the inevitable stranger."

ALMOST THREE DECADES LATER, in 2007, Sean Lennon reached out to meet Jack Douglas. "I was at his show," Douglas reports, "and I got invited to go out with him afterwards, and I was supposed to go out with all of his friends." Before the concert, Douglas ran into Bob Gruen, who invited him over to Yoko Ono's table. Later that night, Douglas went out with Sean's friends to a restaurant and got a message that Sean was held up and couldn't make it. Ono later invited Douglas to work on the elaborate Lennon *Signature* reissues in 2010 to commemorate his seventieth birthday, and appear in the PBS *American Masters* documentary *LENNONYC.*

One of drummer Bun E. Carlos's favorite memories after the Lennon sessions was hearing about Sean Lennon attending a show through some roadies: "We heard all kinds of secondhand stuff, of course, after that. But one time, Sean showed up at one of our sound-checks in 1988 or 1989, and hung out with roadies. They told us later he was saying, 'I can't believe my dad was cool enough to record with Cheap Trick.' We had a laugh about that. 'You know, kid,' we thought, 'you kinda had it backwards.'"

SLOWLY, OVER YEARS of Beatle reissues and a thriving bootleg market, which created a grip on the Internet, a larger symbolism to Lennon's loss came into view, and continues to form our impressions of him. You can sense it in the way that a critic like Mikal Gilmore began his Lennon essay for *Rolling Stone* in 2005 with these words: "It has been nearly thirty years, and it can still stop your mind."[15] Or the way the cultural historian Anthony Elliott laid out the thesis of his provocative *The Mourning of John Lennon*: "It is one of the rich ironies of Lennon's life that he experienced so much loss and mourning and then came to represent mourning, came to symbolize the struggle to mourn, at the level of our general culture."[16] Or when Rosanne Cash sang "I wish I was John Lennon, free as a bird," in her song "World Without Sound" on her *Black Cadillac* album from 2006. The loss Lennon had expressed through songs like "No Reply," "Yer Blues," "Strawberry Fields Forever," "Cold Turkey," and "It's So Hard" finally came to express his audience's loss for the man himself. Fans gathered at annual festivals where sound-alike bands competed for attention: ex-wives, siblings, cousins, ex–Apple staffers, and photographers shared stories; and soon the children of these fans jumped into the Beatle world without any direct experience of the band itself.

It took decades for most outside the music industry to catch on to the material's staying power. Academia didn't start offering courses in Rock History until the millennium, and the publishing industry still concentrates on breezy personal memoirs, like Pattie Harrison's *Wonderful Tonight: George Harrison, Eric Clapton, and Me*, a best seller in the summer of 2008.

Establishment recognition began with George Martin's knighthood in 1996, alongside the American conductor André Previn, which simply extended formal respectability to Martin's work as the highbrow producer behind the popular band. Paul McCartney finally got the royal nod in 1997, alongside Elton John, British conductor Roger Norrington, and jazz singer Cleo Laine, but five years after the musical *Cats* composer Andrew Lloyd Webber. Such distinctions came to reflect the respectability of rock 'n' roll in royalty's eyes, even though McCartney had long since become the richest man in show business. Even after Michael Jackson betrayed their friendship to purchase Northern Songs in 1985, McCartney oversaw diverse holdings that included Buddy Holly's publishing, among others'.

Dealing with rock 'n' roll continued to be a major royal conundrum: on the one hand, Prince Charles depended on acts like McCartney, U2, and Oasis to anchor his annual charity concerts; on the other hand, the crown awarded McCartney a knighthood but not Lennon, Mick Jagger (in 2003) but not Keith Richards, David Bowie (also 2003) but not Jimmy Page (Led Zeppelin). It wasn't until politicians were forced to catch up with Britain's huge boomer voting bulge that Prime Minister Tony Blair declared their rock heroes a piece of "cultural" identity and praised the British contributions to the world's creative industries. As he left office in 2007, Blair, instead of talking about the Iraq War or his status as George W. Bush's "poodle," expounded on how much British identity had changed during the boomer era. If Britain could no longer claim to be an imperial power, it could at least lay claim to a new cultural empire, with significance far beyond its borders. In this new British worldview, the sun never set on the British imagination.

NOBODY SUFFERED MORE THAN Ono or Sean or Julian, but a burden of tremendous complexity visited Paul McCartney, who forged ahead with a solo career while watching his best mate and musical intimate ascend to something beyond even the myth of Beatle John—something like the Prince of Peace, or rock's Great Martyr, a towering omen of all the danger and resentment that fame courts even when it speaks the language of togetherness.

Where Yoko handled widowhood like a savvy pro, Paul McCartney faced unreal expectations about how a former band member should best salute his fallen brother. Following Lennon's death, McCartney put out two critically acclaimed albums, *Tug of War* in 1982 and *Pipes of Peace* in 1983, both produced by George Martin, that grappled with his status as the Beatle left behind. The title song to the first record recounts what anxious competitive threads formed the Lennon-McCartney partnership. "Here Today" became his more explicit tribute, a variation on "Yesterday," which acquired new meanings simply because of its theme (he had already written a song called "Tomorrow," on *Wild Life*). In an odd twist, "Yesterday" became the Beatles' own farewell to Lennon, even as McCartney insisted, inaccurately, that Lennon had never contributed to the number. The song acquired mystical overtones: it was very hard to hear any version of Lennon and McCartney's most recorded song, the centerpiece of their publishing fortune, without thinking of John, the Dakota, and the masses who gathered in his memory. *Tug of War,* however, rode an excruciating hit single, "Ebony and Ivory," which reminded people how effete McCartney could be at his worst. *Pipes of Peace* featured two duets with Michael Jackson, "Say Say Say" and "The Man," which followed their hit "The Girl Is Mine."

McCartney's use of the word "saint" in his *Two Virgins* dedication has grown more poignant since Lennon's assassination. As a rock star, Lennon did his best to flee sainthood. Knocking your songwriting partner about for sainthood status is comic; to survive your "sainted" partner in a knighthood goes beyond anything even Lennon might have imagined at his most surreal. Whatever else you might think of his music, McCartney has had to walk through his later career in Lennon's shadow, "the cute one" who submitted to show business where his partner repeatedly renounced it.

McCartney knew better than anybody the sort of saint Lennon most decidedly was not, only now he had to pretend about Lennon, even endorse his sainthood, lest he be disrespectful of the dead. This became a terrible bind for McCartney, who already carried a great degree of anxiety about his standing in the Beatle pantheon and his image as a cartoon "romantic" next to Lennon's "cynic."

In 1996, when releasing *Anthology 2,* McCartney stopped the press run the week before release to change the song order. Overthinking the final track sequence, and tired of his "cute" persona, McCartney insisted that the set move "I'm Down" up to the third slot to avoid a front-loading of Lennon tracks. And when he collaborated with Elvis Costello on some songs for material that appeared on 1989's *Flowers in the Dirt,* McCartney had to swallow reviews carping on about how much better his writing seemed when he worked with a more capable wordsmith than himself.

Onstage, McCartney slowly reincorporated more and more Beatle material, at first the lesser classics like "Lady Madonna" and "I've Just Seen a Face" for the *Wings Over America* set, then "Hey Jude" and "Let It Be" at 1985's LiveAid concert, and over the years, a shopworn "Drive My Car" at the Super Bowl in 2007, and a raving, madcap "I Saw Her

Standing There" at the Grammy Awards in 2009. He performed best when he took on grief as a theme, as in the 1999 album he released after Linda McCartney died from breast cancer in 1998: *Run Devil Run*. It's a streak through some favorite oldies, and two sparkling originals, which conveys manic loss and desperation, as well as a confidence about how necessary the music can be. In a career typified by crashingly banal work like "Getting Closer" and "Mary Had a Little Lamb," it sounds as if McCartney could have made this album the day after he recorded "Oh! Darling."

PART OF ANY FAN'S homage came in the form of the pilgrimage to Liverpool, which gradually resigned itself to Beatle tourism. Julia Stanley Lennon's unmarked grave in Allerton Cemetery remains among the less traveled sites on the circuit. She never formally married Bobby Dykins, so when her eldest daughter, Julia Dykins Baird, went looking for family records, she was surprised to find them listed under her famous older stepbrother's surname. Julia's plot sits in section 38, number 805, and is often decorated with flowers or trinkets. She was buried there on July 21, 1958, six days after her death.

The payment of £13 7s. and 6d. was made by Norman James Birch and W. F. Williams, on August 20. Few who know the Lennons can figure out who these two men were. They may have been landlord partners for 1 Blomfield Road, Liverpool, Julia's official address, or simply wards of the state looking after a legally unmarried traffic victim with little savings. The second page of Julia Lennon's burial certificate contains the following addendum: "Purchaser, Norman James Birch, 120a Allerton Road, Liverpool, Garage manager," as if to indicate that the payee would be the neighborhood contact should more expenses need to be traced to Julia Lennon's name. (Was she simply friendly with the local mechanic?)

The sprawling Allerton Cemetery lies south of the Allerton Golf Course Lennon walked through to visit McCartney's house, and the local Beatle tour guides all know where to look when asked. It's easy to imagine the young Lennon visiting this spot on his own as a teenager. That same public library shelf contains all the admittance and release records for the Blue Coat Orphanage, where young Alfred Lennon, born December 14, 1912, was signed in by his mother, Mary McGuire, on January 27, 1915. The next entry for Alf appears on April 7, 1924, when he was released at the age of eleven. There seems to have been no contact between Alf and Julia after Blackpool in 1946, when John raced after his mother and returned with her to Liverpool.

CULTURAL TENSIONS CONTINUED to shape Lennon's persona long after his death. Liverpudlians, especially, have an anxious relationship with Yoko Ono. She makes generous donations to local charities, appears at many grand openings and local functions, such as the dedication of Liverpool's John Lennon Airport in 2002. Ono also helps oversee the National Trust's conservancy of Mendips, which sits on the same tourist bus route as Paul McCartney's Allerton house and Strawberry Field. A live-in Beatle scholar stays abreast of research with many like-minded fans and gives personable tours of Aunt Mimi's home three times a day, six days a week.

On the other hand, until Paul McCartney married Heather Mills in 2002, Yoko Ono was the number one Beatles villain, and the myth of her "breaking up" the Beatles is one of the band's more persistent fictions. An early McCartney PR fumble came when he refused to attend the Rock and Roll Hall of Fame's third annual ceremony in 1988, at which Mick Jagger inducted the Beatles. George Harrison, Ringo Starr, Yoko Ono, Sean and Julian Lennon all attended. McCartney sent a message reading: "After twenty years, the Beatles still have some business differences which I had hoped would have been settled by now. Unfortunately, they haven't been, so I would feel like a complete hypocrite waving and smiling with them at a fake reunion." McCartney did appear to induct John Lennon as a solo artist into that hall in 1994, and then lobbied hard to get his own solo spot there five years later.

During this same phase, McCartney approached Ono about a proposed reunion project between the remaining Beatles, and asked her if Lennon had left any song demos behind. She gave him Lennon's demo tapes for two unfinished songs, "Free as a Bird," and "Real Love," for the 1995 *Anthology* project, produced by Electric Light Orchestra's Jeff Lynne. "Free as a Bird" became the lead track. "Real Love" sounded thinner, its sentimentality gapingly unironic.

When the band launched its Las Vegas Cirque du Soleil extravaganza, *Love,* in 2006, the launch featured the two remaining ex-Beatles, and the missing figures represented by their wives. The project sprang from George Harrison's friendship with Cirque's French Canadian founder, Guy Laliberté. Ono and McCartney squabbled as only intimate in-laws could, but they also struck deals like this, the larger Beatle fortunes compelling accord. As if realizing Lennon's biggest fear—appearing in Vegas with the Beatles as an oldies act—they figured out a cheeky way to burnish the band's myth with an exorbitant cash-generating engine without the Beatles having to pick up their instruments. *Love* now plays fourteen times a week at the Mirage Hotel, to capacity crowds who pay up to $150 a ticket for the chance to hear the remixing job George Martin supervised as one of his last projects. The soundtrack, a mash-up of Beatle tracks created by Martin's son Giles, returned the band to the top ten, giving them the status of being the sole rock act to score that honor in its fifth decade of existence. The show features a thin coming-of-age narrative based on a wartime childhood told through gymnastics, tightrope walkers, and rollerblading.

LENNON MAY NEVER HAVE cracked that exasperating Beatle riddle—the constant reunion questions, the sense that he worked in the shadow of his best younger work and that no matter which windmills he tilted at, his audience usually fixed on the most trivial. By now, perhaps even McCartney has learned that it's not wise to try. But in another way, *Double Fantasy* (and *Milk and Honey,* its leftover tracks, including, "Nobody Told Me," a charming answer to the Shirelles' "Mama Said") posed a convincing countermyth about how marriage and parenthood presented the best chance for happiness in the Beatles' wake. By admitting defeat to a show-business legend that was always bigger than celebrity, Lennon seems to have found a stillness worth singing about.

Perhaps, in some atavistic ways, his dilemma reflected a very familiar bind, like the one his parents had set for him that summer day in Black-pool, 1946, when Alf put it to his five-year-old son to choose between his mother or a new life in New Zealand. Lennon had already survived the toughest test any five-year-old could muster, and like any sane kid, he chose twice: first his father, then his mother. He knew exactly what he wanted—both parents, with the certain wisdom born of his experience that at some level, either was essentially out of reach.

This wasn't a choice, but a trap Lennon internalized. The dilemma created emotional roadblocks, but also a profound creative universe that buoyed him through his wildest experiments, darkest free falls, and most elliptical drug rants. This Blackpool trauma doesn't explain every-thing in Lennon's messy life, but it does inflect most of his intimate en-counters, his glaring insecurities, and how certain inscrutable choices seemed, for him, entirely reasonable. Fame was nothing compared to the Gordian knot his parents tied him up in. With the Beatles, he believed the best and worst about himself, sometimes simultaneously, and this almost instinctively pushed rock 'n' roll toward art. In so doing, he used fame's shifting media mirrors to toy with his elastic persona, recording songs too poetic to be contained by an era obsessed with the giant now. If ever a muse might redeem a messy character, it was John Lennon's. And if one song could be said to redeem his retreat, it would be the de-liriously elegant "Beautiful Boy," where he caught the meaning of it all gazing back at him through his own five-year-old son's eyes.

Selected Bibliography

These titles comprise all this text's primary sources. All record chart positions are taken from two registries for consistency: for the U.S., *Joel Whitburn's Top Pop Singles 1955–1990,* and for the UK, *The Complete Book of the British Charts: Singles and Albums* (Warwick, Kutner and Brown, 2004).

Ali, Tariq. *Street Fighting Years: An Autobiography of the Sixties.* New York: Verso, 2005.

Ashton, David. "The Time Capsule: Stories—Age Concern England." *Home/Care Services for Elderly People: Health, Home, Pension & Insurance Cover for Over 50s/Age Concern England,* http://www.thetimecapsule.org.uk/TimeCapsule/ 1960s_D55D7B9D222E4780A856A8F10B4CBAD9.htm.

Babiuk, Andy. *The Beatles Gear: All the Fab Four's Instruments, from Stage to Studio.* San Francisco: Backbeat, 2001.

Badman, Keith. *The Beatles: After the Break-Up 1970–2000: A Day-By-Day Diary.* New York: Omnibus Press, 1999.

———. *The Beatles Off the Record 2: The Dream Is Over.* New York: Omnibus Press, 2000.

Baird, Julia, and Geoffrey Giuliano. *John Lennon, My Brother: Memories of Growing Up Together.* London: Jove, 1989.

Baird, Julia. *Imagine This: Growing Up with My Brother John Lennon.* New York: Hodder & Stoughton Ltd, 2007.

Baker, Nicholson. *Human Smoke: The Beginnings of World War II, the End of Civilization.* New York: Simon & Schuster, 2008.

Bangs, Lester. *Psychotic Reactions and Carburetor Dung.* Edited by Greil Marcus. New York: Alfred A. Knopf, 1987.

Barrow, Tony. *John, Paul, George, Ringo and Me: The Real Beatles Story.* New York: Thunder's Mouth Press, 2005.

Beatles, The. *The Beatles Anthology.* San Francisco: Chronicle Books, 2000.

Beatles, The. *The Beatles Illustrated Lyrics.* Edited by Alan Aldridge. New York: Delacorte, 1969.

Benson, Harry. *Harry Benson: Fifty Years in Pictures.* New York: Abrams, 2000.

Best, Pete, and Patrick Doncaster. *Beatle! The Pete Best Story.* London: Plexus, 1985.

Best, Roag, with Pete and Rory Best. *The Beatles: The True Beginnings.* New York: Thomas Dunne Books/St. Martin's Press, 2003.

Blaney, John. *Listen to This Book.* Guildford: Paper Jukebox, 2005.

Boyd, Pattie, with Penny Junor. *Wonderful Tonight: George Harrison, Eric Clapton and Me.* New York: Harmony Books, 2007.

Bracewell, Michael. *Re-make/Re-model: Becoming Roxy Music.* New York and Washington, D.C.: Da Capo Press, 2008.

Bramwell, Tony, and Rosemary Kingsland. *Magical Mystery Tours: My Life with the Beatles.* New York: St. Martin's Griffin, 2006.

Braun, Michael. *Love Me Do: The Beatles' Progress.* New York: Penguin, 1964.

Bromell, Nick. *Tomorrow Never Knows: Rock and Psychedelics in the 1960s.* Chicago: Chicago University Press, 2000.

Brown, Peter, and Steven Gaines. *The Love You Make—An Insider's Story of the Beatles.* New York: McGraw-Hill, 1983.

Cannon, Lou. *President Reagan: The Role of a Lifetime.* New York: Simon & Schuster, 1991.

Carlin, Peter. *Paul McCartney: A Life.* New York: Touchstone Books, 2009.

Carr, Roy, and Tony Tyler. *The Beatles: An Illustrated Record.* New York: Harmony Books, 1975.

Christgau, Robert. *Any Old Way You Choose It: Rock and Other Pop Music, 1967–1973.* Expanded ed. New York: Cooper Square Press, 2000.

———. *Rock Albums of the Seventies.* New Haven: Ticknor & Fields, 1981.

Clapton, Eric. *Clapton: The Autobiography.* New York: Broadway Books, 2007.

Clayson, Alan. *Beat Merchants: The Origins, History, Impact and Rock Legacy of the 1960s British Pop Groups.* London: Blandford, 1996.

———. *Hamburg—The Cradle of British Rock.* London: Sanctuary Publishing, 1998.

———. *John Lennon.* NY: Chrome Dreams, 2001.

Clayson, Alan, with Barb Jungr and Robb Johnson. *Woman: the Incredible Life of Yoko Ono.* New Malden: Chrome Dreams, 2004.

Clayson, Alan, and Spencer Leigh. *The Walrus Was Ringo*. New Malden: Chrome Dreams, 2003.

Clayson, Alan, and Pauline Sutcliffe. *Backbeat: Stuart Sutcliffe: The Lost Beatle*. Philadelphia: Trans-Atlantic Publications, 1994.

Coleman, Ray. *John Lennon*. New York: McGraw Hill, 1986.

Cording, Robert, ed., with Shelli Jankowski-Smith, E. J. Miller Laino. *In My Life: Encounters with the Beatles*. New York: Fromm International, 1998.

Cotterill, Dave, and Ian Lysaght, directors. *Liverpool's Cunard Yanks*. Souled Out Films, 2007. DVD.

Coupe, Laurence. *Beat Sound, Beat Vision: The Beat Spirit in Popular Song*. Manchester and New York: Manchester University Press, 2007.

Cross, Charles. *A Room Full of Mirrors*. New York: Hyperion, 2006.

Davies, Hunter. *The Beatles—The Authorized Biography*. New York: McGraw Hill, 1968.

———. *The Quarrymen*. London: Omnibus Press, 2001.

Dickstein, Morris. *Gates of Eden: American Culture in the Sixties*. New York: Basic Books, 1977.

Dilello, Richard. *The Longest Cocktail Party: An Insider's Diary of the Beatles, Their Million-Dollar Apple Empire, and Its Wild Rise and Fall*. Edinburgh: Canongate Books, 2005.

Doggett, Peter. *Abbey Road/Let It Be: The Beatles (Classic Rock Albums Series)*. New York: Schirmer Books, 1998.

———. *The Art and Music of John Lennon*. New York: Wise Publications, 2005.

———. *There's a Riot Goin' On: Revolutionaries, Rock Stars, and the Rise and Fall of the '60s*. London: Canongate, 2008.

———. *You Never Give Me Your Money: The Battle for the Soul of the Beatles*. New York: Harperstudio, 2010.

Du Noyer, Paul. *Liverpool: Wondrous Place—Music from Cavern to Cream*. London: Virgin Books Ltd, 2002.

Dyer, Geoff. *The Ongoing Moment*. New York: Vintage, 2007.

Edwards, Henry, and May Pang. *Loving John*. New York: Warner Books, 1983.

Elliott, Anthony. *The Mourning of John Lennon*. Berkeley: University of California Press, 1999.

Emerick, Geoff, and Howard Massey. *Here, There and Everywhere: My Life Recording the Music of the Beatles*. New York: Gotham, 2007.

Emerson, Ken. *Always Magic in the Air: The Bomp and Brilliance of the Brill Building Era*. Boston: Penguin, 2006.

Epstein, Brian. *A Cellarful of Noise*. New York: Doubleday & Company, Inc., 1964.

Everett, Walter. *The Beatles as Musicians: Revolver Through the Anthology*. New York: Oxford University Press, 1999.

————. *The Beatles as Musicians: The Quarry Men Through* Rubber Soul. New York: Oxford University Press, USA, 2001.

————. *The Foundations of Rock: From "Blue Suede Shoes" to "Suite: Judy Blue Eyes."* New York: Oxford University Press, USA, 2008.

Faithfull, Marianne. *Faithfull: An Autobiography.* New York: Cooper Square Press, 2000.

Farrow, Mia. *What Falls Away.* New York: Nan A. Talese, Doubleday, 1997.

Fawcett, Anthony. *John Lennon One Day at a Time.* New York: Grove Press, Inc., 1976.

Fields, Danny. *Linda McCartney.* Boston: Little, Brown, 2000.

Firminger, John, and Spencer Leigh. *Halfway to Paradise: British Pop Music 1955–1962.* Liverpool: Finbarr International, 1996.

Fletcher, Tony. *Moon: The Life and Death of a Rock Legend.* New York: Avon Books, 1999.

Flippo, Chet. *Yesterday: The Unauthorized Biography of Paul McCartney.* New York: Doubleday/Dell, 1988.

Frame, Pete. *The Beatles and Some Other Guys: Rock Family Trees of the Early 1960s.* London: Omnibus Press, 1997.

Freeman, Robert. *Yesterday: The Beatles 1963–1965.* New York: Holt Rinehart and Winston, 1983.

Frith, Simon, and Howard Horne. *Art into Pop.* London: Methuen and Co., 1987.

Frontani, Michael R. *The Beatles: Image and the Media.* Jackson: University of Mississippi Press, 2007.

Garofalo, Steve, and Reebee Chapple. *Rock 'n' Roll Is Here to Pay, the History and Politics of the Music Industry.* Chicago: Nelson Hall, 1977.

Garry, Len. *John, Paul & Me: Before the Beatles: The True Story of the Very Early Days.* Toronto: CG Publishing Inc, 1997.

Geller, Debbie. *In My Life: The Brian Epstein Story.* New York: St. Martin's Press, 2000.

Gilmore, Mikal. *Stories Done: Writings on the 1960s and Its Discontents.* New York: Free Press, 2008.

Goldman, Albert. *The Lives of John Lennon.* New York: Morrow, 1988.

Goldrosen, John, and John Beecher. *Remembering Buddy: The Definitive Biography of Buddy Holly.* New York: Da Capo, 1996.

Gottfridsson, Hans Olof. *The Beatles from Cavern to Star-Club: The Illustrated Chronicle, Discography and Price Guide 1957–1962.* Stockholm: Premium Publishing, 1997.

Gould, Jonathan. *Can't Buy Me Love: The Beatles, Britain and America.* New York: Harmony Books, 2007.

Green, John. *Dakota Days: The True Story of John Lennon's Final Days*. New York: St. Martin's Press, 1983.

Green, Jonathon. *Days in the Life: Voices from the English Underground 1961–1971*. London: Minerva, 1988.

Guralnick, Peter. *Last Train to Memphis*. New York: Little, Brown, 1995.

———. *Careless Love*. New York: Little, Brown, 2000.

Harris, David. *Dreams Die Hard: Three Men's Journey Through the '60s*. New York: St. Martin's Press, 1982.

Harrison, George. *I Me Mine*. New York: Simon & Schuster, 1980.

Harrisson, Tom. *Living Through the Blitz*. New York: HarperCollins Distribution Services, 1975.

Harry, Bill. *Mersey Beat — The Beginnings of the Beatles*. New York: Omnibus Press, 1977.

———. *The John Lennon Encyclopedia*. London: Virgin Publishing, 2000.

Hayes, Harold. *Smiling Through the Apocalypse: Esquire's History of the Sixties*. New York: McCall Publishing, 1969.

Henke, James. *Lennon: His Life and Work*. Cleveland: Rock and Roll Hall of Fame and Museum, 2000.

———. *Lennon Legend: An Illustrated Life of John Lennon*. San Francisco: Chronicle Books, 2003.

Hennessy, Peter. *Having It So Good: Britain in the Fifties*. London: Allen Lane, 2006.

Heylin, Clinton. *All Yesterdays' Parties: The Velvet Underground In Print 1966–1971*. New York: Da Capo, 2005.

Hieronimus, Dr. Robert R. *Inside the Yellow Submarine: The Making of the Beatles' Animated Classic*. Iola, WI: Krause Publications, 2002.

Hoberman, J. *The Dream Life: Movies, Media, and the Mythology of the Sixties*. New York: The New Press, 2003.

Hoffman, Dezo. *The Beatles Conquer America: The Photographic Record of Their First Tour*. New York: Avon, 1984.

Hopkins, Jerry. *Yoko Ono*. New York: MacMillan, 1986.

Ingham, Chris. *The Rough Guide to the Beatles*. London: Rough Guides, 2009.

Kane, Larry. *Ticket to Ride: Inside The Beatles' 1964 & 1965 Tours That Changed the World*. Philadelphia: Running Press, 2003.

Keeler, Christine. *The Truth At Last*. New York: Picador, 2002.

Kehew, Brian, and Kevin Ryan. *Recording the Beatles: The Studio Equipment and Techniques Used to Create Their Classic Albums*. Houston: Curvebender Publishing, 2006.

Kirchherr, Astrid with Max Scheler. *Yesterday: The Beatles Once Upon a Time*. (New York: Vendome Press, 2007).

Kozinn, Allan. *The Beatles (20th-Century Composers)*. London: Phaidon Press, 1995.

Laing, Dave. *Buddy Holly*. New York: Collier, 1972.

Lapham, Lewis H. *With the Beatles*. Hoboken: Melville House Publishing, 2005.

Leaf, David, director. *The U.S. vs. John Lennon*. Lions Gate, 2006. DVD.

Leigh, Spencer. *The Best of Fellas: The Story of Bob Wooler, Liverpool's First DJ, the Man Who Introduced the Beatles*. Liverpool: Drivegreen, 2002.

Lennon, Cynthia. *A Twist of Lennon*. New York: Avon, 1980.

———. *John*. New York: Random House, 2005.

Lennon, John. *The Lennon Tapes: John Lennon and Yoko Ono in Conversation with Andy Peebles, 6 December 1980*. London: British Broadcasting Corporation, 1981.

———. *The Writings of John Lennon: In His Own Write/A Spaniard in the Works*. New York: Simon & Schuster, 1981.

———. *Ai: Japan Through John Lennon's Eyes: A Personal Sketchbook*. Redwood, CA: Cadence Books, 1992.

Lennon, John, Yoko Ono, and David Sheff. *The Playboy Interviews with John Lennon and Yoko Ono*. New York: Putnam, 1981.

Lennon, Pauline. *Daddy, Come Home: The True Story of John Lennon and His Father*. London: Angus and Robertson, 1990.

Lewisohn, Mark. *The Beatles Live!* New York: Henry Holt & Co., 1986.

———. *The Beatles Recording Sessions: The Official Abbey Road Studio Session Notes 1962–1970*. London: Harmony, 1988.

———. *The Beatles: Day By Day, A Chronology 1962–1989*. New York: Harmony Books, 1990.

Liverpool Post and Echo Ltd, eds. *Bombers Over Merseyside: The Authoritative Record of the Blitz, 1940–1941*. Liverpool: Scouse Press, 1983.

MacDonald, Ian. *Revolution in the Head: The Beatles' Records and the Sixties*. New York: Henry Holt, 1994.

Madinger, Chip, and Mark Easter. *Eight Arms to Hold You: The Solo Beatles Compendium*. Chesterfield, MO: 44.1 Productions Ltd, 2000.

Mansfield, Ken. *The White Book: The Beatles, the Bands, the Biz, an Insider's Look at an Era*. Nashville: Thomas Nelson, 2007.

Marqusee, Mike. *Redemption Song: Muhammed Ali and the Spirit of the Sixties*. New York: Verso, 1999.

———. *Wicked Messenger: Bob Dylan and the 1960s*. New York: Seven Stories Press, 2005.

Marsh, Dave. *The Beatles' Second Album (Rock of Ages)*. Emmaus, PA: Rodale Books, 2007.

Martin, George. *All You Need Is Ears*. New York: St. Martin's Press, 1979.

Martin, George, and William Pearson. *The Summer of Love: The Making of* Sgt. Pepper. London: Macmillan, 1994.

Matteo, Steve. *Let It Be.* New York: Continuum, 2004.

McCabe, Peter, and Robert D. Schonfeld. *Apple to the Core: The Unmaking of the Beatles.* New York: Pocket Books, 1972.

McCartney, Mike. *The Macs: Mike McCartney's Family Album.* New York: Delilah Communications Ltd., 1981.

McKinney, Devin. *Magic Circles: The Beatles in Dream and History.* Cambridge, MA: Harvard University Press, 2004.

Mellers, Wilfred. *Twilight of the Gods: The Music of the Beatles.* New York: Schirmer Books, 1975.

Melly, George. *Revolt into Style: The Pop Arts in Britain.* London: Penguin Books, 1972.

Meltzer, Richard. *The Aesthetics of Rock.* New York: Da Capo, 1988.

Miles, Barry. *Paul McCartney Many Years from Now.* New York: Henry Holt & Co., 1997.

———. *The Beatles Diary Volume I: The Beatles Years.* London: Omnibus Press, 2001.

———. *Frank Zappa: The Biography.* London: Atlantic Books, 2005.

Miller, Jim, ed. *The Rolling Stone Illustrated History of Rock & Roll.* New York: Rolling Stone Press, 1976.

Montieth, Sharon. *American Culture in the 1960s.* Edinburgh: Edinburgh University Press, 2008.

Munroe, Alexandra, with Jon Hendricks. *Yes Yoko Ono.* New York: Japan Society and Harry N. Abrams, 2000.

Napier-Bell, Simon. *You Don't Have to Say You Love Me.* London: Ebury Press, 1998.

Norman, Philip. *Shout!: The Beatles in Their Generation.* New York: Simon & Schuster, 1981.

———. *John Lennon: The Life.* New York: Ecco, 2008.

O'Brien, Geoffrey. *Dream Time: Chapters from the Sixties.* New York: Counterpoint, 1988.

O'Donnell, Jim. *The Day John Met Paul: An Hour-by-Hour Account of How the Beatles Began.* New York: Penguin Books, 1996.

Oldham, Andrew Loog with Simon Dudfield. *Stoned: A Memoir of London in the 1960s.* New York: St. Martin's Press, 2001.

———. *2Stoned.* London: Vintage Rand, 2003.

Ono, Yoko. *Grapefruit: Works and Drawings by Yoko Ono.* New York: Simon & Schuster, 1970.

———. *Lennon: His Life and Work.* Cleveland: Rock and Roll Hall of Fame, 2000.

———. *Memories of John Lennon.* Brattleboro: Harper Paperbacks, 2006.

Palmer, Robert. *Blues and Chaos.* New York: Scribner, 2009.

Pang, May. *Instamatic Karma: Photographs of John Lennon.* New York: St. Martin's Press, 2008.

Panowski, Gareth L. *How They Became The Beatles*. New York: E. P. Dutton, 1989.

Parker, Alan, and Phil Strongman. *John Lennon and the FBI Files*. London: Sanctuary Publishing, Ltd., 2003.

Pritchard, David, and Alan Lysaght. *The Beatles: An Oral History*. Toronto: Stoddard, 1998.

Ribowsky, Mark. *He's a Rebel: Phil Spector, Rock & Roll's Legendary Producer*. New York: Dutton, 1989.

Riley, Tim. *Tell Me Why: The Beatles: Album by Album, Song by Song, the Sixties and After*. New York: Alfred A. Knopf, 1988.

———. *Hard Rain: A Dylan Commentary*. New York: Alfred A. Knopf, 1992.

———. *Madonna Illustrated*. New York: Hyperion Books, 1992.

———. *Fever: How Rock 'n' Roll Transformed Gender in America*. New York: St. Martin's, 2004.

Robertson, John. *The Art and Life of John Lennon*. New York: Birch Lane Press, 1990.

Rolling Stone, editors of. *The Ballad of John and Yoko*. Garden City: Doubleday Dolphin, 1982.

Ross, Danny. *A Bluecoat Boy in the 1920's*. Gunnison, CO: Pharaoh Press, 1996.

Salewicz, Chris. *McCartney: The Definitive Biography*. New York: St. Martin's Press, 1986.

———. *Mick & Keith*. London: Orion, 2002.

Saltzman, Paul. *The Beatles in Rishikesh*. New York: Penguin, 2000.

Sandbrook, Dominic. *Never Had It So Good: A History of Britain from Suez to the Beatles*. New York: Little, Brown, 2005.

Sauceda, James. *The Literary Lennon: A Comedy of Letters*. Ann Arbor: Pierian Press, 1983.

Schaffner, Nicholas. *The Beatles Forever*. New York: McGraw-Hill, 1978.

———. *The Boys from Liverpool: John, Paul, George, Ringo*. London, Henley, and Boston: Routledge & Kegan Paul, 1980.

Schultheiss, Tom. *The Beatles—A Day in the Life: The Day-by-Day Diary 1960–1970*. New York: Perigee Books, 1982.

Seaman, Frederic. *The Last Days of John Lennon: A Personal Memoir*. New York: Birch Lane Press, 1991.

Sheff, David and Barry Goulson, editor. *The Playboy Interviews with John Lennon and Yoko Ono*. New York: Playboy Press, 1981.

Shotton, Pete, with Nicholas Schaffner. *John Lennon in My Life*. New York: Stein and Day, 1983.

Solt, Andrew, director. *Imagine: John Lennon* (Deluxe Edition). Warner Home Video, 1988. VHS.

Southall, Brian, with Rupert Penny. *Northern Songs: The True Story of the Beatles Song Publishing Empire*. London: Omnibus Press, 2006.

Spector, Ronnie, with Vince Waldron. *Be My Baby: How I Survived Mascara, Miniskirts, and Madness, or My Life as a Fabulous Ronette.* New York: HarperPerennial, 1990.

Spinetti, Victor, and Peter Rankin. *Up Front . . . His Strictly Confidential Autobiography.* London: Anova, 2006.

Spitz, Robert. *The Beatles: A Biography.* New York: Little, Brown, 2005.

Spitzer, Bruce. *The Beatles' Story on Capitol Records, Part One: Beatlemania & The Singles.* New York: Four Ninety-Eight Productions, 2000.

————. *The Beatles' Story on Capitol Records, Part Two: The Albums.* New York: Four Ninety-Eight Productions, 2000.

————. *The Beatles Are Coming: The Birth of Beatlemania in America.* New York: Four Ninety-Eight Productions, 2003.

————. *The Beatles on Apple Records.* New York: Four Ninety-Eight Productions, 2003.

Stark, Steve D. *Meet the Beatles: A Cultural History of the Band That Shook Youth, Gender, and the World.* New York: HarperCollins, 2005.

Starr, Ringo. *Postcards from the Boys.* Britain: Cassell Illustrated, 2004.

Stokes, Geoffrey. *The Beatles.* New York: Times Books, 1980.

Sulpy, Doug, and Ray Schweighardt. *Get Back: The Unauthorized Chronicle of the Beatles' Let It Be Disaster.* New York: St. Martin's Press, 1997.

Sutcliffe, Pauline. *Stuart Sutcliffe & His Lonely Hearts Club: In The Shadow of the Beatles.* London: Pan Books, 2001.

Sutcliffe, Pauline, and Kay Williams. *Stuart, the Life and Art of Stuart Sutcliffe.* London: Genesis Publications, 1996.

Tashian, Barry. *Ticket to Ride: The Extraordinary Diary of The Beatles' Last Tour.* New York: Dowling Press, Inc., 1997.

Taylor, Alistair. *Yesterday: The Beatles Remembered.* London: Sidgwick & Jackson Limited, 1988.

————. *With the Beatles.* London: John Blake, 2003.

Taylor, Derek. *As Time Goes By.* London: Davis-Poynter Limited, 1973.

————. *It Was 20 Years Ago Today.* New York: Fireside Books/Simon & Schuster, Inc., 1988.

Thomson, Elizabeth, and David Gutman. *The Lennon Companion: Twenty-five Years of Comment.* New York: Da Capo, 2004.

Walker, Christopher, director, with John Midwinter, Janine Polla Werner, and Ed Ward. *John Lennon's Jukebox.* PBS Great Performances and Channel 4 International. First UK broadcast, March 2004. Film.

Warwick, Neil, with John Kutner and Tony Brown. *The Complete Book of the British Charts: Singles and Albums,* third edition. London: Omnibus Press, 2004.

Wenner, Jann. *Lennon Remembers*. San Francisco: Straight Arrow Books, 1971.

Whitaker, Bob. *The Unseen Beatles: Photographs by Bob Whitaker*. San Francisco: HarperCollins, 1991.

Wiener, Jon. *Come Together: John Lennon in His Time*. Urbana: University of Illinois Press, 1990.

Williams, Allan, with William Marshall. *The Man Who Gave the Beatles Away*. Newark: See Notes [sic], 1975.

Williams, Richard. *Out of His Head: The Sound of Phil Spector*. New York: E. P. Dutton & Co., 1972.

Winn, John C. *Lifting Latches: The Beatles' Recorded Legacy, Volume Three—Inside the Beatles Vaults*. Sharon, Vermont: Multiplus Books, 2005.

———. *That Magic Feeling: The Beatles' Recorded Legacy, Volume Two*. Sharon, Vermont: Multiplus Books, 2005.

———. *Beatlemania, Volume One*. Sharon, Vermont: Multiplus Books, 2006.

———. *Way Beyond Compare: The Beatles' Recorded Legacy, Volume One*. New York: Three Rivers Press, 2008.

Womack, Kenneth. *The Long and Winding Road: The Evolving Artistry of the Beatles*. New York: Continuum, 2007.

Wolfe, Tom. *The Electric Kool-Aid Acid Test*. New York: Farrar Straus Giroux, 1968.

SELECTED INTERNET RESOURCES

BAGISM
www.bagism.com/

BEATLE FAN
www.beatlefan.com

BEATLEGS PODCAST
http://dinsdalep.podomatic.com/

BEATLE MONEY
www.beatlemoney.com

BEATLE PHOTO BLOG
http://beatlephotoblog.com/

THE BEATLES (OFFICIAL)
www.beatles.com

THE BEATLES INTERNET ALBUM
www.beatlesagain.com

BEATLES INTERVIEWS
http://www.beatlesinterviews.org/

BEATLES LINKS
www.beatlelinks.net/links/

CHILD OF NATURE'S BEATLE PHOTO BLOG
http://childofnaturebeatles.blogspot.com/

THE FEST FOR BEATLE FANS
http://www.thefest.com/

GEORGE MARTIN
pcug.org.au/~jhenry

IMAGINE PEACE
imaginepeace.com/

JOHN LENNON
www.johnlennon.com/html/news.aspx

JOHN LENNON FBI FILES
www.lennonfbifiles.com/

LENNON FAMILY
http://www.lennon.net/

LIVE: PEACE IN TORONTO
beatles.ncf.ca/live_peace_in_toronto_p1.html

PAUL MCCARTNEY
www.mplcommunications.com/mccartney

PAUL MCCARTNEY CENTRAL
www.macca-central.com

THE QUARRYMEN
www.originalquarrymen.co.uk/

RARE BEATLES
www.rarebeatles.com

SOUNDSCAPES: BEABLIOGRAPHY
http://www.icce.rug.nl/~soundscapes/BEAB/index.shtml

YOKO ONO
www.yoko-ono.com/

Selected Parlophone/
Apple Discography

With the Beatles, John Lennon recorded for the Parlophone label in Britain, a subsidiary of Electrical and Mechanical Industries (EMI) between 1962 and 1970. As the band issued its last recordings on its new company label, Apple, Lennon began his solo career recording with his wife, Yoko Ono, on both Apple and its experimental subsidiary, Zapple, in 1968. During the dissolution of Apple in the early 1970s, Lennon's solo recordings reverted to the Capitol label in America, and EMI throughout Britain and Europe.

This discography updates the Beatles' catalog for the digital era, using all the UK track sequences. However, to correspond with this narrative, the original British release dates and catalog numbers have been used to provide a succinct chronology. All Beatles' songs are by Lennon-McCartney except where indicated. For clarity, bootlegs, repetitions, and unnecessary overlaps between singles, albums, and compilations have been omitted. For a complete Beatle discography, consult Mark Lewisohn's *The Recording Sessions* (Harmony, 1988). The most recent editions, usually referred to as the 2009 Remasters, rank with the best digital mastering, and continue to reward close listening in both mono and stereo.

Lennon's solo singles listing appears at the end, with chart numbers from both the U.S. and the UK to diagram his cross-Atlantic persona. For a complete Lennon solo discography, see Chip Madinger and Mark Easter's *Eight Arms to Hold You* (44.1 Productions, 2000).

THE BEATLES
"Love Me Do" / "P.S. I Love You" (Parlophone R 4949)
October 5, 1962

"Please Please Me" / "Ask Me Why" (Parlophone R 4983)
January 11, 1963

PLEASE PLEASE ME (Parlophone PCS 3042)
March 22, 1963
Side 1
"I Saw Her Standing There"
"Misery"
"Anna (Go to Him)" (Alexander)
"Chains" (Goffin-King)
"Boys" (Dixon-Ferrell)
"Ask Me Why"
"Please Please Me"
Side 2
"Love Me Do"
"P.S. I Love You"
"Baby It's You" (David-Bacharach-Williams)
"Do You Want to Know a Secret?"
"A Taste of Honey" (Marlow-Scott)
"There's a Place"
"Twist and Shout" (Russell-Medley)

"From Me to You / Thank You Girl" (Parlophone R 5015)
April 11, 1963

TONY SHERIDAN WITH THE BEATLES (Polydor EPH21610) EP
July 12, 1963
Side A:
"My Bonnie" (with Tony Sheridan) / "The Saints" (with Tony Sheridan)
Side B:
"Why" (with Tony Sheridan) / "Cry for a Shadow"

WITH THE BEATLES (Parlophone PCS3045)
November 22, 1963
Side 1
"It Won't Be Long"
"All I've Got to Do"
"All My Loving"
"Don't Bother Me" (Harrison)

"Little Child"

"Till There Was You" (Willson)

"Please Mr. Postman" (Holland-Bateman-Gordy)

Side 2

"Roll Over Beethoven" (Berry)

"Hold Me Tight"

"You've Really Got a Hold on Me" (Robinson)

"I Wanna Be Your Man"

"Devil in Her Heart" (Drapkin)

"Not a Second Time"

"Money" (Gordy-Bradford)

"I Want to Hold Your Hand" / "This Boy" (Parlophone R 5084)

November 29, 1963

A HARD DAY'S NIGHT (Parlophone PCS 3058)

July 10, 1964

Side 1

"A Hard Day's Night"

"I Should Have Known Better"

"If I Fell"

"I'm Happy Just to Dance with You"

"And I Love Her"

"Tell Me Why"

"Can't Buy Me Love"

Side 2

"Any Time at All"

"I'll Cry Instead"

"Things We Said Today"

"When I Get Home"

"You Can't Do That"

"I'll Be Back"

"I Feel Fine" / "She's a Woman" (Parlophone R 5200)

November 27, 1964

BEATLES FOR SALE (Parlophone PCS 3062)

December 4, 1964

Side 1

"No Reply"

"I'm a Loser"

"Baby's in Black"

"Rock and Roll Music" (Berry)

"I'll Follow the Sun"

"Mr. Moonlight" (Johnson)

"Kansas City"/"Hey Hey Hey" (Leiber-Stoller/Penniman)

Side 2

"Eight Days a Week"

"Words of Love" (Holly)

"Honey Don't" (Perkins)

"Every Little Thing"

"I Don't Want to Spoil the Party"

"What You're Doing"

"Everybody's Trying to Be My Baby" (Perkins)

"Help!" / "I'm Down" (Parlophone R 5305)

July 23, 1965

HELP! (Parlophone PCS 3071)

August 6, 1965

Side 1

"Help!"

"The Night Before"

"You've Got to Hide Your Love Away"

"I Need You" (Harrison)

"Another Girl"

"You're Going to Lose That Girl"

"Ticket to Ride"

Side 2

"Act Naturally" (Russell-Morrison)

"It's Only Love"

"You Like Me Too Much" (Harrison)

"Tell Me What You See"

"I've Just Seen a Face"

"Yesterday"

"Dizzy Miss Lizzie" (Williams)

RUBBER SOUL (Parlophone PCS 3075)

December 3, 1965

Side 1

"Drive My Car"

"Norwegian Wood (This Bird Has Flown)"

"You Won't See Me"

"Nowhere Man"

"Think for Yourself" (Harrison)

"The Word"

"Michelle"

Side 2

"What Goes On"

"Girl"

"I'm Looking Through You"

"In My Life"

"Wait"

"If I Needed Someone" (Harrison)

"Run for Your Life"

"We Can Work It Out" / "Day Tripper" (Parlophone R 5389)

December 3, 1965

"Paperback Writer" / "Rain" (Parlophone R 5452)

June 10, 1966

REVOLVER (Parlophone PCS 7009)

August 5, 1966

Side 1

"Taxman" (Harrison)

"Eleanor Rigby"

"I'm Only Sleeping"

"Love You To" (Harrison)

"Here, There and Everywhere"

"Yellow Submarine"

"She Said She Said"

Side 2

"Good Day Sunshine"

"And Your Bird Can Sing"

"For No One"

"Dr. Robert"

"I Want to Tell You" (Harrison)
"Got To Get You into My Life"
"Tomorrow Never Knows"

"Strawberry Fields Forever" / "Penny Lane" (Parlophone R 5570)
February 17, 1967

SGT. PEPPER'S LONELY HEARTS CLUB BAND
(Parlophone PCS 7027)
June 1, 1967
Side 1

"Sgt. Pepper's Lonely Hearts Club Band"
"With a Little Help from My Friends"
"Lucy in the Sky with Diamonds"
"Getting Better"
"Fixing a Hole"
"She's Leaving Home"
"Being for the Benefit of Mr. Kite"

Side 2

"Within You Without You" (Harrison)
"When I'm Sixty-four"
"Lovely Rita"
"Good Morning, Good Morning"
"Lonely Hearts Club Band" (reprise)
"A Day in the Life"

"All You Need Is Love" / "Baby, You're a Rich Man" (Parlophone R 5620)
July 7, 1967

"Hello, Goodbye" / "I Am the Walrus" (Parlophone R 5655)
November 24, 1967

MAGICAL MYSTERY TOUR (Parlophone SMMT1/2 MONO) 2 EPs
December 8, 1967
Side A:

"Magical Mystery Tour" / "Your Mother Should Know"
Side B:

"I Am the Walrus" / "No You're Not" (speech)

Side C:

"The Fool on the Hill" / "Flying" (instrumental)

Side D:

"Blue Jay Way" (Harrison)

"Lady Madonna" / "The Inner Light" (Parlophone R 5675)
March 15, 1968

"Hey Jude" / "Revolution" (Apple R 5722)
August 30, 1968

THE BEATLES ("*White Album*") (Apple PCS 7067/8)
November 22, 1968

Side 1/Disc 1

"Back in the USSR"

"Dear Prudence"

"Glass Onion"

"Ob-La-Di, Ob-La-Da"

"Wild Honey Pie"

"The Continuing Story of Bungalow Bill"

"While My Guitar Gently Weeps" (Harrison)

"Happiness Is a Warm Gun"

Side 2/Disc 1

"Martha My Dear"

"I'm So Tired"

"Blackbird"

"Piggies" (Harrison)

"Rocky Raccoon"

"Don't Pass Me By" (Starkey)

"Why Don't We Do It in the Road?"

"I Will"

"Julia"

Side 3/Disc 2

"Birthday"

"Yer Blues"

"Mother Nature's Son"

"Everybody's Got Something to Hide, Except Me and My Monkey"

"Sexy Sadie"

"Helter Skelter"

"Long, Long, Long" (Harrison)

Side 4/Disc 2

"Revolution 1"

"Honey Pie"

"Savoy Truffle" (Harrison)

"Cry Baby Cry"

"Revolution No. 9"

"Good Night"

"Get Back" / "Don't Let Me Down" (Apple R 5777)

April 11, 1969

"The Ballad of John and Yoko" / "Old Brown Shoe" (Apple R 5786)

May 30, 1969

YELLOW SUBMARINE (Apple PCS 7070)

January 17, 1969

Side 1

"Yellow Submarine"

"Only a Northern Song" (Harrison)

"All Together Now"

"Hey Bulldog"

"It's All Too Much" (Harrison)

"All You Need Is Love"

Side 2

"George Martin Orchestra: Pepperland"

"Medley: Sea of Time/Sea of Holes"

"Sea of Monsters"

"March of the Meanies"

"Pepperland Laid Waste"

"Yellow Submarine in Pepperland"

ABBEY ROAD (Apple PCS 7088)

September 26, 1969

Side 1

"Come Together"

"Something" (Harrison)

"Maxwell's Silver Hammer"

"Oh! Darling"

"Octopus's Garden" (Starkey)

"I Want You (She's So Heavy)"

Side 2

"Here Comes the Sun" (Harrison)
"Because"
"You Never Give Me Your Money"
"Sun King"
"Mean Mr. Mustard"
"Polythene Pam"
"She Came in Through the Bathroom Window"
"Golden Slumbers"
"Carry That Weight"
"The End"
"Her Majesty"

"Let It Be" / "You Know My Name (Look Up the Number)" (Apple R 5833)
March 6, 1970

LET IT BE (Apple PXS I)

May 8, 1970
Side 1

"Two of Us"
"Dig a Pony"
"Across the Universe"
"I Me Mine" (Harrison)
"Dig It"
"Let It Be"
"Maggie Mae" (trad.—arr. Lennon, McCartney, Harrison, Starkey)

Side 2

"I've Got a Feeling"
"One After 909"
"The Long and Winding Road"
"For You Blue" (Harrison)
"Get Back"

THE BEATLES ANTHOLOGY series

The Beatles, ANTHOLOGY 1 (Apple CDPCSP 727)

20 November 1995
"Free As a Bird"
"That'll Be the Day" (Allison, Petty, Holly)
"Hallelujah, I Love Her So" (Charles)

"You'll Be Mine"

"Cayenne" (McCartney)

"My Bonnie" (traditional)

"Ain't She Sweet" (Ager-Yellen)

"Cry for a Shadow" (Lennon, Harrison)

"Searchin'" (Leiber-Stoller)

"Three Cool Cats"

"The Sheik of Araby" (Smith, Wheeler, Snyder)

"Like Dreamers Do"

"Hello Little Girl"

"Bésame Mucho" (Velázquez, Skylar)

"Love Me Do"

"How Do You Do It" (Murray)

"Please Please Me"

"One After 909"

"One After 909"

"Lend Me Your Comb" (Twomey, Wise, Weisman)

"I'll Get You"

"I Saw Her Standing There"

"From Me to You"

"Money (That's What I Want)" (Gordy-Bradford)

"You Really Got a Hold on Me" (Robinson)

"Roll Over Beethoven" (Berry)

The Beatles, ANTHOLOGY 2 (Apple CDPCSP728)

March 18, 1996

Disc One

"Real Love"

"Yes It Is"

"I'm Down"

"You've Got to Hide Your Love Away"

"If You've Got Trouble"

"That Means a Lot"

"Yesterday"

"It's Only Love"

"I Feel Fine"

"Ticket to Ride"

"Yesterday"

"Help!"

Blackpool Night Out television broadcast

"Everybody's Trying to Be My Baby" (Perkins)

"Norwegian Wood (This Bird Has Flown)"

"I'm Looking Through You"

"12-Bar Original" (Lennon/McCartney/Harrison/Starkey)

"Tomorrow Never Knows"

"Got to Get You into My Life"

"And Your Bird Can Sing"

"Taxman" (Harrison)

"Eleanor Rigby"

"I'm Only Sleeping"

"I'm Only Sleeping"

"Rock and Roll Music" (Chuck Berry)

"She's a Woman"

Disc Two

"Strawberry Fields Forever" (demo sequence)

"Strawberry Fields Forever" (take 1)

"Strawberry Fields Forever" (take 7 & edit piece)

"Penny Lane"

"A Day in the Life"

"Good Morning Good Morning"

"Only a Northern Song" (Harrison)

"Being for the Benefit of Mr. Kite!"

"Being for the Benefit of Mr. Kite" (take 7 & effects tape)

"Lucy in the Sky with Diamonds"

"Within You Without You" (Harrison)

"Sgt. Pepper's Lonely Hearts Club Band (Reprise)"

"You Know My Name (Look Up the Number)"

"I Am the Walrus"

"The Fool on the Hill"

"Your Mother Should Know"

"The Fool on the Hill"

"Hello, Goodbye"

"Lady Madonna"

"Across the Universe"

The Beatles, ANTHOLOGY 3 (Apple CDPCSP 729)

October 28, 1996

Disc One

"Happiness Is a Warm Gun"

"Helter Skelter"

"Mean Mr. Mustard"

"Polythene Pam"

"Glass Onion"

"Junk" (McCartney)

"Piggies" (Harrison)

"Honey Pie"

"Don't Pass Me By" (Starkey)

"Ob-La-Di, Ob-La-Da"

"Good Night"

"Cry Baby Cry"

"Blackbird"

"Sexy Sadie"

"While My Guitar Gently Weeps" (Harrison)

"Hey Jude"

"Not Guilty" (Harrison)

"Mother Nature's Son"

"Glass Onion"

"Rocky Raccoon"

"What's the New Mary Jane"

"Step Inside Love" / "Los Paranoias"

"I'm So Tired"

"I Will"

"Why Don't We Do It in the Road?"

"Julia"

JOHN LENNON—SELECTED SOLO DISCOGRAPHY

All release dates refer to the original UK issues for consistency, except where noted. Duplicates and significant overlaps have been omitted for compression. All tracks written by John Lennon or John Lennon-Yoko Ono unless indicated.

UNFINISHED MUSIC NO. 1: TWO VIRGINS (Apple (S)APCOR 2)

November 29, 1968

Side One

"Two Virgins No. 1"

"Together"

"Two Virgins No. 2"

"Two Virgins No. 3"
"Two Virgins No. 4"
"Two Virgins No. 5"
Side Two
"Two Virgins No. 6"
"Hushabye Hushabye"
"Two Virgins No. 7"
"Two Virgins No. 8"
"Two Virgins No. 9"
"Two Virgins No. 10"

UNFINISHED MUSIC NO.2: LIFE WITH THE LIONS (Zapple 01)

May 9, 1969
Side One
"Cambridge 1969"
Side Two
"No Bed for Beatle John" (Ono)
"Baby's Heartbeat"
"Two Minutes Silence"
"Radio Play"

WEDDING ALBUM (Apple SAPCOR 11)

November 7, 1969
Side One
"John & Yoko"
Side Two
"Amsterdam"

LIVE PEACE IN TORONTO 1969 (Apple CORE 2001)

December 12, 1969
Side One
"Blue Suede Shoes" (Perkins)
"Dizzy Miss Lizzie" (Williams)
"Yer Blues"
"Cold Turkey"
"Give Peace a Chance" (Lennon-McCartney)
Side Two
"Don't Worry Kyoko (Mummy's Only Looking for Her Hand in the Snow)"
(Ono)

JOHN LENNON / PLASTIC ONO BAND (Apple PCS 7142)

December 11, 1970

Side One

"Mother"

"Hold On"

"I Found Out"

"Working Class Hero"

"Isolation"

Side Two

"Remember"

"Love"

"Well Well Well"

"Look At Me"

"God"

"My Mummy's Dead"

YOKO ONO / PLASTIC ONO BAND (Apple)

December 11, 1970

All songs by Yoko Ono:

Side One

"Why"

"Why Not"

"Greenfield Morning I Pushed an Empty Baby Carriage All Over the City"

Side Two

"AOS"

"Touch Me"

"Paper Shoes"

IMAGINE (Apple PCSP 716)

October 8, 1971

Side One

"Imagine"

"Crippled Inside"

"Jealous Guy"

"It's So Hard"

"I Don't Want to Be a Soldier"

Side Two

"Give Me Some Truth"

"Oh My Love"

"How Do You Sleep?"

"How?"

"Oh Yoko!"

SOME TIME IN NEW YORK CITY (Apple PCSP 716)

September 15, 1972

Side One

"Woman Is the Nigger of the World"

"Sisters, O Sisters"

"Attica State"

"Born in a Prison"

"New York City"

Side Two

"Sunday Bloody Sunday"

"The Luck of the Irish"

"John Sinclair"

"Angela"

"We're All Water"

Side Three

"Cold Turkey"

"Don't Worry Kyoko (Mummy's Only Looking for Her Hand in the Snow)"

Side Four

"Well" (Ward)

"Jamrag"

"Scumbag" (Lennon-Ono-Zappa)

"Aü"

MIND GAMES (Apple PCS 7165)

November 16, 1973

Side One

"Mind Games"

"Tight A$"

"Aisumasen (I'm Sorry)"

"One Day (at a Time)"

"Bring on the Lucie (Freda Peeple)"

"Nutopian International Anthem"

Side Two

"Intuition"

"Out the Blue"

"Only People"
"I Know (I Know)"
"You Are Here"
"Meat City"

WALLS AND BRIDGES (Apple PCTC 253)

October 4, 1974

Side One

"Going Down on Love"
"Whatever Gets You Thru the Night"
"Old Dirt Road" (Lennon, Nilsson)
"What You Got"
"Bless You"
"Scared"

Side Two

"#9 Dream"
"Surprise, Surprise (Sweet Bird of Paradox)"
"Steel and Glass"
"Beef Jerky"
"Nobody Loves You (When You're Down and Out)"
"Ya Ya" (Robinson, Dorsey & Lewis)

ROCK 'N' ROLL (Apple PCS 7169)

February 21, 1975

Side One

"Be-Bop-A-Lula" (Davis, Vincent)
"Stand By Me" (Leiber, Stoller, King)

Medley:

a) "Rip It Up" (Blackwell, Marascalco)
b) "Ready Teddy"
"You Can't Catch Me" (Berry)
"Ain't That a Shame" (Domino, Bartholomew)
"Do You Want to Dance" (Freeman)
"Sweet Little Sixteen" (Berry)

Side Two

"Slippin' and Slidin'" (Bocage, Collins, Penniman, Smith)
"Peggy Sue" (Allison, Petty, Holly)

Medley:

    a) "Bring It on Home to Me" (Cooke)

    b) "Send Me Some Lovin' " (Marascalco, Price)

    "Bony Moronie" (Williams)

    "Ya Ya" (Robinson, Dorsey & Lewis)

    "Just Because" (Price)

SHAVED FISH (Apple PCS 7173)

    October 24, 1975

Side One

Medley:

    a) "Give Peace a Chance" (Lennon-McCartney)

    b) "Cold Turkey"

    "Instant Karma"

    "Power to the People"

    "Mother"

    "Woman Is the Nigger of the World"

Side Two

    "Imagine"

    "Whatever Gets You Thru the Night"

    "Mind Games"

    "#9 Dream"

Medley:

    a) "Happy Xmas (War Is Over)"

    b) "Give Peace a Chance" (reprise) (Lennon-McCartney)

DOUBLE FANTASY (Geffen K 99131)

    November 17, 1980

Side One

    "(Just Like) Starting Over"

    "Kiss Kiss Kiss" (Ono)

    "Cleanup Time"

    "Give Me Something" (Ono)

    "I'm Losing You"

    "I'm Moving On" (Ono)

    "Beautiful Boy (Darling Boy)"

Side Two

    "Watching the Wheels"

    "Yes, I'm Your Angel" (Ono)

"Woman"

"Beautiful Boys" (Ono)

"Dear Yoko"

"Every Man Has a Woman Who Loves Him" (Ono)

"Hard Times Are Over" (Ono)

POSTHUMOUS RELEASES:

MILK AND HONEY (Polydor POLH 5)

January 23, 1984

Side One

"I'm Stepping Out"

"Sleepless Night"

"I Don't Wanna Face It"

"Don't Be Scared"

"Nobody Told Me"

"O' Sanity"

Side Two

"Borrowed Time"

"Your Hands"

"(Forgive Me) My Little Flower Princess"

"Let Me Count the Ways"

"Grow Old with Me"

"You're the One"

JOHN LENNON: LIVE IN NEW YORK CITY (Polydor PCS 7031)

February 24, 1986

Side One

"New York City"

"It's So Hard"

"Woman Is the Nigger of the World"

"Well Well Well"

"Instant Karma!"

Side Two

"Mother"

"Come Together"

"Imagine"

"Cold Turkey"

"Hound Dog"

"Give Peace a Chance"

MENLOVE AVENUE (Parlophone PCS 7308)

November 3, 1986

Side One

"Here We Go Again"

"Rock and Roll People"

"Angel Baby" (Hamlin)

"Since My Baby Left Me" (Crudup)

"To Know Her Is to Love Her" (Spector)

Side Two

"Steel and Glass"

"Scared"

"Old Dirt Road"

"Nobody Loves You"

"Bless You"

Compilations, Soundtracks, Miscellaneous

LENNON (4CD box set) (Parlophone CDS 7 95220 2)

October 30, 1990

Disc One

"Give Peace a Chance"

"Blue Suede Shoes" (Perkins)

"Money (That's What I Want)" (Gordy)

"Dizzy Miss Lizzy" (Williams)

"Yer Blues"

"Cold Turkey"

"Instant Karma!"

"Mother"

"Hold On"

"I Found Out"

"Working Class Hero"

"Isolation"

"Remember"

"Love"

"Well Well Well"

"Look at Me"

"God"

"My Mummy's Dead"

"Power to the People"

"Well (Baby Please Don't Go)"

Disc Two

   "Imagine"

   "Crippled Inside"

   "Jealous Guy"

   "It's So Hard"

   "Give Me Some Truth"

   "Oh My Love"

   "How Do You Sleep?"

   "How?"

   "Oh Yoko"

   "Happy Xmas (War Is Over)"

   "Woman Is the Nigger of the World"

   "New York City"

   "John Sinclair"

   "Come Together"

   "Hound Dog" (Leiber-Stoller)

   "Mind Games"

   "Aisumasen (I'm Sorry)"

   "One Day (at a Time)"

   "Intuition"

   "Out the Blue"

Disc Three

   "Whatever Gets You Thru the Night"

   "Going Down on Love"

   "Old Dirt Road"

   "Bless You"

   "Scared"

   "#9 Dream"

   "Surprise, Surprise (Sweet Bird of Paradox)"

   "Steel and Glass"

   "Nobody Loves You (When You're Down and Out)"

   "Stand By Me" (Leiber, Stoller, King)

   "Ain't That a Shame" (Domino, Bartholomew)

   "Do You Want to Dance" (Freeman)

   "Sweet Little Sixteen" (Berry)

   "Slippin' and Slidin'" (Bocage, Collins, Penniman, Smith)

   "Angel Baby" (Hamlin)

   "Just Because" (Price)

   "Whatever Gets You Thru the Night" (live version)

"Lucy in the Sky with Diamonds"

"I Saw Her Standing There" (Lennon-McCartney)

Disc Four

"(Just Like) Starting Over"

"Cleanup Time"

"I'm Losing You"

"Beautiful Boy (Darling Boy)"

"Watching the Wheels"

"Woman"

"Dear Yoko"

"I'm Stepping Out"

"I Don't Wanna Face It"

"Nobody Told Me"

"Borrowed Time"

"(Forgive Me) My Little Flower Princess"

"Every Man Has a Woman Who Loves Him"

"Grow Old with Me"

ANTHOLOGY (4 CD box set) (Capitol C2 8 30614 2)

November 2, 1998

Side One: Ascot

"Working Class Hero"

"God"

"I Found Out"

"Hold On"

"Isolation"

"Love"

"Mother"

"Remember"

"Imagine"

"Fortunately"

"Well (Baby Please Don't Go)"

"Oh My Love"

"Jealous Guy"

"Maggie Mae"

"How Do You Sleep?"

"God Save Oz"

"Do the Oz"

"I Don't Want to Be a Soldier"

"Give Peace a Chance"

"Look at Me"

"Long Lost John"

Disc Two: New York City

"New York City"

"Attica State" (live)

"Imagine" (live)

"Bring on the Lucie (Freda Peeple)"

"Woman Is the Nigger of the World" (live)

"Geraldo Rivera—One to One Concert"

"Woman Is the Nigger of the World"

"It's So Hard" (live)

"Come Together" (live)

"Happy Xmas (War Is Over)"

"Luck of the Irish" (live)

"John Sinclair" (live)

The David Frost Show

"Mind Games (I Promise)"

"Mind Games (Make Love, Not War)"

"One Day at a Time"

"I Know"

"I'm the Greatest"

"Goodnight Vienna"

Jerry Lewis Telethon

"A Kiss Is Just a Kiss"

"Real Love"

"You Are Here"

Disc Three: The Lost Weekend

"What You Got"

"Nobody Loves You When You're Down and Out"

"Whatever Gets You Thru the Night" (home)

"Whatever Gets You Thru the Night" (studio)

"Yesterday" (parody)

"Be-Bop-A-Lula"

"Rip It Up"/"Ready Teddy"

"Scared"

"Steel and Glass"

"Surprise, Surprise (Sweet Bird of Paradox)"

"Bless You"

"Going Down on Love"

"Move Over Ms. L"

"Ain't She Sweet" (Ager-Yellen)

"Slippin' and Slidin'" (Bocage, Collins, Penniman, Smith)

"Peggy Sue" (Allison, Petty, Holly)

"Bring It On Home to Me" (Cooke)/"Send Me Some Lovin'" (Marascalco, Price)

"Phil and John 1"

"Phil and John 2"

"Phil and John 3"

"When In Doubt, Fuck It"

"Be My Baby"

"Stranger's Room"

"Old Dirt Road"

Disc Four: Dakota

"I'm Losing You"

Sean's "Little Help"

"Serve Yourself"

"My Life"

"Nobody Told Me"

"Life Begins at 40"

"I Don't Wanna Face It"

"Woman"

"Dear Yoko"

"Watching the Wheels"

"I'm Stepping Out"

"Borrowed Time"

"The Rishi Kesh Song"

Sean's "Loud"

"Beautiful Boy"

"Mr. Hyde's Gone (Don't Be Afraid)"

"Only You"

"Grow Old with Me"

"Dear John"

"The Great Wok"

"Mucho Mungo"

"Satire 1"

"Satire 2"

"Satire 3"

Sean's "In the Sky"
"It's Real"

ACOUSTIC (Capitol B000641ZJ0)

November 1, 2004
"Working Class Hero"
"Love"
"Well Well Well"
"Look at Me"
"God"
"My Mummy's Dead"
"Cold Turkey"
"The Luck of the Irish"
"John Sinclair"
"Woman Is the Nigger of the World"
"What You Got"
"Watching the Wheels"
"Dear Yoko"
"Real Love"
"Imagine"
"It's Real"

DOUBLE FANTASY Stripped Down (New Mix & Original Recording Remastered) (Capitol B003Y8YXH6)

John Lennon, Yoko Ono
October 5, 2010

Disc 1

"(Just Like) Starting Over"
"Kiss Kiss Kiss"
"Cleanup Time"
"Give Me Something"
"I'm Losing You"
"I'm Moving On"
"Beautiful Boy (Darling Boy)"
"Watching the Wheels"
"Yes, I'm Your Angel"
"Woman"
"Beautiful Boys"
"Dear Yoko"

"Every Man Has a Woman Who Loves Him"
"Hard Times Are Over"

Disc 2

"(Just Like) Starting Over"
"Kiss Kiss Kiss"
"Cleanup Time"
"Give Me Something"
"I'm Losing You"
"I'm Moving On"
"Beautiful Boy (Darling Boy)"
"Watching the Wheels"
"Yes, I'm Your Angel"
"Woman"
"Beautiful Boys"
"Dear Yoko"
"Every Man Has a Woman Who Loves Him"
"Hard Times Are Over"

JOHN LENNON SIGNATURE BOX SET
(11 CDs) (Capitol B003TVMIDO)

October 5, 2010

Disc 1

"Mother"
"Hold On"
"I Found Out"
"Working Class Hero"
"Isolation"
"Remember"
"Love"
"Well Well Well"
"Look at Me"
"God"
"My Mummy's Dead"

Disc 2

"Imagine"
"Crippled Inside"
"Jealous Guy"
"It's So Hard"
"I Don't Wanna Be a Soldier Mama"

"Gimme Some Truth"

"Oh My Love"

"How Do You Sleep?"

"How?"

"Oh Yoko!"

Disc 3

"Woman Is the Nigger of the World"

"Sisters, O Sisters"

"Attica State"

"Born in a Prison"

"New York City"

"Sunday Bloody Sunday"

"The Luck of the Irish"

"John Sinclair"

"Angela"

"We're All Water"

Disc 4

"Cold Turkey" (live)

"Don't Worry Kyoko (Mummy's Only Looking for Her Hand in the Snow)" (live)

"Well (Baby Please Don't Go)" (live)

"Jamrag" (live)

"Scumbag" (live)

"Aü" (live)

Disc 5

"Mind Games"

"Tight A$"

"Aisumasen (I'm Sorry)"

"One Day (at a Time)"

"Bring on the Lucie (Freda Peeple)"

"Nutopian International Anthem"

"Intuition"

"Out the Blue"

"Only People"

"I Know"

"You Are Here"

"Meat City"

Disc 6

"Going Down on Love"

"Whatever Gets You Thru the Night"

"Old Dirt Road"
"What You Got"
"Bless You"
"Scared"
"#9 Dream"
"Surprise Surprise (Sweet Bird of Paradox)"
"Steel and Glass"
"Beef Jerky"
"Nobody Loves You (When You're Down and Out)"
"Ya Ya" (Robinson, Dorsey & Lewis)

Disc 7

"Be-Bop-A-Lula" (Davis, Vincent)
"Stand By Me" (Leiber, Stoller, King)
Medley: "Rip It Up"/"Ready Teddy" (Blackwell, Marascalco)
"You Can't Catch Me" (Berry)
"Ain't That a Shame" (Domino, Bartholomew)
"Do You Want to Dance" (Freeman)
"Sweet Little Sixteen" (Berry)
"Slippin' and Slidin' " (Bocage, Collins, Penniman, Smith)
"Peggy Sue" (Allison, Petty, Holly)
Medley: "Bring It on Home to Me" (Cooke)/"Send Me Some Lovin' "
    (Marascalco, Price)
"Bony Moronie" (Williams)
"Ya Ya" (Robinson, Dorsey & Lewis)
"Just Because" (Price)

Disc 8

"(Just Like) Starting Over"
"Kiss Kiss Kiss"
"Cleanup Time"
"Give Me Something"
"I'm Losing You"
"I'm Moving On"
"Beautiful Boy (Darling Boy)"
"Watching the Wheels"
"Yes, I'm Your Angel"
"Woman"
"Beautiful Boys"
"Dear Yoko"
"Every Man Has a Woman Who Loves Him"
"Hard Times Are Over"

Disc 9

"I'm Stepping Out"

"Sleepless Night"

"I Don't Wanna Face It"

"Don't Be Scared"

"Nobody Told Me"

"O' Sanity"

"Borrowed Time"

"Your Hands"

"(Forgive Me) My Little Flower Princess"

"Let Me Count the Ways"

"Grow Old with Me"

"You're the One"

Disc 10

"Power to the People"

"Happy Xmas (War Is Over)"

"Instant Karma!"

"Cold Turkey" (single version)

"Move Over Ms. L"

"Give Peace a Chance"

Disc 11

"Mother" (studio outtake)

"Love" (studio outtake)

"God" (studio outtake)

"I Found Out" (studio outtake)

"Nobody Told Me" (home recording)

"Honey Don't" (studio outtake)

"One of the Boys" (home recording)

"India, India" (home recording)

"Serve Yourself" (home recording)

"Isolation" (studio outtake)

"Remember" (studio outtake)

"Beautiful Boy (Darling Boy)" (home recording)

"I Don't Wanna Be a Soldier Mama" (studio outtake)

GIMME SOME TRUTH: THE HITS (Capitol B003Y8YXF8)

October 5, 2010

Disc 1

"Working Class Hero"

"Instant Karma!"

"Power to the People"

"God"

"I Don't Wanna Be a Soldier Mama"

"Gimme Some Truth"

"Sunday Bloody Sunday"

"Steel and Glass"

"Meat City"

"I Don't Wanna Face It"

"Remember"

"Woman Is the Nigger of the World"

"I Found Out"

"Isolation"

"Imagine"

"Happy Xmas (War Is Over)"

"Give Peace a Chance"

"Only People"

Disc 2

"Mother"

"Hold On"

"You Are Here"

"Well Well Well"

"Oh My Love"

"Oh Yoko!"

"Grow Old with Me" (*Anthology* version)

"Love"

"Jealous Guy"

"Woman"

"Out the Blue"

"Bless You"

"Nobody Loves You (When You're Down and Out)"

"My Mummy's Dead"

"I'm Losing You"

"(Just Like) Starting Over"

"#9 Dream"

"Beautiful Boy (Darling Boy)"

Disc 3

"Mind Games"

"Nobody Told Me"

"Cleanup Time"

"Crippled Inside"

"How Do You Sleep?"

"How?"

"Intuition"

"I'm Stepping Out"

"Whatever Gets You Thru the Night"

"Old Dirt Road"

"Scared"

"What You Got"

"Cold Turkey" (single version)

"New York City"

"Surprise Surprise (Sweet Bird of Paradox)"

"Borrowed Time"

"Look at Me"

"Watching the Wheels"

Disc 4

"Be-Bop-A-Lula" (Davis, Vincent)

"You Can't Catch Me" (Berry)

Medley: "Rip It Up"/"Ready Teddy" (Blackwell, Marascalco)

"Tight A$"

"Ain't That a Shame" (Domino, Bartholomew)

"Sweet Little Sixteen" (Berry)

"Do You Want to Dance" (Freeman)

"Slippin' and Slidin'" (Bocage, Collins, Penniman, Smith)

"Peggy Sue" (Allison, Petty, Holly)

Medley: "Bring It on Home to Me"/"Send Me Some Lovin'"

"Yer Blues" (live) (2010 digital remaster)

"Just Because" (Price)

"Bony Moronie" (Williams)

"Beef Jerky"

"Ya Ya" (Robinson, Dorsey & Lewis)

"Hound Dog" (live) (Leiber, Stoller)

"Stand By Me" (Leiber, Stoller, King)

"Here We Go Again"

JOHN LENNON Charting singles:

1969 "Give Peace a Chance" (with the Plastic Ono Band)
#2 UK, #14 U.S.

1969 "Cold Turkey" (with the Plastic Ono Band)
#14 UK, #30 U.S.

1970 "Instant Karma!" (with Yoko Ono and the Plastic Ono Band)
#3 U.S., #5 UK

1971 "Mother" #43 U.S.

1971 "Power to the People" (with the Plastic Ono Band)
#7 UK, #11 U.S.

1971 "Imagine"
#3 U.S.

1972 "Happy Xmas (War Is Over)"
(with Yoko Ono, the Plastic Ono Band and the Harlem Community Choir)
#4 UK

1972 "Woman Is the Nigger of the World"
#57 U.S.

1973 "Mind Games"
#18 U.S., #26 UK

1974 "Whatever Gets You Thru the Night"
(with the Plastic Ono Nuclear Band)
#1 U.S., #36 UK

1975 "Number 9 Dream"
#9 U.S., #23 UK

1975 "Stand By Me" (Leiber, Stoller, King)
#20 U.S., #30 UK

1975 "Imagine"
#6 UK

1980 "(Just Like) Starting Over"
#1 U.S., #1 UK

1980 "Happy Xmas (War Is Over)"
(with Yoko Ono, the Plastic Ono Band and the Harlem Community Choir)
(re-entry)
#2 UK

1980 "Give Peace a Chance"
(with the Plastic Ono Band) (re-entry)
#33 UK

1980 "Imagine" (re-entry)
#1 UK

1981 "Woman"
#1 UK, #2 U.S.

1981 "I Saw Her Standing There"
(Elton John Band featuring John Lennon & the Muscle Shoals Horns)
#40 UK

1981 "Watching the Wheels"
#10 U.S., #30 UK

1981 "Happy Xmas (War Is Over)" (with Yoko Ono, the Plastic Ono Band
and the Harlem Community Choir) (re-entry)
#28 UK

1982 "Love"
#41 UK

1984 "Nobody Told Me"
#5 U.S., #6 UK

1984 "I'm Stepping Out"
#55 U.S.

1984 "Borrowed Time"
#32 UK

1985 "Jealous Guy"
#65 UK

1988 "Jealous Guy"
#80 U.S.

Acknowledgments

Sausage factories make for dreadful tours, but there's this inexcusable myth of the lone author, and it's worth debunking every time.

Let me start with some oversights: Steve Christopher was my first music teacher in Boulder, Colorado, on the snare drum one summer at Boulder High. Later, he led my Base Line Junior High School stage band, where I met guitarist Eric Shreve, John Lovell, and bassist Seth Geltman. We learned most of the Beatle catalog together as teenagers. Mrs. Eddy taught me piano when we lived across the street on Bluebell Avenue; her son, the superb cellist Timothy Eddy, taught my Eastman buddy, Mark Stewart, many, many years later. I've mentioned my Fairview High School choir director Ron Revier before, but his work ethic and powers of self-actualization continue to inspire. At the University of Colorado, I worshipped composer Cecil Effinger, and he gave me far too much latitude.

Several primary piano teachers deserve mention here: Doris Pridonoff Lehnert and Eloise Ristad (author of *A Soprano on Her Head*) in Boulder, Colorado; Eugene Pridonoff at the Eastern Music Festival in Greensboro, North Carolina, and later at Arizona State University in Tempe; Joseph Schwartz at the Oberlin Conservatory; Claude Frank, Charles Wood, and Lee Luvisi at the Aspen Music Festival; and Rebecca Penneys at the Eastman School of Music. Alongside all these pianists and composers came captains of thought like James Hepokoski, whose Oberlin Mahler course has had lasting effects; Richard Gollin, who taught Film Comedy at the University of Rochester; the Juilliard String Quartet cellist Joel Selznick, who gave a riveting lesson on William Schuman's String Quintet at Tanglewood; and Sergiu Luca at Aspen, a baroque violinist who's worth every effort it takes to track down his elegant recordings.

In the congress of Beatle scholars, there are few minds more enjoyable to pick than Jonathan Gould's and Walter Everett's. Gordon Thompson, a new sucker to this whole book racket, brought us all together one weekend at Skidmore in autumn 2008 to talk about the *White Album*, a major gust to this project's sails. We reunited in the fall of 2010 for more. McCartney biographer Peter Carlin shared stories and favorite myths hanging out in Las Vegas, and has remained a constant support and source of solid, reliable contacts.

There are many, many others, mostly critics and editors, who agreed to talk, and helped more than they might imagine, including Kit Rachlis and Bob Merlis in Los Angeles; Jimmy Guterman and Milo Miles in Boston; Joyce Millman in San Francisco; and filmmaker David Leaf (*The U.S. vs. John Lennon*).

In Liverpool, the still active Quarrymen Colin Hanton, Rod Davis, and Len Garry were extremely helpful in the amount of details and song references they brought to the fore. Davis had especially helpful dates to pore over, and vivid memories about Julia Stanley Lennon's grabbing his banjo at rehearsals ("Didn't she have her own banjo?"). Davis also contributed a great lost Lennon photo. Spencer Leigh at Merseyside BBC extended a very generous hand with his address book at several crucial points, as did *The Beatles* author Bob Spitz. All the curators at the National Trust homes in Liverpool extended the warmest courtesies. Derry and Seniors saxophonist, Howie Casey, happily recounted many Hamburg scrapes. And several long talks with Quarry Bank classmate Michael Hill helped illustrate a first-person account of Lennon hearing Little Richard for the first time.

Paul Du Noyer met up with me several times and shared important contacts that led to important finds. All critics should have such thoughtful colleagues. Colin Fallows, Liverpool John Moores University, gave a tour of his pop culture archives, and offered lively debate over the merits of Albert Goldman's approach. (Curiously, the British tend to forgive this American author where the Yanks hold their noses.) Finally, the hospitality and embrace of locals like Terry Heaton made repeated visits to Liverpool not just warm but treasured.

In London, McCartney and Joe Strummer biographer Chris Salewicz always offered helpful feedback, and he put me in touch with his friends, Zapple's Barry Miles and photographer Bob Gruen, both of whom sat for lengthy interviews. The 2006 launch party for *Recording the Beatles* with authors Kevin Ryan and Brian Kehew led to illuminating talks with the venerable EMI engineers Ken Townsend, Richard Lush, and Chris Thomas. EMI house "historian," Lester Smith, spent several hours with me discussing the company's history. Independent producer Joe Boyd provided deep, extensive background on the period, the scene around his UFO club, and many details about recording practice, the appearance of Dylan's *Basement Tapes*, and EMI lore.

Glenn Gass invited me to teach his Indiana University Beatle course in London during the summer term in 2008, and the students in that group proved earnest beyond all reckoning. Quarryman Rod Davis and *Merseybeat* publisher Bill Harry both spoke to the class. Chris Hutchins, who introduced the Beatles to both Little Richard and Elvis Presley, recounted Hamburg's scene vividly, and posed intriguing insights about Brian Epstein. Billy J. Kramer told me the story about Lennon's "P.S. I Love You" demo tape.

Stan Bronstein, Tex Gabriel, and Gary Van Scyoc of the Elephant's Memory band, came up with fresh scenes and quotes from their work with John and Yoko. Rosanne Cash talked about her father's sending signed photographs of the Beatles from the road, and Marshall Crenshaw talked about how humbling it felt to portray Lennon in *Beatlemania* (the only man in show business cast as both Lennon and Buddy Holly?). *The Mike Douglas Show* producer Michael Krauss was both candid and circumspect. Elliot Mintz, the deejay who became a confidant, extended his already generous writings on his time with the Lennons and provided a vivid account of how it felt to greet Ringo Starr and his wife at the Dakota on December 9, 1980.

Cheap Trick drummer Bun E. Carlos had total recall of nearly every moment he spent in Lennon's *Double Fantasy* sessions, including work on tracks that haven't been released. Producer and longtime friend Jack Douglas shared many stories about how it felt to be tapped as the board man for the big comeback project. My sister-in-law, Ann Laschever, lent me her apartment in the fall of 2008 for some hardcore cramming as Wall Street imploded.

IN LONDON, one of the best conversations I ever had about the band took place with Ray Connolly, who reported on and befriended Lennon as the Beatles fell apart. I regret that I came to this project too late to converse in depth with the wonderful British critic Ian MacDonald, author of *Revolution in the Head,* but I treasure his book. Devin McKinney's *Magic Circles* remains a towering piece of inspiration, and one of the best extended arguments about how the Beatles' legacy transcends its era.

Larry Kane gave me several long interviews concerning his books, and put me in touch with Pauline Sutcliffe. Pauline spoke patiently with me and cleared up many misconceptions. Tony Barrow gave me a lengthy interview after his book was published, and then again in Liverpool during Beatle Days at the Adelphi Hotel. Stu Sutcliffe's fiancée, Astrid Kirchherr, spoke with great tenderness about her romance with Sutcliffe, and about how he and Lennon loved to spend the day roaming Hamburg's museums. She still sleeps with his picture at her bedside. Victor Spinetti told me wild stories about producing *In His Own Write* and *Spaniard in the Works* for the London stage, including backstage rants about Laurence Olivier, and followed up with a signed photo of himself as Albert Einstein.

Mark Lapidos and "Fest for Beatle Fans," where I enjoyed Alistair Taylor's friendship in the late 1980s, has provided many provocative forums for discussions with Beatle fans. Other sources from that venue include Wings drummer Denny Seiwell, Neil Innes (songwriter for the Rutles), Robert Freeman, and Peter Asher.

Dave Marsh propped up his book about *The Beatles' Second Album* with far too many quotes from *Tell Me Why*, and my lawyers will be in touch. Robert Christgau and Greil Marcus have turned in sustaining work for a continuous stream of insights and ideas, as has movie critic David Thomson.

For over ten years, Jason Kruppa has become far more than a colleague in the wilds of Beatle scholarship. In many, many phone calls and e-mails, he shamed me out of weak ideas and prodded me toward more and better ones. As photo editor for this project, he yielded his considerable graphic taste and standards over a huge swath of material and returned with choices that reached beyond what my words aimed at. To him I say, "Someday, all this will be yours."

John Winn, Mark Easter, and Chip Madinger eagerly devoured the manuscript for errors and did their jobs a bit too well for this author's pride. Mark Lewisohn's status among Beatle researchers rests on both his scholarship and genial nature. No books are more eagerly anticipated than his three-volume epic. I cannot thank him enough for his gratis photograph, and this book owes a great debt to his prodigious research.

Jon Baldo, University of Rochester, Eastman School, was among the very first to edit my first manuscript, *Tell Me Why*, back in 1984–5, and he pored over an embarrassingly early draft of this book with infinite patience and forgiveness. I cannot thank him enough for his steady encouragements. Another editor who left a huge imprint on my prose has been *Fresh Air*'s Milo Miles, and I'll always feel lucky that I came to Boston in time to meet Mark Moses and hang out with movie critics Charles Taylor and Stephanie Zacharek. Musicians like Clint Conley and Mark Leccese deserve special mention as colleagues of indomitable redoubt.

At Emerson College, I thank the steadfast support of my Journalism department chair, Ted Gup, and dean, Janis Andersen, who make teaching such a pleasant pursuit.

At Hyperion, I thank Gretchen Young for her sensitive and gracious edit, and Elizabeth Sabo for favors both large and small. Cover designer GTC Art and Design, production editor Kevin MacDonald, and copyeditor Rick Willett weeded out many an error with awesome humility and patience.

In Ike Williams, I have an agent whose diligence under abject circumstances is downright miraculous, and whose talent cannot be overstated. His Kneerim and Williams team, with Hope Denekamp and Katherine Flynn, always make me feel a bit spoiled.

There are many, many others—librarians, reporters, Oberlin interns, tour

7 7

guides—who assisted along the way; let my poor memory sit in grand contrast to their contributions.

Finally, there is simply no chance this project would have ever seen completion without my wife Sara Laschever's Olympian endurance. There were so many times when our discussions sharpened my ideas that her influence echoes through every sentence. If I could coax all the chocolate in the world to sing, I would have it sing her virtues to the highest rafters.

As for Moses and Adam, dittos with confetti: this part's all in claymation.—TR

Notes

The following codes have been used to indicate frequently referenced works:

BA   Beatles, The. *The Beatles Anthology*. San Francisco: Chronicle Books, 2000.

BC   Lewisohn, Mark. *The Beatles Chronicles*. London: Hamlyn, 2006.

BJY   *Rolling Stone,* Editors of. *The Ballad of John and Yoko*. Garden City: Doubleday Dolphin, 1982.

BL   Lewisohn, Mark. *The Beatles Live!* New York: Henry Holt & Co., 1986.

CLJ   Lennon, Cynthia. *John*. New York: Random House, 2005.

CLT   Lennon, Cynthia. *A Twist of Lennon*. New York: Avon, 1980.

DCH   Lennon, Pauline. *Daddy, Come Home: The True Story of John Lennon and His Father*. London: Angus and Robertson, 1990.

IT   Baird, Julia. *Imagine This*. London: Hodder & Stoughton, 2007.

JLE   Harry, Bill. *The John Lennon Encyclopedia*. London: Virgin Publishing, 2000.

JLMB Baird, Julia, with Geoffrey Giuliano. *John Lennon, My Brother*. London: Grafton, 1988.

MYFN Miles, Barry. *Paul McCartney Many Years from Now*. New York: Henry Holt & Co., 1997.

PB   Lennon, John, Yoko Ono, and David Sheff. *The Playboy Interviews with John Lennon and Yoko Ono*. New York: Putnam, 1981.

RTB   Kehew, Brian, and Kevin Ryan. *Recording the Beatles*. Houston: Curvebender Publishing, 2006.

SS   Pete Shotton and Nicholas Schaffner. *John Lennon in My Life*. New York: Stein and Day, 1983.

TBRS   Lewisohn, Mark. *The Beatles Recording Sessions: The Official Abbey Road Studio Session Notes 1962–1970.* London: Harmony, 1988.

Chapter 1: No Reply

1. BA, 4.
2. S. Almond and B. J. Marsh, *Home Port: Bootle, the Blitz and the Battle of the Atlantic* (Sefton: Metro Borough of Sefton Education Department, 1993), 7.
3. S. C. Leslie, Ministry of Home Security, *Bombers Over Merseyside: The Authoritative Record of the Blitz, 1940–1941* (Liverpool: Scouse Press, 1983), 8.
4. William Manchester, *The Last Lion: William Spencer Churchill: Alone, 1932–1940* (Boston: Little, Brown and Company, 1988), 679.
5. Isaiah Berlin, with Henry Hardy, Roger Hausheer, *The Proper Study of Mankind: An Anthology of Essays* (New York: Farrar, Straus and Giroux, 1997), 618.
6. CLJ, 29.
7. Jan Morris, "In Liverpool," from *The Ballad of John and Yoko* (Garden City: Doubleday Dolphin, 1982), 4.
8. JLMB, 19.
9. During the Irish potato famine in the 1840s, 9,000 Irish arrived in its ports each day, swelling the population from 286,000 to 376,000 between 1841 and 1851.
10. Danny Ross, *A Blue Coat Boy in the 1920s* (Gunnison, Colorado: Pharaoh Press, 1996). Ross writes about his childhood friend, Alfred Lennon, who gave Danny a mouth organ and taught him how to play.
11. JLE, 474. Harry reports that the Blue Coat orphanage publicly "berated" Alfred, but he seems to be the only source for this incident.
12. JLMB, 8–9.
13. Ibid.
14. DCH, 75.
15. Although it is an important primary source, very few Lennon narratives work in Alf's quotes from *Daddy Come Home* surrounding any of these key events.
16. JLE, 476.
17. DCH, 33.
18. Ray Coleman, *John Lennon* (McGraw-Hill, 1986), 25.
19. The October 10, 1940, edition of the *Liverpool Echo* reported only news about British raids on Germany, especially on its armament factories in Krupps. But there is no mention of raids on the Merseyside area that night of October 9, just a single bomb falling "in a north-west town," again, name withheld for security reasons. On this same night, forty London districts were detailed as

bombed. Aunt Mimi may have been misremembering bombs which fell on the night of October 10 and 11. From author correspondence with Quarrymen member and Lennon confidant Rod Davis.

20. Coleman, 25.

21. JLE, 821.

22. Ibid, 34.

23. DCH, 30–33. This narrative reports that Julia, Alf, and John had shared the apartment with the Stanleys since John was born; others differ as to precisely when the Stanleys gave up the Berkeley Street dwelling. But Anne's death brought about some sort of living readjustments if only because the balance of family chemistry changed radically.

24. Ibid, 40.

25. Ibid, 42.

26. JLMB, 13.

27. Maritime Museum exhibition, Liverpool, May 2008.

28. Walter Everett, *The Beatles As Musicians: The Quarry Men Through* Rubber Soul (New York: Oxford University Press, 2001), 14.

29. Ibid, 369; DCH, 61.

30. Paddy Shennan, "Teenage Teds Without a Care in the World," *Liverpool Echo*, October 3, 2007, http://www.liverpoolecho.co.uk/liverpool-entertainment/the-beatles/the-beatles-news/2007/10/03/teenage-teds-without-a-care-in-the-world-100252-19888187/. If this expulsion came in the spring of 1946, this preceded the Blackpool scene, which signals how boisterous Lennon's temperament had grown in advance of this defining trauma.

31. DCH, 65.

32. JLE, 480. Sydney Lennon claims that he and his wife also took the boy in for nine months when John was four, during this same period.

33. DCH, 67.

34. Founder Alderman William George Bean quoted in 1896, in the same turn-of-the-century park fever that inspired Chicago's White City and later Disneyland. http://en.wikipedia.org/wiki/Blackpool_pleasure_beach.

35. Hunter Davies, *The Beatles—The Authorized Biography* (New York: McGraw-Hill, 1968), 9.

36. DCH, 70.

37. Ibid, 72.

38. Ibid, 75; 110.

39. MYFN, 47.

40. Davies, *Beatles,* 12.

41. Ibid, 44.

Chapter 2: Something to Hide

1. MYFN, 44.
2. JLMB, 15.
3. Author interview with Len Garry, Chicago, 2007.
4. "Leila" seems to be spelled "Liela" on the Liverpool Lennon.net family Web page, http://www.lennon.net, and in IT, but not JLMB.
5. All these Stanley Parkes quotes come from the Lennon.net family Web site, at http://www.lennon.net/reflections/s_parkes.shtml, stories that have not been reproduced elsewhere until now. Mimi and George lived in "The Cottage" before taking over Mendips; her sister Harriet moved in with Leila after the war.
6. JLMB, 28.
7. Coleman, 25.
8. CLJ, 106.
9. Coleman, 30–31.
10. Ibid.
11. SS, 23.
12. Ibid, 27–28.
13. Ibid.
14. David Ashton, *A Woolton Childhood*, unpublished memoir, http://www.beatles ireland.utvinternet.com/John7020Lennon/Woolton.Woolton1.html, 3.
15. SS, 33. Although it's not uncommon for adolescents to fantasize about places more magical and mysterious than their ordinary surroundings, the early ambition to write a work resembling Lewis Carroll's points to Lennon's nonlinear bent that would produce such surreal pop landscapes as "Tomorrow Never Knows," "Strawberry Fields Forever," "Lucy in the Sky with Diamonds," "I Am the Walrus," "Glass Onion," "The Continuing Story of Bungalow Bill," "Happiness Is a Warm Gun," "Across the Universe," and "I Dig a Pony."
16. Ibid.
17. Coleman, 32.
18. Hunter Davies, *The Quarrymen* (New York: Omnibus Press, 2001), 23.
19. Reproduced in James Henke, *Lennon Legend: An Illustrated Life of John Lennon* (San Francisco: Chronicle Books, 2003), 8.
20. Davies, *Quarrymen*, 23.
21. SS, 38–39.
22. Ibid, 29.
23. Ibid, 29.
24. Author interview with Liverpool resident Paul McNutt, 2008.
25. SS, 30.
26. Author interview with Michael Hill, January 2005.

27. Allen Ginsberg, with Bill Morgan, ed., *The Letters of Allen Ginsberg* (New York: Da Capo, 2008), 223.

28. Lisa Philips, ed., *Beat Culture and the New America—1950–1965* (Paris and New York: the Whitney Museum of Art in association with Flammarion, 1995), http://www.lib.berkeley.edu/MRC/Carney.html.

29. CLT, 25.

30. BA, 9.

31. JLE, 72.

32. Davies, *Quarrymen*, 32.

33. Author interview with Rod Davis, Chicago, August 2007.

34. Davies, *Quarrymen*, 23.

35. Ibid, 20.

36. As evidenced in Henke, 8.

37. Author interview with Rod Davis, 2007.

Chapter 3: She Said She Said

1. Paul Johnson, *Modern Times: The Twenties to the Nineties* (revised edition) (New York: Harper Perennial, 1992), 439.

2. Jann Wenner, *Lennon Remembers* (San Francisco: Straight Arrow Books, 1971), 146.

3. Dave Cotterill and Ian Lysaght, directors, *Liverpool's Cunard Yanks* (Souled Out Films, 2007).

4. Tony Bramwell and Rosemary Kingsland, *Magical Mystery Tours: My Life with the Beatles* (New York: St. Martin's Griffin, 2006).

5. Author interview with Colin Hanton, Liverpool, 2005.

6. BA, 11.

7. Pauline Sutcliffe and Douglas Thompson, *The Beatles' Shadow: Stuart Sutcliffe & His Lonely Hearts Club* (London: Macmillan, 2002), 31. Jackson was an innovator as well, stringing together sound effects to create jingles between songs that accented the music's inanity. On Jackson's show, rock 'n' roll sprouted comic leaks; the only thing on the three BBC frequencies that came anywhere close was Lennon's beloved *Goon Show* with Spike Milligan, Harry Secombe, and Peter Sellers, which got considerable comic leeway.

8. John Firminger and Spencer Leigh, *Halfway to Paradise: British Pop Music 1955–1962* (Liverpool: Finbarr International, 1996), 30.

9. Ibid, 29.

10. Alan Clayson, *Beat Merchants: The Origins, History, Impact and Rock Legacy* (London: Blandford Press, 1996), 30–31.

11. Ibid, 18.

12. BA, 28, and MYFN, 19.

13. Author interview with Colin Hanton, Liverpool, 2005.

14. Mark Lewisohn Beatle Days conference interview with Julia Baird, Liverpool Adelphi Hotel, August 2005.

15. JLMB, 25.

16. Ibid, 28.

17. SS, 38.

18. Author interview with Len Garry, Chicago, 2007.

19. JLMB, 23.

20. BA, 11.

21. Ibid.

22. All quotes from this scene from an author interview with Michael Hill, January 2005.

23. BA, 10.

24. Ibid, 11.

25. Ibid.

26. Davies, *Beatles*, 12.

27. JLMB, 27.

28. Stanley Parkes, quoted in a 2002 interview on lennon.net, the Lennon Family Web page, http://www.lennon.net/reflections/s_parkes3.shtml.

29. Ibid.

30. BA, 8.

31. SS, 38.

32. Ibid, 38.

33. JLMB, 49–50.

34. Julia Baird interviewed at Beatle Days conference by Mark Lewisohn, August 2005.

35. Jim O'Donnell, *The Day John Met Paul: An Hour-by-Hour Account of How The Beatles Began* (New York: Penguin Books, 1996), 69.

36. Author interview with Len Garry, 2007.

37. Davies, *Quarrymen*, 39.

38. Ibid, 43.

39. BL, 19. "The 550th Anniversary of King John, who issued the royal Charter 'inviting settlers to take up burgages or building plots in Liverpool, and promising them all the privileges enjoyed by free boroughs on the sea.'" Also, Quarrymen has always been a single word band name.

40. JLMB, 34.

41. BA, 20.

42. Ibid.

43. Author interview with Colin Hanton, 2005. McCartney is alone in remembering Lennon's alcoholic breath; Colin Hanton and Rod Davis swear the

drinking was at a minimum, and have no distinct memories of Lennon chugging at ale or anything else. Others speculate Julia may have bought a pint for him.

Chapter 4: Nobody Told Me

1. This "Auntie Jin" shows up in McCartney's Wings song, "Let 'Em In," in 1976.
2. MYFN, 21.
3. Bob Spitz, *The Beatles: The Biography* (New York: Little, Brown and Company, 2005), 89.
4. Ibid, 90.
5. MYFN, 32.
6. BA, 134.
7. Spitz, 110.
8. MYFN, 46.
9. Author interview with Colin Hall, Mendips curator, 2005.
10. Simon Frith and Howard Horne, *Art into Pop* (London: Methuen and Co., 1987), 73.
11. John Goldrosen and John Beecher, *Remembering Buddy* (New York: Da Capo, 1996), 29.
12. Ibid, 65.
13. JLE, 514.
14. Bramwell, 32.
15. Goldrosen and Beecher, 159.
16. Author interview with Colin Hall, August 2005.
17. Sutcliffe and Thompson, 16. This is yet another important first-person account of the young Lennon that has eluded previous Lennon biographers.
18. Ibid, 18.
19. Ibid, 20.
20. Ibid, 17.
21. Davies, *Beatles,* 65.
22. BL, 20.
23. BC, 16. Lewisohn pegs the date as February 6, 1958.
24. BL, 17.
25. Ibid, 18.
26. Author interview with Colin Hanton in Liverpool. Lewisohn claims Hanton did not participate in the recording. Hanton remembers it vividly.
27. Ibid.
28. JLMB, 51.
29. Ibid, 51–52.

30. Spitz, 146.
31. Paddy Sherman, *Liverpool Echo*, October 5, 2007.
32. JLMB, 52.
33. Ibid, 54–55.
34. JLE, 958.
35. MYFN, 48.
36. Ibid, 49.

Chapter 5: Pools of Sorrow

1. Sutcliffe and Thompson, 44.
2. Frith and Horne, 40.
3. Sutcliffe and Thompson, 40.
4. Ibid, 40.
5. Davies, *Beatles*, 55.
6. Steve Stark, *Meet the Beatles* (New York: HarperCollins, 2005), 72.
7. CLT, 18.
8. Davies, *Beatles,* 57.
9. Ibid, 57–58.
10. Sutcliffe and Thompson, 32.
11. Ibid, 37.
12. Ibid, 39.
13. Davies, *Quarrymen,* 63.
14. Sutcliffe and Thompson, 25.
15. Ibid, 52.
16. Ibid, 122.
17. Spencer Leigh, *The Best of Fellas: The Story of Bob Wooler—Liverpool's First D.J., the Man Who Introduced "The Beatles"* (Liverpool: Drivegreen Ltd, 2002), 160.
18. Sutcliffe and Thompson, 122.
19. BL, 16.
20. Peter Guralnick and Ernst Jorgensen, *Elvis Day by Day: The Definitive Record of His Life and Music* (Chicago: Ballantine Books, 1999), 123. Less than two months later, early on the morning of August 14, his mother died in Methodist Hospital in Memphis. Elvis was granted emergency leave from Killeen to be at Graceland when she passed.
21. John Lennon, *The Lennon Tapes: John Lennon and Yoko Ono in Conversation with Andy Peebles, 6 December 1980* (London: British Broadcasting Corporation, 1981), 203.
22. Patricia Romanowski with Jon Pareles and Holly George-Warren, *The Rolling Stone Encyclopedia of Rock & Roll* (New York: Simon & Schuster, 2001), 72.

A hat-checker in Berry's St. Louis nightclub. She complained to the police when Berry fired her. "After a blatantly racist first trial was disallowed, he was found guilty at a second. Berry spent two years in federal prison in Indiana, leaving him embittered."

23. Sutcliffe and Thompson, 64.

24. Philip Norman, *Shout!: The Beatles in Their Generation* (New York: Simon & Schuster), 1981, 67.

25. Before his recording career, Vincent had suffered a leg injury during a motorcycle accident in the navy, which required a metal brace. Part of his appeal stemmed from his sexual demeanor in spite of this wound.

26. Alan Clayson, *Hamburg—The Cradle of British Rock* (London: Sanctuary Publishing, 1998), 50.

27. Andrew Loog Oldham, *Stoned: A Memoir of London in the 1960s* (New York: St. Martin's Press, 2001), 133. Oldham's remark gets argued through many British band encores, from the Who and T. Rex covering "Summertime Blues" to Led Zeppelin's "C'mon Everybody."

Chapter 6: Well Well Well

1. Paul Du Noyer, *Liverpool: Wondrous Place, From the Cavern to the Capital of Culture* (London: London Virgin, 2002), 32.

2. BA, 46.

3. Norman, *Shout!*, 95.

4. BA, 47.

5. Ibid.

6. Ibid.

7. Pete Best and Patrick Doncaster *Beatle! The Pete Best Story* (London: Plexus, 1985), 111. It's one of those Lennon stories you hope is true, but it's disputed by Harrison, who was probably there.

8. This same Casey later performed with Paul McCartney's Wings *Venus and Mars* tour in 1975–76.

9. Author interview with Howie Casey, 2004.

10. Best and Doncaster, 115.

11. Spitz, 228.

12. Devin McKinney, *Magic Circles: The Beatles in Dream and History* (Cambridge, Massachusetts: Harvard University Press, 2004), 4.

13. Alan Clayson, *John Lennon: The Unauthorised Biography of John Lennon* (New York: Chrome Dreams, 2001).

14. Guralnick and Jorgensen, 41.

15. BA, 49.

16. Ibid.

17. Ibid.
18. Doncaster and Best, 46.
19. Andy Babiuk, *The Beatles Gear: All the Fab Four's Instruments, from Stage to Studio* (San Francisco: Backbeat, 2001), 35.
20. Doncaster and Best, 42.
21. Ibid, 55. Also, Stark, 150. Stark comes up with the best interpretation of this Scouser term: "No translation necessary."
22. Sutcliffe and Thompson, 99.
23. Philip Norman, *Shout!*, 97.
24. Sutcliffe and Thompson, 135.
25. Norman, *Shout!*, 97. A deliciously ironic quote: innocence is not "all-protecting," it *requires* protecting.
26. CLJ, 69.
27. Frith and Horne, 85.
28. "Living together" before marriage was more common among European families than it was in American homes of the period. Cynthia Powell soon moved in to live with John at his aunt Mimi's house later in 1962, strictly as a "boarder" in the adult's mind, but quite something else for the young couple. And Paul famously lived with his girlfriend Jane Asher's family when he settled in London in 1964.
29. Author interview with Astrid Kirchherr, 2008.
30. Paul Goodman, *Growing Up Absurd* (Princeton: Vintage Books, 1960).
31. Doncaster and Best, 58.
32. Ibid, 59.
33. Norman, *Shout!*, 100.
34. Doncaster and Best, 120.
35. Sutcliffe and Thompson, 88.
36. Du Noyer, 32.
37. BA, 45.
38. Author interview with Tony Bramwell, 2006.
39. BA, 49.
40. Ibid.
41. Ibid.
42. Coleman, 132.
43. Bramwell, 4.
44. BA, 56.
45. Doncaster and Best, 85.
46. Clayson, *Hamburg*, 188.

Chapter 7: I Found Out

1. BA, 69.
2. Sutcliffe and Thompson, 121.
3. Ibid.
4. Author interview with Astrid Kirchherr, April 2008.
5. Sir Eduardo Paolozzi received his knighthood in 1989; his sculpture of Sir Isaac Newton (on William Blake's image) sits outside the British Library in London.
6. Sutcliffe and Thompson, 134.
7. JLE, 64.
8. Bill Harry, *Mersey Beat—The Beginnings of the Beatles* (New York: Omnibus Press, 1977), 22.
9. Ibid.
10. Ibid.
11. "One After 909" was recorded during 1963 then held, and later revived as a delirious throwaway during the *Let It Be* sessions in 1969. It remains the largest question hovering over their early set list: apparently, Lennon was never satisfied with the lyric.
12. BA, 67. McCartney: "We would still do our rock act, though we wouldn't get decent money for any gig apart from cabaret. I could pull out 'Till There Was You' or 'A Taste of Honey,' the more cabaret things, and John would sing 'Over the Rainbow' and 'Ain't She Sweet.' These did have cred for us because they were on a Gene Vincent album and we didn't realize 'Rainbow' was a Judy Garland number, we thought it was Gene Vincent, so we were happy to do it."

Chapter 8: A Man You Must Believe

1. Debbie Geller, *In My Life: The Brian Epstein Story* (New York: St. Martin's Press, 2000), 24.
2. Ibid, 23.
3. Ibid, 42.
4. Author interview with Colin Hanton in Liverpool, 2005.
5. Harry, *Mersey Beat*, 10.
6. Ibid, 19.
7. Alistair Taylor, *With the Beatles* (England: John Blake, 2003), 13.
8. Author interview with David Backhouse, Liverpool architect, May 2004.
9. BA, 65.
10. Geller, 37.
11. Taylor, Alistair, 28.
12. Geller, 25.

13. Ibid, 25–26.

14. Ibid, 21.

15. CLJ, 103.

16. Geller, 37.

17. Taylor, Alistair, 29.

18. Ibid, 31.

19. Ibid, 33.

20. Gay conspiracy theories swarm the Lennon-Epstein relationship, to the point where they have them hooking up in Hamburg in 1961, long before Epstein sees Lennon at the Cavern, and postulate Epstein's 1967 death as a suicide at Lennon's break-off of the five-year affair. While unverifiable on any number of levels, it still says a great deal about the alternative sexuality underground that such whispers were fervent throughout Lennon's career, and spoke to their sense of his heroic stature.

21. BA, 98.

22. Ibid, 58.

23. Leigh, 160.

24. Author interview with Spencer Leigh in Liverpool, May 2004.

25. Oldham, 132.

26. Taylor, Alistair, 28.

27. MYFN, 75.

28. BC, 65.

29. Jonathan Gould, *Can't Buy Me Love: The Beatles, Britain and America* (New York: Harmony Books, 2007), 166.

30. Leigh, 158–59.

31. The eleven CDs of this material collected on bootlegs (*The Complete Beatles at the BBC,* on the underground labels Great Dane and Purple Chick) sport a feast of material, and diagram their songwriting, vocal, and ensemble models the way few bands ever get to chart.

32. BA, 69.

33. Some biographies insist Lennon confessed to L.A. session guitarist Jesse Ed Davis, a notoriously unreliable source.

34. Kirchherr in Yoko Ono, *Memories of John Lennon* (Brattleboro: Harper Paperbacks, 2006), 119.

Chapter 9: Isolation

1. At EMI this boiled down to the difference between a regular session, capturing sound for a possible release, and test session, where newly signed acts were recorded at a preliminary session for audio diagnostics, which the producer rarely attended.

2. In 1923, Oscar Preuss founded the label's British branch. Like many labels of this period, it hooked up through leasing arrangements with other small labels, like Okeh Records in the United States. Columbia Graphophone Company UK acquired a controlling interest in 1927, and in 1931, Columbia merged with the Gramophone Company to form EMI.
3. BC, 55.
4. Taylor, Alistair, 81.
5. TBRS, 17.
6. This version appeared on 1995's *Anthology 1,* track twenty-one. See discography. George Martin also found an acetate of "Love Me Do" in his attic while preparing the *Anthology.*
7. TBRS, 17.
8. BA, 71.
9. Steve Garofalo and Reebee Chapple, *Rock 'n' Roll Is Here to Pay, the History and Politics of the Music Industry* (Chicago: Nelson Hall, 1977), 70.
10. CLJ, 90.
11. Ibid.
12. Ibid.
13. Ibid.
14. BA, 71.
15. Ibid, 72.
16. Ibid, 71.
17. Ibid, 49.
18. Leigh, 167.
19. JLMB, 73.
20. BA, 72.
21. Wedding quotes from CLJ, 96. Bolthole, or "fuckpad."
22. Bramwell, 77.
23. There are, however, several versions of "Love Me Do" in "official" circulation. They are easy to distinguish: on Ringo's version, there is no tambourine. Which raises yet another question: if they are that similar in tone and effect, why did Martin sweat the difference?
24. BA, 77.
25. Harry, *Mersey Beat,* January 3–17, 1963, 49.
26. Ibid.
27. Norman, 292.
28. Oldham, 173.
29. Southall, 11–15.
30. John Winn, *Way Beyond Compare: The Beatles' Recorded Legacy, Volume One* (New York: Three Rivers Press, 2008), 21–24.

Chapter 10: Hold On

1. Gould, 91.
2. To Britons this term is derogatory slang for "prostitute."
3. Christine Keeler, *The Truth at Last* (New York: Picador, 2002). Keeler has since claimed she was a patsy for an Anglo-Soviet spy ring.
4. John Lennon, *The Writings of John Lennon: In His Own Write/A Spaniard in the Works* (New York: Simon & Schuster, 1981), 39.
5. Michael Braun, *Love Me Do: The Beatles' Progress* (New York: Penguin, 1964), 52.
6. Leslie Fiedler, *A New Fiedler Reader* (Amherst, NY: Prometheus, 1999), 282.
7. Greil Marcus, "The Beatles," *The Rolling Stone Illustrated History of Rock 'n' Roll* (New York: Rolling Stone Press, 1976), 181.
8. Author interview with Billy J. Kramer, 2005.
9. Oldham, 172. Mark Wynter, Oldham's friend, was also at this rehearsal, and impressed enough to call his agent, Ian Bevan of the Harold Fielding Agency, which handled Tommy Steele. "I'm not interested in handling groups" was Bevan's reply.
10. Oldham had shepherded Dylan and his manager around London during this little-known BBC appearance in 1962.
11. Oldham, 171.
12. Ibid, 182.
13. Helen Shapiro quoted in *Uncut Legends,* No. 7 (2005): 18.
14. BA, 90.
15. Ibid, 92.
16. TBRS, 26.
17. Gould, 103.
18. The songwriting credit reads "Medley-Russell" because Berns sometimes wrote with his partner Phil Medley under the name of "Bert Russell." He went on to refashion "Twist and Shout" into "Hang on Sloopy" for the McCoys, and to write "Here Comes the Night" for both Lulu and Van Morrison's Them. There is no evidence that Lennon ever heard this original Top Notes track, although he probably spoke with Phil Spector about it later on.
19. Notably on a UK TV special called *The Beatles in the Round* from 1964.
20. BA, 95; in TBRS, Lewisohn has "From Me To You" dashed off on February 27.
21. Oldham, 175.
22. Ibid.
23. Bramwell, 101.
24. Geller, 56.

25. Screenplay to *The Hours and Times* by Christopher Munch, unpublished, http://imdb.com/title/tt0104448/quotes.

26. Richard Harrington, review of "The Hours and Times," *Washington Post,* November 17, 1992, http://www.washingtonpost.com/wp-srv/style/longterm/movies/videos/thehoursandtimesnrharrington_a0ab53.htm.

27. SS, 73.

28. Taylor, 72.

29. BA, 94.

30. Author interview with Billy J. Kramer, May 2005. Lennon gave Kramer his faux middle initial: "I went into Brian's office, and he said, 'John's got a suggestion. How about Billy "J" Kramer. It's American sounding, it's catchy, it flows.' And I said 'What do I say if someone asks what it stands for?' And he said, 'Julian.' Now I didn't even know John was married, let alone had a son called Julian, so I said, 'I don't like that name, that's a real poofter's name!'" *Uncut Legends,* No. 7 (2005): 18.

Chapter 11: Thick of It

1. Winn, *Way Beyond Compare,* 91.

2. Oldham, 234–35.

3. Ibid, 235.

4. Ibid, 236.

5. Author interview with Kim Fowley, 2005.

6. Barry Miles, *The Beatles Diary Volume I: The Beatles Years* (London: Omnibus Press, 2001), 118.

7. Oldham, 169.

8. Robert Freeman, *Yesterday: The Beatles 1963–1965* (New York: Holt Rinehart and Winston, 1983), 12.

9. Ronnie Spector with Vince Waldron, *Be My Baby: How I Survived Mascara, Miniskirts, and Madness, or My Life as a Fabulous Ronette* (New York: Harper-Perennial, 1990), 72.

10. D. Lowe and Thomas Whiteside, "Talk of the Town," "Beatle Man," *New Yorker,* December 28, 1963, 23.

Chapter 12: One Sweet Dream

1. BA, 116.

2. Spector, 72.

3. Author interview with Barry Miles, May 2008.

4. Without consulting Epstein, producers of *The Ed Sullivan Show* ran each Beatle's name beneath his head as they performed "Till There Was You," their

second song. Beneath John's name came the message: "Sorry girls, he's married." It won Lennon's argument for him.

5. Spector, 76.
6. J. Hoberman, *The Dream Life: Movies, Media, and the Mythology of the Sixties* (New York: The New Press, 2003), 92.
7. Spitz, 458.
8. Braun, 28.
9. BA, 116.
10. Directors: Albert Maysles, David Maysles; Susan Frömke, *Beatles—The First U.S. Visit* (Capitol, 2001), DVD.
11. Steve Sutherland, editor, *John Lennon: New Musical Express Originals* (October 2003), 17.
12. BA, 119.
13. For the record: Magician Fred Kaps's Card and Salt Shaker Trick, the Broadway cast of *Oliver!* singing "I'd Do Anything," and "As Long as He Needs Me," Frank Gorshin's Hollywood impressions, Olympic athlete Terry McDermott, a show tune medley from Tessie O'Shea, and McCall and Brill's office comedy sketch.
14. Author interview with Richard Meltzer, 2005.
15. BA, 120.
16. Author interview with Marshall Crenshaw, December 2006. Crenshaw played John Lennon on Broadway in *Beatlemania* in the early 1980s.
17. BA, 120.
18. Keith Badman, *The Beatles Off the Record 2: The Dream Is Over* (New York: Omnibus Press, 2008), 87–88.
19. BA, 123.
20. Badman, 88.
21. *All in the Family* producer Norman Lear later adapted this British series for America's early 1970s hit, *Sanford and Son*.
22. BA, 128.
23. Ibid.
24. Braun, 51.
25. Lester Bangs and Greil Marcus, ed., *Psychotic Reactions and Carburetor Dung* (New York: Alfred A. Knopf, 1987), 325.
26. Author interview with Victor Spinetti, August 2007.
27. Taylor, *With the Beatles,* 109. Also DCH, 110–112.
28. BA, 135.
29. Kane, 14.
30. Ibid, 21.
31. Ibid, 28.

32. Spector, 77.
33. Ibid, 80, 84. Ronnie describes how she lost her virginity to Phil several months later when he brought over the test pressing of the new Ronettes record, "Do I Love You?" to her house. "Phil and I made love for the first time listening to that record. And every two minutes and fifty seconds, Phil would reach over from the bed and lift the needle back to the beginning of the record. We must've played that song fifty times, because we made love on that mattress until late into the night."
34. Tony Barrow, *John, Paul, George, Ringo and Me: The Real Beatles Story* (New York: Thunder's Mouth Press, 2005), 66.
35. James Sauceda, *The Literary Lennon: A Comedy of Letters* (Ann Arbor: Pierian Press, 1983), 3.

Chapter 13: Watching the Wheels

1. Michael R. Frontani, *The Beatles: Image and the Media* (Jackson: University Press of Mississippi, 2007), 100.
2. Miles, *Diary,* 189.
3. Author interview with Victor Spinetti, Chicago, August 2006.
4. Ibid.
5. Victor Spinetti, *Up Front . . . His Strictly Confidential Autobiography* (London: Anova Books, 2009), 163.
6. George Harrison, *I Me Mine* (Simon & Schuster, 1980), 47.
7. CLJ, 182.
8. Ibid.
9. Pattie Boyd with Penny Junor, *Wonderful Tonight: George Harrison, Eric Clapton and Me* (New York: Harmony Books, 2007), 101–2.
10. The photo for *Beatles VI* was taken on Lennon's birthday, October 9, 1964, by Robert Whitaker at Farringdon Studio, with all four Beatles holding a carving knife cutting a cake, cropped from the final photo.
11. Winn, *That Magic Feeling*, 103.
12. Author interview with Richard Meltzer, 2005.
13. Kane, 225.
14. The Beatles, *The Beatles Illustrated Lyrics,* Alan Aldridge, ed. (New York: Delacorte, 1969), 33.
15. Coleman, 310.
16. BA, 193.

Chapter 14: Another Kind of Mind

1. Ringo Starr, *Postcards from the Boys* (Britain: Cassell Illustrated, 2004), 49.

2. Maureen Cleave, "How Does a Beatle Live? John Lennon Lives Like This," reprinted in *Read The Beatles: Classic and New Writings on the Beatles, Their Legacy, and Why They Still Matter,* June Skinner Sawyers, ed. (New York: Penguin, 2006), 85–91. Cleave's *Evening Standard* article ran on March 4, 1966.

3. BC, 214–15.

4. Author interview with Barry Miles, May 2008.

5. Author interview with Ken Townsend, Abbey Road Studios, London, November 2006.

6. This was long held to be a Lennon move; more recently, Robert Whitaker has done interviews taking credit. (Web: http://www.rareBeatles.com/album2/openalbm.htm).

7. Author interview with Kim Fowley, 2005.

8. Miles, *Diary,* 234.

9. BA, 216.

10. Robert Cording, ed., with Shelli Jankowski-Smith and E. J. Miller Laino, *In My Life: Encounters with the Beatles* (New York: Fromm International, 1998), 49.

11. Hoji Murayama, a reporter for the *Asahi Shimbun* (Tokyo's *New York Times*), reported to the author that Lennon's Tokyo spree included a $20,000 bill at a specialty antiques store, which revealed a previously unknown interest in Oriental artifacts. This was four months before he met Yoko Ono, who would immerse him in Japanese culture and turn Japan into his favorite refuge from the world during the 1970s.

12. The first two of these performances were taped for Nippon Television (NTV).

13. Cording, 56–57.

14. BC, 212. 74,450 Philippine pesos, or £6,840.

15. Ibid.

16. Ibid, 216; also BA, 205.

17. Walter Everett, *The Beatles as Musicians:* Revolver *Through the* Anthology (New York: Oxford University Press, 1999), 70. Everett notes that Epstein's naïve acceptance of the damage unintentionally gave the Lennon flap legs.

18. BA, 226.

19. Winn, *That Magic Feeling,* 62–63.

20. BA, 227.

21. Ibid, 229.

22. Tom Wolfe, *The Electric Kool-Aid Acid Test* (New York: Farrar Straus Giroux, 1968), 205–6.

23. Mike Evans, ed., *The Beatles Literary Anthology* (UK: Plexus Publishing, 2004), 184.
24. Wenner, 106–7.
25. Evans, 185.
26. JLE, 682, and MYFN, 272. Miles writes that Lennon later contributed some watercolored lyrics to "The Word," which he and McCartney gave to Yoko Ono. Cage featured it in his book *Notations,* among other scores he assembled for the Foundation of Contemporary Performance Arts.
27. Author interview with Barry Miles, May 2008.
28. Badman, 246.
29. BA, 237.
30. MYFN, 306–7.
31. George Martin, *All You Need Is Ears* (New York: St. Martin's Press, 1979), 204.

Chapter 15: In a Play

1. BJY, 143.
2. Greil Marcus, *Interview* magazine, March 1, 2000, http://www.beatlemoney .com/paul6467.html.
3. BA, 255.
4. CLJ, 183.
5. Ibid.
6. Mitchell would later collaborate with Lennon and Victor Spinetti on *In His Own Write*'s stage production in 1968.
7. Most Americans recognize Bach's third "Allegro assai" movement from this Brandenburg Concerto as the theme music to William F. Buckley's *Firing Line* interview show on PBS.
8. BA, 247.
9. Ibid.
10. Bramwell, 191. Bramwell's film still makes the rounds in various forms, for documentaries and among bootleg collectors, but the BBC banned the broadcast of the footage since the song itself had been banned for "drug references."
11. Winn, *That Magic Feeling,* 100.
12. Ibid, 103.
13. Bramwell, 200.
14. Ian MacDonald, *Revolution in the Head, The Beatles' Records and the Sixties* (New York: Henry Holt, 1994), 192.
15. Davies, *Beatles,* 266–67.
16. Alistair Taylor, *Yesterday: The Beatles Remembered* (London: Sidgwick & Jackson Limited, 1988), 108.

17. Simon Napier-Bell, *You Don't Have to Say You Love Me* (London: Ebury Press, 1998), 129.

18. Bramwell, 200–201.

19. Robert Christgau, *Any Old Way You Choose It: Rock and Other Pop Music, 1967–1978.* (New York: Cooper Square Press, 2000), 42.

20. Richard Goldstein, "We Still Need the Beatles, but . . . ," *New York Times,* June 18, 1967, 104.

21. Bramwell, 191. Even the iconic *Pepper* album sleeve, shot by Michael Cooper and with art direction by Peter Blake and Robert Fraser, from McCartney's design concept, was outrageously expensive. The final costs came to a staggering £2,867, a hundred times more than most album covers, and burst EMI's "sleeves" budget. But Lennon insisted that art was beyond price. He cracked, "If you can't stand the art, get out of the kitschen."

22. Charles Cross, *A Room Full of Mirrors* (New York: Hyperion, 2006), 322.

23. BA, 255.

24. Chet Flippo, *Yesterday: The Unauthorized Biography of Paul McCartney* (New York: Doubleday, 1988), 242.

25. Author interview with Barry Miles, May 2008.

26. Many people close to Epstein in this period strongly infer a romantic link without wanting to go on the record. The business deal was far too lopsided to make any other kind of sense.

27. Napier-Bell, 118.

28. Ibid, 120.

29. Ibid.

30. Taylor, *With the Beatles,* 187.

31. Napier-Bell, 124.

32. Marianne Faithfull, *Faithfull: An Autobiography* (New York: Cooper Square Press, 2000), 135.

33. BA, 264.

34. Wenner, 25.

Chapter 16: I Should Have Known Better

1. One of the best parodies of "All You Need Is Love" as a swollen sixties bromide came with Nick Lowe's breezy "What's So Funny 'Bout Peace Love and Understanding?" which Elvis Costello transformed on 1979's *Armed Forces* with reverse irony.

2. Tariq Ali, *Street Fighting Years* (New York: Verso, 2005), 361.

3. BA, 285.

4. Ibid.

5. In *A Twist of Lennon*, Cynthia Lennon reports occasional brief contacts from Alf, including an appearance at the *Magical Mystery Tour* wrap party, 178.

6. CLJ, 206.

7. Ibid, 182.

8. Ibid.

9. Ibid, 207.

10. Ibid, 206.

11. Ibid, 207.

12. Lewis H. Lapham, *With the Beatles* (Hoboken: Melville House Publishing, 2005), 63.

13. Ibid, 71–2.

14. Ibid, 78.

15. Mia Farrow, *What Falls Away* (New York: Bantam, 1997), 137.

16. Ibid, 132–33.

17. Lapham, 84.

18. BA, 291.

19. Ibid.

20. CLJ, 208.

21. BA, 284.

22. CLJ, 209.

23. Ibid, 210.

24. Ibid, 285.

25. Ibid, 211.

26. Ibid, 212.

27. SS, 168.

28. Ibid, 169.

29. CLJ, 213–14.

30. Alexandra Munroe with Jon Hendricks, *Yes Yoko Ono* (New York: Japan Society and Harry N. Abrams, Publishers, 2000), 15.

31. Ibid.

32. Ibid, 17.

33. Ibid.

34. Ibid.

35. Ibid.

36. CLJ, 221.

37. Lennon's theatrical piece opened June 18.

38. CLJ, 222.

39. Ibid, 223.

Chapter 17: How?

1. Peter Carlin, *Paul McCartney: A Life* (New York: Touchstone Books. 2009), 232.
2. CLJ, 225. Also Carlin, 232.
3. Ibid.
4. Spitz, 320. Many years later, band biographer Bob Spitz tracked down McCartney's steady and sometime roommate of Cynthia Powell, Dot Rhone, who claimed McCartney backed out of his informal commitment to her in 1962 after watching Lennon get hitched. She eventually miscarried.
5. Winn, *That Magic Feeling,* 187.
6. Author interview with Victor Spinetti, 2007.
7. Richard Dilello, *The Longest Cocktail Party: An Insider's Diary of the Beatles, Their Million-Dollar Apple Empire, and Its Wild Rise and Fall* (Edinburgh: Canongate Books, 2005). The best book on the Apple office atmosphere from one of Derek Taylor's lackeys.
8. Geoff Emerick and Howard Massey, *Here, There and Everywhere: My Life Recording the Music of the Beatles* (New York: Gotham, 2007), 246–47.
9. Ibid, 225.
10. BJY, 384.
11. Bramwell, 189.
12. RTB, 489. Trident's playback speakers were both trebly and loud, and the American recorder hadn't been tweaked to reproduce properly on EMI's setup.
13. Emerick and Massey, 262. Also BRS, 147. Emerick remembers Lennon, Lewisohn cites McCartney for this quote.
14. Ibid, 260–63.
15. Eric Clapton, *Clapton: The Autobiography* (New York: Broadway Books, 2007), 99–100.
16. RTB, 496.
17. Author interview with Chris Thomas, November 2006.
18. Jon Wiener, *Come Together: John Lennon in His Time* (Urbana: University of Illinois Press, 1990), 61.
19. Editors of *Rolling Stone, The Ballad of John and Yoko* (Garden City: Doubleday Dolphin, 1982), 55.
20. Author interview with Chris Thomas, November 2006.
21. Emerick and Massey, 244.
22. Alan Travis, "The Night Yogi and Boo-Boo Helped Semolina Pilcher Snare a Beatle," *The Guardian*, August 1, 2005.
23. Ibid. Five months later, when Pilcher raided George Harrison's Esher estate, he timed his raid to coincide with Paul McCartney's marriage to Linda Eastman, assuming Harrison's house would be empty. Pilcher's name became synony-

mous with London police corruption. In 1972, he was convicted of "conspiracy to pervert the course of justice" and sentenced to four years' imprisonment.

24. Author interview with Barry Miles, 2008.

25. Miles, *Diary*, 314.

26. The period teems with activity: Lennon's You Are Here art show opened at the Robert Fraser Gallery in July, as did the movie animated feature, *Yellow Submarine*. The movie opened to mixed reviews on November 13 in New York City. Two avant-garde films shot at Lennon's Kenwood home in August, *Smile* and *Two Virgins,* were shown at the Chicago Film Festival during this same month. John and Yoko were also plotting the more ambitious seventy-five-minute *Rape*, which followed the twenty-one-year-old Hungarian actress Eva Majlata around the streets of London.

27. Clayson, *Lennon*, 170. Based on the 1966 Dangerous Drugs Act, Section 42.

28. Peter Doggett, *There's a Riot Goin' On: Revolutionaries, Rock Stars, and the Rise and Fall of the '60s* (London: Canongate, 2008), 200.

29. Winn, *That Magic Feeling*, 249.

30. CLJ, 235.

Chapter 18: Thank You Girl

1. Doug Sulpy and Ray Schweighardt, *Get Back: The Unauthorized Chronicle of the Beatles' Let It Be Disaster* (New York: St. Martin's Press, 1997), 169.

2. Ibid.

3. Ibid, 181.

4. Ibid, 199.

5. Ibid, 169.

6. Preston also likely knew Allen Klein, who had counseled Sam Cooke when he formed his own company in the early sixties.

7. Another layer of Sulpy and Schweighardt's research for *Get Back* involves the innumerable musical fragments the Beatles scatter throughout their rehearsals, not just oldies run-throughs but stray lyrics from old radio hits and appreciative romps through work by sixties contemporaries. Harrison and Lennon attempt John Sebastian's hit with the Lovin' Spoonful, "Daydream," their first morning reunited on January 22 (206), and during a rambling blues improvisation on January 9, they start calling out names to each other, diagramming their Quarrymen heroes. McCartney calls out "Cassius Cleavage," Lennon responds with "Deirdre McSharry," a magazine editor, McCartney answers with "Humphrety Lestouq," the *Whirligig* children's TV show host. The list continues on through Betty Grable, comedian Ronnie Corbett, Radio Luxembourg deejay Emperor Rosko, and many others. This banquet of inside jokes and adolescent references gives a clue as to how they free-associated as they hunted

for song ideas, swapped character names, and killed time while songs took shape. An outline of secretly shared pop history, these references map Lennon and McCartney's songwriting unconscious, and the sheer number of song titles they drop deserves its own compilation.

8. BA, 321.

9. Starr, 25.

10. Author interview with Barry Miles, May 2008. Also Carlin, 95.

11. In the UK, Denmark Street is roughly analogous to "Tin Pan Alley," a literal address where Epstein knocked on Dick James's door in 1962, but also a frame of reference for the older pop tradition it housed.

12. BA, 325.

13. Miles, *Diary,* 337.

14. BA, 286.

15. Lennon quotes from Amsterdam hotel bed; see http://holysmoke.tripod.com/amsterdam.htm/.

16. Miles, *Diary,* 338.

17. Ibid, 339.

18. Ibid.

19. Quentin Tarantino uses "You Never Can Tell" for John Travolta and Uma Thurman's twist contest at Jack Rabbit Slim's in 1994's *Pulp Fiction.* Nick Lowe returned to Berry's tune for "I Knew the Bride (When She Used to Rock and Roll)" in 1985.

20. MYFN, 548.

21. Anthony Fawcett, *John Lennon One Day at a Time* (New York: Grove Press, 1976), 74.

22. CLJ, 234.

23. Winn, *That Magic Feeling,* 294.

24. *Rolling Stone,* June 28, 1969, 6.

25. Ibid.

26. Andrew Solt, director, *Imagine: John Lennon* (Warner Home Video, 1988), DVD.

27. BA, 334.

28. CLJ, 234.

29. Ibid, 236.

30. Ibid, 243.

31. Unpublished Alan White interview, transcript at http://www.quipo.it/mccartney/specials/alanwhite/.

32. Clapton, 118.

33. BA, 184.

34. Ibid, 347.

35. Wenner, 31.
36. Author phone interview with Kim Fowley, 2006.
37. Southall, 81–3.
38. Peter McCabe and Robert D. Schonfeld, *Apple to the Core: The Unmaking of the Beatles* (New York: Pocket Books, 1972), 152.
39. The Northern Songs publishing fortune, centered around Maclen, the Lennon-McCartney song catalog, is considered the most valuable property in rock publishing. It differs from Beatle recording royalties in that it earns money whenever somebody performs a Lennon-McCartney song. It finally fell into Michael Jackson's hands in 1983, after he sought business advice from McCartney himself.
40. David Leaf, director, *The U.S. vs. John Lennon* (Lions Gate, 2006), DVD.
41. Richard Robinson, "Our London Interview," *Hit Parader,* August 1970 (http://www.instantkarma.com/magarchive1_99.html).
42. Interview with Desmond Morris for BBC-TV's *Men of the Decade* (http://homepage.ntlworld.com/carousel/pob02.html).

Chapter 19: Just We Two
1. Mark Moses, "The Late Beatles: Carry That Weight," *Boston Phoenix,* December 4, 1987, 11, 15–18.
2. Braun, 52.
3. Richard Williams, *Out of His Head: The Sound of Phil Spector* (New York: E. P. Dutton & Co., 1972), 149.
4. Cox hung onto the film for another twenty-six years, until several collectors formed a consortium and bought the material from him. Yoko Ono successfully fought to prevent its release in 2008.
5. PB, 216.
6. Williams, 153.
7. Ibid.
8. Miles, 345.
9. BA, 350.
10. Keith Badman, *The Beatles: After the Break-Up 1970–2000: A Day-By-Day Diary* (New York: Omnibus Press, 2000), 4.
11. Ibid, 15.
12. Ibid, 4.
13. Author interview with Ray Connolly, May 2008.
14. Lou Cannon, *President Reagan: The Role of a Lifetime* (New York: Simon & Schuster, 1991), 630.
15. Wenner, 23.
16. Williams, 156–58.

17. Ibid, 159.
18. PB, 104.
19. Fawcett, 109.
20. Arthur Jano to John Harris in *Mojo*, 2000, http://primaltherapy.com/SED/john-lennon.shtml.
21. Wenner, 24.
22. Author interview wth Richard Lush, November 2006.
23. Badman, *After the Break-Up*, 24.
24. Christgau, *Rock Albums of the Seventies* (New Haven: Ticknor & Fields, 1981), 242.
25. Dave Marsh, "John Lennon—Plastic Ono Band, Yoko Ono—Plastic Ono Band," *Creem*, March 1971, http://beatpatrol.wordpress.com/2008/08/26/john-lennon-john-lennonplastic-ono-band-yoko-ono-yoko-onoplastic-ono-band-1970/.
26. Howard Smith, WPLJ interview. See: http://tittenhurstlennon.blogspot.com.
27. Badman, *After the Break-Up*, 25.
28. DCH, 177–81. This is the only account of this scene in the entire span of Lennon literature, and therefore the only quotes of Lennon discussing the choice his parents had him make in Blackpool twenty-five years before. Naturally, the narrative is slanted in favor of Freddie, who behaves with a dignified calm, and against Lennon, even though Pauline recognizes that "following psychotherapy, to experience a death wish towards a parent is part and parcel of the process of freeing oneself from childhood trauma. What was unusual in John's case was the method whereby he had visualized killing his father. By imagining him dumped deep in the ocean he was finally enacting his revenge on his father for the years he had spent at sea while he was a child."
29. The date of this interview assumes prophetic significance. Excerpts from the longer interview are available in BJY. The complete text, along with a new introduction from Ono, came out from Verso publishers in 2000.
30. Wenner, 106.
31. Paul McCartney in *Life*, April 16, 1971, 56.

Chapter 20: I'll Cry Instead

1. Badman, *After the Break-Up*, 19. "A declaration that the partnership business carried on by the plaintiff and the defendants under the name of The Beatles & Co., and constituted by a deed of partnership dated 19 April 1967 and made between the parties hereto, ought to be dissolved and that accordingly the same be dissolved."
2. Ibid, 27.
3. Ibid, 32.

4. Ibid, 24.
5. Wenner, 140.
6. Ali, 381.
7. Badman, *After the Break-Up,* 4.
8. Transcript from the Apple case, the High Court of Justice, Chancery Division, 10:B.
9. Ibid, 26:A.
10. Miles, *Zappa,* 3.
11. Andy Peebles, *The Lennon Conversations* (London: BBC, 1981), 46. The Olympics number was "Well (Baby Please Don't Go)," the B-side to "Western Movies."
12. Badman, *After the Break-Up,* 55.
13. Author interview with Ray Connolly, May 2008.
14. Steve Sutherland, "John Lennon: The Beatles and Beyond," *NME Originals,* Vol. 1, Issue 113, 2003, 84–85.
15. *The Dick Cavett Show—John Lennon & Yoko Ono,* Shout DVD, 2005. Paradoxically, this comment foreshadows the hypnosis treatment Yoko will use to lure Lennon away from May Pang in Los Angeles some three years on.

Chapter 21: You Can't Do That
1. "Another Day" revives McCartney's "A Day in the Life" character as a Professional Skirt on the A-Side, with a hard-boiled Lennon pulp novel on the B-Side, "Oh Woman, Oh Why." Instead, most commentators remark on "Let Me Roll It" as McCartney's best Lennon impersonation.
2. Badman, *After the Break-Up,* 24.
3. Jon Savage, "Imagine" review, *Mojo* (158, 2007), 287–29.
4. Doggett, 454.
5. Williams, 2.
6. Ibid, 4.
7. Author interview with Wayne "Tex" Gabriel, August 2008.
8. Author interview with Gary Van Scyoc, August 2008.
9. Author interview with Michael Krauss, July 2008.
10. Alan Parker and Phil Strongman, *John Lennon and the FBI Files* (London: Sanctuary Publishing, Ltd., 2003), 48.
11. Ibid, 39.
12. Author interview with Bob Gruen, 2008.
13. Wiener, 200.
14. Doggett, 462.
15. John Blaney, *John Lennon: Listen to This Book* Guildford: (Paper Jukebox, 2005), 89.

16. Ibid.

17. John Lennon, "Peace and Love," Letter to the Editor, *New York Times,* December 28, 1971, 28.

18. Doggett, 470.

19. Parker and Strongman, 165.

20. Doggett, 470.

21. "Talk of the Town," *New Yorker,* January 8, 1972, 28.

22. Author interview with Bob Gruen, 2008.

23. Author interview with Tex Gabriel and Van Scyoc, August 2008.

24. Ibid.

25. Dave Marsh, *Cream,* August 1972.

26. Ian MacDonald, *Uncut,* December 1998 (see *Rock's Back Pages* online archive, http://rocksbackpages.com).

27. BJY, 172.

28. All quotes from author interview with Gabriel and Van Scyoc, 2008.

29. Ibid.

Chapter 22: I'm a Loser

1. Ryan's wife had died of cancer. Now largely forgotten, Ryan epitomized the stony male reserve through characters like Deke Thornton in Sam Peckinpah's *The Wild Bunch;* a Hollywood staple in his time, he shared a sensibility with leading men like Robert Mitchum and Sterling Hayden.

2. Philip Norman, *John Lennon: The Life* (New York: Ecco, 2008), 706. Norman drapes the Dakota in faded chic: "Once the acme of luxury, the Dakota was no longer in Manhattan's premier real-estate league and had become the haunt of middle-range actors, film directors, and similar bohemian types."

3. Badman, *The Dream Is Over,* 101.

4. Bangs and Marcus, 214.

5. Chris Charlesworth, *Mind Games* review, *Melody Maker,* November 3, 1973, 37.

6. Badman, *The Dream Is Over,* 117.

7. Ibid, 98.

8. Badman, *After the Break-Up,* 95–96.

9. Ibid, 94.

10. Coleman, 489.

11. Author interview with Jack Douglas, August 2008.

12. Author interview with Bob Gruen, August 2008.

13. Ibid.

14. *New York Times,* September 30, 1973.

15. Ibid.

16. Mark Ribowsky, *He's a Rebel: Phil Spector, Rock & Roll's Legendary Producer* (New York: Dutton, 1989), 266.

17. Author interview with Dan Kessel, June 2007.

18. Ribowsky, 268.

19. Author interview with Dan Kessel.

20. Nicholas Schaffner, *The Beatles Forever*, New York: McGraw-Hill, 1978, 161.

21. Ribowsky, 259.

22. "Random Notes," *Rolling Stone,* Issue 154, February 14, 1974, 24.

23. All Jack Douglas quotes from author interviews, 2008.

24. Badman, *The Dream Is Over,* 127.

25. Ibid.

26. Ibid, 128–29.

27. Ibid.

28. All quotes, CLJ, 255.

29. Author interview with Bob Gruen, 2008.

30. Ben Gerson, "Together Again: *Walls and Bridges,*" *Rolling Stone,* November 21, 1974, 44–46.

31. Author interview with Bob Gruen, 2008.

32. PB, 46.

Chapter 23: Get Back

1. One of the great late themes of Lennon's development is his immersion in blues forms, beginning with "Yer Blues," "Come Together," and "I Want You (She's So Heavy)," and progressing through "Well Well Well," "It's So Hard," and "I'm Losing You."

2. Of the four, Ringo Starr refused to take himself seriously and wound up singing "Yellow Submarine" and "With a Little Help from My Friends" at summer shows for the rest of his days. He remains the band's most underrated musician.

3. Lisa Robinson, *Hit Parader,* December 1975, http://beatlesinterviews.org/db1975.1200.beatles.html.

4. Ibid.

5. Jerry Hopkins, *Yoko Ono* (New York: Macmillan, 1986), 124.

6. Fawcett, 139.

7. Jon Landau, "Lennon Gets Lost in His Rock 'n' Roll," *Rolling Stone*, May 22, 1975, 66.

8. In the continuing song volley between ex-collaborators, McCartney closed side one of *Band on the Run* with "Let Me Roll It," which had the uncanny air of a *Plastic Ono Band* outtake. Turns out McCartney impersonated Lennon far better than the other way around ("One Day at a Time"). At least until "Beautiful Boy."

9. Geoffrey Giuliano, *Lennon in America* (New York: Cooper Square Press, 2000),

71. "Fame" provides the model for the James Brown track "Hot (I Need to Be Loved, Loved, Loved)."

10. Badman, *After the Break-Up,* 153.

11. Ibid, 160.

12. Author interview with Larry Kane, August 2007.

13. PB, 74.

14. Ibid, 73.

15. Ibid, 75.

16. Badman, *The Dream Is Over,* 169–70.

17. Author interview with Bob Gruen, 2008.

18. Elliot Mintz, in Yoko Ono's *Memories of John Lennon,* 170.

19. PB, 75.

Chapter 24: Three of Us

1. CLJ, 256. Robert Christgau also makes this connection in a 1983 review of May Pang's *Loving John,* http://www.robertchristgau.com/xg/bkrev/rockbios-83.php.

2. All Bob Gruen quotes from author interview, September 2008.

3. DCH, 10.

4. Badman, *After the Break-Up,* 181–82.

5. Ibid. Later that fall, when Monty Python's Eric Idle hosted the show, Michaels returned to the gag to introduce Idle's short film, *The Rutles,* which became *All You Need Is Cash.*

6. Ibid, 182.

7. The *Saturday Night Live* story turned into a 2000 Michael Lindsay-Hogg made-for-TV movie called *Two of Us,* much distorted in Mark Stanfield's script.

8. BJY, 165.

9. Ibid.

10. Ibid, 141.

11. Ibid, 166.

12. Dorothy Hansen, ed., *The Art of John Lennon: Drawings, Performances, Films* (Cantz Verlag, 1995). One of the entries in the closing Biographical Notes sounds like it was dictated directly from Ono: "17 November 1980—Lennon and Ono's joint album *Double Fantasy* is released to unprecedented critical acclaim for Yoko Ono: she is applauded for contributing the best tracks."

13. Starr, 82.

14. SS, 190–200. Shotton's memoirs are riddled with calendar errors, but he describes Lennon carrying Sean as an infant, and the Sally Field TV movie *Sybil* dates the visit to 1976.

15. Ibid, 200.

16. BJY, 173.
17. Yoko Ono, *Lennon: His Life and Work* (Cleveland: Rock and Roll Hall of Fame, 2000).
18. Starr, 85.
19. Yoko Ono, *Memories of John Lennon*, 167–69.
20. Dave Marsh, "An Open Letter to John Lennon," *Rolling Stone*, November 3, 1977, 50.
21. "A Love Letter From John and Yoko: To People Who Ask Us What, When, and Why," *New York Times*, Sunday, May 27, 1979, 20E.
22. Dave Marsh, "Another Open Letter to John Lennon," *Rolling Stone*, August 23, 1979, 28.
23. Norman, *Lennon*, 788. In addition, Lennon never mentions his reaction to Paul McCartney's Japanese marijuana bust in January, 1980.
24. PB, 92–93.
25. All Jack Douglas quotes come from author interview, August 2008.
26. All Bun E. Carlos quotes from author interview, July 2008.
27. David Geffen, "A Reminiscence," *Rolling Stone*, Issue 335, January 22, 1981, 59.
28. Ibid, 61.
29. Robert Palmer, *Blues and Chaos* (New York: Scribner, 2009), 251.
30. Geoffrey Stokes, "The Infantalization of John Lennon," *Village Voice*, January 7, 1981, 31.
31. Charles Shaar Murray, in Sutherland, 132.
32. Author interview with Andy Peebles, London, 1985.
33. Annie Leibovitz, *Rolling Stone*, Issue 335, January 22, 1981, 61.
34. David Geffen, "A Reminiscence," *Rolling Stone*, Issue 335, Jan. 22, 1981, 59.
35. Ibid.
36. Yoko Ono, quoted in *New York Times*, December 10, 1980, 1.
37. BJY, 203.
38. Ibid.

Epilogue

1. Author interview with Elliot Mintz, September 2008.
2. JLE, 587.
3. BJY, 205.
4. Ibid.
5. Ibid, 207.
6. Badman, *After the Break-Up*, 276.
7. "Silent Tribute to Lennon's Memory is Observed Throughout the World," *New York Times*, December 15, 1980, 1.
8. Ibid.

9. Jonathan Schell, "Talk of the Town," *New Yorker,* December 22, 1980.

10. BJY, 61.

11. Author interview with Bob Gruen, August 2008.

12. BJY, 291.

13. All Jack Douglas quotes from author interview, September 2008.

14. Harrison had actually started the song before Lennon's death and reworked the lyrics once he decided to issue it as a tribute record. He fought off a knife attack by his own delusional fan in his Friar Park home in late 1999.

15. Mikal Gilmore, "The Mystery of John Lennon," *Stories Done: Writings on the 1960s and Its Discontents* (New York: Free Press, 2008), 158.

16. Anthony Elliott, *The Mourning of John Lennon* (Berkeley: University of California Press, 1999), 6.

Index

Photo Credits

Photo Section 1

Page 1: Dave Trimble/LFI (*top*), Mark and Coillen Hayward/Getty Images (*middle*), Mercury Press Agency/Rex USA (bottom); *page 2*: Rex USA (*top*), Mark and Coillen Hayward (*bottom*); *page 3*: James Davis/Rod Davis (*top*), Geoff Rhind/ LFI (*bottom*); *page 4*: Leslie Kearney/Mark Lewisohn Collection (*top*), Sam Leach/Michael Ochs Archives/Getty Images (*bottom*); *page 5*: Hulton Archive/ Getty Images (*top*), Orbital Media/ LFI (*bottom*); *page 6*: Astrid Kirchherr/Retna; *page 7*: Astrid Kirchherr/Redferns/Retna (*top*), Astrid Kirchherr/Retna (*middle*), Peter Bruchmann/K&K Ulf Kruger OHG/Getty Images (*bottom*); *page 8*: Astrid Kirchherr/Getty Images (*top*), Michael Ochs Archive/Getty Images (*bottom*).

Photo Section 2

Page 1: Frank Apthorp/Daily Mail/Rex USA; *page 2*: Mirrorpix (*top*); John Pratt/Hulton Archive/Getty Images (*bottom*); *page 3*: Bettmann/Corbis; *page 4*: Frank Hermann/Camera Press/Retna (*top*), Hulton Archive/Getty Images (*bottom*); *page 5*: Linda McCartney; *page 6*: Mirrorpix (*top*), David Nutter/Camera Press/Retba (*bottom*); *page 7*: Bettmann/Corbis (*top*), Ron Howard/Redferns/Getty Images (*bottom*); *page 8*: Tom Hanley/Redferns/Getty Images (*top*), Bob Gruen (*bottom*).

Photo Section 3

Page 1: Bob Gruen; *page 2*: Bob John Rodgers/Redferns/Getty Images (*top*), Hulton Archive/Getty Images (*bottom*); *page 3*: Bob Gruen; *page 4*: Bob Gruen (*top*), Ron Galella/Getty Images (*bottom*); *page 5*: Bob Gruen; *page 6*: Bob Gruen; *page 7*: Gene Kappock/Corbis (*top*), Bettmann/Corbis (*bottom*); *page 8*: Bob Gruen.